Administrative Law Facing the Future:
Old Constraints and New Horizons

Administrative Law Facing the Future: Old Constraints and New Horizons

Edited by

Peter Leyland and Terry Woods

BLACKSTONE
PRESS LIMITED

First published in Great Britain 1997 by Blackstone Press Limited,
Aldine Place, London W12 8AA. Telephone 0181-740 2277

ISBN: 1 85431 689 3

British Library Cataloguing in Publication Data
A CIP catalogue record for this book is available from the British Library.

Typeset by Style Photosetting Ltd, Mayfield, East Sussex
Printed by Livesey Ltd, Shrewsbury, Shropshire

Contents

List of Contributors

The Hon. Mr Justice Sedley, Justice of the High Court

Rodney Austin, Senior Lecturer in Law, University College London

Mike Radford, Lecturer in Law, University of East Anglia

Gabriele Ganz, Professor of Law, University of Southampton

Gavin Drewry, Professor of Public Administration, Royal Holloway and Bedford New College, University of London

Linda Mulcahy, Lawfords Reader in Public Law, University of North London

Judith Allsop, Professor of Health Policy, South Bank University

Nicholas Bamforth, Fellow, Robinson College Cambridge

John Alder, Professor of Law, University of Newcastle

Michael Fordham, Barrister, 2 Hare Court and College Lecturer, Hertford College, Oxford

Christopher Himsworth, Reader in Law, University of Edinburgh

Maurice Sunkin, Professor of Law, University of Essex

Peter Cane, Professor of Law, Corpus Christi College Oxford*

Paul Craig, Professor of Law, Worcester College Oxford

David Pollard, Chevalier des Palmes Academiques, University of Leicester

Adam Tomkins, Lecturer in Law, Kings College, London

Fiona Donson, Lecturer in Law, University of Cardiff

Peter Leyland, Principal Lecturer, University of North London

Terry Woods, Senior Lecturer, University of North London

(*Now Professor of Law, Australian National University, Canberra)

Foreword

Modern judicial review of public administration has been, in terms at least of public perception, the principal victim of its own success. It has attracted not only public approbation and a still-growing caseload, but also a political counteroffensive drawing upon constitutional notions of sometimes surprising eccentricity. This is not to say that the judges have been getting it consistently right, even if one shares the Dworkinian belief that there is a right answer to every legal question. The courts themselves, as is the way of the common law, have been tacking in the face of a complex of pressures which include both the demands of legal consistency and the background noise about what they are up to. There has certainly not been the kind of linear movement towards a supremacist goal which their critics claim to fear.

During the 1960s a change of mood and a change of pace without question entered public law. In effect it was rediscovered by a profession which had been educated to believe that there was no such thing. The single court which heard all applications, presided over by the Lord Chief Justice, began to take a gradually greater interest in errors of law and misuses of power. Property developers, who had money to spend, were among the most vigorous initial litigants, but close behind them — with the help of legal aid — came the new law centres whose clients were repeatedly encountering awkward local officials. By the end of the 1960s two major territorial claims had been settled by the courts: the exercise of the royal prerogative (no minor anachronism but a major reservoir of state power) had been brought within their supervisory jurisdiction, and the privative clause had been stood on its head, effectively opening all issues of administrative law to legal scrutiny. The rest is history — that is to say, a succession of events the evaluation of which itself continually changes.

Why, for example, has it happened as and when it has? Legal historians have so far been disconcertingly silent; but political scientists have offered some valuable perceptions. We know that from the time of the First World War until the end of the 1950s judicial intervention in public administration — apart, notoriously, from recalcitrant local authorities — was modest in the extreme. Judicial quietism coincided with what is recognised as the Civil Service's period of unimpeded growth and unchallenged power, a period which embraced the radical reforms of the post-war Labour government. Yet this phenomenon followed a much greater period of judicial interventionism, spanning the later Victorian years, in which legal and procedural challenges to the boards and commissions set up by Parliament to regulate public and private enterprise were entertained by often sympathetic courts, and the Edwardian years when the newly installed Northcote-Trevelyan Civil Service continued to attract judicial suspicion. It was in this era that practically all the modern principles of judicial review were established. Much of the post-1960s flowering of public law has been no more than the rediscovery and reapplication of them.

Yet something sent the courts to sleep in the first part of this century. I have advanced elsewhere the suggestion that it had in part to do with the fact that by 1914 the Civil Service was headed by a remarkable intellectual elite recruited from the same schools and universities as the judges themselves and able, as the old politicians' placemen had not been, to be trusted to run the country soundly while governments came and went. It clearly also had to do initially with a sense that in wartime it would be unpatriotic to rock the boat.

Legal historians have been equally reticent on why it is since the 1960s that public law has rediscovered itself. One can pick out certain barometric events — the Crichel Down affair among them — which may have triggered a judicial sense that government was capable of going out of control. It has also been attributed to a 'never again' reaction towards the statism of post-war administrations, especially the first. Certainly the first great modern stirring, the *Northumberland Case* in 1952, is redolent of judicial resentment of the new welfare state's claim to immunity from legal challenge to its administrative wrongdoing. But it would be unwise to come to any conclusion without a comparative study of other common law jurisdictions. The US, to take a single example, has gone in the last hundred years through a not dissimilar cycle. India, remarkably, seems to have condensed it into little more than the last 10 years. Popular feeling and popular movements undoubtedly play a part, though how these are mediated is complex. The easiest and poorest historiography is that which tries to explain the development of law simply in terms of judicial abstention or interventionism, and which thereby collapses independence into autonomy and effect into cause. It feeds the dangerous assumption that intervention is value-laden while abstention is neutral.

Against this tentative theoretical background, what is happening in public law now? To suggest, as is sometimes done, that it is running out of control is to echo the crassest of the media coverage; but it is nevertheless worth asking why and from where this message has been coming. The time when it might more defensibly have been put out was in the early 1980s when the House of Lords' unexpected decision in the *Fares Fair* case sent local authorities running to their lawyers for fear of challenge and surcharge should they do anything remotely autonomous. It was not then, however, but in the run-up to the Scott Report and the first Nolan Report that the segment of the press which feeds on the lobby system of unattributable departmental briefings undertook regular assaults, some of them abusive, on judges whose decisions were going against central government. The message was that judges were interfering unwarrantably in the business of government. Any doubt that it was a pre-emptive strike from Whitehall at Scott and Nolan has been dispelled by the fading away of the campaign in the wake of publication of the two reports — though not before a series of loaded leaks had greeted every attempt by Sir Richard Scott to be open in finalising his text.

The impulse to resist this loaded coverage makes a balanced account doubly difficult to assemble. Public law *has* made strides in the last 30 years. The fact that these have consisted in large part of the rediscovery of forgotten or occluded doctrines of standing, reviewability and natural justice does not make them any less important, for they are being reapplied in a polity of far greater complexity and in a democracy of much greater sophistication than before. How the courts deal, or decline to deal, with the independent bodies to which significant powers of government are now being devolved will be the next crucial question.

The development of judicial oversight has been part of a centuries-long search for consistent standards of fair and lawful administration in a protean state. To their breadth, which is readily defensible in terms of principle and consistency, modern judicial review has — perhaps most significantly and certainly most controversially — added a new depth. The real sea-change has in my view been the relative rigour with which, compared with say the 1940s, today's courts of judicial review require to be satisfied of proper standards of legality, rationality and fairness in public administration, and it may be that on analysis it is the strongest of *these* cases which have provoked the most noise.

To this wide-ranging debate the present volume makes a handsome contribution. It ebbs and flows, like all legal discourse, between what is and what could or should be: between, in other words, received textual authority and the calls of legal principle in a changing polity. Its greatest virtue is its practical orientation — neither a practice manual nor a textbook of theory, it engages from a variety of positions with what is happening and what could or should be happening in this most dynamic of all contemporary fields of law. I wrote somewhere once that law spends its life stretched on the rack between certainty and adaptability, sometimes groaning audibly but mostly maintaining a stoical silence. A book like this can both soothe some of the groans and speak in the silences, and it will be good to have it on the shelves of all those who think or act (or, praise be, do both) in the arena of public law.

Stephen Sedley
Royal Courts of Justice
September 1997

Introduction

In this collection of essays on administrative law we have set out to offer students a readable and accessible supplement to the textbook they may use on an everyday basis, while at the same time providing academics in the field, as well as those in related disciplines, with an interesting and insightful collection in its own right. In our experience students reading a chapter in a textbook very often find that they wish to undertake further research (or that their tutor advises them to go and look up a number of journal articles). One problem is that such sources are not readily available (or not as readily available as they should be). Another is that they are frequently very academic in style, having been written for other scholars rather than with the needs of the student also in mind. This book has the clear intention of bridging the frequently perceived gap between the two audiences by offering something in the nature of a rigorous yet approachable discussion of a variety of areas of continuing interest and concern to those studying public law in general, or administrative law in particular (as well as busy practitioners seeking analysis of the law and related issues in a relatively short space). There is also a certain logic to the order of the contributions in the collection. The text begins with an overview of the recent transformation in the structure and role of the state. It then moves on to consider the variety of non legal and legal mechanisms available to hold government and governmental bodies to account. The remainder of the book concentrates upon the role of the courts in their practical function as supervisory mechanisms of review and the controversy surrounding the theoretical underpinnings of this function, as well as the place of public law theory in relation to the whole.

Having noted this, it is by no means easy to say in the United Kingdom today just what it is that constitutes the 'field' of public or administrative law, so rapid have changes been in recent years. It is one measure of the pace of these developments that although the focus of the collection remains the courts, today there are many other emphases given to the study of the subject, in particular how the citizen secures a remedy for a grievance at the micro level. For example, Mulcahy and Alsop discuss internal dispute resolution procedures in the National Health Service. Another aspect of the debate centres upon the analysis of empirical data surrounding the efficacy of judicial review itself, discussed here by Maurice Sunkin with reference to the issue of settling.

Indeed, the content and boundaries of the subject are not only debated but the very terms of the debate itself are being constantly re-cast, prompted by changes in the wider society beyond the confines of the law courts or the academic seminar room. For example, we have witnessed since the 1980s the emergence and triumph (at least for the moment) of new models of public administration ('new public management') based on public choice theory, models which assert the priority of efficiency, effectiveness and value for money: parameters set by economists rather than the traditional lawyer's values of justice and the rule of law. Similarly, the proper (public) role of the judiciary has emerged as a matter for debate to an extent that would have been unthinkable before 1980, not least among the judiciary themselves. In fact, the perception has gained hold in some quarters that the courts have over the last 20 years or so become something of a surrogate opposition to the results of executive dominance over Parliament. A number of aspects of the alleged failures of parliamentary scrutiny are dealt with in the chapters by Gabriele Ganz (e.g., regarding the relative ineffectiveness of the available mechanisms for the control of delegated legislation) and Mike Radford (e.g., regarding the ability of the courts to remedy the obvious deficiencies inherent in the convention of individual ministerial responsibility to Parliament). The election of a Labour government with a majority of 179 will inevitably place further strains on these mechanisms of control.

The outcome of this ferment of historical and sociological change, as well as of ethical and legal debate, has been that not only does each subject discussed in this book constitute a field of systematic knowledge and learning practices in its own right, but new contributions embodying fresh approaches to the subject are always being welcomed. The grounds of review, for example, have witnessed some development and refinement over recent decades, which are thematically discussed in an essay by Michael Fordham. The area of standing has also been significantly modified with the apparent acceptance, in a string of cases, of a public interest basis for an application for judicial review by pressure groups (see Christopher Himsworth's chapter on standing). In addition, the scope of public law remedies has been considered by the Law Commission as recently as 1994 as well as being influenced by the jurisprudence of the European Court of Justice (see the chapter by Peter Cane). The utility of the divide between public and private law itself is a topical issue that has also been analysed and debated by many scholars. For example, in relation to the emergence of new kinds of contracting state formation (see the contribution by Rodney Austin) and in terms of the legal-technical necessity of the divide between public and private law made by Lord Diplock in *O'Reilly* v *Mackman* [1983] 2 AC 237 (see John Alder's chapter). Or whether, regarding a number of the more theoretical aspects of the debate, the state itself is an entity so markedly different from any individual citizen as to necessitate a distinct system of remedies for the litigant (for a wide-ranging discussion see the chapter by Nicholas Bamforth).

Another important development of recent decades, reflected in this collection, has been the opening up of many opportunities for the comparative study of public law. (See, for example, the chapters by David Pollard on the use of the prerogative power in Britain and France, and that by Gavin Drewry on the role of the ombudsman institution in a variety of jurisdictions.) At the same time, the contribution by Paul Craig considers the influence on English law, both direct and indirect, of our membership of the European Community since 1973. For example, regarding the doctrine of the sovereignty of Parliament, the availability of remedies for the citizen and the effect on the judiciary of various jurisprudential doctrines of the European Court of Justice, including those of purposive reasoning in the interpretation of statutory provisions and the doctrines of legitimate expectation and proportionality. The steady growth of the increasingly influential case law of the European Court of Human Rights, or of international human rights law, has also been a factor, one now set to have a more immediate impact on this country following the Labour government's decision to incorporate the European Convention on Human Rights into English law. (See in particular the essay by Fiona Donson.)

A further significant matter alluded to above has been the steady growth among lawyers (judges as well as academics) of dissatisfaction with the Diceyan model of administrative law. In particular, the search has been on for a new foundational statement, sometimes based on natural law or human rights principles, sometimes on new principles of public management and theories of the proper role of the state. These dissentients vary, from those who seek to limit the role of the courts to the minimum level of intervention in public affairs and who argue for the development of the democratic process (see Adam Tomkins in relation to demands for more open government and the law of public interest immunity) to those who would like to see the courts and the judiciary take a more principled and interventionist stand in issues of public law. The final three chapters in the book by Fiona Donson and by Leyland and Woods discuss some important aspects of this ongoing debate.

In sum, the whole subject is now more 'up for grabs' than ever before. Indeed, it will soon be apparent that there has been no attempt by us to impose a uniform line on our contributors, other than that of the broad theme of administrative law looking to the future rather than seeking to excavate the past. For this reason the reader will find that topics are discussed from a number of perspectives, ranging from largely court-centred approaches to those of a more socio-legal persuasion, to more abstract philosophical approaches. Looking back over the whole project, perhaps the largest and most problematical question, in the light of the changes charted in the contributions to this volume, is whether a new foundational theory for the subject is needed (or, if it is, what the implications of such a theory would be) as we look towards the 21st century.

We would like to acknowledge here what a pleasure it has been to work with our contributors. The process has at times been a testing one, but it has provided the opportunity to explore our own ideas about the subject with others, often far more knowledgeable than ourselves. We have also had the opportunity to make a number of friends and to build upon our contacts in the field of administrative law.

In particular, we would especially like to thank Sir Stephen Sedley not only for writing a stimulating foreword to the collection, but also for finding the time to read all the chapters so thoroughly.

In regard to our own contributions, we would like thank Caroline McCann, a research student in public law, who was not only efficient and methodical but who also demonstrated considerable initiative in obtaining materials for us. A number of colleagues were also kind enough to read and make helpful comments upon earlier drafts of our chapters. Particular thanks to Bill Bowring, Adam Tomkins and Carol Harlow. All cross-referencing in this volume is the work of the authors. Of course, any remaining defects of style or content are entirely our own responsibility.

Bridget Shersby, the law librarian for the School of Law at the University of North London, was, as ever, extremely helpful. We would also like to thank Bob Wareing MP and Sarah Crabbe for some additional assistance with our research. Last, but by no means least, we would like to express our gratitude to Alistair MacQueen and Heather Saward at Blackstone Press for the support and encouragement they gave to this project from the start.

Peter Leyland
and
Terry Woods
October 1997

1

Administrative Law's Reaction to the Changing Concepts of Public Service

Rodney Austin

SUMMARY

British public administration has been transformed in the last two decades by a series of structural, institutional and process changes, such as privatisation, contracting out, and a number of reforms known collectively as the new public management. The response of administrative law has been largely to ignore these radical new developments which have taken much of government beyond the scope of legal regulation. But administrative law does have a positive role to play, albeit a limited one, in the transformed public services.

INTRODUCTION

British public administration has, in a period of just under two decades, undergone a radical transformation in both structures and processes. The comfortable post-war consensus as to the proper role of the state as collective provider of almost every need, from cradle to grave, of the vast majority of the population, and as engine to the forces of the economy by virtue of its substantial ownership or control of the means of production and distribution, was rudely shattered when the Thatcher government was elected in 1979. The revolution of the Thatcherite right and its Majorist successors was dedicated to the transformation of the state — privatisation, the search for efficiency savings, value for money audit, the new public management, Next Steps executive agencies, public choice and public information, the quest for direct accountability to the consumer, contracting out and the internal market, the Citizen's Charter, and the *Open Government* White Paper. These and other reforms aimed at 'rolling back the frontiers of the state'[1] and empowering the individual have dramatically altered the government's business and the way government goes about it.[2] A new and fundamentally different concept of public service and the manner of its performance has been developed, which transforms the relationship between the individual and the state and completely alters the notions of and mechanisms for accountability of the public services. Many, if not most, of these developments have been carried through without the need for legal change, in the sense that no legislation, either primary or subordinate, was required to effect most of these reforms. Curiously, administrative law, the law which regulates much of the activity of the state and other public authorities, which might have been expected to react dynamically to such a radical transformation, has undergone no such development. This chapter seeks to examine these constitutionally significant changes in the concept of public service and the reaction of administrative law to those changes.

THE HISTORICAL PERSPECTIVE: SUBJECTS NOT CITIZENS: THE TOP-DOWN TRADITION

The historical continuity of British government without a genuine revolution for nearly a millennium (since the Glorious Revolution of 1688 was merely the transfer of absolute legislative sovereignty from the King to another select group of powerful and wealthy men, already institutionalised as part of the existing constitutional structure, i.e. Parliament) has meant that the UK continues to have a top-down system of government, which the advent of popular democracy in the 19th century did not fundamentally change. Indeed, the creation of mass political parties which resulted from the extension of the franchise under the Reform Acts 1820–1867, and the control exercised by the modern party leadership over the party MPs via its immense powers of patronage, the whip system and the payroll vote, have strengthened the executive's power over the legislature and transferred effective sovereignty over to the 'elective dictatorship'[3] of the Prime Minister and Cabinet, creating an even more autocratic and politically top-down system.

Power in the UK constitution springs legally also from the top of the constitutional structure i.e., from the Crown exercising its prerogative powers, and from

---

1 See the Conservative Party's 1979 election manifesto, referred to in McDonald, O., *The Future of Whitehall*, London: Weidenfeld & Nicolson, 1991, p. 2.
2 See McDonald, O., *op.cit.*, for an analysis of the early years of these reforms. See Oliver, D., and Drewry, G., *Public Service Reforms*, London: Pinter, 1996, for the most recent comprehensive analysis of the revolution in public administration.
3 Lord Hailsham, *Elective Dictatorship*, London: British Broadcasting Corporation, 1976.

the Crown in Parliament exercising its legislative sovereignty. Hence all civil servants are not public servants but servants of the Crown. Since by convention or statute almost all powers of the Crown are either vested in, or exercised by or on the advice of ministers of the Crown, the civil servant owes an absolute duty of loyalty to the minister he or she serves,[4] rather than to the Queen or Parliament or some abstract notion of the public interest or the interests of the state,[5] or to the people. The UK has never had a constitutional settlement under which the people delegated their sovereignty to the government, to be exercised in the service of the people and for no other purpose. Nationals of the UK are subjects of the Crown, not citizens of the state. Indeed, the constitution of the UK has no such formal entity or legal concept as the state. The legal status of citizenship, to the extent that it exists, is concerned almost exclusively with immigration and residence rights.[6]

Consequently, the concept of public service is equally undeveloped in the UK.[7] Civil servants are, in legal terms, Crown servants, holding office at the pleasure of, and dismissable at will by, the Crown. The Civil Service Code,[8] the Establishment Officers Guide, the Armstrong Memorandum on the Duties of Civil Servants[9] and the Osmotherly Rules on the Conduct of Civil Servants appearing before Select Committees,[10] all make it abundantly clear that the civil servant's primary and overwhelming duty is to his or her minister as the holder by constitutional convention of the powers of the Crown. The criminal law makes it clear that the civil servant cannot appeal to a concept of acting in the interest of the state or of the public in order to excuse or justify conduct contrary to the civil servant's duty to the minister.[11]

---

4   See *Questions of Procedure for Ministers*, London: Cabinet Office, 1992 (revised 1994 and 1996). See also *Departmental Evidence and Response to Select Committees*, London: Cabinet Office, 1994. (Also known as the Osmotherly Rules).

5   The Official Secrets Act 1911, s. 2 provided that it was an offence to disclose official information to a person other than a person to whom it was in the interest of the state to disclose it. In the prosecution of Clive Ponting, the civil servant who disclosed information about the sinking of the Argentinian warship *Belgrano* to a member of Parliament, the trial judge in his summing up and in his rulings during the trial, indicated that the public interest was synonymous with the interest of the government of the day. See Ponting, C., *The Right to Know*, London: Sphere Books, 1985, pp. 183–94.

6   See the British Nationality Act 1981 and the Immigration Acts 1971 and 1988.

7   For a comparative study of the concepts of public service in European Community/Union countries, see Grard and Vandamme (eds), *Le Service Public Européen*, Brussels: Trans European Policy Studies Association 1995.

8   The Civil Service Code, Hansard HL Deb, 30 October 1995, coll. 146–8, para. 2.

9   *Armstrong Memorandum: The Duties and Responsibilities of Civil Servants in relation to Ministers, 1987/1993–94*, note by the then Head of the Civil Service, Sir Robert Armstrong, Hansard HC Deb, 2 December 1987 and revised HC 27–II, 1993–4.

10 *Departmental Evidence and Response to Select Committees*, London: Cabinet Office, 1994, paras. 38–41.

11 *Chandler* v *DPP* [1964] AC 763; *R* v *Ponting* [1985] Crim LR 318.

Recently, however, certain fundamental changes to the structure of government and the Civil Service, to the ways in which public services are delivered to the public and to the mechanisms of accountability of those serving the public have brought about significant change to the notion of public service. The hiving-off of executive agencies under the 'Next Steps' programme,[12] the creation of hospital trusts and general practitioners' fund-holding budgets under the National Health Service,[13] the creation of the Citizen's Charter,[14] the publication of information about the performance of public service providers,[15] the application of internal market discipline within the public service[16] and the contracting out,[17] through competitive tendering, of the delivery of many public services, have all been intended by the government to create greater accountability to the public *qua* consumers of public services and to the taxpayer as ultimate paymaster for such services.

Efficiency, effectiveness and accountability have been the key motivating forces behind these fundamental reforms. Value for money has been the overriding consideration for the government concerned to reduce the level of public expenditure. Mechanisms have been established or enhanced to ensure closer financial scrutiny of public service providers to Parliament.[18] Financial management systems have been initiated to ensure greater efficiency and effectiveness in securing policy objectives and meeting implementation targets.[19] These reforms have yet to be fully effective, but it is clear that they have wrought a sea-change in attitudes to, and the concept of, public service in the UK.

Ironically, these changes in the notion of public service at the sharp end of provision have not been matched by any comparable revolution in the attitudes of the top echelons of the Civil Service responsible for policy formulation and advice, nor in the position of ministers. The traditional doctrines of Civil Service loyalty to the minister of the day and the accountability of ministers to Parliament remain

---

12 *Improving Management in Government: the Next Steps*, London: Cabinet Office, 1988.
13 Department of Health, *Working for Patients*, London: HMSO, 1989; Department of Health, *Funding and Contracts for Hospital Services*, London: HMSO, 1989; Department of Health, *Contracts for Health Services: Operational Principles*, London: HMSO, 1990.
14 *The Citizen's Charter: Raising the Standard*, CM 1599, London: HMSO, 1991. For analysis of the Charter, see Barron and Scott, 'The Citizen's Charter Programme' (1992) 55 *Modern Law Review* 526; Drewry, G., 'Mr Major's Charter: Empowering the Customer' [1993] *Public Law* 248.
15 See, for example, *The Citizen's Charter (supra)*, pp. 13 and 14, 'A Charter for Parents', and pp. 10–12, 'A Charter for Patients'.
16 See, for example, *Next Steps Review*, Cm 2430, London: HMSO, 1993. See also Lewis, N., *Choice and the Legal Order: Rising above Politics*, London: Butterworths, 1996, Ch. 7.
17 See generally, Harden, I., *The Contracting State*, Milton Keynes: Open University Press, 1992. See also, *Competing for Quality: Buying Better Public Services*, London: HMSO, Cm 1730, 1991.
18 The National Audit Act 1983; see McEldowney, J. F., 'The Control of Public Expenditure', in Jowell, J., and Oliver, D., (eds), *The Changing Constitution* (3rd ed.), Oxford: Oxford University Press, 1994, Ch. 7.
19 See McDonald, *op. cit.* note 1, Ch. 1.

unchanged at the pyramid of United Kingdom government.[20] There is a danger that real political responsibility and accountability to the public through its representatives will fall into this gap between traditional doctrine and the practical realities of the modern structure of government. If the delivery of public services and the implementation of policy are no longer the responsibility of central government departments led or at least headed by elected government ministers but have been 'farmed out' in one form or another, by one method or another, to non elected, appointed bodies, there will be little or nothing for political responsibility or accountability to bite on. What will become much more important will be the systems of direct accountability and responsibility of public service providers, to their consumers, for public service delivery.

The purpose of the first part of this chapter is to chart these changes in the structure of government and in the institutions and systems by which public services are delivered, to examine the changed notions and means of accountability and responsibility for the delivery of services, and to determine whether and to what extent it is accurate to say that the UK has developed a new and distinctive concept of public service.

The historical tradition

As every schoolchild still learns, the Norman conquest of England in 1066 led to a fundamental legal and political revolution — the ownership of all land was vested in the King, hence, under the feudal system, all executive, legislative and judicial power was vested in the King. Although the feudal aristocracy exercised some seignorial and manorial judicial powers, these were soon reclaimed by the Crown through the creation of a central judiciary and the common law. Authority flowed down the pyramid, not upwards.

Despite the gradual democratisation of the British constitution in the centuries that followed, through the creation of Parliament and its eventual legislative supremacy, the monarch retained very extensive and substantial executive powers under the royal prerogative:[21] the power to conduct foreign relations, including the power to conclude treaties with foreign states; the power and duty to defend the realm, including the exclusive power to declare and to conduct war (together with the necessary powers ancillary to war such as conscription, requisition of property, imposition of restrictions on trade and the movement of persons) and to determine the numbers, armaments, equipment and disposition of the armed forces; the power to appoint and dismiss ministers, including the Prime Minister, and therefore to

---

20   See Oliver and Drewry, *op. cit.* note 2, Ch. 1. See also Turpin, C., 'Ministerial Responsibility', in Jowell and Oliver, *op. cit.* note 18, Ch. 5.

21   See generally Bradley, A. and Ewing, K. (eds), *Wade and Bradley, Constitutional and Administrative Law* (12th ed.), Harlow: Addison Wesley Longman, 1997, Ch. 12.

determine who shall form the government; the politically crucial power of prorogation and dissolution of Parliament; the power and duty to maintain public order through the King's peace; the power to maintain the security of the state against sedition, sabotage and espionage by both domestic and foreign enemies; the power to administer justice and to that end to appoint judges; the power to appoint, to determine and alter at will the terms of appointment of, and to dismiss at pleasure, Crown servants, i.e. the permanent Civil Service; the power to pardon criminals and to commute sentences imposed by the courts; the power to issue or to withhold passports to or from subjects; the power to make *ex gratia* compensation payments; the power to grant or withhold Royal Assent to Bills passed by Parliament, thereby giving them the status of Acts of Parliament; all these and more fell within the royal prerogative. Furthermore, since the King could issue orders in Council under the royal prerogative, without Parliamentary authority or approval, the King and his ministers had a source of legislative power independent of, though not superior to, Parliament.

The exercise of these extraordinary powers, being prerogative, (see Pollard, Ch. 13 generally) required no sanction or consent from Parliament or any other body; and until the extension of the franchise in the 19th century, the Crown was not, except in the most negligible sense, accountable or responsible to Parliament for the exercise of these powers. Nor, until 1984, was the exercise of the prerogative subject to judicial control, though its existence and extent were determined by law and hence justiciable in the courts.

Even after Parliament seized the constitutional high ground of control over taxing, spending and legislative powers in the Glorious Revolution and the Bill of Rights 1689, this control was and remains negative and reactive, in the sense that the executive government, i.e. the Crown's ministers, initiates proposals and Parliament's power lies in its right to approve or reject the government's proposals. So over a very wide range of important areas of government, the Crown and its ministers continued to exercise dominant, or in some cases exclusive, power.

Modern times: the unaccountable administrative state

In addition to the extraordinary powers historically retained by the executive, the modern administrative state has necessitated the conferral upon ministers, by statute, of very wide discretionary powers, to take action or to confirm action taken by others, which in the 19th century would have been carried out by legislation, e.g. the compulsory acquisition of land for housing, roads and other major public works. Similarly, Parliament has delegated to ministers by statute extensive legislative powers to implement the policy objectives of the enabling statute through statutory instruments, regulations, orders and rules, not all of which are subject to any form of Parliamentary scrutiny and control, which may vary from apparent and negligible to real and absolute. Ministers may also, in the exercise of their numerous statutory and prerogative powers choose to 'legislate' by circulars, codes of practice, administrative rules, official guidelines and other types of informal 'quasi-legislation'[22] of varying degrees of enforceability, in many, if not most, cases without any parliamentary scrutiny or control, real or apparent.

The Emperor's clothes: ministerial accountability and responsibility

The justification given for conferring such extensive powers upon government ministers is that old constitutional sacred cow, the convention of collective and individual ministerial responsibility to Parliament. According to this convention, a minister is *accountable* to the House of Commons for everything done by his or her department or its civil servants, whether he or she authorised or knew about it or not. He or she is *responsible* only for those actions or policies which he or she personally authorises or knows about, or could reasonably be expected to have known about.[23] A minister is also responsible for his or her own personal indiscretions or misbehaviour while he or she is in office. Being accountable means that the minister must inform the House what has taken place, what steps he or she has taken to rectify matters and to ensure that there is no recurrence of the conduct complained of, who, if anybody, is to blame and whose head, if anybody's, is going to roll. Being responsible means that the minister concerned should resign, but such resignations are rare,[24] even where it is apparent that a minister's policy has failed, that his or her decision was erroneous, or that his or her conduct was reprehensible. Resignation is in theory necessary where a minister has lost the confidence of the House of Commons, but in reality this also will rarely occur, because the minister can rely upon the convention of collective ministerial responsibility to ensure the support of his or her ministerial colleagues, and upon party loyalty via the whips system and the influence of party patronage to ensure the support of his or her own party's back-bench members of Parliament. Since the government by convention must command the support of a majority in the Commons, a minister is secure as

---

22 Ganz, G., *Quasi-legislation: Recent Developments in Secondary Legislation*, London: Sweet & Maxwell, 1987.

23 The origin of the modern rule is said to be found in the statement to the House of Commons by the then Home Secretary, Sir David Maxwell Fyfe, concerning the Crichel Down affair, see 530 HC Deb 5th ser., col. 1285, 20 July 1954. See Wilson, G., *Cases and Materials on Constitutional and Administrative Law* (1st ed.), Cambridge: Cambridge University Press, 1966, pp. 64–73. Following the report of Sir Richard Scott, *Report of the Inquiry into the Export of Defence Equipment and Dual-Use Goods to Iraq and Related Prosecutions*, HC 115, London: HMSO, 1996, in particular its concerns with ministerial accountability and responsibility, the Select Committee on the Public Service set up an inquiry into the issue, reporting in July 1996: see Public Service Committee, 2nd Report 1995–96, *Ministerial Accountability and Responsibility*, HC 313. See also Oliver and Drewry, *op.cit.* note 2, Ch. 1.

24 See Finer, S. E., 'The Individual Responsibility of Ministers' (1956) 34 *Public Administration* 377, the seminal work on this subject. See also Bradley and Ewing, *op. cit.* note 21, Ch. 7.

long as he or she enjoys the backing of his or her own party. It is loss of this backing, through fear of the political damage to the government's electoral prospects which may flow from continuing to back a failed minister, which leads to ministerial resignations, not the formal loss of confidence of the House of Commons. To a considerable extent, the convention of collective ministerial responsibility cancels out the convention of individual ministerial responsibility (see Radford, Ch. 2 generally).

Secret government

Another factor which enables governments in the UK to avoid responsibility and even accountability is the excessive secrecy which shrouds much of the activities of government.[25] Despite a number of recent reforms,[26] the basic position at law is that all official information is secret, i.e. that disclosure will constitute a breach of the criminal law, or the civil law or the Civil Service Code (or all three) unless it has been authorised by a person with the power to do so (usually a minister but in some cases a senior civil servant).

The Official Secrets Act 1989 restricted the scope of the criminal law to a limited range of sensitive information concerning defence, intelligence, international relations, information received in confidence from foreign governments or international organisations, criminal intelligence information and information obtained by the interception of communications. But this long overdue reform of the discredited Official Secrets Act 1911, s. 2 did not make any more government information publicly available.

While criminal sanctions apply after the event and so do not always prevent publication by deterrence, the civil or private law of confidence has the advantage that it operates prospectively so as to prevent publication by court order in the form of the interlocutory injunction, which can be obtained at very short notice and at great speed and which applies' to the world at large, thus warning off any alternative publishers who might feel tempted to print the information in place of the publisher subject to the injunction. Equally, the law of confidence provides for recovery of profits obtained by the publisher in consequence of his publication. This is likely to deter all but the most idealistic of publishers.

The Civil Service Code continues to make it clear that civil servants are bound by the obligation of confidentiality,[27] and that breach of the code can lead to disciplinary sanctions, including dismissal, demotion or reprimand or in the case of retired civil servants, loss of pension rights.

---

25   See Austin, R., 'Freedom of Information: the Constitutional Impact', in Jowell and Oliver, *op. cit.* note 18, Ch. 14.

26   Official Secrets Act 1989; *Open Government*, CM 2290, London: HMSO, 1993 (Code of Practice on Access to Government Information).

27   Civil Service Code, *op. cit.* note 8, para. 10.

In short, government retains the legal powers to determine the extent of its own accountability by reserving to itself the discretion to disclose or keep secret all official information. In recent years central government has sought to use those powers extensively on numerous occasions to maintain secrecy and avoid real accountability and responsibility. At the same time it has imposed on local government, the National Health Service and other semi-autonomous or subordinate governmental bodies obligations of public disclosure which it has been unwilling to accept itself. Most recently it has publicly espoused the doctrine of transparency in government, but the credibility of its commitment to that principle has been severely undermined by the weaknesses of the government's own 1993 White Paper, *Open Government*,[28] together with the inadequate implementation and fulfilment of the right to governmental information promised in that document.

The top-down, centralised, authoritarian state

Thus, despite the apparent trappings of a modern democracy in the UK, real power continues to flow from the top of the pyramid to its base. This authoritarian structure was for most of this century made tolerable by a political culture in which governments sought to achieve consensus between the major political and economic power centres within the UK. In recent times, however, the central government has rejected that political culture and seized greater power by diminishing the power of other authorities such as local government, and the influence of other public institutions such as the universities, the trade unions, the professional bodies and other major representative or issue pressure groups.

In some cases the central government has simply abolished those authorities which opposed or obstructed its policies[29] In others it has used its immense financial powers and resources to control public authorities through the limitation of public expenditure, the reduction or removal of various grants, the capping of local taxing powers,[30] the privatisation of large areas of the public sector,[31] the hiving-off of executive agencies and the imposition of contracting out and the internal market. Through the funding agencies it has imposed control over universities as to the numbers of students to be admitted and to which degree courses. It has imposed strict academic audit and teaching quality assessment

---

28 See note 26.
29 For example, the abolition of the metropolitan counties and the Greater London Council by the Local Government Act 1985. See Loughlin, M., 'The Restructuring of Central-Local Government Relations', in Jowell and Oliver, *op. cit.* note 18, Ch. 10.
30 Loughlin, *op.cit* note 29.
31 See Prosser, T., *The Privatisation of Public Enterprises in France and Great Britain*, Florence: European University Institute, Working Paper No. 88/364, 1988; Graham, C., and Prosser, T., 'Rolling Back the Frontiers? The Privatisation of State Enterprises', in Graham, C., and Prosser, T., *Waiving the Rules*, Milton Keynes: Open University Press, 1988, Ch. 5.

requirements on the universities and publicly ranked them in order of performance. Even research is now heavily influenced by government requirements for the research assessment (formerly selectivity) exercise (the RAE), in which universities must participate if they want a slice of the pie of public money to be paid out by the various research councils. Research ratings are published, universities are ranked, and research funds are allocated to universities from the public purse according to their performance in the ratings.

Trades unions have been subjected to a series of statutory legal restrictions which has broken the power of the unions and employees and shifted the balance firmly in favour of the employer.[32] Trade union immunity in tort for actions taken in pursuance or contemplation of a trade dispute has been so restricted that it has become extremely difficult for a union to take industrial action and remain within the law.[33] The employer has been armed with one of the most lethal weapons in the legal armoury, the injunction, breach of which will lead to crippling fines for contempt of court and sequestration of the union's assets to pay for the fines and any damages and costs awarded to the employer against the union. Public sector unions have had their pay bargaining structures and arrangements swept away, and the government simply decides and announces, without consultation, the level of remuneration for teachers, nurses and other public sector workers. Even where independent machinery has been set up to make recommendations concerning the pay of a particular group of workers within the public sector, the government as often as not will not follow the recommendations of the body concerned, either by awarding less than recommended, or by deferring or phasing payment. Wages councils, which had responsibility for monitoring the pay of the low-paid, have been abolished, enabling employers to reduce wages for the lowest paid sectors of the economy.

Public order law has been drastically revised twice[34] in response to inner city race riots, violence during industrial disputes, violence during public demonstrations against government policy, obstruction of government or public authorities by demonstrators occupying property in protest against proposed road construction, nuclear missile sites, nuclear waste sites, etc., and generally disruptive activities and groups such as New Age travellers, animal welfare protesters and hunt saboteurs. As a consequence of those new statutory provisions, it is now almost impossible to organise or hold a lawful public demonstration without the consent of the police, who can impose highly restrictive conditions on the size, location, time and duration of the proposed demonstration, or seek an order banning it.[35]

---

32   See Ewing, K., 'Trade Unions and the Constitution: the Impact of the New Conservatives', in Graham and Prosser, *op. cit.* note 31, Ch. 8.
33   Trade Union and Labour Relations (Consolidation) Act 1992, s. 220.
34   Public Order Act 1986; Criminal Justice and Public Order Act 1994.
35   Public Order Act 1986, ss. 11–14; Criminal Justice and Public Order Act 1994, ss. 68–71.

Over the past 15 years, then, the UK has seen a transformation in the nature of central government. It has ceased to work by consensus and instead has sought to impose its policies and its will on all other public authorities and institutions by every means available to it. A population either encouraged by the prospect of material benefit in the 1980s or cowed by fear of the consequences of recession in the 1990s, has up until now been willing to accept, or at least not effectively to oppose, the government's measures, with the exception of the community charge (the infamous poll tax). The government has effectively extinguished or rendered impotent all potential opposition to its policies, and in so doing has created an even more highly centralised and authoritarian state, in which power flows down from the top. The Cabinet and in particular the Prime Minister, have become even more powerful, to the point where the UK has moved much closer to a presidential style of government, though retaining the trappings of the parliamentary system. Despite the election in May 1997 of a new Labour government, after 18 years of successive Conservative governments, few if any of these changes are likely to be reversed. This, then is the context in which has occurred the extraordinary transformation of the structures and the processes of public service which is examined in the following section.

THE REVOLUTION OF THE RIGHT: THE CREATION OF THE CITIZEN/CONSUMER, THE PRIVATISATION OF THE STATE AND THE IMPOSITION OF THE MARKET ON THE PROVISION OF PUBLIC SERVICES

Introduction: the ideological programme of economic liberalism[36]

Paradoxically, at exactly the same time as it became more centralised and authoritarian, the previous government sought to reduce the role of the state and the public sector generally, and to that end has adopted measures to promote and increase the role of the individual citizen in the running of his or her own economic life. By reducing the role of the state and by reducing direct taxes on income, the government sought to encourage not only the creation of wealth but also the enlargement of the role of the citizen and the empowerment of the citizen, *qua* consumer of services. With more of their income in their own hands, and with many public services either privatised, contracted out or subjected to the competition of the internal market, citizens can make their own choices and purchase more of their public services from their own resources.

The discipline of the competitive marketplace should ensure that the providers of public services will deliver a better service or lose the trade to a more

---

36 See Oliver and Drewry, *op. cit.* note 2, Ch. 2, for analysis of the ideological underpinning of the reforms to the public service.

competitive provider who is willing and able to deliver the service desired by the citizen/consumer at the price he or she is willing to pay. In order for the citizen to be so empowered, he or she must be informed about the quality of the service which is being provided by the public service providers. To that end, the previous government sought to establish measurable, qualitative and quantitative standards of public service provision, combined with obligations to publish performance data and records. Equally, where the public service provider, whether privatised, contracted out or remaining in the public sector, has a monopoly in the sense that the citizen/consumer has no choice of provider, the government sought to enforce the obligations of quality service provision via the Citizen's Charter, under which failure to meet the standards of service set entitles the citizen to some redress, usually of a financial, compensatory nature, such as a refund or an extension of existing service entitlements, e.g. the public transport passenger's season ticket, or simply the payment of some monetary sum as compensation for the failure. In the case of the privatised natural monopoly public utilities, the government sought to rectify the inevitable absence of competitive pressures to provide quality service at the best price by creating regulatory authorities to achieve the same result. This admixture of the public and private sectors in British government has added a new dimension to the concept of public service in the UK.

The transformation of the state

The new public management: the first steps
After initially seeking and eventually achieving a massive overall reduction in the number of civil servants in central government (from approximately 750,000 to 565,000) the Thatcher government sought not merely the consequent public expenditure savings but also to improve efficiency and effectiveness by improvements in management. To that end a number of management innovations were introduced to ensure better value for money, to improve information systems and to measure performance in the achievement of defined objectives.[37]

The first of these innovations was the Rayner efficiency reviews or scrutinies, which analysed the function costs of implementing particular government policies or programmes with a view to making savings or improving efficiency. Every department was subjected to review via a number of scrutinies of various aspects of its administrative responsibilities. Over a four-year period, over 150 scrutinies were carried out in a series of five review programmes, achieving efficiency savings in excess of £50m per annum, about 50 per cent of the figure for savings identified by the reviews. But the Rayner efficiency programme sought to achieve efficiencies within the existing structure and operation of the government system, and did not attempt to make radical changes in the way government operated and

---

37   See McDonald, *op. cit.* note 1, Ch. 1.

was structured. Many of the scrutiny recommendations were not implemented because of actual or potential political difficulties or because of the internal opposition from civil servants with entrenched positions and vested interests. Rayner did not fundamentally change the ethos of the government machine.

What followed Rayner, however, eventually did lead to quite revolutionary change in the structures and functioning of government. Initially developed in 1979 by the then Secretary of State for the Environment, the Management Information System for Ministers (MINIS) armed ministers and top civil servants with detailed knowledge of what their departments were doing. When combined with a management accounting system, known as the MAXIS or Joubert system, MINIS became the Financial Management Initiative (FMI),[38] strongly backed by the Treasury and the Management and Personnel Office (which replaced the Civil Service Department, abolished by Margaret Thatcher in 1981). The aim of this programme was to map the allocation of and identify responsibilities for particular financial management tasks within departments, and then to require line managers to carry out those operational tasks and responsibilities allocated to them by senior management, who in turn could then concentrate on defining departmental goals and policies. In other words, a clear division was being made between policy and operational functions, a division which was to become of even greater significance at a later stage in the transformation of government, the Next Steps initiative.[39]

The Next Steps Agencies

Shortcomings in the implementation and operation of the FMI, caused by lack of line manager control over budgets and by over-emphasis on value for money rather than effectiveness, led to the belief that greater autonomy was needed if operational functions were to be carried out effectively.[40] Accordingly, it was decided to create executive agencies which would operate with a much greater degree of autonomy than hitherto, with responsibility for discrete functions and for the management of their own staff and budgets, hived off from their parent departments yet still linked by the umbilical cord of ultimate responsibility to the departmental minister and by the drip-feed of finance to the Treasury.[41] The core departmental function would in future be the development of policy, while executive agencies would have the task of implementing or administering those policies on the ground. Framework documents setting up the agencies would indicate their primary functions and duties, together with their performance targets and the systems for monitoring performance. The documents also set out the division of responsibilities between ministers and the agencies.[42]

---

38   *The Financial Management Initiative*, Cmnd 8616, London: HMSO, 1982.
39   Cabinet Office, *Improving Management in Government: The Next Steps*, 1988.
40   McDonald, *op. cit.* note 1, Chs 1 and 2.
41   *The Financing and Accountability of Next Steps Agencies*, Cm 914, London: HMSO, 1989.
42   See Drewry, G., 'Revolution in Whitehall: The Next Steps and Beyond', in Jowell and Oliver, *op. cit.* note 18, Ch. 6.

The perceived advantages of the Next Steps development are twofold. First, the executive agency is free to operate on its own initiative to achieve the maximum or optimal performance on efficiency and effectiveness targets without the dead hand of excessively detailed departmental, parliamentary, ministerial or Treasury scrutiny and control. These same justifications were given for the autonomous public corporation status of the former nationalised industries, but in reality, because of their need for government subsidy for loss-making industries, very considerable Treasury and ministerial control was exercised over those bodies which were central to the government's anti-inflation and wage control policies during the 1960s and 1970s.[43] Since the new executive agencies are heavily dependent on Treasury support and subject to substantial ministerial control, their autonomy may be more apparent than real. It is not as yet clear exactly how far in practice agencies will be able to pursue their performance goals of economic efficiency and effectiveness without some level of interference from ministers and the Treasury.[44]

The second advantage is that ministers, while retaining a reasonable degree of control over executive agencies, will nonetheless be able to shrug off political responsibility by categorising as operational all issues for which they do not wish to bear that responsibility. While this will enable the minister to escape political flak when things go wrong, it is equally clear that the old notion of civil servants' anonymity and lack of political responsibility does not apply to the chief executives of the new executive agencies, who have to appear before select committees to answer questions about their agency's operational performance.[45] This may attract considerable adverse publicity (as was the case with the Child Support Agency and the Prisons Agency), which may eventually lead to a minister's replacing the Chief Executive of an agency. Thus the minister, while retaining overall political responsibility, has been able to pass the buck of operational responsibility to the executive agencies.

The Next Steps programme thus has considerable advantages for ministers; in ideological terms the state machine can be made to function more effectively and efficiently, while at the same time costing the taxpayer less, by bringing in to the public service the cost-conscious and profit-motivated ethos of the private sector, through recruitment of highly-paid former private sector management personnel

---

43   See Foulkes, D., *Administrative Law* (8th ed.), London: Butterworths, 1995, Ch. 2.

44   See Lewis, D., *On the Ropes*, London: British Broadcasting Corporation, 23 May 1996 (radio broadcast tape), for a trenchant account of ministerial interference in the day-to-day running of an executive agency, the Prison Service.

45   *The Financing and Accountability of Next Steps Agencies*, Cm 914, 1989. Several Select Committees have investigated Next Steps agencies, including the Child Support Agency — see Select Committee of the Parliamentary Commissioner for Administration, Third Report (1994–95), *Investigation of Complaints against the Child Support Agency*, HC 135 and *The Child Support Agency*, HC 199.

and the adoption of private sector management practices. In political terms the minister can be isolated from and insulated against accountability for the day-to-day implementation and administration of policy. Failures on the ground will not be laid at his door. In parliamentary terms far less of the government machine will be accountable to the daily scrutiny of the elected legislature, but will instead have to answer to the bottom line of economic efficiency and effectiveness, from time to time before a Select Committee and on a regular and continuing basis to the Treasury.[46]

The new audit regime[47]

Whereas hitherto the Comptroller and Auditor-General had effectively been an in-house Treasury auditor, checking only whether public expenditure was legally authorised, the National Audit Act 1983 transformed his status to that of an officer of the House of Commons,[48] appointed by the Prime Minister with the agreement of the Chairman of the Public Accounts Select Committee.[49] The Comptroller's major function under the Act is to conduct economy, efficiency and effectiveness examinations, better known as 'value for money' audits, with full power to compel production of testimony and documents.[50] His audit powers extend, in addition to central government departments and other public bodies specified as subject to his jurisdiction, to any authority or body receiving more than half of its income from public funds.[51] The Comptroller has thus taken on the task of pursuing greater efficiency in the public service that the Rayner reviews failed to complete. His reports have routinely criticised the waste of public money in the last decade, and departments are far more concerned about an investigation by the Comptroller than about normal parliamentary scrutiny. The Comptroller reports to the Public Accounts Committee and is required to take into consideration any proposals made to him by that committee in deciding whether to conduct an economy, efficiency and effectiveness examination.[52] Audit has become a major weapon in the government's ideological campaign to reduce the level of public expenditure by gains in efficiency.

Privatisation and regulation

The flagship of the previous government's ideological programme of 'rolling back the frontiers of the State' over the past 18 years was the privatisation of

---

46   The government is keeping the Next Steps initiative under constant scrutiny and publishes annual
     reviews: see *Next Steps Review* 1993, Cm 2430; 1994, Cm 2750; 1995, Cm 3164, London: HMSO.
47   See McEldowney, *op. cit.* note 18.
48   National Audit Act 1983, s. 1(2).
49   *Ibid.*, s. 1(3).
50   *Ibid.*, s. 8.
51   *Ibid.*, s. 7.
52   *Ibid.*, ss. 6 and 7.

nationalised industries and public utilities.[53] Thus the steel industry, the coal industry, motor vehicle manufacturing, the gas and electricity supply utilities, the water and sewerage utilities, the public transport and telecommunications providers and much else, have all been privatised by the sale of shares in public limited companies quoted on the Stock Exchange, for all to buy on the open market. But many of these industries, utilities and public service providers enjoyed a statutory monopoly. Equally, in some cases the wasteful duplication of high-cost supply or carrier network dictated national or local monopolies, as in gas, electricity, water and the recently privatised railways industry. Privatisation could not therefore of itself bring to these industries the claimed benefits of competition, such as better services at lower prices to the consumer. Hence regulatory agencies have been created to ensure that the privatised industries provide services efficiently, effectively and at appropriate cost to the consumer. Telecommunications, water supply and treatment, electricity and gas supply, and rail franchising all have regulatory authorities determining prices, standards and conditions of service. These new agencies and their activities are a further facet of the changing face of government and public service in the UK. The *raison d'être* of these regulators is to compel privatised industries to provide quality services at reasonable prices, in an unorthodox new combination of the public and private sectors.

Consumer choice and public information
A major component of the previous government's ideology over the past 18 years was public choice theory,[54] the translation of free market consumer choice from the private sector into the public sector. But free markets depend on perfect information for perfect operation, so the consumer must have access to the maximum possible information about the competing products. Thus in reality most private sector markets are regulated by information publication requirements to enable the consumer to make an informed choice. So too in the public sector, the application of public choice theory has necessitated the imposition on public service providers of duties to publish information about their performance standards in the provision of those services. This represents a fundamental break from the British tradition of state paternalism, captured by the expression 'Nanny knows best', which has in the past meant that government and public service providers decided what was best for the citizen and therefore how much, or more accurately how little, the citizen needed to know about the service being provided. This new doctrine of public choice requires the citizen *qua* consumer of public services to take the decisions hitherto taken by government and public service providers, decisions which cannot be taken without the maximum possible information about those services and their provision.

---

53   See note 31.
54   See Lewis, N., *Choice and the Legal Order: Rising above Politics*, London: Butterworths, 1996;
      Oliver and Drewry, *op. cit.* note 2, Ch. 2.

Thus schools have been required to publish the results of their pupils in public examinations, and these have then been published as a league table of performance, with every school ranked in order of success. Although a crude measure of performance — first because it fails to measure the quality of the input, only the quality of the output, and second because examinations are only one measure of performance (there may be and are many other aspects of education which are not examined by formal state examinations in a limited range of subjects) — such information gives to parents, as the consumers of the education service, some basis for comparison of available schools within their area and for making choices of schools for their children, in addition to the traditional means of visiting the school, inspecting the classrooms and other facilities, talking to teachers and talking to parents of existing pupils at the schools. While one may cavil at the lack of sophistication in the league tables, it is difficult to argue against the principle of informing prospective and existing recipients of the education service of the performance of the schools of which they have a choice, so as to ensure that that choice is as informed as possible. Since the league tables include the results of the private sector, fee-paying schools, they enable comparison with competition from outside the state system, though for most parents the comparison is hypothetical since they cannot afford the cost of private education.

Similarly, hospital trusts, as part of the arrangements to establish the internal market in the National Health Service (see below), are now being required to publish information on clinical performance, including such sensitive material as death rates. Again, this can be an extremely crude and misleading guide to performance because it fails to take into account the particular hospital's patient catchment area, which may have a high proportion of elderly, socially and economically disadvantaged patients living in substandard accommodation. Clearly, such a hospital is likely to have a much higher death rate than one whose catchment area population is younger, socially and economically better off and living in higher standard housing. Output statistics alone are likely to be misleading unless measured against input statistics indicating the impact of such factors. But even if the operation of the principle of publication can legitimately be criticised, it is difficult to oppose the principle of informed patient choice. Of course, in reality that choice is much more likely to be exercised by the patient's doctor, the general practitioner, who as part of a fund-holding practice may seek to maximise the resources available to the practice by choosing the hospital trust able to provide the least expensive treatment. To the extent, however, that a fund-holding doctor's choice of hospital is based on patient welfare and securing the best possible treatment for his or her patients, full and accurate information about the hospital's clinical performance is obviously of crucial relevance. Furthermore, some patients do take considerable interest in the type of treatment offered by particular hospitals, for example in obstetrics where women have to a considerable extent rebelled against 'high-tech', interventionist medical practice in favour of natural child-birth whenever possible. To patients sympathetic to that approach, information about the obstetric medical practices followed by a particular hospital, e.g., the percentage of epidural anaesthetics administered or caesarian sections performed, will be crucial to their choice of hospital in which to receive such treatment. Without that information, patients may find themselves receiving treatment which they would have preferred not to have (see Mulcahy and Allsop, Ch. 5 generally).

The publication of information by public service providers therefore became a key feature of the previous government's public choice ideology, reinforced and given even greater emphasis in the Citizen's Charter, the Open Government White Paper and the Code of Practice on Access to Government Information.

Increased competition

One of the identifying features of the previous government's ideological package was the belief that key aspects of the private sector free market can be adopted even in those areas of the public sector which are not privatised. The idea was thus to seek to increase the opportunities for competition and thereby increase competitiveness, efficiency and effectiveness in the delivery of public services. In the National Health Service, for example, institutional changes were adopted such as creating hospital trusts and general practice fund-holders, in order to apply the internal market under which hospitals have to compete for the available patients by ensuring that their costs are competitive. General practice fund-holders will not wish to exhaust their funds by paying for operations at hospital A which cost more than the same operation at hospital B. Thus they will choose hospital B, which will consequently receive more of the available resources and be able to expand and provide more and better services. Hospital A will not prosper in this manner unless it reduces its costs by becoming more efficient and thus more competitive.

The new Labour government has indicated that the internal market in the NHS is likely to be abolished, but not the remainder of the NHS reforms. General practice fundholding will be retained, but hospitals will no longer give priority to patients from fundholder practices. This means that in practice there will be greater emphasis on price competition for patients, rather than jumping waiting lists. It is difficult to see how this constitutes abolition of the internal market.

Contracting out services

Similarly, in many areas, increased competitiveness has been sought through the media of contracting out and competitive tendering of specific and discrete functions.[55] Thus refuse collection, public housing repairs and maintenance, individual building projects, road repairs, highway construction, prisons, and a vast

---

55   See Harden, *op. cit.* note 17. See also Wood, 'Privatisation: Local Government and the Health Service', in Graham and Prosser, *op. cit.* note 31.

array of other public service functions have been contracted out to the private sector in recent years. This alternative to full privatisation was seen by government as an effective means of bringing to the public sector the benefits of the free market operating in the private sector.[56]

The practice of contracting out has been a mixed success, with some anecdotal evidence of contractors' cartels corrupting the tendering process by agreeing identical or similar bids, or by allocating tenders amongst, and agreeing not to bid against, fellow cartel members. They are then able to inflate their bids, having destroyed the element of competition which is the purpose of contracting out. Some local authority direct labour organisations have proved to be highly effective in tendering for the work, possibly because of their familiarity with the standards and specifications of work required in the public sector. Equally, the costs to the public authorities concerned in preparing the tender documents, considering and choosing between the competing bids, and drafting and agreeing contracts for the work, may well have eliminated any savings which may have been gained by contracting out. On the other hand, there is some evidence to suggest that savings can be made through contracting out and the practice is widespread for certain functions, for example refuse collection, road repairs, highway construction, parks maintenance and public housing construction.

These various means of increasing competitiveness are major features of the centre-piece of the previous government's policies on improving public services, the Citizen's Charter.

The Citizen's Charter[57]

Launched in 1991 as the flagship of the then Prime Minister's government, the Citizen's Charter has been subjected to ridicule and derision in the popular press, but respected political, constitutional and legal commentators have taken the Charter rather more seriously.[58] Combined with the numerous other changes in the structures and processes of the state described above, the Citizen's Charter represents the culmination of the process of transforming the state and its relationship with its citizens more radically than any other change since the post-war creation of the Welfare State. It was intended to build on the Next Steps initiative, in the sense that whereas Next Steps created the management structure for the delivery of public services, the Charter defines the expected output

---

56 The government has put the continued contracting out of public services on a statutory basis in the Deregulation and Contracting Out Act 1994.

57 *The Citizen's Charter: Raising the Standard*, Cm 1599, London: HMSO, 1991.

58 See Barron and Scott, *op. cit.* note 14; Drewry, *op. cit.* note 14; Lewis, N., 'The Citizen's Charter and Next Steps: A New Way of Governing' (1993) 64 *Political Quarterly* 316; Cooper, D., 'The Citizen's Charter and Radical Democracy: Empowerment and Exclusion within Citizenship Discourse' (1993) 2 *Social and Legal Studies* 149; Tritter, J., 'The Citizen's Charter: Opportunities for Users' Perspectives?' (1994) 65 *Political Quarterly* 397.

performance of that reformed structure. Output performance is defined by the following 'Principles of Public Service':[59]

(a) *The setting and improvement of standards* Public service providers must establish and publish explicit standards of service in clear language, which they must maintain. These standards should be prominently displayed at the point of delivery of the service, and should invariably include 'courtesy and helpfulness from staff, accuracy in accordance with statutory entitlements, and a commitment to prompt action'.[60] Independent inspectorates should be established or, if already in existence, strengthened, to monitor compliance with the standards set.[61] Public service providers who meet those standards and the other requirements of the Charter are granted a Chartermark award.[62] Failure to maintain the standards may result in loss of the Chartermark.

(b) *The creation of greater openness and the provision of public information*[63] Public service providers should not only abolish unnecessary secrecy by the removal of restrictions on disclosure of information, but should actively publish full and accurate information about how public services are run, what services are being provided, how much they cost, who is in charge, their performance standards/targets, and the level of their achievements audited and measured against those standards and targets. Staff should not be anonymous, and all those who deal with the public should wear name badges and identify themselves over the telephone and in letters.

(c) *The provision of choice by the public sector wherever practicable*[64] The Charter requires greater responsiveness to customers and their needs as consumers of the service provided, including regular and systematic consultation with people affected by the service. Although the concept of consumer consultation has long been a facet of public service in the UK, as demonstrated by the Consumer Councils set up by statute in respect of the main utility public corporations such as gas, electricity, rail, etc., that concept was significantly different from the Charter concept in that it involved the notion of indirect consumer representative consultation rather than direct consultation with individual customers about their needs. The former reflects the corporatist nature of the former system of public service provision: the latter reflects the atomised, individualistic character of the relationship between the state and the citizen *qua* consumer of public services, as conceived by the Charter and the ideology it represents.

---

59   Charter, p. 5.
60   *Ibid.*
61   *Ibid.*, pp. 40–1.
62   *Ibid.*, p. 6.
63   *Ibid.*, p. 5.
64   *Ibid.*, p. 5.

(d) *The observance of the non discrimination principle*[65] Public service providers must make their services available to all, irrespective of gender, race or ethnic origin. Given that the law, in the form of the Sex Discrimination Act 1975 and the Race Relations Act 1976 (and, since the Charter, the Disability Discrimination Act 1996), already applies to those who provide services to the public or a section of the public, including government bodies, this seems an otiose provision, but the positive obligations included in the Charter, such as the need to print leaflets in minority languages in addition to English, go further than the law and reflect good practice already observed by many public authorities operating in areas with significant ethnic minority populations.

(e) *Accessiblity of services*[66] Public services should be run to suit the convenience of customers, not staff. This requires flexible opening hours and telephone inquiry points to direct callers promptly to someone who can help them.

(f) *The Charter requires public service providers to give a good explanation, or an apology when things go wrong, and to have a well-publicised and readily available complaints procedure*[67] Serious problems should be put right and lessons learnt to prevent repetition of mistakes. Machinery for the redress of grievances should ensure that customers are able to have their complaints properly investigated and, if upheld, adequately remedied. The Charter originally proposed a system of local lay adjudicators to handle grievance claims where internal redress mechanisms failed to provide a satisfactory remedy,[68] but these have not yet been established (see also Mulcahy and Allsop, Ch. 5, p. 15).

An interesting feature of the Charter is its reliance on non legal, non enforceable mechanisms for redress. Despite the utilisation in the new public management of the language and concepts of the private sector free market and the citizen as consumer, the current ideology omits the crucial factor of the legally binding obligation imposed by contractual agreement or by legislative intervention by statute, enforceable through judicial remedy such as damages, or court orders such as injunctions. The Charter even fails to enlist the aid of the ombudsman concept, whose recommendations after an investigation are not legally enforceable yet are almost universally complied with. There thus remains an unwillingness on the part of the Charter's architects to follow the logic of their basic ideology. They retain an element of state paternalism, with the provision of remedies the responsibility of the public service provider, reflecting the previous government's ultimate reluctance to transform the relationship between the state and the individual citizen into one of legally enforceable mutual obligations.

---

65 *Ibid.*, p. 5.
66 *Ibid.*, p. 5.
67 *Ibid.*, pp. 5, 42–4.
68 *Ibid.*, p. 43.

In addition to these general principles, the Charter goes on to establish individual charters for specific public services, including the National Health Service, education, public housing, public transport, the employment service, social services, social security, postal services, revenue services, the police, the criminal justice system and the courts. Each of these charters applies the general principles to the specific context of the particular service.

The Charter went further by establishing future programmes and policies by means of which the objectives of the Charter for better provision of services were to be achieved. Thus further privatisation of public services, the introduction of wider internal competition, further contracting out, the expansion of performance-related pay, and the creation of tougher and more independent inspectorates were all seen as the measures through which the gains sought by the government, in efficiency and effectiveness in the provision of public services, would be achieved.[69]

The Open Government White Paper

As a follow-up to the Citizen's Charter and as a means of blunting the demands of campaigners for freedom of information legislation, the government introduced a Code of Practice on Access to Government Information in the 1993 White Paper on *Open Government*.[70] The code requires government departments and other public authorities to publish factual information and analyses upon which government policies are based and to disclose factual information on request, both obligations being subject to a number of very wide exceptions. It also requires the giving of reasons for administrative decisions. The code is non statutory and although it creates the right of complaint to the Parliamentary Commissioner for Administration when information is wrongly withheld, his recommendation is not enforceable. The code does not create any legally enforceable rights to information or reasons. It has been met with a degree of scepticism by many academic commentators[71] and the record of compliance after more than three years of operation is variable.[72] Nonetheless, the acceptance by the government of the principle of open government is a considerable step, given the UK government's usual obsession with official secrecy.

The new concept of public service

The transformation of the state achieved by the previous government over the past 18 years has in turn radically altered the concept of public service in the UK in a

---

69   *Ibid.*, pp. 28, 29, 33, 35, 38, 40.
70   *Open Government*, Cm 2290, London: HMSO, 1993, Annex A.
71   See, e.g., Birkinshaw, P., '"I only ask for information" — the White Paper on Open Government' [1993] *Public Law* 557.
72   Parliamentary Commissioner for Administration 1994–95, Second Report — Session 1994–95, *Access to Official Information: the First Eight Months*, HC 91.

number of ways. First, public service is no longer the service of the public as a collective, but rather the service of the individual consumer of specific and limited public services. This is reinforced by the weakening or even removal of the traditionally public, institutional and constitutional mechanisms for accountability and redress, such as ministerial responsibility to Parliament, and their replacement by individualised, atomistic relationships between the citizen *qua* consumer and the providers of public services. The citizen must seek individual redress through complaints mechanisms which depend on an educated, informed, highly motivated individual with the means and initiative to pursue a complaint or grievance through the system. The relationship between the public service provider and the individual is equated with the contractual relationship of the private sector, but only partly. The citizen cannot sue the public service provider or the government for their failure to live up to the standards set by the Charter. Unlike the free market where there is freedom of contract between individuals equal in the eyes of the law, there is an inherent inequality between state institutions and the individual, since coercive power is the exclusive preserve of government. The public service provider may on the face of it have duties to the individual, but there are no correlative, Hohfeldian rights to enforce those duties. The individual is seen as liberated by public choice theory to make informed choices and to be entitled to exercise those choices in the services he or she seeks as a consumer. The citizen/consumer is seen by this ideology to be empowered, rather than enslaved, by the state, and not to be as dependent on the state as hitherto. The state in turn has far less to do, but obligations to do that which it still retains within its jurisdiction more efficiently, more effectively and more economically, giving the individual citizen/consumer greater choice of and more information about the public services provided. The public service providers are not seen as delegates or servants of the populace, but rather as paid contractors who perform a service at the request of the individual citizen/consumer. They are of course paid by the taxpayer, but that aspect of their political accountability seems to have been somewhat neglected in the new public management, except to the extent that much of the driving force behind the transformation of the state was the desire to reduce public expenditure so as to reduce the tax burden upon the taxpayer, who is therefore an automatic beneficiary and does not need to be accounted to in any other way.

The consequences of this radical change in the notion of public service is that our concept of representative and responsible government is significantly altered. Traditionally, public officials were seen as responsible to ministers, who in turn were responsible to the elected representatives of the people in Parliament for the performance of public service functions. Now, much of what government formerly performed is in the hands of the private sector and the individual consumer is a citizen no longer when he transacts with the private sector service provider. When he deals with the executive agency or the privatised public utility, it is to the Citizen's Charter he must turn as an individual, to seek redress by way of individual complaint if he has not received the level of service which he is entitled to expect. He can no longer rely on the public mechanisms of redress such as calling upon his MP to raise the matter with the minister or in Parliament, since the minister will simply refer the matter to the executive agency,[73] the privatised industry or the regulatory authorities. What has also become clear in recent years with the privatisation of so much of government's former activities, is that the principal motivation of those privatised industries is not the public service but rather the production of profit for the shareholders and the Board of Directors.

The United Kingdom is not alone in seeking to transform the state and the provision of public services; New Zealand and Sweden preceded this country with substantially similar reforms,[74] and other countries are following suit. This revolution in the nature of government is therefore not some temporary aberration which will be corrected now that the political pendulum has swung the other way. The changes which have occurred are so extensive, of such a fundamental character, and would entail such massive costs and resources to reverse, that this is now a permanent transformation of the state and of our concepts of public service.

The new Labour government has thus far made few changes. Next Steps agencies are to be retained, the Citizen's Charter is to be relaunched, freedom of information legislation may replace the Code on Access to Government Information, and compulsory competitive tendering is to be renamed 'best value' tendering. General practice fundholding will be retained but the rest of the internal market will be abandoned within the NHS. In education, the monitoring of standards and performance is to be even more rigorous. There will be no re-nationalisation of the privatised industries and utilities. Most of the new public management will thus be retained.

THE CONTRACTING STATE AND THE NEW PUBLIC MANAGEMENT: THE IMPLICATIONS FOR PUBLIC LAW

Given the likely permanence of the reforms, it is important to examine their implications for public law. The first — and one of the most striking — features of the revolution in public administration is that most of the changes have been wrought without recourse to legislation, and that even where legislation has been used, the terms of the new regime of public management and accountability fall outside the scope of legal control. Thus the Citizen's Charter is neither a statute nor a statutory instrument, but simply a command paper, as is the White Paper on

---

73   Oliver and Drewry, *op. cit.* note 2, Ch. 1.
74   Oliver and Drewry, *op. cit.* note 2, Ch. 8.

Open Government, which established the Code of Practice on Government Information. Similarly, the Next Steps agencies were envisaged in the report of the Efficiency Unit on the Rayner reviews and the Financial Management Initiative, and created by the simple expedient of the government's exercise of its prerogative power of employment and management of the Civil Service. The framework documents setting out the terms under which the executive agencies operate have no legal status other than as the means of delegation of functions. The performance targets create no legally enforceable standards; failure to meet the targets could give rise to no enforceable remedy.

Contracting out is, in the case of central government, simply the exercise of the power of the Crown as a legal entity to enter into contractual agreements; while in the case of much of local government and other public authorities, it is the exercise of existing general ancillary statutory powers. Contracting out has an important legal consequence for the recipient of the service, the consumer; namely that, because of the doctrine of privity of contract, he has no legal remedy in contract against the contractor for failure to perform the contracted service. Since the contract is an agreement freely arrived at between the public authority and the contractor, its terms fall outside the scope of judicial review,[75] so that even as council tax payer, the consumer has no legal means of challenging the contract or of calling the public authority or the contractor to account. He or she must rely on political accountability alone, a poor substitute for a legally enforceable remedy which the notion of contract implies.

A further consequence of this use of non legislative or informal means of establishing new institutions, machinery and processes for the delivery of public services is that the *public law* system of legal control and accountability is largely excluded. Since the framework documents setting out the structure, jurisdiction and terms of reference of the executive agencies have no formal legal status, no application for judicial review will lie to examine the failure of the agency to meet its performance targets or the minister's intervention in operational matters from which he is excluded by the framework document. Unlike formal statutory delegation of power to statutory authorities, where the powers of the authority and the minister's powers of intervention are set out in the legislation and are thus amenable to judicial intervention, definition and enforcement, the framework document wholly lacks any such justiciability.

Equally, the Citizen's Charter, lacking any formal legal status, provides no legal redress for those who suffer from a failure by an executive agency, public authority or privatised public utility to meet the standards laid down in the Charter. The Charter itself provides no formal mechanisms for redress, such as complaint to the

---

75   *Roy* v *Kensington and Chelsea Family Practitioner Committee* [1992] 2 WLR 239, HL. See, for a critical assessment of the capacity of public law to meet the challenge of contractualisation of public services, Freedland, M., 'Government by Contract and Private Law' [1994] *Public Law* 86.

ombudsmen, either local or parliamentary, legally enforceable compensation, or injunctive, prohibitory or mandatory relief. The Code of Practice on Access to Government Information, while providing for appeal to the Parliamentary Commissioner for Administration, does not confer legal enforceability upon his recommendations. The internal market within the National Health Service is created by means of 'contracts' which are not legally enforceable.

The second public law-related consequence of a number of the reforms set out above as features of the new public management and the shrinking of the state, is that their use, while not excluding the operation of private law, does appear to exclude the public law jurisdiction of the courts and thus to deny both the citizen and the public authority respectively the special benefits and protections which public law offers,[76] such as the greater range of remedies, the broader *locus standi*, the simplified application procedure, the leave stage, the short time limit, the normal absence of oral testimony and cross-examination, the limited use of discovery, and the discretionary nature of the remedies. Contracting out and privatisation both appear to have this effect. The courts have claimed that public law procedures should enjoy exclusive jurisdiction over public law matters because of the peculiar appropriateness of those procedures to such matters.[77] The removal of large areas of public administration from that exclusive jurisdiction by the use of private law forms of ownership and transactional relationships tends to deny or contradict that claim. Equally, the special public law standards imposed by the substantive legal principles of judicial review may be evaded by the use of contracting out, privatisation and the internal market.[78] Fairness, legality (in the public law sense) and rationality[79] simply do not apply to privatised utilities which have become almost wholly commercial enterprises operating in the marketplace as public limited companies. Competitiveness, economic efficiency and profit are the legitimate concerns and objectives of such organisations.

A further, related consequence is that the boundaries between public and private law, already an issue of considerable complexity and confusion (see Bamforth, Ch. 6 and Alder, Ch. 7 generally),[80] are further blurred by the use of the new public management's institutions and processes. The use of contracts to secure the performance of public services combines elements of both private law and public law. Disputes arising between privatised utilities and their regulators over the terms

---

76   Supreme Court Act 1981, s. 31; Rules of the Supreme Court, ord. 53.
77   *O'Reilly* v *Mackman* [1983] 2 AC 237, CA and HL; *Cocks* v *Thanet DC* [1983] 2 AC 286, HL.
78   Freedland, *op. cit.* note 75.
79   The three grounds of judicial review reformulated by Lord Diplock in *Council of Civil Service Unions* v *Minister for the Civil Service* [1985] AC 374.
80   See, for example, Alder, J., 'Hunting the Chimera — the End of *O'Reilly* v *Mackman?*' (1993) 13 *Legal Studies* 183; Tanney, A., 'Procedural Exclusivity in Administrative Law' [1994] *Public Law* 51; Fredman, S., and Morris, G., 'The Costs of Exclusivity: Public and Private Re-examined' [1994] *Public Law* 69.

of franchises and licences in the form of contracts, containing public service obligations and performance standards, are notoriously difficult to classify as either public or private, with the result that expensive and time-consuming litigation may be necessary to determine this preliminary issue.[81] While some contracting out, such as the construction and maintenance of housing, does not raise this problem to any significant extent, since the provision of housing is not an exclusively or even predominantly public function, rather the reverse, other areas of contracting out raise this difficulty in acute form. Contracting out the running of a prison, or the transporting of prisoners, for example, combines the private law of contract with one of the most essentially public functions of the state, the maintenance of law and order. Nor is this merely a jurisdictional, choice of forum issue. The application of the substantive law of tort may depend on whether the defendant is a private person or a public authority. The liability of public authorities has been substantially diminished by the erosion in *Murphy* v *Brentwood DC*[82] of the principles of *Dorset Yacht*[83] and *Anns*,[84] and recent decisions appear to give a broad public policy immunity in negligence, even in the operational sphere, to public authorities.[85] Will that immunity apply to private persons operating prisons and other public services under contract? Similarly, public interest immunity operates where a public function is being performed. In *D* v *NSPCC*,[86] the public function of initiating legal proceedings to protect children at risk of physical or sexual abuse, was conferred by statute upon a private charitable organisation which was thus able to seek the protection of public interest immunity so as to prevent disclosure of the identity of an informer who made false accusations against the plaintiff. If private persons are *contracted* to perform public functions, rather than being authorised by statute, will they too be able to claim the benefit of public interest immunity? One of the historically most significant authorities on public interest immunity, *Duncan* v *Cammell Laird*,[87] concerned exactly this situation, and no question was even raised in the proceedings that because the defendant was a private person, public interest immunity could not be sought to prevent disclosure of documents in the public interest. Of course, in that case it was the Admiralty, with whom the defendant had contracted, which made the actual claim, but there seems no reason in logic or principle to prevent the claim from being put forward by the defendant, provided it was duly supported by ministerial affidavit and certificate.

---

81 *Mercury Communications Ltd* v *Director-General of Telecommunications* [1996] 1 All ER 575, HL.
82 [1991] 1 AC 398.
83 *Dorset Yacht* v *Home Office* [1970] AC 1004.
84 *Anns* v *Merton LBC* [1978] AC 728.
85 *Hill* v *Chief Constable of West Yorkshire* [1989] AC 53; *Alexandrou* v *Oxford* [1993] 4 All ER 328; *Osman* v *Ferguson* [1993] 4 All ER 344.
86 [1978] AC 171.
87 [1942] AC 624.

Equally, the law of contract itself may apply different rules where public authorities are concerned. A public authority cannot bind itself by contract not to exercise its statutory powers or to exercise them in a particular way, particularly where executive necessity requires the authority to act contrary to the terms of the contract.[88] Nor may a public authority be estopped from exercising its statutory powers,[89] though this latter rule has been somewhat tempered in recent years by the judicial development of the doctrine of legitimate expectation.[90] Will private persons contracted to perform functions conferred on public authorities by statute, such as the operation of a prison, be able to claim the benefit of these rules in relation to other parties with whom they contract for the performance of services, or to whom they give assurances or undertakings which would otherwise give rise to an estoppel? If private persons are able to claim the benefits of tort immunity, public interest immunity, the rule against fettering, the doctrine of state necessity and the rule against estoppel, this will create a privileged class of private persons, contrary to one of the basic tenets of the rule of law, the notion of equality before the law.

The administrative law response

We have seen from the above the potential impact upon public law in the broad sense. How has administrative law responded to the new public management? Thus far, hardly at all, it seems. This lack of response is not surprising, however. First, as shown above, many of the reforms, such as the Citizen's Charter, the Code of Practice on Access to Government Information and the Next Steps executive agencies, have been implemented through informal, non legislative, managerial means, which fall outside the scope of judicial review so that the courts lack jurisdiction. Despite the attempts by the courts to abandon the source of power as the basis for the exercise of judicial review,[91] it remains the case that for the courts to intervene there must be some legally enforceable basis for or backing to the powers of the authority under review. Where power is conferred and limits are imposed by non legal means, the courts lack the necessary peg upon which to hang the exercise of their powers. Where contract is involved, the courts expressly reject the use of their judicial review powers.[92]

---

88 *Rederiaktiebolaget Amphitrite* v *R* [1921] 3 KB 500; *Stringer* v *Minister of Housing and Local Government* [1970] 1 WLR 1281; *Ayr Harbour Trustees* v *Oswald* (1883) 8 App Cas 623.

89 *Western Fish Products* v *Penwith DC* [1981] 2 All ER 204; *Lever Finance* v *Westminster London Borough Council* [1971] QB 222.

90 *R* v *Home Secretary, ex parte Asif Khan* [1984] 1 WLR 1337; *R* v *Ministry of Agriculture, Fisheries & Food, ex parte Hamble (Offshore) Fisheries Ltd* [1995] 2 All ER 714; *R* v *Secretary of State for Transport, ex parte Richmond upon Thames LBC* [1994] 1 WLR 74.

91 *R* v *City Panel on Takeovers and Mergers, ex parte Datafin* [1987] 1 All ER 564, CA; *Council of Civil Service Unions* v *Minister for the Civil Service* [1985] AC 374.

92 *Ex parte Datafin (supra)*; *R* v *Lord Chancellor, ex parte Hibbit and Sanders* (1993) *The Times*, 12 March, QBD; *Law* v *National Greyhound Racing Club Ltd* [1983] 1 WLR 1302.

Secondly, even where the reforms have been implemented by statute, the purposes underlying the reforms — of economy, efficiency and effectiveness, measured by compliance with performance targets — are alien to the legal culture, which is largely concerned with principles of good administration such as legality, fairness and rationality. The former purposes are to do with achieving quantified ends, with producing a measurable output, whereas the latter concern the use of proper means, the quality of the process of decision making. Thus the principles of judicial review are likely to have only peripheral relevance or application to the new public management.

Equally, questions of economy, efficiency and effectiveness in the application of government policy and the delivery of public services are issues which the courts are unlikely to regard as justiciable.[93] The courts lack both the expertise and the resources to gather and assess large volumes of statistical, empirical evidence in order to pass judgment on the correctness of conclusions about issues of economic efficiency and effectiveness, or value for money. The judiciary in the UK have neither the political will of their brethren in the USA to evaluate such issues under the doctrine of substantial evidence, nor the training and expertise of their continental brethren in such complex policy issues. With a few notable exceptions which tend to prove the rule, the judiciary are reluctant to intervene in such technically difficult matters, particularly those involving the allocation of scarce resources by highly expert, often professionally qualified decision makers. Such decisions are also frequently, if not invariably, politically sensitive, and the judiciary are normally reluctant to become involved in politically controversial disputes which, by calling into question their political impartiality, may put at risk their judicial independence.

A third reason for judicial abdication is that while judicial review is concerned exclusively with issues of public law, many of the reforms described above have removed the provision of public services from the public sector into the private sector. Privatisation and contracting out have put many public services beyond the reach of judicial review. Although the European Court of Justice may regard a privatised public utility as continuing to fall within the scope of public law,[94] it is unlikely that English courts will apply the same test. The actions of a company selling gas, water, electricity, telecommunications or transport services on a commercial, profit-making basis are a matter for *private law*, and hence beyond the scope of judicial review. Contracts for the supply of public services, such as health care, even fall within the purview of *private law* and thus outwith the reach of judicial review.[95] The courts' acceptance of a distinction between private law

---

93   *Per* Lord Diplock, in *Council of Civil Service Unions* v *Minister for the Civil Service*, note 91 supra.

94   *Foster* v *British Gas* [1990] 3 All ER 897, ECJ; [1991] 2 All ER 705, HL.

95   *Roy* v *Kensington and Chelsea Family Practitioner Committee* [1992] 2 WLR 239, HL.

and public law and their adoption of the doctrine of exclusivity of judicial review, coinciding with the very beginning of the public service reforms, has put many of today's public services beyond the reach of administrative law.

The future for administrative law

In 1959, the late Professor Stanley de Smith, in the first edition of his *locus classicus, Judicial Review of Administrative Action*, stated that:

> In the broad context of the administrative process the role of judicial institutions is inevitably sporadic and peripheral.[96]

In 1995, the editors of the 5th edition of that work claimed that:

> . . . the effect of judicial review on the practical exercise of power has now become constant and central.[97]

While it is undoubtedly the case that the courts have dramatically extended the principles of judicial review in the past three decades and have applied those principles over wide areas of public administration not hitherto subject to judicial review, the law's dominion does appear to have diminished substantially as a consequence of the developments analysed above. Privatisation, contracting out, the internal market, the Citizen's Charter, and other aspects of the new public management have, it is submitted, removed large areas of public administration from the protective and supervisory jurisdiction of the courts. It may be argued that the reforms have enhanced the citizen's position *vis-à-vis* public services by setting performance targets to improve efficiency and effectiveness, providing greater information about their success or failure in achieving those performance standards, direct remedies against those public services for their failure to meet those targets, and better quality services via market mechanisms of greater choice and competition. It is nonetheless a matter for concern that one significant consequence of the reforms has been to reduce one of the citizen's most valuable protections against injustice and error by the state, legal redress. This runs contrary to the sustained progress made by judicial review over the past three decades in expanding and improving the citizen's avenues for redress and supervising administrative action.

---

96   de Smith, S. A., *Judicial Review of Administrative Action*, London: Stevens, 1959, p. 3.
97   de Smith, S. A., Woolf, H., and Jowell, J., *Judicial Review of Administrative Action* (5th ed.), London: Sweet & Maxwell, 1995, p. vii.

How can administrative law respond? How should it respond?

A first and important point to make is that administrative law does not consist of judicial review alone. There are numerous other forms of redress available to citizens for grievances against, and other mechanisms for controlling and holding to account, government and other public authorities. There are ombudsmen for central government, the National Health Service and local authorities, and the institution has spread, both by statute and voluntary arrangement, to large areas of the private sector, such as banking, building societies and insurance. There are numerous administrative tribunals providing appellate remedies covering wide areas of public administration, and in some areas there are adjudicators prior to such tribunals. Public authorities may be liable in damages for tort, including negligence, trespass and breach of statutory duty, where their conduct has been unlawful or in some other way legally improper. Public inquiries may provide the citizen with the opportunity to air his or her grievances in respect of some action taken or proposed by a public authority, or in some cases to appeal against such action. So in seeking to answer the above questions, the scope of the inquiry should not be restricted to judicial review alone. It is also important to remember that judicial review may act in concert with other remedies or controls over public authorities. For example, judicial review has on occasion followed investigation by one of the various ombudsmen, where that investigation has provided the grounds for review.[98] Judicial review has in some cases (including some very high profile *causes célèbres*) gone hand in hand with audit, the auditors having discovered the illegality or irrationality which provided the basis for review.[99] This is an important complementary role for judicial review to play.

In seeking to answer the above questions, it is also important to keep in mind the qualifications of the various institutions of administrative law. Economists, accountants, Treasury and Bank of England officials, and others with financial expertise may be appropriate to determine issues of economic efficiency and effectiveness, but lawyers as presently educated and trained, and courts as presently constituted, may not be. Those with experience in public administration may be appropriate to determine whether maladministration has occurred, or to judge the propriety of decisions concerning the allocation of scarce resources, but lawyers and courts may not be.

A number of possible responses to the above inquiries may be suggested. First, the scope of judicial review could be expanded by broadening the grounds of review to include substantive issues such as value for money, or whether standards of service or performance have been met, or whether there has been compliance with the terms of 'contracts' within the internal markets, or whether resources have

---

98 For example *Congreve v Home Office* [1976] QB 629.
99 For example, *Roberts v Hopwood* [1925] AC 578; *R v Secretary of State for Foreign Affairs, ex parte World Development Movement* [1995] 1 All ER 611.

been appropriately allocated in making provision for public services. But to do so would require our judges to gain expertise in economics and public administration, to become more like the judges of the French *Conseil d'Etat* and other continental European administrative courts. This would necessitate a revolution in the process by which our judges are selected, appointed and trained. It would also require the forensic processes of our courts to be substantially revised to enable the admission and testing of evidence by which such polycentric issues could be satisfactorily determined. Parties to judicial review would have to make very different presentations and submissions from those they now make. The US concept of the Brandeis brief would have to be adopted in this country, with all that that implies not only in terms of political controversy but also in the necessary elongation of judicial review proceedings with all the attendant cost and delay to public administration.

A further and more fundamental objection to judges becoming involved in such questions is the constitutional impropriety of judges deciding the merits of issues of policy over which the executive and legislative branches of government should have exclusive jurisdiction as to substance. Even if the response to this objection is that judicial intervention is at the periphery only, does not occur unless extreme errors have been committed by decision makers, and can be justified by reference to fundamental constitutional principles derived from democratic values and human rights, judicial involvement in policy issues may still put at risk the principle of judicial independence. Intervention in matters of political controversy, even if based on politically neutral grounds, may nonetheless damage the public perception of judges as politically impartial. It is both appropriate and understandable therefore that, with a few exceptions, judges have been reluctant to exercise their judicial review jurisdiction in these areas. Much of the new public management has become and will rightly remain a no-go area for judicial review, except for intervention based on the traditional grounds for review, illegality, irrationality and procedural error. At the same time, it is important to recognise that grievance procedures and remedies devised to redress output failure have very different aims from those of judicial review, which is concerned with the quality of the processes of public administration and with respect for certain fundamental rights and constitutional principles. Judicial review will continue to have a role, to complement other, different mechanisms for the redress of grievances and the control of public administration, and in appropriate cases to exercise supervisory control over those other mechanisms.

Another possible avenue for the courts to explore is the development of a public law of contract,[100] with special rules for contracts in the public services, even where those services have been privatised. Although it is beyond the scope of this chapter to elaborate in detail the possible forms such development might take, it

---

100 Harden, *op. cit.* note 17 and Freedland, *op. cit.* note 75, both suggest that special rules of public law contract need to be developed.

is only necessary to point out that there already exist special rules in public law concerning contracts entered into by public authorities. The doctrine of executive necessity, the rule against fettering discretionary powers by contract, the rule that a public authority cannot be estopped in the exercise of discretionary powers, the statutory limitations on the use of contracts to require the employment of union members or the granting of sub-contracts to contractors employing union members, and the European law restrictions on the terms of procurement contracts,[101] are all examples of a distinctive public law of contract. There is a number of other new notions which the courts might develop in the formation of this area of law. One could be the extension of liability to third parties, i.e. the consumers of public services, for breach of contract involving failure to meet performance targets. This would probably involve, in some cases, the abandonment of the doctrines of privity and consideration. Another possibility is the notion, already existing in competition law, of abuse of dominant position. Many public utilities enjoy effective natural, if not legally protected, monopolies, such as gas, water and electricity. It might be argued that many of the contracts which operate between consumer and supplier are onerous in their terms because the supplier enjoys this dominant position. The notion of unconscionability arising from the inevitable inequality of bargaining power between the individual and the public utility, might also be fertile ground for development of a separate and distinctive public law of contract.

The ombudsman concept could be extended to many areas of the new public management and, given its existing application to the private sector, to the privatised public utilities (see Drewry, Ch. 4 generally). The Citizen's Charter provided the ideal opportunity to expand the jurisdiction of the existing ombuds-men, an opportunity which was not taken. But the Parliamentary Commissioner for Administration has seen the opportunity and stepped in where government declined to tread. The Commissioner will regard a failure by a public service provider over which he has jurisdiction, to meet its Charter performance standards as prima facie evidence of maladministration. But there are now whole areas of public service provision outside the jurisdiction of any of the statutory, public sector ombudsmen. The Citizen's Charter requires the setting up of complaints and grievance pro-cedures and proposed the establishment of independent lay adjudicators, but few of these have materialised. The advantage of such lay adjudicators is that they would provide cheap, expeditious redress for the consumer of a public service and relieve the ombudsman of the primary burden of complaints. They could also operate in those bodies not falling within the Commissioner's jurisdiction, and those bodies might well consider establishing non statutory, voluntary ombudsmen systems, as already exist in the private sector. One might therefore envisage water, gas, electricity or rail services ombudsmen being established to investigate

---

101   See, on the use of contract terms, Arrowsmith, S., 'Public Procurement as an Instrument of Policy and the Impact of Market Liberalisation' (1995) 111 LQR 235.

complaints of failure to comply with Charter performance standards. Equally, the regulators of these privatised public utility industries might have their present limited complaints role expanded to provide redress for individual consumers where appropriate, in addition to their more general regulatory role.

CONCLUSION

The re-invention of the state in the last two decades has transformed the machinery and processes for delivery of public services, from public bureaucracy to the private market. This has led to new mechanisms for control and accountability, rendering obsolete or inapplicable the existing systems, both legal and political. Administrative law, in its widest sense, has shown the capacity to adapt and develop to meet this revolution. It has not been completely sidelined, and still has a vital role to play in the continuing development of modern public administration. In particular, its task is to develop and apply principles of good administration to ensure the fairness, rationality and legality of public decision making processes, and their compliance with fundamental constitutional and human rights values.

2

Mitigating the Democratic Deficit? Judicial Review and Ministerial Accountability

Mike Radford

SUMMARY

Accountability for the exercise of public power lies at the heart of democratic government. In the United Kingdom, this is said to be achieved through ministerial responsibility to Parliament. In recent years, however, concern has grown because of the apparent ineffectiveness of this constitutional convention. In the light of evidence that MPs are failing adequately to control ministers, this chapter considers the suggestion that judicial review can go some way to counteract the problem of accountability. The importance of judicial review is fully acknowledged, but it is argued that the courts cannot compensate for shortcomings in the political process.

INTRODUCTION

Accountability for the way in which public power is exercised is fundamental to the concept of representative democracy. It is only by knowing what government is doing, and on what basis, that the electorate can seek to influence the development and application of policy and, come an election, be in a position to make an informed judgement as to its performance. Equally important, accountability is essential as a means of safeguarding against the abuse and misuse of power: administrative autonomy and executive taciturnity provide fertile conditions for the growth of arbitrary and unconstrained government. The more transparent the decision making process and the greater the opportunity to hold ministers and officials answerable for their actions, the better the means of ensuring that they are performing their duties with propriety and in the public interest.

In the United Kingdom, this function has fallen principally to Parliament, and to the House of Commons in particular. The courts have, of course, long played a vital role in ensuring that those exercising power on behalf of the government have legal authority for their actions,[1] but traditionally the judiciary have regarded their role as being primarily to determine the limits of such power, rather than to become involved in disputes about the way in which (otherwise lawful) power is exercised. Scrutiny of how the executive carries out its functions and chooses to use its powers has been seen as predominantly a political issue, formalised in the well-established constitutional doctrine of ministerial responsibility. Recently, however, there has been a growing awareness, not least amongst the judiciary, that Parliament is no longer effective (assuming it ever was) in holding the executive to account. One High Court judge, for example, has described it as 'too weak to vindicate to the just satisfaction of the citizen its historic power to control the Executive in the name of the people,'[2] while another has observed that 'Parliament has no way and no hope of supervising, through ministerial accountability, the myriad activities which in increasing volume it delegates to the executive'.[3] Significantly, this perceived inadequacy in political control has coincided with a period of considerable judicial activism. Taking full advantage of the opportunities afforded by the combination of procedural changes relating to judicial review of administrative action,[4] the developing jurisprudence of the European Court of Justice (much of which is essentially administrative law), and the novel constitutional position of the domestic courts under the European Community's legal order, a confident and invigorated judiciary (or, to be more precise, a relatively small number amongst their senior ranks) have overseen a sustained and unprecedented development in both the substance and the application of public law. Indeed, the dynamic nature of judicial review is in sharp contrast to the apparent impotence of the House of Commons properly to control the executive and has served to focus attention on the potential of the courts to compensate for at least some of Parliament's shortcomings. MPs themselves have acknowledged that 'the accountability of the Executive to the courts has been enhanced in recent years by the growth of judicial review'[5] and has tended 'to increase the extent to which the public is able to ensure that public services are properly accountable'.[6] These views have

---

1 *Entick* v *Carrington* (1765) 19 St Tr 1030.
2 Laws, Sir John, 'Judicial Remedies and the Constitution' (1994) 57 *Modern Law Review* 223.
3 Sedley, Sir Stephen, 'Governments, Constitutions and Judges' in Richardson, G. and Genn, H. (eds), *Administrative Law and Government Action*, Oxford: Clarendon Press, 1994, p. 42.
4 SI 1977/1955 and SI 1980/2000; see also the Supreme Court Act 1981, s. 31.
5 Treasury and Civil Service Committee, *Role of the Civil Service*, HC 27, London: HMSO, 1993, para. 136.
6 Public Service Committee, *Ministerial Accountability and Responsibility*, HC 313, London: HMSO, 1996, para. 171.

been echoed by other commentators. Lord Irvine of Lairg, for example, writing while 'shadow' Lord Chancellor, and therefore drawing on his experience as both practitioner and parliamentarian, has recently suggested that the consequences of the 'democratic deficit', which he defines as 'the want of Parliamentary control over the executive,' have been, 'to an important degree, mitigated by the rigours of judicial review'.[7] It is beyond doubt that the modern development of judicial review is of profound constitutional significance; whether it can be regarded as an effective or indeed desirable — albeit partial — substitute for ministerial responsibility to Parliament is the subject of this chapter (see Donson, Ch. 15 generally).

POLITICAL ACCOUNTABILITY[8]

By defining the relationship between ministers and Parliament on the one hand, and ministers and their officials on the other, it is incontrovertible that a concept described variously as ministerial responsibility or ministerial accountability is central to the United Kingdom's constitutional arrangements. To state with any precision exactly what it entails is, however, surprisingly difficult in view of its importance. In 1879, Gladstone described it thus:

> In every free state, for every public act, some one must be responsible; and the question is, who shall it be? The British Constitution answers: 'the Minister and the Minister exclusively'.[9]

In broad terms, this remains the gist of the doctrine, but in practice the rigour and consequences of its application can vary enormously. As with so much which lies at the heart of the United Kingdom's constitution, its status is merely that of a convention, meaning that it has evolved over time and is continuing to develop in response to the changing nature of the executive and its relationship with Parliament. As such, the substance of the doctrine is essentially whatever Parliament demands of a minister in the particular circumstances. Although custom and practice are influential, the doctrine's impact inevitably owes rather more to the

---

7   Lord Irvine of Lairg, QC, 'Judges and Decision-Makers: The Theory and Practice of *Wednesbury* Review' [1996] *Public Law* 59.

8   On ministerial responsibility/accountability generally, see further: Marshall, G., *Ministerial Responsibility*, Oxford: Clarendon Press, 1989; *Questions of Procedure for Ministers*, London: Cabinet Office, 1992, amended July 1994 and November 1996; Woodhouse, D., *Ministers and Parliament: Accountability in Theory and Practice*, Oxford: Clarendon Press, 1994; Turpin, C., 'Ministerial Responsibility', in Jowell, J. and Oliver, D. (eds), *The Changing Constitution* (3rd ed.), Oxford: Clarendon Press, 1994; Public Service Committee, *Ministerial Accountability and Responsibility*, note 6 *supra*; Tomkins, A., 'A Right to Mislead Parliament?' (1996) 16 *Legal Studies* 63.

9   Quoted by the Public Service Committee, *Ministerial Accountability and Responsibility*, note 6 *supra*, para. 1.

political exigencies of the situation than the strict application of an immutable constitutional principle; as the Public Service Committee of the House of Commons has recently observed, there have 'always been elements of ambiguity and confusion' about the convention, largely because 'the way it is used in practice tends to be variable and inconsistent'.[10]

Despite this uncertainty, it can be said with confidence that Parliament expects ministers to present, explain and answer for the activities of their respective departments (including taking charge of government legislation which falls within their domain) by means of statements to the House, debates (both on the floor of the House and in standing committee), parliamentary questions, appearances before select committees, and responding to MPs' correspondence and representations. In addition, an increasingly important extra-parliamentary element has developed, in the sense that it has become the norm for ministers to make themselves available to the media in order to be questioned on their areas of responsibility, and there is an important interaction between what they say to journalists and what goes on in the Commons. Indeed, on many occasions journalists appear to be significantly more successful in holding ministers to account than are MPs. For its part, government formally recognises these obligations: *Questions of Procedure for Ministers* (recently revised and reissued as *A Code of Conduct and Guidance on Procedures for Ministers*), the nearest thing the political component of British government has had to binding standards of behaviour, specified that it is a 'principle of ministerial conduct' that ministers are accountable for the policies, decisions and actions of their departments and those executive agencies which fall within their departmental jurisdiction; must not knowingly mislead Parliament; and are required to correct any inadvertent errors at the earliest opportunity. In order to meet these requirements, ministers:

> must be as open as possible with Parliament and the public, withholding information only when disclosure would not be in the public interest, which should be decided in accordance with relevant statute and the Government's Code of Practice on Access to Government Information.

Despite the mandatory tone, there remains considerable scope for personal discretion as it is left to 'individual ministers to judge how best to act in order to uphold the highest standards'.[11] Herein lies a problem. Given the scope of activity undertaken by modern government, the volume of information it generates, the lack of time and resources available to MPs, their relative dearth of expertise, and the degree of autonomy enjoyed by ministers in carrying out their duties, how is

---

10   *Ibid.*, para. 2.
11   *Questions of Procedures for Ministers*, para. 1, as amended (see Public Service Committee, *Government Response to the Second Report from the Committee (Session 1995–96) on Ministerial Accountability and Responsibility*, HC 67, London: HMSO, 1996, Appendix B).

Parliament to ensure that the executive is meeting its own stipulation laid down in *Questions of Procedure for Ministers*, namely, of being 'as open as possible'?

At this point it is necessary to distinguish the notion of *accountability* from that of *responsibility*: to what extent does a minister's obligation to Parliament go beyond being merely a conduit for information, to include some degree of liability both for what goes on within his or her department and for his or her personal conduct? It is the case that a minister's political authority can be fatally undermined by virtue of incompetence or gross misjudgement in relation to ministerial duties, culpability for misleading Parliament, or as a result of extra-ministerial activities, but there remains serious concern that the House of Commons lacks either the means or the will effectively to hold ministers responsible.

Three separate issues arise in this context. First, given the scope of government activity, to what degree is it reasonable to regard a minister as personally responsible for everything that is carried out in his or her name? This is both a legal and a political question for, in the main, legislative powers are conferred upon ministers, not on departments or officials, despite the fact that most departmental functions are carried on without direct reference to, or the personal knowledge of, ministers. For their part, the courts have recognised the reality that ministers can be expected to become personally involved only in the most important decisions and, inevitably, most of the work will be delegated to officials.[12] Provided that they are of suitable grading and experience,[13] this situation is acceptable to the courts, partly out of necessity — 'Public business could not be carried on if that were not the case'[14] — and partly because they recognise that ministers are answerable politically for their departmental responsibilities.

Secondly, what is a minister responsible for? Many of the issues concerning responsibility which arise as a result of changes to the administrative state remain unanswered. Compared to the time when there was a direct line of accountability from the hospital ward, the prison cell and the benefit office to the Secretary of State's desk, the growth of executive agencies,[15] the extensive powers of quangos, the transfer of functions to the private sector through privatisation and contracting out, and the injection of business principles and quasi-markets into the public sector, have all served to increase confusion about who is responsible for what.

---

12 *Carltona Ltd* v *Commissioners of Works* [1943] 2 All ER 560.
13 *Oladehinde* v *Secretary of State for the Home Department* [1991] 1 AC 254, at 303 (Lord Donaldson MR). It was suggested in the same case, at pp. 283–4, that in respect of central government departments, power is devolved to civil servants, rather than delegated: 'The civil servant concerned acts not as the delegate, but as the alter ego of the Secretary of State. "Devolution" might be a better word.'
14 *Carltona Ltd* v *Commissioners of Works*, note 12 *supra*, at 563 (Lord Greene MR).
15 Public bodies which perform at arm's length functions previously carried out directly by a government department. Although ministers continue to lay down the policies to be followed, one of the reasons for their creation was to give managers greater autonomy and responsibility for operational matters.

Against this background, the Public Service Committee has emphasised, in respect of executive agencies, that a minister's duty to give an account can be delegated to the chief executive, but 'the liability to be held to account . . . cannot'. Thus ministers remain under a duty to make investigations in response to concerns raised with them, to put matters right where things have gone wrong, to ensure that if mistakes have been made, those responsible for making them are duly disciplined, and 'if something has gone wrong which they might have been able to prevent, to take some of the blame themselves'.[16] Although such a formulation appears straightforward, it is naïve in assuming that it is possible to make a clear distinction between policy and operational matters, and it has not prevented disputes arising, such as in the Prison Service, as to where exactly the boundaries of responsibility lie. There has also been a growing practice for ministers to attempt to abdicate their executive function by arguing that they were powerless to do anything except follow expert advice, an explanation put forward, for example, by ministers in justifying their response to bovine spongiform encephalopathy (BSE) in the national cattle herd. Another tactic, adopted by defence ministers over the condition known as 'Gulf War syndrome', has been to distance themselves from the decisions of their officials which they have previously endorsed. Such examples increase uncertainty about who is actually in charge, who is making decisions and developing policy, and who is ultimately accountable.

Thirdly, what are the consequences if a minister fails to fulfil his or her obligations to Parliament? What powers and sanctions do MPs possess to hold a minister to account? Ministers are appointed under the authority of the prerogative on the advice of the Prime Minister and they are entitled to remain in office for so long as they retain his confidence. Parliament has no formal power either to dismiss a minister or force his or her resignation, although by convention defeat on a motion of censure of a minister or on a motion to reduce his or her salary will lead to his or her resignation. In holding ministers to account, the problem is not only the relative powerlessness of Parliament, but also the political context. Clearly, either resignation or a weakened minister who clings to office with his or her authority undermined can harm both the government and the governing party. This gives rise to considerable pressure on the government's backbenchers to rally to the support of a minister under threat. It is a characteristic of the British political system that when the future of a minister is in question it will be regarded as first and foremost an aspect of the continuing party political conflict rather than an occasion for the House to act collectively to discipline the executive. It was no surprise, for example, to see in the weeks immediately preceding the 1997 general election, the Minister of Agriculture comfortably surviving a motion of no confidence over his widely criticised handling of the BSE crisis.

---

16   Public Service Committee, *Ministerial Accountability and Responsibility*, note 6 *supra*, para. 112.

In general, no matter how forceful the criticism from the Opposition, the pressure for a minister to go only becomes irresistible once his or her own backbenchers conclude that the political damage caused by resignation is less than that arising from the minister remaining in post. The pivotal role of the government's backbenchers, rather than the Commons, in deciding a minister's fate is recognised by the government:

> Some people talk as if the Party system has killed off accountability to Parliament. This ignores the central part which Parties now play as the medium for democratic argument and debate: in answering to Parliament, a Minister must simultaneously win and hold the confidence of his Party colleagues. Failure to do so ultimately leads to his or her departure from the Government.[17]

If a minister is able to weather the initial onslaught, he or she will generally survive (at least until the next government reshuffle). One of the executive's most potent weapons is the short attention span of the Commons; a minister's future can appear decidedly precarious and become the subject of excited speculation and then, just as suddenly, simply cease to be an issue, the political (and media) bandwagon having moved on to the next heady issue. One only has to look at the aftermath of the Scott Inquiry to appreciate the problem. A long, independent and detailed inquiry culminated in serious, but measured, criticism of the executive, including a finding that ministers had failed to discharge their obligations to Parliament on seven separate occasions.[18] Upon publication of the Report, the government sought to downplay and undermine Scott's conclusions and, in the ensuing debate, a partisan Commons allowed ministers and officials off the hook. Meanwhile, media interest reached fever-pitch for a few days, but soon evaporated when it was apparent that there would be no casualties. The episode represents an appetite for political theatre at the expense of a principled and considered reckoning of the executive's conduct.

For their part, ministers have taken full advantage of the failure by MPs effectively to hold them to account. We have seen that it is a fundamental precept of parliamentary procedure that they should not mislead the Commons, and any minister who is suspected of such behaviour can expect to be subjected to the full wrath of MPs. In general, the only way to save a ministerial career in such circumstances is to make a statement to the House at the earliest opportunity providing a full explanation and offering an abject apology. The gravity of the

---

17 Public Service Committee, *Government Response to the Second Report from the Committee (Session 1995–96) on Ministerial Accountability and Responsibility,* note 11 *supra,* Annex A, para. 20.

18 Sir Richard Scott, *Report of the Inquiry into the Export of Defence Equipment and Dual-Use Goods to Iraq and Related Prosecutions,* HC 115, London: HMSO, 1996, K8.1.

offence is not therefore in doubt, neither is the seriousness of the potential outcome. The weakness of the principle is in establishing what conduct amounts to misleading the House. For example, although the Public Service Committee, in proposing a 'working definition of "ministerial responsibility"', has suggested — and the government has acknowledged — that the executive is obliged 'to provide *full* information about and explain its actions in Parliament,'[19] this is to ignore the realities of modern British party politics. Given the pugilistic nature of so much that goes on in Parliament, where evasiveness, speciosity and crude point-scoring are too often more highly regarded than objectivity and substance, it is inevitable that ministers will regard the management of information as an invaluable weapon in their armoury. The prevailing attitude of ministers and officials towards their duty to 'be as open as possible with Parliament'[20] was exposed as a result of the candid evidence provided by senior civil servants to the Scott Inquiry. A former Permanent Under-Secretary of State in the Ministry of Defence described the activity of seeking and giving information in Parliament as:

> analogous to a game . . . in the sense that it is a competitive activity . . . the Opposition will seek to extract information which they can use to portray the Government in a bad light . . . The Government for its part will be reluctant to disclose information of a kind, or in a form, that will help the Opposition to do so

and he observed that the 'most pervasive pressure' on the government's attitude to providing information was 'the unflaggingly adversarial political context'.[21] On the basis of the evidence before him, Scott concluded that:

> In circumstances where disclosure might be politically or administratively inconvenient . . . the Government comes down, time and time again, against full disclosure.[22]

(For further discussion of the Scott Inquiry in relation to public interest immunity and open government, see Tomkins, Ch. 14, pp. 340 *et seq*).

Parliament's effectiveness in holding ministers to account is further undermined by the fact that a failure to *inform* Parliament is not regarded with anything like

---

19 Public Service Committee, *Ministerial Accountability and Responsibility*, note 6 *supra*, para. 32 (emphasis added); *Government Response*, note 11 *supra*, p. vi.

20 *Questions of Procedure for Ministers*, note 8 *supra*.

21 Sir Michael Quinlan, quoted by Sir Richard Scott, *op. cit.* note 18 *supra*, D4.61 and by the Public Service Committee, *Ministerial Accountability and Responsibility*, note 6 *supra*, para. 41.

22 Sir Richard Scott, *op. cit.* note 18 *supra*, D1.165 and cited by the Public Service Committee, *Ministerial Accountability and Responsibility*, note 6 *supra*, para. 47.

the same seriousness as *misleading* the House. This is a distinction which all too easily descends into semantics. The Cabinet Secretary, for example, argued before the Scott Inquiry that providing Parliament with information which did not give 'the full situation' — what he described as 'a half answer' — and thereby gave a false impression, did not amount to misleading Parliament, so long as the partial information that was made public was 'true' and 'accurate'. *'Very often'*, he said, 'one is finding oneself in a position where you have to give an answer that is not the whole truth, but falls short of misleading.'[23] This echoes previous complaints from MPs. The Foreign Affairs Committee, for example, in its report on the Pergau Dam affair, found that 'ministerial replies to certain questions were literally true, though less open and less informative than the House has a right to expect'.[24] In the light of this situation, the Public Service Committee subsequently recommended to the Commons that it should adopt a resolution on accountability specifically stating that:

> All Members of this House and all witnesses who come before it are obliged not to obstruct or impede it in the performance of its functions . . . Ministers must take special care, therefore, to provide information that is full and accurate to Parliament, and must, in their dealings with Parliament, conduct themselves frankly and with candour. The House recognises that Ministers may need, upon occasions, to withhold information, but believes they should do so only exceptionally.[25]

That a cross-party committee of MPs felt the necessity to propose such a resolution, and in these terms, is a potent indication of the scale of the perceived problem; whether it adequately meets it is another matter. Not only would its implementation, against all recent trends, require a change in the political culture, but, as it stands, it would rely totally on the good faith of ministers. Without a more determined attitude by backbench MPs to hold ministers to account, and an extra-parliamentary check, such as enhanced statutory rights of access to information, the executive will continue to be in a position to determine the flow and presentation of official information. It is against this background that the modern law of judicial review has evolved.

---

23   Sir Richard Scott, *op. cit.* Day 62: Evidence of Sir Robin Butler, 9 February 1994, p. 52; quoted by the Public Service Committee, *Ministerial Accountability and Responsibility*, note 6 *supra*, para. 43 (emphasis added).

24   Foreign Affairs Committee, *Public Expenditure: The Pergau Hydro-Electric Project, Malaysia, The Aid and Trade Provisions and Related Matters*, HC 271, London: HMSO, 1994, para. 44.

25   Public Service Committee, *Ministerial Accountability and Responsibility*, note 6 *supra*, para. 60. See now, Public Service Committee, *op. cit.* note 11 *supra*, Annex C: Guidance to Officials on Drafting Answers to Parliamentary Questions.

ACCESS TO INFORMATION[26]

Clearly, access to information — the ability to find out what the government is doing, and why — is a prerequisite of effective accountability. In this respect, citizens of the UK are seriously hampered by both the absence of a general legal right of access to official information and the associated culture of secrecy which pervades so much of government; secrecy which is underpinned by civil and criminal sanctions for unauthorised disclosure. Although the much criticised 'catch-all' provisions of s. 2 of the Official Secrets Act 1911 have been replaced by the relatively less restrictive terms of the 1989 Act, these remain very broad in respect of security and intelligence, defence, international relations, crime, special investigation powers, and confidential information. Moreover, although the Official Secrets Act 1989 is the most significant single piece of legislation restricting the publication of information, it is only the tip of the secrecy iceberg. In 1993, the government calculated that there were more than 200 other pieces of legislation which made it a criminal offence to disclose specific categories of information.[27] In addition, such statutory protection is reinforced by contractual provisions and common law doctrines which further restrict the flow of official information. Thus, civil servants may not seek 'to frustrate or influence the policies, decisions or actions of government by the unauthorised, improper or premature disclosure' of any information to which they have access;[28] as is the case with all employees, civil servants are under a duty of confidentiality (which in respect of security and intelligence officers is for life[29]); and the Attorney-General may obtain an injunction to prevent the publication of information if its revelation would be against the public interest.[30]

Notwithstanding all these measures, it is acknowledged that a very great volume of official information is placed into the public domain. Legislation has been introduced providing a legal right of access to tightly-defined categories of information; although, typically, these have focused on local and health authorities rather than central government departments.[31] In addition, specific provisions in

---

26 On access to information generally, see further: Austin, R., 'Freedom of Information: The Constitutional Impact' in Jowell, J. and Oliver, D. (eds), *The Changing Constitution* (3rd ed.), Oxford: Clarendon Press, 1994; Birkinshaw, P., *Freedom of Information* (2nd ed.), London: Butterworths, 1996.
27 *Open Government*, Cm 2290, London: HMSO, 1993, Appendix B.
28 *The Civil Service Code*, London: Cabinet Office, para. 10.
29 *Lord Advocate* v *Scotsman Publications* [1990] 1 AC 812; Official Secrets Act 1989, s. 1(1).
30 *Attorney-General* v *Guardian Newspapers Ltd* [1987] 1 WLR 1248; *Attorney-General* v *Guardian Newspapers (No. 2)* [1990] 1 AC 109.
31 For example, Local Government (Access to Information) Act 1985; Community Health Councils (Access to Information) Act 1988; Data Protection Act 1984; Access to Personal Files Act 1987 (provides access to social services and housing records held by local authorities); Access to Health Records Act 1990.

legislation may require ministers to release information, or they may choose to do so voluntarily. In particular, during his period as Prime Minister, John Major promoted a limited but nevertheless discernible change towards greater openness. Thus material concerning the workings of government, such as the existence, membership and terms of reference of Cabinet committees and, perhaps most importantly, *Questions of Procedure for Ministers*, was published; the Citizen's Charter initiative[32] (see Austin, Ch. 1, p. 19 and Himsworth, Ch. 9, p. 210) encouraged the publication of information about services, although the emphasis has been on matters such as service standards rather than policy issues; and, having formally rejected the idea of freedom of information legislation,[33] the previus government introduced in 1994 a Code of Practice on Access to Government Information, the stated aim of which is 'to improve policy-making and the democratic process by extending access to the facts and analysis which provide the basis for the consideration of proposed policy'. Under the Code, government departments and other public bodies are expected to publish the facts and supporting analysis 'which the Government considers relevant and important in framing major policy proposals and decisions'; to publish explanatory material such as rules, procedures and guidance; to give reasons for administrative decisions to those affected; to publish information about the management and performance of public services; and 'to release, in response to specific requests, information relating to their policies, actions and decisions and other matters related to their areas of responsibility'[34] (see Tomkins, Ch. 14, p. 342).

These developments are to be warmly welcomed so far as they go, but the initiative remains very much with the government. The basis of disclosure is still overwhelmingly voluntary, thereby denying any enforceable legal right to such information (although the Parliamentary Ombudsman may investigate complaints of non-compliance by bodies which fall within his jurisdiction and, presumably, there will be situations in which the code can be relied upon as giving rise to a legitimate expectation that its terms will be complied with). Furthermore, the code relates to the provision of information, not access to original documents or data; and material can be withheld where 'disclosure would not be in the public interest', a test which will generally be interpreted and applied by those in possession of the information. In short, in too many situations, it remains the case that it is entirely within the government's discretion to decide what material should be disclosed and the form in which it should be made available. One of the tests of the new government's commitment to freedom of information will be the extent to which this situation is allowed to change.

---

32   *The Citizen's Charter: Raising the Standard*, Cm 1599, London: HMSO, 1991.
33   See further, *Open Government*, note 27 *supra*.
34   Office of Public Service and Science, London, 1994, paras 2 and 3.

THE NATURE OF JUDICIAL REVIEW

Judicial review of administrative action is a 'supervisory jurisdiction'. That is to say, it provides a procedure whereby the courts supervise or oversee those exercising public power, to ensure that they are acting lawfully. In most cases it is retrospective: the courts will be concerned with a decision that has already been made, although it is possible in some circumstances to seek a declaration in advance so as to establish the legal position. Traditionally, the courts have focused principally on the limits of public power, their role being to ascertain whether a decision-maker has acted beyond his or her statutory or common law powers, or applied an otherwise lawful power improperly. This is particularly relevant in the context of the extensive discretionary statutory powers which Parliament is persuaded to place in the hands of public officials, especially ministers. Read literally, many of these seem to impose little restriction on the manner in which they may be used. The courts, however, have adopted the principle that, regardless of how wide and subjective a statutory power might appear to be, it can be used only in accordance with the policy underlying the relevant legislation.[35] By ensuring that powers are used within the boundaries defined by Parliament and strictly for the purpose that Parliament expressly or by implication is assumed to have intended, judicial review plays an essential role in securing the rule of law.

In recent years, however, the courts have extended the ambit of judicial review well beyond this relatively narrow test of illegality to the extent that it is claimed that there has developed:

a new relationship between the courts and those who derive their authority from the public law, one of partnership based on a common aim, namely the maintenance of the highest standards of public administration[36] (see Fordham, Ch. 8 generally).

In the view of the editors of de Smith:

. . . the standards applied by the courts in judicial review must ultimately be justified by constitutional principles, which govern the proper exercise of power in any democracy . . . The concrete application and elucidation of broad constitutional principles are not self-evident or static. It is for the courts to articulate them as rules and standards of good administration.[37]

35 *Padfield* v *Minister of Agriculture, Fisheries and Food* [1968] AC 997.
36 *R* v *Lancashire County Council, ex parte Huddleston* [1986] 2 All ER 941, at 945 (Lord Donaldson MR).
37 de Smith, S. A., Woolf, H., and Jowell, J., *Judicial Review of Administrative Action* (5th ed.), London: Sweet & Maxwell, 1995, para. 1–025.

It can be readily appreciated that these approaches are far-removed from the courts' orthodox role of preventing, to adopt Wade's graphic phrase, 'the powerful engines of authority . . . from running amok',[38] and has served greatly to extend their influence. Increasingly, the focus is not so much on the *extent* of public power but rather on *how* such power is exercised. Acting entirely on their own initiative, the courts have developed common law standards which, in the absence of statutory provisions to the contrary, they will require of public officials. While judicial review remains a means for individuals to seek redress against the state,[39] the procedure has now developed beyond being simply a mechanism for dispute resolution. Indeed, in some circumstances the individual grievance which precipitated the challenge essentially ceases to be relevant.[40] By extending the grounds for judicial review to include 'irrationality' and 'procedural impropriety',[41] the courts have been concerned to structure the use of discretionary power and to shape the way in which public administration is conducted. These terms are not intended to be discrete or even, given the way they have evolved through the case law, particularly precise. Rather, they provide a general indication of the standards that courts expect from public administrators. Thus, 'irrationality' is sometimes used synonymously with the test of '*Wednesbury* unreasonableness'[42] (see Fordham, Ch. 8 p. 189); elements that have been traditionally associated with '*Wednesbury* unreasonableness' may also be regarded as falling within the requirements of 'procedural propriety'; and unreasonableness has been held to include the important European Community law principle of proportionality.[43] Fortunately, the semantics of these doctrines are not important in the present context; they are essentially conceptual, not terms of legal art. Their significance lies in the values and standards which they represent; the courts have indicated that the word which best 'expresses the underlying concept'[44] is 'fairness'. As a former Lord Chancellor observed, 'The purpose of judicial review is to ensure that the individual receives fair treatment'.[45]

Instead of mechanically applying a list of objective criteria, the nebulous concept of fairness allows the court to consider the decision-making process as a

---

38 Wade, W. and Forsyth, C., *Administrative Law* (7th ed.), Oxford: Clarendon Press, 1994, p. 5.

39 The court 'has the constitutional role and duty of ensuring that the rights of citizens are not abused by the unlawful exercise of executive power. While the court must properly defer to the expertise of responsible decision makers, it must not shrink from its fundamental duty to ''do right to all manner of people'': *R* v *Ministry of Defence, ex parte Smith* [1996] 1 All ER 257, at 265 (Sir Thomas Bingham MR).

40 For example, *R* v *Dairy Produce Quota Tribunal, ex parte Caswell* [1990] 2 AC 738.

41 Adopting Lord Diplock's formulation in *Council of Civil Service Unions* v *Minister for the Civil Service* [1985] AC 374, at 410.

42 *Associated Provincial Picture Houses Ltd* v *Wednesbury Corporation* [1948] 1 KB 223, at 229 (Lord Greene MR).

43 *R* v *Secretary of State for the Home Department, ex parte Brind* [1991] 1 AC 696.

44 *Lloyd* v *McMahon* [1987] AC 625, at 702 (Lord Bridge).

45 *Chief Constable of North Wales* v *Evans* [1982] 1 WLR 1155, 1161 (Lord Hailsham LC).

whole and to take account of matters such as the nature of the power, the identity of the decision-maker, the weight given to the respective factors leading to the decision, and the degree of explanation, consultation and consideration involved:

> The principles of fairness are not to be applied by rote identically in every situation. What fairness demands is dependent on the context of the decision, and this is to be taken into account in all its aspects.[46]

It follows that what is required in any particular situation can vary dramatically depending upon 'the character of the decision-making body, the kind of decision it has to make and the statutory or other framework in which it operates'.[47] In broad terms, the courts will generally apply a high threshold when the decision is likely to have a significant adverse effect upon the individual concerned, such as compromising his or her liberty;[48] at the other end of the spectrum, it can be overridden or severely negated by considerations such as protecting national security.[49]

A particular aspect of fairness which the courts have developed is the notion of legitimate expectation. This may arise when a decision leads to the loss of a benefit or advantage which either the decision-maker has permitted in the past and which could legitimately be expected to continue until such time as the person affected has been advised of 'some rational grounds for withdrawing it on which he has been given an opportunity to comment'; or the decision-maker has given an assurance that it will not be withdrawn without providing those affected an opportunity to make representations as to why it should not be withdrawn.[50] By holding a decision-maker to an express promise,[51] or a course of conduct[52] pending consultation with those affected, the courts are not only preventing arbitrary or duplicitous behaviour, they are also promoting accountability by, first, requiring a decision-maker to explain what he intends to do and why and, secondly, providing an opportunity for those affected to participate in the decision-making process through their representations.

---

46   *R v Secretary of State for the Home Department, ex parte Doody* [1994] 1 AC 531, at 560 (Lord Mustill).

47   *Per* Lord Bridge, *Lloyd v McMahon*, note 44 *supra*, at 702.

48   *R v Secretary of State for the Home Department, ex parte Doody*, note 46 *supra*; *R v Secretary of State for the Home Department, ex parte Duggan* [1994] 3 All ER 277.

49   See, for example, *Council of Civil Service Unions v Minister for the Civil Service*, note 41 *supra*; *R v Secretary of State for the Home Department, ex parte Cheblak* [1991] 1 WLR 890.

50   *Council of Civil Service Unions v Minister for the Civil Service*, note 41 *supra*, at 408–9 (Lord Diplock). See further on legitimate expectations, *R v Secretary of State for the Home Department, ex parte Hargreaves* [1997] 1 All ER 397.

51   For example, *Attorney-General of Hong Kong v Ng Yuen Shiu* [1983] 2 AC 629; *R v Secretary of State for the Home Department, ex parte Asif Mahmood Khan* [1984] 1 WLR 1337.

52   For example, *Council of Civil Service Unions v Minister for the Civil Service*, note 41 *supra*; *R v Secretary of State for the Home Department, ex parte Ruddock* [1987] 1 WLR 1482.

A similar consequence results whenever a decision-maker is required to consult before confirming or implementing a decision. There are many situations in which statute requires such an exercise to be undertaken and the legislation will generally indicate who should be consulted and the procedure to be followed. In circumstances where consultation is not mandatory, ministers will often choose voluntarily to undertake such an exercise or, if they do not, the courts may require it, especially when those affected are threatened with losing a significant benefit.[53] Regardless of the basis on which it is undertaken, the courts are concerned to ensure that once a consultation exercise has been initiated, it does not become a pretence; the decision-maker is required to demonstrate that it involves 'a genuine invitation to give advice and a genuine consideration of that advice'.[54] In order to demonstrate that these two criteria have been met, the process must be initiated when the proposals are still at a formative stage, and all those with a relevant interest should be consulted and provided with adequate information in respect of all relevant issues about what is proposed and why.[55] In short, those consulted are entitled to adequate information and time in order that they may respond with 'sufficiently informed and considered information or advice' about the substance of the proposals and their implications for those affected,[56] which 'must be conscientiously taken into account' in arriving at a final decision.[57] There are clearly practical problems in establishing that this latter requirement is fulfilled, particularly if the decision-maker is not under an obligation to provide reasons for his decision. Moreover, there is no requirement to give any particular weight to the responses received, regardless of their force, and in most cases the decision-maker will therefore retain considerable discretion in arriving at the final decision. It is also the case that, despite the detailed and apparently strict procedural requirements for consultation laid down by the courts, a failure adequately to comply with them is not necessarily fatal to the eventual decision if the court considers that to quash it would result in undue administrative inconvenience.[58] While in the view of one commentator this last caveat 'makes a mockery of the requirement of consultation',[59] the growing importance of consultation in the eyes of the courts, and in its absence the possibility of having a decision struck down, does assist in obtaining information, and provides an opportunity to explore and respond to policy options.

---

53   *R* v *Devon County Council, ex parte Baker* [1995] 1 All ER 73.
54   *R* v *Secretary of State for Social Services, ex parte Association of Metropolitan Authorities* [1986] 1 WLR 1, at 4.
55   *R* v *Secretary of State for Health, ex parte United States Tobacco International Inc.* [1992] QB 353, at 371; see also *R* v *Devon County Council, ex parte Baker*, note 53 *supra*, at 91.
56   *R* v *Secretary of State for Social Services, ex parte Association of Metropolitan Authorities*, note 54 *supra*, at 4; see also, *R* v *Secretary of State for Health, ex parte United States Tobacco International Inc.*, note 55 *supra*, at 371.
57   *R* v *Devon County Council, ex parte Baker*, note 53 *supra*, at 91.
58   *R* v *Secretary of State for Social Services, ex parte Association of Metropolitan Authorities*, at note 54 *supra*.
59   Cane, P., *Introduction to Administrative Law* (3rd ed.), Oxford: Clarendon Press, 1996, p. 194.

THE REACH OF JUDICIAL REVIEW

In the same way that the grounds for judicial review are not discrete, neither are the other elements of the judicial review procedure such as leave, scope and remedies. The significance of this is that development in one area will generally have an impact in another. For example, while the courts were primarily concerned with enforcing the *limits* of public power, it was inevitable that attention would be focused on statutory powers and, where there was doubt about their scope and meaning, to look to the perceived parliamentary intention. Once attention turned to *how* public power is exercised then it was to be expected that, eventually, judicial oversight would extend to at least some aspects of the prerogative (see Pollard, Ch. 13 generally), a development which was formally recognised by the House of Lords in *Council of Civil Service Unions* v *Minister for the Civil Service*. Lord Scarman stated 'with confidence' that:

> if the subject matter in respect of which prerogative power is exercised is justiciable, that is to say if it is a matter on which the court can adjudicate, the exercise of the power is subject to review in accordance with the principles developed in respect of the review of the exercise of statutory power.

In his view, the previous limitation on scrutiny by the courts 'has now gone, overwhelmed by the developing modern law of judicial review'. Henceforth, 'the controlling factor' in determining whether the exercise of prerogative power is subject to oversight by the courts is not its source but its subject matter'.[60] This is potentially significant in terms of accountability because, formerly, ministers had been answerable exclusively to Parliament for the way in which they exercised prerogative power, and there was little evidence that Parliament was particularly effective in this regard. By enlarging the scope of judicial review to include at least some aspects of the prerogative, the courts extended accountability for the way in which it is used beyond the political arena, and presented themselves with the opportunity to impose similar procedural requirements as had been developed in respect of statutory powers.

This still begs the question of what the courts would consider to be justiciable. Lord Roskill suggested that the making of treaties, the defence of the realm, the prerogative of mercy, the grant of honours, the dissolution of Parliament, and the appointment of ministers were among the matters carried out under the prerogative

---

60   Note 41 *supra,* at 407. Similarly, Lord Diplock could see 'no reason why simply because a decision making power is derived from a common law and not a statutory source it should *for that reason only* [sic] be immune from judicial review' (at 410) and Lord Roskill was 'unable to see . . . that there is any logical reason why the fact that the source of the power is the prerogative and not statute should today deprive the citizen of that right to challenge to the manner of its exercise which he would possess were the source of the power statutory. In either case the act in question is the act of the executive' (at 417).

which 'because of their nature and subject matter' are not 'amenable to the judicial process'.[61] While it is clear that the courts have remained cautious in reviewing prerogative power, they have been prepared to do so when they consider it appropriate and, despite the Roskill list of non justiciable subjects, the courts have extended their jurisdiction to include consideration of the issue of passports;[62] treaty making;[63] national security;[64] and the prerogative of mercy.[65] Moreover, it is not only in respect of prerogative power that the courts have extended their involvement; any administrative power which they consider in the light of current standards to be appropriate for judicial oversight will be drawn into the net, so that matters such as the decisions of prison governors, which were previously thought to be immune,[66] may now be subject to review,[67] as are the Home Secretary's decisions in respect of the 'tariff' imposed on a prisoner serving a mandatory life sentence.[68]

The reach of judicial review has also been extended as a result of the courts' approach to standing (see Himsworth, Ch. 9 generally). In considering an application for judicial review, the court is under a duty to refuse leave 'unless it is satisfied that the applicant has a sufficient interest in the matter to which it relates'.[69] Clearly the way in which this test is applied has a direct bearing on both the number and the nature of the challenges which will proceed to a substantive hearing. Despite arguments to apply a relatively restrictive test, based on fears of opening the floodgates, the danger of encouraging vexatious litigants, and the traditional view that the courts' primary role is to provide redress for individual grievances, the judges have continued to use the test of sufficient interest as an effective filter, while at the same time adopting enough flexibility in their approach to ensure that potentially meritorious challenges come before the courts. Where the issue of standing is obvious, it may be dealt with at the leave stage; otherwise, it is considered at the substantive hearing together with the legal and factual context.[70] Even when leave is subsequently denied on the basis of a lack of

---

61 At 418.
62 *R v Secretary of State for Foreign and Commonwealth Affairs, ex parte Everett* [1989] QB 811.
63 *Blackburn v Attorney-General* [1971] 1 WLR 1037; *R v Secretary of State for Foreign and Commonwealth Affairs, ex parte Rees-Mogg* [1994] QB 552, at 569–70.
64 *Council of Civil Service Unions v Minister for the Civil Service*, note 41 *supra*; *R v Secretary of State for the Home Department, ex parte Ruddock*, note 52 *supra*; *R v Secretary of State for the Home Department, ex parte Cheblak*, note 49 *supra*. In *R v Ministry of Defence, ex parte* Smith, note 39 *supra*, at 325–6 the policy of not allowing homosexuals to join or remain in the armed forces was held to be justiciable because it did not give rise to 'operational considerations' or have 'security implications' (Simon Brown LJ).
65 *R v Secretary of State for the Home Department, ex parte Bentley* [1994] QB 349.
66 *R v Deputy Governor of Camphill Prison, ex parte King* [1985] QB 735.
67 *Leech v Deputy Governor of Parkhurst Prison* [1988] 1 AC 533.
68 *R v Secretary of State for the Home Department, ex parte Doody*, note 46 *supra*.
69 RSC ord. 53, r. 3(7), given statutory force by virtue of the Supreme Court Act 1981, s. 31(3).
70 *R v Inland Revenue Commissioners, ex parte National Federation of Small Businesses Ltd* [1982] AC 617.

standing, it does not necessarily prevent a decision on the substantive issues.[71] The courts have thereby sought to:

> embrace all classes of those who might apply and yet permit sufficient flexibility in any particular case to determine whether or not 'sufficient interest' was in fact shown.[72]

They appear to have been successful in this regard; it has recently been observed that 'it is difficult to find any case where an applicant has been refused relief on the grounds that he has no *locus standi* where relief would have been granted but for his lack of *locus standi*'.[73] While the concept might suggest that it is necessary to demonstrate an interest in the disputed matter beyond that of the ordinary man in the street, a taxpayer,[74] a journalist acting in the public interest,[75] a television licence-holder,[76] and an individual with 'a sincere concern for constitutional issues'[77] have all satisfied the courts in the context of their particular challenges that they were applicants with a sufficient interest.

Of equal significance has been the courts' attitude towards representative groups. It has been said that a claim to sufficient interest by a group cannot be better than that of the individuals who make up its membership, on the basis that 'an aggregate of individuals, each of whom has no interest, cannot of itself have an interest'.[78] However, the preferable view, and the one which appears now to be more generally adopted by the courts, recognises that a group of persons who combine to make an application may gain 'enhanced authority to speak on a subject on behalf of a section of the public'.[79] Indeed, it is clear that pressure groups are playing an increasingly important part in judicial review proceedings. They often have much greater awareness of the existence and potential of judicial review than the ordinary, even well-informed, citizen and many are more familiar with the procedural requirements than the average lawyer. But their contribution is more than simply tactical. Pressure groups can make an application on behalf of those who are not in a position to do so themselves because of their circumstances; they

---

71   *R* v *Secretary of State for the Environment, ex parte Rose Theatre Trust Co.* [1990] 1 QB 504.
72   *R* v *Inland Revenue Commissioners, ex parte National Federation of Small Businesses Ltd*, note 70 *supra*, at 658 (Lord Roskill).
73   de Smith, Woolf and Jowell, *op. cit.* note 37 *supra*, at para. 2–035.
74   *R* v *Her Majesty's Treasury, ex parte Smedley* [1985] QB 657.
75   *R* v *Felixstowe Justices, ex parte Leigh* [1987] QB 582.
76   *R* v *Independent Broadcasting Authority, ex parte Whitehouse* (1984) *The Times*, 14 April.
77   *R* v *Secretary of State for Foreign and Commonwealth Affairs, ex parte Rees-Mogg*, note 63 *supra*.
78   *R* v *Inland Revenue Commissioners, ex parte National Federation of Small Businesses Ltd*, note 70 *supra*, at 663 (Lord Wilberforce), a view echoed by Schiemann J in *R* v *Secretary of State for the Environment, ex parte Rose Theatre*, note 71 *supra*, at 520: 'The fact that some thousands of people join together and assert that they have an interest does not create an interest if the individuals did not have an interest.'
79   de Smith, Woolf and Jowell, *op. cit.* note 37 *supra*, at para. 2–040.

can step in when there is no obvious individual to do so; and they can bring a degree of expertise and informed argument to the matter in dispute. Accordingly, a group's 'national and international expertise'[80] may be a factor in granting sufficient interest, as may the fact that 'a less well-informed challenge might be mounted which would stretch unnecessarily the court's resources and which would not afford the court the assistance it requires in order to do justice between the parties'.[81] Hence the courts have been willing to countenance groups who represent the interests of third parties;[82] groups seeking to represent the interests of their members;[83] and interest groups seeking to further their own objectives.[84]

THE CONTRIBUTION OF JUDICIAL REVIEW TO GOVERNMENT ACCOUNTABILITY

We have seen that there are serious shortcomings in Parliament's traditional role of holding government to account. Too often, political constraints and considerations take priority over the fundamental function of the House of Commons to scrutinise the executive. This is not to suggest that Parliament is never effective, but at a time when perceptions seem to matter more than substance in politics, the government's party managers are working constantly to present its performance in the best possible light: questions are planted, reliable backbenchers are placed on committees, patronage is dispensed, and loyalty demanded (not always with success). These are clearly factors which do not sully the courts.

Judicial review has been famously described in successive editions of *de Smith's Judicial Review of Administrative Action* as 'inevitably sporadic and peripheral' on the basis that 'the prospect of judicial relief cannot be held out to every person whose interests may be adversely affected by administrative action'. This view has been endorsed by the present editors, but with the caveat that 'caution is now needed before relegating judicial review to a minor role in the control of official power'.[85] This is surely correct. To focus on bare statistics alone fails to provide an accurate picture of its impact. It is inevitable that, despite a significant increase in recent years, the case-load will forever remain minute in comparison to the scale of activity by public bodies, but the effect of judicial review is out of all proportion to its volume. For example, it has provided a unique opportunity for the judiciary

---

80   *R v Secretary of State for Foreign Affairs, ex parte World Development Movement Ltd* [1995] 1 All ER 611, at 620 (Rose LJ).
81   *R v Inspectorate of Pollution, ex parte Greenpeace Ltd (No. 2)* [1994] 4 All ER 329, at 350 (Otton J).
82   For example, the Child Poverty Action Group, Shelter, the Joint Council for the Welfare of Immigrants, and Help the Aged.
83   For example, the Fire Brigades Union.
84   For example, the World Development Movement, Greenpeace, the Royal Society for the Prevention of Cruelty to Animals and the Royal Society for the Protection of Birds.
85   de Smith, Woolf and Jowell, *op. cit.* note 37 *supra*, paras 1–002 and 1–033.

to embark upon a searching analysis of fundamental aspects of the constitution and to develop the common law in a manner appropriate to contemporary standards of government and administration. In more general terms, there is a consensus that judicial review has 'improved the quality of decision making by making it more structured and consistent' and contributed 'to upholding the values of fairness, reasonableness and objectivity in the conduct of public business'.[86] Furthermore, because applications for judicial review come before the High Court, the decisions are binding on lower courts, tribunals, and public administrators, subject to being negated by Parliament (although this is not possible in respect of decisions based on European Community law). The status and authority of the decisions emanating from judicial review can therefore engender an immediate and widespread administrative response. Even where this is not forthcoming, the ripple effect of the case law should not be underestimated, as the standards promoted by the courts become integrated into administrative procedures (see Sunkin generally).

In respect of the relatively small number of cases involving the executive which actually come before the courts,[87] the nature of the judicial process requires the decision maker to justify his conduct before an independent and objective tribunal. This is, in itself, an act of accountability and one whose characteristics are in marked contrast to those of the political arena. It has been suggested that the courts are engaged in an exercise 'to impose upon all decision makers standards that are inherent in a democracy,'[88] an undertaking which gives no weight to the politicians' arts of point-scoring, partisanship, presentation and spin. To this extent, it is reasonable to compare the courts favourably with Parliament, on the basis that 'the judges at least listen to reasoned argument in public and attempt to decide issues according to known and accepted principles'.[89] In a parliamentary debate, there is little opportunity to undertake a detailed examination of a minister's motives and conduct, and a competent politician will generally be able to deflect criticism and minimise embarrassment. Even select committees, the most forensic of parliamentary institutions, face formidable problems. The range of subjects they are able to investigate is small compared with the overall power and responsibilities of the executive; the time available for inquiries is limited; they remain ill-equipped and under-resourced in comparison with the battalion of officials available to brief ministers; and experience suggests that, despite the worthiness of select committee

---

86   Treasury and Civil Service Committee, *op. cit.* note 5 *supra*, para. 136.
87   It has been estimated that challenges to the decisions of government departments make up approximately 25 per cent of the judicial review case-load; the Home Office is the department most often involved. See further, Sunkin, M., Bridges, L. and Mészáros, G., *Judicial Review in Perspective: An Investigation of Trends in the Use and Operation of the Judicial Review Procedure in England and Wales*, London: Public Law Project, 1993; and 'Trends in Judicial Review' [1993] *Public Law* 443.
88   de Smith, Woolf and Jowell, *op. cit.* note 37 *supra*, para. 1–026.
89   Sedley, Sir Stephen, 'Governments, Constitutions and Judges', note 3 *supra*, p. 42.

reports, the government's earnestness in considering their recommendations is often to be doubted. By way of contrast, prevarication is impossible before a court and the eventual decision cannot be ignored:

> No government welcomes scrutiny of its activities by an independent judiciary. It can be highly embarrassing for ministers to have to explain their decisions on affidavit, to be required to disclose documents they would rather keep secret, and to be obliged to give instructions to their counsel to answer questions from a persistent judge that can be evaded in the less demanding forum of the House of Commons.[90]

A further major weakness of looking to Parliament for ministerial accountability is that it severely restricts those who can participate. To play the game, one has to be part of the political or journalistic élite: the general public cannot hold ministers to account directly (expect in relatively exceptional circumstances through private correspondence or having the opportunity to question them on political panel programmes). Even those with particular expertise are effectively excluded: they can challenge through the media, they may be called as witnesses before a select committee (but that will not involve challenging a minister directly), they can enter into correspondence, they may be consulted; but the traditional political process provides no right of direct access to a minister or his officials. Such a situation is to be contrasted with judicial review, where the applicant confronts the minister on an equal footing and, as a result of the flexible application of the test of sufficient interest, not only are those directly affected by a decision able to challenge the executive, but so too are pressure groups (subject to the discretion of the courts). It is striking, for example, that factors such as Greenpeace's 'particular experience in environmental matters, its access to experts in the relevant realms of science and technology (not to mention the law),' enabling it 'to mount a carefully selected, focused, relevant and well-argued challenge,'[91] have been regarded by the judiciary as positive factors in gaining access to the courts, whereas politicians might choose to deny or restrict the formal involvement of such a well-informed organisation in the political process. Indeed, judicial review can be particularly valuable for those groups with whom the government has little sympathy, and who might otherwise have difficulty in getting any hearing, or to whom ministers may be inclined to pay only lip-service.

It is not only by granting access to the courts that judicial review assists in furthering the 'constitutional principle . . . of political participation'.[92] It is central to the concept of fairness underlying the principles of good administration, which

---

90   David Pannick QC, 'Why judges cannot avoid politics', *The Times*, 7 November 1995.
91   *R v Inspectorate of Pollution, ex parte Greenpeace Ltd (No. 2)*, note 81 *supra*, at 350 (Otton J).
92   de Smith, Woolf and Jowell, *op. cit.* note 37 *supra*, para. 1–025.

the courts have been so concerned to promote. While one aspect of increased accountability resulting from judicial review is apparent through the cases which actually advance to a substantive hearing, of much wider practical significance is the ever-widening scope and application of the doctrines which the courts have developed: the provision of information, the opportunity to make representations, legitimate expectation and the other factors which together constitute fairness have the effect of placing a duty on decision makers to justify their actions and allow those affected to contribute to the decision making process. This represents accountability in action, although it would be strengthened further if ministers and their officials were under an obligation to provide reasons for their decisions. Clearly, this would have the advantage of placing the onus on decision makers to explain the basis of their decisions, promote greater transparency, and permit those interested in the outcome to assess whether a challenge is appropriate. It has been said that 'no single factor has inhibited the development of English administrative law as seriously as the absence of any general obligation upon public authorities to give reasons for their decisions'[93] and, according to Lord Woolf, such a development would be 'the most beneficial improvement which could be made to English administrative law'.[94] At present, however, there is no general common law requirement to do so, although a decision maker's conduct may give rise to a legitimate expectation that reasons will be given, or the courts may demand it if they consider the circumstances of the case merit reasons in the interests of fairness. For example, if its importance is such that an unreasoned decision — as if 'the distant oracle has spoken, and that is that' — is inadequate,[95] or to rebut the impression that a decision is aberrant.[96] A trend appears to be developing; indeed, the Divisional Court, while recognising that there remain decisions for which fairness does not demand reasons, has specifically rejected the contention that the circumstances in which such an obligation arises are to be any longer regarded as exceptional.[97] Moreover, once leave for judicial review has been granted, the respondent is under a duty to make 'full and fair disclosure' to the court.[98] Atypically, however, this is an area where the government appears to have moved ahead of the courts, at least for the moment. With the stated aim of protecting the interests of individuals and companies, the Code of Practice on Access to

---

93   Justice/All Souls Committee Report, *Administrative Justice. Some Necessary Reforms*, Oxford: Clarendon Press, 1988, p. 71.

94   Woolf, H., *Protection of the Public. A New Challenge*, London: Stevens, 1990, p. 92.

95   *R v Secretary of State for the Home Department, ex parte Doody*, note 46 *supra*, at 561 (Lord Mustill).

96   *R v Universities Funding Council, ex parte Institute of Dental Surgery* [1994] 1 WLR 242, at 263 (Sedley J).

97   *R v Universities Funding Council, ex parte Institute of Dental Surgery*, note 96 *supra*, at 257 (Sedley J).

98   *R v Lancashire County Council, ex parte Huddleston*, note 36 *supra*, at 945 (Lord Donaldson MR).

Government Information provides that reasons for administrative decisions should be provided 'except where there is statutory authority or established convention to the contrary'.[99]

That judicial review, as a result of its procedure and its doctrines, has greatly increased accountability for the way in which government power is exercised is beyond doubt, but it is not all-embracing. In all except the most extreme cases, the merits of a decision remain immune from challenge; access to information is still a problem;[100] and, most significantly, there are huge swathes of government activity which remain effectively beyond judicial oversight. The courts will be reluctant to become involved if the subject matter is not amenable to the judicial process;[101] concerns matters of political opinion,[102] questions of social and ethical controversy,[103] or the allocation of resources;[104] lacks objective criteria;[105] or involves 'such questions of policy that [the courts] should not intrude because they are ill-equipped to do so'.[106] It is altogether appropriate that the judiciary should be alert to the dangers of straying into areas of policy, but their caution also serves, despite its far-reaching impact, to highlight significant limitations on the legitimate scope of judicial review:

> The greater the policy content of a decision, and the more remote the subject matter of a decision from ordinary judicial experience, the more hesitant the court must necessarily be in holding a decision to be irrational . . . Where decisions of a policy-laden, esoteric or security-based nature are in issue, even greater caution than normal must be shown in applying the test.[107]

Such a statement serves to emphasise that legal accountability augments political accountability, it does not replace it.

---

99 Note 34 *supra*, at para. 2.
100 Without a *prima facie* case for suggesting that an affidavit or other evidence relied on by a minister was false, or at least inaccurate, it will normally be inappropriate for the court to grant discovery in order to allow the applicant to check the accuracy of the evidence in question: *R v Secretary of State for the Environment, ex parte Islington LBC, The Independent*, 6 September 1991, applied in *R v Secretary of State for Foreign Affairs, ex parte World Development Movement Ltd*, note 80 *supra*, at 620–2.
101 *Council of Civil Service Unions v Minister for the Civil Service*, note 41 *supra*, at 418 (Lord Roskill).
102 *R v Secretary of State for the Environment, ex parte Hammersmith and Fulham LBC* [1991] 1 AC 521, at 595–7.
103 *Gillick v West Norfolk and Wisbech Area Health Authority* [1986] 1 AC 112, at 193.
104 *R v Cambridge Health Authority, ex parte B* [1995] 2 All ER 129.
105 *R v Secretary of State for the Environment, ex parte Hammersmith and Fulham LBC*, note 102 *supra*, at 595–7.
106 *R v Secretary of State for the Home Department, ex parte Bentley*, note 65 *supra*, at 363 (Watkins LJ).
107 *R v Ministry of Defence, ex parte Smith*, note 39 *supra*, at 264 (Sir Thomas Bingham MR).

CONCLUSION

The respective constitutional roles of Parliament and the courts in promoting government accountability are separate and distinct; complementary, but not interchangeable. The effectiveness of the one can never compensate for the weakness of the other. In recent years the courts have, by means of judicial review, achieved a significant and unprecedented impact on the way in which government-al power is exercised. Overall, the judiciary have been bold in extending the scope of decisions which they are prepared to review, imaginative in granting access to the courts, and enlightened in their development and application of the adminis-trative standards which they demand. The last is particularly significant as these are matters which have been largely ignored by Parliament. Furthermore, the courts have demonstrated that the question of accountability is not confined to the single issue of resignation. In the political context, debate about the circumstances in which a minister should resign has tended to dominate the wider question of what constitutes effective control and how it can best be achieved. The Chairman of the Public Service Committee has, for example, recently emphasised the view of his Committee that 'proper and vigorous scrutiny . . . may be more important to Parliament's ability to correct error than forcing resignations'.[108] An ultimate sanction is necessary, but in general terms the ability to know how power is being (or not being) exercised and the opportunity to influence the course of events are of at least equal importance.

Secondly, the courts have demonstrated that accountability is not the exclusive concern of Parliament. The government has claimed that 'the proper test of whether our doctrine of accountability is working is the extent to which Parliament is effective in getting policies and systems that are not working changed for the better'.[109] In terms of constitutional orthodoxy this is an accurate statement, but not only have MPs themselves recognised that the Commons is not adequately fulfilling this role, it is also important to appreciate what Lord Nolan has described as 'the very centralist nature of this position'. As he points out, 'It brings the accountability of the Executive down to one very narrow point — the answerability of a hundred Ministers, or twenty Secretaries of State, to Parliament and its Committees'.[110] Judicial review goes at least some way in providing an opportunity for those outside the exclusive confines of the political establishment to become involved in holding the executive to account.

These are all extremely positive achievements. They do not, however, solve the problem of the democratic deficit. The courts cannot compensate for Parliament's

---

108   Giles Radice, 290 HC Deb., 6th ser., col. 274.
109   Public Service Committee, *op. cit.* note 11 *supra*, Annex A, para. 24.
110   Lord Nolan, in a lecture delivered at the University of Warwick, quoted by Dr Tony Wright, MP, 290 HC Deb., 6th ser., col. 286.

shortcomings. If political oversight of the executive in ineffective, the answer lies with the politicians themselves, either by adopting a more rigorous approach or by reforming the relevant institutions. Griffith's contention remains valid: 'Law is not and cannot be a substitute for politics . . . Only political control, politically exercised, can supply the remedy.'[111] If there is a democratic deficit arising from a lack of effective parliamentary oversight — and all the evidence suggests that there is — then it can only be rectified by Parliament, not the courts.

---

111   Griffith, J., 'The Political Constitution' (1979) 42 *Modern Law Review* 16.

3

Delegated Legislation: A Necessary Evil or a Constitutional Outrage?

Gabriele Ganz

SUMMARY

Sir Richard Scott is the latest in a long line of critics accusing successive administrations of abuse of executive power in the use of delegated legislation. Effective parliamentary control is hampered by the party system in the Commons and by the composition of the House of Lords. It is left to the courts to control the executive.

INTRODUCTION

In a passage reminiscent of Lord Hewart's *The New Despotism*,[1] Sir Richard Scott in a little noticed section of his report[2] on the export control system concluded that, 'from 1950 at latest until December 1990 there was, in my opinion, a reprehensible abuse of executive power by successive administrations'.[3] Lord Howe, commenting on this section of the report, characterised it as 'intéressant, mais il ne vaut pas le détour'.[4] Nothing can better illustrate the nonchalant attitude of the executive to the misuse of delegated legislation which is the subject of this chapter and which

---

1 Hewart, C.J., *The New Despotism*, London: Benn, 1929.
2 *Report of the Inquiry into the Export of Defence Equipment and Dual-Use Goods to Iraq and Related Prosecutions* ('the Scott Report'), HC 115, London: HMSO, 1996, section C.
3 Scott Report, C 1.64.
4 *Ministerial Accountability and Responsibility*, Public Service Committee, HC 313, London: HMSO, 1996, Q 260. It seems that the most outrageous statements in this affair had to be made under the cover of French, *cf* 'economical with the *actualité*,' the Scott Report, G 17.29.

is exemplified in so many particulars by the system of export controls exposed in the Scott Report (see Tomkins, Ch. 14, pp. 340 *et seq* for further discussion of the Scott Report).

What makes this exposé uniquely valuable and distinguishes it from Lord Hewart's diatribe is the access that Scott had to government papers. The executive is condemned out of its own mouth in one quotation after another from its own briefing papers. Important constitutional issues relating to delegated legislation were at stake.

The Import, Export and Customs Powers (Defence) Act 1939, which had its second reading on the ominous date of 1 September, 1939[5] gave blanket powers to the Board of Trade by order to make such provisions as it thought expedient for prohibiting or regulating the importation into or exportation from the United Kingdom of all goods or goods of any specified description (s. 1). There was no provision for any parliamentary control over these orders (they did not even have to be laid before Parliament), but the Act was to continue in force only 'until such date as His Majesty may by Order in Council declare to be the date on which the emergency that was the occasion of the passing of this Act came to an end, and shall then expire . . .' (s. 9(3)).

No such Order in Council was ever made. The war-time Act, which passed through all its stages in the House of Commons in 20 minutes, was used to control exports until 1990 and this usage survived three legal challenges.[6] From the contemporary documents Scott makes out a convincing case that this omission to bring the emergency to an end was deliberate and 'prompted by considerations of administrative convenience and political expediency'.[7] This abuse was legitimated rather than ended by the Import and Export Control Act 1990, which was prompted by the prospective reunification of Germany.[8] This made it difficult to sustain the convenient fiction that the 1939 emergency continued.[9] The Gulf crisis added urgency to proposals for the 1990 Bill[10] which did no more than repeal the provision in the 1939 Act for bringing the emergency to an end by an Order in Council. Thus the war-time powers to control imports and exports were made permanent in 1990 and, as Scott points out in another constitutional aside, 'the export control powers exercised by Government since 1950 are, for all practical purposes, indistinguishable in their scope and effect and in the manner of their exercise, from prerogative powers'.[11]

---

5   351 HC Deb, 5th ser., col. 171.
6   *Willcock* v *Muckle* [1951] 2 KB 844; *R* v *Secretary of State for Trade and Industry, ex parte Chris International Foods Ltd,* 4 March 1983, Hodgson J, 21 July 1983; Woolf J, *R* v *Blackledge and Others* CA, 22 May 1995. See Scott Report, C 1.50 *et seq.*
7   Scott Report, C 1.64.
8   *Ibid.,* C 1.68.
9   *Ibid.,* C 1.71.
10 *Ibid.,* C 1.79.
11 *Ibid.,* C 1.150.

The 1990 Act not only legitimated the delegation of blanket powers to the government to make export control orders, it also perpetuated the lack of Parliamentary control over such orders. The first draft of the Bill provided that such orders should be subject to annulment in either House.[12] This procedure was to be used as a bargaining counter with the Opposition to obtain their consent to the quick passage of the Bill through Parliament.[13] Due to a misunderstanding[14] this tactical weapon was not needed and the Bill was passed without opposition through the House.[15] Scott comments that proper Parliamentary supervision should not have been treated as merely an optional extra[16] and even more pointedly, 'The wider the ambit of the powers, the more necessary is the maintenance of Parliamentary scrutiny and control. The neglect of these principles is to give substance to the charge, usually attributed to Lord Hailsham, that the constitution has become an 'elective dictatorship'.[17] In evidence to the Scott Inquiry, the Attorney-General rejected this verdict and accused Scott of 'a lack of understanding of how Parliament really works and of what are the real safeguards within the democratic process'.[18] Scott refutes this with 19 quotations from government sources recognising the need for Parliamentary scrutiny in the form of at least a negative resolution.[19]

Lastly, Scott raises the issue (which has not yet been tested) of whether the absence of any published criteria for interference with the right to the enjoyment of property (which export or import controls clearly are) constitutes an infringement of the European Convention on Human Rights (Art. 1 of Protocol No. 1).[20] Scott returns to this issue in the final section of his report where he expresses his opinion that the absence in the Act of the purposes for which export controls can be used has led to a dangerous confusion between the law and government policy on export controls.[21] He is referring there to the way in which export controls are implemented under the Act.

As Scott points out, there is no mention of the licensing of goods for export in the 1939 Act. No procedure for granting licences is laid down, the only reference to a licence being in the Export Control Orders made under the Act which provide that nothing shall be taken to prohibit the exportation of any goods under the

---

12 *Ibid.*, C 1.81.
13 *Ibid.*, C 1.82 and C 1.83.
14 *Ibid.*, C 1.111.
15 *Ibid.*, C 1.107.
16 *Ibid.*, C 1.110.
17 *Ibid.*, C 1.108.
18 *Ibid.*, C 1.117.
19 *Ibid.* The Conservative government agreed that there should be formal Parliamentary scrutiny of export control orders: *Strategic export control, a consultative document*, Cm 3349, 1996, para. 2.6.1.
20 Scott Report, C 1.119 and C 1.120.
21 *Ibid.*, K 2.1 and C 3.5

authority of a licence granted by the Secretary of State.[22] Ministers, therefore, could literally grant or refuse licences at their discretion subject to judicial review. Detailed guidance for officials[23] dealing with export licences was, unusually for this area, laid down by the notorious Howe guidelines for the sale of defence equipment to Iran and Iraq to which so much criticism was devoted in the Scott Report. They were not legally binding,[24] were based on no statutory authority, were not subject to parliamentary approval, could be changed at any time or applied flexibly without being changed[25] and did not have to be published, though they were published after nearly a year's delay.[26] They were in fact a typical example of quasi-legislation, namely rules which structure administrative discretion but are not subject to the normal safeguards which apply to statutory instruments (see below).

Thus, Scott's analysis of the export control system exposes some of the fundamental problems with regard to delegated legislation. First, it illustrates the use of enabling or skeleton legislation giving blanket powers to ministers to make orders without stating the purposes or criteria limiting the use of such powers. Secondly, it shows the lack of parliamentary control over these orders and, thirdly, it exemplifies the use of informal rules of guidance to structure administrative discretion which blur the line between government policy and the embodiment of that policy in legal rules. Lastly, it shows the use of judicial control to challenge the legality of delegated legislation, though unsuccessfully in this instance.[27] These issues are not confined to export controls and will now be examined more generally.

SKELETON ACTS

The use of enabling or skeleton legislation is not a new phenomenon. Criticism of this type of legislation was amongst the factors which led to the setting up of the Committee on Ministers' Powers which categorised it as falling within the exceptional type of delegated legislation[28] and recommended that it should be granted only on exceptional grounds and that powers to make delegated legislation should be clearly defined.[29] It would not be an exaggeration to say that from being the exception, legislation conferring such powers has become the norm with a consequential shift in the balance of power between Parliament and the executive. This development is constitutionally far more significant than the increase in the

---

22 *Ibid.*, C 1.125.
23 *Ibid.*, D 1.80.
24 *Ibid.*, D 1.82.
25 *Ibid.*, D 3.122 and 123. The difference was one of the main issues in the Scott Report.
26 *Ibid.*, D 1.90.
27 See note 6 *supra*.
28 Cmd 4060, 1932, p. 31. Four categories were listed, including powers to legislate on matters of principle and powers conferring so wide a discretion that it is impossible to know what limits Parliament intended.
29 *Ibid.*, p. 58–9.

sheer volume of delegated legislation.[30] Delegated legislation is used not only for matters of detail,[31] but for matters of policy at the broadest level. Examples of this are legion,[32] including such controversial policies as the assisted places scheme,[33] the Social Fund,[34] student loans[35] and the jobseeker's allowance.[36] Even more disturbing is the use of delegated legislation 'to *change* policies in ways that were sometimes not envisaged when the enabling primary legislation was passed'.[37] The most recent and notorious example is the regulations withdrawing social security benefits from asylum seekers[38] which were successfully challenged in the courts, though not on this ground. In the course of his judgment Simon Brown LJ said, 'I for my part regard the Regulations now in force as so uncompromisingly draconian in effect that they must indeed be held *ultra vires*'.[39] This is not the only occasion on which the courts have criticised the objectionable nature of delegated powers.[40]

HENRY VIII CLAUSES

Probably the most objectionable type of delegated legislation, as its name implies, is the Henry VIII clause.[41] This is the nickname given to clauses in Acts allowing Ministers to amend Acts of Parliament, whether the parent Act or another statute. Again, they are not a new phenomenon but date back to the Local Government Act 1888. The Committee on Ministers' Powers, though it did not endorse Lord Hewart's charge of a conspiracy by the Civil Service to arrogate power to itself,[42] recommended that they should be used only in exceptional cases and only to bring an Act into operation subject to a one-year time limit.[43] Such clauses were not used again till after 1945,[44] but it is the escalation in their use recently that has again

---

30   The numbers grew from 2,350 in 1986 to 3,345 in 1995, which take up two feet, six inches of bookshelf: *Special Report from the Joint Committee on Statutory Instruments*, HC 582, London: HMSO, 1996, para 4.

31   See Renton, Sir David, *The Preparation of Legislation*, Cmnd 6053, London: HMSO, 1975, para. 11.25.

32   See Procedure Committee, *Delegated Legislation*, HC 152, London: HMSO, 1996, 'Evidence' p. 10, n. 8. The Child Support Act 1991 contains over 100 regulation-making powers.

33   Education Act 1980. The scheme is being phased out under the Education (Schools) Act 1997.

34   Social Security Act 1986.

35   Education (Student Loans) Act l990 — virtually an enabling Act.

36   Jobseekers Act 1995, see *op. cit.* note 32, Appendix 4.

37   *Op. cit.* note 32, 'Evidence' p. 27, para. 2 and Q 59.

38   Social Security (Persons from Abroad) Miscellaneous Amendments Regulations (SI 1996/30).

39   *R* v *Secretary of State for Social Security, ex parte Joint Council for the Welfare of Immigrants* [1997] 1 WLR 275, 293C: see 'Judicial control'.

40   *R* v *Secretary of State for Social Security, ex parte Stitt* (1990) *The Guardian*, 10 July (Purchas LJ).

41   King Henry VIII is regarded as the embodiment of autocracy.

42   Cmd 4060, p. 59.

43   *Ibid.*, p. 65, para. IV.

44   *Making the Law*, Report of the Hansard Society Commission on the Legislative Process, London: The Hansard Society, 1992, para. 268.

given rise to concern. As Lord Rippon put it,[45] 'Ministers . . . take power to amend or repeal primary legislation by order almost as a matter of common form' and without any time limit. Henry VIII clauses come in a variety of forms, some merely allowing updating of the original Act but some provisions giving very wide powers to change the substance of policy without limit.[46] Matters came to a head with the Courts and Legal Services Bill 1990 in the House of Lords, when criticism in particular by Lord Simon of Glaisdale, who castigated such clauses as a 'constitutional outrage', forced the Lord Chancellor to give an undertaking that in the case of this Bill those clauses would be subject to the affirmative resolution procedure.[47] Unease about Henry VIII clauses formed part of the pressure to set up the Delegated Powers Scrutiny Committee in the House of Lords to monitor Bills conferring such powers.[48]

DEREGULATION ORDERS

The most extreme example of a Henry VIII clause is to be found in the Deregulation and Contracting Out Act 1994. In fact Part I of that Act can be regarded as one giant Henry VIII clause. It gives power to a minister to repeal or amend any Act which authorises or requires the imposition of a burden affecting any trade, business or profession, where the burden can be removed or reduced without removing any necessary protection. The legislation was called a constitutional outrage in its passage through the House of Lords[49] and Conservative peers invoked shades of the Civil War to which Parliament owes its sovereignty,[50] whilst the House of Lords Delegated Powers Scrutiny Committee said that the provisions were 'unprecedented in time of peace'.[51] The Opposition felt so strongly about the Bill that they refused to give evidence to the Procedure Committee considering parliamentary scrutiny of the orders to be made under the Bill.[52] None of this prevented the Bill becoming law with only one substantial amendment in Part I.[53]

The dire warnings made at the time of the passing of the Bill are in marked contrast to the report on the first year's work by the Chairman of the House of Commons Committee scrutinising deregulation orders.[54] Nearly all amendments to proposals were accepted by the then government, draft orders were unanimously approved and there have been no divisions in the Committee. Only one proposal

45   *Third Commonwealth Conference on Delegated Legislation*, London: HMSO, 1989, p. 38.
46   *Op. cit.* note 32, 'Evidence' p. 60, para. 24.
47   516 HL Deb, 5th ser., col 157, 20 February 1990.
48   See *infra*.
49   555 HL Deb, 5th ser., col. 958, 6 June, 1994, Lord Peston.
50   Lord Beloff, *ibid.*, col. 1018; Lord Cockfield, *ibid.*, col. 972.
51   HL 60, London: HMSO, 1994, para. 1.
52   HC 238, London: HMSO, 1994, paras 4 *et seq.*
53   Increasing the period for Parliamentary consideration of a proposal from 40 to 60 days, see *infra*.
54   *Op. cit.* note 32, Appendix 8.

on Sunday Dancing was rejected and the government accepted defeat.[55] The House of Lords Delegated Powers Scrutiny Committee put it succinctly, 'In our opinion the degree of controversy associated with this proposal makes it unsuitable for a deregulation order'.[56] Apart from this order relatively small and uncontroversial proposals were put forward by the government; the crunch will come, and the parliamentary procedures to scrutinise them will only be tested, when controversial proposals start coming forward. One such was the proposal making small firms exempt from unfair dismissal claims by new employees which was greeted by a storm of protest from Labour and trade union leaders.[57] As the Procedure Committee said in its report on Parliamentary Scrutiny of Deregulation Orders,[58] 'Without serious checks, the balance between the legislature and the executive could be altered'. These special checks will now be considered before turning to the scrutiny of ordinary delegated legislation.

PARLIAMENTARY CONTROL

Deregulation orders

The statutory provisions relating to the parliamentary scrutiny of deregulation orders are very meagre, merely laying down a 60-day period for parliamentary consideration of proposals before they are embodied in a draft order[59] which has to be approved by a resolution of both Houses of Parliament.[60] In fact both Houses have constructed an elaborate two-tier process for considering these orders which has been suggested as the model for other delegated legislation.[61] A new committee, the Deregulation Committee, has been set up in the House of Commons[62] to consider whether the deregulation proposal falls within the criteria laid down in the Act and whether it is an inappropriate use of delegated legislation. In addition the Deregulation Committee fulfils the functions of the Joint Committee on Statutory Instruments[63] for these orders. It can report in three ways — in favour of the proposal, proposing amendment, or against the proposal. Significantly, the Conservative government rejected the Procedure Committee's recommendation that a negative report should prevent the proposal going further.[64] The minister has

---

55   *Ibid.*, para. 20. See now also HC 387 and HC 439, London: TSO, 1997.
56   HL 102 London: HMSO, 1995, para. 22; *cf* HC 817 London: HMSO, 1995, para. 9.
57   *The Guardian*, 24 September 1996. See also the proposal to abolish the Trustee Investment Act 1961, Treasury Consultation Paper, 1 May 1996, HL 70, London: TSO, 1997 and HC 440, London: TSO, 1997.
58   HC 238, London: HMSO, 1994, para. 15.
59   Deregulation and Contracting Out Act 1994, s. 4.
60   *Ibid.*, s. 1(4).
61   See *infra*.
62   Standing Order No. 124A.
63   See *infra*.
64   HC 404 (1993-94) Appendix, paras 15–19.

to have regard to the Committee's report made within the 60-day period.[65] This gives him or her the opportunity to make amendments; and as we have seen, nearly all recommendations for amendments have been accepted. The Committee then has 15 days in which to consider the draft order embodying the proposal against the same criteria as before. Depending on whether it reports in favour of the order — either unanimously or by a majority — or against the order, there will be no debate, a debate for one and a half hours or for three hours on the floor of the House.[66] So far all reports have fallen into the first category.

The orders proceed in parallel through both Houses, but there are differences in the procedure in the House of Lords. It is the Delegated Powers Scrutiny Committee in the House of Lords which fulfils the functions of the Deregulation Committee.[67] In the House of Lords no motion to approve a draft order can be moved till this Committee has reported.[68] At this point a problem arises in the House of Lords which does not exist in the Commons. The Lords were stripped of their veto power over Bills by the Parliament Acts 1911 and 1949. These Acts did not affect their powers to approve or annul delegated legislation which remain intact. Conscious of their constitutional position as the unelected House, the Lords have exercised great self-restraint in the exercise of these powers. Only once since 1945 has an order been voted down — the Rhodesian Sanctions Order in 1968.[69] Since 1982 there had been no direct votes on motions to approve or annul an order[70] until such a vote was held on the motion to approve the Broadcasting (Restrictions on the Holding of Licences) (Amendment) Order 1995[71] which had been rejected by a Committee in the House of Commons.[72] Whether this self-restraint constituted a convention was hotly debated in the House of Lords on a motion by Lord Simon, which affirmed the unfettered freedom of the House of Lords to vote on any subordinate legislation.[73] This debate was precipitated by the Deregulation Bill which was then passing through the Lords. To enable the Lords to vote against a Deregulation Order without breaching the alleged convention, the government agreed that the House could vote instead on the report from its Delegated Powers Scrutiny Committee, and if the vote on such a motion was against approving the order, the government would drop the order.[74] The

---

65 Deregulation and Contracting Out Act 1994, s. 4(4).
66 Standing Order No. 14A.
67 558 HL Deb, 5th ser., col. 332, 20 October, 1994. This Committee has now been renamed the Delegated Powers and Deregulation Committee, see *infra*.
68 Standing Order No. 70 — there is no 15-day time limit.
69 293 HL Deb, 5th ser., col. 594, 18 June 1968. This led to the suspension of all-party discussions on reform of the House of Lords.
70 558 HL Deb, 5th ser., col. 362, 20 October 1994.
71 566 HL Deb, 5th ser., col. 71, 17 July, 1995. The motion was carried.
72 See notes 77 and 97 *infra*.
73 558 HL Deb, 5th ser., col. 356, 20 October 1994.
74 *Ibid.*, col. 352.

government thus conceded the substance of the Lords' veto power over such orders; Lord Simon's motion asserted the formal right to vote on them.

Lord Simon in moving his motion stressed the function of the House of Lords as 'countervailing the power of the Executive'.[75] The Labour peer Lord McIntosh put this into perspective when he pointed out that rejection of delegated legislation was carried only when there was a Labour government.[76] This is literally true as only the Rhodesian Sanctions Order has been defeated in the last half-century in the House of Lords. The fear of what a Conservative House of Lords could do to a Labour government very much affected the conduct of the Labour Opposition in the Lords to the benefit of a Conservative government. The Opposition adhered to the convention that the Opposition front bench does not vote against orders because it accepts the will of the elected House and this was strictly observed on the Broadcasting Order, though the Opposition felt the government was abusing the convention by springing it on the Lords for approval after a Commons Committee had rejected it.[77] The convention was put under even greater strain when the regulations withdrawing social security benefits from asylum seekers were being debated in the Lords. The Opposition were utterly opposed to the regulations which they found morally repugnant, but at the end of the debate they withdrew the motion to annul the regulations in accordance with the convention.[78] This self-denying ordinance applies also to amendments moved to approval motions.[79] This gave the government a narrow victory by five votes on an amendment moved to the motion to approve the regulations introducing the 'no win no fee' scheme for solicitors, though the Opposition supported the thrust of the amendment.[80] Even a defeat of the government on such an amendment would have no legal effect, as neither House has power to amend orders but only to approve or annul them, but it is a means of putting pressure on the government. This is *a fortiori* true of motions in the House of Lords attempting to undo the perceived ill-effects of regulations when they have become law. This device was used after the withdrawal by the Opposition of the motion to annul the regulations on social security for asylum seekers[81] and the Opposition did not observe the convention of abstention on such motions. The government were defeated on such a motion relating to the qualifications of probation officers,[82] but the victory was moral and political rather than legal. Though the Lords affirmed their unfettered freedom to vote on subordinate legislation in Lord Simon's motion and the government made a concession for the approval of deregulation orders, the

---

75   *Ibid.*, col. 358.
76   *Ibid.*, col. 365.
77   566 HL Deb, 5th ser., col. 76, 17 July, 1995.
78   568 HL Deb, 5th ser., col. 1359, 30 January 1996.
79   574 HL Deb, 5th ser., coll. 763, 794, 16 July 1996.
80   564 HL Deb, 5th ser., col. 1589, 12 June 1995.
81   568 HL Deb, 5th ser., col. 1359 *et seq.*, 30 January 1996.
82   567 HL Deb, 5th ser., coll. 923—949, 5 December 1995.

political reality makes this more symbolic than effective because of the composition of the House of Lords.

Super-affirmative procedure

The Procedure Committee of the House of Commons suggested[83] that taking the procedure for deregulation orders as a model, it should be possible for legislation to provide that certain very important orders would be examined in a two-tier process. The Committee suggested that a departmental select committee would first examine the order and could propose amendments within 60 days before it was debated in the House. This procedure, as we have seen in the case of deregulation orders, can lead to amendments being made by the government which cannot be achieved by debate on the floor of the House. This procedure can be, and has already been, used without statutory compulsion. Important delegated legislation has sometimes been considered by the relevant departmental select committee, an outstanding example being the regulations withdrawing social security benefits from asylum seekers. A special sub-committee of the Social Security Committee was set up to take evidence, but the committee was able to report in time for the debate in the House only because the government agreed to postpone the introduction of the regulations.[84] The experience of that committee does not augur well for the use of such a procedure for politically controversial regulations. The committee split along party lines on whether the government should withdraw the regulations[85] and there were many votes on amendments to the report put forward by the Opposition. The Procedure Committee foresaw that a unanimous report on controversial regulations was unlikely, but thought that such a procedure would nevertheless provide an opportunity for 'effective parliamentary input'.[86] This procedure would apply only to a very few regulations and would not affect the vast majority of instruments.

Sifting committee

The parliamentary procedure applicable to delegated legislation depends on the Act which authorises it. The Act may provide for approval by one or both Houses of Parliament (affirmative resolution), or for annulment by either House within 40 days of being laid (negative resolution) or have no provisions for parliamentary scrutiny. The vast majority of statutory instruments[87] are subject to the negative

---

83   *Op. cit.* note 32, para. 9 and Q 8.
84   *Ibid.*, Appendix 5.
85   HC 81, London: HMSO, 1996.
86   *Op. cit.* note 32, para. 9.
87   Defined by the Statutory Instruments Act 1946, s. 1, to include Orders in Council made under statute and where statutory powers are said to be exercisable by statutory instrument.

procedure, over 1,300 in 1994–95 compared to 175 affirmative instruments.[88] There are no criteria for deciding which procedure is applicable and this is often the result of political bargaining rather than based on the importance of the instrument.[89] The Procedure Committee suggested that the inadequacy of parliamentary scrutiny rather than the substance of delegated powers dictated the type of parliamentary control.[90] It was there referring to the startling figures on the lack of debate of negative instruments. All affirmative instruments have to be debated to be approved. They are now automatically referred to a standing committee unless the government agrees to a debate on the floor of the House.[91] For the negative procedure a motion has to be tabled to annul the instrument (called a prayer) and the government may either refer it to a standing committee, or allow it to be debated on the floor of the House for one and a half hours or disregard it. In 1994–5 only 34 of the 172 instruments prayed against were debated in this way and such annulment motions seem now to be the exclusive preserve of the Opposition parties rather than backbenchers.[92] The Procedure Committee was concerned to remedy this situation. It recommended that 20 MPs should be allowed to ask for an annulment motion to be debated in a standing committee and this request should be voted on without debate.[93] More importantly it recommended the setting up of a Sifting Committee, modelled on the European Legislation Committee, which would examine all statutory instruments subject to annulment, recommend those of sufficient political importance for debate in a standing committee and put down a motion to this effect.[94] Debates should be held before the expiry of the time limit for prayers.[95]

The procedure in standing committees where most instruments are now debated, is generally regarded as very unsatisfactory, mainly because the committee can only vote on a motion that it has considered the instrument. The substantive vote on whether to approve the instrument takes place on the floor of the House without debate.[96] Thus, even if the government is challenged to a vote in the standing committee and defeated, as happened in the case of the Broadcasting Order 1995, this has no practical effect.[97] The Procedure Committee recommended that a standing committee should be able to vote on a substantive motion whether to

---

88   *Op. cit.* note 32, 'Evidence', p. 44.
89   *Ibid.*, para. 7.
90   *Ibid.*
91   Standing Order No. 101. A substantial number are still debated on the floor subject to a one and a half hour time limit (*op. cit.* note 32, para. 6 and Standing Order No. 14B).
92   *Op. cit.* note 32, para. 25.
93   *Ibid.*, para. 27.
94   *Ibid.*, para. 33 *et seq.*
95   *Ibid.*, para. 36. The Procedure Committee deplored the practice of delaying debates until the 40-day time limit has expired.
96   Annulment motions do not come back to the House.
97   263 HC Deb, 6th ser., coll. 1485 and 1567, 18 July 1995, and see note 77 *supra.*

approve or annul the instrument and, if the government is defeated on such a motion, this should necessitate an hour's debate on the motion when it returns to the floor of the House.[98] Even if all these recommendations were implemented,[99] as long as a government has a majority, whipping will always ensure victory, other than in extraordinary circumstances, e.g., when it has a very small majority or on a sensitive issue.[100]

A different type of Parliamentary scrutiny is performed by two committees, the House of Lords Delegated Powers Scrutiny Committee and the Joint Committee on Statutory Instruments.

Delegated Powers Scrutiny Committee (renamed Delegated Powers and Deregulation Committee)[101]

As early as 1932, it was recommended by the Committee on Ministers' Powers that the committee which it had advised should be set up to scrutinise delegated legislation should also examine the Bills under which it was made.[102] It took 60 years before this proposal bore fruit in the House of Lords. The enormous increase in the volume and breadth of delegated legislation had given rise to much criticism in the House of Lords in 1990.[103] The proposal to set up such a committee was made by the Jellicoe Committee and was modelled on the Scrutiny of Bills Committee of the Australian Senate.[104] The terms of reference of the Delegated Powers Scrutiny Committee established in 1992 were, however, narrower than those of the Australian committee. They were to 'report whether the provisions of any bill inappropriately delegate legislative power, or whether they subject the exercise of legislative power to an inappropriate degree of Parliamentary scrutiny'.[105] The Australian committee has in addition a brief to consider the impact of Bills on personal rights and liberties. A proposal to allow the House of Lords committee to scrutinise Bills for conformity with the European Convention on Human Rights has not so far been adopted.[106]

The Committee has not laid down a set of criteria by which to judge inappropriate delegation of power, but skeleton Bills and Henry VIII clauses are

98   *Op. cit.* note 32, paras 50 and 54.
99   There were no changes in the last Parliament, 281 HC Deb, 6th ser., col. 636, 11 July 1996.
100   There have been three government defeats on delegated legislation since 1970, see Hayhurst, J. D. and Wallington, P., 'The Parliamentary Scrutiny of Delegated Legislation' [1988] *Public Law* 558.
101   575 HL Deb, 5th ser., col. 231, 29 October 1996.
102   Cmd 4060, pp. 67 *et seq.*
103   515 HL Deb, 5th ser., coll. 1407–1437, 14 February 1990.
104   HL 35, London: HMSO, 1992.
105   540 HL Deb, 5th ser., col. 91, 10 November 1992.
106   558 HL Deb, 5th ser., col. 844, 2 November 1994. The Committee commented on clauses in the Police Bill 1997, which as originally drafted allowed interference with property without a judicial warrant, even though these clauses did not fall within its terms of reference as they did not confer delegated legislative powers (HL 12, London: TSO, 1996).

obvious candidates.[107] Whereas Henry VIII clauses are invariably commented on
by the Committee, though in most cases not critically, other forms of inappro-
priateness are only occasionally drawn to the attention of the House. Apart from
the Deregulation and Contracting Out Bill 1994, the Committee was not happy that
arrangements for railway pensions after privatisation were left to delegated
legislation in the Railways Bill 1993, nor that interference with the freedom of
association of students in students' unions should be left to delegated legislation
by the Education Bill 1994. The provision was later dropped from the Education
Bill but not from the Railways Bill.[108] The Committee's most trenchant criticisms
have been reserved for the Jobseekers Bill 1995, which the Committee castigated
as a skeleton measure, particularly where key terms were left to be defined in
regulations. The government later moved amendments to meet the main points
made by the Committee.[109] The Committee has also not laid down criteria for what
constitutes an inappropriate degree of Parliamentary scrutiny. It has never so far
recommended downgrading an affirmative resolution to a negative one, but has
frequently recommended a higher degree of Parliamentary scrutiny than is provided in the Bill; the government has often (but not invariably) given effect to the
recommendation.[110]

The Committee has no powers except to make a report on a Bill. It is then up
to the government whether to accept its recommendations to amend a Bill, and any
member of the Committee, just like any other peer, can table amendments. The
Committee thinks that it has had a salutary effect in that fewer reprehensible Bills
are coming forward and ministers are sensitive to the likely reaction of the
Committee.[111] The Committee has not so far reported on amendments providing
for delegated powers made to a Bill during its passage through the House.[112] It
would be a difficult burden for the Committee to discharge in the time available.
The power to make regulations withdrawing social security benefits from asylum
seekers, which reversed the decision holding such regulations *ultra vires*,[113] was
contained in an amendment to the Asylum and Immigration Bill 1996 tabled at a
very late stage,[114] which therefore escaped through this loophole.

It is paradoxical that the House of Lords should have established a committee
which functions as the 'constitutional conscience of the House in relation to
delegated powers', while the Procedure Committee of the House of Commons sees
no need to duplicate its function in the Commons and asserts that debate on a Bill

---

107 See generally, *op. cit.* note 32, Appendix 2.
108 *Ibid.*, Appendix 2, paras 13 and 14.
109 *Ibid.*, Appendix 2, Annex I.
110 *Ibid.*, Appendix 2, para. 20 and Annex I.
111 *Ibid.*, Appendix 2, para. 29.
112 *Ibid.*, Appendix 2, para. 10.
113 See note 39 *supra* and note 132 *infra*.
114 573 HL Deb, 5th ser., col 1220, 1 July 1996.

provides sufficient scrutiny of powers of delegation. It added, 'No procedural changes could readily influence the outcome of such debate.'[115] The elected House seems content to abdicate its constitutional function in this respect to the unelected House.

Joint Committee on Statutory Instruments[116]

This committee has its origins in the recommendations of the Committee on Ministers' Powers,[117] although it was not set up until 1944, 12 years after the Committee reported. Originally it was a Committee of the House of Commons, but in 1973 it was established as a Joint Committee of both Houses. Its jurisdiction has been extended several times so that it now covers all general, as distinct from purely local, statutory instruments, whether or not they have to be laid before Parliament. The terms of reference have also been amended over the years, but have not substantially altered the function of the Committee as a watchdog monitoring the legality, procedural regularity and clarity of instruments but which is not concerned with their merits or policy. This is emphasised by having a Chairman from the Opposition party and being advised by Speaker's Counsel and his equivalent in the House of Lords. In fact the main burden of the work of examining the ever-increasing stream of instruments (1,666 in 1995) to see whether they fall within the terms of reference, and therefore should be drawn to the attention of Parliament,[118] falls on these advisers. The former Chairman acknowledged that the Committee acted more like a lay jury.[119] This is because the Committee is charged with the legal issue of whether the instrument falls within the powers given to the minister in the parent Act[120] on which it is difficult to challenge its advisers. There is a grey area between law and politics in one of the grounds on which an instrument must be drawn to Parliament's attention, namely that it makes unusual or unexpected use of the powers conferred in the Act. The Committee has, however, steered clear of party politics. Votes are rare and so is whipping. This may be a measure of its weakness rather than its strength.

The Committee has no powers except to make a report drawing an instrument to the attention of Parliament. It has been a source of constant complaint by the Committee that instruments have been debated in the House of Commons or in a standing committee before it has made a report.[121] It has therefore been frequently

---

115 *Op. cit.* note 32, para. 14.
116 *Ibid.*, 'Evidence' pp. 26 *et seq.*
117 Cmd 4060, pp. 68 *et seq.*
118 About 1 in 10 instruments are reported to Parliament.
119 *Op cit.* note 32, 'Evidence' p. 28, para. 5.
120 Regulations made under the European Communities Act 1972 have to be assessed by reference to European Community law.
121 *Op. cit.* note 32, 'Evidence' p. 27, para. 3.

recommended that the Commons should not make a decision on a statutory instrument until the Joint Committee has considered the instrument. This has not so far been implemented. Where the Committee has reported in time for a debate, the Chairman may participate to draw attention to the report.[122]

The success of the Committee seems to be clearest in matters of procedure, and in particular the drafting of instruments. The Committee and Speaker's Counsel have the impression that drafting has improved overall, though the Committee refers to some regular drafting defects[123] and its former Chairman was appalled at the standard of English.[124] Advisers may also be sounded out in advance about what is acceptable. More importantly, instruments may be withdrawn or the defect remedied so that no report or a report for the record only is made by the Committee. The deterrent effect of the Committee preventing departments making defective instruments is by definition difficult to prove.

Taking all these factors into account, it is nevertheless surprising how little the Committee has done to curb the worst excesses of delegated legislation falling within its terms of reference. This is most evident in the case of instruments whose legality is in doubt, i.e. whether they are *intra vires*. Research by Hayhurst and Wallington[125] has shown that of the few cases which were successfully challenged in the courts for *vires* on substantive grounds between 1914–86 none was spotted by Parliament. The most recent example quoted is the *Cotton* case,[126] where supplementary benefit regulations were declared *ultra vires* by the courts but not commented on by the Joint Committee. Further light may have been thrown on this subsequently by the former Chairman of the Committee. In his memorandum to the Procedure Committee he has revealed:

> I was once asked to let a Social Security SI through in the 1980s so that a pressure group could beat the Government in the courts. On the same occasion the Conservative attendance at the Committee suggested that they had been whipped to get it through. The court subsequently ruled it was *ultra vires* — the Government had bought time and a pressure group claimed a coup.[127]

No such excuse has so far been made for the failure by the Committee to report to Parliament on the regulations withdrawing social security benefits from asylum seekers.[128] The Social Security Committee, which also considered the regulations,

---

122   *Ibid.*, p. 29, para. 8.
123   HC 582, London: HMSO, 1996, para. 9(b).
124   *Op. cit.* note 32, 'Evidence' p. 28, para. 6.
125   *Op. cit.* note 100 *supra*, pp. 568 *et seq.*
126   *R v Secretary of State for Social Services, ex parte Cotton* (1985) *The Times*, 5 August and 14 December (CA).
127   *Op. cit.* note 32, 'Evidence' p. 29, para. 8.
128   HC 34v, London: HMSO, 1996, Annex.

was warned by welfare organisations that a legal challenge would be made,[129] but it was assured by the government that the regulations complied with the United Kingdom's treaty obligations and existing statute law.[130] The Opposition's prayer to annul the regulations predictably failed on a whipped vote with only the Conservative MP, Mr Peter Brooke, declaring in the debate that he would abstain.[131] Thus Parliament abdicated its function to the courts.

JUDICIAL CONTROL

Illegality

R v *Secretary of State for Social Security, ex parte Joint Council for the Welfare of Immigrants*[132] must rank as one of the landmark decisions of judicial control over delegated legislation. The Court of Appeal by a majority reversed the decision of the Divisional Court and held the Social Security (Persons from Abroad) Miscellaneous Amendments Regulations 1996 *ultra vires*. Simon Brown LJ explicitly did not base his decision on the narrow ground (which failed in the lower court) that the withdrawal of social security benefits from asylum seekers amounted to constructive removal (refoulement) of the refugee from this country in breach of the UN Convention on the Status of Refugees 1951. He also declared that, 'So basic are the human rights here at issue that it cannot be necessary to resort to the European Convention on Human Rights to take note of their violation'. After citing a 200-year-old case[133] which stated that, 'As to there being no obligation for maintaining poor foreigners . . . the law of humanity, which is anterior to all positive laws, obliges us to afford them relief, to save them from starving,' Simon Brown LJ held it 'unlawful to alter the benefit regime so drastically as must inevitably not merely prejudice, but on occasion defeat, the statutory right[134] of asylum seekers to claim refugee status'.[135]

Simon Brown LJ recognised that he was carrying existing case law[136] further 'in a field where Parliament has been closely involved in the making of the impugned Regulations'. But he continued, 'Parliamentary sovereignty is not here in question: the Regulations are subordinate legislation only'.[137] However, he rejected counsel's argument that the legislative history of the regulation-making power now contained in the Social Security (Contributions and Benefits) Act 1992, which showed an

---

129   HC 81, London: HMSO, 1996, para. 28.
130   *Ibid.*, para. 4.
131   270 HC Deb, 6th ser. coll. 231, 251, 23 January 1996. For the role played by the House of Lords, see note 78 *supra*.
132   [1997] 1 WLR 275.
133   *R* v *Inhabitants of Eastbourne* (1803) 4 East 103.
134   See Asylum and Immigration Appeals Act 1993.
135   [1997] 1 WLR 275, at 292 F–H.
136   *R* v *Secretary of State for the Home Department, ex parte Leech* [1994] QB 198.
137   [1997] 1 WLR 275, at 292 C.

intention to continue support for asylum seekers, could be used to limit the present scope of the Act. He founded his judgment on the ground that:

> Parliament cannot have intended a significant number of genuine asylum seekers to be impaled on the horns of so intolerable a dilemma: the need either to abandon their claims to refugee status or alternatively to maintain them as best they can but in a state of utter destitution. Primary legislation alone could in my judgment achieve that sorry state of affairs.'[138]

The ball was thus put back firmly in Parliament's court. 'That sorry state of affairs' was achieved by a clause inserted in the Asylum and Immigration Bill 1996 which had reached its final stage in the House of Lords. Though the government suffered a narrow defeat on an Opposition amendment in the House of Lords,[139] it was whipped through the Commons[140] and finally through the Lords.[141] Parliamentary sovereignty triumphed but the court won the moral victory.

Though perhaps the most spectacular example, the asylum seekers case is in line with a number of decisions where the courts have held delegated legislation *ultra vires* by implying limitations in the parent Act from general principles fashioned by the courts. These principles have included not restricting access to the courts and legal advice,[142] not imposing a tax or charge,[143] and not excluding judicial control by judge-proofing decisions.[144] Express power in the enabling Act to contravene these principles is necessary in such cases.

Irrationality

Unreasonableness or irrationality[145] (see Fordham, Ch. 8, pp. 188 *et seq*) is another ground of judicial review, but the courts have applied it with great caution to delegated legislation, particularly when it is subject to parliamentary scrutiny and control and 'in an important area of the national economy and with the legitimate aim of removing an unwarranted burden on public funds'.[146] Neill LJ, dissenting

---

138   *Ibid.*, at 293D.
139   573 HL Deb, 5th ser., col. 1261, 1 July 1996.
140   281 HC Deb, 6th ser., col. 883, 15 July 1996.
141   574 HL Deb, 5th ser., col. 1211, 22 July 1996.
142   *Ex parte Leech* case, note 136 *supra*. A more recent example is the court declaring *ultra vires* rules made by the Lord Chancellor forcing even recipients of income support to pay court fees. This constituted denial of access to the courts: *R* v *Lord Chancellor, ex parte Witham* (1997) *The Guardian*, 8 March.
143   *Attorney-General* v *Wiltshire United Dairies* (1921) 37 TLR 884.
144   *Customs and Excise Commissioners* v *Cure and Deeley Ltd* [1962] 1 QB 340.
145   *Associated Provincial Picture Houses Ltd* v *Wednesbury Corporation* [1948] 1 KB 223.
146   *R* v *Secretary of State for Social Security, ex parte Joint Council for the Welfare of Immigrants* [1997] 1 WLR, 275, at 291A, *per* Simon Brown LJ referring to *R* v *Secretary of State for the Environment, ex parte Hammersmith and Fulham London Borough Council* [1991] 1 AC 521.

in the Court of Appeal in the asylum seekers case propounded a novel test of disproportionality: 'A court is only entitled to intervene where the interference with the other rights is disproportionate to the objects to be achieved.'[147] He held that in this case the threshold of illegality had not been crossed. The converse doctrine of proportionality (that the means must be proportional to the objects to be achieved) is a European legal concept which has not yet been recognised in its own right in English law.[148]

Procedural impropriety

Where the proper procedure has not been followed when making regulations, the courts may hold them *ultra vires*. In some cases Acts provide that before a regulation is made those affected must be consulted.[149] The Consumer Protection Act 1987 so provided in the case of safety regulations. When the Secretary of State proposed to make regulations banning oral snuff on the advice of an expert committee on cancer, he wrote to the sole manufacturer in the UK, who had been encouraged by the government to set up a factory, asking the company to make representations. He refused to disclose the advice or the reasons given by the expert committee. The Divisional Court quashed the regulations.[150] In the words of Taylor LJ (as he then was): 'In view of the total change of policy the Regulations would bring about and its unique impact on the applicants, fairness demanded that they should be treated with candour. To conceal from them the scientific advice which directly led to the ban was, in my judgment, unfair and unlawful.'[151] He pointed out that the regulations were subject to annulment in Parliament but were not so annulled. Parliament would be unaware of any procedural impropriety[152] and therefore resort to the courts would be the only remedy. However, the remedy may be shortlived if the same conclusion is reached after the proper procedure has been observed by the Secretary of State.[153]

The most common procedural requirements are those concerned with laying before Parliament. The vast majority of all general instruments have to be laid

---

147 [1997] 1 WLR 275, at 283A.
148 *R v Secretary of State for the Home Department, ex parte Brind* [1991] 2 WLR 588.
149 For example, the Deregulation and Contracting Out Act 1994, s. 3. In some cases a specific body must be consulted, e.g., the Council on Tribunals or the Social Security Advisory Committee. Mostly consultation is voluntary.
150 *R v Secretary of State for Health. ex parte United States Tobacco International Inc.* [1991] 3 WLR 529. New regulations banning the supply of tobacco for oral use were made in 1992 (SI 1992/3134).
151 *Ibid.*, at p 543D.
152 Parliament also did not know that Neil Hamilton, who lobbied ministers on behalf of US Tobacco, had been paid for introducing the company to lobbyist Ian Greer: HC 30, London: TSO, 1997, para. 836.
153 See *R v Secretary of State for the Environment, ex parte Hackney London Borough Council* [1983] 1 WLR 524.

before Parliament, though, as we have seen, even this minimal control was not required for export control orders.[154] Where an Act provides that a statutory instrument shall be laid before Parliament, the instrument cannot come into operation before being laid unless this is essential and an explanation has been given to the Speaker of the House of Commons and the Lord Chancellor.[155] The Joint Committee on Statutory Instruments has recently complained of failure to observe this requirement.[156] Whether failure to observe these laying requirements makes the instrument invalid has been assumed rather than decided by the courts.[157] It is self-evident that this is the case if the requirement for approval by Parliament has not been observed.

Publication

It is also clear that failure to publish a statutory instrument does not as such invalidate it, even though the Statutory Instruments Act 1946, s. 2 provides that statutory instruments shall be sent immediately to Her Majesty's Stationery Office (HMSO) after being made and copies thereof shall be printed and sold by HMSO as soon as possible. HMSO must publish lists showing the date on which the instrument was issued.[158] If the instrument has not been issued by HMSO, it is a defence to a prosecution for its contravention unless reasonable steps have been taken to bring the instrument to the notice of those likely to be affected (s. 3(2)). This last provision would have been superfluous if failure to publish *per se* invalidated the instrument.[159]

These provisions have recently had to be amended by the Statutory Instruments (Production and Sale) Act 1996, because a loophole in the 1946 Act was discovered as a result of preparations for the privatisation of HMSO. HMSO had been contracting out some of the printing of statutory instruments for over 30 years,[160] but the 1946 Act provided only for printing and sale *by* HMSO not *under the authority of* HMSO, as was provided for Acts of Parliament by the Documentary Evidence Act 1882, s. 2. These words were, therefore, added by the 1996 Act because it was feared that, where someone was charged with an offence under an instrument which had not been printed by HMSO, he or she would have a defence under s. 3(2) of the 1946 Act that it had not been issued by HMSO. The 1996 Act was given retrospective effect to cover existing instruments,[161] but not in respect

---

154   See 'Introduction'.
155   Statutory Instruments Act 1946, s. 4. The Act only applies to statutory instruments as defined in s. 1, note 87 *supra*.
156   HC 582, London: HMSO, 1996, para. 9(d).
157   *R v Sheer Metalcraft Ltd* [1954] 1 QB 586, at 590.
158   Section 3(1) and SI 1948/1, para. 9.
159   *R v Sheer Metalcraft Ltd* [1954] 1 QB 586, at 590.
160   279 HC Deb, 6th ser., written answers, col. 471, 19 June 1996.
161   This is the reason why the loophole was not closed by using a deregulation order, see 280 HC Deb, 6th ser., col. 1004, 3 July 1996.

of proceedings commenced before the date when the Bill was published (21 June 1996) so as not to take away any existing defence. The Bill was politically controversial because of its linkage with the privatisation of HMSO. Though the minister explained that the Bill was not necessary for the privatisation of HMSO, which required no primary legislation,[162] it was necessary to enable the printing of statutory instruments to be contracted out. If the Bill was not passed before the sale of HMSO, which was planned to be completed during the summer,[163] statutory instruments would have to be printed by the residual HMSO[164] in-house. This led to the Bill being rushed through Parliament under strong protest from the Opposition.[165]

Where an Act confers power on a minister to legislate but does not provide for this to be exercisable by a statutory instrument, the Statutory Instruments Act 1946 has no application. The document does not have to be published, therefore, unless there are express provisions for publication in the Act itself. This situation gave rise to much litigation when the breathalyser was first introduced. The Road Safety Act 1967, s. 7(1) gave the minister power to approve the type of breathalyser, but approval did not have to be made by a statutory instrument. Originally approval of a certain device (Alcotest) was contained in a circular to Chief Constables, but in *Scott* v *Baker*[166] the court refused to accept the circular as evidence of approval. It was only when the minister made the Breath Test Device (Approval) Order 1968, copies of which were published and printed by HMSO, that the courts would accept such copies as evidence of approval.[167]

QUASI-LEGISLATION

These cases illustrate the practical problems that can arise when delegated legislation does not take the form of a statutory instrument. This is becoming increasingly common as statutory provisions proliferate giving ministers power to give directions to officials, local authorities and quangos, to make schemes, e.g. for criminal injuries compensation,[168] or to make arrangements, e.g. for making grants in respect of nursery education.[169] In many cases there is no provision for parliamentary control. However, the difference from statutory instruments is one of form, not legal force, as these rules are legally binding.

---

162 *Ibid.*
163 It was sold in September 1996 (*Observer*, 15 September 1996). HMSO is replaced by TSO.
164 In whom Crown copyright remains vested.
165 All the stages of the Bill in the House of Commons were taken in one day. In the House of Lords the Opposition were outraged by the government's behaviour and forced a vote on the Third Reading, a rare event: 574 HL Deb, 5th ser., col. 1385, 24 July 1996.
166 [1968] 3 WLR 797.
167 *R* v *Clarke* [1969] 2 WLR 505.
168 Criminal Injuries Compensation Act 1995.
169 Nursery Education and Grant-Maintained Schools Act 1996. The Labour government has ended the nursery education voucher scheme.

There is a distinction between these examples of delegated legislation and statutory provisions giving power to make codes of practice, guidance or guidance notes to which the decision maker must have regard, or which must be taken into account in legal proceedings or before a tribunal. There is now a plethora of such rules originating with the Highway Code, which has been the model for codes ranging from industrial and race relations and health and safety to education and police custody. Statutory provisions for guidance and guidelines cover disbursements from the Social Fund, provision for the homeless, and are also addressed to Chief Constables. Some of these provisions, especially in the area of industrial relations, have raised constitutional issues. The codes of practice on picketing and the closed shop were called 'unconstitutional legislation' as they contained provisions which were deliberately omitted from the Act but had to be taken into account by courts and tribunals. They were a form of back-door legislation as they avoided the detailed scrutiny to which a Bill is submitted, though they were subject to parliamentary approval.[170] This is by no means true of all such 'twilight' legislation — a marked exception is the guidance to Social Fund officers.

There is even less control over an expanding area of rules which have no statutory basis. Increasingly ministers issue circulars, guidelines, codes of conduct and tax concessions which are extra-statutory but may have some legal force. Planning policy is contained in guidance notes which have to be taken into account as relevant considerations when making planning decisions. The concept of legitimate expectation evolved by the courts has been used so as to make extra-statutory rules binding until they have been changed,[171] or at least until those affected have been given an opportunity to make representations against departing from them.[172] The most common examples of extra-statutory rules are internal departmental rules and guidelines which structure administrative discretion. The most notorious recent example are the Howe guidelines for the sale of defence equipment to Iran and Iraq which were discussed earlier. They illustrate so many of the deficiencies of such rules — uncertainty, secrecy[173] and lack of parliamentary control.

CONCLUSION

Delegated legislation is a necessary evil. The classic reasons for its use, i.e. lack of parliamentary time, its technicality, flexibility and detail, are as valid today as

---

170   Ganz, G., *Quasi-Legislation: Recent Developments in Secondary Legislation*, London: Sweet & Maxwell, 1987, pp. 12 *et seq.*
171   *R v Secretary of State for the Home Department. ex parte Ruddock* [1987] 1 WLR 1482.
172   *R v Secretary of State for the Home Department, ex parte Asif Mahmood Khan* [1984] 1 WLR 1337. See now *R v Secretary of State for the Home Department, ex parte Hargreaves* [1997] 1 WLR 906.
173   The Code of Practice on Access to Government Information (1997), Part I, para. 3(ii) commits the government to publishing internal guidance to officials subject to exceptions, e.g., harm to international relations (Part II, para. 1b).

they ever were. The danger in recent developments is that the exceptional types of delegated legislation threaten to become the norm. The increasing use of skeleton legislation, Henry VIII clauses and, most recently, deregulation orders alters the balance of power between the executive and the legislature still further in favour of the former. The Procedure Committee's report on delegated legislation says, 'there is no prospect of any significant reduction in the volume or significance of delegated legislation'.[174] It continues, 'It is, therefore, crucial that delegated legislation should be subject, and be seen to be subject, to adequate parliamentary scrutiny'. As we have seen, it makes recommendations towards this end, but it does not mention the inherent limitations of such scrutiny. Where the issue is politically controversial, discussion in committee, and even cross-party voting to defeat the government, will not prevent the government imposing its will by a whipped vote on the floor of the House. The House of Lords has a formal veto power over delegated legislation, but as the Opposition front bench observe the convention of abstaining, a defeat of the government is unlikely. The House of Lords Delegated Powers and Deregulation Committee has had some success in achieving modification of government Bills, and the Joint Committee on Statutory Instruments has had a salutary effect on procedural issues, but has not been successful in stopping *ultra vires* instruments. This has been left to the courts, most notably in the asylum seekers case. But as that case graphically illustrates, the courts do not have the last word, which lies with Parliament which is dominated by the executive.

Sir Richard Scott blamed the 'extent to which the executive has come to dominate Parliament'[175] for the export control system. He was shocked to find that for more than 40 years after the end of the emergency, export control orders were made under war-time legislation[176] and that even today there is no provision for parliamentary control over these orders. He was further disturbed by the blurring of law and policy due to the wide discretion conferred on ministers which enables them to grant or refuse licences in accordance with government policy, embodied in guidelines which do not have to be published or scrutinised by Parliament.

The Delegated Powers Scrutiny Committee of the House of Lords prefaced one of its reports with the declaration, 'Democracy is not only about the election of politicians; it is also about setting limits to their powers'.[177] In the absence of a written constitution there are no legal limits to the sovereignty of Parliament, and therefore to the powers of the executive which dominates it. Legally there is nothing to stop Parliament passing an 'enabling law' giving blanket powers to the executive — the classic tool of dictators — and in war-time it has done just that.[178]

---

174   *Op. cit.* note 32, para. 15.
175   *Op. cit.* note 4, Q 451 (Evidence to the Public Service Committee).
176   He has called it 'a cynical evasion by government of its constitutional duties': *ibid.*, Q 442.
177   HL 90 London: HMSO, 1994, para. 1.
178   Emergency Powers (Defence) Act 1939. Tony Benn has argued in the past that renationalisation could be carried out in this way: see Andrew Bennett, *The Guardian*, 25 November 1985.

The only limits on the executive are self-restraint and the power of public opinion. Scott was shocked at the lack of protest over the use of war-time powers for export control for 40 years after the emergency had ended.[179] Apathy is the greatest danger to our democracy.

---

[179]   Note 175 *supra*.

4

The Ombudsman: Parochial Stopgap or Global Panacea?[1]

Gavin Drewry

> The goal of every Ombudsman should be to be put out of work
> for lack of business.[2]

SUMMARY

Ombudsmen, independent investigators of citizens' grievances against the administration, complementing the role of the courts, have become an established feature
of administrative law. Ombudsman systems exist, in a wide variety of forms,
throughout the world. The British Parliamentary Commissioner for Administration
is closely linked to Parliament, and this is a source both of strength and of
weakness. Most individual ombudsman cases have limited significance; but
ombudsmen are a deterrent to maladministration, and cumulatively their decisions
help to propagate principles of good administrative practice.

OMBUDSMEN AND ADMINISTRATIVE LAW

Defining the boundaries of administrative law — a necessary prerequisite for
'facing the future' of the subject — has never been easy, particularly for people

---

1 Parts of this chapter are adapted from the author's essay on 'The Parliamentary Ombudsman', to
   be published in *The World Encyclopaedia of Parliaments and Legislatures*, Washington DC:
   Congressional Quarterly Inc.
2 Parliamentary Commissioner for Administration, Second Report, Session 1990–91, *Annual Report
   for 1990*, London: HMSO, 1991, HC 299, para. 5.

brought up on idiosyncratic English legal, constitutional and political traditions. One issue to be addressed at the outset is whether the office of ombudsman[3] — a Swedish word variously translated as an independent 'grievance' or 'complaints' officer, or in some contexts as a 'solicitor', 'commissioner' or 'representative' — can properly be regarded as part of the territory of administrative law. Legal commentators in many other European countries — with more legalistic administrative traditions, and with ombudsmen appointed overwhelmingly from legal and judicial backgrounds would probably have little hesitation in replying in the affirmative. But in Britain the answer is less clear-cut.

At one level the question may seem of little practical importance. The fact that ombudsman systems have, since the mid-1960s when the office of Parliamentary Commissioner for Administration (PCA) was first established, become familiar features of the institutional landscape in Britain, means that their inclusion in this book, with the phrase 'administrative law' in its title, is hardly controversial. Indeed, given that ombudsmen are nowadays routinely and often extensively discussed in virtually every textbook on UK administrative law, including some of the major works on judicial review, their omission from the present work would look decidedly perverse.

Ombudsmen complement the administrative law jurisdiction of the courts: the latter can do some things (e.g., legally enforce their decisions) that ombudsmen cannot; and *vice versa* (ombudsmen operate in an 'inquisitorial' way and can carry out lengthy in-depth investigations far beyond the scope of 'adversarial' court proceedings). Many ombudsmen (though not those in the UK) can launch investigations on their own initiative. Including ombudsmen in a discussion of administrative law is no odder than discussing other 'alternative dispute resolution' procedures, such as conciliation in the context of divorce law or arbitration in the context of commercial law.

However, in treating the case for inclusion as self-evident we must be careful not to beg some questions about the character of the institution — and the nature of the 'landscape' of which ombudsmen are a feature. These questions are particularly important when we seek to compare the many variants of the institution cross-nationally, in very different constitutional settings.

One familiar and growing difficulty is the blurring of the boundaries between public and private institutions and functions, which produces tensions and ambiguities between public and private law (see Austin, Ch. 1 and Bamforth, Ch. 6 generally). In many developed countries this problem has become ever more acute in recent years in the wake of a 'new public management' revolution which has resulted in the privatisation, agentcification and marketisation of so much public

---

3 This chapter adopts what has now become a fairly standard anglicisation of the word, with a plural
   version, 'ombudsmen'. This usage is, however, gender-neutral. Many ombudsmen throughout the
   world are women, but it is not proposed to do further violence to the Swedish language by referring
   to 'ombudsperson' or 'ombudswoman' — or (as is the practice in some parts of the USA) an
   'ombuds'.

sector activity.[4] There is a massive grey area between 'the state' and 'the market' where the respective territorial claims of administrative law and private law are open to dispute. Ombudsmen have nowadays to extend their reach into the administration of 'contracted out' services; parts of the British ombudsman system — for instance the Insurance Ombudsman and the Banking Ombudsman — are themselves more or less privatised, operating on a non-statutory basis, and funded by a particular industry or sector which undertakes to respect 'its' ombudsman's independence.

In Britain this blurring of the 'public' and the 'private' is compounded by the late and incomplete development — particularly compared with the experience of our continental European neighbours — of a distinctive corpus of administrative law and of a written constitution.

How much blame A.V. Dicey bears for the tardy development of English administrative law has been the subject of much discussion, a rehearsal of which lies far beyond the scope of this chapter (Dicey knew little enough of the French *droit administratif*, and nothing at all of ombudsmen who existed then only in Sweden and, by the end of his life, in Finland) (see Leyland and Woods, Ch. 16, pp. 377 *et seq*). But the fact remains that the theory and the practice of traditional public administration in Britain owes little to law. Some 40 years ago C.S. Sisson wrote that the continental administrator is, in general, 'a lawyer, specialising in that branch of law — namely administrative law — which is mostly concerned with the functions of government.'[5] In contrast, members of the British higher Civil Service, bred in a robust generalist tradition (albeit tempered in recent years by managerialism), are not practitioners of administrative law, though they may of necessity have become more conscious of 'The Judge over Your Shoulder' — and indeed of 'The Ombudsman in Your Files'.[6]

Former Minister of Public Service and Science, William Waldegrave, told the House of Commons Treasury and Civil Service Committee, with reference to the enhanced machinery for redress of citizens' grievances promised by the Citizen's Charter (see below), that 'if we can avoid getting too many lawyers involved in these redress systems, except when issues are very, very serious, so much the better I think.'[7] In saying this the minister was articulating a conventional wisdom among politicians that lawyers are best kept at arm's length from the activities of government. Ministers and their generalist Civil Service advisers, particularly ones bred in the 'can do' culture of Mrs Thatcher's and John Major's 'new public management' revolution, have tended to regard lawyers as a nuisance. Non

---

4   See, for instance, Hood, C., 'A Public Management for All Seasons' (1991) 69 *Public Administration* 3–20; Oliver, D. and Drewry, G., *Public Service Reforms: Issues of Accountability and Public Law*, London: Pinter, 1996.

5   Sisson, C.H., *The Spirit of British Administration*, London: Faber and Faber, 1959, p. 39.

6   See note 39, *infra*.

7   Treasury and Civil Service Committee, Sixth Report, 1992–93, *The Role of the Civil Service: Interim Report*, vol. II 'Minutes of Evidence and Appendices', HC 390-II, Question 27.

ministerial parliamentarians have tended to be wary of allowing lawyers, courts and ombudsmen to trespass too vigorously on the territory traditionally, but largely ineffectually, occupied by ministerial responsibility and the grievance-chasing role of constituency MPs.

In Britain the public accountability of public servants and the redress of citizens' grievances against the state have always — again in contrast with continental Europe — emphasised political and parliamentary mechanisms rather than legal ones. This is a tradition that, as Fred Ridley has observed, 'is deeply embedded in British political traditions and has imprinted itself on British ways of thought'.[8]

As we will see, both these lines of thinking — that law has only a peripheral role in public administration and that every MP carries an 'ombudsman's baton' in his or her knapsack — were reflected in the peculiarly British variant of the ombudsman established in 1967. Thus (to take just two aspects) almost uniquely among ombudsman systems worldwide, all complaints to the PCA have to be 'filtered' through MPs; and, unlike most of his European counterparts, the PCA is not required to have a legal or judicial background — indeed only two of the seven holders of the office to date have been lawyers.

Two points should be made before looking nationally and internationally at ombudsman systems. The first is to take issue with William Waldegrave's view that lawyers should become involved only in the most serious matters: this might be taken to imply that grievances and problems that can be resolved by non legal means are inherently less serious than ones susceptible to legal redress, a view which is open to serious dispute and which implicitly begs serious questions about the importance of ombudsman systems that address *different* but by no means self-evidently *less important* and *less difficult* issues than those addressed by lawyers and administrative courts. Grievance has a subjective as well as an objective dimension, and for every citizen with the persistence to bring a complaint to an MP and thence to the ombudsman, his or her case is of the very highest importance, whatever a minister might think to the contrary. The second point is that ombudsmen do not work in a vacuum and their effectiveness is dependent on many factors — one of which is the institutional context in which they operate. It will be argued later that the attachment of the PCA to the House of Commons is a source both of strength and — given some of the limitations of that institution — of significant weakness.

THE DEVELOPMENT OF OMBUDSMEN: A WORLDWIDE MOVEMENT

The proliferation of ombudsman systems, providing a facility for extra-judicial investigation into citizens' complaints against the administration by an independent

---

8   Ridley, F.F., 'The Citizen Against Authority: British Approaches to the Redress of Grievances' (1984) 37 *Parliamentary Affairs* 4.

and impartial 'citizens' defender', has been a notable feature of political development, almost a worldwide phenomenon, since the mid-1950s. Given the immense
diversity of the constitutions and political cultures of the countries and sub-national
and sectoral contexts in which these ombudsmen have developed, it is not
surprising to discover that the office manifests itself in a wide variety of forms,
though all of them have some definitive characteristics in common.

Given the variety of ombudsmen that exists, the following description, in a
major international reference book on ombudsman systems edited by Gerald
Caiden, probably comes as close as we are likely to get to a generally acceptable
(apart from the author's exclusive references to the male gender) definition of this
diverse institution:

> The ombudsman is an independent and nonpartisan officer . . . often provided for
> in the Constitution, who supervises the administration. He deals with specific
> complaints from the public against administrative injustice and maladministra-
> tion. He has the power to investigate, report upon, and make recommendations
> about individual cases and administrative procedures. He is not a judge or tribunal,
> and he has no power to make orders or to reverse administrative action. He seeks
> solutions to problems by a process of investigation and conciliation. His authority
> and influence derive from the fact that he is appointed by and reports to one of the
> principal organs of state, usually either the parliament or the chief executive.[9]

Ombudsmen can be found operating at different levels of government — central,
state and local. There is at least one international ombudsman, the office of
European Ombudsman, set up under the Maastricht Treaty and appointed by the
European Parliament (his tenure is for the five-year duration of the parliamentary
term) to investigate complaints of maladministration by EU institutions, excluding
the European Court of Justice. Some ombudsmen have a wide jurisdiction; others
specialise in particular areas of public administration, such as health services,
prisons or schools. Most are established by legislative means; many have continuing links with and are sometimes answerable in one way or another to legislative
bodies — hence the frequently used adjective, more apposite in some instances
than in others, 'parliamentary'.

Some ombudsmen are in fact more 'executive' than parliamentary, a feature
which disqualifies them in the eyes of some observers who regard the parliamentary character of the office as essential to its authenticity, and consider that
executive ombudsmen lack the essential quality of independence. Thus Donald
Rowat cites the appointment by the US Postmaster General in 1971 of a postal
ombudsman for business as just one unacceptable instance of the misappropriation

---

9   Caiden, G.E. (ed.), *International Handbook of the Ombudsman*, Westport CT.: Greenwood Press,
    1983, p. 13.

of the term 'ombudsman' by the executive arm of government. More recently, in the UK, the Government's use of the term 'prisons ombudsman' has been criticised both by the PCA and by the Select Committee on the PCA. The latter has also noted general concern 'that the currency of the term "Ombudsman" brought with it the threat of devaluation', and has taken the view that it is 'unacceptable that any person should be described as an Ombudsman if there remains a right of appeal [as is the case with some ombudsmen appointed internally by government departments] to the Parliamentary Ombudsman'. It has recommended 'that the Government take immediate steps to ensure that no complaints officer within the public service use the term "Ombudsman" to describe himself if the body concerned comes within the jurisdiction of the Ombudsman appointed under statute'.[10]

However, the notion of 'executive' ombudsmen is not excluded from the Caiden description, above, and it is surely arguable that in a less than perfect world, having such an ombudsman is better than having no ombudsman at all, particularly in countries where parliamentary government is weak or non existent, as has been the case in some African countries. Moreover, 'executive' ombudsmen have in practice often proved no less robust in dealing with citizens' grievances than their 'parliamentary' counterparts. In any case, the parliaments to which the latter are linked may themselves be dominated by a strong executive — as is the case in the UK — so the distinction may not in practice be as clear-cut as it is in theory.

Sometimes, as with the Swedish and Finnish Chancellors of Justice (see below), an executive ombudsman may co-exist with a parliamentary one. And sometimes an executive ombudsman may be replaced by a parliamentary one,— as with the transformation of the South African office of Advocate General, set up in 1979, into a parliamentary office in 1991 — which in turn was replaced in 1993 by a new parliamentary office of Public Protector.

Some ombudsmen (e.g., those operating in the newspaper or insurance industries, or in trade unions, or in universities) operate outside or on the fringes of core government and have little or no official status. Are they really 'ombudsmen' at all? Does it matter anyway? Perhaps not, but there is some force in the point made by the Select Committee, quoted earlier, about the dangers of devaluing the ombudsman currency: the effectiveness of all ombudsmen depends very much on public confidence, and any disappointment with 'counterfeit' ombudsmen may undermine the credibility of the genuine article.

Ombudsman systems serve several important functions. 'For the public,' as Gerald Caiden and his co-authors point out, 'the ombudsman is a welcome device for assuring that justice is done and that bureaucracies treat their clients fairly, promptly and respectfully.'[11] But an ombudsman's office is not merely an instrument

10   First Report from the Select Committee on the PCA, 1993–94, *The Powers, Work and Jurisdiction of the Ombudsman*, HC 33–I, paras 27 and 28.
11   *Op. cit.* note 9 *supra*, p. 3.

of redress, it also serves an important function of quality control: 'For bureaucracies, it is an additional fail-safe check on their operations to ensure that any mistakes that have not been spotted are eventually caught and rectified, and it also serves to identify unintentional impacts of otherwise well-intentioned procedure'.[12]

More generally, the adoption of an ombudsman scheme signals to citizens and public employees, and to the international community (including funding agencies, dispensing international aid), a recognition by the state of the importance of justice and good government. There is a possible downside to this in the possibility of ombudsmen being appointed and then controlled or manipulated by the executive in order to give a specious impression of democracy and justice — which is why importance is widely attached to harnessing ombudsmen, to a greater or lesser extent, to the democratic legitimacy of a parliamentary system.

PERSUASION VERSUS ENFORCEMENT

Apart from their independence and their impartiality, a definitive characteristic of ombudsmen is that they have no power either to *change* a decision or to *compel* the bodies within their jurisdiction to act in a particular way. Their detailed powers vary from case to case depending upon the legislation under which they operate; but in general they have the power to investigate, to report, to criticise, to say how the matter in question should have been dealt with, and to recommend remedial action in the event of a finding of injustice caused by administrative default or error in the instant case and/or changes in practice (or perhaps in legislation) to avoid a recurrence.

The likelihood of acceptance of their findings and of compliance with their recommendations depends on various factors, including the nature of relevant institutional and political cultures, but is ultimately determined substantially by the measure of esteem in which the office is held. The ombudsman's main weapon is the exercise of moral authority, underpinned by legislation, and backed by the implicit threat of causing political embarrassment to a non co-operative administration — the 'mobilisation of shame'. Wade and Forsyth put it thus:

> an ombudsman requires no legal powers except powers of inquiry . . . His effectiveness derives entirely from his power to focus public and parliamentary attention upon citizens' grievances. But publicity based on impartial inquiry is a powerful lever . . . The consciousness of the ombudsman's vigilance has a healthy effect on the whole administrative system, making it more sensitive to public opinion and to the demands of fairness.[13]

---

12 *Ibid.*
13 Wade, H.W.R. and Forsyth, C.F., *Administrative Law* (7th ed.), Oxford: Clarendon Press, 1994, p. 81.

In this sense ombudsmen are quite different from courts of appeal. However, many ombudsmen are appointed from professional–legal or judicial backgrounds; their role is sometimes formally linked to that of the courts;[14] and as we have already noted, they are often discussed in textbooks on administrative law alongside administrative courts and tribunals. They complement, but in no sense replace, the judicial process.

Some ombudsmen have wider powers than others, and their effectiveness and impact varies from one office to another, over a period of time, between different holders of the same office — and even from one case to the next. Ombudsmen are not formally bound by precedent, but develop, in effect, their own case-law through an accumulation of published rulings; given that the encouragement of consistency in administrative decision making is likely to be part of an ombudsman's mission, arguably the office itself should give a lead in that respect. However, because of the 'parliamentary' character of the office in most countries with ombudsman systems, and its consequent engagement — notwithstanding the non partisan stance of ombudsmen themselves — with the political process and the vagaries of the political climate, some degree of variation over time is inevitable.

SWEDEN: THE BENCHMARK CASE

The word 'ombudsman' is sometimes said to have originated with the early Germanic tribes, as the title given to a person chosen to collect blood money from a wrongdoer on behalf of an aggrieved party.[15] But its modern, and more familiar usage — explained earlier — comes from Sweden. Apart from the parliamentary ombudsman, Sweden has (in common with many other countries) numerous specialised non parliamentary ombudsmen, concerned with, for instance, trade unions, equal opportunities, consumer affairs, the dealings of banks and other financial institutions, the press, etc.

The Swedish parliamentary ombudsman dates back to 1809. However, the office had antecedents in the office of Chancellor of Justice, established in 1713 by King Charles XII while he was in temporary exile in Turkey following a military defeat. In response to civil unrest throughout Sweden, the King decreed that his highest ombudsman, the Chancellor of Justice, should ensure that laws were obeyed and that civil servants carried out their obligations. The Swedish office of Chancellor of Justice, operating from within the administration, still co-exists with that of the parliamentary ombudsmen, who perform a similar role on behalf of the Riksdag.

---

14   For instance, decisions of the Northern Ireland Commissioner for Complaints (dealing with complaints against local authorities and other non central public bodies) can be enforced through the courts, though this facility is rarely used in practice.

15   For an outline history of the Swedish ombudsman, see Ludvik, U., *The Swedish Parliamentary Ombudsman*, Stockholm: JO, 1982.

He tends to be approached less by members of the public than by administrative agencies themselves, seeking an authoritative ruling on the legality of their actions.

In 1809, the Riksdag adopted a new constitution, based on a balance of power between king and parliament. It provided for the appointment by the King of a Chancellor of Justice, and for the election by the Riksdag of an Ombudsman for Justice (*Justitieombudsman*, commonly abbreviated to 'JO'), who was to be 'a man[16] of known legal ability and outstanding integrity'. The parliamentary ombudsman's role, exercised on behalf of the Riksdag, was to ensure compliance with the law by all state officials and judges (not all ombudsmen systems include the judiciary within their jurisdiction).

The office of Swedish parliamentary ombudsman has undergone several important reorganisations since its establishment. In 1915, a separate military ombudsman was established alongside the Ombudsman for Justices but in 1968, in consequence of the imbalance of workload between the two ombudsmen, the offices were amalgamated, and the Riksdag appointed three ombudsmen under the single institution of *Justitieombudsman*; further reorganisations occurred in 1975, and again in 1986. There are now four ombudsmen, one of whom is the Chief Ombudsman, who is responsible for the administration and staffing of the office and for the general distribution of responsibilities among himself and his colleagues.

The ombudsmen are elected at a plenary session of the Riksdag (a unicameral legislature since 1971) for four-year terms, with the possibility of re-election. There is a convention that the ombudsman must enjoy all-party support within the legislature, and in recent years ombudsmen have been elected by acclamation. It is also a convention that ombudsmen should not be members of the Riksdag. In practice, the ombudsmen are always recruited from judicial backgrounds. The annual case-load of the Swedish ombudsman nowadays averages about 4,000 complaints, more than a third of which are dismissed without investigation, about half produce no formal criticism following an investigation, and only about 12 per cent result in a formal admonition or other criticism of the body complained against.

This may be an appropriate point to enter a cautionary note about drawing over-ambitious inferences from ombudsman statistics. It may be tempting, for instance, to conclude that a case-load of 4,000 in a population of about 8.6 million people represents a more effective and highly-regarded ombudsman system than that of (say) the UK, where the Parliamentary Commissioner — as we shall see — receives about half the number of complaints from a population nearly seven times as large. But, while it *might* be arguable that the Swedish system is 'better' than the UK one, that conclusion cannot be drawn solely from the kinds of statistic

---

16   The office was not opened to women until 1941.

just cited.[17] The main problem is that we would not be comparing like with like. For one thing, the PCA is not the only UK ombudsman: a statistical comparison would require an aggregation of figures for several ombudsmen (to include, in particular, those covering local government and health services), and there would have to be adjustments to the Swedish figures too to ensure comparability of jurisdiction. Moreover, as we shall see, the PCA receives complaints via an 'MP filter' whereas the Swedish citizen enjoys direct access to his or her ombudsman. And, as already noted, the British tradition attaches great importance to parliamentary rather than legal forms of redress; Sweden has a much stronger tradition of administrative law, along with a system of public administration that is far more detached from ministerial and departmental control than is the case with the British system (the Next Steps reforms notwithstanding — see Austin, Ch. 1).

The moral is that, even within one ombudsman system, statistics must be interpreted with the utmost circumspection. Using ombudsman statistics as a basis for meaningful cross-national comparison is almost a non starter.

TWENTIETH CENTURY DEVELOPMENTS: THE OMBUDSMAN MOVEMENT

The office of the Swedish ombudsman stood in solitary splendour until 1919, when Finland, shortly after gaining independence from Sweden, appointed its own ombudsman. But the modern ombudsman movement did not begin until the 1950s and 1960s: in 1953, Denmark appointed an ombudsman; Norway and New Zealand followed in 1962, and Tanzania in 1966. In 1967, the United Kingdom established its own variant of the office of ombudsman, in the form of the PCA — an institution which bears little resemblance to the Swedish prototype. An examination of this office, and of the reasons for its being established in this peculiar form, provide an instructive illustration of the truism that every ombudsman's office, if it is to function effectively, must fit comfortably into the relevant constitutional and cultural context. Ombudsmen worldwide are recognisable as variations on a common theme, but when one comes down to matters of operational and jurisdictional detail, there is no such thing as a universally transferable 'ombudsman model'.

However, this issue of transferability seems to have done nothing to inhibit the momentum of what has become a worldwide 'ombudsman movement'. Data compiled by Gerald Caiden and others,[18] record that national ombudsmen were appointed in Mauritius (1970); Israel (1971); Fiji (1972); France and Zambia

---

17 There is useful discussion of this 'comparability' problem in Gregory, R. and Pearson, J., 'The Parliamentary Ombudsman after Twenty-Five Years' (1992) 70 *Public Administration* 469, at pp. 471–5.

18 *Op. cit.* note 9 *supra*.

(1973); Papua New Guinea (1975); Australia, Austria, Portugal and Trinidad and Tobago (1976); Jamaica (1978); The Philippines (1979); Ghana (1980); and Eire, The Netherlands and Spain (1981). In the late 1960s and the 1970s, several ombudsmen appeared in the provinces and states of Canada, the United States, Australia and India. And over the same period many municipal ombudsmen were appointed — for instance in Jerusalem, Haifa, Anchorage, Detroit, Seattle, New York and Zurich.

As will be noted later, in our discussion of the establishment of the PCA in Britain, the appointment of an ombudsman in New Zealand in 1962 neatly answered those who claimed that the office was manifestly incompatible with Westminster-style parliamentary government. Like the PCA in Britain, the New Zealand ombudsman is answerable to Parliament. But there is no MP filter, and the ombudsman's competence extends beyond 'maladministration' to cover any administrative decision, recommendation, act or omission judged to be 'unreasonable, unjust, oppressive or improperly discriminatory' or even simply 'wrong'. The reply to critics who complain that an ombudsman is incompatible with Westminster-style ministerial responsibility is that an ombudsman only has the power to recommend, not to decide; and, far from cutting across the convention of ministerial responsibility, he or she can be seen to reinforce the roles both of the constituency representative and of the minister by adding an extra channel of official accountability over and above the traditional mechanisms already in place. Ministers, whether trying to keep a firm grip on their departments or seeking to relax their grip by devolving managerial responsibility down the line, usually have cause to regard an ombudsman as more of an ally than an adversary.

The cases of France and Spain are of interest for different reasons, in demonstrating that the need for an ombudsman is not obviated by the existence of a well-developed system of specialised administrative courts. In France there was a feeling that an ombudsman would unnecessarily compete with the administrative courts and that the institution had little relevance to the French situation. However, the view that ombudsmen and courts serve usefully complementary functions was the one that prevailed. The French office of *Médiateur de la République* also provides the only other significant instance — apart from the UK — of an ombudsman who is accessible only via members of the legislature.

According to the International Ombudsman Institute, by mid-1981 there were 75 general legislative ombudsman plans in 25 countries — 19 operating at national level, 34 at state or regional level and 22 at local level. These figures excluded large numbers of ombudsmen exercising specialised jurisdictions and a lot more that handled complaints within the executive machinery of government. Twelve years later, the May 1993 edition of the Institute's annually updated *Directory of Ombudsmen and International Ombudsman Offices* — a useful checklist, but like any membership directory, a far from definitive listing — contains entries for 54 countries, embracing 179 individual offices/office holders.

But even a superficial scrutiny of the entries reveals the amorphousness of this group of officials who possess, or see themselves as possessing, the attributes of ombudsmen. This is evident if we look, for instance, at the largest national contingent, 38, from the USA: the offices listed include ombudsmen operating at State/territory level (Alaska, Guam, Iowa, Michigan; Nebraska, Oregon, Puerto Rico); several municipal or local ombudsmen; various schools/education ombudsmen; a long-term care ombudsman; a hospital ombudsman; several ombudsmen for corrections (dealing with prisons); an ombudsman for mental health and mental retardation; an ombudsman attached to the International Monetary Fund in Washington DC; and another attached to the Office of the Administrator of the Panama Canal Commission. The terminology used to describe ombudsman offices, even within a single country, is very variable. One of those listed is Assistant to the City Manager in Roanoke, Virginia; another is listed as an 'Emeritus Ombudsman'.

Ombudsmen have been seen as instruments of good government in many emergent democracies, and are often seen as protectors of human rights and/or as leading the fight against the corruption that is endemic in many developing and transitional economies. The Polish Ombudsman was a prototype in post-Communist Eastern Europe. The 1993 Constitution of the Russian Federation provides for the appointment of an Ombudsman for Human Rights; early reports suggested that the office was to have a staff of 270 and was expected to deal with 160,000 complaints in its first year. (The appointment of ombudsmen in post-apartheid South Africa and in the European Union has already been noted.)

OMBUDSMAN WESTMINSTER-STYLE: THE PARLIAMENTARY COMMISSIONER FOR ADMINISTRATION

Meanwhile, it was halfway into the 20th century before it could plausibly be claimed that British lawyers had shaken off their suspicion — a legacy of Diceyan dogma (though Dicey himself does not bear all the blame) — of a distinctive system of administrative law (see Leyland and Woods, Ch. 16, p. 375). Even as late as 1959, the third edition of *Halsbury's Laws of England* still contained no separate entry on administrative law (subsequent editions have remedied this omission). But by then things were beginning to change. Books, journals and university courses on administrative law had begun to appear. Educative and sensible things had begun to be written in English about the French *Conseil d'Etat*.[19] And legal commentators and law reformers had begun to notice, and to see merit in, the Scandinavian office of ombudsman as something that might provide useful remedies in cases of maladministration by officials — of the kind

---

19   In particular, Hampson, C.J., *Executive Discretion and Judicial Control*, London: Stevens, 1954.

that had emerged in the famous Crichel Down case in the early 1950s.[20] It began gradually to be recognised by some commentators that this hitherto unfamiliar foreign institution, suitably adapted to fit the British context, might usefully complement the administrative law functions of courts and tribunals on the one hand and the grievance-chasing role of MPs on the other. Interest in the idea of ombudsman gained added momentum when the first Danish ombudsman, Professor Hurwitz, visited Britain in 1958 and delivered lectures about his work. But many people, both lawyers and politicians, remained sceptical and, for reasons already mentioned, any parliamentary ombudsman acceptable (as a 'parliamentary' institution must be) to British MPs would have to be designed with some cunning so as to present the office as an adjunct to parliamentary redress through ministerial responsibility rather than as a competitor to such redress.

The original blueprint for the British ombudsman was drawn up in 1961 by a committee of JUSTICE, the British section of the International Commission of Jurists, headed by Sir John Whyatt (who had recently retired as Chief Justice of Singapore). The Whyatt Report regarded its remit and its recommendations as a direct follow-up to the *Franks Report on Tribunals and Inquiries* which had appeared in 1957. It drew an important distinction between complaints about the merits of an administrative decision (in respect of which it advocated extensions of the existing system of administrative tribunals) and complaints of maladministration, involving allegations of inefficiency, delay, negligence, bias, unfairly preferential treatment or dishonesty. The Report concluded, in words that aptly sum up the rationale of most ombudsman systems, that:

> There appears to be a continuous flow of relatively minor complaints, not sufficient in themselves to attract public interest but nevertheless of great importance to the individuals concerned, which gives rise to feelings of frustration and resentment because of the inadequacy of the existing means of seeking redress.[21]

Of the options available as possible remedies against maladministration, the Whyatt Committee dismissed judicial review as too limited and too expensive; it considered parliamentary techniques, like questions to ministers and adjournment debates, as ineffective (a verdict subsequently corroborated by the Scott Report). *Ad hoc* inquiries, such as those conducted from time to time under the Tribunals of Inquiry (Evidence) Act 1921, departmental inquiries and parliamentary investigatory committees, were cumbersome, and quite unsuited to dealing with day-to-day matters of maladministration (the arguments about the appropriateness

---

20 The origins and early history of the UK ombudsman are discussed in: Stacey, F., *The British Ombudsman*, Oxford: Clarendon Press, 1971; Gregory, R. and Hutchesson, P., *The Parliamentary Ombudsman*, London: George Allen and Unwin, 1975.

21 Whyatt, Sir J., *The Citizen and the Administration*, London: JUSTICE, 1961, para. 76.

and effectiveness of the Scott Inquiry come to mind here). The Report proposed the establishment of an independent ombudsman, acting on behalf of Parliament (and with the title of Parliamentary Commissioner) to deal with complaints of maladministration brought by members of the public against central government departments.

This novel but cautious proposal was too radical for the Conservative govern ment of the day, which argued *inter alia* that a 'Parliamentary Commissioner would seriously interfere with the prompt and efficient despatch of public business'. It was left to a Labour government — perhaps encouraged by the fact that another Commonwealth country with a Westminster-style constitution, New Zealand, had introduced its own ombudsman in 1962 — to introduce the legislation that became the Parliamentary Commissioner Act 1967. The first PCA, Sir Edmund Compton, a former Comptroller and Auditor General, was actually appointed in 1966, before the Act governing his office was formally on the statute book.

The cautious flavour of the 1967 legislation reflected a number of concerns, referred to on many occasions while the Bill was going through Parliament. Crucially, as already noted, the ombudsman was to be a *parliamentary* commis- sioner. MPs were, and still are, fiercely protective of their traditional role in dealing with constituents' grievances against central government departments. The new ombudsman was presented from the outset as acting in collaboration with rather than in competition with constituency MPs, and working within the constitutional framework of ministerial responsibility. There was also a good deal of concern about the possible 'swamping' of a small office by a deluge of complaints — a fear that certainly has not been borne out by experience: in recent years the number of cases referred by MPs has steadily increased (986 in 1993, 1,332 in 1994, 1,706 in 1995, 1,933 in 1996), but the incidence of referrals is still a lot lower than some of the more alarmist predictions made in the mid-1960s.

Complaints reach the PCA only if they are referred to him by Members of the House of Commons, and he reports the outcome of his investigations to the referring MP; he also reports annually to Parliament, and may (under s. 10(3) of the 1967 Act) produce special reports if his findings of maladministration are ignored by departments. The existence of an 'MP filter', and the absence of direct public access, has been a matter of continuing controversy throughout the PCA's existence. Numerous external commentators, and some ombudsmen themselves, have suggested abolition of the 'filter'. The German co-authors of a comparative study of ombudsman systems have gone so far as to suggest that 'direct access to the Ombudsman is . . . an essential requirement of the office'.[22] If so, the present discussion of the PCA — as the prototype and centrepiece of the UK 'ombudsman' system would be redundant.

---

22   Kempf, U. and Mille, M., *The Role and Function of the Ombudsman: Personalised Parliamentary Control in 48 Different States*, Freiberg: Pädagogische Hochschule, 1992.

There is a non accidental resemblance between the office of the PCA and that of the Comptroller and Auditor General (C&AG), which dates back to 1866. The C&AG, the head of the National Audit Office, reports to the House of Commons via its most effective and prestigious select committee, the Public Accounts Committee: in a sense his role is to look into financial maladministration (though this phrase is not used in the relevant legislation); and, conversely, the functions of ombudsmen might be said to include the 'quality auditing' of the administrative process.

On similar lines to the C&AG/PCA relationship, the main interface between the PCA and the House of Commons, is a small all-party Select Committee on the Parliamentary Commissioner, comprising nine backbench MPs, and chaired by a prominent backbencher from the Government side of the House, which receives his reports and produces reports of its own, having taken evidence from the PCA and his deputies and (as it considers appropriate) from ministers and officials. After the 1997 General Election the PCA Select Committee was merged with the former Public Services Committee, to form a new Public Administration Committee.

Lastly, mention should be made of the role of the PCA in overseeing the Code of Practice on Access to Government Information, which came into effect in April 1994 (see Austin, Ch. 1, p. 22 and Tomkins, Ch. 14, p. 342). This may be seen as a logical extension of his role, given that so many instances of maladministration boil down in practice to failures of communication. The ombudsman is empowered to consider complaints referred to him by MPs that public bodies have refused to supply information as required by the code. In 1996, he received 44 such complaints: of the 12 cases fully investigated, five were upheld wholly or in part. The ombudsman has expressed surprise at the small number of complaints in this area of his jurisdiction — in contrast to the experience of other countries, particularly Canada, Australia and New Zealand: one factor has been lack of publicity for the code, and some steps have been promised to improve this. In March 1996, the PCA Select Committee published a substantial report on *Open Government*,[23] and some (but not all) of its recommendations for clarifying the code and improving the procedures for disclosure were accepted by the government.

The status and background of the PCA

The PCA is appointed by the government of the day which (since the late 1970s) has adopted the practice of consulting the chairman of the Select Committee on the Parliamentary Commissioner. He is formally treated as an officer of Parliament (though unlike the National Audit Act 1983, which defines the status and functions

---

23   Second Report, HC 84, 1995–96.

of the C&AG, the Parliamentary Commissioner Act 1967 is silent on this point) and he is debarred from being an MP. Like a senior judge, he holds office subject to 'good behaviour' and can be removed only on an address by both Houses of Parliament. The retiring age is 65. He appoints his own staff (about 100 of them, mostly temporarily seconded civil servants, who also serve the PCA in his capacity as Health Service Commissioner, see below), subject to Treasury approval in respect of numbers, pay, etc.

There has been some debate over the years about the most appropriate background from which the PCA should be recruited. The first holder of the office, Sir Edmund Compton (1967–71) had been the C&AG with the task, analogous to that of the PCA (see above), of seeking out financial maladministration in government departments and of reporting to the House of Commons via a select committee (the Public Accounts Committee). The next two incumbents, Sir Alan Marre (1971–76) and Sir Idwal Pugh (1976–79) had been senior civil servants. The next two, Sir Cecil Clothier (1979–85) and Sir Anthony Barrowclough (1985–89) were barristers. The next incumbent, William Reid (1990–97), had been Secretary of the Scottish Home and Health Department, and his successor, Michael Buckley, who took up office in January 1997, also has a Civil Service background, having served prior to his appointment as PCA as a grade 3 in the Department of Energy and then as a member of the Civil Service Appeals Board.

Former civil servants are familiar with the Whitehall system, and with the tricks their former colleagues may get up to; but might they not be too readily disposed to give those colleagues the benefit of the doubt? Lawyers lack first-hand experience of the system, but are perhaps more overtly 'independent' than former officials. Legal skills may in some circumstances be useful to a PCA, e.g., in cross-examining officials about their conduct or unravelling the intricacies of a big business fraud case (like Barlow Clowes, see below); but the PCA is not really there to resolve grievances which are primarily legal in character; he can, where necessary, seek independent legal advice from Treasury Counsel.

Extent of the PCA'S jurisdiction

The PCA's jurisdiction is confined to complaints relating to central departments and agencies, for which ministers are answerable to Parliament: thus his powers do not extend, for example, to public corporations, local government and the police — although, as we shall, see, separate variants of the ombudsman machinery have subsequently been introduced in several of these areas. The Parliamentary and Health Service Commissioners Act 1987 brought some 50 non departmental bodies — like the Commission for Racial Equality, the Arts Council, the Equal Opportunities Commission and the Research Councils — within the purview of the PCA, effectively extending the schedule of relevant departments originally listed in the

1967 Act to more than 100. However, in practice this extension has yielded a small crop of additional referrals.

Next Steps executive agencies are part of government departments and are therefore included in the PCA's remit (see Austin, Ch. 1, p. 12). Indeed, given that many such agencies are in the business of providing services to and/or dealing directly with the public (particularly in the very sensitive areas of paying out welfare benefits and collecting tax), it is not surprising to find that they feature very prominently in the PCA's case-load. Thus in recent years nearly half the cases received by the PCA (834 out of 1,706 in 1995; 908 out of 1,933 in 1996) have concerned the Department of Social Security — and a quarter of the cases received have concerned just one DSS agency, the Child Support Agency.

The PCA is debarred by statute from investigating matters where a complainant has a right of appeal to an administrative tribunal or the possibility of redress in a court of law — though the Act gives him a discretion to conduct an investigation into matters where there may be a remedy in a tribunal or a court 'if he is satisfied that in the particular circumstances it is not reasonable to expect [the complainant] to resort or to have resorted to it'.[24]

The PCA is also debarred from reviewing legal proceedings in the courts — a restriction designed to protect the independence of the judiciary; after some dispute, his jurisdiction was extended in 1991 to allow him to examine complaints relating to the administrative actions of court officials — civil servants who now work in the Courts Service executive agency.

A ruling of the Divisional Court in 1993[25] established that the PCA himself is subject to judicial review, though the judge intimated that the Court would not readily be persuaded to interfere — on grounds of *Wednesbury* unreasonableness — with the PCA's exercise of the wide discretion bestowed on him by the 1967 Act. However, in October 1996, Sedley J referred a case back for reconsideration by the ombudsman, who had ruled in favour of the Department of Transport in a planning dispute.[26]

The various matters excluded from the PCA's jurisdiction are listed in sch. 3 of the 1967 Act (as amended). Particular controversy has surrounded the exclusion of personnel matters in the Civil Service and contractual and commercial transactions. The PCA receives many complaints about such matters, and he and the Select Committee have on several occasions urged that the Act be amended so as to include them within his jurisdiction. Looking at other ombudsman systems, such exclusions are rare — and the Northern Ireland PCA (whose office is modelled closely on that of the mainland PCA) does exercise jurisdiction in this area, without this causing any apparent difficulties.

---

24 Parliamentary Commissioner Act 1967, s. 5(2).
25 *R v Parliamentary Commissioner for Administration, ex parte Dyer* [1994] 1 All ER 375.
26 *R v Parliamentary Commissioner for Administration, ex parte Balchin*; see PCA, *Annual Report for 1996*, HC 386, 1996–97, para. 72.

Apart from the limitations already noted, including those stemming from the parliamentary character of the PCA's office, there are various other restrictions. The PCA's jurisdiction is confined to complaints of injustice caused by 'maladministration' — the latter having been rather cryptically described by Richard Crossman, the minister in charge of steering the 1967 legislation through Parliament, as 'bias, neglect, inattention, delay, incompetence, inaptitude, perversity, turpitude, arbitrariness and so on':[27] he is expressly debarred from questioning the merits of a decision taken by a department without maladministration in the exercise of its discretion. However, he is permitted to review ministerial, as well as Civil Service, decisions, provided that the latter are 'administrative' in character. The difficulty of establishing a clear demarcation line between responsibility for, on the one hand, 'policy' matters and, on the other, 'administrative' (or 'operational') matters is well known and is not peculiar to the study of ombudsmen.[28]

This capacity (seldom exercised) to review departmental decisions in which ministers are directly involved gave rise to three of the PCA's most famous and controversial cases. In the Sachsenhausen case, which arose in the early days of the office's existence, the PCA was very critical of the Foreign Secretary's refusal to depart from rigid and unsatisfactory criteria devised by his department and award compensation to British prisoners of war who had been detained in inhumane conditions in a German prison camp. The minister repudiated the PCA's criticisms but rather grudgingly awarded compensation on an *ex gratia* basis. In the Court Line case, in the mid-1970s, the PCA criticised misleadingly reassuring statements made by the Secretary of State for Trade and Industry about the financial soundness of a travel company, which subsequently went bankrupt. In this instance the minister again repudiated the PCA's criticisms, but many of the aggrieved clients of the company did eventually receive a measure of compensation under the provisions of the Air Travel Reserve Fund Act 1975.

An even more dramatic ministerial response was forthcoming in the Barlow Clowes case in the early 1990s,[29] in which the PCA found that the Department of Trade and Industry was guilty of maladministration in five aspects of its exercise of its regulatory functions in relation to a fraudulent investment company, whose collapse caused serious loss to thousands of private investors. The surprising reluctance of most MPs to refer cases to the PCA has been noted,[30] but every now

27 HC Deb, 18 October 1966, col. 51.
28 The Home Secretary's dismissal of the head of the Prison Service, based on his contention that breaches of prison security had been caused by operational failings rather than by policy decisions (e.g., under-resourcing of the prison system) or by ministerial interference in prison management, is a recent, much discussed, example.
29 Gregory, R. and Drewry, G., 'Barlow Clowes and the Ombudsman' [1991] *Public Law* 192–214 and 408–42.
30 Harlow, C. and Drewry, G., 'A "Cutting Edge"? The Parliamentary Commissioner and MPs' (1990) 53 *Modern Law Review* 745–69.

and then a high-profile case arises in which Members — prompted by angry letters from their constituents — mobilise their indignation through the ombudsman to try to persuade the government to put matters right. The Barlow Clowes case prompted references of complaints to the PCA by no fewer than 159 MPs of all parties (unusually, they were publicly encouraged to do so by the PCA himself). Although the government strongly disputed his findings, the authority of the PCA, backed by strong parliamentary and media pressure, forced a climb-down, and led to the announcement of a generous publicly funded compensation scheme, costing £150m. This would not have come about without the ombudsman's intervention.

More recently, the PCA was engaged in another major tussle — 'the largest single investigation I had undertaken in my time as Parliamentary Commissioner'[31] — this time with the Department of Transport. The case arose from complaints referred by three Kent MPs about the Department's unwillingness to consider paying *ex gratia* compensation in cases of exceptional hardship caused by blight to property values arising from uncertainties over the Channel Tunnel high speed rail link project. Unusually, the Department refused to accept the ombudsman's finding that there had been maladministration, and for only the second time in the history of the office the PCA laid a report before Parliament under s. 10(3) of the 1967 Act, which relates to cases where, in the ombudsman's view, injustice has been caused to a person in consequence of maladministration and that injustice has not been and will not be remedied. In this and the other cases cited the PCA received strong support from his select committee, which took evidence from the Secretary of State and the Permanent Secretary. In the end, the Department, while continuing to deny maladministration, agreed to reconsider the possibility of a scheme for redress in cases of exceptional hardship, 'out of respect for the PCA Select Committee and the Office of the Parliamentary Commissioner, and without admission of fault or liability'. The PCA 'welcomed' this decision.

Variations on the ombudsman theme

After a rather cautious beginning, the UK has embraced the ombudsman concept with growing enthusiasm — though cynics might argue that executive 'enthusiasm' for (or even tolerance of) an ombudsman in any system may give cause for doubting its capacity to make a real nuisance of itself. As Birkinshaw puts it, 'it is a wonder, perhaps, that the PCA has been accepted and has achieved what he has, which probably means that he has not been an unduly burdensome thorn in any important flesh'.[32]

---

31 Parliamentary Commissioner for Administration, Fourth Report, Session 1995–96, *Annual Report for 1995*, para. 7. The details of the case are outlined at paras 109–119.
32 Birkinshaw, P., *Grievances, Remedies and the State* (2nd ed.), London: Sweet & Maxwell, 1994, p. 210.

A Health Service Commissioner (HSC) (the office is in fact held by the PCA — a duplication made possible only by the latter's small case-load) was set up by the National Health Services Reorganisation Act 1973 (see Mulcahy and Allsop, Ch. 5, p. 133). He receives complaints directly from members of the public and reports to the relevant minister (the Secretary of State for Health, or for Scotland, or for Wales), though his reports are laid before Parliament — and the Select Committee on the Parliamentary Commissioner spends a lot of its time looking at HSC issues. The number of complaints received by the ombudsman in his capacity as HSC have been similar (1,784 in 1995–96) to the number he has received (via MPs) as PCA. But some increase in his case-load is likely in consequence of the provisions of the Health Service Commissioners (Amendment) Act 1996 which extend the HSC's jurisdiction to enable him to cover, in particular, family practitioner services and matters of clinical judgment — his exclusion from which has always been a matter of controversy.

A Commission for Local Administration (with three regional Commissioners for England, and one each for Scotland and Wales) was established by the Local Government Act 1974. Since 1988, direct access — rather than access exclusively via reference of a complaint by an elected local councillor — has been allowed and this resulted in a substantial increase in the number of complaints they have received: in 1988/89 the Commissioners received 5,908 complaints; by 1991/92 this had risen to 10,610; and by 1995/96 the total was 15,266. In 1995 a fundamental review of the Commission's work by Sir Geoffrey Chipperfield concluded that the Commission would not be able to handle effectively the increasing volume of complaints and recommended that it should be replaced by a requirement for every local authority to operate its own complaints mechanism, comprising both a process of internal review and an external adjudicator. The prospect of eliminating the ombudsman as a wholly external investigative mechanism was resisted by the Commissioners themselves, by the local authority associations and by bodies which represent complainants, such as citizen's advice bureaux — and the government, while emphasising the importance of local authorities having their own complaints procedures, rejected the view that there is no continued need for the Commission's independent role.[33]

Unlike the PCA and the HSC, the local government ombudsmen suffer from a significant problem of non compliance: of 4,544 reports finding maladministration causing injustice, issued between 1974/75 and 1995/96, 238 are recorded as yielding an 'unsatisfactory outcome'. Although the Local Government and Housing Act 1989 provided some additional mechanisms to put pressure on recalcitrant local authorities, culminating in a requirement for a statement, agreed between the ombudsman and the authority, to be published in the local press, the number of

---

33 Local Government Ombudsman, *Annual Report 1995/96*, 1996, p. 3.

'further reports', indicating the ombudsman's dissatisfaction with the authority's response to the original report, has not noticeably diminished. There may be a case for providing for judicial enforcement — perhaps along the lines of the Northern Ireland Commissioner for Complaints scheme. The contrast between the PCA/HSC and the local ombudsman may be explained in part by the former's reinforcement by the role of the Select Committee: as Wade and Forsyth observe, 'they are not 'Parliamentary' commissioners, except in the sense that their work is of concern to the House of Commons' Select Committee on the Parliamentary Commissioner, who have several times taken evidence from them and given them support'.[34]

The 1980s saw the appearance in the UK of a variety of private sector ombudsmen, particularly in the financial services sector — some, like the Building Societies Ombudsmen (established in 1987), the Legal Services Ombudsman (1990) and the Pensions Ombudsman (1991), being statutory,[35] others, like the Banking Ombudsman (1986) and the Insurance Ombudsman (1981) being non statutory. Such self-regulatory devices have in many cases been adopted by the industries concerned as a preferable alternative to the prospect of more draconian regulation imposed by the government. There is a statutory Broadcasting Standards Commission[36] and a non statutory Press Complaints Commission; many newspapers now have their own in-house ombudsmen. The Citizen's Charter has required public bodies to review their own internal complaints mechanisms, and this has resulted in the establishment of various internal quasi-ombudsmen, including the Revenue Complaints Adjudicator.

THE EFFICACY OF OMBUDSMEN

As indicated earlier, ombudsman statistics are not a reliable basis for cross-national comparison: nor do they constitute a satisfactory or scientific basis for measuring the impact and effectiveness of any given ombudsman system. Much of any such assessment must be based on circumstantial and indirect evidence: the statements of relevant actors — including ombudsmen themselves, whose annual reports often contain thoughtful nuggets of self-assessment — can provide helpful insights.

So far as the UK ombudsman system is concerned, some of the early criticisms of the apparent 'toothlessness' of the PCA 'merely reflected the vague and unrealistic notions of ill-informed critics labouring under the mistaken impression that, in other countries, virtually nothing was beyond the powers of review and direction vested in the ombudsman'.[37] However, there is continuing criticism of the

34   *Op. cit.* note 13 *supra*, p. 142.
35   Building Societies Act 1986; Courts and Legal Services Act 1990; Pensions Schemes Act 1993.
36   By the provisions of the Broadcasting Act 1996, the Broadcasting Complaints Commission merged with the Broadcasting Standards Council in April 1997 to form the Broadcasting Standards Commission.
37   Gregory *et al.*, *op. cit.* note 17 *supra*, p. 469.

low-profile of the office and of the unwillingness of most MPs to make much use of it: '. . . it is not so much that the watchdog is thought to lack teeth; the feeling is rather that he is too infrequently asked to make use of them.'[38] There is continued questioning of the need for an MP filter, though most MPs themselves (including members of the Select Committee) have continued to argue for its retention. The 'parliamentary' character of the office — particularly the role of the Select Committee — is an undoubted source of strength. But in the end the effectiveness and the credibility of a Parliamentary ombudsman is substantially bound up with the effectiveness and credibility of the parliament to which it is linked: the depressing revelations in the Scott Report about the impotence of the Westminster Parliament in the face of ministerial cynicism and duplicity, and the numerous 'sleaze' revelations in the run up to the 1997 general election, are a depressing reminder of the fragile health of parliamentary government.

The office gets intermittent — and largely favourable — publicity through its so far mainly successful confrontations with the government in big cases like Barlow Clowes and the Channel Tunnel rail link. However, it must be remembered that for every one of these cases, there are hundreds of much smaller cases, involving familiar bureaucratic delinquencies such as discourtesy, lost files and lack of urgency, and the cumulative effectiveness of an ombudsman in dealing with such cases and winning apologies and small *ex gratia* sums by way of compensation is every bit as important a measure of 'efficacy' as are his relatively few headline-hitting successes in winning large remedies from stubborn ministers.

One of the most valuable legacies of an ombudsman system is in the cumulative small print of its reports — which amount to an illuminating casebook of administrative practice, good and bad. And, in the British system, where so much of the traditional administrative process is cloaked in secrecy, and where so little has been codified, the ombudsmen's reports — taken together with the many charters, framework documents and performance indicators that have appeared in consequence of the new public management revolution — are an invaluable source of good administrative practice and due process. It is interesting to note that in response to a recommendation by the Select Committee, the Cabinet Office has produced, with the help of the PCA's office, a document for civil servants called *The Ombudsman in Your Files*, as a guide to the ombudsman's role and highlight-ing — with cautionary examples — ways of avoiding maladministration.[39]

The Commission for Local Administration has issued a substantial guidance note on *Good Administrative Practice*.[40] This draws upon recommendations of the

---

38 *Ibid.*, p. 471.
39 London: Cabinet Office, December 1995. This document is a companion to an earlier Cabinet Office publication, *The Judge Over Your Shoulder* (revised edition, 1994), which alerts civil servants to the principles and pitfalls of judicial review.
40 London: CLA, August 1993; re-issued February 1995.

Committee of Ministers of the Council of Europe and upon practical experience of local ombudsman investigations, containing 42 principles or axioms of good administration illustrated with real-life examples.

CONCLUSION

In summary, the UK ombudsman system is now firmly established, and it has expanded and diversified, but there remains a feeling that its profile is much too low and that there is a good deal of potential that remains unrealised.

What of the global picture? Caiden's cross-national study concludes in rather lukewarm terms that, in general, given the constraints, 'the institution of ombudsman has fulfilled limited expectations'.[41] Certainly the speed at which and extent to which the ombudsman institution has spread throughout the world is hardly suggestive of any widespread perception of failure. However, the Caiden study does also note some negative features, which may be summarised as follows:

- some ombudsmen receive few complaints, 'barely enough to justify their existence';

- some offices have very limited jurisdiction and/or take a deliberately narrow view of their powers;

- some are reluctant to deal with big issues like corruption, fraud and official or political intimidation;

- some tend to be over-bureaucratic, legalistic and cumbersome, 'possibly because in reality they constitute protection for the administration, not the public';

- lack of publicity, a factor that contributes to the small case-loads noted above;

- in some instances ombudsmen who have challenged powerful figures have not been reappointed at the end of their terms of office, or have even been forced to resign.

Concluding a chapter on ombudsmen in developing countries, Donald Rowat observes that while it may be true that the office is not very well equipped for hunting lions, 'it can certainly swat a lot of flies'.[42] If one can hazard a verdict about an institution like the ombudsman that manifests itself in so many different guises, this slightly lukewarm verdict seems apt — albeit subject to two reservations. First, the pile of 'dead flies' that has built up through the collective endeavours of ombudsmen throughout the world .has now reached mountainous

---

41 *Op. cit.* p. 19.
42 Rowat, D. (ed.), *The Ombudsman* (2nd ed.), London: Allen and Unwin, 1985, p. 170.

proportions. Secondly, it must be borne in mind that swatting one delinquent bureaucratic fly may be a small act in itself, but it does often help to concentrate the minds of its companions on important matters like quality of public service and due process.

5

A Woolf in Sheep's Clothing? Shifts Towards Informal Resolution of Complaints in the Health Service

Linda Mulcahy and Judith Allsop

SUMMARY

The Woolf Report heralded a move away from formal grievance procedures and a burgeoning of interest in 'alternative' dispute resolution. The new GPs complaints system captures the spirit of the Woolf proposals by placing a firm emphasis on informal service level resolution of disputes. But whether the rhetoric of informalism serves the needs of procedural justice remains the subject of some debate.

INTRODUCTION

In this chapter we discuss the shift from formal systems for the redress of citizen grievances to more informal ways of resolving disputes. Informal dispute resolution procedures are defined here as those which have a non bureaucratic structure and make minimal use of legal professionals. They have a tendency to eschew official law in favour of substantive and procedural norms which are vague, unwritten, commonsensical, flexible and *ad hoc*.[1] We use the case of how complaints against general medical practitioners (GPs) are dealt with to illustrate more general trends in the United Kingdom (UK) civil justice system towards informalism. In recent months, a tribunal designed to adjudicate disputes between

---

1 See Abel, R., 'The Contradictions of Informal Justice', in Abel, R. (ed.) *The Politics of Informal Justice*, New York: Academic Press, 1982.

GPs and their patients, the Medical Service Committee, has been largely replaced by a system which seeks to resolve dissatisfaction and grievances informally before they harden into disputes. First set up in 1911 to oversee the performance of GPs under contract to provide medical services within the public health service, Medical Service Committees were one of the many tribunals or 'lower courts' which existed to redress citizens' grievances. We look at the particular circumstances in which such a shift from formal adjudication to local resolution of dissatisfaction has been made and explore what the new procedures aim to achieve as compared to the old. This assessment is made from three perspectives: the state, which is responsible for the regulation of medical services and the provision of systems for the redress of grievances; the person with the grievance who wants it resolved; and the doctor who has been criticised.

Any state-sanctioned redress system performs a number of functions and is subject to a variety of demands. Silbey[2] has argued that the lower courts can be understood only if they are seen as institutions moderating the tensions between substantive and procedural justice, between enforcement and responsiveness, and between universalist and particularist values. She suggests that they must be viewed within the context of a multiplicity of conflicting social, legal and organisational demands to which they respond. In short, the lower courts need to be seen as occupying a unique position at the boundaries of several social systems.

The discussion will draw upon the findings of empirical studies of disputes conducted by the authors and others. In particular, we seek to address the issue of whose interests are best served by the shift towards informal resolution. We argue that judging the effectiveness of informalism is dependent on the perspective from which it is viewed. In our discussion we draw on a number of ideal types of redress system which explore the various standpoints from which the question of 'effectiveness for whom' might be addressed.

NEGLECT OF THE LOWER STRATA OF THE CIVIL JUSTICE SYSTEM

Traditionally, the redress of citizens' grievances has been seen as a core function of the state and is one of the rights contained in the Magna Carta. In their attempt to fulfil this obligation, policy makers have introduced a plethora of formal dispute resolution mechanisms in the UK. These have tended to be introduced on an *ad hoc* basis rather than as part of a grand design. Thus, redress systems do not necessarily reflect a rational approach to the management of disputes or to the development of a balanced justice system.

Procedures for the resolution of grievances between citizens and GPs take a number of forms, ranging from conciliation at GP practices to statutory tribunals subject to review by the Council on Tribunals. To date, public lawyers have

---

2   See Silbey, S., 'Making Sense of the Lower Courts' (1981) *Justice System Journal*, Vol. 6, No. 1, p. 276.

expressed little interest in complaints systems or other lower-level dispute resolution systems in the National Health Service (NHS) or elsewhere.[3] Instead, emphasis has been placed on formal adjudicatory forums such as the higher courts and, in particular, on the process of judicial review. This emphasis is not without its critics. In 1987, Rawlings, in his review of the literature on grievance procedures and administrative justice for the Economic and Social Research Council, criticised the lack of interest in the lower end of the civil justice 'hierarchy'. He suggested that the existing socio-legal literature should be expanded to enhance our understanding of less formal internal mechanisms for the handling of disputes between the citizenry and public sector organisations.[4] He commented:

> The focus has been on the visible tip of the iceberg, especially as regards central government. Certain tribunals and inquiries have been heavily researched, others less so . . . Within the various institutions researchers have often opted for soft targets, leaving complex and/or controversial issues such as efficiency, administrative impact and appointments unstudied.[5]

The criticism has also been made that inadequate attention has been paid to the *dynamics* of individual tribunal systems. In the words of Genn:[6]

> Despite the potential significance of tribunals as scrutinizers of administrative decisions the writers of leading textbooks appear to have some difficulty in coping with tribunals . . . Discussion of tribunals generally tends to be relegated to a separate chapter which has little theoretical content and which follows a conventional pattern . . . and a final declaration, on the basis of meagre argument, that tribunals are a 'good thing'.[7]

When the oversight has been recognised, it has been justified on two main grounds. First, that the respect in which the courts are held gives their decisions an influence

---

3 But see, Mulcahy, L., Lickiss, R., Allsop, J. and Karn, V., *Small Voices — Big Issues: An Annotated Bibliography of the Literature on Public Sector Complaints*, London: University of North London Press, 1996; Lewis, N. and Birkinshaw, P., *When Citizens Complain: Reforming Justice and Administration*, Buckingham: Open University Press, 1993; Allsop, J., 'Two Sides to Every Story: Complainants' and Doctors' Perspectives in Disputes about Medical Care in a General Practice Setting' (1994) *Law and Policy*, vol. 16, No. 2, pp. 149–84; Mulcahy, L. and Lloyd-Bostock, S., 'Managers as Third-party Dispute Handlers in Complaints about Hospitals' (1994) *Law and Policy*, vol. 16, No. 2, pp. 185–208; Hanna, J., 'The Time Limit Hurdle: Ruling Out Patient Complaints' (1992) *New Law Journal* 1098 (July).

4 See Rawlings, R., *Grievance Procedure and Administrative Justice — A Review of Socio-Legal Research*, Swindon: Economic and Social Research Council, 1987.

5 *Ibid.*, p. 84.

6 See Genn, H., 'Tribunal Review of Administrative Decision-making', in Genn, H. and Richardson, G. (eds), *Administrative Law and Government Action: The Courts and Alternative Mechanisms of Review*, Oxford: Oxford University Press, 1994, pp. 249–87.

7 Ibid. pp. 249–50

out of proportion to the number of cases with which they deal. According to this argument their decisions have a direct impact on the way public officials handle subsequent cases. Galanter[8] has referred to this as the 'radiating effect' of the courts. Secondly, that the decisions of the higher courts are elaborately reasoned in public. This is crucial in developing the rules of law which define the positive principles which should be adhered to and the limits of lawful administrative action. The courts are seen as having a 'declaratory' role or as bestowing a 'regulatory endowment'.[9] In the words of Galanter:

> This contribution includes, but is not exhausted by, communication to prospective litigants of what might transpire if one of them sought a judicial resolution. Courts communicate not only the rules which would govern adjudication of the dispute but also remedies and estimates of the difficulty, certainty and costs of securing particular outcomes.[10]

Criticising the proliferation of forms of private dispute resolution, Fiss has argued that the declaratory role of the courts provides a key reason why formal and public adjudication should be encouraged. Where decisions are made privately or more informally, the weaker party may be coerced into settlement. Similarly, Fuller[11] has argued that private dispute resolution is the antithesis of rule-based systems of law and that formal adjudication should be the standard process.

It becomes clear from these arguments that, when discussing the courts, emphasis is placed not just on their ability to resolve the dispute for particular individuals, but on the court's ability to set legal boundaries and relay public messages which serve the more general public interest. We will argue that these two functions — redress and regulation — are not always compatible.

The 'top-down' approach to redress in the public sector has a number of shortcomings. It tends to create the illusion that non court-based procedures are relatively unimportant. In fact, it is clear that far more people use internal complaints procedures than courts or tribunals, prompting the National Consumer Council to label public complaints systems the mass end of the disputes.[12] Similarly, Kagan[13] has argued that the greatest number of official decisions in the

8   See Galanter, M., 'The Radiating Effect of the Courts', in Boyum, K. and Mather, L. (eds), *Empirical Theories about Courts*, New York: Longman, 1983.
9   See Fiss, O., 'Against Settlement', *Yale Law Journal*, 1984, April/July, pp. 1073–90 and note 9 *supra*.
10 *Op. cit.* note 8, p. 121.
11 See Fuller, L. 'Mediation — Its Forms and Functions', *South California Law Review*, 1971, vol. 44, p. 305.
12 See National Consumer Council, *Putting Things Right for Consumers*, London: National Consumer Council, 1996.
13 See Kagan, R., Book Review, 'Inside Administrative Law', 84 *Columbia Law Review* 1984, 816.

legal system of the modern state are not made by judges but by front-line administrative staff and assorted other bureaucrats.

Arguments about the primary importance of the courts' work in developing meaningful legal concepts and regulatory frameworks are convincing if the courts receive the most serious, typical or complex cases. Disputes between doctors and patients raise a number of important public law issues, such as the proper level of skill to be expected of doctors, the extent of health authorities' duty to provide healthcare and the appropriateness of the priorities set by them. However, there is much evidence to suggest that cases which proceed to formal adjudication are unrepresentative of the range of serious issues which arise in the citizen's interface with state authority.[14] There are a number of reasons for this. Gatekeepers within organisations may not recognise a grievance brought to them as legitimate, or they may narrow it to fit into a recognised cause of action.[15] It is also the case that many service users do not pursue grievances, for instance because they are not aware of their interests having been compromised or of the existence of a procedure through which they can channel a grievance. Alternatively, they may not have the resources to pursue the matter, or they may choose to 'lump it', to remain 'loyal' to the service provider or to avoid the dispute by changing their service provider. In their survey of 1,640 householders for the Department of Health in 1994, Mulcahy and Tritter[16] found that however accessible or well designed complaints systems are, they will not be used by many dissatisfied service users. In particular, they found that grievances about policy issues tended not to be voiced as complaints.

The radiating effect of court decisions and their role in the setting of regulatory frameworks has not gone unquestioned. The top-down approach assumes a 'rational' reaction to rules — administrators and others not only taking their lead from formal systems, but also responding to the directions given to them by those in authority. But while lawyers have tended to assume the link between standard setting and compliance, sociologists have focused on the study of 'avoidance' techniques.[17]

---

14 See Felstiner, W.L., Abel, R.L. and Sarat, A., 'The Emergence and Transformation of Disputes: Naming, Blaming, Claiming . . . ', *Law and Society Review*, 1980–81, vol. 15, Nos 3–4, pp. 631–54; Harris, D., Maclean, M., Genn, H., Lloyd-Bostock, S., Fenn, P., Corfield, P. and Brittan, Y., *Compensation and Support for Illness and Injury*, Oxford: Clarendon Press, 1984; Brennan, T., Leape, L., Laird, N., Herbert, L., Localio, A., Lawthers, A., 'Incidence of Adverse Events and Negligence in Hospitalised Patients: The Results from the Harvard Medical Malpractice Study I'(1991) 324 *New England Journal of Medicine*, pp. 370–6.

15 See Serber, D., 'Resolution or Rhetoric: Managing Complaints in the California Department of Insurance', in Nader, L. (ed.), *No Access to Law — Alternatives to the American Judicial System*, London: Academic Press, 1980, pp. 317–43; Mather, L. and Yngvesson, B., 'Language, Audience and the Transformation of Disputes', *Law and Society Review*, 1980–81, vol. 15, No. 3, pp. 775–833.

16 See Mulcahy, L. and Tritter, J., 'Hidden Depths', *Health Service Journal*, 1994, July, pp. 24–6.

17 See Hawkins, K., *The Uses of Discretion*, Oxford: Clarendon Press, 1992, and Galanter, M., 'Compared to What? Assessing the Quality of Disputes Processing' (1986) 66 *Denver University Law Review*, pp. xi–xiv.

ALTERNATIVE MODELS OF GRIEVANCE HANDLING

We have already argued that the effectiveness of a complaint handling procedure is dependent on the purpose for which it has been designed. In this section we outline a number of models of social organisation and functioning which place the Family Health Service Authority and Medical Service Committees within a framework of expectations. These draw implicitly on particular theories about human behaviour and motivation. They are a device for simplifying complex interrelated phenomena and they capture the extremes of what may in reality be continua. Later in the chapter, we discuss the different interests of stakeholders within NHS primary care. Discussion of both models and interests allows us to set the criteria for evaluation and to predict the likely success of the recent shift towards informalism.

We identify five models for dealing with grievances and disputes which are based on the *form* of the dispute resolution agency: the legal model; the bureaucratic model; the managerial model; professional self-regulation; and the grass roots model. These operate along two continua involving degree of formality and locus of control. These are ideal types which we have found useful for the purposes of analysis.

The legal model

The legal model is essentially rule-bound. Grievance handlers are able to respond to and fashion solutions, but in highly defined and limited ways. Grievance procedures which exhibit features of the legal model tend to be amongst the most formal of those available and to be adjudicatory and court-based.[18] All issues have to be initially presented and finally resolved in terms of the language of individual rights and duties which limits what a decision maker can 'see' and do. A high status is given to rules in such systems and, in particular, to notions of procedural fairness and impartiality. The rules are deemed to reflect the rights possessed by, and the duties owed to, the parties and to the members of society. They form what amount to organising concepts for the legal account of the world itself. The main aims of the model are to set the boundaries of what is acceptable behaviour and to allow for the ritualistic closure of a dispute rather than its resolution to the satisfaction of the parties involved.

---

18   This vision of a legal model is ethnocentric in that the Anglo-American legal systems have been used as a reference point in its evolution. Alternative versions of the legal model may exist in states with different political ideologies (see, in particular, on this point Damaska, M., *The Faces of Justice and State Authority — a Comparative Approach to the Legal Process*, London: Yale University Press, 1986).

The bureaucratic model

The legal model for handling disputes can be compared to the bureaucratic one. State bureaucracies operate within a much more flexible rule-making system than the courts. In defining problems, setting policies and establishing regulations, policy makers have a greater choice of ends and means than the judiciary. Moreover, since the turn of the century, much legislation delegates authority to public servants to interpret policies, establish regulations, and even define problems. Bureaucratic rules tend to be more instrumental than legal ones and, where bureaucratic agencies have complaints procedures, their grievance machinery is an administrative method for ensuring that the state's duty to the public is fulfilled. The organisation providing the service investigates the complaint. The rules used place more emphasis on setting work directives for administrators and on obtaining value for money than on maintaining the rights of citizens.

A particular tension arises in the pure bureaucratic model when professionals or other experts are employed or under contract to provide services. Complaints systems in this context are often legal–bureaucratic–professional hybrids and take the form of a reactive disciplinary procedure.[19] Because of the expert group's need to regulate membership, emphasis swings away from system as contributing to an untoward event failure and is placed instead on whether individuals have failed to demonstrate a particular level of skill. This allows the expert group to distance itself from culpability for individual error and maintain credibility. It is likely that the issues which can be looked at by such a redress system will be narrowed and the discourse changed from what the complainant wants to be considered to what the organisation requires to establish fault. Fellow professionals may be involved in the process to give expert opinions. Each complaint is taken as a discrete event and there tends to be a concentration on the few complaints which can be taken as exemplary. Data on complaints may not even be recorded.

The managerial model

With reform of the public sector, the bureaucratic model has been replaced by a more managerial model. As attempts have been made to impose the discipline of the market on the provision of public service, an expectation that such services should be more business-like has arisen. Managers are expected to use complaints to learn what their customers think of the service. The rhetoric of contract, rather than the notion of public duty, is used to explain relationships between service-users and providers. The work of all staff, including professional groups, is managed and the main aims of providers are to ensure continuous improvement in

---

19 See Allsop, J. and Mulcahy, L., *Regulating Medical Work*, Buckingham: Open University Press, 1996.

the quality of service and 'customer' satisfaction. Dissatisfaction may even be sought out and complaints encouraged as part of a consumer feedback programme. Adversarial situations and publicity are avoided, and resolution and redress are used as a way of maintaining the relationship between the user and the organisation rather than distributing rights. As a result, emphasis is placed on informal service-level handling of grievances in private. The mechanisms for dealing with complaints will be pervasive and complaints seen as a corporate responsibility. There are no separate complaints systems for particular groups of staff, such as professionals. Data are collected on the substance of complaints and staff groups are expected to reflect on and learn from complaints through monitoring and audit.

The professional model

The professional model offers a fourth ideal type based on complete self-regulation of work and grievance handling. The primary goal here is to protect the interests of the group. Historically, professional groups have been able to self-regulate in areas of work where training is necessary to acquire a high degree of specialised knowledge and expertise. Typically, the application of this knowledge requires not only technical skill, but also the exercise of expert judgement within a personal service. It has been argued that self-regulation is the only appropriate form of control in such circumstances because only the experts themselves have the expertise to judge a colleague.[20] Professional models display many formalistic features, such as dependence on strict rules and protocols. The limitation of issues to be considered may be used to restrict the impact of proceedings on the profession while lending a certain credibility to the process. For example, the General Medical Council disciplines a small number of errant doctors in public but in doing so demonstrate that some self-regulation is occurring. Otherwise, the profession itself controls its own members through largely internal methods of investigation and inquiry. In addition, by making, judging and monitoring standards of practice internally, the professional group could be said to maintain its 'contract' with the state to protect the public interest.

The grass roots model

To these four models can be added a fifth which we call the 'grass roots model'. This places greater emphasis on the needs of service users and like the managerial model displays many informal characteristics. The emphasis is on empowering users by allowing them to maintain control over the issues to be considered. Because the parties to disputes have a great variety of aims and objectives, resolution mechanisms allow discretion in choice of resolution technique and

---

20   See Jamous, H. and Peloille, B., 'Professions or Self-perpetuating Systems? Changes in the French University Hospital System', in Jackson, J. (ed.), *Professions and Professionalism*, Cambridge: Cambridge University Press, 1977.

outcome to service users themselves. Procedures are flexible and tend to be mediatory. Their aim is to resolve the dispute to the satisfaction of the parties involved, but particular emphasis is put on the needs of service users who are recognised as being in a weaker position than providers. The emphasis is on indigenous norms, rather than formal standardised rules, and on the ability of service users to contribute to the definition of what constitutes an acceptable standard of behaviour. The approach is exemplified in, for example, patient-run complaints systems in GP practices.[21]

THE CURRENT CONTEXT: GENERAL SHIFTS TOWARDS INFORMALISM

In recent years, policy makers in the UK and elsewhere have shown increasing interest in the promotion of state-sanctioned informal mechanisms for the resolution of disputes. The Lord Chancellor, the Bar Council and Law Society have all pledged support for the move away from formal adjudicatory systems for the resolution of disputes.[22] Most recently, the Woolf Report has argued that alternatives to formal adjudication and more cooperative attitudes to the resolution of disputes should be actively encouraged,[23] and the Department of Health has recently launched a pilot scheme to test the case for mediation of medical negligence claims.

At the same time, policy makers have been paying more attention to complaints systems across the public sector and have suggested that more attention be paid to informal resolution of disputes at service level. In 1991, the Conservative government's Citizen's Charter mechanism saw complaint handling as a key mechanism in encouraging service users to voice their concerns and contribute to the evaluation of local services[24] (see Austin, Ch. 1, p. 21). In 1993, a Citizen's Charter Unit task force was set up to investigate complaint handling in public sector services and was instrumental in setting specific standards of performance for complaints procedures.[25]

---

21 See Pietroni, S. and De Uray-Ura, S., 'Informal Complaints Procedures in General Practice: First Year's Experience' (1994) 308 *British Medical Journal* 1546.

22 See Law Society, *Alternative Dispute Resolution*, Second Report, London: Law Society, 1992; Brown, H., *Report on ADR for the Courts and Legal Services Committee*, London: Law Society, 1991; Bar Council, *Report by Committee on ADR*, Chair: Rt Hon Lord Justice Beldam, London: Bar Council, 1991.

23 See Lord Chancellor's Department, *Access to Justice — The Final Report*, London: HMSO, 1996.

24 See Citizen's Charter Unit, *The Citizen's Charter: Raising the Standard*, Cm 1599, London: HMSO, 1991.

25 See Citizen's Charter Complaints Task Force, *Effective Complaint Handling: Principles and Checklist*, London: HMSO, 1993; Citizen's Charter Complaints Task Force, *Access, Speed and Simplicity, Fairness, Information, Attitude and Motivation, Redress, Discussion*, Papers 1–6, London: HMSO, 1995a; Citizen's Charter Complaints Task Force, *Putting Things Right: Main Report*, London: HMSO, 1995b.

The burgeoning of interest in informalism has been a response to criticism of the formal systems for the redress of grievance. It has occurred in parallel to an increasing interest in 'alternative' or 'appropriate' dispute resolution (ADR). The notions of informalism and of ADR are not synonymous but are often treated as such. Although simplification and informality are achieved through many forms of ADR, this is not necessarily the case. Private mini-trials, for example, may be extremely rule-bound.[26]

As there is no universally accepted definition of either informalism or what constitutes an 'alternative' to formal adjudicatory processes, and supporters of these approaches are an ill-assorted group.[27] Murray, Rau and Sherman[28] suggest that two main categories are discernible — the 'hot' and 'cold' protagonists. The former see the advantages of informalism as being increased efficiency. They focus on three issues: the expense to the state and disputants of the civil litigation system; the ways in which the courts have become clogged with cases; and delays involved in obtaining adjudication. In contrast, 'cold' protagonists see informalism as more appropriate to satisfying the needs of the parties. Those in this camp argue that formal adjudicatory systems are inaccessible and narrow the issues in the dispute unnecessarily, involve specialists and complex rituals and encourage the escalation of hostility and impose judgments on the disputing parties. Furthermore, formal systems fail to respect indigenous norms and emphasise conflict of interest over values. In doing all these things, formal systems disable and disempower the parties involved. Such criticisms are not just a reaction against the courts. Abel argues that informalism is better viewed as a part of a much broader reaction against *all* formal institutions in complex modern states and state intervention in the lives of the citizenry.[29]

Informal dispute resolution has also been criticised.[30] Flexibility is seen as being capable of promoting unfairness amongst groups of disputants. Decision making can be unpredictable and decisions in similar cases irrational and inconsistent. Those who make decisions are less likely to be accountable, and issues of public importance are less likely to be openly debated. It has been argued that public debate is particularly important in countries where the courts play a role as guardians of the constitution. For instance, in democratic societies, few would wish to see important public cases involving human and civil rights being resolved by private mediation.[31] Concern has also been expressed that an increasing emphasis

---

26   See Brown, H. and Marriot, A., *ADR Principles and Practice*, London: Sweet & Maxwell, 1993.
27   *Ibid.*
28   See Murray, J., Rau, A. and Sherman, E., *The Process of Dispute Resolution: The Role of Lawyers*, New York: Foundation Press, 1989.
29   *Op. cit.* note 1 *supra.*
30   See notes 1 and 27 *supra.* Also, Grillo, T., 'The Mediation Alternative: Process Dangers for Women' (1991) 100 *Yale Law Journal* 1545.
31   See Freeman, M. (ed.), *Alternative Dispute Resolution*, Aldershot: Dartmouth, 1995; Green, E., 'The Complete Courthouse', in *Dispute Resolution Devices in a Democratic Society*, New York: Roscoe Pound Foundation, 1985, and *op. cit.* note 26 *supra.*

on informalism could lead to an erosion of people's right to seek a judicial determination and a consequential rationing of procedural justice.[32] Lastly, critics have commented on the extent to which informal procedures have a tendency towards creeping formalisation.

Other, more fundamental criticisms of the purpose behind state sanctioning of informalism have also been made. Rather than viewing the shift towards informalism as a victory for common sense and access to justice, Abel[33] has argued that it is designed to deflect attention from oppressive state policies. Abel also believes that informalism is in danger of allowing the judiciary to divert low status non commercial cases away from the courts; and that somewhat paradoxically state-sanctioned informality also allows for expansion of state control in areas where it might not previously have been involved. He summarises the concerns of commentators by posing a catalogue of important questions for consideration:

Does the growth of informal institutions represent an expansion or contraction of the apparatus of state control? Do they grant redress to more individual complainants or do they withdraw state support from grievants? Do they equalize the positions of disputing parties or do they aggravate existing inequalities? Do they provide greater opportunity for popular participation in handling disputes and redressing grievances or do they curtail citizen involvement? Do they introduce new substantive standards for behaviour and if so are these preferable? . . . Do they close the gap between the promises of liberalism and the reality or do they widen it? Do they enhance or undermine the legitimacy of the state? The answer to virtually every question will be both.[34]

THE SHIFT TO INFORMALISM IN NHS COMPLAINT SYSTEMS

The general shift towards informalism favoured by policy makers has been reflected in changes made to NHS complaints systems in April 1996. These must be seen in the context of broader changes introduced by the National Health Service and Community Care Act 1990 which had a radical effect on NHS organisations. The reforms reflect a desire to regulate public expenditure through the application of private sector discipline. A split has been introduced between the functions of providing services and purchasing them, through a contractual relationship between agencies. A key feature of the changes is that certain GP practices have been allowed to hold funds to purchase hospital, community and mental health services, drugs and practice staff on behalf of their practice population. This is part of a much wider strategy to shift the provision of care from

---

32 See Davis, G., *Partisans and Mediators*, Oxford: Oxford University Press, 1988, and note 6 *supra*.
33 *Op. cit.* note 1 *supra*.
34 *Ibid.*, pp. 269–70.

the secondary to primary care sector, and means that GPs have considerable leverage over providers.[35] One result of these changes is that health care provision is now increasingly diverse and fragmented, and many of the formal links within a traditionally hierarchical service have been abandoned. Regional health authorities have been absorbed into the policy arm of the service, the NHS Executive, and the functions of Family Health Service Authorities (responsible for purchasing primary care services) and district health authorities (responsible for purchasing secondary care services) have been integrated to form joint commissioning authorities. In terms of regulatory principles, the reforms have attempted to increase local accountability through the introduction of the purchaser–provider split. This inevitably means that there will be greater variety in the way rules are applied in the NHS, and that systems of accountability are concentrated at the level of increasingly autonomous local service providers.

Historically, a number of different complaints procedures have been available in the health service. Until April 1996, there were five core systems in operation administered by three separate organisations. The General Medical Council dealt with complaints about gross professional misconduct; individual hospitals dealt with complaints about their service in line with the Hospital Complaints (Procedure) Act 1985;[36] and Family Health Service Authorities managed complaints about GPs which might constitute a breach in the practitioner's contract. These systems had varying degrees of 'formality' and 'informality' depending on the sector and the type of complaint.

The Family Health Service Authority had three main ways of dealing with complaints from members of the public. First, Family Health Service Authority administrators could discuss minor non contractual matters, such as grumbles about appointment systems, with the GP concerned. Secondly, if they thought the dispute between the service user and the doctor could be dealt with informally, they could draw on the services of a conciliator appointed by the Family Health Service Authority to try to resolve such matters. Thirdly, a complaint could be referred to the lay chair of a Medical Service Committee, if it appeared to an administrator that there was a *prima facie* case of breach of the contractual terms of service. It was this last procedure which formed the core of the complaints system. (See 1988/89 Family Health Service Authority service indicators — final version DoH 1990.) Formal regulations placed most emphasis on it, as did commentators. In the last year for which figures are available on average Family Health Authorities dealt with 16 written complaints administratively to every two through conciliation and six through service committee hearings.

Since April 1996, there has been a shift from formalism to informalism, and the primary responsibility for dealing with complaints now falls on front-line

---

35 See note 19 *supra*.
36 This is a short Act containing two sections. The main guidance until April 1996 was contained in Health Circular (88) 37.

providers. In the primary care sector, these are the doctors in GP practices. Family Health Service Authorities, now incorporated into local health authorities, have a role in facilitating practice-based procedures, assisting with conciliation and, only rarely, in using the Medical Service Committee tribunals for cases which are strictly disciplinary. The remainder of this section looks at the features of Medical Service Committees. We then go on to consider the reduction in their role and justifications for this.

Prior to 1996, the regulations governing Family Health Service Authority complaints procedures were lengthy and detailed. As we have already suggested, the guidelines provided by the Department of Health (DoH) concentrated, almost exclusively, on the formal quasi-judicial procedures of Medical Service Committees. These tribunals were composed of three lay members who were nominated from, or by, the Family Health Service Authority, and three medical members nominated by the local medical committee — a professional association of doctors — from among its members. There was a lay chair, who might or might not be legally qualified, again nominated by the Family Health Service Authority. If a breach was found, a Medical Service Committee was able to discipline the doctor by issuing a warning, imposing a withholding of remuneration or referring the matter to another tribunal which could dismiss the doctor from NHS employment. Although rarely used, this last sanction was a powerful one as the NHS has a virtual monopoly in employing GPs.

Medical Service Committees represented the most formal, legalistic and rule-bound end of the complaints procedure. They operated according to guidelines and procedures laid down in statutory instruments drafted by the DoH and agreed by Parliament which reflected the general principles of natural justice. There were elaborate rules about who decided whether there was a *prima facie* case for a hearing which safeguarded the rights of both parties; a system of rules about what cases could be heard; rules which gave guidance as to the sort of evidence which had most weight; and rules of procedure for the committee itself. The stated aim of the Medical Service Committee was to establish the facts of the complaint made, listen to both sides of the case according to an ordered procedure at a 'hearing', and reach a decision as to whether there had been a breach of the terms of service or not. Reasons for the decision were given in a report with recommendations for action. The activities of Medical Service Committees were overseen by the Council on Tribunals which had a responsibility to ensure that they were operating in a fair and impartial way.

But their formality was also tempered. Medical Service Committees operated with a certain amount of discretion. Although it was for each party to conduct its case in terms of calling witnesses and getting documentary evidence, the committee could assist the parties to the dispute if they had difficulties in obtaining information by writing to the people concerned. Moreover, like many other administrative tribunals, cases were required to be considered on their merits and there was technically no system of case law.[37]

In the period up to 1996, Medical Service Committees were the major way of dealing with complaints. While the regulations made reference to the possibility of informal resolution, official statistics show that more cases were formally adjudicated by Medical Service Committees then conciliated. Conciliation was allowed but the regulations gave no indication of how it should operate. Practice varied from one Family Health Service Authority to another. In a few cases, the job of conciliator was advertised, but in other instances conciliators were appointed through personal recommendations. A few conciliators were paid but most Family Health Service Authorities merely engaged the service of someone prepared to undertake the work.[38] At a national level, there was neither monitoring of conciliation services nor the setting of standards as to the type of person and qualifications suited to this work.

A full appreciation of the emphasis on formal procedures is possible only if the nature of the Family Health Service Authority's relationship with the state and practitioners is fully understood. Unlike most hospital-based doctors, GPs enjoy self-employed status. Their contract of employment with the NHS is negotiated nationally and co-ordinated by health authorities. The arrangement reflected a health insurance scheme rather than a national health service, in that Family Health Service Authorities merely administered contracts fulfilled by independent contractors. They still do not manage practitioners directly. They pay practitioners and help them develop services but do not manage their budgets. In recent years, there has been a shift from the fulfilment of a pay and rations function towards more active management of standards and quality, but Family Health Service Authorities are still hampered in their regulation of doctors by the nature of their legal relationship.

In general, Family Health Service Authorities attempted to regulate doctors' behaviour through negotiation, persuasion, bargaining and advocacy, since they had few formal sanctions at their disposal. This explains the attraction of Medical Service Committees which provided one of the few opportunities to enforce the terms of a practitioner's contract. But the balance to be achieved between the safeguarding of standards as a result of complaints and the provision of redress to aggrieved service users was a fine one. It reflected the tensions, touched upon above, between bureaucratic and professional models. If Family Health Service Authorities used their sanctions too freely, they were unable to maintain their role as encouragers and persuaders.[39] At the same time, they were expected to

---

37 But see Elcock, H., *Administrative Justice*, London: Longman, 1969.
38 See Hogg, C., *Complaints about Family Practitioners — Community Health Councils and FHSA Complaints*, London: GLACHC, 1992.
39 See Allsop, J. and May, A., *The Emperor's New Clothes*, London: King Edward's Hospital Fund for London, 1986.

reconcile the interests of the state (for whom they acted as agents), individual practitioners and local professional leaders with those of the patient community for whom they had to ensure that a service was provided. They could be seen, then, as the focus for the interplay of various interest groups. This inevitably created tensions of the sort identified by Silbey[40] in relation to her discussion of the lower courts.

CRITICISMS OF THE PROCEDURE

From the late 1980s, NHS complaints systems received an increasing amount of attention from policy makers, practitioners and academics'[41] and in the early 1990s criticisms of existing complaint procedures mounted.[42] Interest groups representing consumers, doctors and NHS managers were all concerned about the existing arrangements, including Medical Service Committees.[43] The Council on Tribunals devoted more and more space in its reports to the conduct of these committees and was increasingly outspoken in its comments. Its report for 1988–89 voiced its concerns thus:

> Over the past 12 years or so we have visited service committees on some 120 occasions. That practical experience is, we would claim, of unique value in assessing whether what takes place at service committee hearings can properly be regarded as fair to all those present by comparison with the standards prevailing generally in tribunal systems under our jurisdiction. Based on our observations, we can with confidence assert that very many service committees are well run and dispense justice to complainants and practitioners in an entirely proper fashion within the limits provided by their constitution. But in a significant minority of cases, we are equally confident that there are grounds for concern.[44]

---

40 *Op. cit.* note 2 *supra.*
41 See Association of Community Health Councils for England and Wales, *NHS Complaints Procedures: A Review*, London: ACHCEW, 1990; National Association of Health Authorities and Trusts, *Complaints Do Matter*, London: NAHAT, 1993; Steele, K., 'National Health Service Complaints Procedures: The Way Forward', *Public Money Management*, 1993, Oct/Dec, pp. 45–52; NHS Executive, *Being Heard: The Report of the Review Committee on NHS Complaints Procedures*, Chair: Professor Alan Wilson, London: HMSO, 1994; Allsop, J. and Mulcahy, L., 'Dealing with Clinical Complaints', (1995) 4 *Quality in Health Care*; and Citizen's Charter Unit, *op. cit.* note 25, 1993.
42 See NHS Executive *op. cit.* note 41; Mulcahy, L. and Lloyd-Bostock, S., 'Complaining — What's the Use?', in Dingwall, R. and Fenn, P. (eds), *Quality and Regulation in Health Care*, London: Routledge, 1992; Steele, K., *op. cit.* note 41; ACHCEW, *op. cit.* note 41; and Hanna, J., *op. cit.* note 3.
43 See General Medical Services Committee, *Evidence to the Wilson Committee*, unpublished, 1993; and ACHCEW, *op. cit.* note 41 and NAHAT, *op. cit.* note 41.
44 See Council on Tribunals, *Annual Report*, London: HMSO, 1989, pp. 5–6.

Criticism of the Family Health Service Authorities procedures centred on three main issues. First, the system was said to be biased towards doctors. Secondly, the procedures were thought to be opaque. Lastly, it was said that too much attention was placed on disciplining doctors rather than on resolving disputes. It is significant that while the first two criticisms suggest the need for a move towards more formal protection of the complainant's position, the last reveals a desire for a move away from a formalised legal model.

Bias towards doctors

Inequality of bargaining power
A number of critics suggested there was an inequality of bargaining power between the practitioner and the complainant in the service committee procedure. From their inception, Medical Service Committees represented medical interests to ensure these were protected. They provided a good example of a process which has been called corporatism through which professional interest groups are drawn into government administration to meet the needs of the profession and the state. It has been argued that the profession is more likely to accept that decisions are reasonable if its representatives have taken part in decision making, while government can reach agreement about what is acceptable without public conflict.[45] The fact that doctors were decision makers in Medical Service Committees, albeit in a minority, reflects this. Moreover, lay members were usually appointed by agreement with the Local Medical Committee (LMC). Lastly, professional channels of communication were secured by the fact that the medical members could report back to the LMC and that this has strong links with the GPs' negotiating body, the General Medical Services Committee, a committee of the British Medical Association.

Use of medical networks
Medical influence is also exerted at a less formal level. In a recent study of how GPs respond to complaints, Mulcahy, Allsop and Shirley[46] found that doctors tend to make extensive use of their medical networks. They are most likely to discuss a complaint with medical colleagues within their own practice, but also commonly contacted their medical defence organisation and LMC secretary for advice,

---

45 See Day, P. and Klein, R., *Inspecting the Inspectorates: Services for the Elderly*, London: Joseph Rowntree Memorial Trust, 1990. Interestingly, in Sweden, the Medical Responsibility Board, which performs similar tasks to the MSC, does not contain doctors. See, Rosenthal, M., *Dealing with Medical Malpractice — the British and Swedish Experience*, London: Tavistock Publications, 1987.

46 See Mulcahy, L., Allsop, J. and Shirley, C., *The Voices of Complainants and GPs in Complaints about Healthcare*, Social Science Research Papers, No. 3, London: South Bank University, 1996.

emotional support and help in preparing a formal response. The secretaries are repeat players in the system with an intricate knowledge of the terms of service and a clear understanding of how best to present a defence. Secretaries interviewed for this study estimated that only about 5 per cent of doctors failed to make any contact with them. The secretaries went to some lengths to let doctors know they were there to support and advise them. In two health authorities, information about the LMC secretary was sent out to the GP with a copy of the initial complaint letter. Another health authority routinely informed the LMC that there was a complaint about a particular doctor and sent out a factsheet to the doctor about what to do and whom to contact. Secretaries provided doctors with help by writing letters for them and by providing various types of support at hearings. This could include anything from help in constructing a defence to actual presentation of their case, despite the fact that representation by paid advocates was not permitted by official guidance. In the words of one LMC secretary: 'I do think I help doctors to make the most of their case . . . I always defend them because that's what they're paying me for.'

Mulcahy, Allsop and Shirley also reported that complainants, too, were extremely resourceful in identifying people who could help them to prepare for the service committee. But those who were *most* successful were those who had 'insider knowledge' of the Family Health Service Authority, NHS or other complaints systems. In their study it was noted that the sources that complainants used included a partner who worked in a hospital casualty department and an acquaintance who was a paramedic. But, in contrast to doctors, making contact with 'insiders' was more haphazard. What we cannot tell from these data is how many potential complainants were deterred by a lack of 'insider' support or knowledge.

Closing of ranks and imbalance
Complainants' views of the tribunal process also reveal concerns about bias. What emerged clearly from the research conducted by Mulcahy, Allsop and Shirley[47] was the complainants' sense of impotence, regardless of the help they received. All the complainants felt that doctors closed ranks to protect one another and that this occurred throughout the medical hierarchy. In the words of one, 'The complaint was a fight with the medical profession. Medics are a very closed shop.' Complainants perceived themselves to be less well supported than the doctor. Many referred to the impression that GPs had a 'professional' or 'experienced' representative to present their case. Despite the impartiality with which the service committee was thought to be conducted, there was a universal feeling amongst complainants that the support of GPs by the medical defence organisations and LMC weighed against complainants who did not have these advantages.

---

47   *Ibid.*

Concern has also been expressed in other quarters about the imbalance in the representation available for hearings.[48] The Council on Tribunals noted that service committees were the only tribunals under its jurisdiction where paid lawyers were barred. This was seen as a problem as doctors were generally more articulate than complainants. Mulcahy, Allsop and Shirley found that while complainants said that they had had no trouble preparing for the hearing, the majority said that it was much more formal than they had anticipated. One complainant said: 'All the questions were abrupt. To me, they were all too miserable, too serious. There were no conversations. It was very formal.' Significantly, it was felt that their misconceptions had had a detrimental effect on their performance on the day. Even a complainant whose complaint was upheld felt on reflection that she had been underprepared. Although she had taken a representative from the Community Health Council to present the case, she was perturbed by having to give her evidence in her own words.

Interestingly, complainants as well as doctors considered the conduct of Medical Service Committees to be fair and well organised.[49] GPs also thought that all the parties to the hearing, including the lay members of the panel, played a full role although there was a recognition that these views might not be shared. In the words of one doctor:

> Yes [it was fair]. I don't think the patient thought it was fair, as she appealed unsuccessfully to the Secretary of State and took legal proceedings. I don't think she understood or cared that it was a hearing about terms of service for the GP.

Opaque procedures

Another criticism of the old Medical Service Committee system was its opacity. If grievance systems are to serve the common good and contribute to the development of a framework of rules understood and acted upon by the relevant communities and known to the public, then Medical Service Committees did not serve their purpose. Hearings were held in private and records of proceedings were not made available to the public. Nor did they appear to have a radiating effect on other doctors. Mulcahy, Allsop and Shirley[50] found that LMC secretaries reported little feedback to the LMC as a whole, or to rank and file doctors, on the substance and outcome of complaints brought before the Medical Service Committee. In three of the authorities studied, the only information available was an annual report giving overall data on the numbers of complaints but not their substance. In the fourth, a system for discussing anonymous reports from service committees has only just been introduced.

---

48   See note 45 *supra*.
49   *Op. cit.* note 36.
50   *Ibid.*

Discipline rather than resolution

Medical Service Committees were not concerned to redress the complainant's grievances but rather to discipline doctors if fault was found. They narrowed the issues at stake to focus on contractual obligations, yet for a dispute to be resolved all the issues of concern to the disputants need to be aired and discussed. The fact that the main purpose of the procedures was disciplinary had three main implications.

First, the procedure could not offer a full range of remedies to the parties. The outcomes of the procedure were disciplinary measures such as financial penalties rather than compensation, apologies or explanations. Mulcahy, Allsop and Shirley's study[51] reported that all the complainants interviewed, even those whose cases had been successful, thought the *outcome* was unfair; conversely, all the GPs contacted in a parallel study felt that the outcome was fair, even where the complaint against them had been upheld.

Secondly, the procedure encouraged a defensive response to complaints in which positions became entrenched rather than resolution possibilities explored. If complaints about clinical care are taken as an attack on the professional judgement and professional integrity of a clinician, then it is not surprising that strong feelings are aroused. In her study of complaints reaching a Family Health Service Authority service committee, Allsop[52] found that 92 per cent of doctors responded to complaints by denying responsibility. Examples of defensive strategies included claims that: the matter fell outside contractual responsibilities; events were due to the disease process and uncertainty in medical practice; or the failure was due to other people, to external events or to some fault on the part of the complainant or patient.[53] Another reason for defensiveness is the personal cost to doctors if the complaint escalates. This may lead to inquiries by senior colleagues which can threaten reputation, promotion and livelihood. In his study of doctors with problems in the NHS, Donaldson[54] suggests that certain criticisms are much more likely to be upheld than others through peer review processes.[55] For example, clinical complaints taken to the final stage of the clinical complaints procedure in hospitals were much more likely to be upheld if they concerned communication

---

51 *Ibid.*
52 *Op. cit.* note 3 *supra*, 1994.
53 See also Mulcahy, L., 'From Fear to Fraternity: Doctors' Construction of Accounts of Complaints' [1996] *Journal of Social Welfare and Family Law* 397 and Lloyd-Bostock, S. and Mulcahy, L., 'The Social Psychology of Making and Responding to Hospital Complaints: An Account Model of Complaint Processes', *Law and Policy*, 1994, vol. 16, No. 2, pp. 123–47.
54 See Donaldson, L., 'Doctors with Problems in an NHS Workforce' (1994) 308 *British Medical Journal* 1277.
55 See Donaldson, L. and Cavanagh, J., 'Clinical Complaints and their Handling: A Time for Change' (1992) 1 *Quality in Health Care* 21.

and behaviour. The author suggests that these were more acceptable and less threatening aspects of professional practice on which to base a peer rebuke.[56]

Ironically, defensive responses tend to exacerbate complaints rather than encourage resolution. One study of GPs showed that if, following a complaint, a GP removed a patient from the practice list, showed lack of sympathy, was hostile or failed to address the issues raised, these then became issues in the dispute. The length of time taken to deal with the complaint, a lack of openness and an unwillingness by those involved to take action when incompetence is revealed, can also induce disillusionment and a determination to pursue the complaint.[57] A breakdown in the relationship between the doctor and patient was a common effect of complaints that went as far as a Medical Service Committee. In their study, Mulcahy, Allsop and Shirley[58] found that, most commonly, this occurred at the instigation of the complainant and was more likely to be prompted by complaints that had reached a Medical Service Committee than by those which had been conciliated.

Despite the propensity for defensiveness, doctors in the same study accepted that complainants' motivations for bringing the complaint were not of the type to endanger the GP's career. Most doctors believed that complainants wanted a social response such as an explanation (26 per cent); an apology (22 per cent); an investigation (21 per cent). Only 17 per cent thought that complainants wanted doctors to be reprimanded, and 2 per cent that they wanted compensation. Paradoxically, their parallel study of complainants revealed that a desire for a doctor to be disciplined was an important motivation for pursuing a complaint, although only a minority wanted a doctor struck off.

The third and final reason why complaints might not be resolved to the satisfaction of the parties was that the issues which could be considered by Medical Service Committees were narrowly defined and did not permit an airing of all the disputant's concerns. The self-employed status of GPs confined investigations to the consideration of whether they had breached their terms of service and, consequently, the processing of complaints had the potential to leave many issues unresolved. For instance, complaints about attitude and behaviour could not be heard, despite the fact that they constituted a significant proportion of allegations made.[59] Yet, Mulcahy, Allsop and Shirley's study[60] demonstrated that what doctors were prepared to define as a complaint went way beyond the issues which could

---

56   See Bosk, C., *Forgive and Remember: Managing Medical Failure*, Chicago: University of Chicago Press, 1979.
57   See Allsop, J., *op. cit.* note 3 *supra*, 1994.
58   *Op. cit.* note 46 *supra*.
59   See Nettleton, S. and Harding, G., 'Protesting Patients: A Study of Complaints Submitted to a Family Health Service Authority', *Sociology of Health and Illness*, 1995, vol. 16, No. 1, pp. 38–61; and see Allsop, J., *op. cit.* note 3 *supra*, 1994.
60   *Op. cit.* note 46 *supra*.

be considered under the Medical Service Committee procedures. Fourteen per cent of doctors and all complainants mentioned attitude, behaviour and communication problems as being at the crux of the dispute. In summary, the limited research on formal service committee procedures suggests that a mismatch of expectations exists between those making complaints and those responding to them. This reflects the different orders of priority of the disputing parties, which needs to be taken into account if the dispute is to be resolved rather than just managed.

REFORMING THE COMPLAINTS SYSTEM

By 1993, criticisms of Medical Service Committees and the hospital complaints procedure led to the Secretary of State for Health setting up a review committee, chaired by Professor Alan Wilson, which reported and made recommendations for change in May 1994.[61] The report signalled a shift in emphasis from a formal rule-bound procedure to informal resolution for the vast majority of disputes and was couched in the language of user empowerment. In line with the grass roots and managerial models discussed above, it argued that one of the main aims of the procedures was to satisfy the complainant. The report outlined nine key principles which should be incorporated into any procedure: responsiveness; quality enhancement; cost effectiveness; accessibility; impartiality; simplicity; speed; confidentiality; and accountability.

While recognising the tensions between the needs for both formality and informality, a major tenet of the report was that, in the majority of cases, resolution and satisfaction could be achieved most effectively by the provision of rapid, personal and informal responses to complaints. Training in complaints handling was recommended for all NHS staff likely to be in contact with patients. A further contribution to developing informal procedures in the public sector was made by the Complaints Task Force report in 1995.[62] This focused on the steps which managers should take to ensure that complaints were used to improve practice.

In contrast to the recommendations of these reports, the Council on Tribunals has demonstrated greater concern for the type of procedural fairness enshrined in the legal model. It has consistently argued for increased formalism in complaints handling. By the end of the 1980s, the Council was devoting more space to Medical Service Committees and was increasingly outspoken in its comments. It has also recommended the appointment of legally qualified chairs and has argued for the introduction of rules which will give Medical Service Committees greater powers, for instance, that they should be able to subpoena witnesses and order the production of documents. It criticised what were to become the 1990 revised guidelines, on the grounds that they permitted a continuance of a bias in favour of

---

61   See NHS Executive, *op. cit.* note 41 *supra.*
62   *Op. cit.* note 25 *supra*, 1996.

practitioners to whom the availability of professional assistance gave a substantial advantage which it had witnessed at hearings.

Following the Wilson Report, a Government White Paper, *Acting on Complaints*,[63] laid down policy which was broadly in line with the Wilson recommendations and new guidelines were published for implementation in April 1996.[64] The spirit of the new policy also marks a shift towards a more informal, conciliatory approach and away from the legal/bureaucratic/professional models described earlier. There are elements of the grass roots model in that emphasis is placed on the needs of the complainant. But managerial needs are also reflected. Rather than simply following and interpreting rules, in the new business-like NHS, managers must ensure that complaints are used to improve the service and satisfy the customer. In their review of submissions to the Wilson Committee, Stacey and Moss contend that the approach reflects a reformist rather than a radical approach to change.[65]

The new guidelines require trusts, GP practices, and health authorities (which now incorporate Family Health Service Authorities) as purchasers to develop a simplified two-stage structure for complaint handling.[66] In the primary health care setting, at stage one, complaints handling is seen as the responsibility of GPs, with a view to early resolution. This stage displays many of the hallmarks of informality. Guidelines are not prescriptive about the precise stage one procedures to be adopted, although they must comply with minimum national standards. The guidelines place emphasis on principles rather than procedures: flexibility and understanding what the complainant wants are the key issues. They suggest that: 'Rigid, bureaucratic and legalistic approaches should be avoided at all stages of the procedure, but particularly during local resolution.'[67]

In order to comply with their obligations at stage one, GP practices are required to have a system for complaint handling with a designated complaints officer who may be a doctor. Some core standards have been laid down. Each practice must keep within time limits, publicise the procedure and the further stages a complainant might pursue if he or she remains dissatisfied. It is anticipated that the complaint will be resolved informally by the complaints officer and that the complainant will be sent a letter outlining the practice's response to his or her concerns. It is not known how such systems will operate nationally, but a study of practice-based complaints procedures in one Family Health Service Authority

---

63 See NHS Executive, *op. cit.* note 41 *supra*, 1994.

64 NHS Executive, *Complaints — Listening . . . Acting . . . Improving*, Leeds: Department of Health, 1996.

65 Stacey, M. and Moss, P., Report to the Health Committee of the House of Commons, Coventry: University of Warwick, 1994.

66 See Department of Health, *Guidance on New Complaints Procedures*, Leeds: Department of Health, 1996. It is now a requirement of the GPs' contract with the health authority that they set up a practice-based complaints procedure.

67 *Ibid.* p. 17.

found that 84 per cent of practices already had procedures in place. Typically, they were co-ordinated by a practice manager, and required records of complaints to be kept and used for feedback about the quality of the service. Attempts had also been made by the local Family Health Service Authority to oversee these systems by accrediting those which met specific good practice guidelines.[68] Health authorities are responsible for providing support for GP practices and ensuring that they comply with the regulations. They may also provide access to a conciliator if either party wishes.

A second, more formal, stage is available for those complainants who remain dissatisfied. A panel with a lay chair and a majority of lay members can be set up by the health authority to review the complaint afresh. Independent panels are to be composed of three members: an independent lay chairperson, the convenor and a third person nominated by the regional office. Where a clinical complaint is being considered, these members will be joined by two independent clinical assessors.

As is the case with the first stage procedure, the emphasis at the second stage is also on flexibility. The guidelines make it clear that:

> The panel should be proactive in its investigation, always seeking to resolve the complainant's grievance in a conciliatory manner, while at the same time taking a view on the facts it has identified. The panel should be flexible in the way it goes about its business, choosing a method or procedure appropriate to the circumstances of the complaint. It should not allow confrontational situations to arise.[69]

Thus, NHS staff are encouraged to respond to complaints in an open and non defensive way.

The new procedure allows for a considerable amount of discretion to be exercised by service providers in the operation of the procedure. At practice level, this appears almost unbounded. Moreover, the second stage review of the procedure is not available to complainants as of right. Instead, a case for referral has to be made to a designated panel convenor within 28 days of completion of attempts at local resolution. The convenor is expected to consult with a lay representative identified from a regional list and to take advice from two clinical assessors where appropriate, but the convenor's use of discretion remains pivotal. He or she will decide whether there is a case for a panel being set up; whether a complaint is about clinical judgment or not; and the panel's terms of reference.[70]

---

68 See Mulcahy, L., Allsop, J. and Shirley, C., 'Diplomatic Service', *Health Service Journal*, 1996, January, pp. 26–7.

69 *Ibid.*, p. 31.

70 The convenor is expected to take into account whether the GP against whom the complaint is made could take any further action short of an independent review panel to satisfy the complainant; whether the GP has taken all practical action so that the establishment of an independent review panel would serve no further purpose; and whether the complainant intends to pursue the matter in the courts.

Within this context, variation amongst cases — a concern of those who are wary of discretionary powers — is actually encouraged. As the guidance makes clear:

> The Guidance is not designed to be all-embracing and to cover every contingency: trusts, health authorities and family health service practitioners are expected to design and operate their complaints procedures in the spirit of the Guidance, while adhering to the legal requirements of the appropriate Directions and Regulations. It is recognised that size and complexity of organisations will result in different models emerging for the management of complaints, and it is hoped that in due course different experiences will be exchanged so that lessons can be learned.[71]

Nonetheless, attempts at visibility have been made. Where recourse to an independent review panel is refused, the convenor is expected to be fully accountable to the complainant as to the reasons why. If the complainant continues to be dissatisfied, he or she can refer his or her complaint to the Health Service Commissioner who, since April 1996, has been empowered to review the handling of both clinical and non-clinical complaints.

But essentially the procedures make a shift towards privatised justice. At practice level, where most complaints are now to be handled, the content of the complaints handled remains confidential to the practice. The confidentiality of the conciliation is stressed and conciliators are not required to provide information gathered during their session for those involved with subsequent stages. At the second stage, copies of the report of the panel are available only to those specified in the guidelines and are not public documents. A case might be made for privacy contributing to a more relaxed environment for the resolution of a dispute. Given the concerns about formality voiced by complainants in our study of Family Health Service Authority complaints procedures, this clearly has the potential to advantage the complainant. But privacy and informality are not synonymous. It might also be argued that the new procedures aim to ensure the co-operation of the professional stakeholders by preserving confidentiality. Information which is not passed from one stage to another will not prompt open or public discussion. It will not allow external checks on medical behaviour.

Moreover, the health authority now performs an even more marginal role in the regulation of medical work through complaints. Under the new procedures, the Medical Service Committee has not been abolished but it has only a residual disciplinary part to play. If, in trying to resolve the complaint, the health authority, which remains responsible for managing the contracts of GPs, believes there has been a breach in the terms of service and the matter should be pursued in the

---

71   *Op. cit.* note 71 *supra.*, p. 15.

interests of maintaining the standards of service, it may set up a Medical Service Committee which would operate in accordance with the guidelines discussed above. The committee's role is clearer in that it will now take the part of complainant with the service user acting as a mere witness. But given its general lack of control over doctors' work, it is doubtful whether this provides a sufficient residue of power. Anecdotal evidence to date suggests this regulatory tool will be underutilised.

A WOOLF IN SHEEP'S CLOTHING?

In this section, we consider how well the interests of three of the major stakeholders in GP complaint systems — the state, doctors and complainants — are served. We turn to a discussion of the way in which a different, more informal, hybrid model is replacing the old, and to the advantages and disadvantages for stakeholders. Paying attention to the complainant's perspective has become increasingly popular in recent years. Consumer groups have emerged as a significant political force demanding improved conditions and rights for the population. Patient choice, information for patients and exploration of their views have all become more important. A better-educated population also has higher expectations of care, while universal suffrage and the drive for equity have led to policies which appeal to a greater proportion of the public at large. At the same time, the intimacy of the doctor–patient relationship, the potential for exploitation and the serious consequences of medical mistakes have all been given as justifications for regulation from a consumer protection perspective.

For doctors as experts in an area of work, complaints have been shown to have a strong emotional impact, although there are strategies for distancing and denial.[72] These may be the consequence of a culture in which it is accepted that there is a high degree of uncertainty in diagnosis and treatment, and where doctors take individual responsibility for clinical decisions within the framework of self-regulation. Doctors have tended to resist lay involvement in regulation, although the pressure to include lay persons to ensure accountability has increased. In this sense, the structure of Medical Service Committees in the GP complaint system, prior to 1996, was something of an anomaly. A panel with a majority of lay members which could make judgments about whether a doctor had acted reasonably in providing a service and decide whether there were disciplinary consequences was unusual. Arguably, given the power of the medical profession, the system was tolerated only because the process was relatively hidden, reports were anonymous and the audience limited to sections within the health department. Moreover, the links into other disciplinary systems were weak, the incidence of

---

72   See Allsop, J., *op. cit.* note 3, 1994 and Mulcahy, L., *op. cit.* note 53, 1996.

cases was low and sanctions limited. In the 1980s, as the numbers of complaints rose, so did pressure for change within the profession itself.

The state has long had an interest in the resolution of grievances and the handling of conflict between citizens and between citizens and the state. It has addressed this by establishing various frameworks of rules. Prior to 1996, Medical Service Committees were an uncomfortable mix of a grievance handling forum for disputes between doctors and patients and a way of holding GPs to account for providing poor service. In practice, they had to attempt to manage the tension between the various interests. During the last two decades the concerns of government have changed. In the NHS reforms, much greater responsibility has been devolved to managers at the local level for purchasing services within limited budgets. The disciplines of the business sector in solving problems and pleasing the customer have replaced notions of entitlement and of rights. In the framework of this analysis, flexible, local-level complaint handling is simply an aspect of the new public sector management.

We have shown that the old-style complaint procedure had disadvantages for the stakeholders in the system. For complainants, it could narrow and obfuscate issues. It was long-winded, seen to be biased and redress was, in practice, limited to the satisfaction of holding the doctor to account. But will the new system provide greater opportunities for complainants? The rhetoric used in official documentation suggests that the new complaint systems will be accessible, user-friendly, informal and flexible. Whether this is the case depends largely on the approach of staff in the general practices, the quality of their training, their attitudes towards patients, and their administrative and managerial skills. If successful and implemented as planned, the new system has greater potential for satisfying the needs of complainants. Early studies of practice-based complaint systems suggest that they can be developed to allow concerns to be resolved in a way that strengthens relationships within the practice.[73] However, there is to be little accountability to health authorities for the practice-based systems. There are few guarantees that the system will operate as it should. The health authority's powers to accredit and monitor systems are sketchy in outline and likely to depend on the influence and energy of the health authority concerned. Moreover, the informality of the procedures leaves considerable scope for 'cooling out' the complainant, especially for those who are disadvantaged.

Behind every institutional structure or procedure there are power relationships. Traditionally, the legal system has attempted to redress such imbalance through the use of procedural guidelines. The new procedures do nothing to enhance the power of the service user who is still in a weak position of being at the receiving end of a monopoly service. The new arrangements mean that complaints should be raised

73 See *op. cit.* note 21 *supra.*

in the first instance with the doctor with whose service the person is dissatisfied. While there is a certain commonsense logic in this, in practice, the service user is at a disadvantage in relation to the expert provider on whom they may depend. Our research on the views of complainants indicated that for those with a serious grievance, the support of a Family Health Service Authority administrator and the formality of the Medical Service Committee procedures were seen as advantages.

For GPs, the new arrangements appear to have considerable benefits. GPs now have the opportunity of early notification of dissatisfaction and time to resolve issues before they escalate. Emphasis has been placed on the privacy of dispute resolution. At the second stage, the independent review panels can take a more informal and less adversarial form than the Medical Service Committees. Professional advisers give their view on the papers before them and there is less opportunity for questioning which could elicit further information. The additional options to resolve the complaint and the separation of complaint resolution and discipline are likely to result in the Medical Service Committee hearing being a rare event.

For the state, the new arrangements have the advantage of distancing complaints. Complaint handling is now the responsibility of local providers and the health authorities as purchasers. The new procedures herald a shift not only towards informalism, but also towards the devolution of the state's responsibility to provide for the redress of citizen grievances. The appellate role of the Secretary of State largely disappears. The new complaint systems are likely to be a considerable administrative burden. But the costs of running the system fall on the local level authorities which, under the health service reforms, are more clearly responsible for the quantity and quality of service. Furthermore, in running the second-stage procedures, it will be the health authorities' responsibility to resolve the tension between professionals and service users. They have the incentive to do this well as there is a right of appeal to the Health Service Commissioner. However, there is little guidance as to what ought to be defined as good practice. Instead the emphasis is on flexibility.

With the expansion of his remit to cover the review of clinical complaints, the Health Service Commissioner's role as regulator of complaints procedures has been strengthened considerably (see also Drewry, Ch. 4, p. 102). It is too early to assess the style of the new Health Service Commissioner, Michael Buckley, in performing this function, but his recently-retired predecessor, William Reid, frequently demonstrated his willingness to push the boundaries of his jurisdiction in order to protect disadvantaged complainants. But however proactive his approach, the Commissioner can only react to problems which are referred to him and can do nothing about complaints which are 'lost' at local resolution level when complainants are discouraged from pursuing them. The new procedures have created a 'black hole' at practice level and it is virtually impossible for any regulator to know what goes missing within it. GP practices are required to report only the bare number of complaints they receive each year and are under no obligation to reveal the outcome of complaints or the style of complaint handling. Relationships in the NHS may have shifted from trust to contract, but it is trust upon which we are forced to rely if we are to be confident that the informal procedures are being operated in the spirit of the Wilson Report and new regulations.

The new procedures reveal a tension between the needs of individual complainants disadvantaged by formalised grievance systems, providers of medical services and the needs of the general public and the state in regulating medical work. Regulation of powerful groups in society has always been a somewhat daunting task for the state and one which has been boldly attempted as part of the shift towards marketisation of the public sector. But in their attempts to encourage informalism, responsiveness and flexibility in the consumer interest, the Department of Health may have got the balance between competing interests wrong and provided insufficient checks on internal activity. While it has employed the rhetoric of consumerism, it may actually have reinforced self-regulation by allowing complaint handling to 'go underground' at practice level.

CONCLUSION

While health authorities continue to be hampered in their regulation of GPs by the nature of their legal relationship with them, the new procedures undermine even further their ability to call GPs to account. Their attempts at standardisation of practice-based complaints systems by the introduction of systems of accreditation, are worthy of praise, but are still based on voluntary participation of GP practices. It would seem that health authorities are even more reliant on their ability to cajole and encourage good practice than previously. They continue to be able to set up Medical Service Committees but, it could be argued, are even less likely to use this device to effect if they do not have the excuse of an incensed complainant to cloak or prompt their proactivity.

Our major concern is reflected in the adage that justice must not only be done but be seen to be done. It is the invisibility of the new procedures which is most likely to concern public lawyers. This is a particular worry when notions of what is 'public' are being intensely debated. In allowing an emphasis on private informal justice, there is little doubt that the state has devolved its responsibility for redress of citizen grievances to a powerful professional group. The pursuit of public discussion of issues has been left to the small percentage of complainants prepared to push their case beyond the first stage of the new procedures. The complainant is hindered at every threshold by discretionary powers granted to state agents to decide whether the issue ought to be pursued. An optimist might hope that the professional standards of doctors and the caring nature of their role will prompt the more satisfactory resolution of grievances and repair fractured doctor–patient relationships. Those interested in the effective resolution of disputes to the satisfaction of those involved will welcome the potential provided by the new procedures to do this. But the questions for public lawyers are whether the new procedures contribute to the regulation of doctors' behaviour or provide an adequate opportunity for their behaviour to be questioned and standards to be set. These issues raise fundamental questions about the role of law, the impact of theories of new public sector management and the dangers of privatised justice which need to be addressed.

6

The Public Law – Private Law Distinction: A Comparative and Philosophical Approach

Nicholas Bamforth

SUMMARY

This chapter argues that it is a mistake to talk about whether there should be a substantive public law–private law distinction. Such distinctions are in fact presupposed both by the distinctive functions of the state in modern constitutional democracies and by the philosophical presumption that a sound normative justification must be provided for state action to be legitimate. The real questions are therefore when public law-private law divides should come into play and where they should be set. These questions can only be answered by reference to normative theories of the proper role and definition of state bodies and functions.

INTRODUCTION

Discussion of the distinction between 'public law' and 'private law' has — at least in English law — typically focused on the possibility, the desirability or the positioning of an open, substantive boundary line of this sort in relation to the application for judicial review. As such, the debate has generally been concerned with the merits or demerits of cases like *R* v *Panel on Take-overs and Mergers, ex parte Datafin plc*[1] and *R* v *Disciplinary Committee of the Jockey Club, ex parte Aga Khan*,[2] together with the now-diluted exclusivity rule.[3] Some commentators

---

1 [1987] QB 815.
2 [1993] 1 WLR 909.
3 For analysis of the position in Scots law, see Wolffe, W.J., The Scope of Judicial Review in Scottish Law' [1992] *Public Law* 625.

are happy — in this context — to retain a conceptual distinction between public and private law, but wish to eliminate the possibility that such a division will give rise to wasteful procedural litigation;[4] others, by contrast, have advocated the complete abandonment of the distinction as a substantive matter.[5] For, despite the recent watering-down of the exclusivity rule in *Roy* v *Kensington and Chelsea and Westminster FPC*[6] and *Mercury Communications* v *Director General of Telecommunications*,[7] the distinction remains of substantive analytical and practical significance in cases concerning the boundaries of judicial review: after all, the prerogative remedies (together with the 'public law' declaration and injunction) are nowadays used only in relation to 'public law' decisions and actions,[8] while the application for judicial review is governed by special time limits and standing rules.[9] When fully applied in *O'Reilly* v *Mackman*,[10] exclusivity provided a harsh incentive to the litigant correctly to categorise his case as public or private at the outset; the dilution of the exclusivity rule simply weakens that incentive rather than changing the nature or positioning of the public law–private law distinction (see also Alder, Ch. 7 generally for further discussion of the case law).

It is not my intention in this chapter to reiterate the many well-known arguments raised by cases of this sort. The debate about whether particular bodies and decisions are — or should be — susceptible to judicial review (the substantive issue in *ex parte Datafin, ex parte Aga Khan* and *O'Reilly* v *Mackman* — despite the focus of the last case on the apparently 'procedural' question of exclusivity) will instead be placed in a broader context: for it will be suggested that the focus of any debate about the merits and workings of a substantive distinction between public and private law is seriously distorted by concentrating only on the amenability of particular bodies and decisions to judicial review. In fact, English law, EC law, and Canadian and US constitutional law are littered with other examples of differential treatment of public authorities and private citizens — such distinctions generally serving to reflect the differing roles of the state and the private citizen in modern constitutional democracies. Areas of law which entail the

---

4   *Cf.* Fredman, Sandra, and Morris, Gillian, 'The Costs of Exclusivity: Public and Private Re-examined' [1994] *Public Law* 69 at pp. 84–5; 'Public or Private? State Employees and Judicial Review' (1991) 1 *Law Quarterly Review* 298 at pp. 315–16.

5   Harlow, Carol, '"Public" and "Private" Law: Definition Without Distinction' (1980) 43 *Modern Law Review* 241; Allison, J.W.F., *A Continental Distinction in the Common Law: A Historical and Comparative Perspective on English Public Law*, Oxford: Clarendon Press, 1996.

6   [1992] 1 AC 624.

7   [1996] 1 WLR 48.

8   A clear indication of the on-going practical significance of the public law–private law divide is provided in *British Steel plc* v *Customs and Excise Commissioners* [1996] 1 All ER 1002, at 1012–3.

9   *Cf.* Harlow, Carol, 'Why Public Law is Private Law: An Invitation to Lord Woolf', in Zuckerman, A.A.S. and Cranston, Ross (eds), *Reform of Civil Procedure: Essays on 'Access to Justice'*, Oxford: Clarendon Press, 1995, Ch. 11 at p. 204.

10   [1983] AC 237.

drawing of substantive distinctions between citizen and state include, for example, the rules governing public interest immunity in English law, as well as the EC law provisions on direct effect of directives and the 'public service' exceptions to the EC Treaty rules regulating the free movement of workers, services and freedom of establishment. It is hard to escape the conclusion that modern legal systems reflect the fact that the state (however this term is ultimately defined) exercises a whole array of distinctive functions.

The distinctive nature of the state is equally evident if we consider the normative argument that state action requires special justification — an idea which might be said to form the basis of political philosophy as a distinctive discipline.[11] If one subscribes to the widely-held philosophical view that the state — unlike the private citizen — exercises power in a special capacity and in a distinctly coercive fashion, and as such must have a sound normative justification in order legitimately to exercise that power, then an adequate justification can legitimise the existence of differential rules governing public authorities and private citizens. The idea that the state's power must be limited and exercised only where justifiable has been advanced from both liberal and conservative standpoints. From a liberal perspective, Professor Hart has defended the 'general critical principle that the use of legal coercion by any society calls for justification as something *prima facie* objectionable to be tolerated only for the sake of some countervailing good'.[12] From a rather more conservative position, Professor John Finnis has stressed the desirability of limited government and the fact that principled debate about whether particular laws should be created 'involves a number of explicit or implicit judgments about the proper role of law and the compelling interests of political communities'.[13] The notion that citizen and state may differ in their responsibilities is clearly evident in Finnis's suggestion that 'The government of political communities is rationally limited not only by constitutional law and by the moral norms which limit every decent person's deliberation and choice, *but also by the inherent limits of its general justifying aim, purpose or rationale*'.[14]

Despite their differing political standpoints, both Hart and Finnis therefore support the idea that the moral legitimacy of laws (or proposed laws) turns on a convincing philosophical justification being found for them. As a matter of logic,

---

11   This assertion is not intended to contract the entirely valid analytical observation that political and moral philosophy frequently interact with or blend into one another — see Nozick, Robert, *Anarchy. State and Utopia*, New York: Basic Books, 1974, p. 6; Kymlicka, Will, *Contemporary Political Philosophy: An Introduction*, Oxford: Clarendon Press, 1990, pp. 5–8.

12   Hart, H.L.A., *Law, Liberty and Morality*, Oxford: Oxford University Press, 1963, p. 20.

13   Finnis, John, 'Law, Morality and "Sexual Orientation"' (1993–4) 69 *Notre Dame Law Review* 1049 at p. 1055.

14   Finnis, John, 'Is Natural Law Theory Compatible with Limited Government?', in George, Robert (ed.), *Natural Law, Liberalism and Morality*, Oxford: Clarendon Press, 1996, Ch. 1 at p. 4 (emphasis added). It should be noted that by referring to 'moral norms', the political community's 'general justifying aim' *and* its 'constitutional law', Finnis would appear to be running the normative into the descriptive.

any such justification will rest on a theory of justice — that is, a theory concerning rightful and wrongful distributions of entitlements among members of society — which will be closely connected with a theory of political morality, concerning the principles which should guide the exercise of public power (including the creation and enforcement of laws) by state institutions. And although neither theorist was addressing the question of a substantive public law–private law distinction, their arguments must presuppose the existence, at a normative level, of a distinction between the role of the state and that of the citizen, for there would otherwise be no need to find a special justification for the exercise of state power.[15] Such reasoning can also be inferred from communitarian theories of justice and political morality. For while communitarian theories are commonly assumed to envisage a closer affinity between individuals and the communities to which they belong than do their liberal counterparts, communitarians characteristically rank any such affinity as both a good in its own right and as a measure of the *legitimacy* of the political institutions of the community concerned. Taking affinity as a measure of legitimacy would make no sense, within the structure of communitarian thought, unless community institutions were presumed to have a distinctive role in promoting the common good.[16]

It might therefore be suggested that the state's distinctive functions, together with the belief that exercises of state power require special justification, make it unsurprising that substantive distinctions have emerged in the law's treatment of public authorities and private citizens. This is reflected in Laws J's suggestion at first instance in *R v Somerset County Council, ex parte Fewings* that:

Public bodies and private persons are both subject to the rule of law. . . . But the principles which govern their relationship with the law are wholly different. For private persons, the rule is that you may do anything you choose which the law does not prohibit. It means that the freedoms of the private citizen are not conditional upon some distinct and affirmative justification for which he must burrow in the law books. . . . But for public bodies the rule is opposite, and so of another character altogether. It is that any action to be taken must be justified by positive law. A public body has no heritage of legal rights which it enjoys for its own sake; at every turn, all of its dealings constitute the fulfilment of duties which it owes to others; indeed, it exists for no other purpose.[17]

---

15   The most famous liberal formulation of the notion of limited government is to be found in J.S. Mill's 'harm principle' — *cf*. Mill, J.S., *On Liberty and Other Writings*, Collini, Stefan (ed.), Cambridge: Cambridge University Press, 1989, p. 13. Finnis's notion of limited government — whereby the government has responsibility for the 'public' moral environment — is considerably less limited than Mill's.

16   For further discussion, see Kymlicka, *op. cit.* note 11 *supra*, pp. 224–32; Etzioni, Amitai (ed.), *New Communitarian Thinking: Persons, Virtues, Institutions, and Communities*, Charlottesville: University of Virginia Press, 1995, essays 8–12.

17   [1995] 1 All ER 513 at 524. Laws J's decision was affirmed on other grounds by the Court of Appeal: [1995] 3 All ER 20.

This distinction — necessary, according to Laws J, to guard citizens against arbitrary interference by public authorities — has important consequences for the way in which we evaluate the public law–private law distinction in cases like *ex parte Datafin, ex parte Aga Khan* and *O'Reilly* v *Mackman*. For any argument about these cases cannot plausibly maintain that *all* public law–private law distinctions are undesirable or unworkable (to do so would be to ignore the wide range of such distinctions in each of the legal systems mentioned, as well as the notion that the state is — as a general matter — subject to a special regime of justification). Rather, any analysis must take account of the broader philosophical and practical grounds on which distinctions between citizen and state are drawn. Consideration of this broader canvas will in turn help to determine *which* public law–private law distinctions should be seen as legitimate (see Leyland and Woods, Ch. 17, pp. 423 *et seq*).

This chapter therefore seeks to build on Geoffrey Samuel's suggestion that rather than focusing on whether public law can be analysed as 'an autonomous set of rules' — an exercise which takes the existing case law as its starting point — we should instead 'think more positively about the relationship between individual and state.'[18] It is not my intention to offer support for the positioning or operation of the public law–private law distinction in cases such as *ex parte Datafin* or — by contrast — *ex parte Aga Khan*,[19] nor does my argument depend for its validity upon the adoption either of an *ultra vires*-based[20] or a control of public power-based view[21] of the function of judicial review. My aim is instead to re-cast the debate about distinctions between public and private law: for if it is to be intellectually coherent, the debate should turn not on *whether* any such distinction is necessary or desirable, but rather on *which* distinctions merit support. Building on the points made so far, I aim to rebut the claim that *all* types of distinction between public and private law are unnecessary or conceptually redundant. My argument rests on a combination of two claims — one descriptive, the other normative. After outlining these claims more fully, I will examine some possible counter-arguments.

THE DESCRIPTIVE CLAIM

My first, descriptive claim is that in a modern constitutional democracy, certain duties and functions are generally entrusted to the state rather than to the private

---

18   Samuel, Geoffrey, 'Public and Private Law: A Private Lawyer's Response', (1983) 46 *Modern Law Review* 558 at pp. 558 and 582. Samuel's argument was drafted in response to Carol Harlow's seminal article ' "Public" and "Private" Law: Definition Without Distinction', note 5 *supra*. As Samuel acknowledges in his article, Harlow was not herself arguing that 'public' and 'private' could be defined solely in terms of the cases (*cf.* Harlow, Carol, 'Changing the Mindset: The Place of Theory in English Administrative Law' (1994) 14 *Oxford Journal of Legal Studies* 419).

19   For criticism of the reasoning in *ex parte Aga Khan*, see Bamforth, Nicholas, 'The Scope of Judicial Review: Still Uncertain' [1993] *Public Law* 239.

20   *Cf.* Forsyth, Christopher, 'Of Fig Leaves and Fairy Tales: the *Ultra Vires* Doctrine, the Sovereignty of Parliament and Judicial Review' (1996) 55 *Cambridge Law Journal* 122.

21   *Cf.* Oliver, Dawn, 'Is the *Ultra Vires* Rule the Basis of Judicial Review?' [1987] *Public Law* 543.

citizen — devising frameworks for education, social security and policing, for example. The word 'frameworks' is used to make the point that even if some sort of 'opting-' or 'contracting-out' regime is in operation — so that central or local government does not actually provide or administer the services concerned — the state still devises and administers the overall (usually statutory) framework within which the service provision takes place.[22] Indeed, it seems fair to suggest that the whole rationale for having state bodies is that they discharge special functions of some sort — however broadly or narrowly such functions are defined. Unless state bodies could discharge functions which private individuals could not — or could not effectively — there would be no logical reason for creating, maintaining or financing such bodies. The very nature of the state's work thus suggests that some or all of the state's functions can logically be categorised as 'public' in that they are not — and many would say cannot effectively be — discharged by private citizens.

If we look beyond the standard cases on amenability to judicial review — principally *ex parte Datafin* and *ex parte Aga Khan* — we can find many situations in which the English, EC, US and Canadian legal systems treat public authorities and private citizens in substantially different ways, such divergences reflecting the different roles performed by the actors concerned. A classic example in English law can be found in the rules concerning public interest immunity. There has been much argument about whether the state must — or simply may — claim immunity in the public interest from the obligation to disclose documents to a court, and whether judges should merely take the word of the minister that documents should not be disclosed rather than forming a conclusion after examining the documents for themselves.[23] However these questions are ultimately answered — and whatever the exact policy justification advanced in favour of public interest immunity[24] — it should be clear that such a concept would not be thought necessary *unless* the state was clearly perceived to be playing a special role, in the public interest, which required it to keep secret certain documents which ought otherwise to be made public.[25] This is reflected in the existence of limitations on the range of bodies which may claim public interest immunity. For while the House of Lords confirmed in *D v NSPCC*[26] that such claims were not restricted to situations where

---

22   One of the more prominent examples relates to health-care provision: *cf.* Barker, Kit, 'NHS Contracts, Restitution and the Internal Market' (1993) 56 MLR 832; see, more generally, Freedland, Mark 'Government by Contract and Private Law' [1994] *Public Law* 86.

23   For general discussion of such issues, see the *Report of the Inquiry into the Export of Defence Equipment and Dual-Use Goods to Iraq and Related Prosecutions,* London: HMSO, 1996, vol. III, pp. 1781–94. Particular controversy has been caused in these regards by *Air Canada v Secretary of State for Trade* [1983] 2 AC 394; *Makanjuola v Commissioner of Police* [1992] 3 All ER 617; see also *R v Chief Constable of the West Midlands Police, ex parte Wiley* [1994] 3 WLR 433.

24   Contrast *Conway v Rimmer* [1968] AC 910; *Burmah Oil v Bank of England* [1980] AC 1090.

25   See *Ex parte Coventry Newspapers* [1992] 3 WLR 916.

26   [1978] AC 171.

the effective functioning of *central* government departments or activities was at stake — thus suggesting a relatively flexible approach to the boundaries of public interest immunity — their Lordships were nevertheless clear that immunity could not apply *regardless of* the nature of the body[27] (see Tomkins, Ch. 14 generally for further discussion of public interest immunity).

The constitutional law systems of both the United States and — in the wake of the enactment of the Charter of Rights and Freedoms — of Canada are affected by boundary problems concerning the reach of special *constitutional* review of government action. In a style somewhat reminiscent of English cases such as *ex parte Datafin* and *ex parte Aga Khan*, constitutional review in both jurisdictions is confined to decisions and actions falling within the governmental or public sphere. Comparing the constitutional law of the two jurisdictions, Dale Gibson observes that:

> The text of the Constitution of the United States is much clearer than the language of the Canadian Charter in restricting the operation of most constitutional guarantees to the public sector. American courts have become unavoidably involved, therefore, in efforts to distinguish between governmental and non-governmental activities for constitutional purposes.[28]

Such a distinction has traditionally been made, in US law, using the somewhat amorphous concept of 'state action'. There is some controversy as to whether it is possible to derive any coherent principles from the cases on which to base a definition of this concept: Professor Laurence Tribe, for example, argues that in so far as it is possible to make sense of the concept, its boundaries may depend more upon the type of constitutional right or value at stake in each case than upon the type of body which has taken the impugned decision.[29] This formulation is nevertheless subject to the over-arching point that 'Nearly all of the Constitution's self-executing, and therefore judicially enforceable, guarantees of individual rights shield individuals only from government action'.[30] In similar vein, s. 32(1) of the Canadian Charter makes clear that 'the Parliament and government of Canada' are bound by the rights guarantees contained in the instrument — a definition which appears broad enough to cover the activities of bodies acting under statutory authority.[31] But, as McIntyre J ruled for the majority of the Supreme Court of Canada in *Retail, Wholesale and Department Store Union* v *Dolphin Delivery*, 'where . . . private party "A" sues private party "B" relying on the common law,

---

27 See also *British Steel Corporation* v *Granada Television* [1981] AC 1096.
28 Gibson, Dale, *The Law of the Charter: General Principles*, Toronto: Carswell, 1986, p. 89.
29 Tribe, Laurence, *American Constitutional Law*, (2nd ed.), New York: Foundation Press, 1988, pp. 1699–1703. See also Gibson, *op. cit.* note 28 *supra*, at pp. 89–93.
30 *Ibid.*, p. 1688.
31 Hogg, Peter, *Constitutional Law of Canada* (3rd ed.), Toronto: Carswell, 1992, pp. 836–9.

and where no act of government is relied upon to support the action, the Charter will not apply'.[32] Whatever test is actually adopted for determining where the boundary between public and private law lies in such cases, any distinction of this sort clearly relates, at root, to differing normative perceptions of the *roles* of government and private citizen in the societies concerned. Defending the inapplicability of the Canadian Charter to private bodies, for example, Professor Hogg points out that 'a private corporation is empowered to exercise only the same proprietary and contractual powers that are available to a natural person. It does not possess the coercive power of governance to which the Charter applies'.[33] While Dale Gibson calls, by contrast, for an extension in the scope of Charter liability, he nevertheless relies upon the *functions* of government and private bodies as the basis for his argument, stressing the many shared *responsibilities* owed to the community by public authorities and private citizens.[34]

Perhaps the most dynamic examples of differential functions can be found in EC law (for present purposes, EC law and English law will be treated as composite legal systems in their own right): for the question how far EC law operates in a 'federal' as opposed to an 'inter-state' fashion — that is, how far it constitutes an over-arching superstructure within which the legal systems of the member states are incorporated, rather than being a set of rules enforceable principally between the governments of the Member States — turns largely on how strong a role is given to citizens and private bodies as users, enforcers and subjects of EC law. As a general matter, it is clear — as Van Gerven A-G noted in Case C-188/89, *Foster* v *British Gas* — that 'some notion of public authority' plays a role in many areas of EC law, so that the 'most important general conclusion to be drawn . . . is that an interpretation is sought of each measure [giving the notion of public authority a special role] which is most in keeping with its place in the Treaty and thus with the purpose of the concept of public authority which is used'.[35] In other words, public authorities are allocated a special role, in most substantive areas of EC law, in adhering to and furthering the aims of the EC Treaty (together with the Treaty on European Union), requiring the rules governing each area to be interpreted so as to reflect these distinctive functions.

This can be illustrated in the case law on the free movement of goods, the free movement of workers, the freedom of establishment and the freedom to provide services. As an obvious example, we might consider the member states' responsibility under Article 30 of the Treaty to promote the free movement of goods by eliminating quantitative restrictions on imports, together with measures having

---

32   [1986] SCR 573 at 603. For argument in favour of a broader application of the Charter, see Gibson, *op cit.* note 28 *supra*, pp. 110–18.
33   Hogg, *op. cit.* note 31 *supra*, p. 837.
34   Gibson, *op. cit.* note 28 *supra*, p. 117.
35   [1990] ECR I-3313, para. 11.

equivalent effect to such restrictions. In order to enforce this Article, it was necessary for the European Court of Justice to define what counted as a measure adopted by the state (effectively, the governing authorities of the member state concerned) so as to test whether it amounted — or had equivalent effect — to a quantitative restriction. In Case 249/81, *Commission* v *Ireland*,[36] a wide, purposive interpretation was adopted by the Court, which ruled that a promotional campaign for Irish goods, organised by the Irish Goods Council — technically a private company — fell within the scope of the Article. The members of the Council's Management Committee were appointed by the government, which granted it substantial public funding and defined the aims and broad outline of the Council's campaigning work in promoting the sales of Irish goods within Ireland. The fact that the Council was only engaged in a promotional campaign and lacked the authority to issue binding rulings (of a 'governmental' nature) to companies or consumers in Ireland did not matter given that the potential effect of the Council's campaign could be comparable to that resulting from binding government measures. The national government's distinctive responsibility under Article 30 — that is, its function in promoting the free movement of goods — thus precluded it even from supporting the type of 'arm's length' activity carried out by the Council.

The 'public service' exception to the rules on free movement of persons (Articles 48 to 51 of the EC Treaty), together with the parallel 'official authority' exception to the rules on freedom of establishment (Articles 52 to 58) and freedom to provide services (Articles 59 to 66), illustrate an attempt by the Treaty drafters to strike a *balance* between the distinctive functions of state authorities under EC law and the national laws of member states. The public service exception — set out in Article 48(4) — provides that the freedom of movement of workers provisions in Article 48 'shall not apply to employment in the public service' — an exception defined in Case 149/79, *Commission* v *Belgium*, as covering posts which 'in fact presume on the part of those occupying them the existence of a special relationship of allegiance to the State and reciprocity of rights and duties which form the foundation of the bond of nationality'.[37] Article 48(4) pinpoints an important clash between two rival functions of the governing authorities of the member states. On the one hand, they are charged under EC law with abolishing discriminatory national measures affecting access to employment in their territory by nationals of other member states, and with allowing such persons to enter and remain within their territory in search of work.[38] In the eyes of EC law, therefore, it is one function of the governments of member states to promote the free movement of workers — as part of a broader function, nowadays, of making progress towards the single European market. The public service exception is,

---

36   [1982] ECR 4005.
37   [1980] ECR 3881, para. 10.
38   *Cf.* Case C-292/89, *R v Immigration Appeal Tribunal, ex parte Antonissen* [1991] ECR I-745.

however, designed to cover those posts 'which involve direct or indirect participation in the exercise of powers conferred by public law and duties designed to safeguard the general interests of the State or of other public authorities'.[39] As Professor David O'Keeffe has noted, the public service exception is thus, 'geared to a conception of the State performing certain essential activities related to its function as the State, where the legitimate interests of the State can best be served and protected by the recruitment of the State's own nationals to perform certain tasks on its behalf'.[40] In other words, state governments' function as protectors of their own national interests must sometimes prevail over their function as promoters of freedom of movement under EC law. The fact that Article 48(4) is a *public* service exception simply reflects the fact that both of the functions in question are functions of the *governments* of the member states. The drawing of this particular public–private distinction reflects, then, not merely the fact that state authorities have distinct functions of their own, but also that such distinctive functions can potentially conflict.

A similar observation can be made about the workings of the analogous Articles 55 and 66 exception to the provisions on freedom of establishment and freedom to provide services. The exemption covers activities which, in the relevant member state, are 'connected, even occasionally, with the exercise of official authority'. The notion that such authority is something unique to the state was made clear by Mayras A-G in Case 2/74, *Reyners v Belgium*, where the Advocate-General stated that it arises from the sovereignty and majesty of the state, and that 'for him who exercises it, it implies the power of enjoying the prerogatives outside the general law, privileges of official power and powers of coercion over citizens'.[41] The concept of official authority thus reflects the state's distinct functions and powers, and can potentially clash with the state's function in EC law as a guarantor of freedom of movement. Any move towards a fully federalised Europe would, of course, most likely involve the withering away of the official authority and public service exceptions, consequent upon a decline in the distinct functions of member states' governments to which they related.

Turning to the more directly 'constitutional' aspects of EC law, the case law on direct effect provides a striking demonstration of how the on-going *development*

---

39 European Court of Justice, *Commission v Belgium*, note 37 *supra*, para. 10. See also Case 149/79, *Commission v Belgium* (No. 2) [1982] ECR 1845; Case 307/84, *Commission v France* [1986] ECR 1725; Case 66/85, *Lawrie-Blum v Land Baden-Wurttemberg* [1986] ECR 2121; Case 222/85, *Commission v Italy* [1987] ECR 2625; Case 419/92, *Scholz v Opera Universitaria di Cagliari* [1994] ECR I-505.

40 O'Keeffe, David, 'Judicial Interpretation of the Public Service Exception to the Free Movement of Workers', in Curtin, Deirdre, and O'Keeffe, David (eds), *Constitutional Adjudication in European Community Law and National Law*, London: Butterworths, 1992, p. 89 at p. 105.

41 [1974] ECR 631 at 664. See also Case C-306/89, *Commission v Greece* [1991] ECR I-5863; Case C-272/91, *Commission v Italy* [1994] ECR I-1409; Case C-49/92, *Thijssen v Controledienst voor de Verzekeringen* [1993] ECR I-4047.

of a legal concept can both affect and be influenced by perceptions of the respective roles of state authorities and the private citizen. Direct effect[42] entitles private individuals and companies to invoke (in a variable range of circumstances) EC Treaty Articles, Regulations and Directives before national courts and the European Court of Justice, with the consequence that contradictory provisions of national law must be 'disapplied'.[43] Prior to the decision of the European Court of Justice in Case 26/62, *Van Gend en Loos* v *Nederlandse Administratie der Belastingen*,[44] the enforcement of EC Treaty requirements lay in the hands of the European Commission, which was charged under Article 169 of the Treaty with bringing member states who had failed to comply with their obligations before the European Court of Justice (other member states could also do so, under Article 170, provided that they had first submitted the matter to the Commission). As Professor Paul Craig has observed, this purely 'public' mode of enforcement was both too weak and confronted the Commission with potential conflicts of interest.[45] In *Van Gend en Loos*, the European Court of Justice sought to overcome these weaknesses by agreeing that private individuals might also take action against states — using the Article 177 reference procedure — for breaches of Treaty articles which laid down a sufficiently clear and precise obligation.

This decision certainly created a more powerful incentive for member states to comply with their Treaty obligations than had existed hitherto.[46] Its importance for present purposes lies in its confirmation that private citizens have a role to play in EC law. For the Court of Justice made clear that the EC Treaty is 'more than an agreement which merely creates mutual obligations between the contracting states', and that:

> the Community constitutes a new legal order . . . for the benefit of which the states have limited their sovereign rights, albeit within limited fields, and the subjects of which comprise not only Member States but also their nationals.

---

42   Uncertainty dogs the precise distinction between direct effect and direct applicability: contrast Schermers, Henry and Waelbroek, Denis, *Judicial Protection in the European Communities* (5th ed.), Deventer: Kluwer, 1992, paras 219–23; Pescatore, Pierre, 'The Doctrine of "Direct Effect": An Infant Disease of Community Law' (1983) 8 *European Law Review* 155; Winter, J.A., 'Direct Applicability and Direct Effect: Two Distinct and Different Concepts in Community Law' (1972) 9 *Common Market Law Review* 425; Steiner, Josephine, 'Direct Applicability in EEC Law — A Chameleon Concept' (1982) 98 *Law Quarterly Review* 229.

43   The concept of 'disapplication' was laid down by the European Court of Justice in Case C-213/89, *R* v *Secretary of State for Transport, ex parte Factortame* [1990] ECR I-2433. Note, however, Pescatore's observation that the primacy of EC law over national law depends on the notion of direct effect only in the legal systems of some member states — *op. cit.* note 42 *supra*, at p. 157.

44   [1963] ECR 1.

45   Craig, Paul, 'Once Upon a Time in the West: Direct Effect and the Federalization of EEC Law' (1992) 12 *Oxford Journal of Legal Studies* 453 at pp. 454–7.

46   For discussion of later developments in the context of effectiveness, see Steiner, Josephine, 'From direct effects to *Francovich*: shifting means of enforcement of Community law' (1993) 18 *European Law Review* 3.

Independently of the legislation of Member States, Community law therefore not only imposes obligations on individuals but is also intended to confer upon them rights which become part of their legal heritage.[47]

This development was crucial. As Craig has argued:

Granting rights to individuals which they can enforce in their own name transformed the very nature of the EEC Treaty. No longer would the Treaty be viewed solely as the business of nation states in the manner of many other international treaties. It was to be a form of social ordering in which individuals were involved in their own capacity.[48]

In similar vein, Pescatore sees the Court as suggesting that 'the Treaty has created a Community not only of States but also of peoples and persons and . . . therefore not only Member States but also individuals must be visualised as being subjects of Community law'.[49] *Van Gend en Loos* recognised, in other words, that the enforcement of Treaty obligations was no longer a solely 'public' function: private individuals were affected by the Treaty, and as such deserved to have the legal right to enforce appropriate provisions of it.

Subsequent case law has confirmed the integral involvement of private individuals in enforcing EC law before the European Court of Justice and the national courts of member states, and debate about how direct effect *should* develop can be seen as turning largely on the questions how strong a role the private citizen or body should be given in enforcement, and how wide a range of bodies should be subject to the requirements of EC law. An important political issue shelters behind these questions. For if, throughout the member states, citizens have as strong a role as governments in bringing proceedings, and if private bodies are subject to EC law in the same way as governments, it becomes plausible to talk of the EC legal system as having developed into a federal structure in all but name — for all would be treated directly as players in and subjects of the one super-national system, regardless of the national rules of their own member states.

At present, the European Court of Justice has effected a compromise falling slightly short of such a position. While Case 43/75, *Defrenne* v *Sabena (No. 2)* found that Treaty Articles could, if sufficiently clear and precise,[50] have direct

---

47 [1963] ECR 1 at 12.
48 Craig, Paul, *op. cit.* note 45 *supra*, at p. 458.
49 Pescatore, Pierre, *op. cit.* note 42 *supra*, at p. 158. See also Dashwood, Alan, 'The Principle of Direct Effect in European Community Law' (1978) 16 *Journal of Common Market Studies* 229 at p. 232.
50 In 'Once Upon a Time in the West: Direct Effect and the Federalization of EEC Law', note 45 *supra*, Craig traces the gradual dilution of the standards of clarity and precision which are deemed necessary before direct effect can apply.

effect in litigation between two private parties ('horizontal direct effect') as well as in actions between private parties and public authorities ('vertical direct effect'), the European Court of Justice ruled in Case 152/84, *Marshall* v *Southampton and South-West Hampshire Area Health Authority*, that Directives, being 'addressed' only to the member states, are to have vertical direct effect only.[51] The strength of this restriction has, however, been diluted by two methods.[52] First, a notion of 'indirect effect' has been developed. In Case C-106/89, *Marleasing SA* v *La Comercial*, the Court of Justice ruled that national courts must, 'in applying national law, whether the provisions in question were adopted before or after the directive,' interpret national law 'so far as possible, in the light of the wording and the purpose of the directive in order to achieve the result pursued by the latter'.[53] Obviously the phrase 'so far as possible' checks the ambit of the *Marleasing* interpretative obligation, as does the need for a relevant directive covering the same area as national law.[54] Nevertheless, the Court's ruling that the interpretative obligation arises in cases (such as *Marleasing* itself) involving only private parties *as well as* in 'vertical' cases might be said to supply a 'backdoor' route for horizontal direct effect.

Secondly, the European Court of Justice has adopted a broad definition of an 'emanation of the state' — that is, of the bodies which are sufficiently 'public' or 'governmental' to be subject to the vertical direct effect of Directives. In *Marshall* v *Southampton and South-West Hampshire Area Health Authority* itself, the Court found that:

> where a person involved in legal proceedings is able to rely on a directive as against the State he may do so regardless of the capacity in which the latter is acting, whether [as] employer or public authority. In either case it is necessary to prevent the State from taking advantage of its own failure to comply with Community law.[55]

This was taken further by the European Court of Justice in Case C-188/89, *Foster* v *British Gas*, where it was ruled that:

> a public body, whatever its legal form, which has been made responsible, pursuant to a measure adopted by the State, for providing a public service under

---

51   [1986] ECR 723.
52   The ever-widening damages liability of member states for failure to comply with EC law obligations may well constitute a third (although it is not directly relevant for present purposes) — a point well illustrated in Case C-91/92, *Faccini Dori* v *Recreb Srl* [1994] ECR I-3325.
53   [1990] ECR I-4135, para.8.
54   For a sceptical view of the width of *Marleasing* v *Là Comercial*, see Maltby, Nick, '*Marleasing*: What Is All the Fuss About?' (1993) 109 *Law Quarterly Review* 301.
55   [1986] ECR 723, para. 49.

the control of the State and has for that purpose special powers beyond those which result from the normal rules applicable in relations between individuals is included in any event among the bodies against which the provisions of a directive capable of having direct effect may be relied upon.[56]

In other words, a public authority acting in the apparently 'private' capacity of employer will fall within the scope of vertical direct effect — even if it happens to be as far removed from the machinery and workings of central government as a local health authority — as will a privatised utility, or indeed any provider of a public service under the control of the state.[57] The sheer width of this formulation must undermine the utility of the horizontal/vertical direct effect distinction as a means of restricting the range of liability under EC law.

How widely an 'emanation of the state' is defined is also significant when considering the distinctive functions of public bodies in EC law. A significant justification advanced by the Court of Justice for allowing Directives to have vertical but not horizontal direct effect is the wording of Article 189 of the EC Treaty, which states that 'A directive shall be binding, as to the result to be achieved, upon each Member State to which it is addressed.' In *Foster v British Gas*, the Court asserted that:

where the Community authorities have, by means of a directive, placed Member States under a duty to adopt a certain course of action, the effectiveness of such a measure would be diminished if persons were prevented from relying upon it in proceedings before a court and national courts were prevented from taking it into consideration as an element of Community law. Consequently, a Member State which has not adopted the implementing measures required by the directive within the prescribed period may not plead, as against individuals, its own failure to perform the obligations which the directive entails.[58]

In *Marshall v Southampton and South-West Hampshire Area Health Authority*, the Court reasoned that as Directives were only addressed to member states, they could be binding only upon member states and not private individuals. Direct effect is thus inherently connected with the distinctive functions of public bodies. The failure of a member state government to pass a Directive into national law — its failure to perform the function given to it under Article 189 — justifies the

---

56 [1990] ECR I-3313, para. 20.
57 For related case law development, see Case 222/84, *Johnston v Constable of the Royal Ulster Constabulary* [1986] ECR 1651; Case C-262/88, *Barber v Guardian Royal Exchange Assurance Group* [1990] ECR I-1889; *Enderby v Frenchay Area Health Authority* [1992] IRLR 15; *R v British Coal Corporation and Secretary of State for Trade and Industry, ex parte Vardy* [1993] IRLR 104; *British Coal Corporation v Smith* [1994] IRLR 342.
58 [1990] ECR I-3313, para. 16

imposition of direct effect in the first place. Since passing a Directive into national law involves the enactment or amendment of primary or secondary legislation, it constitutes a legislative function which private citizens cannot perform. It is, in other words, a function distinct to the state authorities, and allowing Directives to assume horizontal direct effect would ignore the fact that private citizens and bodies are in no way responsible for the state's failure to discharge its special function.[59] As previously suggested, however, it may be the case that this general argument against horizontal direct effect has been undermined for the future by the wide range of bodies which the Court of Justice is prepared to count as 'emanations of the state': in relation to the facts of *Marshall* v *Southampton and South West Hampshire Area Health Authority,* for example, it is far from clear that the Area Health Authority — against which the Directive was found to have vertical direct effect — has any greater responsibility (whether causally or otherwise) for Parliament's failure to pass a directive into national law than would a private company.

The real significance of the horizontal/vertical direct effect issue can now be spelt out: if horizontal direct effect is to be given to Directives, the significance of the state's distinctive function under Article 189 will be diminished. In an ideal world, member states would continue of their own accord to incorporate Directives into national law, thus assisting the national courts in interpreting and applying them. Ultimately, however, such an exercise would matter little — for once the time limit for incorporating a Directive had expired, it would take direct effect anyway and be determinative of *all* relevant litigation. Individuals would then have just as strong a role as the state in enforcing the provisions of Directives, and would be subject to them just as widely. The argument about direct effect is, therefore, an argument about whether the practical effect of the member states' distinctive legislative responsibility for Directives should continue to be seen as particularly significant.

The examples discussed in the preceding paragraphs are intended to serve simply as illustrations of the fact that all of the legal systems under discussion employ — and employ a wide variety of — rules which draw important distinctions between public authorities and private individuals or bodies. One might, of course, choose to argue that some or all of these distinctions are unnecessary or undesirable, whether as a general matter or when set against the circumstances of the legal system concerned. Any such argument, however, would have at some level to employ normative criteria relating to the proper roles of the state and the private citizen or body; and, as was shown earlier, no relevant normative argument conceives of a totally identical role for the state and its citizens. All presuppose, to a certain extent, some sort of public–private distinction.

---

59   For further discussion of the rationales for direct effect, see Dashwood, *op. cit.* note 49 *supra.*

At a conceptual level, this point is unaffected by disputes as to whether particular companies or bodies should count as public or private, for such disputes go only to who should bear the special responsibilities of the state, rather than to whether such responsibilities should exist at all. Countless normative accounts of the proper size and functions of the state exist — and it is according to such accounts that we must decide whether or not a specific body or function is public in nature.

THE NORMATIVE CLAIM

The argument can now be joined with my second, normative claim — which rests on an appeal to political legitimacy — in order to show which functions should properly be seen as 'public'. As was suggested earlier, a hallmark of non-totalitarian regimes is support for the idea that the state should have a monopoly over the legitimate exercise of certain types of coercive power — in particular the creation and enforcement of laws — but that, to exercise these powers in a morally legitimate fashion, the state must have a sound normative justification for its actions.[60] More particularly, the need to justify the use of law can be explained by reference to the law's coercive potential — its capacity, as an instrument of social regulation, directly to affect the behaviour of at least some of those who are subject to it, to provide a standard whereby people can make normative judgments about each other's behaviour (via comments such as 'that action is wrong because it breaks the law'), and to instil fear in citizens concerning the possibility of state intervention in their lives should they break the law.[61] This last point was acknowledged by the European Court of Human Rights in its acceptance, in *Norris v Ireland*,[62] that a litigant might have standing to challenge the compatibility of a state law with the European Convention on Human Rights even where that law had not been enforced against him or her, on the basis that the mere existence of that law singles him or her out — whether individually or as a member of a group — for treatment of a type which is prohibited under the Convention. An analogous (even if, on the facts, less intense) coercive potential may be present in the use of other types of state power — such as administrative rule-making and the distribution of grants or discretionary benefits — given the state's vast resources,

---

60 The existence of an entrenched constitution or Bill of Rights would, by contrast, be used to test the legal legitimacy — according to the standards laid down in those instruments — of new laws created by the state. The boundary between political/moral and legal legitimacy can often be opaque, however, as is shown by the debate about how far judges should take particular views of political legitimacy into account in deciding 'hard' cases.

61 For discussion of the connections between models of democracy and legitimacy, see Held, David, *Models of Democracy* (2nd ed.), Oxford: Polity Press, 1996; Anthony Birch, *The Concepts and Theories of Modern Democracy*, London: Routledge, 1993, Chs. 3, 4. For a further attempt to develop the notion of legitimacy, see Allan, T.R.S., 'Citizenship and Obligation: Civil Disobedience and Civil Dissent' (1996) 55 *Cambridge Law Journal* 89, esp. at pp. 93–8.

62 (1989) 13 EHRR 187.

its potential ability to control the direction of the economy and national life, its power to tax citizens, the special functions which it discharges, and its ability to alter the law.[63] A proper justification will therefore be needed to show that the exercise of any type of state power is permissible according to a vision of how the state ought, legitimately, to act in a constitutional democracy. Such a vision will explain the interests which state action may properly protect and override, and the social ends which it should serve. It is thus concerned — as Professor Neil MacCormick has argued — with specifying:

> the right exercise of the public powers vested in agencies of state — legislators, governments, judges, police, and prosecutors. Whoever attempts to give a general answer to the question about the right exercise of such powers is necessarily committed to stating practical principles for the guidance of those who exercise them. And practical principles of right conduct are moral principles.[64]

As Raymond Plant has argued, any background political theory will be concerned with 'justifying the right way or ways and identifying the wrong ways in which political power is to be exercised and the nature of the claims which citizens can make on the state and on each other'.[65] The precise range of situations in which one believes that the state may act — for example, through law (i.e., which set of functions one believes the state may properly use coercion to pursue) — will vary according to one's background political theory: libertarian believers in a minimal state may wish to confine the state's responsibilities to maintaining 'law and order' and defending the nation against enemy attack; welfarist liberals might, by contrast, argue that the state should be responsible for compulsory redistributive taxation in order to fund a social security system to support the poor. In addition, one's background vision of how state power ought to be used need not always be expressed in terms of a *single* normative value such as liberty — Professor Tribe's interpretation of the ' state action' cases in US law, for example, rests on the idea that constitutional rights against the government:

> rest on a *series of distinct if related values* which the Supreme Court has found to be implicit in the constitutional plan. These values take the form of a series of judgments: about the identity of those choices which are peculiarly individual and thus shielded from government frustration or usurpation; about the dimen-

---

63 *Cf.* Fredman Sandra, and Morris, Gillian *op. cit.* note 4 *supra* at pp. 309–12.
64 MacCormick, Neil, *Legal Right and Social Democracy: Essays in Legal and Political Philosophy*, Oxford: Clarendon Press, 1982, p. 18. See also Raz, Joseph, *The Morality of Freedom*, Oxford: Clarendon Press, 1986, pp. 2–3.
65 Plant, Raymond, *Modern Political Thought,* Oxford: Basil Blackwell, 1991, p. 2.

sions of individual difference which government must generally ignore; and about the required structural characteristics of government decision making processes.[66]

The major purpose of any non-totalitarian political theory is therefore to explain why it is morally legitimate for the state to discharge a particular range of functions, given that the state requires justification in order legitimately to act (a totalitarian theory would, by its very nature, deny that the state needed any moral justification), in contrast to private citizens, who are presumed to be free to act unless there is a sound justification for stopping them.[67] This provides the normative basis for distinguishing between exercises of 'public' power and ordinary 'private' activities: for the former need special justification to count as morally legitimate; the latter presumptively do not. At a practical level, Professor Hogg has thus argued in relation to the *Retail, Wholesale and Department Store Union* v *Dolphin Delivery* decision in Canada that 'In deciding that the Charter does not extend to private action, the Supreme Court of Canada has affirmed the normal role of a constitution. A constitution establishes and regulates the institutions of government, and it leaves to those institutions the task of ordering the private affairs of the people'.[68] Given, therefore, that the state's 'public' functions are public because they cannot be carried out by private actors (our descriptive claim) — and that they are specially circumscribed by the need for justification (the normative claim) — they must surely be characterised as being of a substantively different order from 'private' activities.

This does not tell us where any boundary line between public law and private law ought to be drawn in practice, nor whether the procedural aspects of public law litigation (rules as to time limits, standing, etc.) should differ from those applicable in private law. This is a task for the individual political theories, each of which will have its own view as to where the proper boundary between state and private action should lie, and how rigorously it should be policed by the courts.

---

66   Tribe, *op. cit.* note 29 *supra*, p. 1699, emphasis added.

67   A point accepted at the level of constitutional law rather than political philosophy by Laws J in *R v Somerset County Council, ex parte Fewings,* note 17 *supra.* While communitarian political theories do not, as a rule, draw such a sharp distinction between citizen and state, they still presuppose — as noted above — the existence of certain distinct functions for state bodies (promoting the common good, for example) and of a space within which citizens can determine the direction of their own lives, albeit with reference to or influenced by the requirements of the common good.

68   Hogg, *op. cit.* note 31 *supra*, p. 848. Hogg's 'task of ordering the ordinary affairs of others' caveat allows him to escape the charge that he believes in a legally unregulated private sphere. Rather, as Hogg goes on to show, his distinction is between a 'public' sphere which is regulated by constitutional norms, and a private sphere which may — so far as the constitution allows — be regulated by ordinary legislation. It need not be the case, therefore, that a distinction between public and private *law* will necessarily be offensive to feminist critics of the separation between the social *spheres* of family and market.

As Peter Cane has suggested: . . . 'different attitudes to the public-private distinction can be related, at a very abstract level, to different accounts of the role of the individual in political life and hence to different accounts of the nature of democracy and the state.'[69] So, while our general argument suggests that some sort of public law–private law distinction is inevitable, the details of how that distinction should work in any legal system will vary according to one's background political theory.

TWO CRITICISMS

We must now consider two important types of criticism of a substantive divide between the legal rights and obligations of public authorities and private individuals. Both types of criticism contain descriptive and normative elements of their own, the main difference between them relating to their respective normative elements. Supporters of the first criticism believe that a public law–private law divide undermines their (normative) vision of the state's proper constitutional role; while the second criticism turns on the idea that in English law, such a divide undermines certain standards of rationality and effectiveness to which the legal system should adhere. Each line of criticism is open to attack using a variety of normative and descriptive criteria.[70] The main argument in this section of the chapter, however, will simply be that neither criticism actually challenges the claim that some sort of public law–private law distinction — in the sense of differential legal treatment of the state and private citizens — is inevitable. Neither can therefore serve as a rebuttal of the argument deployed in this chapter.

The first type of criticism has been advanced by Professors A.V. Dicey and Carol Harlow. While their arguments appear related at surface level, it is important to note that they rest on very different normative views of the proper role of the state[71] (see Leyland and Woods, Ch. 16, pp. 37 et seq). I will briefly outline Dicey's and

---

69   Cane, Peter, 'Public Law and Private Law: A Study of the Analysis and Use of a Legal Concept', in Eekelaar, J. and Bell, J. (eds), *Oxford Essays in Jurisprudence: Third Series* Oxford: Clarendon Press, 1987, Ch. 3 at p. 78.

70   In relation to the first criticism, see the reconceptualisation of Dicey's view — and discussion of various attacks on Dicey — in Jowell, Jeffrey, 'The Rule of Law Today' in Jowell, Jeffrey and Oliver, Dawn (eds), *The Changing Constitution* (3rd ed.), Oxford: Clarendon Press, 1994, Ch. 3. For criticism/analysis of Harlow's account, see Samuel, Geoffrey, *op. cit.* note 18 *supra*; Cane, Peter, *op. cit.* note 69 *supra*. In relation to the second criticism, see — for a review of Allison's account — Bamforth, Nicholas [1996] *Public Law* 716.

71   While Dicey has been categorised as a 'conservative normativist' by Professor Martin Loughlin, Harlow may be felt to fit more neatly within the category of 'functionalists' — *cf.* Loughlin, Martin, *Public Law and Political Theory*, Oxford: Clarendon Press, 1992, Chs. 6–8. For further discussion of Dicey's political theory, *cf.* Craig, Paul, *Public Law and Democracy in the United Kingdom and the United States of America*, Oxford: Clarendon Press, 1990, Ch. 1. It is, of course, arguable whether any theory can ever be 'purely' descriptive in the sense of not being, to an extent, influenced by its author's underlying normative perspective.

Harlow's views before explaining why they should not really be seen as contradicting the argument developed in this chapter. Dicey famously categorised — as the second of the three elements making up his idea of the rule of law — the idea of formal equality of government and citizen before the law, as a result of which any distinction between public law and private law — as existed in France — was alien to the English legal system. 'In England,' Dicey argued, 'the idea of legal equality, or of the universal subjection of all classes to one law administered by the ordinary courts, has been pushed to its utmost limit. With us every official, from the Prime Minister down to a constable or a collector of taxes, is under the same responsibility for every act done without legal justification as any other citizen.'[72] Because of this normative commitment to formal equality before the law, the rule of law excluded:

> any exemption of officials or others from the duty of obedience to the law which governs other citizens . . . from the jurisdiction of the ordinary tribunals; there can be with us nothing really corresponding both to the 'administrative law' (*droit administratif*) or the 'administrative tribunals' (*tribunaux administratifs*) of France.[73]

No special regime of public law could thus exist, applicable only to the state.

Harlow believes that Dicey's view of equality before the law still provides an ideal towards which the courts should strive.[74] She goes on to argue that a public law–private law distinction is undesirable because, *inter alia*, it would be difficult or impossible in practice to separate 'public' from 'private'. 'No activity is typically governmental in nature nor wholly without parallels in private law',[75] Harlow suggests, so that a public law–private law distinction merely serves to promote 'sterile jurisdictional litigation'[76] and inflexibility.[77] Indeed, Harlow argues, the idea of an autonomous body of public law is 'wholly incompatible with the English tradition and is unlikely to contribute in any meaningful way to the solution of the many problems which modern administrative law has to overcome'.[78]

Dicey's and Harlow's arguments must immediately appear suspect in the light of our discussion of the role of government in modern constitutional democracies.

---

72 Dicey, A.V., *An Introduction to the Study of the Law of the Constitution* (10th ed.), London: MacMillan, 1959, p. 193.
73 *Ibid.*, at pp. 202–3.
74 Harlow, *op. cit.* note 5 *supra*, at p. 250.
75 *Ibid.*, at p. 257.
76 *Ibid.*, at p. 250.
77 *Ibid.*, at p. 258. See also Allison, *op. cit.* note 5 *supra* esp. Chs. 3, 5–8. Allison doubts (pp. 243–5) whether political philosophy can, in practice, help in resolving boundary disputes; but as Peter Cane observes (*op. cit.* note 69 *supra*, at pp. 65–6) in response to Harlow, this is to commit the logical error of using pragmatism to deflect an argument of political principle.
78 Harlow, *op. cit.* note 5 *supra*, at p. 242.

For many of the distinctions between 'public' and 'private' which we have examined are plainly the product of the distinctive functions of the modern state, together with such classic functions as law-making. Dicey and Harlow are thus faced with a choice: to continue, on the one hand, to oppose *all* such distinctions would seem to deny the very nature of modern government, a position which would appear to be out of touch with reality. Yet the only obvious alternative would be for Dicey and Harlow to concede that they are opposed only to some such distinctions. The selection of the 'some' to which they are opposed would inevitably have to rest, however, upon their own normative views of the proper function of the state. Quite apart from the fact that any such normative views are again likely to entail an analytical distinction between the ideas of 'state' and 'citizen' (for political philosophy is, as we noted above, concerned with specifying a measure by which the acts of the state may be assessed and sometimes justified), Dicey and Harlow would effectively have conceded the issue by acknowledging that they are opposed only to a certain proportion of public–private distinctions. For I have already suggested that while the existence of a certain range of public–private distinctions is inevitable in any modern legal system, theorists will differ in their views as to which are normatively justifiable.

The second type of criticism of a public law–private law distinction has been developed by John Allison.[79] The normative element in Allison's theory relates not to the proper role of state action,[80] but instead to the need for a legal system to operate in a rational and effective way — something which the English legal system cannot do, Allison claims, given the existence of the type of substantive public law–private law distinction present in cases such as *ex parte Datafin* and *ex parte Aga Khan*. Allison suggests that for a public law–private law distinction to work satisfactorily, four characteristics must be present, without any one of which the distinction will be problematical. First, there must be a well-developed theory of the state, which appreciates the distinctness of the state administration — something which, in turn, would justify the application of a special set of rules to the state administration and special bodies to administer those rules. Allison suggests that without such a theory, any public law–private law distinction will 'be reduced to a rhetorical tool'.[81] This is the case in English law which, Allison argues, embodies no clear conception of the state, instead using 'various vague conceptions, such as the Crown, officials, political superiors, officers of the Crown, and public or political persons'.[82] And since English law lacks norms clearly delimiting state administration, it is difficult to determine the proper scope of judicial review or amenability of the Crown to contempt; as such, Allison argues,

---

79 See Allison, *op. cit.* note 5 *supra*.
80 *Ibid.*, p. 39.
81 *Ibid.*, p. 38.
82 *Ibid.*, p. 79.

the term 'public law' does not adequately describe the area of law it is intended to signify.[83]

Allison's second characteristic is that law would need to be approached in a categorical fashion — that is, it would need to be seen as a system, with exclusive and clearly-defined categories and sub-categories. Without a clear sense of system, a public law–private law divide could not generate coherent boundaries around each category, so that borderline cases cannot be placed in one category or another with confidence. Allison suggests that in English law, legal categories tend to be ordered on a pragmatic rather than a systematic basis, producing uncertainty.[84] The third characteristic is that there would need to be a separation of powers between the judiciary and administration. The courts dealing with public law would need to be both independent — so as to prevent one branch of the state being seen to regulate the other — and expert in the process of public administration, to allow them to intervene confidently and in a way which the administration would respect. Again, Allison argues, this is not the case in English law. What commitment there is to a separation in English law is just too vague to sustain an adequate institutional division. The final characteristic is that courts handling public law cases would need to use inquisitorial rather than adversarial procedures. With adversarial procedures, courts are informed only by the representations of the parties to the immediate dispute, leaving them unable properly to investigate the consequences of a ruling one way or another. Given the range of interests involved in public law disputes, Allison ventures that if courts are inadequately informed, they cannot intervene confidently in a case — yet the procedure in English law is adversarial rather than inquisitorial.

For present purposes, two points must be made about Allison's account. First, it should be noted that Allison is not criticising the idea of a public law–private law split *per se*. Rather, he is claiming that the substantive distinction *in English law* in the *ex parte Datafin/ex parte Aga Khan category* of cases does not work effectively. In this respect, his argument is not incompatible with this author's: he appears to be attacking only one particular public law-private law distinction. He does not claim to be attacking other distinctions in other legal systems, although he may doubtless try to apply his methodology to them. The second point is that Allison's own normative criteria for measuring whether a public law–private law divide is 'satisfactory' or 'unsatisfactory' go to whether it measures up to his goal of achieving systematic rationality in the legal system. Given the general philosophical presumption that it is necessary to justify state action, however, it may well be asked whether criteria which go to the efficacy of a legal system *alone* are sufficient to measure that system's desirability (and hence the desirability of any public law–private law divide within it). Allison explicitly confines his attention to

---

83   *Ibid.*, p. 99.
84   *Ibid.*, p. 131.

his efficacy-related criteria[85] — and to that extent, it could well be said that he is simply addressing a different question from those considered in this chapter. On this interpretation, it would be quite logical to claim both that a particular public law–private law distinction does not work effectively *and that*, on the type of normative basis discussed in this chapter, some such distinction remains necessary (in which case, the existing distinction would simply need to be refined to make it work effectively). From the standpoint of day-to-day speculation about the role of the state, however, it would seem strange to advance a theory which is based solely on considerations of effectiveness. For in day-to-day speculation, it seems unlikely that effectiveness-related criteria are likely to count for much on their own: rather, in assessing whether any feature of an existing legal system is 'desirable' or 'undesirable', their most likely role is as an extra reinforcement, using a different standpoint from the main philosophical argument, for the claim that a particular public law–private law distinction is unjustifiable according to one's background theories of justice and political morality.

CONCLUSION

The argument can now be brought back to the public law–private law divide as it operates in the English law of judicial review. In its most recent examination of judicial review (including the exclusivity rule and the special 'procedural' aspects of the jurisdiction), the Law Commission stressed that

> policy is a continual theme in the public law sphere. Judicial review often involves values and policy interests, which must normally be balanced against and may transcend the individual interests, which are normally the subject of litigation between private citizens.[86]

Relevant policy interests to be placed in the balancing exercise included the need to vindicate the rule of law 'so that public bodies take lawful decisions and are prevented from relying on invalid decisions'; the need for speed and certainty in administrative decision making where large numbers of people are affected by a public body's decision; the private interest of litigants in obtaining a remedy for their grievance; and the need for prompt adjudication of disputes through the courts.[87] The Law Commission largely omitted, however, to discuss how much weight should, as a general matter, be given to *each* of these considerations.[88] It

---

85   *Ibid.*, pp. 39–40.
86   Law Commission, *Administrative Law: Judicial Review and Statutory Appeals* (Law Com. No. 226), 1994, para. 2.1.
87   *Ibid.*, para. 2.3.
88   See, for example, the treatment of the policy considerations in relation to exclusivity in Law Com. No. 226, *supra*, paras 3.4 and 3.13.

was therefore left uncertain whether the rule of law should always — or should sometimes, or should never — trump the need for speed and certainty. The argument of this chapter should (it is hoped) show that the resolution of such issues can occur only by reference to a detailed normative argument concerning the proper role and functions of state bodies. It should be added that such an argument need not be inflexible. While Professor Tribe has observed that the problematical US 'state action' cases may not be explicable by reference to a single normative theory of liberty, he is nonetheless clear that constitutional rights:

> instead give legal expression to a series of distinct if related values which the Supreme Court has found to be implicit in the constitutional plan. These values take the form of a series of judgments: about the identity of those choices which are peculiarly individual and thus shielded from government frustration or usurpation, about the dimensions of individual difference which government must generally ignore, and about the required structural characteristics of government decision making processes.[89]

Each of these values is of course normative. Public law–private law distinctions may well be inevitable in modern legal systems, but it is normative arguments concerning the entitlements of the citizen *vis-à-vis* the state which will determine — whether singly or as part of a group of such arguments — their positioning and rigidity from area to area.

---

89   Tribe, *op. cit.* note 29 *supra*, section 18–3, p. 1699.

7

Obsolescence and Renewal: Judicial Review in the Private Sector

John Alder

SUMMARY

The court's supervisory or review jurisdiction derives from basic common law ideas of justice and is a unitary jurisdiction which historically has applied to private bodies exercising monopoly power as well as to public bodies. The introduction of the special application for judicial review procedure has led the courts to drive a wedge between the public and private law aspects of the supervisory jurisdiction. This is unnecessary and undesirable. There are important political and moral differences between the powers of public and private bodies, but these can be met through the flexibility and sensitivity to context that is a prominent feature of the law of judicial review.

INTRODUCTION

Senior members of the legal establishment have recently called for an extension of judicial review into the activities of powerful private bodies.[1] These bodies include trade and professional associations, sports regulatory bodies, and religious and educational organisations, all of which exercise monopolistic powers affecting large numbers of people. Such bodies currently fall outside the scope of the application for judicial review (AJR) procedure governed by the Supreme Court

---

1   Woolf, Lord, *Droit, Public* — English Style [1995] *Public Law* 57, 'Public Law, Private Law: Why the Divide? A Personal View' [1986] *Public Law* 220 at 224–5, 'Judicial Review: A Possible Programme for Reform' [1992] *Public Law* 221 at 236; Borrie, Sir G., 'The Regulation of Public and Private Power' [1989] *Public Law* 552.

Act 1981, s. 31. The reason for this exclusion depends upon the assumption — for which there is no express foundation in the legislation — that the AJR applies only to public law bodies, and upon a restrictive approach to the meaning of public law which excludes bodies that have no direct link with the government irrespective of their public importance and the extent of their power over individuals.[2]

The weight of authority suggests that to count as a public law body, a body must first have a direct connection with the central government. It is not apparently enough that the body exercises important powers affecting the public interest. Secondly, although the cases are not entirely consistent, if the particular power that is being exercised derives formally from contract or the agreement of those subject to it, the matter is one of private law.[3] A broader but overlapping approach is taken in European Union law to the question whether a body is part of the state. This requires that its activities are under the policy control of the central government, and to a lesser extent whether the body has special powers not possessed by ordinary persons.[4] It is therefore a question of degree whether a body that provides a service regulated by government is itself a public body for this purpose. The European aim appears to be the casting of a wide net, while English law's aim appears to be to restrict the application of judicial review. Fear of the floodgates opening seems to be a grave concern.[5]

English law offers no theory as to the nature of the state, or as to the kinds of body or activity properly to be regarded as matters of public law. The question of what activities are appropriately assigned to the private or to the public sector is in English culture a political question on which the constitution offers no guidance. Anything can be assigned to either sector according to the dominant politics of the day, and the boundaries of the public and private sectors are constantly shifting (see Bamforth, Ch. 6 for further theoretical analysis).

It does not follow that once a matter is assigned to the public sector there are no special public law perspectives to be applied. It is a truism that public bodies and public functions may be subject to different moral and legal constraints from private bodies even though the same general law sometimes does duty in both spheres. Public bodies use private law mechanisms such as contract to serve public purposes,[6] and special public law principles are interspersed throughout the law. For example, the law of confidentiality requires a public body to show a public interest in secrecy whereas in private law the public interest acts as a defence to justify disclosure.[7]

---

2   *R* v *Panel on Takeovers and Mergers, ex parte Datafin plc* [1987] QB 815; *R* v *Disciplinary Committee of the Jockey Club, ex parte Aga Khan* [1993] 2 All ER 853.
3   *Ex parte Datafin plc*, note 2 *supra*; *ex parte Aga Khan*, note 2 *supra*.
4   *Foster* v *British Gas* [1990] ECR 1–3313; *British Coal Corporation* v *Smith* [1994] IRLR 342.
5   *R* v *Football Association, ex parte Football League* [1993] 2 All ER 833 at 845.
6   See *Mercury Communications* v *Director General of Telecommunications* [1996] 1 WLR 48; *R* v *Legal Aid Board, ex parte Donn* [1996] 3 All ER 1.
7   *Attorney-General* v *Guardian Newspapers (No. 2)* [1988] 3 All ER 545 at 640.

On the other hand, despite Laws J's *dictum* in *Fewings*,[8] it is *not* peculiar to public law that powers must be specifically conferred by law and that there is no residual freedom. This is also true of corporate bodies in the private sector. Indeed the *ultra vires* doctrine, which is fundamental to judicial review, was in its application to local authorities influenced by 19th-century company law. Also the Crown, a public body, has the same residual common law freedom as an adult human being.

In this chapter I do not intend to deny the validity of a distinction between public and private law, although I am saying that from the perspective of judicial review the distinction is not always important. I want to argue that the scope of judicial review within the AJR procedure governed by RSC ord. 53 should not depend on the distinction between public and private law but should depend on the notion of monopoly power, of which the state is of course a prime example. Within this broad canvas public bodies will often attract special public law principles, just as they do in other branches of the law, but these should not exhaust the concerns of judicial review. Current political fashion favours the use of regulated private bodies to achieve public purposes, so that for this reason as well a narrow approach to the scope of judicial review may be undesirable because the public and the private are intertwined.

I shall argue that, because of a public interest element, some bodies that are formally private bodies should be reviewable under the AJR procedure. I shall suggest that the purpose of judicial review is to provide a remedy against abuse of power by public and private bodies alike. Judicial review exists on the one hand to protect the individual against the abuse of power, and on the other hand to safeguard the general interest in the effective use of power. On this basis the public law–private law distinction should not be the determining factor. It does not follow, of course, that all exercises of private power should be subject to judicial review. Judicial review is a remedy of last resort, so that where there is another private law remedy — for example in contract — judicial review would not be available.

I shall suggest that in their enthusiasm for trying to restrict judicial review to public law, the courts may have underestimated older doctrines relating to the supervisory jurisdiction over private bodies. Until the procedure for judicial review was reformed in 1977, there was a common body of law covering not only natural justice but also abuse of discretion which was applicable both to private and public bodies. This common heritage is sometimes denied, for example, by claiming against the evidence that the doctrine of 'legitimate expectation' is a purely public law doctrine[9] and assuming that unless a matter falls within the AJR or is contractual the individual has no remedy. The legitimate expectation doctrine has been used in private law contexts and the same principles have cross-fertilised each

---

8 *R v Somerset County Council, ex parte Fewings* [1995] 1 All ER 513 at 524.
9 *O'Reilly v Mackman* [1983] 2 AC 237; Forsyth, 'The Provenance and Protection of Legitimate Expectations' (1988) 47 CLJ 238.

other irrespective of the public–private divide[10] (see Craig, Ch. 12, pp. 284 *et seq* for further discussion of legitimate expectation). The courts possess an inherent and unitary supervisory jurisdiction which applies both to public and private bodies. This applies flexibly in relation to particular contexts in respect of which the public–private divide is too crude to be helpful. The AJR is a procedure designed to reflect the special nature of the court's supervisory jurisdiction. By requiring a distinction to be made between public and private law, the courts have artificially separated process from substance.

THE COURTS' SUPERVISORY JURISDICTION

The purpose of the supervisory jurisdiction is not to vindicate rights as such, but to ensure that powers are exercised in accordance with basic standards of legality, fairness and rationality. The public interest in effective decision making is also important, and the judicial review procedure is designed to reflect this in that it relies heavily on the court's discretion at every stage.[11]

In the private law jurisdiction, by contrast, the court determines the rights of the parties *de novo*, for example by interpreting a contract. This can be displaced by an arbitration clause in favour of a quasi-supervisory approach, but in the absence of such a clause the court imposes supervisory jurisdiction by means of the doctrine of implied terms in favour, for example, of the court's view of natural justice. In this context the idea of an implied term seems to be a fiction contrived to bridge the gap between the supervisory and the original jurisdiction, a far more important gap than that alleged to exist between public and private bodies.

Does the public–private divide reflect the concerns of the supervisory jurisdiction? The Law Commission considers that the primary rationale for requiring the use of the AJR procedure is to take account of public interest factors in 'purely public law cases'[12] (see Bamforth, Ch. 6, p. 158). These include ensuring that the law is observed, redressing grievances, and 'the need for speed and certainty in administrative decision making especially where a large section of the community will be affected by a decision'. These factors may also apply to decisions by private bodies. For example, comparing *R* v *Panel on Takeovers and Mergers, ex parte Datafin*[13] (public) and *R* v *Insurance Ombudsman, ex parte Aegon Life Insurance Ltd*[14] (private), it is apparent that both bodies form part of the government's

---

10 For example, *Breen* v *AEU* [1971] All ER 1148; *McInnes* v *Onslow-Fane* [1978] 1 WLR 1520; *Barnard* v *National Dock Labour Board* [1953] 2 QB 18 at 40; *Malloch* v *Aberdeen Corporation* [1971] 1 WLR 1578 at 1596; *Russell* v *Duke of Norfolk* [1949] 1 All ER 109.
11 See *IRC* v *Rossminster* [1980] 1 All ER 80 at 104, and see below p. xx.
12 Law Commission, *Administrative Law: Judicial Review and Statutory Appeals*, Law Com. No. 226, London: HMSO, 1993, para. 3.13.
13 See note 2 *supra*.
14 [1994] COD 426.

regulatory network and that both exercise important powers for the public benefit. The only significant difference between the two is that insurance companies opt by agreement into the ombudsman system, while the Takeover Panel's power is based upon assumed acquiescence. Nevertheless, the insurance ombudsman is not subject to judicial review. Similarly in *R* v *Fernhill Manor School*[15] it was held that a decision by a private school regulated by the government to expel a child was not reviewable even though in breach of natural justice. The child had no remedy in private law either since she had no contract with the school. Conversely, in *R* v *Governers of Haberdashers' Aske's Hatchem College Trust, ex parte Tyrrell*,[16] it was held that the school was sufficiently public law in character to justify judicial review. The key difference between the two cases was that in *Tyrrell* the school was a City Technology College receiving a grant from the Secretary of State which entitled him to place conditions on admissions to the school. In *McLaren* v *Home Office*,[17] Woolf J held that a formal disciplinary procedure should attract judicial review to ensure proper standards of fairness, but limited this to cases where the employee was a public body. He also thought that judicial review should apply where broad policy issues going beyond the rights of the parties were involved. The public dimension of the Jockey Club has been recognised by the courts,[18] although review was refused because the matter was one of private law. By contrast a New Zealand case[19] which concerned a decision by a rugby club to tour South Africa during the apartheid era raised major public interest issues, and the plaintiff was granted an injunction despite having no private law cause of action.

THE INTERPENETRATION OF THE PUBLIC AND THE PRIVATE

Despite the rhetoric of the contracting state and the assumption that in a liberal democracy there is a dividing line between the state and civil society, there are numerous bodies that are intermediate between the state and the private sector. The sectors interpenetrate, the state being one organisation, albeit a very powerful one, among many. These bodies include the voluntary and charitable sectors as well as regulatory and representational bodies. There are no general provisions governing the links between such bodies and the government. Sometimes there is a statutory relationship (e.g., in relation to housing associations): sometimes informal arrangements are preferred (as in the case of the Press Council and the Takeover Panel). Many of these bodies are self-selecting in that they appoint their own membership and determine their own processes. The members of the governing body owe

---

15 [1993] 1 FLR 620.
16 (1994) *The Times*, 19 October. See Batey, E. (1996) 3 *Education and the Law* 191.
17 [1990] ICR 824. See also *Leech* v *Deputy Governor of Parkhurst Prison* [1988] AC 533 at 578.
18 *Ex parte Aga Khan*, note 2 *supra*.
19 *Finnigan* v *New Zealand Rugby Football Club* [1995] NZLR 159.

fiduciary duties, but only to the body itself. Charities and housing associations are regulated by the Charity Commissioners and by the Housing Corporation respectively, but the fact that a body is regulated is not in itself enough to place it within the sphere of public law *vis-à-vis* people over whom it exercises power. Judicial review is a remedy of last resort. The absence of other means of accountability is therefore a reason for seeking to extend the supervisory jurisdiction of the courts to such bodies.[20]

Private power-holding bodies operating for public purposes are an important part of a democracy. They provide checks and balances against a concentration of power in the central state, and supplement the electoral process by providing a mechanism for interest representation. Because they often operate outside formal processes of democratic accountability and are not subject to market or shareholder constraints, there is a need for accountability. This can be partly supplied by the courts, although it is desirable that there be multiple kinds of accountability.

The example of housing associations

Housing associations provide an example of a body constituted in a private law mode, as an industrial and provident society, company or trust, but exercising functions in the public interest with governmental support. Because the powers of a housing association over its tenants or prospective tenants derive from the private law mechanisms of landlord and tenant, it has been held that a housing association is not a public body and therefore not subject even to the substantive principles of judicial review.[21] Housing associations interact with central government in the form of the Housing Corporation which, under the Housing Act 1996, has stringent regulatory powers. They also relate to local authorities, but mainly through non statutory mechanisms such as policy or nomination agreements, or by including local authority representatives on their governing bodies. Housing associations look to private lenders for roughly half their funding and relate to financial institutions through private law commercial devices. The other half of their funding comes from grants made by central government or local authorities. Thus the policy of these ostensibly private bodies can be centrally directed. There are also relationships between housing associations and statutory health and welfare agencies. Housing associations have a statutory duty to assist local authorities in relation to their homelessness responsibilities.[22]

Housing associations exercise considerable power in relation to tenants who are unable to afford to enter the private market. Whether they are sufficiently monopolistic to attract judicial review is debatable, but it does not seem helpful to

---

20   *R* v *Panel on Takeovers and Mergers*, note 2 *supra.*
21   *Peabody Housing Association* v *Greene* (1978) 38 P and CR 644.
22   Housing Act 1996, s. 170.

tackle the problem by seeking to pigeonhole a given activity of a housing association as public or private. The network of vertical and horizontal relationships that characterise housing association activity is intended to form an integrated whole focusing upon the powers entrusted to the association's governing body comprised of self-selected volunteers. Legal accountability of the governing body depends upon private law fiduciary duties which are owed only to the association itself, the membership of which is often coterminous with the governing body which is concerned narrowly with standards of care and conflicts of interest and does not substitute for the supervisory jurisdiction of the courts.

THE COURTS' APPROACH TO THE PUBLIC–PRIVATE DISTINCTION

The search for a requirement of 'publicness' added on to the public importance of the body being challenged is odd, in that the closer the body is to the central government the more likely is it to be subject to judicial review. It could be argued that judicial review is also important when a body is further away from central government. This is because the further a body is removed from democratic controls, the fewer are the alternative channels of redress.

One argument in favour of different treatment for private bodies is the desire for private bodies to be autonomous. It is important in a pluralistic democracy that there be voluntary associations over which the law is not too heavy-handed. However, the court's review jurisdiction is discretionary and highly sensitive to context, as the *Takeover Panel* case itself illustrates.[23] Having held the Takeover Panel to be a public law body susceptible to judicial review, the Court of Appeal went on to emphasise that, because the Takeover Panel was a self-regulating body operating in a context of trust and the need for speed and certainty, the intensity of review should be low. For example, the court would impose enforceable sanctions only in clear cases of unfairness or abuse of power. Similar considerations applied in the private context. In *McInnes* v *Onslow-Fane*[24] for example, Megarry J emphasised that the British Boxing Board of Control carried out its activities in the public interest and that the court should not lightly interfere. Although this was a private law case, the reasoning and underlying concerns are essentially the same as in public law.

Rather than a clear public–private divide, there is what Lord Hailsham in a different but related context described as a 'spectrum of possibilities' open to the court.[25] At one extreme there may be bodies — for example, religious bodies dealing with specialised doctrinal issues (as in *Ex parte Wachman*[26]) — with which

---

23 [1987] QB 815 at 840–42.
24 Note 10 *supra*.
25 *London and Clydeside Estates Ltd* v *Aberdeen DC* [1980] 1 WLR 182.
26 [1992] 1 WLR 1036.

the courts should rarely if ever interfere. Dressing this up in the language of public and private obscures the issue, which is one of justiciability — whether judicial intervention does more harm than good. This applies both in the public and the private sector. Other factors which may affect the level of review in both public and private sectors include the specialised nature of the subject matter, its social or political sensitivity, the expertise and independence to be expected of the decision making agency, the need for speed, and the impact on third parties.[27]

As long ago as 1919, in *Weinberger* v *Inglis*,[28] Lord Parmoor recognised that there is no rigid barrier between the public and the private. He emphasised, in relation to a refusal to re-admit the plaintiff to the Stock Exchange, that where a private body exercises judicial functions affecting a person's 'whole business status' there is a duty similar to that imposed upon public bodies to 'observe the fundamental principles of just action'. In *Weinberger* the House of Lords emphasised the supervisory nature of the court's jurisdiction. Review was not limited to natural justice but included irrelevant considerations and irrationality. As Lord Woolf has pointed out, albeit using the language of public and private,[29] the driving force behind judicial review is the supervisory as opposed to the original nature of the courts' jurisdiction. In both the public and the private sphere this requires deference to the primary decision maker.

I shall not try to analyse in depth the present state of the law as it struggles with the public law–private law distinction. However, before discussing the basis of judicial review of private bodies, it might be helpful to summarise the range of judicial approaches to the public–private distinction, if only to suggest that the search for a general distinction between public and private law may be sterile. The cases are divided. Despite the potentially liberating decision of the Court of Appeal in *R* v *Takeover Panel, ex parte Datafin Plc*,[30] which opened the way to a broadly-based functional approach, the distinction between public law and private law has been made formalistically.

The impact on the public of the decision maker's powers has been discounted in favour of an approach which is a strange mixture of formalism and pragmatism. Statutory bodies are usually regarded as public bodies. Non statutory bodies might also be public bodies if, like the Takeover Panel or the Advertising Standards Authority, they were created to benefit the public at large and are linked to a governmental system of regulation.[31] However, apparently overriding these

27 See below p. xxx. see also *Calvin* v *Carr* [1980] AC 574; *Currie* v *Barton* (1989) *The Times*, 12 February; *R* v *Secretary of State for Defence, ex parte Smith* [1996] 1 All ER 257; *R* v *Visitors to the Inns of Court, ex parte Calder* [1993] 2 All ER 876.
28 [1919] AC 606.
29 *Op. cit.* note 1 *supra*, 1986.
30 Note 2 *supra*.
31 *R* v *Panel on Takeovers and Mergers, ex parte Datafin plc*, note 2 *supra*; *R* v *Advertising Standards Authority* [1993] 2 All ER 202.

concerns, powers, such as those of the Jockey Club, which derive from contract or the consent of those subject to them are private law powers, even where there is a public purpose and even where those subject to them have no real choice but to submit.[32] This formalistic use of contract is odd since contractual devices are used by government bodies to achieve public purposes, and in that context the courts have taken a more flexible approach which requires them to analyse the substance of the issue to see whether there are public policy implications.[33] Where there is a contract the citizen may have a private law remedy, but where there is neither a contract nor a governmental connection the citizen may be without remedy at all. In the *Aga Khan* case this possibility received a mixed response. Bingham MR and Farquharson LJ left the matter open, while Hoffman LJ appeared to face the prospect with equanimity.[34] In seeking the elusive quality of 'publicness', different judges give different weight to and favour different permutations of the basic ingredients of statute, government connection, contract, consent and public interest. The notion of public interest, in particular, is unreliable. As I tried to show in the previous section, public interest also plays a part in private law. Bodies such as the Jockey Club and the Takeover Panel — the functions of which benefit a 'private' constituency of people involved in the industry and also the general public in helping to ensure quality standards — are not convincingly segregated merely because, in the case of the Jockey Club, the government has decided not to play a direct role itself.

Some judges have followed the formalistic approach with reluctance — for example, being held back from extending the AJR process to the Jockey Club only by the weight of authority.[35] Other judges have seized upon a restrictive approach with relative enthusiasm, being motivated by the fear of a flood of applications.[36] It has been remarked many times that contracts made by large monopolistic bodies acting without the market are closely analogous to legislation, there being no real element of agreement, just as in *Datafin* submission to the Takeover Panel was voluntary only in theory. The Takeover Panel and the Jockey Club are similar in terms of the impact of their powers and their public importance. Both serve public purposes and benefit those involved in the industry. The former is reviewable and the latter is not, on the basis of the lines of communication between the Takeover Panel and the government.

---

32   *Ex parte Aga Khan*, note 2 *supra*; see also *ex parte Datafin plc*, note 2 *supra* at 838 and *CCSU* v *Ministry for the Civil Service* [1985] AC 374 at 409.

33   See *McLaren* v *Home Office* [1990] ICR 824 at 836; *R* v *Lord Chancellor's Department, ex parte Nangle* [1992] 1 All ER 897 at 908 and cases cited in note 5 *supra*. Cf. Arrowsmith, S., 'Judicial Review and the Contractual Powers of Public Authorities' (1990) 106 LQR 277. See further below.

34   [1993] 2 All ER 853 at 867, 873, 875–76.

35   *R* v *Jockey Club, ex parte Massingberd-Mundy* [1993] 2 All ER 207; *R* v *Disciplinary Committee of the Jockey Club,* ex parte RAM Racecourses Ltd [1993] 2 All ER 225.

36   *R* v *Football Association, ex parte Football League* [1993] 2 All ER 833. See also *R* v *Code of Practice Committee of the British Pharmaceutical Association* [1991] Admin LR 697 at 718.

In *R v Jockey Club, ex parte RAM Ltd Racecourses,*[37] Simon Brown J put the argument in favour of a unified supervisory jurisdiction. He emphasised the flexibility of the judicial review procedure and the public importance of private regulatory bodies. He said of the older cases applying principles of fairness to private bodies, that 'had they arisen today and not some years ago [they] would have found a natural home in judicial review proceedings'. In *R v Jockey Club, ex parte Massingbird-Mundy,*[38] Roch J (as he was then) would have extended judicial review to the Jockey Club's non contractual powers, but he too felt constrained — even if not strictly bound — by the tenor of previous cases. Roch J clearly found the distinction between contractual and non contractual powers less than compelling. Indeed, judicial attempts to draw the line between the public and the private without considering the substantive law seem inadequate. The decision of Simon Brown J in *R v Chief Rabbi, ex parte Wachman*[39] illustrates this. A rabbi applied for judicial review of a disciplinary decision of the Chief Rabbi to suspend him from rabbinical activities. This was a matter of considerable public interest and concern but was held not to be susceptible to judicial review. It would have been open to the court to argue — as it did in public law with a University Visitor in *Page v Hull University Visitor*[40] — that the special nature of the powers in question meant that for reasons connected with autonomy the matter should be at least partly non justiciable. However, the decision in *Wachman* was based upon the proposition that there was no governmental connection with the Chief Rabbi, either actual or implied. Simon Brown J rightly emphasised the dangers inherent in the courts straying into religious disputes and crossing the boundaries between church and state, so that the categorisation as private law seems superfluous.

Sometimes the courts have used the concept of surrogate government, in the sense that if the body in question did not exist the state would have to step in.[41] This test has never been decisive and seems too speculative to be of much help except to emphasise the importance of the body concerned. A similar approach has sometimes been taken in the USA for the purpose of protecting fundamental rights by extending the idea of 'state action', but has been condemned as incoherent.[42]

In contrast to their rigid attitude towards non governmental bodies, the courts have been flexible in deciding whether a decision of a central government body falls within the AJR or whether the AJR must be used. Activities which are regarded as in substance analogous to private activities have been excluded, and the exceptions to the 'exclusivity' doctrine of *O'Reilly v Mackman*[43] have been

---

37   *Op. cit.* note 35 *supra.*
38   *Op. cit.* note 35 *supra.*
39   [1993] 2 All ER 249.
40   [1993] 1 All ER 97.
41   *Ex parte Aga Khan,* note 2 *supra,* at 866; *R v Football Association,* note 36 *supra,* at 848–9.
42   See *Shelley v Kraemer* 334 US 1 (1948); *Burton v Wilmington Parking Authority* 365 US 715 (1961); *Flagg Bros v Brooks* 436 US 149 (1978); *cf* (1982) U Pa L Rev 1278.
43   [1983] 2 AC 237.

exploited to allow proceedings begun in other courts to be continued unless to do so would be an abuse of process.[44] Only where there is no possible private law cause of action — admittedly a contested zone — do the courts insist that the citizen resorts to the AJR, reducing the scope of the AJR to a truism. If private bodies were to fall within the AJR there would therefore be scope for flexibility where the issues raised were not appropriate to the supervisory jurisdiction. In this context the Law Commission's proposal that there should be transfers into as well as transfers out of the AJR process is a useful one.[45]

In the governmental context, contracts have not been decisive and the courts have been flexible and pragmatic. In *R* v *Legal Aid Board, ex parte Donn*,[46] a decision to grant a legal aid franchise to a firm of solicitors was held to be a public law matter because of the public consequences of the contract. In *McLaren* v *Home Office*,[47] an employment issue was held on its facts to be a private law matter, but Woolf LJ (as he was then) suggested that where the case raised general public issues, going beyond the interests of the particular parties, an employment contract could be dealt with as a matter of public law.

The Law Commission has remarked that private rights 'trump' the policy considerations that justify the use of the AJR.[48] This may make sense in the context of basic human rights or property rights, but contracts are often used merely as technical tools for the implementation of government policies. For example, *Mercury Communications* v *Director General of Telecommunications*[49] was treated as a private law case because the Director General implemented his public regulatory responsibilities by means of requirements imposed in a contract between British Telecom and Mercury. Admittedly this was an 'exclusivity' case. Mercury could, apparently, have brought judicial review proceedings. In *Mercury*, the House of Lords took the pragmatic approach that the forum of choice should be followed unless it was clearly inappropriate, but it seems odd that the apparently grave reasons for the distinction between public and private law given by Lord Diplock in *O'Reilly* v *Mackman*, to do with keeping people off the government's back, should be discounted because of the way a decision making process happens to be structured.

In the case of private bodies, many decisions — for example, a refusal to admit a person to membership or a refusal to grant a licence — do not involve existing private rights. There is therefore no private law cause of action. Unless judicial review were available the citizen would have no remedy.

---

44   *Roy* v *Kensington, Chelsea and Westminster Family Practitioner Committee* [1992] 1 All ER 705.
45   *Op. cit.* note 12, *supra*, paras 3.16 to 3.23.
46   Note 6 *supra*.
47   Note 33 *supra*.
48   *Op. cit.* note 12 *supra*, para. 3. 14.
49   Note 6 *supra*.

THE SUBSTANTIVE LAW OF JUDICIAL REVIEW

Until the AJR was invented, the courts applied the same body of doctrine to private and public bodies without distinguishing between them as such. For example, despite being hijacked by Lord Diplock for the purpose of demonstrating public law jurisprudence, the doctrine of legitimate expectation does not provide a remedy only in public law. The legitimate expectation doctrine has been used as an aspect of fairness in private law cases. Indeed in *Breen* v *AEU*,[50] a private law case, Lord Denning MR, employing the doctrine, was moved to remark that 'we now have a developed system of administrative law'. Judicial review principles are broad, and their application depends on the particular context. The existence of a contractual relationship is only one of many factors affecting the level of natural justice. In *Calvin* v *Carr*,[51] for example, the Privy Council, in deciding whether a failure by the Australian Jockey Club to give a hearing at first instance was cured by an appeal hearing, took into account the voluntary nature of the arrangement. The desirability of a body being independent and its decisions final has also been stressed in both public and private contexts.[52] The AJR procedure is designed to give the court considerable flexibility of response, and arguably this would be useful in the case of private bodies. I shall discuss this later.

The distinction between governmental and private bodies does not govern the scope of the substantive law. The supervisory jurisdiction over private bodies has included error of law unreasonableness, irrelevant considerations, fettering discretion and irrationality, although natural justice cases have pre-dominated. The scope of review over private bodies has been assimilated with that over public bodies.[53] The level of review is based upon the seriousness of the decision, the nature of the decision making body and the availability of other channels of redress. At one end of the spectrum a purely domestic or commercial relationship, or a power that does not seriously disadvantage a citizen, may fall outside the court's supervisory jurisdiction.[54] In the middle of the spectrum, decisions of clubs and bodies not affecting vital interests may be subject to a limited level of review based upon *ultra vires*, natural justice and good faith.[55] In cases involving higher stakes, such as bodies controlling livelihood or affecting the public interest, principles of reasonableness, fettering discretion, errors of interpretation and relevance may apply, including a stricter application of natural justice.[56]

---

50   [1971] 1 All ER 1148 at 1153–4. See also *McInnes* v *Onslow-Fane*, note 10 *supra*.
51   [1980] AC 574.
52   *McInnes* v *Onslow-Fane*, note 10 *supra*; *R* v *Panel on Takeovers and Mergers* [1987] QB 815 at 839–42.
53   *Breen* v *AEU*, note 50 *supra*, at 1153–54.
54   *Currie* v *Barton*, note 27 *supra*, but see *R* v *Tower Hamlets London Borough Council, ex parte Chetnic Developments* [1988] AC 858 at 872.
55   *Breen* v *AEU*, note 50 *supra*; *cf. Faramus* v *Film Artistes Association* [1964] AC 925, *Dawkins* v *Antrobus* (1881) 17 ChD 615 at 630.
56   *Lee* v *Showmans Guild* [1952] 2 QB 329; *Nagle* v *Fielden* [1966] 2 QB 633; *Abbot* v *Sullivan* [1952] 1 KB 189; *Weinberger* v *Inglis* [1919] AC 606 at 626, 636.

The basis of judicial review

I have tried to argue, first, that there is nothing in the political or conceptual basis of the law to limit judicial review to public law matters; secondly that the courts have not developed a coherent rationale for the purpose of identifying a public law issue; and thirdly that the substantive law of judicial review is highly context-sensitive so as to respond to the many different forms of decision making power, both public and private.

Underlying the proposition that the judicial review process does not apply to private bodies is the view expressed by Hoffman LJ in the *Aga Khan* case,[57] that the court's power to intervene in the affairs of a private body depends upon the legal peg of a private law cause of action. This is not true of the application for judicial review, which focuses upon the nature of the activity being challenged subject to a broad and discretionary *locus standi* requirement.

There is a corresponding debate in public law as to whether the *ultra vires* doctrine is the basis of judicial review, or whether judicial review is a free-standing creation of the common law albeit subject to parliamentary supremacy[58] (see Donson, Ch. 15 generally). These issues are important because they affect the remedies available to the citizen. For example, without a private law peg, damages cannot be awarded,[59] and the grounds of judicial review and the consequences of an unlawful act are affected by the *ultra vires* theory. It is common ground, of course, that the *ultra vires* doctrine is a part of the court's supervisory jurisdiction. However, the *ultra vires* doctrine cannot explain the modern extension of judicial review to non statutory bodies such as the Takeover Panel. Indeed it is sometimes argued that the *ultra vires* doctrine is inadequate even in the setting of statutory powers. For example, the corollary of the *ultra vires* doctrine — that an *ultra vires* decision is a nullity — is not applied strictly, at least in judicial review proceedings,[60] and many of the grounds of judicial review can only by means of a 'fairy tale' or 'fig leaf' be regarded as based on parliamentary intention.[61] An equivalent fairy tale has been told in relation to private bodies, when it is argued that the application of the court's supervisory jurisdiction in all its subtlety and

---

57 [1993] 2 All ER 853 at 875–76.
58 See Oliver, D., 'Is the *ultra vires* rule the basis of judicial review?' [1987] PL 543; Forsythe, C., 'Of Fig Leaves and Fairy Tales: The *Ultra Vires* Doctrine, the Sovereignty of Parliament and Judicial Review' [1996] CLJ 12; Woolf, note 1 *supra*.
59 *Abbot* v *Sullivan*, note 56 *supra*; *Dunlop* v *Whoolhara Municipal Council* [1981] 1 All ER 1202.
60 see *Crédit Suisse* v *Allerdale District Council* [1996] 4 All ER 129 at 156 — private law proceedings, see below p. 179; *R* v *Panel on Takeovers and Mergers* [1987] QB 815 at 840.
61 See Woolf, *op. cit.* note 58 *supra* at 65–6; Laws, Sir J., 'Law and Democracy' [1995] *Public Law* 72 at 79, Oliver, *op. cit.* note 58 *supra*; *cf. Page* v *Hull University Visitor* [1993] AC 680 at 701; *Council of Civil Service Unions* v *Minister for the Civil Service* [1984] 3 All ER 935 at 950; *Mercury Energy Co. Ltd* v *Electricity Corp. of New Zealand* [1994] 2 NZLR 385 at 388; *Cook* [1988] NZLR 158.

contextual sensitivity depends upon an implied term in a contract formed by the governing rules of the body in question.

Neither the *ultra vires* doctrine nor contract theory is capable of providing an adequate explanation of the court's supervisory jurisdiction. In the absence of a written constitution, the supervisory jurisdiction can derive only from the inherent nature of the common law. In *Nagle* v *Fielden*,[62] for example, a private law case, Salmon LJ said 'one of the principal functions of our courts is whenever possible to protect the individual from injustice and oppression', and Danckwerts LJ said 'the courts have the right to protect the right of a person to work when it is being prevented by the dictatorial exercise of powers by a body which holds a monopoly'.[63] The same sentiments were expressed in a public law context by Lloyd LJ in the *Datafin* case.[64] He distinguished the Takeover Panel from a club essentially on the basis that a club has less power: '[The Panel] wields enormous power. It has a giant's strength. The fact that it is self-regulating makes it not less but more appropriate that it be subject to judicial review.' It is significant that in deciding that the AJR procedure should apply to the Takeover Panel, Lloyd LJ regarded the governmental connection point only as a fall-back position.

The continuing debate in US jurisprudence over the basis of judicial review since *Marbury* v *Madison*[65] shows that *ultra vires* cannot in itself justify judicial intervention. In *Marbury*, the US Supreme Court decided that the courts could intervene in respect of the constitutionality of a government act even though the Constitution did not expressly provide for judicial review. It does not logically follow that because a body exceeds statutory limits, its actions are invalid in a sense relevant to a court. A further assumption, even if this is only an appeal to a theory about the inherent judicial function, must justify judicial intervention. Similarly, even if we concede for the moment that the powers of a private body depend on contract, it does not follow that the *court's* powers also derive from the law of contract. *Marbury* depended upon a particular political theory about the place of the courts in the constitutional system and was a manifestation of the political conflict between Jeffersonian republicans and the Marshall court of the day.[66]

In the English context, as we have seen, the same substantive principles of judicial review have been applied to public and private bodies. The principles themselves vary with the context between different kinds of public body as well as between public and private bodies, but display a coherent underlying structure common to both, embodying the concepts of jurisdiction, of natural justice, of good

---

62   Note 56 *supra*, at 654–5.
63   *Ibid.* at 650.
64   [1987] 1 All ER 564 at 582.
65   1 Cranch 137 (1803). See Rakove, J.N., 'The Origins of Judicial Review: A Plea for New Contexts' (1997) 49 *Stanford LR* 1031.
66   Gunther, G., and Dowling N., *Constitutional Law Cases and Materials* (Mineola: NY Foundation Press, 1970).

faith and rationality. The underlying rationale in respect of both public and private bodies is arguably the court's power to do justice by protecting individuals against the abuse of monopoly power, whether that power be public or private.[67] Because the common law derives from the superior courts and not from Parliament, it is independent of the state and its content is potentially unlimited.

It has been suggested that the 'self validating jurisdictional power of the superior courts' gives them 'a corresponding responsibility for the individual citizen rather than for government (or Government)'.[68] In *R* v *Barker*,[69] Lord Mansfield said of *mandamus*, which is an important judicial review remedy, that 'it was introduced to prevent disorder from a failure of justice and defect of police. Therefore it ought to be used upon all occasions where the law has established no specific remedy and where in justice and good government there ought to be one'. Consistently with this, in the *Aga Khan* case,[70] both Bingham LJ and Farquharson LJ were prepared to bridge the public law–private law divide by admitting the possibility that a non governmental body might be susceptible to judicial review where there was no redress in private law. This reflects the broad and self-justifying common law basis for intervention.

Confusion over the nature of the court's supervisory power is compounded by confusion between the questions of what remedies are appropriate and the court's power to intervene as such. For example, the debate about the scope of the AJR has been influenced by a belief that the scope of the declaration and injunction in the AJR was limited to that of the prerogative orders. The latter have always been purely public law remedies. The knot tying the two groups of remedies has now been cut,[71] so that there is no conceptual reason why the AJR should not apply to private bodies using the declaration or injunction.

The basis of the private law jurisdiction
The idea that the court's supervisory jurisdiction over private bodies must be anchored to a private law cause of action has forced the courts to use strained and artificial contrivances. From the middle of the last century until the 1930s, property theory was in the ascendant. This was premised upon the members of an organisation having a future right to the assets of the organisation in the event of its solvent dissolution.[72] The property theory had a strong air of fiction and the relationship between the proprietary right and the remedies which were needed was

---

67 *Ipswich Tailors' Case* (1614) 11 Co Rep 534; *Dr Bonham's Case* (1610) 8 Co Rep 534; *Entick* v *Carrington* (1765) 19 St Tr 1030. Hale *Treatise de Portibus Maribus* 1 Harg 1 Tr 78 (1787).
68 See Detmold, M.J., *Courts and Administrators*, (London: Weidenfeld & Nicholson, 1989, p. ix and Ch. 6.
69 (1762) 3 Burr 1265 at 1267.
70 Note 2 *supra*.
71 *Equal Opportunities Commission* v *Secretary of State for Employment* [1994] 1 All ER 910.
72 *Baird* v *Wells* (1890) 44 ChD 480, *Rigby* v *Connol* (1880) 14 ChD 480. See Lloyd, D., 'The Right to Work' [1957] *Current Legal Problems* 36, (1950) 13 MLR 281, (1958) 21 MLR 661; Summers, C.W., 'Legal Limitations on Union Discipline' (1951) 64 *Harv Law Rev* 1049.

unclear. In *Young* v *Ladies Imperial Club*,[73] for example, property had to be supplemented by the notion of implied contract. There were also flirtations with fiduciary duties[74] and interference with reputation[75] as the basis of the court's intervention.

From the 1930s, property theory was replaced by a free standing-contract theory under which the rules of an organisation could be regarded as a contract between the organisation and the members if the organisation was corporate, or, less convincingly, as a contract between the individual members if the organisation was an unincorporated association. Into this contract — rather as in the case of the *ultra vires* doctrine — the courts, using the concept of implied terms, could imply principles of natural justice, good faith or rationality. For example, a distinction was made between social clubs and professional or trade bodies which exercised monopoly power over people's livelihoods.[76] Natural justice would be implied only into the latter.

The contract notion was artificial in that it made the members of the committee, the decision of which was being challenged, agents for all the members, so that the plaintiff was attempting to sue himself.[77] The contract was also problematic when the body in question was a subsidiary of another body. In *Currie* v *Barton*,[78] Scott LJ refused the invitation to untangle this kind of situation 'much as the academic lawyers might enjoy some words from this court'. *Faramus* v *Film Artistes Association*[79] is a case where an explicit contrast was made between the powers of a domestic body as such and the 'by-laws' of a corporation, and illustrates a clash between the supervisory and contractual models of the court's powers. Lord Evershed based the court's power to intervene on the narrow ground of restraint of trade. Lord Pearce, however, recognised that unreasonableness can apply to domestic bodies on the grounds of public policy overriding any contract. In *Lee* v *Showmans Guild of Great Britain*,[80] Scrutton LJ emphasised the supervisory nature of the court's function. The legislative nature of what are formally contractual rules has often been emphasised, as has the policy basis — in the need to control monopolies — of the court's intervention.[81]

---

73 [1920] 2 KB 523. see also *Osborne* v *Amalgamated Society of Railway Servants* [1911] 1 Ch 540, at 562; *Weinberger* v *Inglis* (1918) 1 Ch 517, at 543, 547, 555.

74 Weinberger and Inglis, *supra*.

75 *Fisher* v *Keane* (1878) 11 ChD 353.

76 *Lee* v *Showmans Guild of Great Britain* [1952] 2 QB 329; *Russell* v *Duke of Norfolk* [1949] 1 All ER 145; *Enderby Town Football Club* v *FA* [1971] 1 All ER 215; *Abbot* v *Sullivan* [1952] 1 All ER 226; *Byrne* v *Kinematograph Renters Society* [1958] 1 WLR 762.

77 *Bonsor* v *Musicians Union* [1954] Ch 479.

78 Note 27 *supra*.

79 [1964] AC 925.

80 Note 76 *supra*.

81 For example *Lee* v *Showmans Guild*, note 76 *supra*, at 343, 347, 350; *Enderby Town Football Club* v *FA*, note 76, *supra*; *Bonsor* v *Musicians' Union*, note 77 *supra*; *Davies* v *Carew-Pole* [1956] 1 WLR 833; *Abbot* v *Sullivan*, note 76 *supra*; cf *R* v *Disciplinary Committee of the Jockey Club, ex parte Aga Khan* [1993] 2 All ER 853 at 867.

The contract theory raises more fundamental problems The notion of a contractual jurisdiction is inconsistent with the nature of the court's supervisory jurisdiction. A supervisory court does not determine the rights of the parties as such, although this may occasionally be the effect of its decision. The court acts as a quality control mechanism, focusing upon the decision making process so as to ensure that the decision conforms to the remit given to the body and to common law concepts of fairness, good faith and rationality. The provisions of the AJR which restrict the parties power to introduce evidence of primary fact fortify this. This might answer an objection that has been made to extending judicial review to contractual powers, that there are adequate remedies available by means of a declaration or an injunction in private law. Assuming that this is true, nevertheless in substance the issues will be dealt with as supervisory issues[82] so that it would be preferable to stick to the forum which is tailor-made for the supervisory jurisdiction.

The contract theory raises difficulties in respect of remedies, for example, whether or not for the purposes of damages a term could be implied that individual decision makers would not act unfairly.[83] This is a different issue from the award of a declaration that a decision is *ultra vires* the contract. The notion of a void act in the contractual context is also difficult, since a decision in breach of contract may still have legal effect but a void decision (being outside the contract) would not attract contractual remedies.[84] The flexible declaratory judgment which in judicial review cases does not require a private law cause of action therefore serves a useful purpose.

Conflicts have arisen between the implied term theory and express terms in the contract that purport to exclude, for example, the rules of natural justice. The courts have disagreed as to whether a contract can exclude natural justice. The power to override provisions excluding natural justice has been justified on the basis of public policy, sometimes by analogy with the doctrine of restraint of trade.[85] The conflict between the supervisory and original models of the court's role lies at the heart of this issue, albeit muddied by the use of the restraint of trade doctrine. *Enderby Town Football Club* v *Football Association*,[86] however, was not a restraint of trade case. The Court of Appeal held that, in the circumstances, fairness did not entitle the club to legal representation before an FA tribunal, but Lord Denning MR and Fenton Atkinson LJ, following the legislative model of such institutions, would have struck out a rule that purported to exclude legal

---

82 For example *R* v *BBC, ex parte Lavelle* [1983] 1 All ER 241.
83 *Abbot* v *Sullivan*, note 76 *supra*; *Edwards* v *SOGAT* [1970] 3 All ER 689. *Cf.* Lloyd, D., 'Damages for Wrongful Expulsion from a Trade Union' (1956) 19 MLR 121.
84 See *White* v *Kuzych* [1951] AC 585; *Lawlor* v *Union of Post Office Workers* [1965] Ch 712 at 734.
85 For example, *Lee* v *Showmans Guild of Great Britain* [1952] 2 QB 329 at 343, 347, 350; *Enderby Town FC* v *FA*, note 76 *supra*; *Maclean* v *Workers' Union* [1929] 1 Ch 602 at 623–4.
86 Note 76 *supra*.

representation absolutely. Cairns LJ would not have done so, although he appeared to agree that a rule excluding natural justice as such would be invalid. In *Lawlor v Union of Post Office Workers*,[87] a case involving expulsion from a trade union, Ungoed Thomas J took a private law approach. Natural justice could be ousted by contract although very clear language would be necessary to do so. The court's jurisdiction itself could not be excluded by contract, but a contract could require the exhaustion of domestic remedies.

This question of exhaustion of domestic remedies illustrates a difference between the supervisory approach under the AJR procedure and in its private law guise. In private law it seems that, unless there is a rule requiring exhaustion of domestic remedies, a plaintiff is absolutely entitled to go straight to the courts. Under the AJR this is a matter for the court's discretion. Judicial review is a remedy of last resort and will normally be refused if there is an alternative, equally appropriate remedy available.[88] Given the goal of autonomy within a domestic body, the latter approach is surely preferable even in a private law context.

The contractual theory also raises the problem that was encountered in the Jockey Club cases, and on which conflicting views were expressed — that of decisions made outside a contractual framework, for example, a decision to refuse a person membership of a body where membership gives access to an important resource, or where there is no agreement to accept the rules of the organisation as such. The problem here is that there is no private law cause of action on which to hang a challenge. In *Edwards v SOGAT*,[89] for example, Sachs LJ distinguished between expulsion cases and admission cases in relation to the irrationality principle. In *Datafin*[90] there was no contract as such and in a strict sense submission to the takeover panel's jurisdiction was voluntary. In practice, however, all who wished to participate in takeovers or mergers had to accept the jurisdiction. Had the Takeover Panel been classified as a private body the citizen would have had no remedy. In the *Aga Khan*[91] case, by contrast, there was a contract; but this is not always so in relation to the Jockey Club, for example where a person is refused membership. In each case the need for supervision by the courts is the same irrespective of the technical relationship between the decision maker and the individual and the various permutations of governmental link. In *Aga Khan*, Bingham MR recognised the anomaly of this and left open the possibility of judicial review, but Hoffman LJ was not willing to 'patch up the remedies available against domestic bodies by pretending that they are organs of government'.[92] The artificial device of treating submission to the jurisdiction of the decision making

---

87 Note 84 *supra.*
88 *R v Merseyside Chief Constable, ex parte Calverly* [1986] 1 QB 424.
89 Note 83 *supra.*
90 Note 2 *supra.*
91 Note 2 *supra.*
92 *Ibid.*, at 876.

body as an implied contract has sometimes been used, thus exposing the poverty of the contractual rationale.[93]

In a few private law cases — of which *Nagle v Fielden*,[94] an interlocutory decision, is probably the most important — the courts have based their supervisory jurisdiction upon the general notion of fairness, or upon the public policy goal of protecting people against the abuse of monopoly power, without requiring a contractual basis. In *Nagle v Fielden*, drawing upon a stream of authority going back to the 17th century,[95] the Court of Appeal held that the test of unreasonableness could be applied to a Jockey Club decision to refuse to grant trainers' licences to women. Both Salmon and Danckwerts LJJ emphasised that the juridical basis of the court's power to intervene lay in the inherent common law jurisdiction to protect individuals. This has been linked specifically to the supposed existence of a 'right to livelihood', and indeed has been limited to that kind of case. However, if it is accepted that the supervisory jurisdiction is an inherent jurisdiction based upon the court's fundamental duty to do justice, and applying to public and private bodies alike, the limitation to livelihood seems unnecessary. There is no reason why other basic interests should not be protected. In *R v Jockey Club, ex parte RAM Racecourses*,[96] Simon Brown J linked this right to work jurisdiction with the AJR, treating cases such as *Nagle v Fielden*[97] as evidence of a unity between the public and private law supervisory jurisdictions.

The monopoly theory in its private law setting faces the problem of remedy. A declaration was made in *Nagle v Fielden*,[98] but in the light of *Gouriet v Union of Post Office Workers*[99] it seems that, except in judicial review proceedings, a person seeking a declaration or injunction must establish either the existence of a private law right or special damage. It is not clear whether the right to work qualifies as a 'private right' in the strict sense. However, a person whose interests have been specifically affected by a decision might fall within the special damage category. In *Royal College of Nursing v DHSS*,[100] the College challenged a DHSS circular in private law proceedings. The circular concerned the possible criminal liability of nurses who assisted in abortions. Woolf J (as he was then) thought that judicial review proceedings would have been more appropriate, but held that he had jurisdiction because the College had a special interest in looking after its members' interests. This was endorsed by the House of Lords.

---

93   *Davies v Carew-Pole*, note 81 *supra*.
94   [1966] 2 QB 633. See also *McInnes v Onslow-Fane* [1978] 1 WLR 1528; *Weinberger v Inglis*, note 73 *supra*.
95   *Ipswich Tailors' Case* (1614) 11 Co Rep 534; *Allnut v Inglis* (1810) 12 East 527; *R v Benchers of Lincoln's Inn* (1825) 4 B and C 855. See Craig, P.P., 'Constitutions, Property and Regulation' [1991] *Public Law* 538.
96   [1993] 2 All ER 225.
97   Note 94 *supra*.
98   *Ibid*.
99   [1978] AC 435.
100 [1981] AC 800. See also *Finnigan v New Zealand Rugby Club*, note 19 *supra*.

Can the AJR extend to private bodies?

I have tried to show that the court's supervisory jurisdiction over public and private bodies has the same legal basis, this being the court's inherent duty to supervise the activities of monopolistic bodies affecting important interests. There is nothing expressly in the legislation governing the AJR that limits its scope to public law matters. The application is for 'judicial review' and is designed so that no specific cause of action is required. Instead there is a leave requirement and the need to show sufficient interest in the matters to which the application relates. The court has a choice of remedies including the prerogative orders, which have a public law history, and the declaration and injunction, which have a private law history but which also apply in public law.

The Law Commission in its 1976 Report,[101] which led to the introduction of the AJR, took the view that judicial review was a matter of public law but left the matter to be decided on a case by case basis. In its 1995 review of the operation of the AJR, the Law Commission broadly approved the 'exclusivity' doctrine of *O'Reilly* v *Mackman*,[102] but surprisingly did not discuss the more fundamental question of the boundaries of public law.

The initial justification for excluding private bodies from the AJR was a fixation with the prerogative orders. The AJR process is essentially a reformed prerogative order process, bringing the declaration and injunction under the same procedural umbrella and making some reforms in the process. These latter remedies previously applied both to public and private bodies, whereas it has always been the case that the prerogative orders lie only against public bodies. Judges were therefore persuaded that, under the AJR, the declaration and injunction were available only against bodies sufficiently public to fall within the prerogative orders.[103] The legislation itself treats the prerogative orders merely as a factor that must be taken into account in determining the scope of the declaration and injunction.[104] The fallacy that the two groups of remedies must be tied together has now been exposed.[105] There is, therefore, no necessary reason to limit the AJR to public bodies.

The AJR has the advantage of a flexible approach to remedies that, first, avoids the need to establish a private law cause of action and, secondly, can select the most appropriate remedy or refuse a remedy in its discretion where the justice of the case requires. The recent decision of the Court of Appeal in *Crédit Suisse* v

---

101 Law Com No. 83, London: HMSO, 1976.
102 [1983] 2 AC 237; Law Com No. 226, p. 24.
103 *Law* v *National Greyhound Racing Club* [1983] 3 All ER 139; *R* v *BBC, ex parte Lavelle*, note 82 *supra*.
104 Supreme Court Act 1981, s. 31(2).
105 *R* v *Equal Opportunities Commission, ex parte Secretary of State for Employment* [1994] 1 All ER 910 at 919.

Allerdale District Council[106] provides a good illustration of the different approaches of private and public law to the question of remedy. The plaintiff claimed
in private law against a local authority under a guarantee which the local authority
had given in respect of a loan made by the plaintiff to a company. The company
had been formed by the local authority in order to finance a leisure complex by
avoiding statutory limitations upon its own borrowing powers. The defence was
that the arrangement was *ultra vires*. The authority was thus relying upon its own
illegality. The local authority's arrangement was held to be *ultra vires* because the
existence of a statutory financial regime meant that the authority had no capacity
to enter into other arrangements. The guarantee was therefore void against the
Council and could not be enforced. Since this was not a public law action the
court's hands were tied. One result of this strict approach is that financial
institutions are likely to be wary of dealing with local authorities.

Had the matter arisen in a judicial review context, the court would have had
more options. Even where a decision is *ultra vires* the court has a discretion not
to give relief or to give selective relief, despite the conceptual incoherence thereby
involved. This applies even where a body acts without capacity. The *locus
classicus* is probably the judgment of Donaldson MR in *R* v *Panel on Takeovers
and Mergers, ex parte Datafin plc*,[107] where he referred to:

> a very special feature of public law decisions such as those of the panel, namely
> that however wrong they may be, however lacking in jurisdiction they may be, they
> subsist and remain fully effective unless and until they are set aside by a court of
> competent jurisdiction. Furthermore, the court has an ultimate discretion whether
> to set them aside and may refuse to do so in the public interest notwithstanding that
> it holds and declares the decision to have been made *ultra vires*.

As Cane pointed out in discussing the first instance decision in *Allerdale*,[108] there
is a tension within the *ultra vires* doctrine between the goal of protecting the
individual against an abuse of power and that of protecting the public against an
improper use of public money. This is equally true of public money entrusted to
private bodies such as housing associations. There are also tensions between
protecting the victim of an abuse of power and protecting third parties who rely
upon official action, avoiding disruption to the administrative process, and
safeguarding the autonomy and responsiveness of decision makers. Unlike private
law, the AJR process is specifically designed to cater for these concerns.

It is submitted that these protective provisions and the more flexible approach
of the AJR are appropriate in relation to private monopolistic bodies as well as to

---

106   [1996] 4 All ER 129.
107   [1987] QB 815 at 840.
108   [1994] 110 LQR 514 at 517.

public bodies. They reinforce the supervisory nature of the court's jurisdiction and respect the autonomy of the decision maker. For example, the court's discretionary powers to control the use of evidence of primary fact and to require internal remedies to be exhausted seem equally applicable to private bodies, as do the flexible time limit provisions of the AJR. This was recognised by Slade LJ in *Law v National Greyhound Racing Club*,[109] even though, because of the mystique of contract, he held that the AJR could not apply. Where a private law cause of action is essential to the case, a plaintiff can still bring proceedings in an ordinary court under the exception to the *O'Reilly* v *Mackman* principle recognised in *Roy* v *Kensington, Chelsea and Westminster Family Practitioner Committee*.[110]

Apart from the practical issue of the judicial case-load, which is irrelevant to the question of what is desirable in principle, two main objections can be raised to the extension of the AJR to private bodies. The first objection, based upon a remark of Lord Donaldson in *Datafin*, is that an aspect of public law decisions is that 'such decisions affect a very wide public which will not be parties to the dispute and that their interests have to be taken into account as much as those of the immediate disputants'. This is not necessarily true in the case of private bodies. However, this is not necessarily true even in the case of public bodies and may sometimes apply to private bodies. The rationale for the court's intervention into the affairs of monopolistic private bodies is that the monopoly is impressed with the public interest in order to prevent an abuse of power.

The other main argument strikes at the supervisory jurisdiction itself. The argument asserts that the autonomy of private bodies should be respected. Voluntary bodies are a crucial aspect of the checks and balances necessary in a democracy and should not, even indirectly, be treated as part of the state. It is submitted, first, that this argument goes too far in that it denies the possibility of the accountability of voluntary bodies. This is also an essential feature of democracy. Secondly, as I have stressed, the substantive principles of judicial review both in the public and the private sector are highly context-sensitive and can balance legitimate claims to autonomy against the interests of the applicant. There can be different levels of review depending upon the nature of the body, the nature of the issue, and the identity and conduct of the applicant.

Selective use of particular grounds of review is one technique that can be used to define a zone of autonomy. The *Datafin*[111] case is a clear example in the public sector. The Court of Appeal thought that only a serious irregularity, such as a breach of natural justice, would justify issuing enforceable remedies, because the Takeover Panel was a self-regulating body. Similarly in *Calvin* v *Carr*[112] (a private

---

109   [1983] 1 WLR 1302 at 1311, 1315.
110   [1992] 1 AC 624 at 628–9, 639, 640, 643–5.
111   Note 2 *supra* at 842.
112   [1980] AC 574.

body case), the fact that a sports regulatory regime was based on contract was a matter not of jurisdiction, but to be taken into account in determining the specific requirements of natural justice. Moreover, the extent of the right to a hearing was affected by the public interest in the ability of the regulator to take effective and speedy action. Other examples include the bias rule, which caters for internal dynamics and loyalties within an organisation,[113] and *Page* v *Hull University Visitor*[114] where the House of Lords would not interfere with the decision of a University Visitor in matters concerning the interpretation of the University's internal rules, except on grounds of natural justice or lack of jurisdiction (in the narrow sense). The level of review is also restrained in respect of closed communities such as prisons and the military.[115] In the New Zealand case of *Mercury Energy Ltd* v *Electricity Corporation of New Zealand*,[116] the Privy Council, dealing with a state-owned utility, recognised that judicial review is not excluded merely because a body acts as a business; but also that, in the case of the commercial activities of state enterprises, review would probably be limited to cases of fraud, corruption or bad faith.

Another technique might be to apply a 'rationality' threshold, so that the court would interfere not because *it* thinks that a decision is wrong in law or in breach of natural justice (the usual test), but only if there is no rational basis upon which the decision could be regarded as proper. The principle that internal remedies must be exhausted, *locus standi*, and the court's inherent discretion in relation to choice of remedy — for example, making a declaration with prospective effect without any enforceable sanction, or issuing *certiorari* but not the more ferocious *mandamus* — would also meet autonomy concerns.

CONCLUSION

The old law relating to the courts' supervisory jurisdiction reveals a unity between the public law and private law aspects of the jurisdiction. This is important today when government services are sometimes delivered by private bodies. Private bodies that carry out public functions, or those which are monopolies in respect of highly valued interests or resources, are impressed with a public interest that imposes obligations upon them that go beyond self-interest. This attracts the supervisory powers of the courts which derive from basic common law values, and distinguishes them from other powerful private bodies such as landlords who, subject to the rights of others, are free to act selfishly, unfairly and irrationally.

---

113 *White* v *Kuzych* [1951] AC 585; *Hannan* v *Bradford Corporation* [1970] 1 LR 937.
114 [1993] 1 All ER 97.
115 *R* v *Secretary of State for Defence, ex parte Smith* [1996] 1 All ER 611; *Leech* v *Deputy Governer of Parkhurst Prison* [1988] AC 533 at 583.
116 Note 61 *supra*. See Taggart, M., 'Corporation, Contracting Out and the Courts' [1994] *Public Law* 351.

The AJR is designed to cater for the special features of the supervisory jurisdiction and is flexible enough to respond to the circumstances of particular kinds of body, including the claims of voluntary bodies to be autonomous. Demarcation disputes about the boundaries of the AJR are pointless unless they serve a valuable social goal, and the criteria used by the courts to distinguish the public from the private bear little relation to the purposes of judicial review. Judicial review has been one of the outstanding common law creations of the postwar period. Its potential for further development should not be fettered without very good cause.

8

Surveying the Grounds: Key Themes in Judicial Intervention

Michael Fordham

SUMMARY

This chapter considers the grounds of judicial review from a thematic point of view and seeks to identify the key distinctions which lie behind the conventional threefold classification into illegality, irrationality and procedural impropriety. The chapter goes on to explore some of the key influences which shape the developing law.

INTRODUCTION

It was 1984 when the late Lord Diplock took off for the third time in as many years to map the shifting terrain of the brave new world of judicial review.[1] His first two survey trips, in *National Federation* and *O'Reilly* v *Mackman,* had been concerned with the procedural implications of the 1977 and 1981 reforms. On this third occasion, in *GCHQ*, he was anxious to scan the contours of substantive public law: the grounds for judicial intervention with public decision making.

From an altitude befitting to his status in the legal world, Lord Diplock was able to make out three distinct and well-developed areas. He said this:

---

1 The three cases are *R* v *Inland Revenue Commissioners, ex parte National Federation of Self-Employed and Small Businesses Ltd* [1982] AC 617; *O'Reilly* v *Mackman* [1983] 2 AC 237 and *Council of Civil Service Unions* v *Minister for the Civil Service* [1985] AC 374 (the '*GCHQ* case').

Judicial review has I think developed to a stage today when . . . one can conveniently classify under three heads the grounds upon which administrative action is subject to control by judicial review. The first ground I would call 'illegality', the second 'irrationality' and the third 'procedural impropriety'.[2]

In more user-friendly language, we can refer to Lord Diplock's three areas as representing public bodies' basic duties of 'lawfulness, reasonableness and fairness'.

Lord Diplock was aware that he was surveying shifting sands. By the time of his first trip, domestic public lawyers had already witnessed the 'progress towards a comprehensive system of administrative law' which he regarded as 'the greatest achievement of the English courts in my judicial lifetime'.[3]

The public law terrain, and the way in which it is described, has continued to change in a dramatic manner and at a disarming pace. Yet, surprisingly perhaps, from a high altitude Lord Diplock's 'three counties' will appear largely intact. There are emergent, trendier labels ('want of due process' for procedural impropriety; 'abuse of power' for irrationality), but the basic threefold classification remains the most helpful outline. That is something which might have surprised Lord Diplock himself. Indeed, he thought he had glimpsed a fourth area of barren terrain ripe for development under the heading of 'proportionality'. That land is evidently still a place over the rainbow, waiting to be properly chartered.

Lord Diplock's picture remains a reliable satellite scan, but closer to ground level the picture may begin to scramble. Here we find what we thought were localised landmarks making cross-border appearances. The closer we get, the more the map begins to look like a jumble of disparate features. Each of these is rather elusive to classify, but easier to recognise in practice. As with Jowitt J and the test for standing, judges might say that a flaw warranting the court's intervention is 'like the horse . . . difficult to define but not difficult to recognise when one sees it'.[4]

Perhaps most interesting of all is not the way things appear from (different altitudes) above, but what we find when we burrow below the surface. There are, as ever, forces lurking *beneath* the crust, which are responsible for the emerging and developing shape of the common law. In surveying the grounds for judicial review we can identify several significant and distinct themes.

VIGILANCE AND RESTRAINT

The law of judicial review can be said to be the product of competing judicial concerns of proper 'vigilance' and proper 'restraint'. The courts have to hold an intricate constitutional balance (see also Pollard, Ch. 13, p. 306 and Donson,

---

2 *GCHQ* case, note 1 *supra*, at 410D.
3 *Ex parte National Federation*, note 1 *supra*, at 641C.
4 *R v Legal Aid Board, ex parte Bateman* [1992] 1 WLR 711, *per* Jowitt J at 721D.

Ch. 15, p. 355). On the one hand, judges must ensure that public bodies are accountable to law, and that abuses and excesses of power do not go unchecked. On the other hand, the courts cannot and must not interfere by second-guessing a decision for which the relevant public body, and not they the judiciary, has the primary function and responsibility. The intricate balance was identified by Sir Thomas Bingham MR in the 'gays in the military' case, when he said:

> It is not the constitutional role of the court to regulate the conditions of service in the armed forces of the Crown, nor has it the expertise to do so. But it has the constitutional role and duty of ensuring that the rights of citizens are not abused by the unlawful exercise of executive power. While the court must properly defer to the expertise of responsible decision makers, it must not shrink from its fundamental duty to 'do right for all manner of people' . . .[5]

It is faithfulness to these dual concerns of vigilance and restraint which produces that unique 'supervisory' jurisdiction of judicial review, by which the courts decide when it is appropriate to interfere with public decision making. The courts say, time and again, that they will not interfere on the basis that they simply 'disagree' with the 'merits' of an impugned decision. It is not enough that the decision appears to the court to be 'wrong'. Before the Court will interfere, there must be a 'wrong' of a kind recognised by administrative law. The grounds for judicial review are simply a list of recognised 'public law wrongs'.

As midwives at the birth of new 'public law wrongs', the courts are motivated by the same concerns of appropriate vigilance and appropriate restraint. As to vigilance, if the rule of law requires an addition to the judicial armoury then the courts (and not just the appellate ones) will fearlessly stake their claim. And even where the courts decline to introduce new 'public law wrongs', it is fascinating that they do not say 'no', but 'not yet'. Take two perceived judicial road-blocks, *Brind* and *Doody*, in relation to general and self-standing grounds of disproportionality and the failure to give reasons, respectively. *Brind* was simply 'not a case in which the first step can be taken'; *Doody* recognition for the fact that 'the law does not at present recognise a general duty to give reasons for an administrative decision'.[6] Judges are undoubtedly alive to the suggestion that 'in the developing field of judicial review it is usually unwise to say "never"'.[7]

As to restraint, on the other hand, it is striking how the courts prefer a two-stage process whereby a new 'public law wrong' is first recognised by reference to an old one, and then liberated from it. The classic example is *Anisminic,* credited with introducing 'error of law' as a ground for judicial review, deleting the superadded

---

5   *R v Ministry of Defence, ex parte Smith* [1996] QB 517, at 556D–E.
6   *R v Secretary of State for the Home Department, ex parte Brind* [1991] 1 AC 696, *per* Lord Roskill at 750E; *R v Secretary of State for the Home Department, ex parte Doody* [1994] 1 AC 531, *per* Lord Mustill at 172D.
7   *R v Panel on Takeovers and Mergers, ex parte Fayed* [1992] BCC 524, *per* Steyn LJ at 536C.

requirement that the error appear 'on the face of the record'.[8] This was achieved only by making use of the available ground of 'jurisdictional error', neatly circumventing a statutory ouster clause (in rather the same way that 'fundamental breach' was once used to get round contractual exemption clauses). The same pattern can explain why courts currently identify 'disproportionality' as a species of 'irrationality', failure to give reasons as a species of 'procedural fairness' or an indicator of 'irrationality' (in the case of an 'aberrant' decision); and perhaps 'fundamental error of fact' as a species of 'error of law'.[9]

The tension between vigilance and restraint is also evident in the space deliberately left between the formulation of grounds for judicial review and their operation in individual cases. The courts deliberately choose open-textured language to enable judges in future cases to balance all the particular circumstances of an individual case. The grounds for judicial review are entirely contextual, and this famous *dictum* of Lord Bridge in truth applies not just to procedural fairness but to all grounds for judicial review:

> My Lords, the so-called rules of natural justice are not engraved on tablets of stone. To use the phrase which better expresses the underlying concept, what the requirements of fairness demand when any body, domestic, administrative or judicial, has to make a decision which will affect the rights of individuals depends on the character of the decision making body, the kind of decision it has to make and the statutory or other framework in which it operates.[10]

A final example of the tension between vigilance and restraint lies in the concept of 'materiality' or 'prejudice'. On the one hand, the courts reserve the capacity to interfere to ensure decision making propriety, irrespective of whether there has been a discernable 'prejudice'. On the other hand, judges are pragmatic enough to hesitate before entertaining futile challenges, in cases where there is no prospect of the impugned decision having been, or any fresh decision being, decided differently in substance. After all, relief in judicial review is discretionary and it is said that 'good public administration is concerned with substance rather than form'.[11] The tension, and care with which a balance is struck, is evident from this passage from a recent natural justice case:

---

8 *Anisminic Ltd* v *Foreign Compensation Commission* [1969] 2 AC 147; as interpreted notably in *In re a Company* [1981] AC 374; *O'Reilly* v *Mackman*, note 1, *supra*; and *R* v *Hull University Visitor, ex parte Page* [1993] AC 682.

9 See *Brind*, note 6 *supra* (proportionality); *R* v *Higher Education Funding Council, ex parte Institute of Dental Surgery* [1994] 1 WLR 242 (reasons); *Edwards* v *Bairstow* [1956] AC 14 (error of fact).

10 *Lloyd* v *McMahon* [1987] AC 625, at 702H.

11 *R* v *Monopolies and Mergers Commission, ex parte Argyll Group plc* [1986] 1 WLR 763, *per* Sir John Donaldson MR at 774E.

[T]he notion that when the rules of natural justice have not been observed, one can still uphold the result because it would not have made any difference, is to be treated with great caution. Down that slippery slope lies the way to dictatorship. On the other hand if it is a case where it is demonstrable beyond doubt that it would have made no difference, the court may if it thinks fit, uphold a conviction even if natural justice had not been done.[12]

SUBSTANCE AND PROCEDURE

Returning to Lord Diplock's high altitude and the lasting nature of his threefold classification, it is worth asking what it is in the axes between 'lawfulness, reasonableness and fairness' which makes these boundaries a helpful delineation. In answering that question, we find two fundamental distinctions.

The first fundamental distinction is that between matters of substance and matters of procedure. It is the difference between the conclusion upon which a public body has seized and the process by which that conclusion has been reached. This distinction underpins Lord Diplock's classification because it explains why 'procedural impropriety' (unfairness) is distinct from 'illegality' and 'irrationality'.

The area of 'procedural impropriety' is distinct, then, because it concerns the characteristics of the decision making process, rather than the decision itself. I may not be able to complain, on judicial review, about the substantive 'merits' of the decision taking away my taxi licence or authorising my deportation, but the court will come to my assistance if I can show that the procedure adopted denied me what Lord Russell once called 'a fair crack of the whip'.[13]

Procedural fairness fits, by its very nature, within the notion of a truly supervisory jurisdiction precisely because the court is not by any means interfering with the 'substance' of the decision, the 'merits'. It is, then, no surprise that this leading expression of the proper role of judicial review was coined in a procedural fairness context:

> Judicial review is concerned, not with the decision, but with the decision making process. . . . Judicial review, as the words imply, is not an appeal from a decision, but a review of the manner in which the decision was made.[14]

Moreover, because by definition the courts are not here interfering with decisions but only decision making processes, it is in procedural fairness contexts that they

---

12 *R v Ealing Magistrates' Court, ex parte Fanneran* (1996) 8 Admin LR 351, *per* Staughton LJ at 356E.
13 *Fairmount Investments Ltd v Secretary of State for the Environment* [1976] 1 WLR 1255 at 1266A.
14 *Chief Constable of the North Wales Police v Evans* [1982] 1 WLR 1155, *per* Lord Brightman at 1173F and 1174G.

feel able to apply some of the most rigorous court-set standards, seizing the opportunity to augment procedural provisions contained in primary legislation.

Grounds which relate to 'substance' do not carry this inherent, self-evident comfort (see Radford, Ch. 2, p. 47). They must find their supervisory nature in their formulation, which is the very point of a threshold like *Wednesbury* 'irrationality' (whereby the decision must be far more than 'wrong'). In this way, procedural fairness and irrationality each have a built-in merits-avoidance mechanism: procedural fairness because it is by nature only procedural, irrationality because its formulation is designed to acknowledge a margin of appreciation.

On closer examination, however, what begins as a simple distinction between substance and procedure begins to blur. Take the *Wednesbury* principles for judicial review of an exercise of discretion. Clearly, the argument that the decision maker has come to a 'irrational' conclusion is 'substance'. But what of the argument that, in coming to a conclusion, the decision maker has failed to have regard to some relevant consideration, or has had regard to some irrelevant one? If a failure to consult is procedural, why not the failure to have regard to relevant views? If being influenced by a predisposition (i.e. actual bias) is procedural, then why is not being influenced by some irrelevant policy interest? The truth is that certain aspects traditionally associated with 'irrationality' have a procedural flavour. An alternative distinction may be that drawn in the context of applications for discovery of documents, between a decision maker's 'terminus' (where they ended up) and their 'route' (how they got there).

This brings us to the analytical challenge presented by the doctrine of legitimate expectation. This challenge has two aspects. The first has to do with the distinction between substance and procedure. The question which arises is whether 'legitimate expectation' operates solely as a procedural doctrine, feeding into procedural unfairness, or whether it can also have a substantive flavour. The *Hamble Fisheries* case took the latter approach.[15] This dovetails with an important line of authority including the *Preston* case and culminating in a notable success in the Court of Appeal for Unilever,[16] where the courts have overtly accepted that notions of 'fairness' are not limited to procedural obligations, such as the duty to consult before acting in a particular way. English law has acknowledged that fairness can involve 'substantive obligations', where a proposed course of conduct is itself unfair, independently of the procedural rigour by which it is sought to be brought into effect. The analytical challenge is this. Would it be better now to acknowledge a single area of 'fairness', in which natural justice orthodoxy and the *Preston* (and

---

15   *R v Ministry for Agriculture, Fisheries and Food, ex parte Hamble Fisheries (Offshore) Ltd* [1995] 2 All ER 714.

16   *R v Inland Revenue Commissioners, ex parte Unilever Plc* [1996] STC 681; after *R v Inland Revenue Commissioners, ex parte Preston* [1985] AC 835 and *R v Inland Revenue Commissioners, ex parte Matrix-Securities Ltd* [1994] 1 WLR 334.

substantive legitimate expectation) cases sit together? Or do we make 'legitimate expectation' and 'fairness' a recurrent theme (perhaps like 'causation' in private law), capable of cropping up in different places; here, on both sides of an important border between substantive and procedural challenges? The answer depends on a second aspect of the picture, having to do not with substance and procedure, but with soft and hard-edged questions (see Craig, Ch. 12, pp. 288 *et seq.*

SOFT AND HARD-EDGED QUESTIONS

The second fundamental distinction which explains why Lord Diplock's threefold classification works, and has aged, so well is that between ordinary (or, for contrast, 'soft') questions and what have been termed 'hard-edged' questions.[17]

In the case of a 'soft' question, the courts adopt the restraint typified by *Wednesbury* irrationality. The court does not intervene on the basis of imposing ('substituting') its own conclusion for that of the public body. The classic examples of 'soft' questions are matters of 'fact', 'judgment' or 'discretion'. The court will not grant judicial review by accepting an invitation to conclude for itself that a finding of fact should have been made, or a judgment or discretion exercised. It is and remains for the public body to decide such questions, and the court exercises a 'secondary' function. The judge does not intervene on the basis of whether the respondent body's conclusion is the 'right' or 'correct' one; more is required. Moreover, the reviewing court restricts itself to material that was before the decision maker. This is how judicial review retains, for questions of 'substance', its truly supervisory character.

A 'hard-edged' question is fundamentally different. Here, the court *does* impose its own conclusion. The classic example concerns questions of 'jurisdictional fact', sometimes called 'precedent fact' or 'antecedent fact'. In essence, a question of fact may be characterised as 'jurisdictional' when it is regarded as 'triggering' the public body's decision making function. In the classic case of *White and Collins,* the public body had power to make a compulsory purchase order, but not where the land was part of a 'park'. This 'trigger' question was characterised as 'jurisdictional', so that the court simply asked for itself (and on all available material), as a matter of objective fact, 'is this a park?'.[18]

The distinction between 'soft' and 'hard-edged' questions presents judges with a fundamental choice which radically affects 'the proper function of the courts'.[19] In *Khawaja,* the House of Lords characterised the question whether a person was

---

17 The term 'hard-edged' was coined by Lord Mustill in *R* v *Monopolies and Mergers Commission, ex parte South Yorkshire Transport Ltd* [1993] 1 WLR 23, at 32D–F.

18 *White & Collins* v *Minister of Health* [1939] 2 KB 838.

19 See *R* v *Monopolies and Mergers Commission, ex parte South Yorkshire Transport Ltd* [1993] 1 WLR 23, *per* Lord Mustill at 32D–F.

an 'illegal entrant' as a precedent fact, reversing its contrary analysis of the same question a few years earlier.[20] In *Bennett*, the House of Lords decided that judicial review should lie to prevent the continuance of criminal proceedings facilitated by an abuse of extradition procedures, which meant that the question whether there had been such an abuse was a question of fact for the reviewing court to decide for itself.[21]

The 'soft' and 'hard-edged' distinction explains the difference between Lord Diplock's 'legality' and his 'rationality'. Questions of *Wednesbury* reasonableness are the paradigm of 'soft' questions. Questions of 'legality', on the other hand, are regarded as 'hard-edged'. If a decision maker gets the law wrong, or misunderstands the nature or extent of its powers, it is no answer that these are questions for the decision maker and the court should not substitute its own view. As Forbes J once put it:

At one stage in his argument I detected a suggestion from [counsel] that in considering the decision of a lay tribunal it could not be said to have misdirected itself in law unless the court came to the conclusion that no reasonable tribunal could so have misdirected itself, in accordance with the *Associated Provincial Picture Houses Ltd* v *Wednesbury Corporation* doctrine. I do not consider this is right . . . A tribunal either misdirects itself in law or not according to whether it has got the law right or wrong, and that depends on what the law is and not what a lay tribunal might reasonably think it was. In this field there are no marks for trying hard but getting the answer wrong.[22]

While 'irrationality' preserves that 'margin of appreciation' which allows judicial review to retain its supervisory nature, 'hard-edged' modes of review show the courts at their most vigilant. Here, the court is overtly deciding a question of substance, and doing so by substituting its own view.

Like the substance/procedure distinction, that between 'soft' and 'hard-edged' questions can become blurred in practice. Take relevancies and irrelevancies again. A public decision maker owes a duty to have regard to relevant, and disregard irrelevant, considerations. But is it for the decision maker, or the court, to decide whether a matter is relevant or irrelevant? If a consideration is relevant, is it for the decision maker or the court to decide to what extent regard should be had to it? There are various approaches which seek to strike an appropriate balance. The two main ones distinguish between obligatory and discretionary relevance, and between relevance and weight, respectively:

---

20 *R* v *Secretary of State for the Home Department, ex parte Khawaja* [1984] AC 74; overruling *R* v *Secretary of State for the Home Department, ex parte Zamir* [1980] AC 930.
21 *R* v *Horseferry Road Magistrates' Court, ex parte Bennett* [1994] 1 AC 42.
22 *R* v *Central Arbitration Committee, ex parte BTP Tioxide Ltd* [1981] ICR 843, at 856B–C.

It is important to bear in mind, however, as . . . [both counsel] accepted, that there are in fact three categories of consideration. First, those clearly (whether expressly or impliedly) identified by the statute as considerations to which regard must be had. Second, those equally clearly identified by the statute as considerations to which regard must not be had. Third, those to which the decision maker may have regard if in his judgment and discretion he thinks it right to do so. There is, in short, a margin of appreciation within which the decision maker may decide just what considerations should play a part in his reasoning process.[23]

It is for the courts, if the matter is brought before them, to decide what is a relevant consideration. If the decision maker wrongly takes the view that some consideration is not relevant, and therefore has no regard to it, the decision cannot stand and he must be required to think again. But it is entirely for the decision maker to attribute to the relevant considerations such weight as he thinks fit, and the courts will not interfere unless he has acted unreasonably in the *Wednesbury* sense.[24]

There are other hybrids of 'soft' and 'hard-edged' questions too. In *Bugdacay*,[25] the House of Lords rejected the argument that whether an asylum-seeker was in fact a 'refugee' was a question for the court, but adopted 'anxious scrutiny' of the Secretary of State's conclusion, an approach which has come to be recognised as more exacting than conventional *Wednesbury* review. In the *South Yorkshire Transport* case, Lord Mustill accepted that the identification of the relevant criterion ('substantial part of the United Kingdom') was 'hard-edged', but its application 'softer':

Once the criterion for a judgment has been properly understood, the fact that it was formerly part of a range of possible criteria from which it was difficult to choose and on which opinions might legitimately differ becomes a matter of history . . . But this clear-cut approach cannot be applied to every case, for the criterion so established may itself be so imprecise that different decision makers, each acting rationally, might reach differing conclusions when applying it to the facts of a given case. In such a case the court is entitled to substitute its own opinion for that of the person to whom the decision has been entrusted only if the decision is so aberrant that it cannot be classed as rational. . . . Even after

---

23 *R* v *Somerset County Council, ex parte Fewings* [1995] 1 WLR 1037, *per* Simon Brown LJ (dissenting, though not on this point) at 1049H–1050A; after *In re Findlay* [1985] AC 318, at 333H–334C.

24 *Tesco Stores Ltd* v *Secretary of State for the Environment* [1995] 1 WLR 759, *per* Lord Keith at 764G–H.

25 *R* v *Secretary of State for the Home Department, ex parte Bugdaycay* [1987] AC 514.

eliminating inappropriate senses of 'substantial' one is still left with a meaning broad enough to call for the exercise of judgment rather than an exact quantitative measurement. Approaching the matter in this light I am quite satisfied that there is no ground for interference by the court, since the conclusion at which the commission arrived was well within the permissible field of judgment.[26]

If illegality is hard-edged and irrationality soft, what about procedural impropriety? It has been suggested that the court does not, or should not, interfere to correct a procedural approach unless satisfied that no reasonable decision maker could have adopted such a conception of what was procedurally fair. The emergent view, however, is that the courts decide for themselves how to set standards of procedural fairness:

> Natural justice or fairness is a requirement that the common law through the judges has grafted on to statutory provisions which give powers to persons or bodies which can adversely affect individuals. It is for the court in any given case to decide what fairness requires.[27]

Which brings us back to the analytical challenge of substantive unfairness and substantive legitimate expectations. It being the case that the court can intervene to protect a substantive legitimate expectation, this second aspect arises. Is the court entitled to substitute its own view of whether the expectation could properly be dishonoured? Is there here a hard-edged question for the court? The *Hamble Fisheries* case had suggested so. The Court of Appeal has decided in the *Hargreaves* case[28] that the test is that of irrationality. Whether to honour a substantive expectation is for the decision maker, and the court's role is the 'soft' *Wednesbury* one. But this is unlikely to be the final word on the matter. For one thing, the Court of Appeal did not cross-analyse the *Preston* line of (substantive unfairness) cases. In those cases, substantive unfairness was treated as requiring an 'abuse of power', but this was without reference to the *Wednesbury* threshold of irrationality. For the time being, though, the position in relation to 'fairness' cases can be said to be this. The second fundamental distinction (between soft and hard-edged questions) is what sustains the first (between substance and procedure). This is because review for substantive unfairness is soft, and for procedural unfairness hard-edged (see Craig, Ch. 12, pp. 290–2.

---

26 *R v Monopolies and Mergers Commission, ex parte South Yorkshire Transport Ltd* [1993] 1 WLR 23, at 32F–33A.

27 *R v Monopolies and Mergers Commission, ex parte Stagecoach Holdings plc* (1997) *The Times*, 23 July (transcript), *per* Collins J.

28 *R v Secretary of State for the Home Department, ex parte Hargreaves* [1997] 1 All ER 397.

FUNCTIONAL INSIGHT

In addition to the general tension between judicial vigilance and restraint, and the fundamental distinctions between substance and procedure and soft and hard-edged questions, there are a number of further discernible features having important roles in shaping the formulation and operation of the grounds for judicial review. Three themes are perhaps worthy of special mention. The first is functional insight.

The grounds for judicial review are not, and deliberately not, tightly-drawn formulae. The way in which they operate in any given case will depend on the particular circumstances in question. The preference for a narrow contextual analysis, and the incremental legal change which complements it, is not judicial shyness or some unspoken conspiracy with the lawyers to promote litigation. Behind it lies an important truth. The types of decisions and decision making functions with which the public law court comes into contact are many and various, and the appropriateness of intervention on a particular basis can properly be assessed only when the reviewing court understands who the respondent body is, and what its true role is.

Take the doctrine of 'jurisdictional error'. This is something designed to identify whether a question is one which the decision maker has the function of deciding for itself, in which case the court should intervene only on a 'soft' basis. The point fits well with classic statements of 'soft' review, like this one:

> My Lords, it is, in my opinion, a pure question of fact whether, in any particular case, the two conditions to which I have just referred are satisfied or not. It is, moreover, a question of fact of a kind which insurance officers, local tribunals and the commissioner are, by reason of their wide knowledge and experience of matters pertaining to industrial relations, exceptionally well qualified to answer.[29]

Public law has always been underpinned by functional insight, though historically the tendency was to draw broad distinctions between bodies of different functional types. Most familiar is the distinction between 'judicial' (or quasi-judicial') and 'administrative' functions. Long abandoned as a touchstone of amenability to judicial review, the judicial/administrative distinction persisted for some time as an indicator of different approaches to the grounds of judicial review, but is now almost entirely discredited. The current mood is well illustrated by the *Kirkstall Valley* case, in which Sedley J confirmed that the *Gough* 'real danger' test for bias applies to administrative functions too.[30]

---

29 *Presho v Insurance Officer* [1984] 1 AC 310, *per* Lord Brandon at 318F.
30 *R v Secretary of State for the Environment, ex parte Kirkstall Valley Campaign Ltd* [1996]
     3 All ER 304; applying *R v Gough* [1993] AC 646.

Another favoured functional distinction is the line between 'courts of law' and other public decision makers. This has been used as a key distinction when it comes to error of law as a ground for judicial review, under *Anisminic* (as interpreted). Here, the courts have tended to favour a superadded requirement in the case of a 'court of law', that the error 'goes to the jurisdiction' or is 'on the face of the record', whereas in relation to other bodies it will suffice that there has been a (material) error of law.[31]

Bright line distinctions between different functional types have to a very great extent been replaced with a spectrum of different shades, but the functional dimension of any given case remains vital. The point is that the court can decide whether intervention is warranted only when it has understood why the public decision making body is there is the first place; what purpose it serves.

An excellent example is the *Perestrello* case, where Woolf J rejected the argument that the existence of a predisposition on the part of DTI inspectors vitiated their activities, on grounds of 'bias'. He said this:

When one considers the functions of those officers, it really is wholly inappropriate to talk about them not being regarded as biased if they are performing their functions properly. Take this very case — it is, in my view, almost inevitable that before the powers under [the Act] . . . are exercised, the officers concerned, and through his officers, the Secretary of State, must regard the situation as one where there are matters to be investigated. They are acting in a policing role. Their function is to see whether their suspicions are justified by what they find, and that being so, it is wholly inappropriate for the case to be approached in the same way as one would approach a person performing a normal judicial role or quasi-judicial role; a situation where the person is making a determination.[32]

The functional insight applies generally. To take an example relating to 'illegality', one need look no further than error of law itself. The simplest justification for why 'courts of law' are allowed to make 'errors of law' must be because it is the very function of a 'court of law' to decide questions of law. As for 'irrationality', an illustration arises from the cases involving judicial review of ACAS. There, the courts emphasised that one should not ask whether ACAS had acted as would a reasonable body, the question was whether a 'reasonable advisory, conciliation and arbitration service . . . could have [acted] as it did.[33]

---

31 See, e.g., *R v Hull University Visitor, ex parte Page*, note 8 *supra*, at 693B–D, 703E–F; *cf. R v Bedwellty Justices, ex parte Williams* [1996] 3 WLR 361, at 367C.

32 *R v Secretary of State for Trade, ex parte Perestrello* [1981] QB 19, at 35A–C.

33 *United Kingdom Association of Professional Engineers v Advisory Conciliation and Arbitration Service* [1981] AC 424, *per* Lord Scarman at 442E–F.

BEYOND *VIRES*

The grounds for judicial review have sometimes been framed as the courts merely enforcing the will of Parliament. A public body could not do something which Parliament never intended it to do. To act unlawfully, unreasonably or unfairly was to exceed its powers. Indeed, Lord Browne-Wilkinson has paraphrased Lord Diplock's threefold classification in this way:

> If the decision maker exercises his powers outside the jurisdiction conferred, in a manner which is procedurally irregular or is *Wednesbury* unreasonable, he is acting *ultra vires* his powers and therefore unlawfully.[34]

No doubt this emphasis on *ultra vires* worked particularly well in a world where judicial review was invariably concerned with scrutinising the activities of statutory bodies wielding statutory powers. It also had the conceptual advantage that the courts could tap into the supremacy of Parliament and avoid suggestions that they, unelected judges, were setting the standards.

As administrative law has continued to mature, the courts appear to have distanced themselves from the orthodoxy of *ultra vires*.[35] To some extent, no doubt, this came with the recognition that judicial review was now available in relation to non statutory bodies wielding non statutory (and even non prerogative) powers[36] (see Alder, Ch. 7 and Bamforth, Ch. 6 generally). Plainly, it would never do to pretend that the courts were enforcing the will of Parliament when considering the accountability to law of non statutory decision making functions.

Indeed, the courts had always been setting the standards, as the law of natural justice amply demonstrates. From *Cooper and Wandsworth* in 1863 to the *Fayed* case in the present day, standards of procedural fairness have been court-imposed, not court-discerned and Parliament-imposed, with the courts themselves 'suppl[ying] the legislative omission' of procedural requirements, and doing so by drawing on 'the justice of the common law'.[37]

The interesting question is whether the courts will become more, or less, interventionist as they venture beyond 'legislative will'. Could it be that, stripped of this comfort blanket, many judges will feel exposed and become more reticent? One thing is for sure: there is boldness and intellectual honesty in the courts exposing the myth and 'owning' the standards which they enforce.

---

34 *R* v *Hull University Visitor, ex parte Page*, note 8 *supra*, at 701E.
35 For a defence of the orthodoxy, see Forsyth, C., 'Of Fig Leaves and Fairy Tales: the Ultra Vires Doctrine, the Sovereignty of Parliament and Judicial Review' (1996) 55 *Cambridge Law Journal* 122.
36 In particular, post-*R* v *Panel on Takeovers and Mergers, ex pate Datafin plc* [1987] QB 815, in which the non statutory Takeover Panel was held amenable to judicial review.
37 *Cooper* v *Wandsworth Board of Works* (1863) 14 CB (NS) 180, *per* Byles J at 194; *R* v *Secretary of State for the Home Department, ex parte Fayed* [1997] 1 All ER 228 (HL awaited).

FUNDAMENTAL RIGHTS

Now to the third and final feature, which exerts a powerful influence on the grounds for judicial review and is worthy of special mention. It is the notion of fundamental rights and freedoms. The law is clear that 'when fundamental human rights are in play, the courts will adopt a more interventionist role'.[38] What this means in practice is perhaps not so much that the grounds for judicial review are differently stated, but that their in-built flexibility is used to require more exacting standards. As to 'illegality', cases such as *Anderson* and *JCWI* show that a decision or rule will the more readily be found to be *ultra vires* where it involves an infringement of fundamental human rights.[39] As to 'procedural impropriety', in a fundamental rights context 'only the highest standards of fairness will suffice'.[40] And in relation to 'irrationality', the *Wednesbury* principle applies in a modified way, as reflected in this proposition:

> The court may not interfere with the exercise of an administrative discretion on substantial grounds save where the court is satisfied that the decision is unreasonable in the sense that it is beyond the range of responses open to a reasonable decision maker. But in judging whether the decision maker has exceeded this margin of appreciation the human rights context is important. The more substantial the interference with human rights, the more the court will require by way of justification before it is satisfied that the decision is reasonable in the sense outlined above.[41]

It is in this area that we glimpse the awesome potential of the common law. Fundamental rights are common law rights, which is why inspiration can be drawn from the European Convention on Human Rights without it having yet been incorporated into domestic law. As Sedley J said in *McQuillan* (see Donson, Ch. 15, p. 357):

> [T]he principles and standards set out in the Convention can certainly be said to be a matter of which the law of this country now takes notice in setting its own standards. . . . Once it is accepted that the standards articulated in the European

---

38 *R v Coventry City Council, ex parte Phoenix Aviation* [1995] 3 All ER 37, at 62g; and see especially *R v Secretary of State for the Home Department, ex parte Bugdaycay*, note 25 *supra*, at 531E–G and 537H.

39 *R v Secretary of State for the Home Department, ex parte Anderson* [1984] QB 778; *R v Secretary of State for Social Security, ex parte Joint Council for the Welfare of Immigrants* [1996] 4 All ER 385.

40 *R v Secretary of State for the Home Department, ex parte Sittampalam Thirukumar* [1989] Imm AR 402, *per* Bingham LJ at 414.

41 *R v Ministry of Defence, ex parte Smith* [1996] QB 517, at 554D–G, 563A, 564H–565B.

Convention are standards which both march with those of the common law and inform the jurisprudence of the European Union, it becomes unreal and potentially unjust to continue to develop English public law without reference to them.[42]

Moreover, fundamental rights are 'constitutional' rights.[43] This important insight allows us now to contemplate what would perhaps be public law's most dramatic development yet, namely judicial review of primary legislation in a non EU law case.[44] The concept of balancing the 'two conflicting principles' of safeguarding fundamental rights and enforcing the 'expressed intention of the legislature'[45] by favouring the former was foreshadowed by Lord Atkin's 'classic dissent' in *Liversidge* v *Anderson*.[46] It can now be suggested that the courts could, by tapping into rights recognised at common law as enshrined in our unwritten constitution, assert the jurisdiction to strike down as unconstitutional a legislative provision which, say, sought to curtail judicial review itself.[47] This could be fortified by a second reinterpretation of *Anisminic*, namely that that case concerned a disapplication of plain statutory language which was indeed inconsistent with the fundamental right of access to the courts.

Many will unquestioningly assume that no domestic court could contemplate doing other than applying plain statutory words, however grave the infringement of fundamental rights. But it is worth noting some comments in the existing case law. Take these two. First, the *Witham* case, where the Divisional Court emphasised that the *present position chosen by the common law* was to defer to a plain statutory restriction on constitutional rights.[48] This is another example of the 'not-yet' rather than 'never' approach. Secondly, ponder these tantalising words of Lord Mustill:

[O]n the view which I have formed of the English law there is no need to engage the important general question which *would have arisen if* the conclusions impelled by the English legislation and decided cases had differed in important

---

42 *R* v *Secretary of State for the Home Department, ex parte McQuillan* [1995] 4 All ER 400, at 422f–j. See also *R* v *Mid Glamorgan Family Health Services, ex parte Martin* [1995] 1 WLR 110, *per* Evans LJ at 118H.

43 *R* v *Secretary of State for the Home Department, ex parte Leech* [1994] QB 198; also *R* v *Governor of Pentonville Prison, ex parte Azam* [1974] AC 18, at 73H–74A; *R* v *Lord Chancellor, ex parte Witham* [1997] 2 All ER 779.

44 I.e. beyond *R* v *Secretary of State for Employment, ex parte Equal Opportunities Commission* [1995] 1 AC 1 (declaration of incompatibility with EU law).

45 *Barnard* v *Gorman* [1941] AC 378, at 389.

46 *Liversidge* v *Sir John Anderson* [1942] AC 206; see *R* v *Secretary of State for the Home Department, ex parte Khawaja* [1984] AC 74, at 110F.

47 Contemplated, notably, in Woolf, Lord, 'Droit Public — English Style' [1995] *Public Law* 57.

48 *R* v *Lord Chancellor, ex parte Witham, op. cit.* note 43 *supra per* Laws J at 783j.

respects from the jurisprudence of the [European Commission and Court of Human Rights] . . .[49]

CONCLUSION

The grounds for judicial review are court-recognised rules of good administration: the judges' way of explaining when a public authority has overstepped the mark and when judicial intervention is warranted. They reflect a careful balance between appropriate vigilance and appropriate restraint. It was Lawton LJ who said that in judicial review:

> I regard myself as a referee. I can blow my judicial whistle when the ball goes out of play; but when the game restarts I must neither take part in it nor tell the players how to play.[50]

Lord Diplock's classification of judicial review grounds identifies three categories which have at their axes vital distinctions: between substance and procedure, and between 'soft' and 'hard-edged' review. What is more, they form a framework which allows judges to acknowledge the application of court-set as well as Parliament-set standards, and one which permits flexibility of response, tailored to such mattters as the public authority's precise function and the importance of fundamental rights.

Dramatic, if incremental, change is axiomatic in the law of judicial review. However, the threefold classification is a helpful overview which deserves its continued prominence.

---

49   *In re D (Minors) (Adoption Reports. Confidentiality)* [1996] AC 593, at 613H (emphasis added).
50   *Laker Airways Ltd* v *Department of Trade* [1977] QB 643, at 724D–E (in fact, those proceedings were in form a pre-exclusivity action for a declaration of *ultra vires*).

9

No Standing Still on Standing

Chris Himsworth*

SUMMARY

The starting assumption in this chapter is that, after a period of some turmoil, the rules on standing in relation to applications for judicial review have acquired a degree of stability. What the chapter then goes on to explore, however, are ways in which pressure for further change may grow. In particular, the influence of the changing function of courts in judicial review, of environmental litigation and, above all, of the European Community are considered.

INTRODUCTION

There is always a temptation to blame history. When difficulties arise in our legal analysis we wish for a clean slate. We wish that the rules from an earlier age did not continue to rule us from their graves. So it once was with the question of standing, the question of who is or should be entitled to initiate an application for judicial review. There were real problems, it was argued, in other areas too. In particular, the grounds of review were expanding and there were genuine issues to be resolved about how far the process should go. There was room for a real debate which involved questions which, though quite technical at their core, rapidly led to others about the function of judicial review itself, and the relationship between judicial review and other mechanisms for seeking redress for individual grievances and the quality and accountability of government.

Discussion of standing was, however, more difficult to liberate from the technicalities of its origins in the rules which historically had governed access to

---

* My thanks to Colin Munro who commented most helpfully on a draft of this chapter.

the remedies available in proceedings against public authorities. There were, in particular, the divisions which had opened up between those remedies (especially the declaration) which remained faithful to their origins in private law and therefore to a private law test of standing and, on the other hand, the prerogative orders to which different rules on standing applied. The position was further confused by the impact on the general rules of standing of the shadowy role of the Attorney-General, whether *ex proprio motu* or in relator actions.

Various other problems used to accompany the analysis of *locus standi* and, to an extent, they still do. These concern the definition of standing rules properly so called and their relationship to other mechanisms for curbing and channelling access to a reviewing court. In his magisterial treatise on US administrative law of 40 years ago, Professor K. C. Davis opened his chapter on standing as follows:

> The five major questions about judicial review of administrative action are whether, when, for whom, how, and how much judicial review should be provided. The question of who may challenge administrative action — the third of the five major questions — is customarily discussed by the courts in terms of 'standing' to challenge. The problem of standing merges with and often seems to overlap the problems of whether and when administrative action may be reviewed.[1]

The overlap is illustrated by reference to the rules adopted by courts to restrict access, one of which is the rule against the use of courts for obtaining an 'advisory opinion' (see Cane, Ch. 11, pp. 266 *et seq*. The courts should not be used for the solution of law mooting issues where a point on which nothing presently turns and where there is not, in US terminology, some sort of a 'case or controversy'.[2] Although the application of this test may raise issues quite separate from those which determine the standing of any particular individual, there are some situations in which there is an overlap. What is merely a mooting issue and would provide no more than an advisory opinion for many would-be litigants, may be a live 'case or controversy' for someone else, who should be given standing to raise it. Similarly, there is some acknowledgement of a need for what in the US would be called 'ripeness'.[3] Parties should not jump the gun and seek an answer to a question which has not really yet crystallised into an issue suitable for judicial resolution. Quite obviously this is an idea closely related to that of locus. 'Ripeness' is not something easily to be decided without reference to the position of the person seeking to challenge the decision or proposed decision. It leads in turn to the

---

1   Davis, K.C., *Administrative Law Treatise*, St Paul, Minn: West Publishing, 1958, vol. 3, p. 208.

2   But, for a recommendation that courts *should* be able to make 'advisory declarations', see Law Commission, *Administrative Law: Judicial Review and Statutory Appeals* (London: HMSO, No. 226) Law Com., 1993, paras 2.12–2.13. See too Jaconelli, J., Law Com., 'Hypothetical Disputes, Moot Points of Law, and Advisory Opinions' (1985) 101 *Law Quarterly Review* 587.

3   See, for example, the Scottish case of *Shaw v Strathclyde Regional Council* 1988 SLT 313.

related but much broader issue of justiciability itself, the question of whether a particular type of dispute is appropriate for resolution by a court at all. Important examples of non justiciability were provided when the scope of judicial review expanded to embrace the review of the 'prerogative' acts of government,[4] and it was acknowledged that *some* prerogative-based decisions such as treaty-making and the appointment of ministers, would nevertheless remain unreviewable.[5] They would not properly be adjudicated upon by a court, regardless of who might seek to initiate the proceedings.

One further preliminary complication which arises is that of the question of the role of the court in deciding these overlapping questions of justiciability, ripeness and standing. It is clear that if the court is to protect itself from a collusive attempt by parties to abuse the court's jurisdiction by seeking what amounts to an advisory opinion, the court must be prepared to take the initiative and, on its own motion, dismiss the action or prevent it from proceeding. Perhaps the same is true of some aspects of justiciability and ripeness. Consent of the parties should not be enough to lure the court into the determination of issues which are not thought fit for resolution by a court, whether at that particular stage or at all. The question of whether standing issues fall into the same category is much more problematic. There can be little doubt that, in practice, standing issues are not raised by respondents who are anxious not to appear obstructive on a technical issue and who do, in any case, want the dispute between the parties to be resolved. In such situations it appears that the courts tend not to intervene. If the respondent is content to join issue with the applicant, the courts have not prevented it and this would not, on the face of it, appear to be offensive in principle provided that collusion by parties over standing does not also amount to a collusive request for an advisory opinion. The suggestion has, however, been made that 'the question of *locus standi* goes to the jurisdiction of the court' and that 'parties are not entitled to confer jurisdiction, which the court does not have, on the court by consent . . .'[6]

The remainder of this chapter divides into three sections. First, there is a summary of the present rules on standing.[7] The primary emphasis is on the position in England and Wales although there is some comparative reference to Scotland, and the main suggestion to be made will be that, although not all the problems of principle have been resolved, a pragmatic accommodation has been reached for the

---

4   *Council of Civil Service Unions* v *Minister for the Civil Service* [1985] AC 374.
5   *Ibid.*, p. 418, Lord Roskill.
6   *R* v *Secretary of State for Social Services. ex parte CPAG* [1990] 2 QB 540 at 556 (Woolf LJ).
7   For full accounts see Woolf, Lord, and Jowell, J., *Judicial Review of Administrative Action* (5th ed.) London: Sweet & Maxwell, 1995, Ch. 2; Craig, P. P., *Administrative Law* (3rd ed.) London: Sweet & Maxwell, 1994, Ch. 13; Wade, H. W. R., and Forsyth, C., *Administrative Law* (7th ed.) Oxford: Clarendon Press, 1994, Ch. 19; Cane, P., *An Introduction to Administrative Law* (2nd ed.), Oxford: Clarendon Press, 1992, Ch. 3. See also JUSTICE/All Souls, *Administrative Law: Judicial Review and Statutory Appeals* (Consultation Paper No. 126 (Law Com.), London: HMSO, 1993 pp. 55–65.

time being. Subsequently, however, there is some discussion of the ways in which that accommodation may come under some stress as pressures build for further change. The last section contains some brief conclusions.

STANDING NOW

Important changes occurred in the law of standing in English judicial review when the procedural reforms were introduced in 1977 and placed on a statutory basis in 1981.[8] These provided the opportunity for a new start. No attempt was made, however, to prescribe a new code of rules on standing. The development of such rules was left in the hands of the courts, but they were assisted in this direction by the provision of a new enabling formula on standing — any applicant for judicial review must have a 'sufficient interest' in the matter to which the application relates. It is a formula which goes no further in defining the nature of the interest required or in how to measure its sufficiency. The new form of words did, however, provide the opportunity for the courts to make a break with the past if they wished to do so. They would be able to use the new instruction to require an applicant to identify his or her 'sufficient interest' rather than satisfy some technically burdened test from the past. The courts would, in particular, be free if they wished to use the new formula to eliminate the differences which had developed between the different prerogative orders and then between those 'public law' remedies of declaration and injunction. All these remedies would be available under the new procedure and accessible, therefore, by way of the same application for judicial review. The courts were enabled, but not expressly compelled, to complete the procedural merger by interpreting the common formula on standing in the same way, regardless of the remedy sought or eventually awarded. Finally, the courts would be able, if they wished, to push the interpretation of standing in a generally liberalising direction. In other ways the courts would be able to defend the boundaries of justifiability. They would be able to repel frivolous or vexatious litigants by denying them leave to apply for judicial review on those grounds. In the meantime, however, they would be able to use the broad concept of sufficiency of interest to extend access to judicial review and ensure that deserving applicants were not denied access on merely technical grounds.[9]

In most respects these aims have been achieved. The courts have managed to cast off most of the shackles of history and begun to construct a new jurisprudence around the 'sufficient interest' language of the new rule. In the process of doing so they have avoided drawing distinctions between the nature of the probable remedy sought — at least in the preliminary stages of proceedings — and, in any event, without regard to a remedy's 'public law' or 'private law' origins. Perhaps

8 See ord. 53 r. 3(7) and the Supreme Court Act 1981, s. 31(3).
9 The avoidance of an 'undesirable rigidity' was an aim of the Law Commission in its *Report on Remedies in Administrative Law*, Cmnd 6407 (1976), para. 48.

most importantly of all, the general conclusion is being drawn that 'the term "sufficient interest" is being given a generous interpretation by the courts'.[10] This is a conclusion which may be based not only upon specific instances where the question of *locus* has been tested and the commitment shown to a broad interpretation, but also on the countless cases where standing has not been raised as an issue between the parties.

Three issues have, however, attracted attention since the English procedural reforms. The first relates to the stage in judicial review proceedings at which any standing question should be resolved. On the one hand, the rules themselves require that the 'sufficient interest' test be applied at the application for leave stage. This is readily coupled with an instinctive view that standing is a threshold procedural question to be resolved positively as a prerequisite of further progress on the application. This is not, however, a historically sound approach, and we have seen that questions of *locus standi* have been viewed as aspects of the substantive case to be made in pursuit of a particular remedy. More importantly, it is clear that the statutory rules, while enabling standing to be raised at the leave stage, do not require it to be dealt with finally at that stage; neither do they preclude the raising of standing issues at a later stage. The point has, furthermore, been taken that standing issues are intertwined with — and may indeed be the same as — issues of substance. Most obviously, the same circumstances of fact and law which establish a person's 'legitimate expectation' to a procedural benefit may also form the basis of the same person's argument for standing in the case. Thus one of the principal conclusions reached by the majority in the famous *IRC* case[11] was indeed that standing will usually need to be decided in the light of the legal and factual context.[12] The point was also taken that a person's standing may become relevant at the time at which the court exercises its discretion whether to award a remedy and, if so, which. A person may need to establish a different relationship to the subject matter of the case to be awarded an injunction or order of *mandamus* than for the award of a declaration. Thus the 'common' approach to standing, which may be acceptable and indeed desirable at the outset of the litigation, is much less appropriate at its close.[13]

A second feature of the standing literature (to which Peter Cane has made the most substantial contribution)[14] has been a developing sophistication in the schematic categorisation of the principles to be applied in decisions on the standing

---

10   Woolf and Jowell, *op. cit.* note 7 *supra*, p. 111. The one (temporary) exception to the 'generous' approach — in relation to representative standing — is discussed below.

11   *R v Inland Revenue Commissioners, ex parte National Federation of Self-Employed and Small Businesses Ltd* [1982] AC 617.

12   *Ibid.*, at 630 (Lord Wilberforce).

13   *Ibid.*, at 631.

14   In particular his 'Standing up for the Public' [1995] *Public Law* 276 and 'Standing, Representation, and the Environment' in Loveland, I. (ed.), *A Special Relationship? American Influences on Public Law in the UK*, Oxford: Clarendon Press 1995. See also Hilson, C., and Cram, I., 'Judicial Review and Environmental Law — is there a Coherent View of Standing?' (1996) 16 *Legal Studies* 1.

of different types of applicant. Thus Cane has distinguished those who establish standing on the basis of their own personal interests from those who seek standing on the basis that they represent the interests of others. Those claiming such 'representative standing' are then divisible into three groups. 'Associational standing' is typified by the organisation suing on behalf of its members. 'Public interest standing' is asserted by those who claim to represent not a group with identifiable membership but a wider 'public interest'.[15] Cane's third category, which is more formal in nature, is that of 'surrogate standing' where a nominal applicant represents the interests of the real party to the proceedings. Such an analysis may be used to explain why it is insufficient simply to claim that standing in public law proceedings should be treated differently from its private law counterpart: account should be taken of the different ways in which litigants may make legitimate use of judicial review and, therefore, of the different tests of standing which may be appropriately laid down.

The third general issue of note is that, adopting the Cane analysis, it is possible to conclude that while those applicants for review in the categories of 'personal' and 'associational' standing have benefited from the generosity of approach already referred to, there were initial difficulties with the treatment of applicants of the 'public interest' type which have only more recently been resolved, at least for the time being. These difficulties were demonstrated in the infamous *Rose Theatre* case,[16] where Schiemann J denied standing to a company formed to challenge the refusal of the minister to list an archaeological site. Incorporation could not of itself increase the sufficiency of interest of the individuals concerned and it had to be anticipated that, in some circumstances, there might be no one at all with an interest sufficient to challenge an unlawful decision. It has been argued that, on its particular facts, *Rose Theatre* was defensible.[17] Whether viewed as a claim to 'associational standing' or to 'public interest standing' in circumstances in which the public interest had already been adequately accommodated, the applicant's case may have been appropriately denied. On the whole, however, it has been interpreted as a case in which a very ungenerous attitude to standing was, rather provocatively, adopted.

Be that as it may, there have been more recent signs of an apparently liberalising shift of approach. Two cases in particular are interpreted as illustrating this trend.[18]

---

15 See also Jaffe, L. L., 'The Citizen as Litigant in Public Actions: the Non-Hohfeldian or Ideological Plaintiff' (1968) 116 U of Penn LR 1033.

16 *R v Secretary of State for the Environment, ex parte Rose Theatre Trust Ltd* [1990] 1 QB 504.

17 See, e.g., Cane, P., 'Statutes, Standing and Representation' [1990] *Public Law* 307 and 'Standing, Representation and the Environment', note 14 *supra*, at p. 148. See too Schiemann, Sir Konrad, 'Locus Standi' [1990] *Public Law* 342.

18 See also *R v Secretary of State for Foreign and Commonwealth Affairs, ex parte Rees-Mogg* [1994] QB 552 and *R v Secretary of State for Employment, ex parte Equal Opportunities Commission* [1995] 1 AC 1.

The first was that involving a challenge by Greenpeace to the regulation of the Sellafield site.[19] Otton J in a judgment in which he expressly declined to follow *Rose Theatre,* granted Greenpeace standing (although not the decision it sought on the merits). It was an organisation of national and international status with a large membership (including many in the Cumbria region); it was a serious and responsible body; the issues in the case were serious and, if standing were denied to Greenpeace, there might be no effective way of bringing the issues before the court. The second was the *World Development Movement* case,[20] in which the Movement was given standing to challenge the minister's decision to grant aid to fund construction of the Pergau dam in Malaysia. Factors considered included the importance of vindicating the rule of law and the likely absence of any other responsible challenger. Recalling much earlier examples of liberality of approach to standing,[21] Sir Stephen Sedley has spoken of a:

> contemporary shift in the perception of public law from a system which merely offers a different path to the vindication of private rights to a system of invigilation of the legality of governmental action. It focuses attention, in particular, on the fact that public law is concerned not necessarily with rights (which inhere in individuals) but with wrongs in the conduct of the state (which may but do not necessarily invade individual rights).[22]

It is important that brief mention also be made of the position in Scotland, where there was no division of remedies between those awardable in ordinary actions and those made pursuant to a petition to the supervisory jurisdiction of the Court of Session, which since the procedural changes of 1985[23] has been made by way of application for judicial review. The different remedies, however, attracted different standing rules,[24] but they were all expressed in terms of a person's 'title and interest' to sue. The procedural reform of 1985 did not, unlike the English reform, seek to make any changes in the rules of standing, although — rather paradoxically

---

19 *R* v *HMIP, ex parte Greenpeace Ltd (No. 2)* [1994] 4 All ER 329.
20 *R* v *Secretary of State for Foreign Affairs, ex parte World Development Movement* [1995] 1 All ER 611.
21 See especially *R* v *Speyer* [1916] I KB 595; 2 KB 858.
22 1996 Radcliffe Lecture, 'The Common Law and the Constitution'. The version of the lecture quoted is that reproduced in the *London Review of Books*, Vol. 19, 8 May 1997, p. 10.
23 SI 1985/500. See now Act of Sederunt (Rules of the Court of Session 1994) 1994 (SI 1994/1443).
24 See Bradley, A. W., 'Administrative Law' in the *Stair Memorial Encyclopaedia*, vol. 1, paras 308–323. This provides the most substantial account of the law of judicial review in Scotland. See also Reid, C. T., 'Legal Standing in Scotland' in Robinson, D., and Dunkley, J. (eds), *Public Interest Perspectives in Environmental Law*, London: Chancery Law Publishing, 1995; Himsworth, C. M. G., 'Judicial Review in Scotland' in Supperstone, M., and Goudie, J., *Judicial Review*, London: Butterworths (2nd ed., forthcoming); Cram, I. 'Towards Good Administration — The Reform of Standing in Scots Public Law' 1995 JR 332 and Munro, C., 'Standing in Judicial Review' 1995 SLT (News) 279.

and with much less apparent justification than in England, there is some authority for the view that rules of standing in relation to the general application for judicial review have converged and become a single rule.[25] As in England, the question of standing is raised in relatively few cases, but there has been some interesting restatement of the law, in particular at the hand of Lord Clyde in the cases of *Scottish Old People's Welfare Council (Age Concern), Petitioners*[26] and *Air 2000 Ltd v Secretary of State for Transport (No. 2)*.[27] In both cases, Lord Clyde relied on *dicta* of Lord Dunedin in *D & J Nicol v Dundee Harbour Trustees*[28] to hold that the question of standing must be treated as requiring satisfaction of the separate tests of 'title' and 'interest'. Furthermore, rejecting the view of the majority in the *IRC* case, Lord Clyde took the view that standing should normally be treated as a separate threshold question and one which was 'logically prior to and conceptually distinct from the merits of the case'.[29] The application of these tests led in *Air 2000*[30] to a holding that *Air 2000* did, as an established air traffic operator, have title and interest to challenge new air traffic distribution rules. On the other hand, in the *Age Concern* case, the pressure group was denied standing on the grounds that, while it had title, it did not have the required interest. It was not itself a potential claimant for benefit and the group's own campaigning objectives would not be hindered by the allegedly *ultra vires* action of the respondents.

On one view, this leaves Scotland with a much less developed and less generous concept of representative standing.[31] This point was indeed taken in a recent English case in which Popplewell J was persuaded that, although a token individual applicant might be nominated in its place, Greenpeace would itself be likely to encounter 'very real difficulties in . . . establishing a right of interest, as such, before a Scottish court'.[32] This was, he said, not a criticism but merely an observation on what might be a substantial difference in practice between the jurisdictions.

This view of the limitations of the Scots law of standing should, however, be qualified in two ways. On the one hand, it may be argued that Scots law merely remains frozen at a *Rose Theatre* stage with the need for further litigation upon which to hang arguments for the full adoption of a 'public interest' rather than

---

25 See the *Age Concern* case, note 26 *infra*.
26 1987 SLT 179.
27 1990 SLT 335.
28 1915 SC (HL) 7.
29 1987 SLT 179, at 184.
30 See also *Air 2000 Ltd v Secretary of State for Transport* 1989 SLT 698.
31 It is, at the very least, a different concept of standing which draws on a quite different historical underpinning. It is, for this reason, odd to see it noted in *R v Secretary of State for Social Services, ex parte CPAG* [1990] 2 QB 540, at 556, that, had the Department felt it necessary to raise a standing issue, it would have done so in reliance on *Age Concern*!
32 *R v Secretary of State for Scotland, ex parte Greenpeace Ltd,* 24 May 1995, unreported.

'associational' model.[33] Secondly, it should be noted that, although the equivalent
of a relator action by the Attorney-General is unknown, Scots law has historically
given some recognition to a broad right in individual citizens to challenge the
infringement of a public right by means of an *actio popularis*.[34] In *MacCormick* v
Lord Advocate,[35] however, one of the several reasons why the petitioners failed in
their challenge to the Queen's title as 'Elizabeth II' was lack of standing, despite
a claim that their action was an *actio popularis*. They could not have been accorded
title to sue 'without conceding a similar right to almost any opponent of almost
any political action to which public opposition has arisen'.[36]

STANDING AHEAD

The conclusion to be drawn from this survey of recent developments in the law of
standing in judicial review is that a certain stability has been achieved. If there is
a tension between the purposes which rules on standing serve, they are now in
some sort of an equilibrium. It is true that there is the apparent lingering curiosity
of the differences between the rules in Scotland and England, but as far as England
itself is concerned there is the sense of a firm commitment to the new broadening
of the rules on representative standing. The *Rose Theatre Trust* has been put behind
us and there is an understanding that the more liberal approach to standing is the
correct road to take. Although there are some continuing pressures in the direction
of further change — most radically in the direction of substantially greater rights
of third-party intervention in 'public interest' cases[37] — there seems to be a
consensus forming around the consolidation of the position now reached, perhaps
by means of statutory reconfirmation of the judge-made rules.[38]

A few years ago Lord Woolf, drawing on developments in Canadian jurisprudence during the 1980s, and in advance of the more recent English developments,
described[39] the approach adopted by the Supreme Court in *Finlay* v *Minister of
Finance*.[40] This was a two-track approach which conferred standing as of right to
the litigant who was personally adversely affected by the decision to be reviewed.

---

33 See also now *Cockenzie and Port Seton Community Council* v *East Lothian District Council* 1997
    SLT 81 and *E.I.S.* v *Robert Gordon University* (1 July 1996) 1996 GWD 26–1511.
34 Bradley, *op cit.* note 24 *supra*, para. 309.
35 1953 SC 396.
36 *Ibid.*, at p. 413 (Lord Cooper).
37 For substantial discussion of *inter alia* the advantages of opening up access to proceedings to
    additional 'public interest' parties, see Rawlings, R., 'Courts and Interests' in Loveland, I. (ed.),
    A Special Relationship? American Influences on Public Law in the UK, Oxford: Clarendon Press,
    1995. See also JUSTICE/Public Law Project, *A Matter of Public Interest: Reforming the Law and
    Practice on Interventions in Public Interest Cases* (1996).
38 See *op. cit.* note 7 *supra*., Law Commission.
39 Woolf, Sir Harry, 'Judicial Review: A Possible Programme for Reform' [1992] *Public Law* 221,
    at 232–33.
40 [1986] 2 SCR 607.

In the second track, on which access was granted in the discretion of court, were other potential litigants whose success would depend on the view taken by the court in the light of the following considerations:

(a) the allocation of scarce judicial resources,

(b) the need to screen out the mere busybody;

(c) the concern that in the determination of issues the courts should have the benefit of the conflicting points of view of those most directly affected by them; and

(d) a concern as to the proper role of the courts and their constitutional relationship to the other branches of government.

These considerations are not without their problems. There are sound objections to the idea that access to justice in vindication of the rule of law should depend on the availability of judges and courts.[41] There is scepticism about the existence of busybodies with so little else to do and in such numbers as to be the cause of much difficulty.[42] It does, however, seem reasonable that, in a system in which access is granted in the deliberate exercise of judicial discretion, these factors should at least be borne in mind. They are also the factors, however, which may be taken to have influenced the consensus which has emerged around the meaning of a 'sufficient interest' in English law. Under the present conditions of demand for judicial review and present perceptions of the 'proper role of the courts and their constitutional relationship to the other branches', the existing accommodation has been reached. If, therefore, we are to speculate about the ways in which rules on standing might come under pressure for change in the future, it would be helpful to consider the conditions which might bring about an increase in the nature and level of business, or a change in the role of reviewing courts or both. As far as the level of business is concerned, it is not the numbers of cases involving individual, directly-affected litigants that would be of primary interest. Their standing would be assured and, all other things being equal, the great majority of 'homeless' or 'immigrant' litigants would, for example, be granted standing. Of course, other things might turn out not to be equal and, for instance, rules restricting access to legal aid might tend to turn individual applications into applications by pressure groups, therefore placing them in the representative category.

Looking more broadly at the ways in which the role of reviewing courts may change and bring consequential changes for rules on standing, it may be helpful to consider them under three broad heads:

---

41 See, e.g., Cranston, R., 'Reviewing Judicial Review' in Richardson, G., and Genn, H., *Administrative Law and Government Action*, Oxford: Clarendon Press 1994, pp. 59–60; Harlow, C., 'Why Public Law is Private Law' in Zuckerman, A. A. S. and Cranston, R., *Reform of Civil Procedure: Essays on 'Access to Justice'*, Oxford: Clarendon Press, 1995, at 213.

42 See discussion in Woolf and Jowell, *op. cit.* note 7 *supra*, p. 100.

The constitutional role of courts in judicial review

It may be that the significance of judicial review will, after a long rise, go into decline. A wider availability of other forums in which to challenge decisions of government, or a wider access to statutory appeals[43] in the courts, might reduce pressure on judicial review. Perhaps the conditions for an increased reliance on political rather than judicial resolution of disputes may return? Perhaps the period from 1979 *was* different. Perhaps *The Judge over Your Shoulder* (or indeed the *Citizen's Charter*) will work. Perhaps a new era of openness will produce accountable government by other means (see Radford, Ch. 2, p. 45 and Tomkins, Ch. 14, p. 342). Perhaps, in ways which are difficult to imagine, there will be new developments in the internal review of official behaviour, which might take the pressure off all forms of external review. This might reduce business in the courts. It would also alter the purpose of judicial review in significant ways if it became less important as a means of monitoring the general quality of administrative performance and the balance tipped back firmly in the direction of the redress of individual grievances with consequences in turn for the rationale of *locus standi*.

While it is, for a variety of reasons, not unthinkable that judicial review should go into decline or change its character in these ways, and thus alter the way in which the role of reviewing courts is understood, it must be more likely that change will come about as a result of the further expansion of the scope and practice of review. We have, in the last couple of years, seen Lord Mustill's reconfirmation of a strengthening rationale of contemporary judicial review in which he blamed the failure of parliamentary remedies against the executive for the increased need for judicial review. The vacuum had to be filled in order not to leave the citizen without protection, and the 'courts have had no option but to occupy the dead ground in a manner, and in areas of public life, which could not have been foreseen 30 years ago'.[44] Closely related is that broader phenomenon in the literature of constitutional law which has been the presentation of the case for a general strengthening of the judicial role.[45] Commitment to a new judicial activism includes advocating a broadening and deepening of the grounds of review in the pursuit of a wider vision of fair administration,[46] an important component of which would be the adoption of the doctrine of proportionality (see Craig, Ch. 12, pp. 278 *et seq*) and a rejection of the cautionary words of, amongst others, Lord

---

43   *Cf.* Law Commission, *op. cit.* note 7 *supra.*

44   *R* v *Secretary of State for the Home Department, ex parte Fire Brigades Union* [1995] 2 AC 513, at 567.

45   Laws, Sir John, 'Is the High Court the Guardian of Fundamental Constitutional Rights?' [1993] *Public Law* 59; Lester, A., 'English Judges as Law Makers' [1993] *Public Law* 269.

46   On this, see, in particular, *R* v *MAFF, ex parte Hamble (Offshore) Fisheries Ltd* [1995] 2 All ER 714 (Sedley J); but *cf. R* v *Secretary of State for the Home Department, ex parte Hargreaves* [1997] 1 All ER 397.

Lowry in *Brind*.[47] There he warned that such a development would lead judges beyond the limits of their supervisory jurisdiction as previously understood and beyond the limits of their training and experience. It would also jeopardise stability and relative certainty in judicial decision making, as well as greatly expanding the business of the courts.[48] But such an expansion of the scope of review may nevertheless occur; and so too may the expansion of the rights-based underpinning of judicial review and, to accommodate it, increased discretionary powers of the judges.[49] The point here is not to address the merits of developments in pursuit of these forms of judicial activism, but simply to remind that these would not be brought about without consequences for both the quantity of judicial review business in the courts and, just as importantly, inter-institutional relations. If the starting assumption is right — that principles governing the proper role of *locus standi* derive from these wider aspects of the operation of judicial review — then changes may be expected with some confidence. And if such changes affecting *locus standi* are indeed a predictable, though indirect, result of changing judicial attitudes towards the role of courts, how much greater might be the changes which would follow a more direct intervention by Parliament legislating for constitutional reform? What will the incorporation of the European Convention on Human Rights bring? What will be the consequences of establishing a Scottish Parliament and the expansion of judicial review to embrace challenge to the *vires* not only of statutory instruments but of Acts of the new Parliament?

The impact of environmental law

There is another quite separate factor which may yet force further revision of our thinking about *locus standi*. We have already seen that some of the more recent developments in English law have arisen in cases with an environmental focus, and it seems certain that we have not in this respect heard the last of the environment.[50] As the environmental threat deepens and more regulatory powers are conferred on governmental bodies the more likely it is that the exercise of those powers will fall to be challenged both by those who are regulated and by those much wider groups on the other side, the side of the environment, who wish to compel a more enthusiastic use of regulatory power. It is difficult to forecast trends in this direction, but substantial recourse to the courts is perfectly foreseeable. The only reason for doubting this would be an abrupt change of environmental policy from

---

47   *R* v *Secretary of State for the Home Department, ex parte Brind* [1991] 1 AC 696.
48   *Ibid.*, at 766–67.
49   See, in particular, *R* v *Secretary of State for the Home Department, ex parte Bugdaycay* [1987] AC 514 and *R* v *Ministry of Defence, ex parte Smith* [1996] QB 517.
50   For a very helpful article see Grosz, S., 'Access to Environmental Justice in Public Law' in Robinson, D., and Dunkley, J., *op. cit.* note 24 *supra*. And, for a more recent account focusing in particular upon US/UK comparisons, see Cane, P., 'Standing, Representation, and the Environment', *op. cit.* note 14 *supra*.

increasingly tough 'command and control' mechanisms towards an expanded use of incentive-based techniques which might, in turn, lead to less concern about regulatory failure and thus to reduced scope for challenge by judicial review[51] — a point, of course, of broader application to administrative law in general.

Judicial review will not be the only expanding area. Provision for new forms of civil liability for environmental damage may produce much additional litigation in that field too. However, unless a response comes in the form of a new environmental court — which seems improbable at present — an increase in judicial review seems inevitable. The statutory codes for integrated pollution control, for waste management licensing,[52] for access to information,[53] to take three of many examples, are still in their relative infancy and so too are the new environment agencies.[54] There is much more to come, including the implementation of the complex new provisions for the remediation of contaminated land.[55]

As the existing case law has begun to show, environmental judicial review has the potential to raise very interesting issues in representative *locus standi*. The problems of how far an organisation claiming to represent the interests of a much wider group of people should be granted *locus* are well known. In general, the broader the group the greater the problem. Courts have tended to be intolerant of groups which expand to become all taxpayers, all citizens, the public at large. Even more problematic is the question of how far future, unborn generations could or should be represented in proceedings where powers conferred ostensibly for their benefit are challenged? Not to mention the problem of the representation of trees[56] and other nonhuman life-forms; and, for the very deep ecologists, rocks.

Even if an anthropocentric consensus has formed round the idea that these more distant interests are too fanciful for legal recognition,[57] or that they can reasonably be subsumed within the representation of existing human interests, this still implies a continuing commitment to a very broadly-based approach to representative *locus standi*.[58] If Greenpeace and similar organisations are to assume this responsibility, this cannot be made conditional upon, for instance, individual members being resident in a particular area, as in the Sellafield case; nor presumably upon their respectability as representative bodies. Pressure towards expansion of the existing rules in the direction of citizen suits seems inevitable, and an important question

---

51 See Sunstein, C. R., 'What's Standing after *Lujan*? Of Citizen Suits, "Injuries", and Article III' (1992) 91 Michigan LR 163, at 222.
52 Parts I and II of the Environmental Protection Act 1990.
53 Environmental Information Regulations 1992 (SI 1992/3240).
54 Environment Act 1995, Part I.
55 Environmental Protection Act 1990, Part IIA (as inserted by the Environment Act 1995).
56 See Stone, C., 'Should Trees have Standing?' (1972) 45 S Calif LR 451.
57 See, e.g., Krämer, L., 'Public Interest Litigation in Environmental Matters before European Courts' (1996) 8 JEL 1, at 15.
58 For a recent US account, see Farber, D. A., 'Stretching the Margins: The Geographic Nexus in Environmental Law' (1996) 48 Stanford LR 1247.

which may yet have to be addressed is whether the general rules of *locus standi* can readily accommodate such an expansion in a single area. It may be that, within the general class of representative standing, some especially broad rules will be needed for environmental issues, but for reasons which do not readily apply to other areas of decision making. Rules justified in the environmental sector might skew the pattern of rules overall.

The growing impact of European Community law

If some of these changes affecting the development of judicial review — whether as a result of constitutional or environmental developments — are a little speculative, there is one respect in which the future is already with us. The United Kingdom became a member of the European Community a quarter of a century ago and, if it is true that rules of standing in judicial review are, or should be, affected by a changed relationship between courts and Parliament — and Lord Lester has written of EC membership 'profoundly altering the constitutional role of British judges by widening the scope of substance and merits as well as of form and procedure',[59] then one might have imagined that, with the arrival of the first really serious opportunity to disapply (and, in effect, declare invalid) Acts of Parliament,[60] this would have forced a review of the rules. That there appears to have been no particular discussion of this point may be because it has taken most of the 25 years of membership for its constitutional consequences to sink in. The eye-opening cases of *Factortame*[61] and *Equal Opportunities Commission*[62] took a long time to appear and are still quite recent phenomena. We return to the 'constitutional' consequences of these cases for *locus standi* shortly, but we should first consider two other EC-related developments having an impact on standing.

The first is a very obvious point, but one which has consequences for both the type of judicial review and the quantity of judicial review we should expect to develop in relation to EC issues. In *R v Greater London Council, ex parte Blackburn*,[63] Lord Denning spoke of the 'high constitutional principle that if there is good ground for supposing that a government department or a public authority is transgressing the law or is about to transgress it in a way which offends or injures thousands of Her Majesty's subjects, then anyone of those offended or injured can draw it to the attention of the courts of law'.[64] One effect of the Community is, however, to extend this principle well beyond 'Her Majesty's subjects' and to necessitate a much wider view of citizenship and, therefore, of legitimate access

---

59 Lester, A., *op. cit.* note 45 *supra*, at 288.
60 The opportunity to exploit the Treaty of Union at 1707 in this way has never been fully taken.
61 *R v Secretary of State for Transport, ex parte Factortame Ltd (No. 2)* [1991] 1 AC 603.
62 *R v Secretary of State for Employment, ex parte Equal Opportunities Commission* [1995] 1 AC 1.
63 [1976] 3 All ER 184.
64 *Ibid.*, at 192.

to the courts. If it is a British minister or other public authority which is alleged to be acting in breach of some EC obligation, it is, in principle, just as likely that the applicant for review will be a national of another member state. Although Factortame Ltd and the other companies involved in the litigation brought under its name were British companies, the companies' directors (who were also parties to the application for review) were Spanish and the case raised was, in reality, in defence of a Spanish interest. If it had not involved a peculiarity of the fishing quota regime, the case would simply have been one challenging abuse of the rules of the common market by active discrimination against a non UK citizen. A failure by the UK government to impose on UK enterprises some form of EC-required regulation may also attract challenge from a company in another member state. Some international judicial review of this sort has already begun.[65] It can be expected to grow, and within it the 'citizenship' basis for standing.

There is a second, more direct form of impact which EC membership may have upon judicial review and specifically upon the rules of standing. The appreciation is growing that the development of a common market and the uniform imposition across the Union of rules not directly related to the market (e.g., environmental rules) require a legal regime which provides not only for substantive rules which apply equally across Europe, but also for closely harmonised rules on procedures and remedies. The enforcement of EC rules depends almost entirely upon their application in national courts, and therefore upon national procedural rules. Since, in all sorts of ways, these display a very great diversity, there is the perfectly credible possibility that all the energy devoted to the harmonisation of substantive rules may be undermined by procedural divisions. Treating standing loosely for a moment as a 'procedural' issue, rights to protection against market discrimination would be rendered useless if there were no guarantee of non discriminatory access to courts to enforce them.

If there is indeed a need to achieve procedural harmonisation (and assuming a continuing commitment to reliance upon national courts for the enforcement of EC rules), two alternative strategies are available. One is the promulgation of a Europe-wide procedural code which national courts would then be obliged to apply, at least in EC-related cases. On a number of occasions the European Court of Justice has called for such a code, or at least has appeared to regret its absence,[66] but the political and technical barriers to such a project are formidable[67] and it

---

65 Instances so far would include *Van Duyn* v *Home Office* [1975] Ch. 358; *R* v *Home Secretary, ex parte Dannenberg* [1984] QB 766; *R* v *Ministry of Agriculture, Fisheries and Food, ex parte FEDESA* [1988] 3 CMLR 661; *R* v *IRC, ex parte Commerzbank AG* [1993] ECR I-4017; and *R* v *Home Secretary, ex parte Gallagher* [1996] 2 CMLR 951.

66 See, e.g., Case 130/79 *Express Dairy Foods Ltd* v *Intervention Board for Agricultural Produce* [1980] ECR 1887, at 1900.

67 But see the preliminary moves made in this direction by the group invited by the EC Commission to consider the 'approximation' of laws of procedure. Storme, M. (ed.), *Approximation of Judiciary Law in the European Union*, Dordrecht: Nijhoff, 1994.

seems at present unlikely to be pursued. The other harmonising strategy is to rely on the Court's insistence — maintained more or less consistently since the *Rewe* case in 1976[68] — that there be 'effective protection of Community rights'. The principle of subsidiarity will normally require procedural rules to be left in the hands of member states, but these rules must yield if they would frustrate Community rights by making it impossible or excessively difficult for such rights to be enforced. This was the principle which in the *Factortame* case required that the rule against interim injunctions against the Crown be suspended, and the Court of Justice has taken the same approach to ensure the modification of other procedural and remedial rules.[69] It is not a very satisfactory line of approach for the Court because it invokes the application of a rather clumsy and unpredictable test; and it is also a test which is very one-sided in its operation. It serves to protect the holder of a 'Community right'. It cannot, it seems, be invoked by a person seeking protection from some over-zealous enforcement of such a right.

Despite these deficiencies, it seems quite possible that the need to ensure the effective protection of Community rights will require the Court of Justice to insist on some base standards for rules of standing. It would be shown to undermine the enforcement of Community rules if standing were denied in the courts of any member state to someone who, in the view of the Court of Justice, ought to have access for that purpose. Uniformity of application of the law across the Community would be as much affected by locally defective rules of standing as by an uneven application of the substantive rules.

It may be that, if the Court of Justice did begin to insist on minimum standards for rules on standing, representative standing might be a principal target — although it may be noted, in passing, that the standards the Court has itself imposed in actions brought before it to review the legality of the actions of Community institutions themselves have not been noted for their liberality. In *Greenpeace* v *EC Commission*,[70] following a long line of earlier cases, the Court of First Instance denied standing to both individuals and to Greenpeace in their attempt to challenge the Commission decision to fund power station construction in the Canaries. In the language of Article 173 of the Treaty, they were not 'directly and individually concerned'.[71] Although there is nothing which formally requires the standards which the Court of Justice imposes on national courts dealing with national

---

68 Case 33/76 *Rewe* v *Landwirtschaftskammer Saarland* [1976] ECR 1989.
69 For recent instances, see Case C-312/93 *Peterbroeck van Campenhout & Cie* v *Belgium* [1995] ECR I-4599, [1996] 1 CMLR 793; Case C-430-431/93 *Jeroen van Schijndel and another* v *Stichting Pensioenfonds voor Fysiotherapeuten* [1995] ECR I-4705, [1996] 1 CMLR 801. See Himsworth, C. M. G., 'Things Fall Apart: The Harmonisation of Community Judicial Procedural Protection Revisited' (1997) 22 EL Rev 291.
70 Case T-585/93 [1995] ECR II-2205.
71 For a note on the case see Gérard, N., 'Access to Justice on Environmental Matters — a case of Double Standards?' (1996) 8 JEL 139; and see Krämer, L., *op. cit.* note 57 *supra*.

institutions to reflect those it adopts in its own proceedings in relation to Community institutions, it would not be surprising if this were the case and it might be thought to be fair. The other possibility is, however, that either the existing restrictive approach of the Court will, in due course, be modified, or that it will, in any event, insist on more generous standards for *locus standi* in national courts when they are involved in protecting Community rights. It would, for instance, be interesting to speculate about how the Court of Justice would have reacted to a reference from the *EOC* case if a majority of the House of Lords had been disposed to refuse rather than grant standing to the Equal Opportunities Commission.

Certainly a target for the Court of Justice might be a reference from a Scottish court if an EC-related case arose in which the court sought to apply the stern test adopted in the *Age Concern* case to a representative body seeking judicial review. What looks like an anomalous parting of the ways between the two national legal systems might be held to be unacceptable by the Court of Justice on the ground that the Scottish test of title and interest is inadequate to enable protection of a Community right.[72]

There is one particular field in which there has been a European initiative not from the Court of Justice but from the Commission, and for this we return to the environment. It has already been noted that there appears to be no enthusiasm at a Community level for the promulgation of general procedural rules which would bind national courts in relation to EC-related cases. However, in a Communication in 1996, 'Implementing Community Environmental Law',[73] the Commission made a number of proposals for the better implementation and enforcement of EC environmental rules in member states of the Community, and some of these were specifically related to access to justice.[74] Whereas in areas where powerful economic interests are at stake it may be reasonable to assume that enforcement of legislation will be sufficiently encouraged by the economic operators themselves, this is not necessarily the case in relation to ecological or environmental interests: 'Enforcement of environmental law, in contrast to other areas of Community law such as the internal market and competition, therefore mainly rests with public authorities, and is dependent on their powers, resources and goodwill.'[75] What this in turn requires is that there are supplementary avenues for improving enforcement of the law and, in particular, actions by non governmental organisations and/or citizens. The Communication recalls the problems of environmental protection caused by the 'lack of a private interest as an enforcement driving force',[76] but it observes that:

---

72   It is of interest here to note that the Council in *Kincardine and Deeside District Council* v *Forestry Commissioners* 1992 SLT 1180, was held to have title and interest to challenge the implementation of the EC Environmental Assessment Directive.

73   COM (96) 500.

74   See also the Community's Fifth Action Programme, *Towards Sustainability* (1993) OJ 1993 C138.

75   *Ibid.*, para. 37.

76   *Ibid.*, para. 38.

the ability of the public, as such, to take part in legal actions regarding application and enforcement of Community environmental laws differs widely throughout the Community. . . . It can however be stated that the public and public interest groups do not as a general rule have sufficient access to the national courts of the Member States in environmental matters.[77]

Restrictions on access arise partly because of standing rules which require a 'special interest' to be established, and partly because the cost of enforcement actions may be prohibitive.

The 'access to justice' section of the Communication concludes with consideration of a number of options for taking the issue forward. Prominent among them is the Commission's view that:

a possible way towards achieving improved application and enforcement of Community environmental law would be to ensure that environmental NGOs recognised by Member States are given the necessary *locus standi* to bring judicial review actions, which would be against public authorities in the Member States. If such a scheme proves desirable, a first step towards this direction could be a recommendation encouraging Member States to broaden access to justice for non governmental organisations.[78]

After the publication of the Communication, it became apparent that the then UK government had no enthusiasm at all for this part of the Commission's proposals. It pointed out that the English High Court had already liberalised its approach and it was, in any event, a matter for national governments to decide on the scope of actions in national courts rather than for Community institutions.[79]

Whatever becomes of that particular initiative, there is clear pressure in the direction of EC harmonisation, whether by single issue (environmental) legislation or under guidance from the Court of Justice for the protection of Community rights. There is, however, a further stage to be considered, and that is the question of the consequential effects of specific EC-driven changes upon other aspects of judicial review in a member state. When the Court of Justice requires procedural or remedial change to achieve the better enforcement of a Community rule, that

---

77   *Ibid.*, para. 39.
78   *Ibid.*, para. 43. At an earlier stage, the Commission had been considering the possibility of a Directive to ensure extended access to the courts and substantial work was undertaken by independent researchers to produce a draft Directive. See Fuhr, M., Gebers, B., Ormond, T. and Roller, G., 'Access to Justice: Legal Standing for Environmental Associations in the European Union' in Robinson, D., and Dunkley, J. (eds), *op. cit.* note 24 *supra.*
79   See Explanatory Memorandum on EC Legislation (114 18/96), 9 December 1996 and HL Evidence on 27 November 1996. See Second Report of the House of Lords Select Committee on the European Communities, 'Community Environmental Law; Making it Work' (1997–98) HL Paper 12.

does not in itself compel a general change of the domestic law where no Community issue is at stake and to which the Court's jurisdiction does not extend. That does not mean, however, that there are not good reasons why, in the interests of coherence *within* the domestic system, the influence of the EC rule should not spread more widely. In *Factortame*, the Court of Justice insisted on the availability of an interim injunction against the Crown in circumstances where the enforcement of a Community right demanded it. That could not, in itself, require wider access to remedies against the Crown. There could be one rule for EC-related cases and another where there was no EC connection. The point was, however, taken in *M v Home Office*[80] that it would be preferable to avoid the emergence of a dual system of administrative law and that the domestic rule should, for all purposes, be brought into line and the internal coherence of the system restored.[81] If this approach is adopted, we may expect that any EC developments that do occur will penetrate more deeply into national systems than might at first have been imagined.

Lastly in relation to the EC, we should remember the single most important constitutional consequence of membership, which must be the supremacy of the Treaty and its law and the new-found role of the courts in disapplying and invalidating UK statutes. If, as earlier assumed, the role of the courts *vis-à-vis* other organs of government may be determinative of their attitude to *locus standi,* one would imagine that this new function of constitutional adjudication might bring the greatest changes. We shall have to wait and see. Having taken 25 years to be persuaded that the old rules of parliamentary supremacy do no longer apply, it may take a while for any new approach to standing to evolve. Perhaps, however, the changes may be less than might be supposed. A glance towards the North American jurisdictions shows no great distinctions being drawn between 'constitutional' and 'administrative' standing. Indeed, *Finlay* was a case in which non constitutional challenge in Canada was being deliberately aligned with its constitutional counterpart; and in the United States, when specific statutory guidance is absent, the test of 'injury' is applied regardless of whether it is ultimately a constitutional issue and the validity of legislation which is at stake. There are familiar tensions over confining standing to the vindication of private rights or special interests, although since *Lujan*,[82] it seems that the Supreme Court can claim constitutional justification for holding that Congress has itself sought to extend standing (in the direction of 'citizen suits') beyond limits implicitly laid down in the Constitution.[83]

---

80 [1994] 1 AC 377, at 422 (Lord Woolf).
81 The problem of the 'gap' which may open up between EC-related aspects of domestic systems of administrative law and the non-EC aspects (whether procedural or substantive) is one which has been most exhaustively explored by van Gerven, W., at *inter alia* 'Bridging the Gap between Community and National Laws: Towards a Principle of Homogeneity in the Field of Legal Remedies' (1995) 32 CML Rev 679.
82 *Lujan* v *Defenders of Wildlife* (1992) 504 US 555.
83 See Sunstein, *op. cit.* note 51 *supra.*

Despite claims increasingly made that the EC Treaty has a 'constitutional' status within the Union, parallels with countries with 'real' constitutions should be drawn with care. The common feature, however — the power of the courts to strike down legislation — is of the highest importance, and in the United Kingdom a great novelty. In a country in which sufficiency of interest to challenge the validity of an Act of Parliament would have been a meaningless concept a few years ago, it will be a matter of some fascination to see how meaning comes to be injected into it.

CONCLUSION: NO STANDING STILL

There is no doubting that standing retains its status as a major question in the UK systems of administrative law. Shedding much of its technically burdened past, its significance is now more easily seen and there is a greater clarity about how changes in the approach adopted by courts have moved in the direction of a liberalisation of 'public interest' standing which is underpinned by the same principles which have guided the development of judicial review as a whole. On this basis, it has been suggested that the rules on standing have become better integrated within judicial review doctrine and have acquired a certain stability. It has become clearer who are the individuals and bodies with an interest justifying recognition by the courts as 'stakeholders'.

Of course, no rules should be expected to remain in a state of complete stability and it would be strange if the rules on standing were not to develop further in familiar, incremental ways at the hands of the judges. What has been suggested, however, in this chapter is that there are some influences bearing upon judicial review which may produce more than merely incremental change in the standing rules. It is hoped that in the identification of those influences by reference to the constitutional role of courts, environmental litigation and the European Union, the easy part of forecasting future change may have been achieved. One can see that the 'Old Constraints' may come to be lifted.

'New Horizons' are, however, less clearly seen. The second aspect of forecasting change — the prediction of actual outcomes — is very much more difficult. It is, in particular, difficult to see how the different influences bearing upon standing will interact. It may be that we shall lose the unity of existing rules. The need for 'effective protection' of EC rights may produce a hiving-off, if only temporarily, of rules of standing applicable to the enforcement of EC law. Specifically in relation to EC environmental law, pressure groups may have to be given added recognition. Even if not EC-driven, the enforcement of environmental law may compel solutions specific to that sector.

Other predictions are complicated because, although the idea is attractive that the rules on standing be aligned with the general principles in forming the overall functioning of the courts, the particularities of its application are much less clear and perhaps counterintuitive. A broadening constitutional role for courts in adjudicating upon the *vires* of legislation — whether Westminster Acts or Act of a devolved Scottish Parliament — might imply a broadening of standing rules to embrace the broadening of the interests involved. On the other hand, it may be more likely that, just because of the broadening of the courts' jurisdiction, it will be necessary for them to look more restrictively at the interest asserted by an applicant for judicial review and to consider it more closely in relation to the actual remedy sought. The one confident prediction must be, however, that standing will not, as an issue in the progress towards 'New Horizons' in administrative law, stand alone.

10

Withdrawing: A Problem in Judicial Review?

Maurice Sunkin

SUMMARY

This chapter considers problems associated with the withdrawal of applications for judicial review, particularly once leave has been obtained. Approximately half of applications granted leave are withdrawn before a final hearing. Withdrawal is therefore important in terms of case-load management, but it raises other issues as well. While it is generally desirable for parties to resolve their disputes without the need for a court hearing, withdrawal is problematical for two main types of reason. First, there is a concern based on research in other fields of law that cases may be withdrawn when litigants are coerced by a more powerful opposition into accepting settlements which are unfair. Whether this occurs in judicial review is as yet unknown. However, withdrawal may also be undesirable when courts are prevented from scrutinising the legality of public actions and developing public law. This chapter considers these concerns and argues that reforms will be needed to ensure that the phenomenon of withdrawal remains compatible with the developing public functions of judicial review.

INTRODUCTION

This chapter concerns an aspect of judicial review which rarely receives the attention of students of public law. Our interests are usually monopolised by the content of judgments delivered after a formal adjudication has occurred. Sometimes we consider the problems associated with gaining access to the judicial review system, such as standing[1] and the operation of the leave requirement;[2] more rarely we are concerned with the impact of judgments.[3] As students of the system we are hardly ever concerned with those applications for judicial review which are withdrawn before they proceed to a full hearing. Yet very large numbers of applications are withdrawn, often after leave has been obtained and often following a settlement between the parties.[4] As well as being important numerically, the phenomenon of withdrawal raises key issues of principle. This chapter focuses on withdrawals after leave. Its aim is to introduce some of these issues of contention in the hope of stimulating more debate about withdrawal in the public law context.

The vast majority of civil claims are settled without the need for a court hearing. This is widely considered to be a good thing, to be encouraged and generally applauded. Out of court settlement is seen to be convenient and efficient; it saves the parties time and expense, and avoids the paraphernalia of a court hearing. It also saves public money and avoids a waste of judicial resources.[5] Nonetheless, there is a growing literature, much of it empirically based, which indicates that out of court settlement may be far more problematical than these assertions imply.[6] First, there is evidence that the process of settlement — and consequently the outcomes of settlements themselves — may unfairly prejudice some litigants, particularly those confronted by an opposition which is substantially better resourced and more experienced. In this situation settlement out of court may deprive the weaker side of the formalities of the courtroom which may serve to create a more level playing field. Secondly, there are reasons to doubt that settlement out of court is necessarily as efficient and cost-effective as it is widely assumed to be. Settlements themselves take time and absorb resources. They also incur hidden costs. It has been argued, for example, that by restricting the generation of judicial opinions and precedents, settlements deprive the public of the benefits that flow from clarifications of, and developments in, the law.[7] Thirdly,

---

1   See Ch. 9: No Standing Still on Standing.
2   See generally Le Sueur, A.P., and Sunkin, M., 'Applications for Leave: The Requirement of Leave' [1992] *Public Law* 102.
3   On the impact of judicial review, see Richardson G., and Sunkin, M., 'Judicial Review: Questions of Impact' [1996] *Public Law 79*.
4   In the present context the term settlement is being used to refer to situations where the parties have agreed that the matter should not be pursued. Bearing in mind that judicial review is often concerned with matters of procedure, it does not necessarily imply that the applicant's substantive grievance has been satisfactorily resolved.
5   Genn, H., *Hard Bargaining*, Oxford: Clarendon Press, 1987, p. 1. Encouragement of settlement is an important element of Lord Woolf's proposals for reforming the civil justice system: *Access to Justice: Final Report to the Lord Chancellor on the Civil Justice System in England and Wales*, London: HMSO, 1996.
6   Much of the current writing is North American. For a recent review of the literature, see Cranston, R. 'Social Research and Access to Justice' in Zuckerman, A.A.S, and Cranston, R., (eds), *Reform of Civil Procedure: Essays on 'Access to Justice'*, Oxford: Clarendon Press, 1995.
7   Coleman, J.L., *Markets, Morals and the Law*, Cambridge: Cambridge University Press, 1988.

it can be argued that as well as stifling the flow of information from the courts, procedures and attitudes which encourage settlement may operate to insulate powerful litigants from adjudication thereby ensuring that their actions, policies and procedures are not subject to judicial scrutiny and possible criticism and sanction. In such situations norms and standards of conduct in effect become the product of private and informal bargaining between unequal parties with the minimum degree of judicial oversight, rather than the result of the more open and formal judicial process. Where the powerful party is a public body — and particularly where it is a branch of executive government — such concerns clearly raise further and deeper questions about the effect of settlements on the rule of law itself. Lastly, some also argue that encouragement of settlement trivialises the task of the courts by assuming it to be concerned with the resolution of private disputes rather than the articulation of public values embodied in the law.[8]

Despite this growing literature, very little has yet been written specifically about withdrawal following settlement in judicial review proceedings;[9] and little is yet known about why applications are withdrawn, on what terms and with what consequences for the parties. The paucity of writing and the level of ignorance should not be taken to indicate that withdrawal is unimportant in this area of law, however. On the contrary, this phenomenon of withdrawal raises some of the least considered but most interesting and difficult problems associated with modern public law litigation.

When applications are withdrawn the consequences extend beyond the particular parties involved or the specific issues raised by the case. As well as having implications for court waiting lists, the withdrawal of judicial review proceedings raises many of the broader problems to which I have just referred with particular intensity. Few today would argue that judicial review can be considered to be exclusively — or even mainly — concerned with resolving individual disputes, and most would accept that judicial review has a broader role to play in providing a system of legal scrutiny and developing public law principles. Where withdrawal prevents the courts from reviewing governmental actions or procedures which are of dubious legality, this aspect of its role will not be performed. For this and other reasons the phenomenon of withdrawal raises one of the central tensions in contemporary public law litigation, namely that between the dispute resolution

---

8   Fiss, O., 'Against Settlement' (1984) 93 *Yale Law Journal* 1073. *Cf.* Cranston, *op. cit.* note 6 *supra*, at pp. 46–7.

9   I am not aware of any standard student work on UK public law dealing with withdrawal or settlement in judicial proceedings. Certainly this is not an issue addressed in de Smith, S.A., Woolf, H. and Jowell, J., *Judicial Review of Administrative Action* (5th ed.), London: Sweet & Maxwell, 1995. Even the practitioners' guides provide only very short accounts. See, e.g., The Public Law Project, *Applicant's Guide to Judicial Review*, London: Sweet & Maxwell, 1995, pp. 140–1; Clayton, R., and Tomlinson, H., *Judicial Review Procedure*, Chichester: John Wiley, 1996 pp. 171–3.

function of judicial review and those broader functions which are associated with calling government to account. I shall return to this tension later in the chapter.[10]

As well as issues of principle there are also important issues of practice. Research has revealed that approximately half of all applications for judicial review are withdrawn after leave has been obtained and prior to a full hearing.[11] Indeed, in some classes of application withdrawal has constituted the dominant form of disposal of cases.[12]

Further research will throw more light on why so many applications are not proceeded with.[13] However, it is already clear that there are various reasons why applications are withdrawn once leave has been obtained.[14] It may be, for example, that a grant of interim relief stopping the immediate implementation of a decision adverse to the applicant is sufficient to satisfy the applicant's interest in the case. If a leave decision has been made on a purely *ex parte* basis, without the respondent having been represented, it will be only at the post-leave stage that the respondent's side of the case will be made known and be fully considered by the applicant's legal advisers.[15] If they advise that the application stands little chance of success in the light of the respondent's evidence, the applicant may decide to withdraw; or the applicant may be forced to withdraw by having legal aid withdrawn.[16]

Respondents may also decide, at this stage, to settle the case at least partially in favour of the applicant. The grant of leave may have attracted adverse publicity for the body concerned, which it is thought can best be dissipated by an early settlement. The respondent may also consider that the grant of interim relief to the applicant makes the case less worthwhile or economical to pursue to a full hearing. For example, where the court orders that a homeless applicant be allowed to stay in temporary accommodation at the respondent authority's expense pending the

10   See Fiss, *op. cit.* note 8 *supra.*

11   Applications may be withdrawn after leave has been obtained with the consent of the Crown Office Master or a judge. For the relevant *Practice Directions* see [1982] 1 WLR 979 (civil proceedings) and [1983] 1 WLR 925 (criminal proceedings).

12   Bridges, L., Meszaros, G. and Sunkin, M., *Judicial Review in Perspective*, London: Cavendish, 1995, pp. 122–3.

13   Lee Bridges, George Meszaros and I are currently conducting ESRC-funded research on judicial review litigation. The fieldwork for this research is still in progress and nothing in this chapter should be taken to reflect in any way the provisional or final findings of this project.

14   As Sedley J has observed '. . . while the full range of reasons for [withdrawal after leave] is the subject of continuing research, attrition and surrender must account for some cases' (*R* v *Camden BC, ex parte Martin* [1997] 1 All ER 307, at 312g).

15   Lawyers representing applicants must give further careful consideration to the merits of the application once they have received notice of the respondent's evidence and may be subjected to a wasted costs order if they proceed with a weak application: *R* v *Horsham DC, ex parte Wenman* [1995] 1 WLR 680, at 701.

16   A standard limitation placed on many grants of legal aid in judicial review proceedings is that on receipt of the respondent's evidence, counsel's opinion should be obtained on the merits of continuing. See further Bridges *et al., op. cit.* note 12 *supra*, Ch. 5.

outcome of the case, the authority may decide that it is more economical to offer cheaper permanent accommodation immediately. Where the applicant is legally-aided, the respondent public authority is unlikely to be able to recover the costs of pursuing the case to a full hearing, even if eventually successful, and this factor may also render it more economical to settle the matter once leave has been granted.

The public body may consider that, on further consideration and in the light of any comments made by the judge when granting leave, the applicant's case is justified or does not raise important issues of principle worth pursuing to a full hearing; or that given the risks and the delays which will be incurred settlement is worthwhile from a purely pragmatic point of view. By the same token, the respondent may feel that the application does indeed threaten a key policy or procedure which it hopes to continue in general application. In this situation a settlement of the particular applicant's case may be seen as desirable because it will insure against a court finding the policy or procedure to be unlawful, and thereby forcing the public body in question to undertake more radical reforms.

Whatever the precise reasons for their occurrence, debate about the merits of withdrawal and settlement is likely to become more intense as the pressure on the judicial review system continues to grow and as judges become increasingly drawn into case-load management issues. The current discussion should therefore be placed in the context of some of the more general trends in the use of judicial review and the various proposals for reform which are currently on the table.

THE BACKGROUND: THE GROWTH IN LEGAL CHALLENGE

The growth in the use of judicial review to challenge the legality of the exercise of public power is widely regarded as being one of the most significant legal trends of the past decade or so. Between 1981 and 1996, the number of applications for leave to seek judicial review each year increased from 533 to 3,901.[17]

This growth is widely thought to be indicative of the growing importance of judicial review, and hence of the courts, lawyers and the law within our system of government.[18] Certainly eminent commentators have taken the statistics to 'show a convincing picture of an increased need to resort to the courts for protection against alleged abuse by public bodies of their public duties'.[19] However, this growth has also had its costs. In particular the growing case-load placed this part of the court system under tremendous pressure, and by the early 1990s non

---

17 Crown Office figures to December 1996.
18 The authors of the latest edition of de Smith say that 'the effect of judicial review on the practical exercise of power has now become constant and central': de Smith *et al., op. cit.* note 9 *supra*, p. vii.
19 Woolf, Sir H., 'Public law–private law: why the divide?' [1986] *Public Law* 220, at 222.

expedited judicial reviews were often taking over two years to be heard. As the Law Commission noted, this scale of delay was almost universally condemned as being 'completely unacceptable', 'intolerable', 'reaching scandalous proportions', and 'likely to defeat the purpose of taking proceedings'.[20]

In order to try to cope with the problems associated with overload, judges and administrators have felt forced to introduce a series of reforms that have chipped away at principles previously regarded as being central to the running of the system.[21] Thus since the early 1980s leave decisions have usually been made on the basis of the papers by a single judge, rather than following oral argument in open court;[22] whereas in the early 1980s the dominant approach was to grant leave to proceed to those able to show that their case was potentially arguable, during that decade judges began to insist that applicants show actual arguability, and even then applicants were sometimes excluded if their cases were not exceptional in some way;[23] more recently the idea that judicial review should be the province of an elite specialised Bench has been forsaken as non specialist High Court judges and Deputy High Court judges are increasingly drawn in to help handle the case-load.

The statistics therefore reflect two very different and potentially incompatible images of judicial review. On the one hand there is a popular external image of judicial review as a dynamic jurisdiction of growing importance to citizens and government, and indeed to the constitution itself. But there is also an internal image often seen only by those working with the system and by those trying to use it as litigants. This is an image of a process under continual and possibly mounting stress.

There is no doubt that there has been a marked growth in resort to judicial review, but research has warned us to treat the statistics with a degree of caution.[24] One reason is that the general figures do not necessarily reflect trends in particular subject areas. The vast bulk of the increase in litigation, for instance, has been due to the use of judicial review in two main areas of 'mass' use, namely immigration and homelessness.[25] When these two areas are excluded the increase in the growth in judicial review has been far less striking. Looking more closely at the particular

---

20 Law Commission, *Administrative Law: Judicial Review and Statutory Appeals* (Law Com No. 226), London: HMSO, 1993, para. 2.15.

21 Delays have been greatly reduced. In December 1996 the Crown Office projected that waiting times from entry into Part B of the lists as at the end of October 1996 will be 4.3 months for the Divisional Court and 5.7 months for trials by single judges.

22 The new procedure was part of a package of reforms introduced by SI 1980/2000. Prior to these reforms it was thought to be important, in order to safeguard applicants, that leave decisions be given by three judges in open court, especially if leave was to be refused: Law Commission, *Remedies in Administrative Law* (Law Com. No. 73), London: HMSO, 1976, para. 40.

23 See generally Le Sueur and Sunkin, *op. cit.* note 2 *supra*.

24 Sunkin, M., 'What is Happening to Applications for Judicial Review?' (1987) 50 *Modern Law Review* 432; Sunkin, M., 'The Judicial Review Case-load 1987–1989' [1991] *Public Law* 490; Bridges *et al., op. cit.* note 12 *supra*.

25 During 1996 there were 1,748 immigration applications to seek leave and 340 homelessness applications: Crown Office figures.

subject areas involved in challenges, we find that many aspects of governmental activity affecting vital rights and interests of individuals and groups, attract very few — and even declining numbers of — challenges. For instance, in the mid-1980s there were approximately 100 prisoner applications per year, whereas by the end of the decade fewer than 20 applications were made by prisoners annually.[26] Similarly, while millions of decisions are taken concerning the allocation of welfare benefits, between 1987 and 1989 inclusive fewer than 30 applications involving welfare benefits were made annually. Even in areas of 'mass' use, much of the litigation focuses on very particular activities. For example, during the mid-1980s approximately 20 per cent of all civil applications for leave to seek judicial review involved one type of immigration decision, namely those by immigration officers to refuse permission to enter on the grounds that people were not genuine visitors. More recently refusal to grant asylum has been the most common target for challenge.[27]

Whatever these figures mean, it is not self-evident that they indicate a dynamic jurisdiction widely used by citizens to force the rule of law on government. On the contrary, they may be more indicative of a jurisdiction which is largely irrelevant to most who are adversely affected by actions of government. Certainly these figures suggest that it is premature to stop asking why judicial review is so rarely used in so many areas of governmental activity impinging upon the rights and interests of individuals and groups. Amongst the several answers that may be given, one is that access to the judicial review system is more problematical than the general case-load figures appear to imply.[28]

A second reason for being cautious when using generalised data on the growth in judicial review, flows from the first. We should not assume that the figures are evidence that government in general is becoming more or less directly accountable to the courts. We have just seen that much of the growth in the use of judicial review has focused on particular areas of decision making. It is a corollary to this that judicial review subjects only a narrow range of institutions to regular challenge. Since challenges to central government have usually involved immigration, the respondent in most of these cases has been either the Immigration Appeal Tribunal or the immigration section of the Home Office. This is one reason why the Home Office has been attracting approximately 75 per cent of all challenges to central government decision making.[29] The result is that, despite the huge growth

---

26 Bridges, et al., op. cit. note 12 supra, pp. 18–19.
27 See further ibid., pp. 20–6.
28 See Sunkin, M., 'The Problematical Nature of Access to Judicial Review' in Hadfield, B. (ed.), Judicial Review: A Thematic Approach, Dublin: Gill & Macmillan, 1995.
29 The next most frequently challenged departments were the Department of the Environment (7 per cent of the applications against central government) and the Inland Revenue (4 per cent). Only three other central government departments were subject to 10 or more judicial review challenges during the period 1987–1989 — the Department of Social Security, the Department of Transport, and the Welsh Office: Bridges et. al., op. cit. note 12 supra, pp. 42–3.

in the overall case-load, challenge by judicial review has remained a relatively infrequent occurrence for most central government departments, often happening no more than a handful of times a year. Moreover, even leaving aside immigration and homelessness, it has been local rather than central government which is most often the focus for challenge in areas such as town and country planning, education and licensing. But here too judicial review litigation appears to have been highly centralised, with few local authorities outside London finding themselves being regularly the subject of applications to seek leave.[30]

There is also a third reason for being cautious in the way we view the data on judicial review litigation that is of particular pertinence to this chapter. The statistics which are usually taken to indicate the growth in public law litigation are based on the numbers of applications for leave to seek judicial review rather than on the numbers of judicial reviews themselves. This distinction is important both in scale and in principle. Each year significant numbers of applications are withdrawn even before the leave stage is reached.[31] Of those applications which proceed to the leave stage, approximately 40 per cent will be unsuccessful and will be rejected having been refused leave.[32] Of those applications which succeed in surmounting the leave hurdle, only about half will proceed to be dealt on their merits by a judge after a full hearing, and the rest will be withdrawn. In other words, looking at the way applications for judicial review proceed through the system, we find that roughly half fall at the leave stage and that roughly half of those which are granted leave are later discontinued, usually with only formal judicial involvement. The result is that only 25 per cent or so of the applications originally filed at the Crown Office (and upon which the general statistics are based) result in scrutiny by the courts of the legality of governmental action.[33]

It is worth noting in passing that withdrawal following the grant of leave is particularly common in the two areas of 'mass' use of judicial review. This factor suggests that the profile of the case-load (the incidence and type of application) at the leave stage does not exactly mirror the profile of the case-load being handled

---

30   *Ibid.* pp. 38–40 and 43–4. This is not to say that authorities were not regularly threatened, or that they did not feel regularly threatened.

31   In these cases the applicant will have filed an application at the Crown Office but will have withdrawn it before any formal step has been taken. During the years 1987, 1988 and 1989, 14 per cent, 5 per cent and 8 per cent respectively of applications were withdrawn at this stage: Bridges *et al., op. cit.* note 12 *supra*, p. 117.

32   The actual success rates during 1987–1989 were 65 per cent, 64 per cent, and 66 per cent. Note that the official statistics tend to show lower success rates, probably because they do not take account of applications which are withdrawn before the leave stage. Here too caution is needed as success/failure rates can vary greatly between subject areas. According to Crown Office figures, in 1994 only 18 per cent of immigration cases were granted leave, whereas research shows that approximately 80 per cent of homelessness applications were granted leave: Bridges *et. al., op. cit.* note 12 *supra*, p. 121.

33   In approximately half of these the applicant will be at least partially successful. For a more detailed breakdown, see the diagrams in Bridges *et al., op. cit.* note 12 *supra*, at pp. 116, 118–19.

by the courts at the substantive hearing stage. It also means, incidentally, that while there have been relatively large numbers of immigration and homelessness applications, these cases are not necessarily the ones which have been contributing most to the delays, or to the pressures on court space and judge time. After all, in the past the majority of these cases have dropped out of the system relatively early on. One implication is that steps taken to redirect or exclude immigration or homelessness applications from the judicial review process by, for example, establishing alternative appeal procedures and insisting that appeals be exhausted before judicial review is used, may have less effect on relieving the court system than expected. This is not to suggest that steps should not be taken to improve complaints procedures and appeal systems; only that the motivation for doing so must be the desire to enhance opportunities for redress and improve the quality of decision making, rather than the expectation that this will necessarily relieve pressure on the courts. There is indeed some evidence following the enactment of the Immigration and Asylum Act 1993 that the creation of new statutory appeals does not lead to a reduction in the scale of judicial review litigation and may even have the reverse effect. This might occur where the quality of the appeal procedures themselves gives rise to complaint. It might also arise for other reasons, such as because the creation of rights of appeal further stimulates the involvement of lawyers and a culture of legal challenge.[34]

WITHDRAWALS, DISPUTE RESOLUTION AND ACCOUNTABILITY

The view that where possible litigation should be settled without the need for trial is contentious, essentially for two types of reason. The first is concern that where parties are confronted by an opposition which is stronger and better resourced, out of court settlements may produce outcomes which are unfair to the weaker side. The second is concern that the encouragement of settlement may be contrary to the public interest not only because it enables parties to exploit their superiority, but also because it detracts from the role courts play in developing the law and promulgating legal values. The first type of concern is essentially about the nature and quality of settlements and is capable of empirical investigation and analysis. The second type of concern expresses a view about the role of courts in society. It carries with it the implication that the task of courts is not solely, or even principally, to resolve individual disputes and for this reason that task is not completed when litigation is settled prior to trial. This view has been most famously expressed by the American, Owen Fiss:

> The dispute-resolution story makes settlement appear as a perfect substitute for judgment . . . In that story, settlement appears to achieve exactly the same purpose as judgment — peace between the parties — but at considerably less

---

34 *Ibid.*, pp. 24–6.

expense to society . . . In my view, however, the purpose of adjudication should be understood in broader terms. Adjudication uses public resources, and employs . . . public officials . . . [who] . . . possess a power that has been defined and conferred by public law, not by private agreement. Their job is not to maximise the ends of private parties, nor simply to secure the peace, but to explicate and give force to the values embodied in authoritative texts such as the Constitution and statutes: to interpret those values and to bring reality into accord with them. This duty is not discharged when the parties settle.[35]

While Fiss is writing from the perspective of a North American lawyer, his view has relevance for public lawyers here who argue that the task of judicial review proceedings extends beyond private dispute resolution. In this section of the chapter I shall consider the two concerns outlined above, dealing first with the issue of equality and fairness of settlements to the parties and then with the view that settlement detracts from the public function of the courts.

Settlement, equality and fairness

There is much evidence from other fields of litigation that while settlements out of court appear to benefit litigants, where litigants are confronted by an adversary who is better resourced and far more experienced they will tend to find themselves coerced into settling their dispute on terms which are less favourable than they deserve and less favourable than they could expect to achieve had the matter gone on to trial. Such inequality of bargaining power, it has been argued, calls into question the justice and moral acceptability of settlement.[36]

Inequalities are most apparent in the context of plea bargaining before a criminal trial. Plea bargaining is the process by which defendants agree to plead guilty, either to a lesser offence to that with which they are charged or to achieve a lower sentence, rather than insist that their guilt be proved by trial. Plea bargaining therefore leads to a determination of guilt without providing defendants with the formal protections offered by formal adjudication, such as the presumption of innocence, the rules of evidence and jury trial. Given systemic inequality between defendant and prosecution, without these formal protections defendants are especially vulnerable to pressures to plead guilty. These pressures are imposed, researchers argue, by the system as a whole, for plea bargaining is a function of an overloaded court system — a system within which all parties are driven to seek bargained outcomes rather than expensive and time-consuming trials.[37]

---

35   Fiss, *op. cit.* note 8 *supra*, p. 1085.
36   Coleman, *op. cit.* note 7 *supra*, Ch. 9, p. 208.
37   See Baldwin, J. and McConville, M., *Negotiated Justice*, London: Martin Robertson, 1977; Baldwin, J., *Pre Trial Justice*, Oxford: Basil Blackwell, 1985; Bottoms, A.E., and McLean, J.D., *Defendants in the Criminal Process*, London: Routledge & Kegan Paul, 1976.

Systemic inequalities, however, are not limited to the criminal justice system and are evident in areas of civil justice as well. Hazel Genn's work on settlement in personal injury litigation, for example, shows the pervasive nature of the inequality between inexperienced plaintiffs confronted by defendants backed by experienced and well-resourced insurance companies.[38] She shows, for instance, how plaintiffs tend to find themselves using generalist rather than specialist solicitors. These generalists — for a variety of reasons that are partly to do with the way they are financed and their systems for processing work — tend to adopt a non combative style of litigation which is geared to settlement rather than fighting a trial. Their strategy differs markedly from the much more aggressive pro-litigation approach adopted by specialists and by insurance companies.[39] Genn argues that a non combative approach may compromise the ability of plaintiffs to mount a strong case and force them to bargain from a position of weakness rather than strength. She shows also how the rules and procedures of court contribute to this inequality, with the result that strong defendants can force a settlement on a plaintiff in much the same way as the prosecution in a criminal matter is able to mobilise its vast resources to extract a guilty plea from the defendant to avoid a full hearing.[40] In so arguing she echoes Fiss's view that settlement is 'the civil analogue of plea bargaining' where 'consent is often coerced': like plea bargaining it reflects 'capitulation to the conditions of mass society and should neither be encouraged nor praised'.[41]

Does this research mean that we should be concerned about the scale of withdrawal and sceptical about the quality of settlements in judicial review cases? Judicial review also typically involves a clash between unequal parties. As in criminal proceedings, that clash is typically between an individual and public power.[42] As in personal injury cases, individuals will almost always be 'one

---

38 Genn, *op. cit.* note 5 *supra*; Wheeler, S., *Reservation of Title Clauses*, Oxford: Clarendon Press, 1991. See also Davis, G., *Partisans and Mediators: The Resolution of Divorce Disputes*, Oxford: Clarendon Press, 1988. Galanter would characterise the typical plaintiff in a personal injury case as a 'one shotter'. Defendants, on the other hand, are typically 'repeat players'. Galanter argues that repeat players will almost always come out ahead in litigation, because being frequent users of the system they are likely to have access to skilled and specialised legal services and better systems for processing and handling cases. He also argues that court procedures themselves work to the advantage of repeat players and against the interest of the 'one shotter': Galanter, M., 'Why the Haves Come Out Ahead: Speculations on the Limits of Legal Change' (1974) 9 *Law and Society Review,* 347; Galanter, M., 'Reading the Landscape of Disputes: What we Know and Don't Know (and Think we Know) about our Allegedly Contentious and Litigious Society' (1983) 31 *UCLA Law Review* 40.
39 Genn also shows that the Bar does not iron out these inequalities either because barristers are not instructed, or because the quality of instructions when given are poor: see *op. cit.* note 5 *supra*, pp. 78–81.
40 *Ibid.,* p. 23.
41 Fiss, *op. cit.* note 8 *supra.*
42 Most judicial review fit this pattern, but not all. For example, judicial review is used by public bodies against other public bodies.

shotters', using the system for the first and perhaps only time, with limited financial, psychological and other resources. Their opponents, on the other hand, will be public bodies with access to financial, legal, economic, informational, managerial and other resources which are inevitably beyond the capacity of most applicants. Here too the weaker party carries the burden of proof and must establish the facts as well as marshal the legal arguments. From the outset applicants are at a forensic disadvantage. Not only must they obtain the leave of the court to proceed, and in so doing reveal their arguments, but they must do so with limited access to potentially relevant factual information. There are no obligations upon respondents to disclose documentary evidence in advance, and no general obligation even to provide applicants with reasons for decisions. While courts have called upon respondents to lay their cards on the table,[43] judges have created what the Law Commission described as a 'climate considered unfavourable to applications for discovery'.[44] Furthermore, as in personal injury cases, many applicants will also find themselves being represented by lawyers with little expertise or experience of judicial review. Very few firms specialise in judicial review, and most solicitors who handle judicial review do so as part of a general practice and deal with only a small number of judicial reviews each year. Lastly, as we have seen, judicial review is a system under considerable stress and the environment is now one which encourages withdrawal by applying pressure on applicants and their advisers to proceed very cautiously.[45]

The procedural obstacles confronting applicants extend beyond the process itself to influence the way potential parties act long before a judicial review challenge is made. There is now much anecdotal evidence, for example, that the leave requirement operates as a shield for public bodies not only filtering weak cases from the system, but also deterring those who lack the energy or the resources from even commencing litigation. Those who do seek leave are the applicants who have persevered with their complaints, exhausted other remedies, and obtained legal aid. Unknown numbers of others, perhaps with similar grievances, will not have persevered or surmounted these obstacles. Indeed, the ability of public authorities to do nothing but wait for the complainant to exhaust the various potential avenues of redress including obtaining leave, can itself be coercive and exhausting. It is probably impossible to know how many potential applicants are coerced into accepting outcomes which are unjust, or what proportion of applications for judicial review are made because public authorities simply have not looked seriously at the grievance to see if a resolution is possible until they are forced to

---

43   *R* v *Lancashire CC, ex parte Huddleston* [1986] 2 All ER 941.
44   *Op. cit.* note 20 *supra*, para. 7.7.
45   That pressure is largely exerted by the fear of an adverse costs order against applicants. See, for example, *R* v *Horsham DC, ex parte Wenman* [1995] 1 WLR 680, at 701.

do so once leave has been obtained; but the numbers are likely to be significant.[46]

There are, then, many ways in which inequality pervades the judicial review process and further empirical research will help to show how this affects the parties. However, judicial review litigation differs very markedly from both personal injury and criminal proceedings. While most cases fit the typical 'David and Goliath' mould, the judicial review case-load is heterogeneous. Despite its areas of concentration, litigation covers a very diverse range of subject matter and involves a variety of litigants. While most applicants are typical 'one shotters', many of those who represent them are becoming more experienced. Several pressure groups are also acknowledged to be expert users of the system. Moreover, as we have seen, many public bodies do not find themselves forced to respond to judicial review very often; and while comparatively well-resourced, it should not be assumed that they are necessarily well-equipped to react to legal challenges. Certainly it is well known that during the 1980s central government recognised that it was vulnerable to judicial review, and even comparatively expert departments such as the Departments of Social Security and the Environment experienced difficulties handling individual cases.[47] Some of the problems were to do with the sheer scale and complexity of organisational systems. Others were associated with low levels of legal awareness amongst administrators, staff turnover, working relationships between government lawyers and administrators, conflicting policy priorities within departments, and the relative speed of judicial review litigation compared with other procedures such as the ombudsmen (see Drewry, Ch. 4 generally) and litigation under the European Convention on Human Rights.[48] Judicial review is now more widely understood within local and central government, but it cannot be assumed that public bodies necessarily have efficient and expert systems enabling them to respond to actual or threatened challenge and to assess the risks and consequences involved, a factor which might be particularly pertinent when public bodies are considering whether to settle or fight a case. For these reasons it cannot be assumed that public bodies as a class are as expert as,

---

46 Proposals were put to the Law Commission by the Public Law Project and others, designed to oblige public bodies to exchange information earlier and to provide details of the reasons and background to challenged decisions. These were aimed at forcing authorities to review their decisions and settle before individuals were forced to seek leave. Unfortunately the Law Commission did not accept the proposals. See further Bridges *et. al., op. cit.* note 12 *supra,* pp. 156–7.

47 See generally, Kerry, Sir Michael, 'Administrative Law — The Practical Effects of Developments over the Past 25 Years on Administration in Central Government' (1986) 64 *Public Administration* 163.

48 Sunkin, M., and Le Sueur, A.P., 'Can Government Control Judicial Review?' (1991) 44 *Current Legal Problems* 161 which discusses the Department of Health and Social Security's handling of *R* v *Secretary of State, ex parte Cotton* (1985) *The Times,* 5 August (Div Court) and *The Times,* 14 December (Court of Appeal). See further Le Sueur, A., and Sunkin, M., *Public Law,* London: FT Law & Tax, 1997.

say, insurance companies who deal with personal injury litigation or prosecuting authorities in criminal proceedings.

The nature of the arguments in judicial review and the procedure itself also distinguish this process from fields such as crime and personal injury litigation. Applicants may be using judicial review because they want to secure a tangible result, such as an offer of housing or a licence to trade, which a public authority is refusing to provide. However, the issues before the court are not immediately concerned with the merits or otherwise of the authority's decision. They are principally arguments about matters of process rather than substance. More to the point, unlike questions of quantum or the issues in a criminal trial, in judicial review the disputes focus on issues of law rather than fact. Decisions about withdrawal and settlement therefore tend not to rest on an assessment of how evidential issues will be resolved by the court, or whether witnesses will come up to proof at trial. In this situation it may be that applicants, at least those represented by competent lawyers, are less vulnerable to the coercion found in plea bargaining or personal injury settlements.[49]

The procedure is also significant for the way it appears to 'empower' applicants. The existence of the leave requirement might be a shield for public authorities, but once leave has been obtained it becomes a potentially valuable bargaining weapon to be used against them. At this stage authorities know that they must respond either by fighting the case, or by reconsidering the matter and offering a partial or complete surrender. Applicants are therefore now furnished with advantages of formal adjudication which are denied to those who are obliged to settle altogether outside the courtroom. In particular, provided they make a proper assessment of the strength of their case in the light of the respondent's arguments following leave, they now proceed with the authority of the court behind them, and in an environment which is consequently far less coercive and oppressive than that confronting defendants awaiting criminal trials.

Research, then, alerts us to the possibility that applicants are being coerced by more powerful public bodies into withdrawing applications for judicial review and settling for outcomes which are less than they could expect to obtain following a full hearing. It does not necessarily follow, however, that judicial review litigation is influenced by the sort of inequalities which are apparent in other fields of law. An informed view on this and related questions will have to wait until we have more empirical data. Even if settlements are fair to applicants, however, there are reasons to question whether settlement and its encouragement is compatible with the broader tasks of judicial review. It is to this issue that I now turn.

---

49   Note that Genn's research concerns situations where lawyers are pitched against each other in negotiations which are principally concerned with issues of quantum of compensation, rather than with liability and law.

Settlement and the tasks of judicial review

Fiss objects to the encouragement of settlement because he believes that the task of courts extends beyond resolving private disputes to include the public function of explicating and giving force to legal values. This function, he argues, cannot be performed when parties settle. Not surprisingly his view is controversial.[50] It may also have less general relevance to litigation here than it has to litigation in the United States where it is accepted that courts play a prominent role in enunciating and applying general policy.[51] Having said this, public lawyers in this country will be familiar with the distinction he draws as one that echoes two of the principal demands made on the judicial review system. Judicial review is clearly concerned with resolving particular disputes and providing redress, but it also has a more public function associated with accountability and securing good administration. As the Law Commission put it: 'Judicial review often involves values and policy interests, which must be balanced against and may transcend the individual interests, which are normally the subject of litigation between private citizens'.[52] How these interests should be balanced is often controversial and '[m]any of the problematical issues concerning the present procedure reflect the tensions between differing interests'.[53] The best known examples of such issues include the debates over standing (to which I shall return p. 236), procedural exclusivity, approaches to discovery and cross-examination, and in particular whether they should be reformed so as to enable judges to take more account of matters which have not been presented by the parties,[54] the involvement of third parties, and costs[55] (see Himsworth, Ch. 9 generally).

At present these debates are conducted within the context of procedural arrangements which are still dominated both by the fact that the judiciary is a passive institution that can only handle problems which are brought to it and by the theory that litigation should be party-driven. This implies that the judge's task is to resolve conflicts which have been identified and defined by the parties on the basis of argument and evidence supplied by the parties. If the parties choose not to fight a case through to trial, that is normally regarded as being a matter for the

---

50 *Cf.*, for example Menkel-Meadow, H.C., 'For and against settlement: uses and abuses of the mandatory settlement conference' (1985) 33 *UCLA Law Review* 485.

51 *Cf.* Cranston, *op. cit.* note 6 *supra*, p. 47. Public interests may override the interests of parties wishing to discontinue proceedings, even private law litigation. See, for example, *dicta* of Steyn J in *Chapman* v *Chief Constable of South Yorkshire* (1990) 134 SJ 726 (discontinuance of complex multi-party litigation).

52 *Op. cit.* note 20 *supra*, p. 7.

53 *Ibid.*, p. 8. *Cf.* Harlow, C., 'Why Public Law is Private Law: An Invitation to Lord Woolf' in Zuckerman, A.A.S., and Cranston, R. (eds) with Lord Woolf, '*Droit Public* — English Style' [1995] *Public Law* 57.

54 Griffith, J.A.G., 'Judicial Decision-making in Public Law' [1985] *Public Law* 564.

55 JUSTICE/Public Law Project, *A Matter of Public Interest*, London: JUSTICE, 1996.

parties. It is true that once leave has been obtained, permission to withdraw may be refused if the Master or judge is not satisfied with the quality of the settlement, the reasons given for it by the parties, or that the settlement will serve the public interest. In practice, however it appears that Masters only very rarely refuse to grant consent orders; and while judges do sometimes seek clarification of the reasons for a withdrawal, it appears to be rare for them to refuse to allow the parties to withdraw. Anecdotal evidence therefore seems to indicate that the requirement of consent before withdrawal is normally little more than a formality.[56]

Given the dominant theory, broader public interests in accountability and scrutiny of government find expression when parties fight challenges to trial, but not otherwise. Inevitably this is a sporadic occurrence which carries the risk that illegality and wrongdoing may remain free from scrutiny if they are not challenged by those qualified to litigate,[57] or (and it is this which is of particular relevance to us) if a challenge is withdrawn before trial. How we respond to this very much depends on whether we are content with the current emphasis on the dispute resolution function of judicial review, or whether we seek to emphasise its more public roles. The difference of approach is clearly presented in the recent debates over whether standing requirements should or should not be liberalised.

On the one hand, those arguing for a public interest approach draw on Lord Diplock's warning that if the courts are prevented by narrow rules of standing from examining issues of legality there will be a 'grave lacuna in our system of public law'.[58] On the other hand, we have Schiemann J's view in the *Rose Theatre* case[59] that 'the law does not see it as the function of the courts to be there for every individual who is interested in having the legality of administrative action litigated'. His message is very much influenced by the private dispute resolution approach: the courts are to be concerned with issues of legality only when these are brought to the court's attention by those who have particular legal rights and interests at stake. Schiemann J accepts that this might result in unlawful decisions of government being unchallenged; but while unfortunate, for him this is an inevitable consequence of an adjudicative system which is concerned with specific disputes and which necessarily imposes limits on access.

Where does this lead in the present context? The issue of withdrawal is also likely to be contentious and our attitudes to whether it should or should not be encouraged — and the terms on which it should be permitted — will vary

---

56   Further research might reveal this not to be the case. Evidence of the way judges approach the leave stage suggests that the principles applied by the judges at the leave stage are inconsistent: Bridges *et al., op. cit.* note 12 *supra*, Ch. 8. It would be interesting to know whether there is greater consistency in their approach to withdrawals.

57   For example, because the applicant is out of time or lacks standing.

58   In *IRC* v *National Federation of the Self-employed and Small Businesses Ltd* [1982] AC 617, at 644.

59   [1990] 1 QB 504. See also Schiemann, Sir K., 'Locus Standi' [1990] *Public Law* 342.

depending on how we balance the various tensions inherent in the judicial review system. From a management perspective withdrawal is usually thought to be a good thing because it enables judicial resources to be concentrated on handling those disputes which remain intractable, but whether these are the most important problems for judicial review to handle is not necessarily clear. Those emphasising the dispute resolution perspective will tend to argue that the key questions are to do with whether the matter is resolved. They will tend to view withdrawal as being unproblematic provided there are some controls over the reasons for withdrawal and the quality of settlements. The current system of requiring consent to withdraw after leave may be thought to satisfy this.

Those who emphasise the public interest roles of judicial review in providing accountability and scrutiny, however, should be less sanguine about the benefits of withdrawal. From this perspective judicial review proceedings are distinctive and cannot be equated with ordinary private law litigation. In part this is because judicial review provides the ultimate mechanism for imposing legal accountability upon public bodies. By enabling judges to scrutinise the legality of governmental actions, judicial review operates to identify wrongdoing, define legal obligations and establish standards for future conduct. For these reasons judicial review cannot be understood solely, or even principally, in terms of its role in dispute resolution in particular cases. Nor can public law litigation be adequately understood as a series of isolated, one-off disputes to be bargained over and settled by the parties as they see fit. To view it in this way obscures the broader constitutional dimensions of its functions.

Moreover, once leave has been obtained an important hurdle has been surmounted: a High Court judge has now accepted that it is at least arguable that the respondent public body has exceeded or abused its legal powers. The matter therefore now enters the public domain and can no longer be regarded as solely, or even principally, a dispute between individual parties. It may be argued that issues of legality and general principle now arise which ought to be adjudicated upon following full argument and scrutiny in open court. If cases are to be withdrawn this should occur only if the withdrawal can be justified as being in the public interest, having regard to the possibility that it may insulate public bodies from scrutiny and leave them free to continue to apply policies, or adopt procedures or approaches to decision making which may be unlawful.

Arguably, adopting a private dispute resolution-based approach to withdrawal might also have other undesirable consequences. When cases are withdrawn, for example, later judges, the public, and public bodies in general may be deprived of the benefits which could have flowed from a judgment in the case. Coleman, using the language of economics, says that judicial opinions and precedents:

. . . are public goods because they are sources of information about things that can and cannot lawfully be done in a society. Lawyers and others whose lives are affected by law use them when planning their affairs and when advising others . . . settlements do not increase the amount of information or the number and variety of legal precedents available to the public, and policies that encourage settlements decrease the rate at which these public goods are produced.[60]

Galanter's approach is sociological rather than economic, but he also emphasises the role that courts play in disseminating information in the form of messages: 'These messages are resources that parties use in envisioning, devising, pursuing, negotiating, and vindicating claims (and in avoiding, defending, and defeating them).'[61] From yet another perspective Raz adopts a similar theme to argue that implicit in the basic idea of the rule of law is the requirement that laws should be open and clear so that people are able to know what the law is and be guided by it.[62]

The educational role of the courts has particular pertinence in the context of judicial review. After all, development of this jurisdiction is often presented as having been one of the greatest achievements of the English courts over the past two or three decades.[63] Although there is little empirical support for the view, much of this importance is thought to be due to the influence public law principles have in guiding government and in promulgating good administrative practice. Indeed, one of the reasons why the judicial review jurisdiction is uniquely important within our system is because it is to judicial review judgments that both citizens and public bodies must look to discover the common law constraints on the exercise of public power.

Moreover, despite their rapid evolution many of the grounds of review are still in their infancy and their scope remains uncertain. Witness, for example, recent decisions on reasons, legitimate expectations and proportionality. Even where principles are well established, considerable uncertainty still surrounds their application in particular situations. Also, much often rests on how statutory obligations are to be interpreted. It is not surprising, then, that uncertainty of the law is given as one of the main difficulties facing public authorities. More judicial decision making may not lead to greater clarity of the law (and may lead to the

---

60   Coleman, J.L., *Markets, Morals and the Law*, Cambridge: Cambridge University Press, 1988, Ch. 9, p. 211–12.
61   Galanter, M., 'The Radiating Effects of Courts' in Boyum, K.O., and Mather, L. (eds), *Empirical Theories About Courts*, London: Longman. Galanter emphasises the way in which judicial messages influence the settlement process itself both by providing the backcloth against which settlements occur and by providing negotiators with bargaining counters. On this see Mnookin, R.H. and Kornhauser, L., 'Bargaining in the Shadow of the Law: The Case of Divorce' (1979) 88 *Yale Law Journal* 950. From this perspective settlement may well be a consequence of the way the public are utilising the 'public goods' generated by the courts rather than a cause of their restriction.
62   Raz, J., 'The Rule of Law and its Virtue' (1977) 93 *Law Quarterly Review* 195.
63   See *dicta* of Lord Diplock in *R* v *IRC, ex parte NFSE* [1982] AC 617, at 641C–D.

reverse), but given the status of judicial review and the state of its development there may be reasons to fear that large-scale withdrawal could be having a stultifying effect on the law in this area.

A further, more general concern is that the encouragement of withdrawal might also stimulate what can be described as a culture of 'negotiated or bargained legality'[64] where legal liability becomes increasingly dependent on private bargaining between parties rather than the result of open adjudication following full argument. Within this culture disputes are treated as isolated one-off events from which two sets of norms or standards emerge. One set is promulgated by open judgments and the other evolves as an aspect of bargaining and negotiation. Whereas judgments are the result of processes which are formally fair, the messages generated by bargained outcomes, as we have seen, may be generated by processes which are infused with inequality. Moreover, compared with the lessons to be derived from judgments, those flowing from bargained outcomes are likely to be received by a very limited audience, principally consisting of the parties and their lawyers in the instant case. These lessons might, for example, indicate to the respondent the factors which are more or less likely to encourage applicants to withdraw, or to lawyers representing applicants the sort of strategies that might force respondents to concede. In this way negotiation and bargaining provide a body of experience about how to manage judicial review litigation, including a feel for what deals can be reached and what bargains struck. A feel, in other words, for the terms upon which issues of legality can be negotiated. Since the messages which flow from withdrawals are not widely articulated or officially reported, knowledge of what is acceptable and possible may be shared only by those most regularly involved in judicial review litigation, including those respondents which are most regularly challenged and those solicitors and barristers who are specialists in the field. This body of knowledge and experience will remain largely hidden to those who are not regularly involved.[65]

CONCLUSION: A NEW APPROACH TO WITHDRAWAL

My purpose in this chapter has been to highlight an issue which is rarely discussed or debated in the academic literature, but which is of considerable practical importance and which raises key issues of principle.

Substantial numbers of judicial review challenges are withdrawn, often after leave has been obtained. Research currently underway will throw more light on

---

64 *Cf.* the discussion of consensual regulation in Jowell, J., 'The Rule of Law Today', in Jowell, J. and Oliver, D. (eds), *The Changing Constitution* (3rd ed.), Oxford: Clarendon Press, 1994, at p. 67.

65 The importance of being part of the 'club' in judicial review has been noted in other contexts of the process as well: see Sunkin and Le Sueur, *op. cit.* note 2 *supra*, at p. 119; Loughlin, M., 'Courts and Governance', in Birks, P. (ed.), *The Frontiers of Liability*, Oxford: SPTL, 1994.

why this is happening and what effect it has on the parties. It can be assumed, however, that substantial numbers of cases are not proceeded with because the parties have reached a settlement. It is widely believed that parties should be encouraged to settle their disputes without the need for trial. This should have benefits both for them and for the overall operation of the court system. However, discontinuance of litigation is problematic for two main types of reason.

First, research in other fields of law has shown that settlement can be unfair, particularly when weak litigants are coerced by more powerful opponents into accepting outcomes which may be less than they could reasonably obtain in court. Although inequality pervades judicial review, this area of litigation has characteristics which distinguish it from other fields and it is not self-evident that settlement following leave necessarily operates to the disadvantage of applicants. On this further research is needed.

Withdrawal in public law, however, is problematical for reasons which extend beyond the quality of settlements. While some continue to emphasise the task of judicial review in resolving particular disputes, it is now widely accepted that judicial review is expected to play a more extensive role associated with imposing accountability on government and the development of public law principles for the general benefit of the community and public bodies. Where cases are settled these functions are not performed, illegality may go unchecked and the educational role of the courts may be restricted.

Current attitudes to withdrawal seem to be dominated by the private law model of adjudication reinforced by the belief that withdrawal should be encouraged as being in the interests of court efficiency as well as being in interests of the parties. As the public law jurisdiction matures these views will need to be re-evaluated. The challenge will be to develop an approach to withdrawal and settlement which protects both the interests of parties (and especially of the applicant in securing an adequate outcome as speedily and cheaply as possible) and wider public interests. The current system of requiring applicants to obtain consent to withdraw recognises that there is a balance to be struck, but anecdotal evidence suggests that obtaining consent is usually a formality if the parties are in agreement.

If public interests are to receive greater emphasis new approaches will therefore be needed. These could take various forms. A minimalist approach would be to encourage the Crown Office Master and judges to pay more explicit regard to certain public interest factors when considering applications for consent to withdraw. Where withdrawals occur following settlement, these could be registered in a form designed to give them greater public prominence. Another approach would be to identify those applications which raise public interest matters to ensure that these are dealt with by judges even when the particular issue has been resolved to the satisfaction of the parties (this approach would, of course, require a system of funding which absolved the parties from the costs of the public interest hearing).

A further possibility would be to borrow from the 'friendly settlement' procedure under the European Convention on Human Rights. This permits applicants to withdraw complaints against a state where a settlement has been reached, but only when that settlement is in the public interest and the solution envisaged is based on respect for human rights as defined in the Convention. Both the Committee of Ministers and the Court may continue to deal with a matter where there has been a 'friendly settlement' if they are not satisfied that these conditions have been met.[66] A similar attempt to balance the interests of the parties and the public interest in effective accountability and scrutiny of government would fit well with the current movement towards a more public interest model of judicial review.

Whether or not these ideas are taken forward, it seems clear that the growing pressure on legal aid and strategies such as Lord Woolf's advocacy of alternative means of dispute resolution in public law cases will increase the incentive for litigants to seek bargained outcomes of their disputes rather than to use judicial review. If so, the issues raised in this chapter will become more hotly debated than they have been up to now.[67]

---

66   I am grateful to A.R. Mowbray for this suggestion made at the 1997 SPTL Public Law Group Conference.

67   An earlier version of this Chapter was presented to the SPTL Public Law Group at Birmingham University, April 1997. As well as to members of that group I am grateful to: Lee Bridges, Tom Cornford, Stephen Grosz, George Meszaros, Bob Watt, and to Joanne Dixon of the Crown Office. They have helped me but are not responsible for the views expressed.

11

The Constitutional Basis of Judicial Remedies in Public Law

Peter Cane

SUMMARY

Remedies are the means by which the courts enforce compliance by public bodies with the rules and principles of administrative law, and they are important regulators of the relationship between the courts and the other branches of government. Starting with the doctrine of separation of powers, this chapter analyses public law remedies in terms of their 'intrusiveness' or, in other words, the extent to which particular remedies leave the respondent free to decide how to comply with the remedy. The more intrusive a remedy, the greater the control it enables the court to exercise over the respondent.

THE PUBLIC LAW REMEDIES

One side-effect of the relatively informal and non legalised nature of the UK constitution[1] is that many questions about constitutionality are or very quickly become questions of political or constitutional 'principle', as opposed to questions about the interpretation of legislative texts or the scope and meaning of common law rules. Vague and malleable concepts such as separation of powers, the rule of law and ministerial responsibility figure largely in the way we think about the relationships *inter se* of the various institutions of government. In this chapter I am concerned with one aspect of the relationship between the judicial branch of

---

1 But for a caveat about the notion of a 'UK constitution' see note 12 *infra*.

government on the one hand and the legislative and executive branches on the other. By the term 'judicial branch', I refer primarily to courts (particularly the High Court) and appellate tribunals. There are some legal rules dealing with the relationship between the judicial and the other branches of government; for example, Article 9 of the Bill of Rights 1689[2] and the related common law rule that proceedings in Parliament enjoy absolute privilege in the law of defamation. On the whole, however, the constitutional position of the judicial branch in Britain is defined by concepts, principles and understandings which lack authoritative, let alone canonical, written form.

The aspect of the relationship between the judicial branch and the other branches of government examined in this chapter is that of remedies available from the judicial branch in respect of decisions and actions of the other branches, in cases where breach of some rule or principle of public law forms the basis of or is relevant to the applicant's claim. My main concern will be with English judicial institutions; but it is no longer possible to discuss judicial remedies in English public law without making some reference to decisions of the European Court of Justice.

Judicial remedies fall into the following categories:

(a) mandatory orders;
(b) prohibitory orders;
(c) quashing orders;
(d) orders for the payment of money;
(e) substitutionary orders (such orders are made by judicial bodies in the exercise of appellate jurisdiction; a substitutionary order replaces the decision of the body appealed from with the decision of the appellate body); and
(f) declarations, which are of two types. Sometimes a declaration is sought (and granted) as a non coercive alternative to some other remedy, such as an injunction or *mandamus*. Such a declaration I shall call a 'surrogate declaration'. On the other hand, rather than standing in for another remedy, a declaration may simply state what the law is on a particular topic, or what legal rights or obligations a person has. Such a declaration I shall call an 'autonomous declaration'.

Mandatory and prohibitory orders I shall refer to collectively as 'peremptory' orders. Quashing orders and substitutionary orders I shall refer to collectively as 'executory' orders, that is orders by which the court achieves a particular result rather than ordering someone to bring about a particular state of affairs.

Another important type of remedy in public law is the recommendation. The power to make recommendations is typical of the office of ombudsman. The

---

2 'Freedom of speech or debates or proceedings in Parliament ought not to be impeached or questioned in any court or place out of Parliament.'

recommendation is not a judicial remedy in English law,[3] and so it falls outside the scope of this chapter. Also outside the scope of this chapter are what might be called 'internal remedies', that is remedies resulting from the review of decisions by the original decision maker.

The constitutional basis of each of the above six categories of judicial remedies will be discussed below. Some of the terminology I have used is that recommended by the Law Commission.[4] Unfortunately, however, the Commission did not see fit to take the mildly radical step of abolishing the order of *mandamus* (which the Commission renames 'mandatory order') in favour of the mandatory injunction, and the order of prohibition (which the Commission renames 'prohibiting order') in favour of the prohibitory injunction. For the purposes of this chapter, however, I shall assume that there is only one mandatory and one prohibitory remedy, and I will call the mandatory remedy a 'mandatory order' and the prohibitory remedy a 'prohibitory order'.

THE PLACE OF REMEDIES IN THE LAW

It is trite to say that English law in general and English public law in particular is 'remedies-orientated'. To quote Sir John Laws:

[S]ubstantive law grows out of adjectival law . . . principles are born of procedures . . . the nature of a jurisdiction is conditioned by the remedies that can be granted within it.[5]

I would argue, however, that this received wisdom is true only to the extent that remedies are viewed in much the same way as the old forms of action were viewed, as a sort of procrustean bed into which life has to be forced before the law can deal with it. The public law remedial system certainly has an archaic aspect, with its meaningless retention of the prerogative orders and its tolerance of multiple remedies performing the same function (prohibition and injunction, for instance). The importance of remedial law is also increased by the fact that issues such as standing and time limits are seen as going to remedy rather than liability. However, while it is true that a right without a remedy for infringement or a duty without a remedy for breach has no legal force, it is equally true that remedies have no legal significance in the absence of rights and duties.

Our attitude to public law remedies has largely escaped the revolution in legal thought and practice which replaced the forms of action with causes of action and which made facts central to pleading one's case. We do not think of public law

---

3   But see *R v Secretary of State for the Home Department, ex parte Bentley* [1994] QB 349.
4   Law Commission, *Administrative Law: Judicial Review and Statutory Appeals* (Law Com No. 226), London: HMSO, 1993.
5   Laws, Sir J., 'Judicial Remedies and the Constitution' (1994) 57 *Modern Law Review* 194, at 213.

remedies as tools designed to achieve a variety of ends, but more as a limited repertoire of techniques which the law offers for vindicating rights and duties. We do not allow litigants to say 'this is what I want to be done; please give me a remedy to achieve it'. Rather we require the litigant to pick one of the law's limited repertoire of remedies, often hedged about with technical restrictions, in the hope that the chosen remedy will achieve the desired end. Typical of such traditional thinking is the Law Commission's failure[6] to go beyond a renaming exercise and to recommend a thorough rationalisation of the system of public law remedies. The very distinction between public law and private law remedies may itself be seen as a symptom of the traditional approach. For instance, it is usually said that damages are a private law remedy not available for interference with public law rights or breach of public law duties. But are there arguments of principle (as opposed to technical or practical arguments) which support this statement? Why should an order to pay an unliquidated sum not be available as a remedy in public law?

Just as, under the modern system of pleading, claimants plead facts and ask the court to recognise those facts as giving rise to a cause of action in law, so public law claimants should be free to specify the result they want to achieve by their claim and ask the court to provide an appropriate remedy. A claimant should not be required to specify which remedy is sought; rather it should be for the court to decide if a remedy is available to achieve the claimant's desired end. It is in this spirit that I will discuss judicial remedies in public law.

A CRITERION FOR ASSESSING THE CONSTITUTIONAL BASIS OF JUDICIAL REMEDIES

Intrusiveness

In his book *Suing Government*[7] Peter Schuck suggests that we might think about remedies for government torts in terms of the concept of 'judicial intrusiveness' and its correlate 'official freedom'. Official freedom refers to the extent to which a judicial remedy 'leaves officials and their superiors free to decide whether and how to reduce or eliminate the [tortious] misconduct'. Although Schuck applies these concepts to the analysis of remedies for government torts, I think that they also provide a useful framework for thinking generally about remedies in public law. For the purposes of the following analysis I shall define the intrusiveness of a judicial remedy as being inversely related to the extent to which the remedy leaves government free to decide what to do in order to comply with the remedy.

---

6 In *op. cit.* note 4 *supra*.
7 Schuck, P., *Suing Government: Citizen Remedies for Official Wrongs*, New Haven: Yale University Press, 1983, Ch. 1.

My concept of intrusiveness has three dimensions. The first relates to the substance of the remedy; for instance, a peremptory order is more intrusive than a declaration because it requires its addressee to act or to refrain from action. The second dimension relates to the enforceability of the remedy; in this respect, too, a peremptory order is more intrusive than a declaration because a person who disobeys such an order may be found guilty of contempt of court. The third dimension of intrusiveness relates to the feasibility of bargaining around any particular remedy by agreement with the applicant. For instance, the addressee of a peremptory order may be able to bargain around it, whereas executory orders are not susceptible to bargaining. I will discuss these three dimensions of intrusiveness in relation to each type of remedy.

Intrusiveness and the separation of powers

The value of the concept of intrusiveness in constitutional analysis derives ultimately from its relationship to the idea of separation of powers. Here I wish to interpret this idea in terms of what might be called 'decision-making hierarchies'. For instance, the High Court, the Court of Appeal (Civil Division) and the House of Lords constitute a hierarchy for the purposes of the making and revision of certain types of decisions. Again, social security adjudication officers, social security appeal tribunals and the Social Security Commissioners constitute a hierarchy for the purposes of the making and revision of certain types of decisions. And so on. The defining feature of a decision-making hierarchy is that the units of the hierarchy which have the power to revise decisions of units lower in the hierarchy have the power to make substitutionary orders. Of all the types of remedies listed above, substitutionary remedies are the most intrusive because they give the inferior decision maker no freedom to decide how to comply with the remedy. Indeed, a substitutionary remedy renders the inferior decision maker redundant. The reason why the power of superior units in a decision-making hierarchy to make substitutionary orders is the hallmark of such hierarchies is that in terms of the idea of separation of powers (or 'functions'), the inferior and superior units in a decision-making hierarchy are exercising an exactly similar function at different levels, whether at first instance, at a first-tier appellate level or at a second-tier appellate level. By contrast, when a body has the power to revise decisions of a decision maker who performs a different function from that performed by the reviser, so that the two bodies are not seen as belonging to the same decision-making hierarchy, it is much less appropriate that the reviser should have the power to make orders in substitution for decisions of the inferior decision maker.

It does not follow from this that non substitutionary remedies play no part as between units in decision-making hierarchies; or, conversely, that substitutionary remedies play no part as between units in different decision-making hierarchies. For instance, the procedure by which a magistrates' court or the Crown Court may state a case for the opinion of the High Court can end in the making of a non substitutionary order even though all the courts involved would normally be treated as belonging to the same decision-making hierarchy. Conversely, on an appeal under s. 11 of the Tribunals and Inquiries Act 1992 from a tribunal to the High Court, the Court has power to make a substitutionary order even though the High Court and tribunals would not normally be treated as belonging to the same decision-making hierarchy. Nevertheless, substitutionary remedies are most appropriate when the revising body and the original decision maker belong to the same decision-making hierarchy.

The underlying logic of the proposition that the power of substitution is most appropriate within decision-making hierarchies is that the power to revise a decision by making a substitutionary order is, in effect, a power to make that decision. Units within a decision-making hierarchy share qualifications, experience and competences which units outside the hierarchy may not have. To the extent that the power to make particular types of decisions has been given to a decision maker because it possesses certain qualifications, experience and competences, it would be wrong to give a power to revise that type of decision by making a substitutionary order to a body in a different decision-making hierarchy which lacked some or all of those qualifications, experience and competences. On the other hand, to the extent that the original decision maker and the revising body share qualifications, experience or competences, the fact that they belong to different decision-making hierarchies would not be a conclusive objection to giving the latter power to revise decisions of the former by making a substitutionary order. This helps to explain why the High Court has been given the power under s. 11 of the Tribunals and Inquiries Act 1992 to make a substitutionary order to resolve an appeal on a point of law from a tribunal.

The principle of restrained intrusion

My basic thesis, then, is this: the constitutional basis of judicial remedies in public law is to be found in the idea of separation of powers or functions. Positively, this idea can be used to justify checking by the judicial branch of the other branches of government; and negatively, it demands that bodies with the power to give judicial remedies in public law should not intrude too far into the affairs of decision makers in decision-making hierarchies different from their own, performing functions different from those they perform, and possessing qualifications, experience and competences different from theirs. The more intrusive the remedy (at least in terms of its substance and its enforceability), the less appropriately may it be awarded against a decision maker in a decision-making hierarchy different from that of the body giving the remedy. This I shall call 'the principle of restrained intrusion'. Remember that the criterion of intrusiveness of a remedy is the extent to which it leaves to the person to whom it is addressed freedom to decide how to comply with it (compare Drewry, Ch. 4 for the ombudsman remedy).

In the discussion which follows I shall assess the intrusiveness of the six types of judicial remedies listed above relative to each other, and the extent to which the rules about their use conform to the principle of restrained intrusion.

MANDATORY AND PROHIBITORY ORDERS

It is useful to deal with mandatory and prohibitory orders together because they share certain important features.

Substantive intrusiveness

So far as their substance is concerned, mandatory orders as a class are relatively intrusive because they specify, with more or less precision, what the law requires the addressee of the order to do. The more precise the terms of the order, the more intrusive it is because the less freedom it leaves to the addressee to decide how to comply with the terms of the order. The intrusiveness of any particular mandatory order will depend on its actual terms. In terms of substance, prohibitory orders are more intrusive than mandatory orders because, to be effective, they must make it clear precisely what conduct is prohibited. A well-drafted prohibitory order gives the person to whom it is addressed no freedom to decide what to do in order to comply with it — the addressee must simply refrain from the prohibited action.

Enforceability

The availability of injunctions against the Crown
Concerning the enforceability of peremptory orders, we must begin by looking at *R v Secretary of State for Transport, ex parte Factortame Ltd*,[8] in which the applicants sought interim relief pending determination by the European Court of Justice of the compatibility of certain UK legislation with European Community law. The interim relief sought was, in effect, a mandatory order requiring the UK government to register certain Spanish-owned fishing vessels as British vessels. The respondent was, of course, part of the Crown, and the central question was whether interim relief could be granted against the Crown. By virtue of the provisions of RSC ord. 53, r. 3(10), any interim relief available would have been 'such as could be granted in an action begun by writ', namely an interim

---

8   [1990] 2 AC 85.

injunction. There was authority to the effect that neither interim nor final injunctions were available against the Crown, but it was argued by the applicants that EC law required interim relief to be available so as to give effective protection to rights under EC law. The House of Lords referred this issue to the European Court, which held that if the only obstacle to the granting of interim relief in the circumstances of the case was a rule of English law, the court had an obligation under EC law to set that rule aside. The practical result of the decision of the European Court in *Factortame* was that (interim) injunctions became available against the Crown in order to protect rights under EC law but not rights under English law. This anomaly was addressed and removed by the House of Lords in *M* v *Home Office.*[9] Amongst other things, this latter case establishes that injunctions and other peremptory orders are available against the Crown in judicial review proceedings under RSC ord. 53 to protect rights in English law.

Judicial review proceedings are to be contrasted with proceedings based on private law causes of action such as a tort or breach of contract. Actions of the latter type are 'civil proceedings' as defined in ss. 23(2) and 38 of the Crown Proceedings Act 1947. By virtue of s. 21 of the 1947 Act, injunctions are not available in civil proceedings against the Crown (s. 21(1)(a)), or against an officer of the Crown 'if the effect of granting the injunction . . . would be to give any relief against the Crown which could not have been obtained in proceedings against the Crown' (s. 21(2)).[10] Instead the court has the power to make a declaration *in lieu* of such an order. The meaning of s. 21(2) was discussed by Lord Woolf in *M* v *Home Office.*[11] According to his Lordship, the effect of the subsection is that officers of the Crown (including ministers) are liable to be sued *in a personal capacity* for civil wrongs committed or authorised by them *in an official capacity*; and they are amenable to injunctions when so sued. But s. 21(2) prevents injunctions being awarded against officers of the Crown who are sued *in a representative capacity*. Thus, an injunction could not be awarded against a minister sued in respect of a tort committed, in an official capacity, by another officer of the Crown employed in the minister's department simply on the basis that the minister was legally and politically responsible for the conduct of that officer.[12]

It follows from this interpretation that the ban on the awarding of injunctions against the Crown in civil proceedings can be evaded by identifying the officer of

9   [1994] 1 AC 377.
10 The same applies to other peremptory orders such as orders of specific performance or for the recovery (possession) of land or the delivery of property.
11 [1994] 1 AC 377, at 409–15.
12 In Scotland, judicial review proceedings are 'civil proceedings' for the purposes of the Act: *McDonald* v *Secretary of State for Scotland* 1994 SLT 692. The meaning of s. 21(2) in its application to Scotland has not been settled. This shows that even in matters of constitutional law, the United Kingdom cannot be treated as a fully unitary system.

the Crown who committed or authorised the wrong and suing that officer in a personal capacity. In such a suit, an injunction could be awarded against the officer, and the officer would be personally obliged to comply with it even if the effect of such compliance would be the enjoining of action which, if done by the officer, would be done in an official capacity on behalf of the Crown. By virtue of s. 2(1)(a) of the 1947 Act, the Crown would be vicariously liable for a tort committed by such an officer (provided that the tort was not committed in the discharge or purported discharge of any responsibilities 'of a judicial nature vested in him' or 'which he has in connection with the execution of judicial process').[13] In such an action, damages could be awarded against the Crown; but an injunction could not be awarded against the Crown when sued vicariously in respect of the tort of its officer, because s. 21(1)(a) of the Act prohibits the awarding of injunctions 'in any proceedings against the Crown'.

Whereas injunctions may not be awarded in civil proceedings against ministers in their representative capacity, *M v Home Office* makes it clear that injunctions and other peremptory orders may be awarded in judicial review proceedings against ministers in their representative capacity; that is, regardless of whether the relevant conduct was that of the minister or of some other official in the minister's department. This is because the minister in his or her official capacity is constitutionally responsible for the conduct of government business by the minister personally and by all civil servants employed in the minister's department.

The Crown and contempt of court

Failure to comply with a peremptory order may constitute a contempt of court. In *M v Home Office*[14] it was held that a department of central government which is capable of being sued in accordance with the provisions of s. 17 of the Crown Proceedings Act, can be held guilty of contempt. It was also held that a minister of the Crown can be held to be in contempt of court. If a minister (or any other officer of the Crown), acting in an official capacity, personally disobeys a peremptory order or authorises another to disobey it, the minister (or other officer) may be held to be personally in contempt of court. A minister may also be held to be in contempt of court in a representative capacity if a peremptory order is disobeyed by an officer of the Crown employed in the minister's department for whose conduct the minister is legally and constitutionally responsible. A minister may be held in contempt in a representative capacity for disobedience of a peremptory order even if the minister did not personally disobey the order or authorise another to disobey it. Conversely, unless the minister personally disobeyed a peremptory order or authorised another to do so, the minister could not be held to be personally in contempt of court.

---

13 Crown Proceedings Act 1947, s. 2(6).
14 [1994] 1 AC 377.

By virtue of the provisions of RSC ord. 77, r. 15, there is a crucial difference between a holding of contempt against a minister in his or her representative capacity or against a department of central government, on the one hand, and, on the other, a similar holding against any other governmental body or official acting as such. The difference is that a respondent in the former category cannot be punished for contempt of court, while a respondent in the latter category can be.[15] In the words of Lord Woolf in *M* v *Home Office*:

> the Crown's relationship with the courts does not depend on coercion . . . the object of the exercise [of making a finding of contempt of court against the Crown] is . . . to vindicate the rule of law.[16]

In relation to a minister sued in a representative capacity, a holding of contempt, according to Lord Woolf, is a means of enforcing ministerial responsibility:

> By making the finding against the minister in his official capacity the court will be indicating that it is the department for which the minister is responsible which has been guilty of contempt.[17]

Although it would be 'inappropriate to fine or sequest the assets of the Crown or a government department or an officer of the Crown in his official (i.e. representative) capacity', a finding of contempt against a government department or minister is not 'pointless' because 'the very fact of making such a finding would vindicate the requirements of justice' and could lay the basis for an award of costs against the government.[18]

Summary

To summarise so far:

(a) An officer of the Crown (including a minister) who personally commits a civil wrong in an official capacity may be sued personally in civil proceedings; and an injunction or other peremptory order may, in appropriate circumstances, be made in such proceedings. If the officer personally disobeys such an order, a finding of contempt of court may be made against the officer, and the officer may be punished for the contempt.

(b) A minister or government department may be sued in civil proceedings as representative of the Crown on the basis of the vicarious liability of the Crown for

---

15 Concerning officers of the Crown see *M* v *Home Office* [1994] 1 AC 377, at 427.
16 *Ibid.*, at 425–6.
17 *Ibid.*, at 426.
18 *Ibid.*, at 424–5. Note, however, that an order for the payment of costs by the Crown cannot be executed: RSC ord. 77, r. 15(2).

the tort of an officer of the Crown committed in an official capacity. In such an action, no injunction may be awarded.

(c) In judicial review proceedings, an injunction or other peremptory order may be awarded against a minister as representative of the Crown in relation to things done or to be done by the minister or by officers of the Crown for whom the minister is constitutionally responsible. If the minister personally disobeyed such an order, a finding of contempt could be made against the minister and the minister would be liable to be punished personally for the contempt. If an officer of the Crown for whom the minister was constitutionally responsible disobeyed such an order, a finding of contempt could be made against the officer personally (and the officer could be punished for contempt), or against the minister in a representative capacity (in which case the minister could not be punished for the contempt).

Analysis
These rules prompt several observations:

(a) Distinction between civil and judicial review proceedings   Why should there be a distinction between civil proceedings and judicial review proceedings such that in the latter, but not in the former, peremptory orders are available against ministers in their representative capacity?

(b) Peremptory orders against the Crown are non coercive   The effect of these rules is that as against central government (that is, the Crown), peremptory orders are non coercive because at the end of the day the courts will not allow orders made against the Crown to be executed. In effect, peremptory orders and findings of contempt made against the Crown are merely declaratory, and any force they have over and above that of a declaration is symbolic. It follows, in theory at least, that peremptory orders against the Crown are, in respect of their enforceability, less intrusive than peremptory orders against other government bodies and officials. The traditional explanation for the unamenability of the Crown to coercive judicial orders is that the Crown is the 'fount' of the 'justice' which the courts dispense, so that it would 'be inappropriate for the judges to seek to coerce the source of their power. This explanation is now seen as being both anachronistic and untenable (except, perhaps, in relation to the monarch personally). Even though we still speak of 'Her Majesty's judges', this should be interpreted as a reference to the Monarch as apolitical head of state and as the embodiment of a national ideal, and not as a reference to the politicians who make up the government which is the heir of most of the powers once exercisable by the monarch personally. How, then, are we to explain in modern constitutional terms the unamenability of central government to the execution of court orders made against it?

One way of approaching this question may be to ask another: if, as Lord Woolf said in *M* v *Home Office*, the basis of the relationship between the courts and central government is not coercion, what is it? From the courts' point of view, the answer appears to be that the judges *trust* central government to comply with court orders without having to be coerced into doing so. Such trust is, no doubt, based on experience of respect for and compliance with court orders by organs of central government. What incentive does central government have, in the absence of coercion, to comply with court orders? At the end of the day, it is the fear of adverse political consequences which provides the only incentive. In other words, under the British constitutional system, compliance with the law by central government is guaranteed, if at all, by the exercise of political, not legal, power. On this basis we might conclude that in making non coercive orders against central government, the courts are, in an important sense, not vindicating the rule of *law*[19] but are merely providing the government's opponents with ammunition for use in the arena of politics. The immunity of central government from the execution of judicial orders against it may be said, in an important sense, to put it above and beyond the law. From one point of view, this conclusion is not surprising because it is consistent with the largely non-legal nature of the British constitution. It is, nevertheless, a significant conclusion because it suggests that we should not put too much weight on decisions, such as that in *M* v *Home Office*, which, on the surface, seem to signal a significant strengthening of the role of law and the courts in Britain's constitutional arrangements.

(c)   The Crown and other governmental bodies   It remains true, nevertheless, that compliance with court orders made against governmental bodies other than the Crown can be enforced by legal processes of execution. How are we to explain the different treatment of the Crown and other governmental bodies? Hogg mentions 'the possibility of a damaging or even irreconcilable constitutional confrontation'[20] as a basis for Crown immunity from execution. In the British constitutional regime, central government has a special and superior status relative to all other governmental bodies. The chief legal manifestation of this special position is the fact that some of the powers of central government are non-statutory. Although the non-statutory powers of central government derive their legal force from their being recognised by the courts, they do not depend on the courts for their existence in the same sense in which the statutory powers of non Crown governmental bodies depend on Parliament for their existence. Central government, by virtue of being the premier governmental institution in the country, wields certain powers which

---

19   Although even a non enforceable declaratory remedy is based on law in a way in which a mere recommendation is not.

20   Hogg, P.W., *Liability of the Crown* (2nd ed.), Agincourt, Ontario: The Law Book Company, 1989, p. 27.

are in some sense fundamental to the governmental process. Central government also claims a democratic legitimacy greater than that of any other governmental body. These facts might justify the conclusion that any confrontation between the courts and central government is bound to have more serious constitutional ramifications than any confrontation between the courts and other governmental bodies; and, therefore, that courts are right to avoid such confrontations.

Several arguments pull in the opposite direction, however. First, although execution of orders made against government is more intrusive than the mere making of the order, it might be said that the place for giving effect to the principle of restrained intrusion is in deciding which, if any, remedy to award against the government. Once a peremptory order has been made, execution of that order at the suit of the applicant should be seen as no more than the effectuating of that remedy and not as a further encroachment on the autonomy of the respondent. Secondly, we should, perhaps, resist the implication in arguments against the execution of court orders against the Crown that the courts are subordinate in a relevant sense to central government in a way that they are not subordinate to other governmental bodies. The judicial power is a fundamental feature of the constitution of any democratic state, and if the rule of law is to mean anything, it must empower the custodians of the law to enforce the law for the time being against all law breakers. In my view, it is not satisfactory to leave it to Parliament to discipline ministers who break the law, if only because Parliament is, to all intents and purposes, a tool of the government. Thirdly, the fear of constitutional confrontation perhaps assumes that disobedience to court orders by central government will typically be the result of deliberate decision making by ministers. In fact disobedience is more likely to result from inefficiency or stubbornness on the part of minor officials than from ministerial intransigence, especially since the government will usually be able to neutralise the effect of any court decision at least for the future. For such reasons, the distinction between central government and other governmental bodies in respect of the execution of court orders seems hard to justify.

(d) EC law and the position of the Crown It is at least arguable that the unenforceability of court orders against the Crown is contrary to the requirements of Article 5 of the EC Treaty and the principle of effective protection. The obligations of member states under EC law are legal obligations, not just political obligations; and as such, they should be enforceable in the same way as other legal obligations.[21] If it were established that the Crown was not immune from execution of court orders in cases involving rights under EC law, it would seem intolerably

---

21   *Cf.* Article 171 of the EC Treaty which empowers the European Court of Justice to impose a pecuniary penalty on a member state which fails to comply with a judgment of the Court in which the state was found to be in breach of Treaty obligations.

anomalous that it should be so immune in cases involving rights under English law in the same way that the anomaly generated by the decision of the European Court in the *Factortame* case was felt intolerable. An important side-effect of our membership of the EC is the gradual legalisation of the UK constitution and, in particular, of the relationship between the courts and central government (see Craig, Ch. 12 generally).

(e) Personal and representative responsibility Underlying the rules summarised above is a sharp distinction between personal responsibility and representative or constitutional responsibility. The immunities of the Crown from peremptory orders in civil proceedings and from the execution of process enure for the benefit of officers of the Crown who are sued in a representative capacity, but not for the benefit of officers of the Crown who are sued in a personal capacity, even in respect of things done in an official capacity as officers of the Crown. This distinction is a by-product of the fact that the legal concept of the Crown as it refers impersonally to the government is infected by the personal nature of the monarchy from which the powers of the Crown are derived. If officers of the Crown were servants of a person (the monarch), it might make sense to distinguish between them and their master for legal purposes. But since officers of the Crown are not servants of a person but an integral part of the government, it makes little sense to distinguish for legal purposes between officers of the Crown and the Crown itself.[22] If it is thought right that the Crown should enjoy immunities from judicial process, it should not be possible to evade those immunities by proceeding against an officer of the Crown in a personal capacity for things done in an official capacity. To the extent that this is possible, it seems to be based on an anachronistic and undesirable constitutional theory of the nature of government. I believe that the Crown should not be immune from peremptory orders in civil proceedings or from the execution of judicial process, and that it is undesirable for the law to allow individual civil servants to be held responsible for things done in their official capacity unless, perhaps, the individual deliberately committed a wrong without authority.

It might be argued that it would be unfair to hold ministers legally responsible in their representative capacity for conduct over which they had no personal control. However, I think it would be perfectly appropriate for a court, for instance, to fine a minister for a contempt committed by a civil servant because in this way it could give strong symbolic support to the rule of law. The courts should certainly defer to Parliament as lawmaker, even though it is effectively controlled by the government; but they should not leave it to Parliament to enforce the law against the government.

---

22 For this reason, I disagree with Lord Woolf's criticism in *M* v *Home Office* [1994] 1 AC 377, at 415 of the judgment of Upjohn J in *Merricks* v *Heathcote-Amory* [1955] Ch 567, and with his treatment of *Town Investments Ltd* v *Department of Environment* [1978] AC 359.

QUASHING ORDERS

Quashing orders (that is, common law or statutory orders of *certiorari*) are a form of executory order.[23] In one sense executory orders are extremely intrusive because the decision maker whose decision is under review plays no part at all in the achieving the result ordered by the court. On the other hand, a quashing order unaccompanied by any instruction as to what the decision maker is to do in reaction to the order is very unintrusive because, in theory at least, it leaves the decision maker free to decide how to react to the order. However, if a decision is quashed, the decision maker will usually be under a legal obligation to make a fresh decision, and the grounds on which the decision was quashed will often constrain the decision maker in making the fresh decision. For instance, if a decision is quashed for error of law or fact, and if it is clear what the decision would have been if the decision maker had not made the error of law or fact, there may be only one decision which the decision maker can now legally make. In such a case, a quashing order is, in effect, a substitutionary order. This is obvious in cases where the court exercises its power to remit with directions under RSC ord. 53, r. 9(4). Again, if a decision is quashed for breach of natural justice, and the court specifies precisely in what respect(s) the procedure followed by the decision maker fell short of the requirements of natural justice, the decision maker will be constrained to follow a particular procedure in making a fresh decision.

The only judicial body with the power to make quashing orders is the High Court. Quashing orders represent the archetypal judicial review remedy because a quashing order is the antithesis of a substitutionary order, which is the hallmark of appellate jurisdiction. When the High Court makes a quashing order against a component of the executive branch of government it recognises that the respondent decision maker does not belong to the court's decision-making hierarchy, and that relations between the court and the respondent should be regulated by the principle of restrained intrusion.

Because a quashing order does not require anyone to do anything in order to give effect to the order, questions of the sort discussed previously about liability for failure to implement the order do not arise. However, implementation of a quashed decision would, presumably, justify a finding of contempt of court; and this conclusion makes relevant in this context the discussion above about the liability of government bodies and officials to punishment for contempt.

---

23 Because decisions which breach rules of public law are, in theory, void *ab initio* and legal nullities, it may be thought that *certiorari* merely declares the legal status of the decision. However, public law decisions enjoy a presumption of validity (*Hoffman-La Roche* v *Secretary of State for Trade* [1975] AC 295); and in practical terms, *certiorari* performs the executory function of stripping decisions of the benefit of this presumption.

ORDERS FOR THE PAYMENT OF MONEY

Damages not a public law remedy

Orders for the payment of money may relate to claims for unliquidated damages or for liquidated sums. As a matter of English common law, claims for un-liquidated sums cannot be based on breach of public law rules as such. Only if breach of a public law rule gives rise to a claim under some private law head such as tort[24] or breach of contract, can a claim for an unliquidated sum be based on breach of public law rules.[25] By contrast, if a payment of money is made by a citizen to a governmental body in satisfaction of a demand for payment which is in breach of a public law rule, the payer may obtain restitution of the amount paid.[26] In other words, breach of a public law rule may provide a ground for restitution of a liquidated sum but not for an award of damages. Can this difference between restitution and damages be explained in terms of the principle of restrained intrusion? It seems not. All orders for the payment of money are equally intrusive in that they require the respondent to take precisely defined action, namely to pay a specified sum of money to the applicant; and all such orders are enforceable by execution of process, except against the Crown.[27] The intrusiveness or unintrusiveness of an order for the payment of money does not seem to depend in any way on whether the claim underlying it was for a liquidated or for an unliquidated sum.

There is, however, an important sense in which damages are a 'stronger' remedy than restitution. Restitution only requires the defendant to return to the plaintiff amounts paid by the latter to the former, whereas an order for damages will typically require the defendant to pay to the plaintiff amounts which never passed from the latter to the former. The fact that the stronger remedy of damages is not available as a remedy for public law wrongs suggests that public law rights are seen as being relatively weak and not as worthy of strong protection as private law rights; or, put another way, that public law wrongs do not call for redress as loudly as private law wrongs. Something more than a 'mere' breach of public law is therefore needed to attract damages as a remedy. At first sight, there is a problem with this explanation arising from the fact that in the tort of misfeasance in a public

---

24   There is one tort which can only be committed by public officials, namely misfeasance in a public office. For discussion of this tort, see below.

25   If breach of a public law rule gives rise to a private law claim for 'damages', the private law claim may be tacked on to an application for judicial review under RSC ord. 53, r. 7. It is unclear whether the term 'damages' covers a claim for an unliquidated sum. If it does not, ord. 53 should be amended so as to enable claims for liquidated sums to be tacked on to applications for judicial review. See *op. cit.* note 4 *supra*, paras 8.5–8.

26   *Woolwich Equitable Building Society* v *Inland Revenue Commissioners (No. 2)* [1993] 1 AC 70.

27   Crown Proceedings Act 1947, s. 25.

office, the tortious conduct is defined in terms of public law illegality. However, liability will be imposed in this tort only if the defendant acted with 'malice' which, in this context, means intention to injure the plaintiff or knowledge that the conduct involved was illegal. This requirement of malice ensures that the wrong done is not just a breach of public law but a fundamental interference with the rights of the applicant as an individual.

Ironically, although this section began by pointing out a difference between damages and restitution, I think that the availability of restitution for breaches of public law is actually not incompatible with this explanation of the unavailability of damages. This is because illegal demands for money are not mere breaches of public law — they offend the fundamental constitutional and legal principle of no taxation without parliamentary approval; and this is the something more which justifies the award of the monetary remedy of restitution. The proper conclusion to be drawn from the above discussion is, therefore, that 'mere' breaches of public law attract neither damages nor restitution as a remedy. A breach of public law will provide a basis for the making of an order for the payment of money only if it also amounts to a breach of private law, or was done with malice or offended against an especially basic constitutional principle. Of these three grounds for the making of orders for the payment of money, the last is potentially the most important. The strength of the rule of no taxation without parliamentary approval lies in the fact that it is of fundamental democratic importance, but also that it is contained in a document (the Bill of Rights 1689) which unequivocally has the status of law. If more of the principles of the British constitution were contained in legal documents, the courts might be more willing to give to rights and interests protected by those principles the protection offered by orders for the payment of money, including damages.

The impact of EC law

Important questions arise in this context about the impact of EC law. A factor which influenced the majority of the House of Lords in the *Woolwich* case[28] to recognise a right to claim restitution of payments made by citizens in response to illegal demands by government, was that such a right exists in EC law. And as we have seen, EC law tends to have spillover effects, so that if a particular remedy is available to remedy breaches of EC law, pressure is likely to develop for the same remedy to be available in analogous situations to remedy breaches of English law. An important question, then, concerns when damages are available against institutions of the EC and governments of member states in respect of breaches of EC law. In *R v Secretary of State for Transport, ex parte Factortame Ltd (No. 4)*,[29]

---

28   See note 26 *supra.*
29   [1996] QB 404.

the European Court held that a member state could be liable to pay damages for loss directly resulting from a serious breach of EC law (such as action contrary to a provision of the EC Treaty; or non implementation or incorrect implementation of a Directive)[30] provided that the relevant provision conferred rights on individuals. Such liability could arise out of the actions of any branch of government, whether the legislature, the executive or the judiciary. It is for national legal systems to create an appropriate head of liability; but the rules governing member state liability for breach of EC law must be no less favourable to plaintiffs than the rules relating to similar domestic claims, and they must not be such as to make it impossible or excessively difficult to obtain compensation. The Court expressly held that any rule requiring malice on the part of the member state (as in the English tort of misfeasance in a public office) would make it too difficult to obtain compensation; as would any rule which totally excluded liability for consequential loss of profits and any rule requiring fault greater than a serious breach of EC law. The 'decisive' test of whether a breach is serious is whether it involves a 'manifest and grave disregard' of the limits of its powers by the institution in question. In applying this test, relevant factors are the clarity and precision of the rule breached, the width of the discretion left by the law to the institution in question, whether the breach was 'intentional or voluntary', whether any error of law which led to the breach was 'excusable', and whether the conduct of any EC institution contributed to the breach. It seems clear that the concept of 'serious breach' imports some element of fault, but the precise nature of this fault element is uncertain.

The upshot of the decision in *Factortame (No. 4)* is that English law must now recognise governmental liability to pay damages for serious breaches of EC law by the legislature, the executive, the judiciary or, indeed, any other organ of the state, provided that the relevant provision of EC law conferred rights on individuals and regardless of whether the breach of EC law constitutes a civil wrong recognised in English law. What impact, if any, is the introduction of such liability likely to have on the English law of government liability to pay damages?

The most recent pronouncement on this subject by the House of Lords is contained in *X v Bedfordshire CC*.[31] This case makes it clear that damages liability for breach of statutory duty or for negligence in the exercise of a statutory power can arise only if the relevant statute, properly interpreted, confers a private law right of action on individuals. This condition is analogous to the *Factortame* requirement that the relevant provision conferred rights on individuals. However, in the *Bedfordshire* case Lord Browne-Wilkinson said that duties contained in 'regulatory and welfare legislation' are not actionable in private law; nor, more

---

30   Concerning directives see *Dillenkofer* v *Federal Republic of Germany* [1997] 2 WLR 253.
31   [1995] 2 AC 633; discussed by Cane, P, 'Suing Public Authorities in Tort' (1996) 112 *Law Quarterly Review* 13.

generally, are duties relating to the performance of 'general administrative functions . . . and involving the exercise of administrative discretions' (as opposed to 'very limited and specific' duties).[32] The same is true in relation to statutory powers by virtue of the rule that a duty of care will not be imposed if the exercise of the power by the public authority involved considerations of 'policy' or 'non-justiciable' issues. It is perhaps unlikely that the European Court will apply the *Factortame* test as restrictively as English courts apply the analogous English tests. In *Factortame (No. 4)* itself, the provisions of EC law which had been breached were Articles 30 and 52 of the EC Treaty, both of which are very general in their terms and leave member states with considerable discretion as to how to comply with them.[33] In *Bourgoin v Ministry of Agriculture, Fisheries and Food*,[34] the Court of Appeal had held that breach of Article 30 was not actionable in English law under the head of breach of statutory duty.

The *Factortame* requirement of serious breach finds its counterpart in the rule, laid down in the *Bedfordshire* case, that an action for damages for negligence in the exercise of a statutory power will lie only if the authority's conduct was *Wednesbury* unreasonable. Although there is no requirement of seriousness of breach in the tort of breach of statutory duty, the unreasonableness condition probably applies to actions for breach of vaguely-worded or 'target' duties.[35] Moreover, breach of a clear and precise duty would probably meet the EC test of seriousness. But while the relevant EC and English tests are conceptually similar, they are sufficiently vague and flexible that courts with different attitudes to the desirability of governmental damages liability could use them to achieve quite different results in factually similar cases.

At first sight, EC law and English law might seem to diverge greatly in this area: in EC law, damages are available for government conduct which is illegal in a public law sense, whereas in English law they are available only if conduct constitutes a breach of private law. On closer inspection, however, the situation is more complicated. At the conceptual level, the ideas underlying EC and English law are similar, and English domestic law could be brought into line with 'English EC law' without too much difficulty. However, the rules of both systems give the courts so much room for manoeuvre that conceptual convergence would not necessarily produce similar results in similar cases. It must also be remembered that in English domestic law, parliamentary legislation and decisions of superior courts are effectively immune from challenge on grounds of illegality.

---

32 [1995] 2 AC 633, at 732.
33 See also *R v Ministry of Agriculture, Fisheries and Food, ex parte Hedley Lomas (Ireland) Ltd* [1996] 3 WLR 787.
34 [1986] QB 716.
35 See Cane, P., *An Introduction to Administrative Law* 3rd edn, Oxford: Clarendon Press, 1996, pp. 32–4.

SUBSTITUTIONARY ORDERS

Substitutionary orders are a variety of executory orders. Like quashing orders, they are very intrusive in that they do not require any action or cooperation on the part of the original decision maker to have their effect. They are much more intrusive than quashing orders in that they do not leave the original decision maker any freedom to make a fresh decision. Substitutionay orders, which are the hallmark of appellate jurisdiction, are the most intrusive form of judicial remedy in public law. Appellate jurisdiction is most commonly exercised by one body in a decision-making hierarchy over another body in the same hierarchy: for instance, by a social security appeal tribunal (SSAT) over an adjudication officer, or by the Social Security Commissioners over an SSAT. In such cases, the jurisdiction of the revising body to make a substitutionary order is usually co-extensive with the jurisdiction of the original decision maker. Any issue which can be decided by the original decision maker can be decided again by the revising body. By contrast, when a body in one decision-making hierarchy has power to make a substitutionary order in respect of a decision made by a body in a different decision-making hierarchy, the power of substitution typically relates only to certain of the issues over which the original decision maker has jurisdiction. These issues will typically be ones in respect of which the revising body is thought to have some special qualification, competence or experience. Most importantly, appeals to the courts from decisions of tribunals and components of executive government are typically restricted to questions of law or to questions of law and fact. Such issues are thought to fall particularly within the competence of the courts.

Because substitutionary remedies are the hallmark of appellate jurisdiction and non-substitutionary remedies are the hallmark of supervisory (review) jurisdiction, it is circular to argue that a body exercising supervisory jurisdiction should not have the power to make substitutionary orders. In my view, there is no reason why a court exercising supervisory jurisdiction should not have the power to make a substitutionary order in appropriate circumstances, namely where it is clear what the decision would have been if the original decision maker had not acted in breach of public law. The power given by RSC ord. 53, r. 9(4) is, in effect, a power to make a substitutionary order; and the Law Commission has recommended that such a power be explicitly given.[36] The Commission's recommendation is limited to cases in which the ground of review is error of law. The Commission specifically declines to extend the power to errors of fact on the ground that, even if it were clear what the decision would have been if the error of fact had not been made, to extend the power of substitution to such cases 'could risk the court going beyond its reviewing function'.[37] This is an unnecessary limitation. Because substitutionary

---

36   *Op. cit.* note 4 *supra*, paras 8.15–16.
37   *Ibid.*, p. 76, n. 23.

orders are very intrusive, they should be issued against bodies in different decision-making hierarchies from that of the issuer only in instances where the issuer has some special qualification, competence or experience relevant to the making of the decision in question. It is certainly arguable that courts are especially well-qualified to decide issues of fact; and there is no reason why a court should not, in appropriate circumstances, make a substitutionary order against a decision maker in a different hierarchy in relation to an issue of fact.

In addition to the requirement that a substitutionary order should be made only in cases where it is clear what the decision would have been if the decision maker had not erred, there must also be a proviso that a substitutionary order should be made only where it 'fits' the applicant's claim. Thus, for example, a substitutionary order would not be appropriate in a case where a decision was challenged on procedural grounds, or on the basis that it had been made by the wrong person or that the decision maker had taken an irrelevant consideration into account. A successful challenge on such grounds could not establish that the decision should and would have been otherwise if the error in question had not been made, because the ground of the challenge does not go to the correctness of the decision. This proviso is not an application of the principle of restrained intrusion. Rather, it follows from a proper analysis of the relationship between the applicant's claim and the content of a substitutionary order.

DECLARATIONS

As noted earlier, declarations are of two broad types. Surrogate declarations are declarations the substance of which is essentially the same as that of one of the other remedies we have already considered. Autonomous declarations merely make a statement of law. As far as substance is concerned, any surrogate declaration is as intrusive or as unintrusive as the type of remedy which it 'shadows'. As far as enforceability is concerned, surrogate declarations are non coercive in the sense that by itself, a declaration cannot provide the basis for a finding of contempt of court. In some contexts, the unenforceability of a declaration may be seen as an advantage if, for instance, the applicant is concerned not to take too aggressive a stance towards the respondent and is prepared to trust the respondent to do (or to refrain from doing) whatever the court declares should be done (or not done). The non coercive nature of declarations and their consequent non intrusiveness explain why they have long been available against the Crown.

Autonomous declarations

Autonomous declarations are, from a constitutional point of view, more important than surrogate declarations. The acceptance by the courts that declarations can be used to make general statements of legal and constitutional principle has radically altered the courts' perception of their role in controlling government; and it has the potential to change the relationship between the courts and government in a fundamental way. It has long been recognised that a declaration can be made even if the applicant has no cause of action in private law. For this reason, the declaration was seen as suitable for use in public law, and in the 1960s and 1970s it was much utilised as a way of evading the restrictive procedural rules which applied to applications for a prerogative order under RSC ord. 53. Since 1978, declarations (and injunctions) have been available as remedies in public law both under and outside RSC ord. 53. A complicated case law has developed concerning the proper procedure for seeking declarations in public law matters. The uses of the declaration with which I am primarily concerned can, as we shall see, be achieved only under ord. 53 because the standing required to obtain a declaration outside ord. 53 is quite narrowly defined.

Four factors have been particularly important in the development of the autonomous declaration:

(a) The addition of the declaration to the list of remedies which could be obtained by way of an application for judicial review under RSC ord. 53.

(b) Liberalisation of the rules of standing to make applications for judicial review. So far as the declaration is concerned, this liberalisation reached its zenith in *R* v *Felixstowe Justices, ex parte Leigh*.[38] The decision in this case turns on the fact that the substance of a declaration may be much less intrusive than that of either a peremptory or an executory order because it need not relate to any particular past decision or future action of the respondent. The applicant sought both an order of *mandamus* requiring the chair of the justices to disclose a particular item of information, and also a declaration that the policy of refusing to disclose information of the category into which the particular item fell was contrary to public policy and illegal. The Court held that although the applicant lacked a sufficient interest in the particular item of information sought by the order of mandamus, as a representative of the public he had a sufficient interest in the making of the declaration. The decision in *Felixstowe JJ* established the declaration as the prime remedy in public interest litigation.

(c) The holding in *R* v *Secretary of State for Employment, ex parte Equal Opportunities Commission*[39] that declarations may be awarded under RSC Ord. 53 even in cases where no prerogative order (*certiorari, mandamus* or prohibition) would be available. Thus, in that case it was held that primary legislation could be declared inconsistent with EC law even though an order of *certiorari* would not lie to quash primary legislation.

---

38   [1987] QB 582.
39   [1995] 1 AC 1.

(d) The willingness of courts to make what might be called 'prospective' and 'constitutive' declarations.[40] Such declarations are appropriate where a court refuses to make an order of *certiorari* to quash a decision or to make a (surrogate) declaration of invalidity *in lieu* of such an order even though the decision was in breach of public law. A prospective declaration states, for the future guidance of decision makers, the respect(s) in which the respondent's decision was in breach of public law. A constitutive declaration announces the challenged decision to have been in breach of public law, but not that it was invalid. The prime purpose of such a declaration is to enable the applicant or third parties to rely on the fact that a decision was in breach of public law without depriving it of effect *vis-à-vis* the applicant. Both types of declaration perform functions which no other remedy could perform.

The fact that a declaration may be awarded in public law at the suit of an applicant with no personal interest in the subject matter of the declaration, and despite the fact that no other remedy would be available *in lieu* of the declaration, has established the declaration as a tool by which the courts can entertain applications for judicial review the only aim of which is to establish that the government has acted contrary to principles of public law. The approach to the function of judicial review which is implicit in such use of the declaration is quite different from the traditional view, which sees judicial review as primarily designed to protect the rights of individuals (whether in private law or public law) against encroachment by government. Emphasis on individuals can be seen as a way of preventing judicial review from becoming a 'surrogate political process'.[41] Once the focus of attention shifts from the applicant's rights to the respondent's conduct, the line between law and politics becomes much more difficult to draw. It is much easier to characterise an interference with the rights or interests of an individual as a breach of law than it is so to characterise governmental action in which no individual has a special personal interest.

Nevertheless, there now seems to be a widely (although certainly not universally)[42] held opinion amongst judges and commentators that the high-powered judicial resources devoted to judicial review are most appropriately used to deal with disputes of broad constitutional and institutional significance. On the one hand, the judges see decisions such as those in *M* v *Home Office*,[43] *R* v *Secretary of State for the Home Department, ex parte Fire Brigades Union*[44] and *R* v

---

40 Law Commission Consultation Paper No. 126, para. 14.5; *op. cit.* note 4 *supra*, para. 8.22; Lewis, C., 'Retrospective and Prospective Rulings in Administrative Law' [1988] *Public Law* 78.

41 Allan, T.R.S., *Law, Liberty and Justice: The Legal Foundations of British Constitutionalism*, Oxford: Clarendon Press, 1993, esp. Chs 8 and 9.

42 See, importantly, Irvine, Lord, 'Judges and Decision-Makers: The Theory and Practice of *Wednesbury* Review', [1996] *Public Law* 59; and 'Response to Sir John Laws' [1996] *Public Law* 636.

43 [1994] 1 AC 377.

44 [1995] 2 AC 513.

Secretary of State for Foreign and Commonwealth Affairs, ex parte World Development Movement[45] as exemplifying a new-found constitutional role for the courts in controlling the exercise of government power. On the other hand, it is widely accepted that judicial review in the High Court is not the best avenue for dealing with immigration and homelessness cases, which currently account for a significant proportion of civil judicial review applications. Many believe that such cases, which focus on the rights and interests of individuals, should be dealt with by a tribunal, in the first instance at least. The process of rationing the judge-power allocated to the Crown Office List can also be observed in *Chief Adjudication Officer* v *Foster*,[46] in which the House of Lords held that the Social Security Commissioners have power to pronounce upon the legality of regulations when this issue arises incidentally to the resolution of an appeal against a refusal of social security benefit. Leaving aside criminal judicial review, increasingly the role of the High Court in its judicial review jurisdiction is seen as that of policing law-observance by the executive (and the legislature in the EC context); and even, in the words of Sedley J, 'to fill some of the deficits in political democracy'.[47] This 'new theory of judicial review' (as it might be called) is intimately associated with the development of the declaration as a remedy.

In some ways, autonomous declarations are very non intrusive. Such a declaration creates no enforceable rights and it may not relate specifically to any decision or action of the respondent. But in other respects, autonomous declarations may be seen as extremely intrusive. First, such a declaration may relate to governmental conduct which no traditional judicial remedy could reach. Secondly, autonomous declarations lend themselves to the making of broad pronouncements of a legislative as opposed to an adjudicative nature. Thirdly, courts have utilised such declarations as a medium for making statements of fundamental constitutional (or, some might say, political) principle which the respondent would find it extremely difficult to marginalise or evade. An autonomous declaration may be much more substantively intrusive than any of the more traditional public law remedies exactly because it is autonomous. The autonomous declaration has the potential to alter radically the traditional balance between the courts and the other branches of government.

Advisory declarations

Once the declaration is freed of any requirement of personal interest or independent cause of action, the inevitable next step is to ask whether the use of the

---

45   [1995] 1 WLR 386.
46   [1993] AC 754.
47   Sedley, Sir S., 'Governments, Constitutions and Judges' in Richardson, G., and Genn, H. (eds), *Administrative Law and Government Action*, Oxford: Oxford University Press, 1994, pp. 35, 43.

declaration should be limited to the resolution of actual disputes as opposed to abstract questions (see Himsworth, Ch. 9, p. 201). In other words, is there any reason why the High Court should not award what are often called 'advisory declarations'? Since there appears to be no jurisdictional bar to the award of such declarations,[48] the important question is: in what circumstances, if any, should the High Court decline to award a declaration on the ground that the declaration would be advisory? Woolf and Woolf[49] list a number of factors relevant to the exercise of the court's discretion, but in essence they seem to revolve around two issues:

(a)   Is there a dispute which a declaration may help to resolve? *and*
(b)   Does the dispute have a factual basis?

Is there a dispute?
The importance of this factor rests not so much on a view about the constitutional position of the courts, but more on a political theory about the function of the state. It is widely accepted as proper for the state to provide its citizens with dispute-settling facilities. It is much less widely accepted that the state ought to provide its citizens with a legal advisory service. In the absence of a dispute to which the declaration sought is relevant, an application for a declaration amounts to little more than a request for legal advice. Complications arise, however, when the reason why there is no dispute in existence at the time the declaration is sought is either that an earlier dispute has ended, or that an anticipated dispute has not yet arisen.

In situations of the former type, a court may be asked to make a declaration about a question which is moot in the sense of being relevant to a dispute which is no longer alive but has been resolved or overtaken by events. In *R v Board of Visitors of Dartmoor Prison, ex parte Smith,*[50] a prisoner was charged with doing gross personal violence to a prison officer. At the close of the prosecution case, the Board accepted a submission of no case to answer but directed that the prisoner be charged with the lesser offence of assault. On judicial review, the judge held that the Board had no power to do this. The Board thereupon decided to proceed no further against the prisoner. On appeal from the judge's decision, the Court of Appeal held that even though the prisoner was at no risk of further disciplinary proceedings and so had no personal interest in the outcome, it would decide the appeal because it raised an issue of general public interest. A declaration on a moot question may give parties useful guidance about how to behave in similar circumstances in the future, and may resolve issues which affect large numbers of people.

---

48   Woolf, Lord, and Woolf, J., *The Declaratory Judgment* (2nd ed.), London: Sweet & Maxwell, 1993, para. 4.042.
49   *Ibid.*, paras 4.053*ff.*
50   [1987] QB 106.

A court may, alternatively, be asked to decide issues relevant to a dispute which has not yet arisen (which is not yet 'ripe', to use an American term[51]) but which is anticipated. In principle, there seems good reason why courts should be prepared to make declarations in cases of anticipated disputes if, by so doing, the dispute may be forestalled to the benefit of both parties. The difficult issue is how to define 'anticipated'. Should the court intervene only if the dispute is 'inevitable or very highly probable',[52] or should it be prepared to act on the basis of some lesser likelihood that a dispute will materialise? It seems to me that it may not be necessary to answer this question directly, provided the court refuses to grant declarations *ex parte*. If someone is interested enough in the outcome of the case to oppose the granting of the declaration sought by the applicant, the court would be justified in assuming that the declaration was of potential practical importance. Sir John Laws argues that the court should be more willing to make a declaration concerning future disputes at the suit of public bodies seeking to clarify the limits of their powers and duties than at the suit of individuals seeking to further their own interests.[53] He treats the issue of finding a respondent as essentially a practical problem.[54] On the one hand, I am not sure that the courts should provide a legal advisory service to public bodies any more than to private individuals; and on the other hand, if someone is prepared to oppose the making of a declaration, the fact that the declaration sought will refer to the future should not normally discourage a court from making it, even at the suit of an individual.

I suggested above that caution about the making of declarations in the absence of an existing dispute is not based on constitutional principles. Sir John Laws does not agree.[55] He says that a willingness to make declarations about the future exercise of powers and the future performance of duties by public bodies would imply a view of the role of the courts:

less in terms of battle joined between contesting litigants in the matrix of an individual dispute, but rather as the medium by which new laws are impressed with rigorous legal standards of constitutional propriety.

He goes on to argue that part of the role of the courts is to protect the fundamental rights of individuals, and that 'the use of advisory declarations may be an important tool to be pressed into service' to this end.[56] However, the constitutional innovation which Sir John seeks is not greater use by the courts of declarations as to the future,

---

51 Davis, K.C., 'Ripeness of Governmental Action for Judicial Review' (1955) 68 *Harvard Law Review* 1122.
52 Laws, *op. cit.* note 5 *supra*, p. 215.
53 *Ibid.*
54 *Ibid.*, p. 218.
55 *Ibid.*, pp. 222–7.
56 *Ibid.*, p. 227.

but a new power in the courts to review primary legislation. As he says, the
protection of fundamental rights 'cannot be presumed to be left safely in the
hands of a Legislature with unlimited power, however respectable its democratic
credentials'.[57]

Factual basis

Even if it were logically possible, it is highly unlikely that a court would ever be
asked a question which had no basis in actual or hypothetical facts. However, the
inductive method of the common law is hostile to the statement of general
principles which refer to few facts and inclines to the making of statements of
narrow scope in relation to situations described in considerable factual detail. This
approach does have a constitutional dimension because the more general a
statement, the more it smacks of legislation as opposed to adjudication. The
declaration lends itself to the making of broad, general and abstract statements, and
for this reason some would see it as a dangerous weapon in the hands of the courts.

In practice, however, there is perhaps little danger that courts will often be asked
to make highly abstract declarations. The more abstract a declaration, the less
likely it will be of any use to the applicant. Engaging the judicial process is
sufficiently difficult and expensive that a person is unlikely to do so unless the
result will be of practical use to that person.

The Law Commission has recommended the enactment of a provision expressly
empowering the High Court to make 'advisory' declarations.[58] The Commission
defines an advisory declaration as one about 'an issue of law which is made in
circumstances where the applicant is not seeking review of an existing decision'.
It also recommends that an advisory declaration should not be made unless the
court 'is satisfied that the application raises a point of general public importance'.
It seems to me that this formulation is apt to lure the courts into precisely that
territory which some would say they should avoid — namely the making of
abstract statements of law with minimal reference to existing or hypothetical facts.
In fact, the more abstract the statement, the wider and more 'general' its
significance is likely to be.

BARGAINING AROUND JUDICIAL REMEDIES

The third dimension of the intrusiveness of judicial remedies mentioned above[59]
concerns the ability of the parties to bargain around them (see also Sunkin, Ch. 10
generally). The easier it is for the respondent to avoid the implementation of a
judicial remedy by agreement with the applicant, the less intrusive that remedy is

---

57   *Ibid.*, p. 226.
58   *Op. cit.* note 4 *supra*, para 8.14 and p. 128.
59   See p. XX.

in relation to that respondent. In this respect, executory remedies are the most intrusive because they do not require any action on the part of the decision maker in order to be effective. By contrast, peremptory orders, orders for the payment of money and declarations will be effective only if the respondent acts (or refrains from acting) in accordance with the remedy. For this reason, it will always be possible, in theory at least, for the respondent to bargain with the applicant to waive enforcement of the remedy wholly or partly in return for some other benefit. In this light, a declaration may be seen as nothing more than a bargaining counter in the hands of the applicant. In practice, however, an autonomous declaration on an issue of high constitutional principle may leave the respondent with no room for manoeuvre. The ability of a government body to bargain around a judicial remedy may be as much a function of the political context in which the remedy operates as of its normative force.

In cases where the respondent is a private individual, bargaining around judicial remedies is widely regarded as acceptable, subject to general concerns about the impact of inequality of bargaining power. We may be much less happy about allowing public bodies to bargain around remedies for breaches of public law rules. There is certainly a strong constitutional principle inhibiting the avoidance of judicial remedies by retrospective legislation; and in a governmental system such as the British, in which the legislature is normally under the effective control of the executive, it would seem undesirable that central government (at least) should be free to bargain around a judicial remedy and thereby avoid the effect of a judicial remedy. More generally, it might be argued to be an undesirable use of government contracting power to allow any government body to bargain around a judicial remedy based on breach of a rule of public law. The weakness of this argument is, perhaps, that taken to its logical conclusion it could throw doubt on the propriety of the settlement out of court of public law claims against governmental bodies, since this, too, involves the exercise of bargaining power in relation to alleged breaches of public law. In the end, whatever the constitutional proprieties, it is probably impractical to prevent bargaining around judicial remedies by governmental bodies. As a matter of general principle, however, the exercise of contracting power by a public body — either to settle a claim out of court or to bargain around a judicial remedy — should be subject to some sort of public scrutiny or accountability.

CONCLUSION

The concept of intrusiveness and the principle of restrained intrusion are useful tools for analysing the constitutional basis of judicial remedies in public law. It should be remembered, however, that remedies are only one aspect of the relationship between the judicial branch of government and the other branches. In order fully to measure the intrusion of the judicial branch into the affairs of the other branches, we would need also to examine the grounds on which judicial remedies may be granted; and (much more ambitiously) the practical impact of actual judicial remedies and the effect of judicial remedies on the behaviour of the other branches. Even so, a narrower focus on remedies casts important light on the role of the judicial branch in our constitutional arrangements.

12

The Impact of Community Law on Domestic Public Law

Paul Craig

SUMMARY

EC law has had, and will continue to have, a considerable influence upon domestic administrative law in the UK. The object of this chapter is to provide an overview of the ways in which Community law has had this impact. The analysis will be divided into three sections. The first section will briefly address the implications of Community law for basic constitutional law doctrine. Constitutional and administrative law are intricately interconnected and it is, therefore, necessary to address the impact of EC law on constitutional law as a necessary step to understanding the way in which it has influenced administrative law. The second section will analyse and evaluate the ways in which EC law has affected procedural and substantive doctrines of judicial review. The final section of this chapter will focus upon the law of remedies, concentrating in particular upon the changes in the law relating to damages as a result of the European Court of Justice's (ECJ's) jurisprudence in this area.

EC LAW: THE IMPACT ON CONSTITUTIONAL DOCTRINE

It is readily apparent that there will be clashes between Community law and national law. These will often be inadvertent. More intentional recalcitrance on the part of the member states will be less common, though it is not by any means unknown. In any event some rules must exist for such cases. Not surprisingly, the

ECJ has held that EC law must be supreme should any such conflict arise. This principle was first enunciated in *Costa* v *ENEL*,[1] where the ECJ responded to an argument that its preliminary ruling would be of no relevance to the case at hand because the Italian courts would be bound to follow national law. It held:

> By creating a Community of unlimited duration, having . . . powers stemming from a limitation of sovereignty, or a transfer of powers from the States to the Community, the Member States have limited their sovereign rights, albeit within limited fields, and thus have created a body of law which binds both their nationals and themselves.

The Community's supremacy was given added force by the ECJ's ruling in the *Simmenthal* case,[2] where the Court made it clear that Community law would take precedence even over national legislation which was adopted after the passage of the relevant EC norms. The existence of Community rules rendered automatically inapplicable any contrary provision of national law, *and* precluded the valid adoption of any new national law which was in conflict with the Community provisions:

> It follows from the foregoing that every national court must, in a case within its jurisdiction, apply Community law in its entirety and protect rights which the latter confers on individuals and must accordingly set aside any provision of national law which may conflict with it, whether prior or subsequent to the Community rule.

The supremacy of Community law poses particular problems for legal systems such as our own which are wedded to the idea of parliamentary sovereignty. The leading decision on this issue is now *R* v *Secretary of State for Transport, ex parte Factortame Ltd*[3] (see also Cane, Ch. 11, pp. 248–54). The background to the case was as follows. The applicants were companies which were incorporated under UK law, but the majority of the directors and shareholders of these companies were in fact Spanish. The companies were in the business of sea fishing and their vessels were registered as British under the Merchant Shipping Act 1894. The statutory regime governing sea fishing was radically altered by the passage of the Merchant Shipping Act 1988 and the regulations made pursuant thereto. Vessels which had been registered under the 1894 Act now had to register once again under the new legislation. Ninety-five vessels failed to meet the criteria in the new legislation, and they sought to argue that the relevant parts of the 1988 Act were incompatible with Articles 7, 52, 58, and 221 of the EC Treaty.

---

1   Case 6/64, [1964] ECR 585, at 593.
2   Case 106/77, [1978] ECR 629.
3   [1990] 2 AC 85.

The UK government responded by advancing two arguments. First, it was argued that nothing in Community law prevented a member state from defining for itself who was to be regarded as a national of that state. Secondly, the government contended that the 1988 legislation was not in fact in breach of Community law and that it was consistent with the Community policy on fisheries.

Whether the 1988 statute was in fact in breach of EC law was clearly a contentious question. All the UK courts involved in the case agreed that a reference should be made to the ECJ under Article 177. The question which remained for decision in the first *Factortame* case concerned the status of the 1988 Act pending the decision on the substance of the case by the ECJ. Lord Bridge gave the judgment of the House of Lords and reasoned as follows:

(a) His Lordship rejected the applicants' argument that the 1988 Act should be disapplied pending the final determination of the matter by the ECJ. An Act of Parliament was presumptively valid and this presumption would be displaced only if a challenge to the Act was upheld.

(b) Lord Bridge decided that in any event there was no jurisdiction under English law to grant interim injunctions against the Crown, and that this provided an additional reason why the relief sought by the applicants could not be granted.

(c) Lord Bridge then considered the applicants' argument that the absence of any interim relief against the Crown was itself a violation of Community law. Lord Bridge was unsure whether this was indeed so, but since the point was clearly contentious and of importance a preliminary ruling was requested from the ECJ. The ECJ was therefore in effect being asked to rule on whether a 'gap' in the availability of administrative law remedies in UK law was itself a breach of EC law, at least in so far as this 'gap' affected actions which had an EC element to them.

The ECJ decided in favour of the applicants.[4] The reasoning was founded on the earlier judgment in the *Simmenthal* case.[5] In that case, as we have seen, the ECJ held that provisions of Community law rendered 'automatically inapplicable' any conflicting provision of national law. The *Simmenthal* decision had given a broad construction to the idea of a 'conflicting provision' of national law, interpreting it to cover any legislative, administrative or judicial practice which might impair the effectiveness of Community law.[6] With this foundation the ECJ in the *Factortame* case concluded that:[7]

. . . the full effectiveness of Community law would be just as much impaired if a rule of national law could prevent a court seised of a dispute governed by

4 Case 213/89, *R v Secretary of State for Transport, ex parte Factortame Ltd* [1990] 3 CMLR 867.
5 *Amministrazione delle Finanze dello Stato v Simmenthal SpA* [1978] ECR 629.
6 *Ibid.*, paras 22 and 23.
7 [1990] 3 CMLR 867, para. 21.

Community law from granting interim relief in order to ensure the full effectiveness of the judgment to be given on the existence of the rights claimed under Community law. It follows that a court which in those circumstances would grant interim relief, if it were not for a rule of national law is obliged to set aside that rule.

The case then returned to the House of Lords to be reconsidered in the light of the preliminary ruling given by the ECJ: *R v Secretary of State for Transport, ex parte Factortame Ltd (No. 2)*.[8] A number of interesting issues emerge from their Lordships' decision, including the availability of interim relief against the Crown. Suffice it to say for the present that their Lordships accepted that, at least in the area covered by EC law, such relief would be made available against the Crown. The present discussion will focus upon the approach taken by the House of Lords to the issue of sovereignty and the EC.

Factortame (No. 2) contains *dicta* by their Lordships on the more general issue of sovereignty, and the reasons why these *dicta* are contained in the decision are not hard to find. The final decision on the substance of the case involved a potential clash between certain norms of the EC Treaty itself, combined with EC rules on the common fisheries policy, and a *later* Act of the UK Parliament, the Merchant Shipping Act 1988, combined with regulations made thereunder. One aspect of the traditional idea of sovereignty in the UK has been that if there is a clash between a later statutory norm and an earlier legal provision the former takes precedence. The strict application of this idea in the context of the EC could obviously be problematic, since the ECJ has, as we have seen, repeatedly held that Community law must take precedence in the event of a clash with national law. Earlier UK cases had exemplified a variety of approaches to the issue of a potential clash between the two legal systems. Some authorities appeared to stick to the traditional orthodoxy of giving precedence to national law.[9] Others appeared to be more willing to apply a rule of construction, under which it would be assumed that Parliament had not intended there to be any inconsistency between UK law and EC law, unless Parliament had expressly stated its intent to derogate from the norms of EC law. The *dicta* of the House of Lords in *Factortame* (No. 2) are therefore clearly of importance. Lord Bridge had this to say:[10]

Some public comments on the decision of the Court of Justice, affirming the jurisdiction of the courts of the member states to override national legislation if necessary to enable interim relief to be granted in protection of rights under

8 [1991] 1 AC 603.
9 Craig, P.P., 'Sovereignty of the United Kingdom Parliament after *Factortame*' 11 *Yearbook of European Law* 1991 221, at 240–43.
10 [1991] 1 AC 603, at 658–59.

Community law, have suggested that this was a novel and dangerous invasion by a Community institution of the sovereignty of the United Kingdom Parliament. But such comments are based on a misconception. If the supremacy within the European Community of Community law over the national law of member states was not always inherent in the EEC Treaty it was certainly well established in the jurisprudence of the Court of Justice long before the United Kingdom joined the Community. Thus, whatever limitation of its sovereignty Parliament accepted when it enacted the European Communities Act 1972 was entirely voluntary. Under the terms of the 1972 Act it has always been clear that it was the duty of a United Kingdom court, when delivering final judgment, to override any rule of national law found to be in conflict with any directly enforceable rule of Community law. Similarly, when decisions of the Court of Justice have exposed areas of United Kingdom statute law which failed to implement Council directives, Parliament has always loyally accepted the obligation to make appropriate and prompt amendments. Thus there is nothing in any way novel in according supremacy to rules of Community law in areas to which they apply and to insist that, in the protection of rights under Community law, national courts must not be prohibited by rules of national law from granting interim relief in appropriate cases is no more than a logical recognition of that supremacy.

It is clear that Lord Bridge was speaking in broad terms about the general relationship between EC law and UK law. His *dictum* represents a general statement concerning the priority of Community law over national law in the event of a clash between the two. The foundation for this reasoning is essentially contractarian: the UK knew when it joined the EC that priority should be accorded to EC law, and it must be taken to have contracted on those terms. If, therefore, 'blame' was to be cast for a loss of sovereignty then this should be laid at the feet of Parliament and not the courts.

Space precludes a thorough analysis of the effects of the second *Factortame* decision on the traditional concept of sovereignty as it operates in the UK. This can be found elsewhere.[11] At the very least the decision means that the concept of implied repeal, under which inconsistencies between later and earlier norms were resolved in favour of the former, will no longer apply to clashes concerning Community and national law. If Parliament ever does wish to derogate from its Community obligations then it will have to do so expressly and unequivocally. Whether our national courts would then choose to follow the latest will of Parliament, or whether they would argue that it is not open to our legislature to pick and choose which obligations to subscribe to while still remaining within the Community, remains to be seen.

---

11 Craig, *op. cit.* note 9 *supra*, and 'Administrative Law, Remedies and the EEC' (1991) 3 *European Review of Public Law* 521.

The *EOC* case[12] does, however, serve to demonstrate the ease with which the highest national courts have slipped into their new role. The case concerned the compatibility of UK legislation on unfair dismissal and redundancy pay with EC law. Under the relevant UK law[13] entitlement to these protections and benefits operated differentially depending upon whether the person was in full-time or part-time employment. Full-time workers were eligible after two years; part-time workers only after five. The great majority of part-time workers were women, and the Equal Opportunities Commission (EOC) took the view that the legislation discriminated against women, contrary to Article 119 of the Treaty and to certain Community Directives. The EOC sought a declaration that the UK legislation was in breach of EC law. The House of Lords found for the applicant. It held that the national legislation was indeed in breach of Article 119 and the Directives.

The reasoning of the House of Lords is instructive. Not only did it grant the declaration that the primary legislation was in breach of Community law, it also refused to take the opportunity to avoid the issue afforded by the way in which the question was framed by the applicant. The EOC had sought to argue that the decision which should be subject to judicial review was not the primary legislation itself, but a letter from the minister in which he had denied that the UK statute was in violation of Community norms. This way of framing the argument was doubtless based on the applicant's fear that the national courts might be wary of undertaking the novel task of actually declaring the primary legislation to be incompatible with EC law. The House of Lords declined to avoid the matter in this manner. As Lord Keith stated:[14]

> The real object of the EOC's attack is these provisions themselves. The question is whether judicial review is available for the purpose of securing a declaration that certain United Kingdom primary legislation is incompatible with Community law.

Having affirmed that judicial review could be used in this manner, the House of Lords went on to make it crystal clear that this power to review primary legislation resided in national *courts*. It was not only the House of Lords itself which was to have this species of authority; the Divisional Court could itself exercise this power.[15] Now it may well be the case that such a court would feel loath to exercise this power unless the case was especially clear, preferring instead to leave such heady matters to the Court of Appeal or the House of Lords. Time will tell. The

---

12   *R* v *Secretary of State for Employment, ex parte Equal Opportunities Commission* [1994] 1 All ER 910.
13   Employment Protection (Consolidation) Act 1978.
14   [1994] 1 All ER 910, at p. 919.
15   *Ibid.*, at p. 920.

fact remains that such lower courts have the authority in formal terms to exercise this type of control.

Their Lordships did not therefore shrink from recognising and acting upon the reality of the dispute which was presented to them. The effect of the case is to affirm that the national courts can themselves issue a declaration that primary legislation is in breach of our Community Treaty obligations. The sanctity of such legislation from challenge *by the national courts* themselves was formally denied.

EC LAW AND JUDICIAL REVIEW

It is common to think of the principles of Community administrative law having been fashioned solely by the ECJ as part of its creative jurisprudence under the general heading of 'general principles' of Community law. There is a measure of truth in this. The ECJ *has* played a major role in fashioning the Community's own principles of judicial review. It would, nonetheless, be mistaken to see this body of jurisprudence as having been solely the work of the Court. As with many areas of EC law, the development of administrative law principles has been affected by provisions laid down in primary Treaty articles, subsequent legislation enacted by the Commission, Council and European Parliament, and the case law of the ECJ. Thus, for example, the existence of an extensive duty to give reasons is to be found in Article 190 of the EC Treaty, and important provisions concerning freedom of information are to be found in Council and Commission decisions.

The object of this chapter is not, however, to provide a succinct analysis of all the main doctrines of Community administrative law. It is rather to consider the impact of those principles on judicial review of administrative action in the UK. To this end it is important to bear in mind a simple, but important, distinction: in cases which have a Community law component our national courts are under a *duty* to apply the relevant norms of EC law; in other cases there is no such obligation as such, but our national courts may, nonetheless, draw inspiration from the ECJ's jurisprudence. EC law may well, therefore, have a direct impact and also a spillover impact on domestic administrative law doctrine.

There are certain aspects of Community administrative law which do not differ markedly from domestic jurisprudence. Thus, for example, EC doctrine will lead to the annulment of the exercise of discretionary power where that power has been used for improper purposes. The Community heads of substantive review which are likely to have the most major influence upon domestic administrative law are proportionality, legitimate expectations/legal certainty, and fundamental rights. It is in relation to these doctrines that EC law is more developed than domestic doctrine, and it is therefore these doctrinal principles which applicants are most likely to seek to draw upon when challenging governmental action at national level. They will be considered in turn.

Proportionality

Proportionality is one of the general principles of Community law, and therefore our courts are obliged to have regard to it in those cases which have a Community law dimension.[16] These general principles have been developed by the ECJ and draw their inspiration from the laws of the member states. They can be relied upon in actions to contest the legality of Community measures, or national measures designed to implement Community law. The cases to which the principle of proportionality has been applied can be broadly divided into three categories.

There have been a number of cases falling within the *first category*, which deals with proportionality in the context of *rights* granted by the Community Treaties. One common scenario is where the member state seeks to take advantage of a public policy exception to, for example, the free movement of workers. The right to free movement is guaranteed by Article 48 of the Treaty, and the public policy exception finds expression in Article 48(3). The ECJ has, however, insisted that derogation from the fundamental principle of Article 48 can be sanctioned only in cases which pose a genuine and serious threat to public policy, and then only if the measure is the least restrictive possible in the circumstances.[17] A similar approach is evident in cases concerning the right to free movement of goods. Thus in the famous *Cassis de Dijon* case,[18] the ECJ considered whether a German rule which prescribed a minimum alcohol content for a certain alcoholic beverage constituted an impediment to the free movement of goods under Article 30 of the EC Treaty. Having decided that the rule could constitute such an impediment, the Court assessed the defence that the rule was necessary in order to protect consumers from being misled. The Court rejected the defence, because the interests of the consumers could be safeguarded in other, less restrictive ways, by displaying the alcohol content upon the packaging of the drinks.

Application of proportionality can also be seen in cases where individuals claim that Community regulations infringe their fundamental rights. Thus in the *Hauer* case[19] the ECJ held that the validity of a regulation which restricted the areas in which wine could be grown, and thus limited the applicant's property rights, must not constitute a disproportionate and excessive interference with the rights of the owner.

The principle has been often applied in a *second category* of case, where the applicant claims that the *penalty* which has been imposed is disproportionate to the offence which has been committed.[20] This is exemplified by *R v Intervention*

16 Wyatt, D. and Dashwood, A. *European Community Law* (3rd ed.), London: Sweet & Maxwell 1992, pp. 88–103.
17 Case 36/75, *Rutili* [1975] ECR 1219; Case 30/77, *Bouchereau* [1977] ECR 1999.
18 120/78, [1979] ECR 649; 178/84, *Commission v Germany* [1987] ECR 1227; Case 40/82, *Commission v United Kingdom* [1984] ECR 2793.
19 Case 44/79, [1979] ECR 3727.
20 Schwarze, J., *European Administrative Law*, London: Sweet & Maxwell, 1992, pp. 729–46.

Board, ex parte Man (Sugar) Ltd.[21] The applicant was required to give a security deposit to the Board when seeking a licence to export sugar outside the Community. The applicant was then late, but only by four hours, in completing the relevant paperwork. The Board, acting pursuant to a Community regulation, declared the entire deposit of £1,670,370 to be forfeit. Not surprisingly the company was aggrieved. The ECJ held that the automatic forfeiture of the entire deposit in the event of any failure to fulfil the time requirement was too drastic given the function performed by the system of export licences.[22] In addition to cases dealing with penalties *stricto sensu*, the ECJ has applied proportionality in the field of economic regulation, scrutinising the level of charges which have been imposed by the Community institutions. Thus in *Bela-Muhle*[23] the Court held that a scheme whereby producers of animal feed were forced to use skimmed milk in their product, in order to reduce a surplus, rather than soya, was unlawful because, *inter alia,* skimmed milk was three times more expensive than soya: the obligation to purchase the milk therefore imposed a disproportionate burden on the animal feed producers.

Proportionality has likewise been applied in a *third category* of case, where no rights as such are at stake, nor is there any claim that a penalty is over-burdensome. The essence of the claim in this type of case is that a policy choice made, for example by the Commission, is challengeable because the ends being pursued could be attained in some less disproportionate manner. What is of interest is the meaning given to the concept in many of the cases which are of this kind.

Fedesa[24] provides a good example. The applicants challenged the legality of a Council Directive which prohibited the use of certain substances which had a hormonal action in livestock farming. The challenge was based on a number of grounds including proportionality. The ECJ stressed that the Community institutions must indeed pursue their policy by the least onerous means, and that the disadvantages must not be disproportionate to the aims of the measure. It then continued as follows:[25]

> However, with regard to judicial review of compliance with those conditions it must be stated that in matters concerning the common agricultural policy the Community legislature has a discretionary power which corresponds to the political responsibilities given to it by Articles 40 and 43 of the Treaty. Consequently, the legality of a measure adopted in that sphere can be affected only if the measure is manifestly inappropriate having regard to the objective which the competent institution is seeking to pursue.

---

21   Case 181/84, [1985] ECR 2889.
22   *Ibid.*, para. 29; Case 240/78, *Atalanta* [1979] ECR 2137; Case 122/78, *Buitoni* [1975] ECR 677.
23   Case 114/76, *Bela-Muhle Josef Bergman* v *Grows-Farm* [1977] ECR 1211.
24   Case C-331/88, *R* v *The Minister of Agriculture, Fisheries and Food and the Secretary of State for Health, ex parte Fedesa* [1990] ECR I-4023.
25   *Ibid.*, p. 4063; Case 265/87, *Schrader* [1989] ECR 2237.

What is readily apparent is that if the ECJ wishes to adopt a standard of review which is less intensive in a particular area then this will carry across to proportionality, as well as to other grounds of illegality. A decision will be overturned only if it is 'manifestly inappropriate' to the objective which the institution is seeking to pursue. When proportionality is given this meaning then there will be little difference between it and review for *Wednesbury* unreasonableness.

The case law furnishes, moreover, interesting insights into why the ECJ has adopted this more limited form of review. Space precludes any detailed consideration of this issue, but in essence it is because it does not wish to be continually faced with challenges to Community norms in an area where the Community institutions possessed of discretionary power have to balance a number of variables which can often conflict among themselves. If the ECJ countenanced a more intensive review for proportionality in this sphere then it would be continually faced with challenges by groups which believed that the variables should have been balanced in some other way. The Court would be in danger of second-guessing the policy choice made by the Community institutions. Evidence of this reluctance to overturn the Community's choices in relation to agriculture is evident in other, similar cases[26] and in the secondary literature.[27]

The relative intensity with which proportionality is applied in the agricultural sphere may not necessarily be indicative of how the concept will be used in other cases which come within this third category. There may be other areas where the ECJ is willing to intervene with a more searching form of inquiry, particularly where the area is one in which the administrative authorities possess a narrower discretionary power, or one which is more clearly circumscribed. This third category of cases may, therefore, have to be broken down into more discrete categories to reflect this fact.

The leading authority on the status of proportionality in the UK is still the decision of the House of Lords in *R* v *Secretary of State for the Home Department, ex parte Brind*.[28] The Home Secretary issued Directives under the Broadcasting Act 1981, requiring the BBC and the IBA to refrain from broadcasting certain matters by persons who represented organisations which were proscribed under legislation concerning the prevention of terrorism. The ambit of this proscription was limited to direct statements made by the members of the organisations. It did not, for example, prevent the broadcasting of such persons on film, provided that there was a voice-over account paraphrasing what had been said. The applicants sought judicial review on a number of grounds. The arguments which related to a breach

---

26 See among many, Case 5/73, *Balkan Import-Export* [1973] ECR 1091; Case 138/78, *Stolting* [1979] ECR 713; Cases 197–200, 243, 245, 247/80, *Walzmuhle* [1981] ECR 3211; Case C-8/89, *Zardi* [1990] ECR I-2515,at 2532–33; Case 98/78, *Racke* [1979] ECR 69.
27 Vajda, C., 'Some Aspects of Judicial Review within the Common Agricultural Policy — Part II' (1979) 4 *European Law Review* 341, at 347–48.
28 [1991] 1 AC 696.

of the European Convention will be considered below. The present analysis will be directed towards the other main ground of challenge, which was that the Directives were disproportionate to the end sought to be attained. This objective was both to deny such organisations any appearance of political legitimacy, and also to prevent intimidation.

Their Lordships rejected the argument based upon proportionality. Lord Bridge held that the restrictions on freedom of speech were not unreasonable in scope, and did not believe that the applicants' case could be improved by invoking the idea of proportionality.[29] Lord Bridge did, however, hold that proportionality could be of relevance in establishing *Wednesbury* unreasonableness, and agreed with Lord Roskill that proportionality might at some time be incorporated within our law. Lord Roskill himself acknowledged that Lord Diplock had, in the *GCHQ* case,[30] held this open as a possible future development, but Lord Roskill did not consider that this was an appropriate case for such a development, believing that this would lead the courts into substituting their view for that of the Home Secretary on the particular issue before the court.[31] Similar concerns are apparent in the judgments of Lord Ackner and Lord Lowry. Thus Lord Ackner[32] reasoned that if proportionality was to add something to our existing law, then it would be imposing a more intensive standard of review than traditional *Wednesbury* unreasonableness. This would mean that an 'inquiry into and a decision upon the merits cannot be avoided', in the sense that the court would have to balance the pros and cons of the decision which was being challenged.[33] Lord Lowry was equally wary of overstepping the boundary between a supervisory and an appellate jurisdiction. He felt that the judges are not well equipped by training or experience to 'decide the answer to an administrative problem where the scales are evenly balanced'.[34] His Lordship also feared that stability would be jeopardised because 'there is nearly always something to be said against any administrative decision', and that recognition of proportionality would, therefore, lead to an increase in the number of applications for judicial review, with a consequential increase in costs both for litigants and in terms of court time.[35]

The cogency of these objections will be considered in due course, but before doing so it should be recognised that the courts have in the past applied a concept of proportionality, or something closely analogous thereto, whether as an independent concept or as part of a finding of *Wednesbury* unreasonableness. Precisely *which* cases should be regarded in this light is, however, a more controversial

---

29   *Ibid.*, pp. 748–9.
30   [1985] AC 374, at 410.
31   [1991] 1 AC 696, at 749–50.
32   *Ibid.*, pp. 762–3.
33   *Ibid.*, p. 762.
34   *Ibid.*, p. 767.
35   *Loc. cit.*

question. Advocates of the recognition of proportionality within our law wish, not surprisingly, to categorise a large number of cases in this manner.[36] Others disagree, arguing that many of the cases placed within this category would not be classified in this way in, for example, France.[37] Three types of case can be distinguished:

(a) those decisions which do unequivocally make reference to proportionality;[38]

(b) decisions which make no explicit reference to proportionality as such, but which are said to reflect that concept;[39]

(c) cases which are said to provide some support for proportionality, which do not mention that concept and where one has to dig considerably deeper to find any implicit presence of the idea.[40]

Notwithstanding the decision in *Brind*, it is clear from the preceding discussion that UK courts have an obligation to apply proportionality in cases which do have a Community law dimension. The live question is therefore whether they will proceed to apply proportionality as an independent head of review in cases which do not have a Community law element. There are a number of reasons why this development is likely to occur.

The first reason why this is so is a consequence of the changing judicial attitudes to fundamental rights. Developments in this area will be charted below. Suffice it to say for the present that if we do recognise certain interests as being of particular importance, and are willing to categorise them as fundamental rights or something akin thereto, then this renders the application of proportionality more likely and easier. Proportionality is *more likely* to be applied because the very denomination of those interests as fundamental rights means that any invasion of them should be kept to the minimum. Society may well accept that these rights cannot be regarded as absolute and that some limitations may be warranted in certain circumstances. Nonetheless, there is a presumption that any inroad should interfere with the right as little as possible, and no more than is merited by the occasion. In this sense the recognition of some idea of proportionality is a natural and necessary adjunct to the regard for 'fundamental rights. Proportionality is also *easier* to apply in conditions such as these. The reason why this is so is that in such cases a difficult

---

36   Jowell, J., and Lester, A., 'Proportionality: Neither Novel nor Dangerous', in Jowell, J., and Oliver, D. (eds), *New Directions in Judicial Review*, London: Sweet & Maxwell, 1988, pp. 51–73.

37   Boyron, S., 'Proportionality in English Administrative Law: A Faulty Translation' (1992) 12 *Oxford Journal of Legal Studies* 237.

38   *R v Barnsley MBC, ex parte Hook* [1976] 1 WLR 1052, at 1057.

39   Jowell and Lester, *op. cit.* note 36 *supra*, p. 61. *Wheeler v Leicester City Council* [1985] AC 1054, is said to be one such case.

40   See, e.g., Bromley LBC v *GLC* [1983] 1 AC 768.

aspect of the proportionality calculus has already been resolved: one of the interests, such as freedom of speech, has been identified *and* it has been weighted or valued. We do not have to fathom out this matter afresh on each and every occasion, precisely because the fundamental nature of the right has been acknowledged. Now to be sure we will still have to decide whether the invasion of the right was proportionate, and this may well be controversial. But, as will be seen, this is much less problematic than in cases of the third type considered below. It is natural in cases concerning rights to apply proportionality in the sense of asking whether the interference with these fundamental rights was the least restrictive possible in the circumstances.

The second reason why proportionality is likely to emerge as an independent head of review, and indeed may already have assumed this status, is that the concept is relatively easy to apply in cases where the allegation is that it is the punishment or penalty which is disproportionate to the offence committed. Once again, people may well disagree as to the precise penalty which is appropriate for a particular offence. Yet we know the penalty which has been imposed; we know the offence; and we know also the interest which has been affected by the penalty. This interest may be personal liberty in the case of imprisonment, or it may be loss of livelihood as in *Hook*. It *is* a recognised principle of justice that penalties should not be excessive, as acknowledged in the Bill of Rights 1689. A court is unlikely to intervene unless the disproportionality is reasonably evident,[41] and judicial review of this kind is to be welcomed.

The third reason why proportionality is indeed likely to emerge as a distinct principle within domestic administrative law is that it does contain a more structured methodology through which to decide whether an exercise of discretion should be struck down, as compared with the blunt tool of *Wednesbury* unreasonableness. While this is so one should not underestimate the difficulties of applying proportionality in cases which do not involve fundamental rights or penalties. In such cases a public body will decide to exercise its discretion in a particular manner, which necessitates the balancing of various interests, and a person affected argues that the balancing was disproportionate in some way. There are two reasons why these cases present particular difficulties. On the one hand, there is the fact that it may be harder to apply the steps required by a proportionality inquiry. How do we, for example, weight the respective values of ratepayers and transport users in a *Fares Fair*[42] type of case? What precisely would a balancing or cost–benefit analysis entail in such circumstances? On the other hand, there is the problem of the division of function as between the administration and the judiciary. Many decisions involve just the sort of balancing described above. It is of the very essence of political determinations and also of many

---

41 *Commissioners of Customs and Excise* v *P&O Steam Navigation Co.* [1993] COD 164.
42 [1983] 1 AC 768.

administrative choices. Given that this is so, it cannot be right for the judiciary to overturn such a decision merely because the court would have balanced the conflicting interests differently. This would amount to substitution of judgment by any other name.

Now this should not be taken to mean that proportionality has no role to play in this type of case, and it may well be advantageous for administrative policy choices to be susceptible to scrutiny in the courts.[43] It could be argued that the problems identified above would be alleviated if we were to break down this third category into at least two more discrete sections: those areas in which the administration has a broad discretion might be subject to a less intensive form of proportionality review, while those in which the discretion was more narrowly confined would be subject to a more searching inquiry, albeit one which did not amount to substitution of judgment. A division along these lines would be plausible, although the difficulty of assigning cases to particular categories should not be underestimated.

What it does mean is that if scrutiny is to be via proportionality then we have some further choices to make. We must decide upon the sense of proportionality which is to be used, *and* the intensity with which it will be applied. In those cases where the courts wish to engage in searching review under the guise of a cost–benefit analysis or one of the other tests which have been set out, we must be willing to confront the problems outlined above. Alternatively, a less intensive form of review can be utilised for some of the cases which arise in this area. Precisely what this means can be appreciated by considering proportionality within the EC.

Legitimate expectations

The connected concepts of legal certainty and legitimate expectations (see also Fordham, Ch. 8, p. 189) are to be found in all the legal systems of the member states which make up the Community, although their precise legal content may vary from one system to another.[44] These concepts are applied in a number of different ways in Community law.[45]

One of the most obvious applications of legal certainty is in the context of rules which have an *actual retroactive effect*. Following Schwarze,[46] actual retroactivity covers the situation where a rule is introduced and applied to events which have already been concluded. Retroactivity of this nature may occur either where the

---

43   Harden, I., and Lewis, N., *The Noble Lie: The British Constitution and the Rule of Law*, London: Hutchinson, 1987.
44   Schwarze, *op. cit.* note 20 *supra*, Ch. 6.
45   Craig, P.P., and de Burca, G., *European Community Law: Text, Cases & Materials*, Oxford: Clarendon Press, 1995, pp. 349–56.
46   Note 44 *supra*, p. 1120.

date of entry into force precedes the date of publication; or where the regulation applies to circumstances which have actually been concluded before the entry into force of the measure.

The arguments against allowing measures of this nature to have legal effect are simple and compelling. A basic tenet of the rule of law is that people ought to be able to plan their lives, secure in the knowledge of the legal consequences of their actions. This fundamental aspect of the rule of law is violated by the application of measures which were not in force at the time that the actual events took place. Small wonder then that legal systems have tended to take a very dim view of attempts by legislators or administrators to apply their rules in this manner. The Community is no different in this respect.[47] The normal presumption is against the validity of retroactive measures.[48] This manifests itself in both procedural and substantive terms.

In procedural terms, the Court has made it clear that it will interpret norms as having retroactive effect only if this clearly follows from the manner in which they are expressed, or from the objectives of the general scheme of which they are a part. The general principle of construction is, therefore, against giving rules any retroactive impact.[49] In substantive terms, the Court will strike down measures which do have a retroactive effect where there is no pressing Community objective which demands this temporal dimension, or where the legitimate expectations of those affected by the measure cannot be duly respected.[50]

Of more direct concern to the present analysis are the problems presented by cases of *apparent retroactivity*[51] and the way in which the ECJ deals with those problems. A person may have planned his or her actions on the basis of one policy choice made by the administration, and seeks redress when the chosen policy alters, even though this alteration is only prospective and not retrospective. The moral arguments against allowing laws to have actual retroactive effect are powerful and straightforward. The category of apparent retroactivity is more problematic because the administration must obviously have the power to alter its policy for the future, even though this may have implications for the conduct of private parties which has been planned on the basis of the pre-existing legal regime.

---

47   Case 98/78, *Firma A. Racke* v *Hauptzollamt Mainz* [1979] ECR 69. See also, Case 99/78, *Weingut Gustav Decker KG* v *Hauptzollamt Landau* [1979] ECR 101.

48   Where there is a pressing Community objective and where the legitimate expectations of those concerned are duly respected, then retroactivity may, *exceptionally,* be accepted by the Court in the non criminal context: Case C-331/88, *R* v *Ministry of Agriculture, Fisheries and Food and Secretary of State for Health, ex parte Fedesa* [1990] ECR I-4023.

49   Cases 212–217/80, *Salumi* [1981] ECR 2735.

50   Case 224/82, *Meiko-Konservenfabrik* v *Federal Republic of Germany* [1983] ECR 2539; Case 63/83, *Regina* v *Kent Kirk* [1984] ECR 2689.

51   The distinction between actual and apparent retroactivity is sometimes expressed alternatively in terms of a division between primary and secondary retroactivity: *Bowen* v *Georgetown University Hospital* 488 US 204 (1988).

The ECJ has dealt with this problem in a number of its decisions. Its initial conceptualisation of the problem recognises that there are conflicting interests at stake — that of the individual, who may have detrimentally relied on the earlier policy choice, and that of the public body, which needs to develop its policy. Its jurisprudence provides guidance as to when an individual will be deemed to have a legitimate expectation derived from the earlier governmental policy. It has recognised that there can be what we would term substantive legitimate expectations. Indeed, it has not seen difficulties in principle with recognising this concept, such that the adjectives 'procedural' and 'substantive' are not to be found attached to legitimate expectation within Community law. Provided that the legitimacy of the expectation can be proven, and provided that the public interest will not be unduly harmed by allowing an individual to rely on an earlier norm, or through the modification of the later norm, the ECJ will uphold the claim even though it is to some substantive benefit. The ECJ will, moreover, normally consider the legitimacy of the expectation separately from whether there are valid policy reasons for departing from that expectation.[52]

The case law of the ECJ indicates that the individual must be able to point either to a bargain of some form which has been entered into between the individual and the authorities, or to a course of conduct or assurance on the part of the authorities which can be said to generate the legitimate expectation. Cases of this nature will be examined below. If the applicant does manage to show the existence of some legitimate expectation, the ECJ's case law provides guidance as to how this is then balanced with the needs of the relevant public body to alter the law.

Thus, in the *Sofrimport* case[53] the applicant sought to import apples from Chile into the Community. A licence was required in accord with Regulation 346/88. By a later Regulation, 962/88, the Commission took protective measures and suspended all such licences for Chilean apples. The parent Regulation, 2707/72, which gave the Commission power to adopt protective measures, specifically stated in Article 3 that account should be taken of the special position of goods in transit, for the obvious reason that such measures could have a particularly harmful effect on traders. The applicant's goods were already in transit when Regulation 962/88 was introduced, but they were refused entry to the Community. In an action for annulment the ECJ held that the failure of the Commission to make any special provision for goods in transit as required by the parent Regulation was an infringement of the applicant's legitimate expectations. A similar theme is apparent in the *CNTA* case.[54] The case centred on monetary compensation amounts (mcas), which were payments designed to compensate for fluctuations in exchange rates.

---

52   Craig, P.P., 'Substantive Legitimate Expectations in Domestic and Community Law' (1996) 55 *Cambridge Law Journal* 289.
53   Case C-152/88, *Sofrimport Sarl* v *Commission* [1990] ECR I-2477.
54   Case 74/74, *CNTA SA* v *Commission* [1975] ECR 533.

The applicant was a firm which had made export contracts on the supposition that mcas would be payable. After these contracts had been made, but before they were to be performed, the Commission passed a Regulation abolishing mcas in that sector. The applicant suffered loss, since it had made the contracts on the assumption that the mcas would be payable. The ECJ held that while mcas could not be said to insulate exporters from all fluctuations in exchange rates, they did have the effect of shielding them from such risks, with the consequence that even a prudent exporter might choose not to cover himself against it. The ECJ then stated:[55]

> In these circumstances, a trader might legitimately expect that for transactions irrevocably undertaken by him because he has obtained, subject to a deposit, export licences fixing the amount of the refund in advance, no unforeseeable alteration will occur which could have the effect of causing him inevitable loss, by re-exposing him to the exchange risk.

In the absence of some overriding public interest, the Commission should have adopted transitional measures to protect those in the position of the applicant.[56]

As is common with all principles of Community law, UK courts have an obligation to apply those principles in cases which contain a Community law component. Our courts may also, if they are so inclined, advert to Community law principles in cases which do not have a link with EC law if they find the principles contained therein to be helpful.

The current state of UK law in this area can be summarised broadly as follows. The concept of legitimate expectations has been recognised in the procedural context, either as the reason for according process rights or as the reason for increasing the quantum of such rights.[57] The courts have, however, been more reluctant to recognise that legitimate expectations can have a substantive impact, fearing that to accept that this can be so would lead to the ossification of administrative policy. The case law of the ECJ indicates that this fear is unwarranted and that it is perfectly possible to recognise that legitimate expectations can have such a dimension without thereby preventing policy change when this is deemed to be desirable. The attitude of UK courts in this respect is, however, undergoing a transformation, with a growing willingness to accept a substantive dimension to legitimate expectations. What is particularly interesting in this context is that some of the key decisions in this area have been clearly influenced by the ECJ's jurisprudence, even where the relevant fact situation did not in and of itself raise a Community law issue. This exemplifies the point made earlier concerning the possible spillover impact of Community law.

---

55 *Ibid.*, para. 42.
56 *Ibid.*, para. 43.
57 Craig, P.P., *Administrative Law* (3rd ed.), London: Sweet & Maxwell, 1994, pp. 293–6.

This can be seen in *R. v Ministry for Agriculture, Fisheries and Foods, ex parte Hamble (Offshore) Fisheries Limited*,[58] the facts of which were as follows (see Fordham, Ch. 8, p. 189). In 1987, Hamble Fisheries (HF) purchased a trawler with a view to taking advantage of a policy published by the Ministry of Agriculture, Fisheries and Food (MAFF), allowing the transfer of pressure stock licences[59] from one vessel to another. HF also obtained the transfer of certain other licences which enabled it to fish for non pressure stocks. In 1990 MAFF decided to allow capacity aggregation. This was a system under which similar types of licences could be transferred from existing vessels to a larger vessel, on the condition that the total capacity of the fleet was not increased. On this basis HF then bought two vessels which had beam trawl licences, with the intention of transferring those licences to the larger trawler which it owned. However, in March 1992, MAFF announced an immediate moratorium on the transfer and aggregation of pressure stock licences on to beam trawlers which were fishing in certain areas in order to reduce overall catch. This change of policy was followed by a letter written to the applicant in June 1992, stating that HF's trawler would not qualify for a beam trawl licence for the North Sea because the vessel currently owned by HF had no previous record of North Sea beam trawling.

HF claimed that there had been a breach of its legitimate expectations. It was argued that having acquired North Sea pressure stock licences, and having expended considerable money in the process, the applicant should be able to exploit such licences without hindrance from MAFF; that although policy could of course be changed for the future, the introduction of severe measures such as a moratorium with immediate effect constituted a breach of HF's legitimate expectation in that there should have been appropriate transitional provisions, or provisions to cover transactions which were already in progress.

It was clear that the case raised directly the question as to whether there could be substantive legitimate expectations: the applicant's claim was not based on the denial of any procedural rights as such, but on what HF took to be the unjust refusal to allow it to fish with the licences which it had obtained up to the change of policy in March 1992. Sedley J accepted that this was the point at issue and did not seek to avoid deciding this important point of principle. The judgment is forceful and the reasoning incisive. This reasoning may, for the sake of convenience, be broken down into a series of stages.

Sedley J began by holding that there was some *precedent* in favour of a doctrine of substantive legitimate expectations. He interpreted the *Ruddock* case[60] to be just such a decision. This is surely correct. What was at stake in *Ruddock* was the claim for a substantive benefit: that individuals who did not fall within the government's

---

58 [1995] 2 All ER 714.
59 Pressure stocks were those species of fish which were incapable of sustaining unrestricted fishing.
60 [1987] 1 WLR 1482.

publicised criteria for telephone surveillance would not have their phones tapped by the security services.[61]

He then buttressed this reasoning from precedent with an argument of *principle* in favour of the recognition of substantive legitimate expectations. The essence of the argument is contained in the following extract:[62]

> . . . the real question is one of fairness in public administration. It is difficult to see why it is any less unfair to frustrate a legitimate expectation that something will or will not be done by the decision maker than it is to frustrate a legitimate expectation that the applicant will be listened to before the decision maker decides whether to take a particular step. Such a doctrine does not risk fettering a public body in the discharge of public duties because no individual can legitimately expect the discharge of public duties to stand still or be distorted because of that individual's peculiar position.

Having decided that there might, as a matter of principle, be substantive legitimate expectations, Sedley J then considered *how one decided whether an expectation was indeed legitimate:* what was the 'legal alchemy which gives an expectation sufficient legitimacy to secure enforcement in public law'.[63] He accepted[64] that a specific public promise made by the government could suffice in this respect,[65] but felt that where the expectation was based upon a practice the issue was rather more difficult:[66]

> A promise is, precisely, a representation about future conduct, making it relatively straightforward to decide whether the promisor should be held to it. Practices may, but do not necessarily have the same character. Where the material practice is generated by a policy which is itself liable to change, the practice cannot be logically expected to survive a policy change, and policy change may not be able to be withheld consistently with the statutory duties or powers under which the policy has been brought into existence.

For Sedley J the decision as to whether an expectation was indeed legitimate in this type of case was itself to be decided by a balancing process: legitimacy was not an absolute, but rather 'a function of expectations induced by government and of policy considerations which militate against their fulfilment'.[67] Thus the concept

---

61   [1995] 2 All ER 714, at 723.
62   *Ibid.,* at p. 724.
63   *Ibid.,* at p. 728.
64   *Ibid.,* at pp. 728–9.
65   Citing *Attorney General of Hong Kong* v *Ng Yuen Shiu* [1983] 2 AC 629 by way of example.
66   [1995] 2 All ER 714, at 729.
67   *Ibid.,* at p. 731.

of legitimate expectations was to be reserved for expectations which were not only reasonable, 'but which will be sustained by the court in the face of changes of policy'.[68] This balance was to be struck initially by the relevant policy-maker, but this did not serve to render judicial review otiose or irrelevant. If the balance which was struck by the initial decision maker was then challenged in the courts, it was for the judge, while recognising the constitutional importance of ministerial freedom to reformulate policy, to protect the individual by deciding whether the individual's 'expectation of different treatment has a legitimacy which in fairness outtops the policy choice which threatens to frustrate it'.[69]

Applying this approach to the facts of the case, Sedley J decided against the applicant: it was not unfair, in the light of the government's policy objectives, to exclude from the policy's transitional provisions firms which were in the position of the applicant, notwithstanding the fact that they had expended funds in anticipation of being able to acquire the licence which was being sought. Moreover, the very existence of transitional provisions within the new policy was itself a factor to be taken into account when deciding whether the policy-maker had taken sufficient account of the need for qualifications to the new policy, more particularly where the creation of any further 'single exception' would in reality generate a new class of firms to whom the reformulated policy would not apply.

The reasoning of Sedley J contains a considerable amount of reference to the ECJ's case law on this topic, as well as to secondary literature by academic writers. It is clear that this case law and literature had some considerable impact on his willingness to accept that legitimate expectations can have a substantive impact within domestic administrative law. The status of a doctrine of substantive legitimate expectations within domestic law, is, however, uncertain because of two subsequent decisions of the Court of Appeal.

In *Hargreaves*,[70] the applicants were prisoners who, when admitted to prison in 1994, were informed that they could apply for home leave after serving one-third of their sentences. In 1995 the system changed, with the result that eligibility for home leave became available only after a prisoner had served one-half of the sentence. The applicants sought judicial review, claiming that their legitimate expectations had been frustrated by the change of policy. This claim was rejected by the Court of Appeal. It was held, following *Findlay*,[71] that there was no legitimate expectation enforceable by judicial review on the facts of the case since the discretion of the Home Secretary to change policy within this area could not be fettered. The Court of Appeal also held that, since the deferment of eligibility

---

68   *Ibid.*, at p. 732.
69   *Ibid.*, at p. 731.
70   *R v Secretary of State for the Home Department, ex parte Hargreaves* [1997] 1 All ER 397. For detailed discussion see Craig, 'Substantive Legitimate Expectations and the Principles of Judicial Review' (forthcoming).
71   *Findlay v Secretary of State for the Home Department* [1985] AC 318.

for leave was a matter of substance and not of procedure, the court was not required to conduct any balancing exercise based on fairness or proportionality when deciding upon the lawfulness of this policy change. The *dictum* of Sedley J in *Hamble Fisheries*, suggesting that the court could engage in such a balancing exercise, was overruled. The correct test was, said the Court of Appeal, whether the decision to change policy was unreasonable in the *Wednesbury* sense. On the facts of the case the decision by the Home Secretary to change the policy was not found to be unreasonable in this sense.

Two aspects of this decision must be distinguished: what are the implications in general for a doctrine of substantive legitimate expectations; and what does the decision have to tell us about the test to be applied should such a doctrine still exist as a matter of domestic law?

On the first of these questions, it seems, although it is not entirely clear, as if a doctrine of substantive legitimate expectations does in fact still exist, in principle at least, for the following reason. Given that the applicants' claim was unequivocally substantive in nature, the very fact that the court considered whether such an expectation could be sustained at all on the facts of the case is indicative that such a claim is possible in principle. If it were not then the applicants' claim would have failed *in limine*. This view is reinforced by the fact that the court in *Hargreaves* discussed the test to be applied to determine whether a change of policy could be open to challenge: if substantive legitimate expectations could never be pleaded in principle, this second inquiry would have been otiose.

On the second of these questions, it is clear from the *Hargreaves* case that the court will not sanction a balancing approach as broad as that posited by Sedley J in *Hamble Fisheries*. A change of policy will be struck down only if this change is *Wednesbury* unreasonable, and it is readily apparent from the judgment that the court will not lightly find that this is so.

That a doctrine of substantive legitimate expectations does exist, in principle at least, within domestic law seems to be further reinforced by the decision in the other recent Court of Appeal case, *Unilever*.[72] Space precludes a full analysis of the complex facts in this case. Suffice it to say for the present that the applicant challenged a decision by the IRC to refuse to allow it tax relief for trading losses incurred in a particular tax year when the applicant had made a late claim. The Court of Appeal held that it would be unfair and an abuse of power for the IRC to rely on the time limit, and that this was so notwithstanding that the court also found that the IRC had not made an unambiguous representation on the matter of late claims. Richard Gordon is of the view that the case does unequivocally settle the point that substantive legitimate expectations are a part of domestic law, given that the applicant's claim was entirely substantive in nature.[73] We will, however,

---

72   *R* v *Commissioners of Inland Revenue, ex parte Unilever plc* [1996] STC 681.
73   Gordon and Ward, 'The Billowing Fog' (1996) 146 *New Law Journal* 1663, 1664.

have to await further case law before matters can be regarded as entirely clear, given the decision in the *Hargreaves* case.

The position at present can be summarised as follows. A claim will not be struck out merely because it amounts to a substantive legitimate expectation. However, before the court will hold a public body to a previous policy it will be necessary for the applicant to show both that he or she has the expectation which is being claimed, and also that the change of policy really was unreasonable in the *Wednesbury* sense, or something similar thereto. The latter hurdle will not be an easy one to surmount. It could well be argued that the second hurdle is being set too high, given that the applicant will already have had to prove that he or she does possess the legitimate expectation on the facts of the case.

Fundamental rights

One of the most significant developments in recent years has been the growing recognition by the UK courts that there are fundamental rights (see also Donson, generally and Fordham, Ch. 8, p. 197) which will, at the very least, affect the intensity of judicial review. The decision of the House of Lords in *Derbyshire CC v Times Newspapers Ltd*,[74] that the rights contained in the European Convention on Human Rights also exist within the common law, was a seminal step in this development.[75] Those who seek to present rights-based arguments within the context of judicial review actions can, however, also make use of the ECJ's jurisprudence on fundamental rights in two different ways.

On the one hand, individuals can gain rights from the provisions of the Treaty or norms made thereunder via the concept of direct effect. This concept has been applied to an increasing number of Community norms. Certain provisions of the Treaty which are directly effective deal with subject matter which would undoubtedly merit inclusion in any list of constitutional or fundamental rights. One obvious example is to be found in Article 119 of the Treaty, which is concerned with equal pay and sex discrimination. This was held to be directly effective in the seminal case of *Defrenne*.[76] Defrenne was employed as an air hostess with Sabena. She argued that her conditions of service were discriminatory as compared with those of male cabin stewards who performed the same tasks. The ECJ held that Article 119 was directly effective, in some cases at least, that Defrenne therefore derived rights from the Treaty and that these were enforceable against the airline. Many other cases have followed. For example, in *Johnston*[77] a provision in a UK statutory instrument which, in effect, differentiated between men and women as to

---

74 [1993] 1 All ER 1011.
75 For general discussion see Craig, *op. cit.* note 57 *supra*, pp. 421–32.
76 Case 43/75, *Defrenne* v *Sabena* [1976] ECR 455.
77 Case 222/84, *Johnston* v *Chief Constable of the Royal Ulster Constabulary* [1986] ECR 1651.

the nature of the judicial remedies which they possessed, was held to be in breach of Article 6 of Directive 76/207 on Equal Treatment.

On the other hand, there is the Community concept of fundamental rights which has been developed by the ECJ.[78] The EC Treaty contains no list of traditional fundamental rights as such, in large part because the original rationale for the Treaty was principally economic. The catalyst for the creation of such rights was the threat of revolt by the courts of some member states. Individuals who were dissatisfied with the provisions of, for example, a regulation would challenge it before their national court and contend that it was inconsistent with rights in their own national constitutions, and moreover that these rights could not have been given away by the state when acceding to the Community. An argument of just this kind was made before the German courts in *Internationale Handelsgesellschaft*.[79] The threat which this posed to the supremacy of Community law was not lost on the ECJ, and it stated that Community norms could not be challenged in this manner. However, in order to stem any possible national rebellion, the ECJ declared that fundamental rights were indeed part of the general principles of Community law, and that the compatibility of a Community norm with such rights would be tested by the ECJ itself.[80] Three points concerning the fundamental rights' doctrine are of particular relevance here:

(a)   Although the EC is not formally bound by the decisions of the European Court of Human Rights, the ECJ has referred to specific provisions of the Convention on a number of occasions.[81] In so far as it does so this provides the Convention with a peremptory force in national courts which it would otherwise lack.[82]

(b)   Fundamental rights have been used principally to attack Community norms, such as regulations or decisions. However, if a national provision is based upon a Community norm then the former may not survive a challenge to the latter. Thus in *Kirk*,[83] the ECJ held that the retroactivity of a Community regulation could not validate *ex post facto* national measures which were penal in nature, where these measures imposed penalties for an act which was not punishable at the time that it was committed.

(c)   The third point is the most important, and is potentially of far-reaching significance. While, as noted above, the principal thrust of the fundamental rights doctrine has been to attack Community norms, it is not so limited. The logic of

---

78   Craig and de Burca, *op. cit.* note 45 *supra*, Ch. 7.
79   Case 11/70, [1970] ECR 1125.
80   *Ibid.,* at p. 1134.
81   See, e.g., Case 136/79, *National Panasonic* [1980] ECR 2033 at 2057.
82   Grief, N., 'The Domestic Impact of the European Convention on Human Rights as Mediated through Community law' [1991] *Public Law* 555. This must of course now be read subject to the charges in domestic law being put through by the Labour government concerning the ECHR.
83   Case 63/83, [1984] ECR 2689.

the doctrine would dictate that it can apply against national action too, provided that this action can in some way be connected with Community law. This logic can be simply stated: fundamental rights are part of Community law, and therefore they should be capable of being used not only when the Community authorities act in contravention of these rights, but also when it is a member state which has done so in an area covered by the Treaties. This is indeed now so, as exemplified by the decision in the *ERT* case:[84] where national legislation falls within the field of application of Community law the ECJ, when requested to give a preliminary ruling, must provide the national court with all the elements of interpretation which are necessary in order to enable it to assess the compatibility of that legislation with the fundamental rights — as laid down in particular in the European Convention on Human Rights — the observance of which the ECJ ensures.

EC LAW AND REMEDIES

The impact of Community law on the remedies (see Cane, Ch. 11 generally) which must be made available within national legal systems in order to secure the effective implementation of Community rights has undergone a considerable transformation. The original approach of the ECJ was minimalist: it did not demand that national systems created any new remedies which did not exist hitherto, but only that existing remedies were applied evenly as between domestic cases and those which had a Community law component. The effect of Community law in this respect is now more far-reaching.[85]

The jurisprudence in this area demonstrates, moreover, the two ways in which EC law can lead to changes in domestic law. This will occur directly as a result of the need to bring domestic law into conformity with EC law in cases which have a Community law component. It can occur indirectly as a result of national courts deciding that the changes made in cases where there is an EC element should be extended into purely domestic jurisprudence. This is exemplified by the changes in the availability of interim relief against the Crown. We have already seen in the discussion of sovereignty that the ECJ held that the absence of such relief was itself to be regarded as a breach of Community law. The initial reaction of the UK courts was to modify domestic law in cases which had an EC element and to accept that interim relief could be sought against the Crown in such instances. Within a few years the courts had taken the second step of extending the availability of such relief to cases which were purely domestic in nature.[86]

The most important developments in relation to remedies have, however, occurred in the sphere of damages. In *Brasserie du Pecheur SA v Germany, R v*

---

84   Case C-260/89, [1991] ECR I-2925, para. 42.
85   Craig and de Burca, *op. cit.* note 45 *supra*, Ch. 5.
86   *M v Home Office* [1993] 3 All ER 537.

Secretary of State for Transport, ex parte Factortame Ltd,[87] the ECJ reaffirmed its ruling in *Francovich*,[88] that a state could be liable in damages for losses caused by failure to implement a Directive. It confirmed also that this principle of liability existed irrespective of whether the relevant provision of Community law had direct effect. It held that the right of individuals to rely on directly effective provisions of Community law before national courts constituted only a minimum form of protection:[89] direct effect could not necessarily ensure that individuals would not suffer damage as a result of a breach of Community law which was attributable to a member state. The right to reparation was seen as a corollary of direct effect.[90] The decision of the Court in these joined cases also made it quite clear that damages liability could exist in relation to breaches of Community law other than non implementation of a Directive. Thus breaches of primary Treaty articles could serve to found liability.

The conditions which must exist before liability attaches are clearly of vital importance. The right to damages is dependent upon three conditions:[91]

(a)   the rule of law which was infringed must have been intended to confer rights on individuals;

(b)   the breach of this rule of law must have been sufficiently serious;

(c)   there must have been a direct causal link between the breach of the obligation imposed on the state and the damage which was sustained by the injured parties.

The first of these conditions was held to be satisfied in both of the cases before the Court.[92] In relation to the second condition, the decisive test for deciding whether the breach was sufficiently serious was whether the Community or the member state had manifestly and gravely disregarded the limits of its discretion.[93] The following factors could, said the ECJ, be taken into account when deciding upon this issue:[94] the clarity and precision of the rule which had been breached; the measure of discretion left by the rule to the national or Community authorities; whether the breach and consequential damage were intentional or voluntary; whether any error of law was excusable or inexcusable; whether the position adopted by a Community institution contributed to the act or omission causing loss committed by the national authorities; and whether on the facts the national measures had been adopted or retained contrary to Community law.

---

87   Cases C-46 & 48/93, [1996] 1 CMLR 889, [1996] All ER 301 (ECJ).
88   Cases C-6 & 9/90, *Francovich & Bonifaci v Italy* [1991] ECR I-5357.
89   Note 87 *supra*, para. 20.
90   *Ibid.*, at para. 22.
91   *Ibid.*, at para. 51.
92   *Ibid.*, at para. 54.
93   *Ibid.*, at para. 55.
94   *Ibid.*, at para. 56.

A breach of Community law would, the ECJ said, be sufficiently serious if the state persisted in its behaviour notwithstanding the existence of a judgment by the ECJ which found the infringement of Community law to have been established. It would be equally so where there was settled case law of the Court making it clear that the action by the member state constituted a breach of Community law.[95]

As to the third condition, that of causation, the ECJ held that it was for national courts to determine whether the requisite causal link had been established.[96]

It is clear that the UK courts have an obligation to apply this decision of the ECJ in cases which have a Community law dimension. It remains to be seen what is the precise form of the cause of action which is adopted for these purposes. The two most likely 'candidates' are to utilise breach of statutory duty or to create an autonomous cause of action for this species of liability. On balance there are distinct advantages in pursuing the latter route.[97] What remains to be seen is whether our courts will draw upon the ECJ's case law in order to modify our domestic law on damages liability in cases where there is no EC law element. I have argued elsewhere that there could be advantages in pursuing such a strategy. Time will tell whether EC law has a spillover impact in this area in the way in which it has done in others.

CONCLUSION

There is but little doubt that Community law has had, and will continue to have, a marked impact upon domestic law. This is so both in relation to constitutional doctrine, and also in relation to aspects of administrative law. The impact may be direct and immediate, as when EC law mandates a particular result. It may be more indirect, as when UK courts choose to apply Community law doctrine in cases which have no EC component. This should not be taken to mean that all that emanates from the ECJ or the Community is necessarily worthy of importation. What it does mean is that we should be willing to consider the Community approach and determine whether it may be of help in a domestic context.

---

95   *Ibid.*, at para. 57.
96   *Ibid.*, at para. 65.
97   Craig, P.P., 'Once More Unto the Breach: The Community, the State and Damages Liability' (1997) 113 *Law Quarterly Review* 67, at 87–89.

13

Judicial Review of Prerogative Power in the United Kingdom and France

David Pollard

SUMMARY

This chapter examines the judicial control, by the courts of the United Kingdom and France, of executive power which was formerly the sole prerogative of the monarch and which still remains in the hands of the head of state (King, Queen or President) and ministers. In both countries, the judiciary has admitted that certain actions are so connected with the exercise of high political activity which is vital to the interests of the state and its current political ideology, that approval or disapproval of that activity must, in order to avoid government by non elected judges, be left to the political forum whose participants are elected by and accountable to the people. In both countries, however, there has been a remarkable chronology of judicial intervention in matters once automatically labelled as sacrosanct 'high policy', and doctrines once accepted as immutable have changed almost out of recognition. Issues raised in the United Kingdom include the employment rights of civil and military personnel, the issuing of passports, and the prerogative of mercy; and issues raised in France include the interpretation of treaties, extradition, the employment rights of civil and military personnel, and testing nuclear weapons. In both countries, the courts have been influenced by principles and concepts emanating from the laws of Europe (both Community and Human Rights).

INTRODUCTION

Certain key perspectives of the developing administrative law of the United Kingdom have presented themselves very forcibly to the author of this chapter during a study of public law that has lasted longer than he cares to remember. First — and this is something often ignored by those to whom administrative law is synonymous with judicial review — there has been the developing creation of judicial and political institutions specifically designed to redress grievances in the modern administrative state (the appellate jurisdictions of courts and specialist tribunals, and the investigation and review functions of ombudsmen). Secondly, there has been the complementary creation of statutory rules of procedural fairness which must be followed by administrative authorities. Thirdly, there has been a remarkable chronology of judicial intervention in matters once automatically labelled as sacrosanct, and doctrines once accepted as immutable have changed almost out of recognition. Fourthly, the development of administrative law has been given a helping hand by comparative public law study (in particular from common law jurisdictions of the Commonwealth and the United States of America, and from the civil law jurisdiction of France). Fifthly, the development of domestic administrative law has been and will be increasingly influenced by principles and concepts emanating from the laws of Europe (both Community and Human Rights). Many of these factors form or influence the subject matter of this chapter.

This chapter examines one aspect of administrative law, namely, the control of executive power which was, in times past, the sole prerogative of the monarch. However, this will not be undertaken solely in the context of the royal prerogative as currently exercised within the United Kingdom, but will also be examined in the context of the equivalent presidential power in France, together with the context, perhaps at the moment in embryonic form, of the public law of what may form part of the laws of a European Federation.

At one time monarchs had absolute control over their subjects. Gradually, through revolutions, both bloody and relatively peaceful, much royal power was taken away and vested in political institutions elected or appointed in accordance with more modern precepts of democratic government and accountability. The increasing governmental interference with the everyday affairs of the citizen (as opposed to the subject) which commenced in the late 19th century and continued with dramatic impact in the second half of the 20th century, was based on rules emanating from those democratic institutions in the form of legislation and delegated legislation, leaving a limited amount of the former royal power in the hands of the head of state (King, Queen or President) and ministers. In both countries, the exercise of the legislative function was, during earlier constitutional settlements, accepted as sovereign (although, in France, the control of constitutionality of statutes is now governed by a Constitutional Council[1]), but the rise in modern governmental regulatory power and its exercise was paralleled by a rise in

---

1   On the *Conseil constitutionnel*, see Pollard, D., 'France's *Conseil constitutionnel*' [1991] *Irish Jurist* 2; Pollard, D., *Sourcebook on French Law*, London: Cavendish Publishing, 1996, pp. 331–2 (further reading sources).

the supervision of that power by the judiciary (the High Court and the *Conseil d'État*).

Statutes governing the creation and exercise of the modern administrative functions of the state tend to be specific and detailed, because it is essential for government to spell out the derogations it wishes to make from presumed freedoms of person and property and to regulate with care the benefits it wishes to confer. This is, in one sense, a two-edged weapon. On the one hand, courts in either country cannot replace statutory wording with wording of their own; but, on the other hand, specific wording grants those courts the opportunity to regard the statute as a bench mark against which they can measure and control executive action. The power to measure executive action against the presumed or explicit will of the legislature has been used with dramatic effect in both countries, especially over the last 40 years or so. There is, therefore, a temptation for government to govern either by granting itself — through its control of the legislature — wide, discretionary and possibly judge-proof statutory powers or, instead, by basing executive action on non statutory powers, either on common law powers (in the United Kingdom) or on certain wide statements in the written Constitution (in France). A government which understandably and constitutionally possesses such power may then seek to maintain the exercise of it by stating to the judiciary that, because of the source of that power (in both cases that of the head of state), the judiciary cannot control its exercise. The purpose of this chapter is to examine these more recent constitutional tensions between government and judiciary in the modern state.

In both countries, the judiciary has admitted that certain actions are so connected with the exercise of high political activity which is vital to the interests of the state and its current political ideology, that approval or disapproval of that activity must, in order to avoid government by non elected judges, be left to the political forum whose participants are elected by and accountable to the people. Obviously the creation of boundary lines between matters justiciable and non justiciable is in itself a part of both constitutional law and administrative law, if there is now any legal or logical reason for perpetuating such a distinction, and the crucial questions for public law are to what extent, in matters long governed by a developing administrative law, the constitutional barrier of 'high policy' can be used to disguise the fact that what the executive is doing is not really so connected with high policy and whether that barrier should be turned aside. It is self-evident that the opportunity for exercising a review jurisdiction depends on the accident of a group or an individual seeking that jurisdiction, and the opportunity of extending that jurisdiction to meet novel situations depends on those situations being litigated. In each country, the accident of litigation has not been identical and, in addition, the constitutional backgrounds of the two countries and their respective legal methodologies of judicial control are *prima facie* so disimilar that the question of comparing chalk with cheese may arise. Consequently, this chapter will, first of all, deal with the issues separately, country by country, before examining whether there are common themes and influences from which both systems of law may profit.

THE UNITED KINGDOM

Prerogative powers

In the United Kingdom, unlike France, there is no specific list of the prerogative powers laid down in a written Constitution. That prerogative power is residual — in that it consists of all those powers originally claimed by the monarch which have not been taken away by statute and that no new prerogative powers can be claimed — is uncontroversial, as is the fact that the prerogative is recognised as part of the common law.[2] There has been mild controversy as to whether the term 'prerogative' should be limited to those acts which only a head of state or government may perform (such as declaration of war or dissolution of Parliament) (the 'strict' interpretation), or whether the term 'prerogative' should include all exercise by head of state or government of non statutory power (such as regulating the employment of Crown servants and the provision of non statutory forms of compensation by way of bounty) (the 'wide' interpretation).[3] That controversy seems to have been settled by the courts in that they have labelled the exercise of any common law power by government as 'prerogative'.[4] This is, of course, of great importance, because had the courts divided the common law powers into a first and a second division and then definitively specified the membership of those divisions, the courts might have found it more difficult to justify any relegation or promotion manoeuvres; and this assumes even more importance when coupled with the determination that, in certain circumstances, the manner of exercise of 'prerogative' power will be controlled by the judiciary and is not immune from such control merely because of its legal source. This latter proposition stems, of course, from the two 'landmark' decisions in *R* v *Criminal Injuries Compensation Board, ex parte Lain*[5] and *Council of Civil Service Unions* v *Minister for the Civil Service*[6] (referred to below as the '*GCHQ* case'). Both cases, significantly, related

---

2   *Attorney-General* v *De Keyser's Royal Hotel Ltd* [1920] AC 508; *Burmah Oil Co. Ltd* v *Lord Advocate* [1965] AC 75; *BBC* v *Johns* [1965] Ch 32; *R* v *Scretary of State for the Home Department, ex parte Northumbria Police Authority* [1988] 2 WLR 590; *R* v *Secretary of State for the Home Department, ex parte Fire Brigades Union* [1995] 2 AC 513.

3   In *R* v *Panel on Takeovers and Mergers, ex parte Datafin* [1987] 1 QB 815, Lloyd LJ referred to a 'certain imprecision in the use of the term "prerogative"'.

4   *R* v *Criminal Injuries Compensation Board, ex parte Lain* [1967] 2 QB 864; *Council of Civil Service Unions* v *Minister for the Civil Service* [1985] AC 374; *R* v *Secretary of State for the Home Department, ex parte Fire Brigades Union* [1995] 2 AC 513.

5   [1967] 2 QB 864.

6   [1985] AC 374.

to a 'wide interpretation' power (although in *GCHQ* issues of national security were involved) and both cases demolished the constitutional gospel stated in the texts studied assiduously by the author as a student that, whereas the existence of the royal prerogative could be defined by the courts (which would determine whether the power existed at common law and had not been abrogated by statute). On the other hand, the courts did not have the power to determine whether or how prerogative power should be exercised. *Lain* and *GCHQ* are now water under the bridge. What is proposed is to consider, first, what exercises of prerogative power have been excluded by the courts themselves from control (what is often referred to as the justiciability issue) and, secondly, to what extent the courts have applied the same principles of judicial review, developed (and developed very strongly in recent years) by them in relation to the exercise of statutory power, to the exercise of common law power (what is often referred to as the irrationality issue). These two issues are, of course, inextricably involved.

The justiciability issue

In *GCHQ*, Lord Roskill — having stated that if the executive, instead of acting under a statutory power, acts under a prerogative power so as to affect the rights of the citizen, the citizen should be able to challenge that exercise of power — referred, as did other members of the House, to certain 'exceptions', such as the making of treaties, the defence of the realm, the prerogative of mercy, the grant of honours, the dissolution of Parliament and the appointment of ministers (i.e., the 'strict' interpretation). With regard to the conduct of foreign affairs, the negotiation and making of treaties (but not the interpretation of, and the enforcement of treaty rights conferred by, the instrument incorporating a treaty into the laws of the United Kingdom), the recognition of foreign states, the declaration of war, the operational deployment of the armed forces, and decisions whether or not to prosecute, there is consistent and well-known case law as to self-denial of both jurisdiction and justiciability.[7] However, to the House of Lords the 'non strict' powers would (subject, in that and other cases, to national security considerations) be treated as analogous to powers whose source was statutory.

The *GCHQ* case itself concerned an area of law where a common law power was exercised in circumstances analogous to those where the source of power was statutory, namely the employment of Crown servants, where the common law still deems such servants to hold office during the pleasure of the Crown.[8] At one time

---

7   See, *inter alia*, *Rustomjee* v *R* (1876) 2 QBD 69; *Blackburn* v *Attorney-General* [1971] 1 WLR 1037; *Maclaine Watson* v *Department of Trade and Industry* [1990] 2 AC 418; *Fothergill* v *Monarch Airlines Ltd* [1981] AC 251; *Mighell* v *Sultan of Johore* [1894] 1 QB 149; *Chandler* v *Director of Public Prosecutions* [1962] AC 763; *R* v *Bottrill, ex parte Kuechenmeister* [1947] KB 41; *Gouriet* v *Union of Post Office Workers* [1978] AC 435; *R* v *Secretary of State for Foreign and Commonwealth Affairs, ex parte Rees-Mogg* [1994] QB 552.

8   *Riordan* v *War Office* [1959] 1 WLR 1046; *McLaren* v *Home Office* [1990] ICR 824; *R* v *Lord Chancellor's Department, ex parte Nangle* [1992] 1 All ER 987.

no one would have considered that point of view remarkable, because for so long most people who were employed (as distinct from holding an office) were also dismissible at the will of the steel master, domestic service employer or landowner. Today, extensive employment protection rights are granted by statute and, occasionally, statute has intervened to grant to civil servants legal rights analogous to those employed in service other than under the Crown (such as statutory maternity pay). The conditions of service of Crown servants (both civil and military) are governed by codes analogous to the employment protection legislation (but with modifications deemed necessary). It will be remembered that the *GCHQ* case related to the decision that certain civil servants would no longer be permitted to belong to national trade unions, and that civil servants affected by this decision claimed that the decision was taken without the consultation which they had come to expect. The House of Lords treated the relevant Order in Council (issued under the prerogative) as being on a par with the employment protection legislation applicable to persons employed otherwise than under the Crown, and agreed that, if no question of national security had arisen, the decision making process would have been unfair. One part of the 'employment protection system' for civil servants is the Civil Service Appeals Board, established, of course, under the prerogative. The courts have resisted any claims that the Board is immune from judicial review, at least as far as procedural propriety is concerned. In *R v Civil Service Appeals Board, ex parte Cunningham,*[9] it was simply accepted that the Board was susceptible to judicial review. The Court of Appeal held that the Board was a fully judicial body exercising public law functions amenable to judicial review at the instigation of a person aggrieved, and that the principle of fairness required a tribunal such as the Board to give sufficient reasons for its decisions to enable the parties to know the issues to which it had addressed its mind and to question whether it had acted lawfully.

R v Criminal Injuries Compensation Board, ex parte Lain[10] concerned an organisation described as 'a servant of the Crown charged by the Crown, by executive instruction, with the duty of distributing the bounty of the Crown'. That description did not prevent the court from determining that the Compensation Board was not immune from judicial review as it was exercising a public law function directly affecting the interests of victims of criminal acts (a scheme analogous to existing statutory schemes for, for example, social security and land compensation). Since then, decisions of the Compensation Board have been subjected to judicial review where it has been alleged and found that the Board incorrectly interpreted the individual rules of the compensation scheme,[11] or

---

9   [1991] 4 All ER 310.
10   [1967] 2 QB 864.
11   *R v Criminal Injuries Compensation Board, ex parte Lain* [1967] 2 QB 864; *R v Criminal Injuries Compensation Board, ex parte Clowes* [1977] 1 WLR 1353.

applied those rules in a manner which breached the *Wednesbury* principles of unreasonableness.[12] In *R* v *Criminal Injuries Compensation Board, ex parte P*,[13] the court was faced with a bolder proposition. Under the compensation scheme, compensation for offences committed against a member of the offender's family living with him or her at the time of the offence was originally excluded. Subsequent revision to the scheme removed the complete exclusion of claims in respect of family violence incurred on or after 1 October 1979 (the date of the revision) and this rule was continued in a subsequent revision in 1990. The applicants claimed compensation for acts of sexual abuse committed by their stepfathers when they were children, but the Board rejected the claims which related to acts occurring before 1 October 1979. The applicants alleged that the decision of the Home Secretary to continue the time-bar was irrational, was unjust to women and children and was based on no objective evidence. The court, naturally, accepted jurisdiction, re-affirming that the distribution of bounty on behalf of the Crown did not preclude the courts from exercising their 'constitutional powers' of judicial review, but categorised the issue as non justiciable because the issue involved a balance of competing claims on the public purse and the allocation of economic resources with which the court was ill-equipped to deal. A similar approach had been taken with regard to the analogous scheme for compensating persons, by means of *ex gratia* payments, for hardship suffered as a result of being imprisoned following conviction when that conviction was subsequently quashed, and it was held that it was not for the courts to monitor or control the method by which such payments were made.[14] In two other sets of circumstances, the making of *ex gratia* payments can be of great importance to the citizen, namely, the granting of 'concessionary payments' where the spirit of social security legislation would appear to have intended to give a right to payment but the specific wording did not, and the granting of compensation (for expenses incurred, for loss of money sustained and for the effects of maladministration) following an investigation by the Parliamentary Commissioner for Administration. The actual policy governing the making of such payments does not appear to have been subjected to judicial review but, it is suggested, that as both involve balancing competing claims on the public purse and the allocation of economic resources, the courts will, at least for the present, deem themselves ill-equipped to deal with that policy.

At one time in the past the decision to grant a passport to a citizen (or rather a subject of the monarch) would have been regarded as a high matter of state. Monarchs wanted to monitor the presence of influential citizens within the realm and a personal application to the monarch or Secretary of State was needed.

---

12   *R* v *Criminal Injuries Compensation Board, ex parte Thompstone and Crowe* [1984] 1 WLR 1234.
13   [1995] 1 All ER 870.
14   *R* v *Scretary of State for the Home Office, ex parte Harrison* [1988] 3 All ER 86.

Furthermore, in times past, the monarch could use the high prerogative writ of *ne exeat regno*. Today, the monarch's interest in those going on package tours is minimal and the passport application process has been automated. However, in *Secretary of State for Foreign Affairs, ex parte Everett*,[15] counsel for the Secretary of State 'sought to put the grant of passports under the umbrella of foreign affairs and thereby elevate it to that level of high policy which would preclude the intervention of the courts', because it involved a request in the name of the Queen to a foreign power to grant free passage. This argument was rejected as the grant of a passport was an administrative decision affecting the right of free movement of the citizen who had a normal expectation of the ready issue of a passport, and was just as justiciable as the analogous (but statute-based) scheme for controlling immigration. While the court accepted that passports are issued under prerogative powers and that the Secretary of State could devise and operate a policy of refusing to issue a passport to certain classes of persons, that policy must be implemented in accordance with basic rules of procedural propriety and, possibly, irrationality (see further, below). However, as the policy itself was not in issue the court made no pronouncement as to the justiciability of the policy itself. One presumes that, should the issue of the justiciability of the policy arise, the nature of the policy would be examined and that any policy based on security grounds or on international cooperation in crime prevention would be declared non justiciable. In the possibly analogous (but statute-based) circumstances of exclusion orders under the prevention of terrorism legislation, there is an undoubted derogation from rights of free movement, and other 'more fundamental' human rights (such as the right to life) may be at issue. Here, the courts (with a varying degree of reluctance) have accepted statements to the effect that it was not possible to give detailed reasons for making exclusion orders (because to do so might well lead to the discovery of sources of information available and so possibly compromise police operations and/or put at risk the lives of informants and their families) as sufficient to halt any further scrutiny of the Secretary of State's decisions on exclusion orders.[16] The question of an allegedly 'irrational' policy (the hypothetical example may be used of refusing passports to those wishing to travel to a country to whose policies the United Kingdom had reacted by implementing an international boycott) is one for the future.

One of the matters placed in the high policy list by Lord Roskill in *GCHQ* was the 'prerogative of mercy'. At one time this was in reality a matter of high policy — in that it suspended the normal operation of a criminal law and criminal justice system which frequently used the death penalty — and, for a long time, whether or not to save someone from the block or gallows was a personal decision of the

---

15   [1989] QB 811.
16   *R v Secretary of State for the Home Department, ex parte Adams* [1995] All ER 177 (EC); *R v Secretary of State for the Home Department, ex parte McQuillan* [1995] 4 All ER 400.

monarch. A convention developed whereby the prerogative of mercy was exercised on the advice of the Secretary of State, but possibly because of the proximity of the decision to the person of the monarch, possibly because of the opportunity for statements by the Home Secretary and debate in Parliament, and possibly because it was a matter of mercy rather than legal right or legitimate expectation, it was long held to be outside the competence of the courts to question the exercise of a purely discretionary act.[17] The criminal justice system has altered in nature from that which pertained before. Although the terms 'prerogative of mercy' and 'royal pardon' are still used, with the virtual abolition of the death penalty, the development of the criminal appeals system and the opportunity to refer alleged miscarriages of justice to the courts for review, it may be better to think in terms of a common law power to correct such miscarriages when the statutory machinery turns out to be inadequate for that purpose, as much a part of, and on the same level within, the criminal legal system as decisions relating to sentencing and parole.[18] In *R v Secretary of State for the Home Department, ex parte Bentley*[19] (which related to an application for judicial review of a decision not to recommend a posthumous free pardon), Watkins LJ referred to 'our developed state of public law' and the *GCHQ* case, and stated that the question of justiciability related to whether the courts are qualified (whatever that might mean) to deal with the matter or did the decision involve such questions of policy that the courts should not intrude because they are ill-equipped to do so. As with the 'creation of the policy' issue with regard to passports (see above), it was accepted that the formulation of the criteria for the exercise of the prerogative by the grant of a free pardon was entirely a matter of policy which was not justiciable. However, any misapplication of those criteria in the form of an aberrant decision (such as to refuse to grant a pardon because of a person's race, religion or sex) would be reviewable (see further, below). Such outrageously aberrant considerations were not present and what was alleged was that there had been a non aberrant error of judgement occasioned by a misinterpretation of the appropriate criteria (an 'illegality' rather than an 'irrationality' question). It was emphasised that there were three forms of the corrective machinery — namely, a free pardon, where an innocent person was wrongly convicted, a conditional pardon, which substitutes one punishment for another (in the *Bentley* circumstances this could have been a term of imprisonment rather than hanging), and a remission of sentence, which frees someone from imprisonment. It was alleged that the Home Secretary had failed to recognise this wide scope of the prerogative of mercy and to consider the form of pardon which might be appropriate to meet the facts of the present case. The Court accepted the policy that a free pardon be reserved for cases where it is established that a

---

17   *Hanratty v Butler* [1971] 115 SJ 386 (CA); *de Freitas v Benny* [1976] AC 239.
18   Cf. *R v Secretary of State for the Home Department, ex parte Doody* [1994] AC 531.
19   [1994] QB 349.

convicted person was innocent (and presumably accepted that Bentley's innocence had not been established). With regard to a conditional pardon, the court was far from satisfied that the Home Secretary had given sufficient consideration to recommend that other form of pardon, but refrained from directing the Home Secretary to so recommend (as this would be tantamount to assuming a power which was not theirs) and 'invited' him to look at the matter again and to examine whether it would be just to exercise the prerogative in such a way as to give full recognition to the strongly held view that Bentley should have been reprieved. The Home Secretary accepted that invitation.

   R v Ministry Defence, ex parte Smith and others[20] is a case of great significance (see Donson, Ch. 15, p. 353). It related to the claimed defence interests of the state and national security; to the growing recognition of 'fundamental human rights' and the influence on that recognition of standards laid down by international conventions; unlike *Bentley* or *Everett*, it related to a direct attack on the creation of government policy and not merely to the manner of exercise of a policy with whose formulation the courts would not interfere; and it related to the question of 'irrationality'. The applicants had been discharged, in accordance with Ministry of Defence policy, from the armed forces because of their homosexual orientation and claimed that, even though the operation of such a policy had as its source the prerogative power, that policy was reviewable and should be reviewed on the grounds of irrationality. The Divisional Court had no hesitation in holding the challenge to the policy justiciable and stated that, today, only the rarest cases will be held outside the courts' review jurisdiction. Such cases would be those involving 'national security properly so-called' (such as, *inter alia, Chandler*[21] and *GCHQ*) and where the courts did indeed lack the expertise or material to form a judgment on the point at issue. Although *Smith* related to the armed forces, it did not relate to the 'disposition of the armed forces' (a matter still excluded by *China Navigation* v *Attorney-General*[22]), because no operational considerations were involved in the policy. Furthermore, given that there were no real national security issues involved, if there were no forum in which the fundamental human rights issues of sexual orientation could be entertained, the applicants would be denied an effective remedy under the terms of the European Convention on Human Rights.[23] The Court of Appeal agreed that the issue was justiciable, adding that this did not mean that a court is thrust into the position of the primary decision maker and that it was not the constitutional role of the courts to regulate the conditions of service in the armed forces of the Crown, as the courts did not have the necessary expertise so to do. However, the Court of Appeal held that courts have

---

20　[1995] 4 All ER 427 (DC); [1996] 1 All ER 257 (CA).
21　[1962] AC 763.
22　[1932] 2 KB 197.
23　Article 13.

the constitutional role and duty of ensuring that the rights of citizens are not abused by the unlawful exercise of executive power and that, although the courts must properly defer to the expertise of responsible decision makers, they must not shrink from the fundamental duty to 'do right to all manner of people'.[24]

The irrationality issue

Given that the Ministry of Defence policy was justiciable, the Divisional Court and the Court of Appeal in *Smith* then had to face, head on, the extent to which they would interfere with that policy on the grounds of 'irrationality'. It was not a question of 'illegality' (as in *Bentley*) as there was no misapplication of the policy — that had been truly applied — and it was not a question of procedural impropriety (as in *Everett*). We must return to *GCHQ*, where, having taken the first step of holding that prerogative power was reviewable if the courts deemed the matter justiciable, and having taken the second step that, security considerations apart, the applicants would have had the legitimate expectation of the procedural propriety of advance consultation, the House was, understandably as the issue was not relevant, hesitant to pronounce unequivocally on the question of irrationality. While noting no *a priori* reason to rule out irrationality as a ground for review, Lord Diplock found it

> . . . difficult to envisage in any of the various fields in which the prerogative remains the only source of the relevant decision making powers a decision of a kind that would be open to attack through the judicial process on this ground. The decisions will generally involve the application of government policy. The reasons for the decision maker taking one course rather than another do not normally involve questions which, if disputed, the judicial process is adapted to provide the right answer.[25]

There is a risk in exercising judicial review of imprecisely defined common law powers by means of the '*Wednesbury* principles' (widely used to review executive action in fields governed by detailed statutory schemes, such as immigration, planning and homelessness), in that certain common law powers may relate to matters of government policy based on government ideology in the fields of foreign affairs and economic strategy, and the courts may be accused of — and indeed seen to be — interfering with matters which are claimed by politicians to be within the province of political *persona* and institutions. Because of this risk, it has been asserted that in order to review an undoubted prerogative power on the ground of irrationality, the irrationality must be a very extreme case of abuse of power,

---

24 *Per* Sir Thomas Bingham MR [1996] 1 All ER 257, at 264–5.
25 [1985] AC 374, at 411.

something outrageously aberrant, and that the application for judicial review must pass a 'super-*Wednesbury* test'. In the context of statute-based exercises of power, this view was given an element of support in *Nottingham County Council* v *Secretary of State for the Environment*[26] and in *Hammersmith and Fulham LBC* v *Secretary of State for the Environment*,[27] but was not accepted in *R* v *Parliamentary Commissioner for Administration, ex parte Dyer*.[28] In the *Hammersmith* case, it was held that the formulation and implementation of national economic policy were entirely dependent on political judgment, the decisions were for politicians to take, and the proper forum where such policies were to be debated, approved or disapproved was the House of Commons.

Did the applicants in *Smith* therefore have to prove that the Ministry of Defence policy was so aberrant that it was more than a policy determined by an evenly balanced evaluation of factors (the defence of the realm and fundamental rights) in which the dominant factor was a political judgement which was best left to political institutions? To the Divisional Court, the human rights dimension in the case was a 'powerful countervailing weight when considering both the level at which the irrationality test should be fixed and the intensity of review appropriate'[29] and that court, therefore, determined to apply the 'conventional, well-established and pure' *Wednesbury* test, adapted to a human rights context. However, the terms in which that test was defined appear to the author to be, at the very least, closely approaching a 'super-*Wednesbury*' test. Asking whether the minister could show an important competing public interest sufficient to justify the policy, the Divisional Court stated that 'only if his purported justification outrageously defies logic or accepted moral standards' could the court strike down the policy. The competing public interest was the delivery of an operationally efficient and effective fighting force, and the question was whether it was 'reasonable for the minister to take the view that allowing homosexuals into the force would imperil that interest'. The courts were bound to remain within their current 'constitutional bounds' and only 'if it was plain beyond sensible argument that no conceivable damage could be done to the armed services as a fighting unit would it be appropriate for this court to remove the issue entirely from the hands of both the military and the government'.[30] Although the minister's reasons for the policy were 'unconvincing', it was not 'outrageous' or 'wholly incompatible' with accepted moral standards. The 'super-*Wednesbury*' test was also rejected by the Court of Appeal, since the conventional *Wednesbury* test was sufficiently flexible to cover all situations. However, the Court of Appeal introduced a note of caution:

---

26   [1986] AC 240.
27   [1991] 1 AC 521.
28   [1994] 1 All ER 375.
29   *Per* Simon Brown LJ [1995] 4 All ER 427, at 447.
30   *Per* Simon Brown LJ, *ibid.*, at 448.

The greater the policy content of a decision, and the more remote the subject matter of a decision from ordinary judicial experience, the more hesitant the court must necessarily be in holding a decision to be irrational. That is good law and, like most good law, common sense. Where decisions of a policy-laden, esoteric or security-based nature are in issue, even greater caution than normal must be shown in applying the test.[31]

With regard to the instant case, it was held that the Ministry policy could not

be stigmatised as irrational at the time when these appellants were discharged. It was supported by both Houses of Parliament and by those to whom the Ministry properly looked for professional advice. There was [no] evidence before the Ministry which plainly invalidated that advice. The threshold of irrationality is a high one. It was not crossed in this case.[32]

FRANCE

In France, the revolutionary settlement was heavily influenced by the doctrine of the separation of powers[33] and the executive power was expressly delegated to Kings, Consuls, Emperors and Presidents by the various Constitutions from 1791 to 1958. The current 1958 Constitution gives wide 'prerogative' powers to the President and to ministers, and these are dealt with *seriatim* below. In order to implement these powers and to apply them to given situations, the President and Prime Minister issue decrees. These may relate to an individual (such as a decree nominating someone to a particular office), to a specific situation (such as putting a matter to a referendum), or they may be more of a legislative nature (such as laying down the conditions of service of civil servants) where they are at least comparable to the Order in Council which was the subject of the *GCHQ* case.

The *Conseil d'État*

The judicial control of executive power is vested in a series of special administrative courts, but in the context of 'prerogative' power cases are invariably brought before the highest such court, the *Conseil d'État* (and very often before the highest judicial body, the *Assemblée Plénière* of the *Conseil d'État*),[34] which has, in that part of *droit administratif* known as the '*recours pour excès de pouvoir*', developed

---

31   *Per* Sir Thomas Bingham MR [1996] 1 All ER 257, at 264.
32   *Per* Sir Thomas Bingham MR, *ibid.*, at 266.
33   *Déclaration des Droits de l'Homme*, 1789, article 16.
34   On the *Conseil d'État*, see Brown, L.N. and Bell, J.S., *French Administrative Law* (4th ed.), Oxford: Clarendon Press, 1993; Pollard, *op. cit.* note 1 *supra*, 1996, Ch. 2 and pp. 333–5 (further reading sources).

an extensive administrative law jurisdiction over acts taken under statutory enactments and delegated legislation. In the context of this jurisdiction, it is more convenient to discuss, first, the grounds on which the *Conseil d'État* may find an *excès de pouvoir* in that the administration or executive has not acted in accordance with the powers granted to it by statute or delegated legislation and, with regard to 'prerogative' power, in accordance with the powers granted by the written Constitution.

In each case, executive action is measured against 'the law' and the *Conseil d'État* has developed a number of grounds for review which, in varying degrees, find their counterparts in the common law. A decision may be annulled if it has been made by an authority not invested with that power (*incompétence*); if it has been made contrary to an established rule of procedural propriety (such as a duty to grant a fair hearing or to give reasons) (*vice de forme* or *vice de procédure*); if it has been made contrary to superior norms of constitutional significance, emanating from the Constitution, its Preambles and from '*principes généraux du droit*' (which are norms of any democracy, such as equality of access to public office and employment, equal treatment of welfare state beneficiaries, the right to live a normal family life and freedom of expression, conscience or religion) (*violation de la loi*); or if it has been made for a purpose other than that granted by the enabling power (*détournement de pouvoir*). These grounds approximate to lack of jurisdiction, illegality and procedural impropriety in the common law and examples are given below. However, of greater significance to the context of this chapter is the approach of the *Conseil d'État* to situations where it is alleged that the executive has taken a 'wrong' view of, or made an error of judgement as to, inferences which should be drawn from established facts and the appropriate legal consequences. If the *Conseil d'État* considers that a decision is so wrong or that the error of judgement is so serious and obvious that it speaks for itself (*une erreur manifeste d'appréciation*), that decision will be annulled. The *Conseil d'État* is, in effect, stating to the executive that that original decision is contrary to the principle of legality and that no similar future decision can be made. The ground of *erreur manifeste*, therefore, closely resembles the common law ground of irrationality, and there are suggestions from the cases that there may be degrees of judicial intervention and intensity of review. It may be that, where a power grants a wide discretion to the executive and the *Conseil d'État* feels that the executive is better equipped to exercise a more political judgement, if the *Conseil d'État* finds that there is no error of judgment as to the facts themselves, any alleged misjudgement of the inference to be drawn from those facts must be blatantly wrong before the executive's judgment will be overturned. When so adjudging, the *Conseil d'État* may use phrases such as the decision '*ne saurait utilement discuté devant le juge administratif*' (i.e., there is no purpose in bringing before the court a case where there can be no relief). Examples of this include the decision of a minister to ban the distribution of a newspaper deemed to be contrary to the public interest[35] and the refusal to make someone a member of the *Légion d'Honneur*.[36]

With regard to the review of 'prerogative' power — in particular with the extent to which that review is based on the ground of *erreur manifeste* — one is not helped by an analysis of the reasoning which one finds in the judicial decisions of common law jurisdictions. It must be emphasised that this part of this chapter will be concerned with the results of the reasoning of the *Conseil d'État*, rather than with the reasoning itself, since the decisions are almost always expressed in terse, laconic language and much has to be read between the lines. One is aided in this task by the submissions of the *Commissaire du Gouvernement*[37] who, rather like the Advocate-General of the European Court of Justice, presents a reasoned submission to the court.

Acte de gouvernement

On occasions, when requested to intervene to declare illegal acts based on the wide powers given to the executive directly by the Constitution, the *Conseil d'État* has been met with challenges to its '*compétence*' or jurisdiction invoking the doctrine of '*acte de gouvernement*' (the comparable equivalent of raising the issue that an act is a prerogative one). An *acte de gouvernement* is a term used not literally, because the *Conseil d'État* exercises jurisdiction over many activities of the government, but as a specific, shorthand way of denoting an act which is reserved to the politicians and which, it is claimed, is completely outside the control of the *Conseil d'État*. The *Conseil d'État* had been faced with the conflict between controlling government activity and claims of *acte de gouvernement* from the commencement of its existence and, early on, the *Conseil* refused to intervene if an act taken by the government was taken for political reasons (*motivé par un mobile politique*). However, in 1872, at the commencement of the Third Republic, the *Conseil d'État* became established in its own right, empowered to speak and to act in the name of the French people. In 1875,[38] the *Commissaire du Gouvernement* argued that in 'order to present an exceptional character which makes it outside and above control by the courts, it is not sufficient that an act taken by the government has been taken for political reasons'. This was accepted by the *Conseil d'État*, which, speaking in the name of the French people, laid down that it could determine the existence and extent of an *acte de gouvernement*. This statement of constitutional principle has not been contradicted by statute law or by

---

35 Important decisions of the *Conseil d'État* are published in the *Recueil Lebon* ('Rec.'); CE 2 November 1973, Rec., p. 611.
36 CE 10 December 1986, Loredon, Rec., p. 516.
37 On the *Commissaire du Gouvernement*, see Brown and Bell, *op. cit.* note 34 *supra*, pp. 101–2; Pollard, *op. cit.* note 34 *supra*, p. xiii.
38 CE 19 February 1875, Prince Napoléon, Rec., p. 155.

any subsequent written Constitution. It is noticeable that the *Conseil* very rarely uses the term *'acte de gouvernement'* in its decisions — it will usually say that it cannot intervene or that it can intervene, and then decide the case.

The academic commentators[39] have grouped the cases into two. First, there are acts concerning the relationship between the political institutions of the Constitution (President, Government and Parliament) (such as whether to present a Bill to Parliament,[40] the decision to dissolve the National Assembly[41] and the investigations of the *Médiateur*, who exercises functions similar to those exercised by the Parliamentary Commissioner for Administration).[42] Secondly, there are acts concerning the relationship between France and other states or international institutions (e.g., the European Community and Union). Foreign affairs are again divided into acts relating to the negotiation, creation and execution (including, at one time (below), the interpretation) of an international treaty, acts relating to diplomatic activity and acts relating to the defence of the Republic.

Acte de gouvernement and foreign affairs

If every act of the President or a minister which concerned foreign affairs (taking this phrase literally) were to be classified as an *acte de gouvernement*, an awful lot of things would be outside any form of judicial control (and, as will be adverted to later, outside any political control). As with the United Kingdom, there may be considerable justification for the courts leaving to politicians such decisions relating to high matters of state (declaration of war, creation of empires or recognition of foreign states). However, the *Conseil d'État* has recognised that, in France, much domestic law comes from international law, and international law now concerns itself with economic matters, social matters, and international rules relating to human rights. Therefore the *Conseil d'État* has developed the legal technique of *'acte détachable'*. In other words, it examines the specific act to see whether it is an indispensable attribute of the treaty-making process, of diplomacy, or whether it could be independent of those activities and therefore *détachable* or severable. The question often asked is whether an act goes to the very core of relations between France and other countries. This would mean that the *Conseil d'État* would be substituting its own opinion as to a state of affairs for those of the government. In 'ordinary domestic matters' of conflict between the citizen and the state, it has already been seen that the *Conseil d'État* has developed the concept of *'erreur manifeste d'appréciation'* and has substituted its view of both facts and

---

39   See, e.g., de Laubadère, A., Venezia, J.-C., and Gaudemet, Y., *Traité de Droit Administratif* (13th ed.), Paris: Librairie générale de droit et de jurisprudence, Tome 1, pp. 612–19.
40   CE 29 November 1968, Tallegrand, Rec., p. 607.
41   CE 22 February 1989, Allain.
42   CE 10 July 1981, Retail.

law for that of administrative authorities. How far, therefore, would the *Conseil d'État* extend this concept in matters containing a foreign element?

The academic commentators and the *Commissaires du Gouvernement* have attempted to distinguish between something which they should control and something which is best left to the politicians by dividing matters into those which truly relate to the conduct of foreign affairs and diplomacy (*'tournées vers l'ordre international'*) and those which are really matters of domestic concern (*'tournées vers l'ordre interne'*). As examples of the former, one can cite, first of all, the treaty-making prerogative. The Constitution[43] gives the President of the Republic power to negotiate and ratify treaties. Certain types of treaty — including those which have a commercial or financial impact, or which affect the status of individuals — can be ratified only if a statute so states; and if the Constitutional Council declares that a treaty or international agreement is contrary to the Constitution, such a treaty or agreement cannot be ratified unless the Constitution is amended (as happened with the Treaty on European Union[44]). The negotiation and ratification of treaties has been accepted by the *Conseil d'État* as an *acte de gouvernement* which may be controlled only by the legislature (or, in the case of unconstitutionality, by the Constitutional Council). Relatively recently, the *Conseil d'État* accepted that a treaty between France and Morocco, which granted certain dispensations from immigration formalities to Moroccan citizens, could be unilaterally suspended by the Foreign Ministry and, consequently, during that suspension, the treaty had no effect in domestic law granting rights to Moroccans. By implication, the *Conseil d'État* accepted the submissions of the *Commissaire du Gouvernement* that the decision to suspend a treaty was, like the decision to make the treaty, an *acte de gouvernement*.[45]

International agreements may, of course, create rights and impose obligations within the domestic legal forum and which may turn on the interpretation of treaty provisions. In the context of European Community and Union provisions, the *Conseil d'État* is bound by the European Court of Justice (although acceptance of this took a not inconsiderable time).[46] With regard to other treaties, the *Conseil d'État* for a long time held the view that the interpretation of a treaty was a matter for the Foreign Ministry. In 1969, in *Moraly*,[47] which concerned a claim for compensation for damage to property in Algeria and was based on a Franco-Algerian agreement, the *Conseil d'État* held that it could not interpret the agreement, posed to the Foreign Ministry specific questions as to the meaning of the agreement, and accepted the interpretation answers of the Foreign Ministry

---

43   Articles 52–54.
44   See the decisions of the *Conseil constitutionnel* of 9 April and 2 September 1992, published respectively in the *Journal officiel* of the French Republic on 11 April and 3 September 1992.
45   CE, Ass., 18 December 1992, Préfet de la Gironde c Mhamedi, Rec., p. 446.
46   See Pollard, D., 'European Community Law and the French *Conseil d'État*' [1995] *Irish Jurist* 79.
47   CE 31 January 1969.

without question. Since the Foreign Ministry unequivocally stated that the agreement gave no compensation rights, the *Conseil d'État* dismissed the action. However, in 1990, the *Conseil* altered this long-established case law. *GISTI (Groupe d'information et de soutien des travailleurs immigrés)* concerned the interpretation, in another Franco-Algerian agreement, of the phrase 'minor children' and whether this meant those under 18 (French law) or those under 21 (Algerian law). The Minister of the Interior had, in a circular, referred to 'minor children under 18 years of age'. Instead of simply accepting this interpretation without question, the *Conseil d'État* determined that it had power to examine and interpret the Franco-Algerian agreement as to the meaning of the contested phrase. That the *Conseil d'État* in fact held that the Ministry had exactly and correctly interpreted the terms of the agreement, although not to the plaintiffs' liking, is of far less importance than the fact that treaty interpretation is now within the jurisdiction of the *Conseil d'État*.[48]

Other examples of matters '*tournées vers l'ordre international*' include the decision of France to institute an exclusion area to ships around the Mururoa Atoll (which was held to be an assertion of French sovereignty over the high seas, undoubtedly affecting the relationship between France and other states and the nationals, such as shipowners, of other states, which cannot be detached from France's conduct of diplomatic affairs);[49] the refusal to submit a case to the International Court of Justice;[50] the refusal to control the vote of the French Minister in the European Community Council of Ministers;[51] and the suspension of educational cooperation with Iraq during the Gulf War.[52]

Examples of matters which are '*tournées vers l'ordre interne*', where the *Conseil d'État* will intervene, include the granting of a building permit to construct an embassy (this being treated as a decision taken in conformity with the ordinary internal law of building control, which can be the subject of an action in the same way as permission to build a house);[53] the reimbursement of money owed by Zaire to an agent acting under a Franco-Zaire partnership agreement;[54] whether a commune could refuse to have foreign troops billeted on them under NATO arrangements;[55] and the destruction of an abandoned foreign ship on the high seas.[56] In such cases, the *Conseil d'État* has taken a wide view of 'internal order', stressing the effect of the decision on ordinary people in France who might have

---

48 CE 29 June 1990, Rec., p. 171.
49 CE 1 July 1975, Paris de Bollardière, Rec., p. 423.
50 CE 9 June 1959, Gény, Rec., p. 19.
51 CE 23 November 1984, Les Verts, Rec., p. 382.
52 CE 23 September 1992, GISTI, Rec., p. 346.
53 CE 22 December 1978, No Thanh Nghia, Rec., p. 523.
54 CE 14 May 1993, Ministre de la coopération c Bonn.
55 CE 13 July 1967, Commune d'Auboué.
56 CE 23 October 1987, Société Nachfolger.

their rights harmed if, for instance, the building of an embassy were not able to be controlled. One illustration of this was the decision to hold that the government's resolution to institute the European laboratory SYNCHROTON elsewhere than at Strasbourg undoubtedly concerned the good burghers of Strasbourg, even though the resolution had been taken by a minister after agreeing a common position with Germany.[57]

In particular, the *Conseil d'État* has recognised the inevitable fact that France, like any other state, has been increasingly affected by treaties which are multi-lateral and that France is bound by such treaties, some of which are very detailed indeed. In times past, if France made a treaty with one other state, France would conclude only the treaty it wanted; but nowadays, France, although she will do her best to fix things in her favour, must often accept the constraints imposed by a majority of treaty-making powers. This means that the French government no longer has complete freedom to act as an independent nation — the absolute prerogative is whittled down, not by internal law itself, but by international law which holds a superior position to internal law.[58] If the French courts are, as enjoined by international law, bound to uphold international law, they must therefore apply international law as a norm with which to measure the legality of acts claimed to be *actes de gouvernement*. It is as if the *Conseil d'État* has been given *locus standi* by international law to circumscribe executive action and to diminish executive privilege, and to diminish the effect of *acte de gouvernement*.

Extradition is a matter which would appear very much to be connected with diplomatic activity between states as it relates to the direct request from one state to another. The decision to extradite someone has long been held to be not an *acte de gouvernement*, to relate to the rights of someone inside France, and to be subjected to control by the *Conseil d'État*. For example, in *Bereciatua-Echarri*, an extradition order was quashed on the grounds that the applicant was a refugee according to the terms of the Geneva Convention on the Status of Refugees and that the Minister of Justice had not given evidence that the extradition was based on grounds of national security.[59] In recent years, the *Conseil d'État* had to consider the question of a refusal to extradite someone at the request of another state. In 1992, the United Kingdom government requested the extradition to Hong Kong of a person accused of certain financial offences. The request was rejected by the Foreign Ministry and the United Kingdom brought an action before the *Conseil d'État* to annul that rejection, the action being immediately met with the claimed defence that refusing to extradite was an *acte de gouvernement*. Here the

---

57   CE 8 January 1988, Ministre chargé du plan et de l'aménagement du territoire c Communauté urbaine de Strasbourg, Rec., p. 2.
58   Constitution, article 55.
59   CE 1 April 1988, Rec., p. 135. See also CE 24 June 1977, Astudillo Caleja, Rec., p. 290; CE 27 February 1987, Fidan.

submissions of the *Commissaire du Gouvernement* are most important when he described the progress from an act undoubtedly outside the jurisdiction of the *Conseil d'État* ('*l'acte souveraine*') to an act whose legality the *Conseil d'État* can review ('*l'acte administratif contrôlé*'). He argued that the refusal to extradite someone was not an unilateral sovereign act, but rather a judicial act within a scheme of international cooperation for the prevention of crime, and certain international conventions referred to an 'obligation' to extradite. It was not a sovereign unilateral act because France's room for manoeuvre was circumscribed by the rules of the treaty to which France was a party. It was submitted that the *Conseil d'État* should treat a refusal to extradite in the same manner as a request to extradite and consider the applicability of the normal grounds for review of administrative action (and in the context of extradition this would include the wording of the appropriate extradition treaty and general principles of the law of extradition). This was accepted by the *Conseil d'État* which ruled, very briefly, that a decision rejecting a request for extradition was '*détachable*' from the conduct of diplomatic activity between the two states concerned. On the legality of the decision to reject, the *Conseil d'État* held that the Minister of Justice had misinterpreted the terms of the Franco-British extradition treaty of 1876 and the appropriate French procedural laws implementing extradition matters.[60] Subsequently, the *Conseil d'État* confirmed its decision on jurisdiction and held that the French government had misapplied the European Convention on Extradition.[61]

Parallel developments

There have been parallel developments in matters which do not relate to foreign affairs and where no claim of *acte de gouvernement* has been raised, but which do relate to 'prerogative' powers of a similar nature to those already discussed with regard to the United Kingdom. The President of the Republic is granted by the Constitution[62] a wide power to nominate civil servants, as, subject to the power conferred on the President, is the Prime Minister.[63] It is accepted that the power of nomination entails a complementary power of dismissal and that this latter power is equally a discretionary power which can be exercised '*dans l'intérêt du service*'. In *Leclerc*,[64] which related to a Presidential decree dismissing Leclerc from the post of '*chef du service de l'Inspection générale de la police nationale*', for example, it was accepted, using a long-established formula, that '*le gouvernement pouvait à tout moment . . . décider de mettre fin à ses fonctions*' (i.e., the

---

60   CE 15 October 1993, Rec., p. 267.
61   CE 14 December 1994.
62   Article 13.
63   Article 21.
64   CE 17 June 1992.

government may at any time decide to dismiss someone from the civil service). If, however, the President or Prime Minister (or other competent authority) bases a decision not on the national interest but on the alleged conduct of the civil servant, the *Conseil d'État* reserves the power to determine whether the conduct was proved and was sufficiently serious to warrant dismissal.[65] Furthermore, the *Conseil d'État* will subject the decision to dismiss to the normal tests of illegality. For example, the dismissal can be effected only by the authority with jurisdiction to nominate,[66] the civil servant must be given the opportunity to see his or her internal file in order to present his or her case,[67] and this must be done in '*temps utile*' (i.e., the civil servant must be given sufficient time within which to prepare that case).[68] With regard to the maintenance of discipline in the armed services, at one time the *Conseil d'État* held that placing a member of the armed forces in detention was a matter internal to the functioning of the armed services and not susceptible to its review jurisdiction.[69] However, recently the *Conseil d'État* has recognised that disciplinary action can have consequences for the career prospects of members of the armed services similar to those affecting the career prospects of civil servants (already subject to the review jurisdiction) and has held that such disciplinary actions are susceptible to review — in particular, review with regard to the proportionality of any punishment inflicted.[70]

The nuclear tests issue

In 1995, the *Conseil d'État* was faced with a difficult situation, when President Chirac announced his decision to resume nuclear tests in the Pacific. He regretted the decision but said that events forced him to reverse the moratorium of President Mitterand in 1992 which had left a planned series of tests uncompleted. He said that completing the series was urgent, because in the autumn of 1996 there would be an international test ban treaty and France intended to sign that treaty unreservedly. In order to be in a position to sign the treaty, France had to be able both to ensure that the safety and viability of her nuclear force was complete and to have the capacity, as had the United Kingdom and the United States of America, to develop nuclear weapons by way of simulation. President Chirac pointed out that there were no ecological consequences of such tests. Greenpeace France brought an action before the *Conseil d'État*, asking it to determine that the President's decision was illegal. The tests were to be held on an atoll which is

---

65   CE 13 March 1953, Teissier; CE 27 October 1981, Bréart de Boissanger.
66   CE 10 April 1959, Fourré-Comeray, Rec., p. 233.
67   *Leclerc*, note 64 *supra*.
68   CE 2 February 1966, Torrès, Rec., p. 70.
69   For a relatively recent example, see CE 27 January 1984, Caillol.
70   CE 17 February 1995, Hardouin. For a parallel development with regard to discipline in prisons, see CE 17 February 1995, Marie.

French territory (although a long way from Paris) and Greenpeace was principally concerned with the ecological effects of testing, which would have first (and probably most dangerous) effect on the people on the atoll and the landscape and life of the atoll. Greenpeace wanted the *Conseil d'État* to substitute its appreciation of threats to the ecology of France for that of the President. They were met with the argument that their action was directed against an *acte de gouvernment* and was therefore non justiciable. Given the developments chronicled above, a question of immense importance with regard to judicial intervention was therefore raised.

The *Commissaire du Gouvernement* advanced two main arguments by which the *Conseil d'État* could determine whether the President's decision to re-start the series of nuclear tests was or was not '*détachable*', and in each case he came to the conclusion that it was not '*détachable*' and was intimately connected with the prerogative powers of the President. It was submitted, first, that the possession by France of a nuclear capability was different to other aspects of France's armed forces. It was a nuclear deterrent which had direct consequences on France's diplomatic independence, on France's foreign policy, and on France's position as a world power. The decision to test the nuclear capability directly affected France's credibility as a nation which could effectively deliver a nuclear strike. (One could perhaps question whether a decision to test a new tank or a new gun on an artillery ground in Normandy should now to be classed as an *acte de gouvernement*?) It was submitted, secondly, that the President's decision was taken precisely in the context of France's relations with other states in that, at that time, negotiations were taking place with regard to a comprehensive test ban treaty which, in future, would bind France. The President had clearly and expressly stated that whether France would sign this treaty or not would depend on the successful conclusion of the series of tests which would ensure that France's nuclear strike force would be effective. Since France was still conducting these negotiations, the settled case law of the *Conseil d'État* was that it could not intervene in such negotiations. Since France was not yet bound by a treaty, there was nothing to measure the President's decision against international norms.

The *Conseil d'État* was convinced by the second submission of the *Commissaire du Gouvernement* and held itself unable to accept jurisdiction in the matter.[71] The international context of the negotiations on the test ban treaty, and the timing of the tests so as to enable France to bind herself in the future with the other nuclear powers, were decisive. The President had made it clear that whether or not France signed depended exclusively and unconditionally on the success of the series of tests. In one sense, one would have been surprised if the *Conseil d'État* had decided otherwise (as one would have been surprised at any other decision than was reached in the United Kingdom case of *Chandler*). The disposition of the armed forces is traditionally reserved to the head of state, and this is granted to the

---

71   CE, Ass., 29 September 1995, Rec., p. 347.

President by the Constitution itself.[72] Until the test ban treaty was signed, France was under no international law obligation to surrender her freedom of action.

There remains a question for the future once a test ban treaty has been signed. Since, as has been shown, the *Conseil d'État* has recently been very ready to keep governmental action within the boundaries imposed by a treaty, such as the Treaty of Rome, the various treaties on extradition and the various international conventions on human rights, once France had signed and ratified the test ban treaty, what would the *Conseil d'État* do if France were, in breach of her international legal obligations, to resume more tests. Would the *Conseil* intervene?

CONCLUSION

In the United Kingdom, the courts will apply the term 'prerogative' to all common law powers of the executive, and the fact that an exercise of power has as its source the prerogative will not alone oust the jurisdiction of the courts. However, the subject matter of certain such powers will be deemed non justiciable in the sense that they are of such a high level of national policy that the proper forum for control is Parliament rather than the ill-equipped and non elected judges. The list of non justiciable exercises of power has been whittled down somewhat, although this has mainly occurred with regard to the application of established governmental policy rather than its formulation. Lastly, although the grounds of illegality and procedural impropriety will, national security considerations apart, be applied to the exercise of prerogative power in the same way as they are applied to the exercise of statutory power, and the 'ordinary' *Wednesbury* standard of irrationality will be applied to cases where justiciability is clear and there is a fundamental human rights dimension, there may well be applied a 'super-*Wednesbury* test' of 'outrageous or aberrant conduct' where the justiciability issue is not so clearly determined and the citizen's fundamental rights are not so directly impugned.

In France, the *Conseil d'État*, being bound by the terms of a superior written Constitution, has to accept that it cannot alter the list of prerogative powers granted to the executive by that Constitution. It has, however, refused to accept that a claim of *acte de gouvernement* automatically ousts its jurisdiction to review executive action, whilst itself determining that certain matters of institutional importance and certain matters of diplomatic activity and defence are not justiciable. It has applied the same grounds of review to prerogative power deemed justiciable as it applies to non prerogative power, while leaving a larger margin of appreciation of judgement in certain matters best left to the politicians. It has been very willing to utilise the incorporation of international law as a bench mark against which to measure the legality of executive action.

---

72   Article 15.

Although, as stated above, the differing constitutional backgrounds and the differing legal methodologies make it difficult (and, perhaps, not entirely suitable) to compare specific issues in each country with each other directly, three principal administrative law perspectives are apparent in each system. In each country, individuals have become more conscious of the availability of seeking judicial redress and have been increasingly aided in their endeavours by the formation of pressure groups. In each country, control of the executive by the legislature has been radically diminished by the dominance within the legislature of the political party which forms the government. In the United Kingdom, the former safety valve of ministerial responsibility is virtually non existent; and the creators of the 1958 French Constitution deliberately drafted that Constitution to ensure the dominance of government over Parliament (as a reaction to the perceived instability of governments in earlier Republican régimes). In recent years, the diminishing employment in practice of parliamentary remedial activity has left something of a vacuum in the constitutional regulation of prerogative power and an important principle of both domestic and the ever-increasing European legal scheme of things has, perhaps, subconsciously or not, led the judiciary to assume an opposition role. In this task, both High Court and *Conseil d'État* have invoked adherence to both the letter and the spirit of norms which the executive itself has incorporated, by varying constitutional mechanisms, into the domestic legal order as a consequence of its treaty-making prerogative powers. The treaties of the European Community and Union, together with European secondary legislation, are an integral part of the domestic law of both the United Kingdom and France. The *Conseil d'État* has been enabled to apply directly other international treaties, notably the European Convention on Human Rights, and recent cases tend to suggest that the High Court is being increasingly influenced by such treaties. It is not simply a question of the reception of extra-domestic law which will be important in the future (a matter of no mean importance), but the export of domestic principles which can be used as a base for the creation of universally recognised perspectives within which executive power operated by both national and international organisations may be subject to the rule of law.

14

Public Interest Immunity: Freedom of Information and Judicial Discretion

Adam Tomkins

SUMMARY

This chapter explores the doctrine of public interest immunity (PII) and the implications which PII has for administrative law. The focus is on the two common administrative law themes of discretion (in this case judicial discretion) and secrecy. In narrating the story of the judiciary's development of the modern law of PII, the chapter raises questions about the appropriateness of granting to courts responsibility for ensuring that government is open and that information is free. It welcomes the announcement in 1996 by the Conservative government of a new approach to PII, and considers the changes in the practice of PII brought about as a result of the Scott Inquiry in the light of the government's commitment to open government as expressed in the *Code of Practice on Access to Government Information*. Lastly, initial experience under the Code is reviewed in the light of the continuing debate as to the desirability of a Freedom of Information Act (now promised by the Labour government).

PUBLIC INTEREST IMMUNITY AND ADMINISTRATIVE LAW

Public interest immunity (PII) is a doctrine of the law of evidence which has significant implications for constitutional law and is also of central importance to administrative lawyers.[1] This chapter seeks to explore the ways in which PII is a

---

1 For a treatment of some of the constitutional implications of recent developments in PII, see Leigh, I., 'Public Interest Immunity' (1997) 50 *Parliamentary Affairs* 55.

matter of interest and concern to administrative law. Two major themes of administrative law are prominent in the modern development of PII. The first is lack of information and the second is judicial discretion. If administrative law is the area of law which seeks to control or regulate the exercise of power by public administrators, or if administrative law is part of the law which aims to hold public administration to account, then it is clear that such control, regulation or account-ability can be effective only if the controller, regulator or accountant has sufficient information. PII is a control device which affects the ebb and flow of information from the arena of public administration into that of the court. It is as a mechanism for controlling the freedom of information in court that PII first raises concerns for administrative law.

PII is a doctrine created and policed by judges. While it is (usually) public administrators who claim PII, it is (now) the court which determines the outcome of the claim. Over the past 50 years, the judges have instituted significant changes to the law and procedure of PII, changes which this chapter will outline in the following sections. The reason why these reforms are of interest to administrative lawyers lies in what they tell us about judicial discretion: both the judicial discretion which is employed in the making of the changes, and the judicial discretion which is left by the changes that have been made.

While some of the leading cases on PII which are considered in this chapter may already be familiar to some readers of a volume such as this, too often PII is treated by public lawyers as an arcane and somewhat abstract area of law. It is neither of these things. While the legal rulings of some of the cases which are revisited in the earlier sections of this chapter may be relatively well known, there are several gaps in the story of PII as it is habitually told in the textbooks, gaps which this chapter seeks to begin to fill. There are strangely forgotten cases and conveniently ignored precedents which are here resurrected — not just for their own sake, but for what they tell us about the present law — and their contribution to the development of the contemporary position has often been significant. Moreover, focusing in the usual black-letter way on the detached, rather isolated, narrow legal rulings of the major House of Lords decisions tends to distort the true picture of PII by obscuring the more human side of the story. Here, therefore, considerable emphasis is given to the facts of the cases in which PII has played an important part. It is by giving greater emphasis to the facts, incomplete and truncated as they might be, which allows the more human elements of the PII story to be revealed. By narrating the development of the modern law of PII in a chronological way, and by stressing the factual situations which gave rise to the changes in the law as well as those changes themselves, we will be able to construct a picture of PII which reveals what is often hidden and highlights what is usually ignored or forgotten.

The narrative style employed in this chapter attempts to use 'bits of the past to unsettle the present and to deprive it of peace of mind',[2] in part as a way of trying to lend meaning and understanding to the legal action of PII and in part to encourage not the moral response of more traditional textbook approaches (passivity and acceptance) but rather a degree of outrage and maybe even of resistance.[3] This will lead us to make some conclusions about PII which are somewhat different from the usual, rather lazy assumption that even if *Duncan* v *Cammell Laird* represented a black moment, subsequent judicial decisions such as *Conway* v *Rimmer* and *Burmah Oil* have put things rights and there really is nothing to worry about now — we can trust the judges. The argument here is that, on the contrary, when it comes to seeking ways of guaranteeing open government and freedom of information, we should do no such thing.

PUBLIC INTEREST IMMUNITY AND MINISTERIAL DISCRETION

Before examining in more detail the development of the modern law of PII, something needs first to be said as to its general nature. As indicated above, PII is a doctrine of the law of evidence. It does not affect freedom of information generally: it concerns only information which might be relevant and material evidence in a trial in court. A normal stage of pre-trial procedure is discovery and disclosure. Each side in litigation will disclose to the other the evidence on which it seeks to rely. There are several legal immunities which restrict the scope of the basic obligation to disclose, of which PII is one. The doctrine of PII allows for evidence to be withheld if it would be contrary to the public interest for it to be disclosed. Initially this was a privilege granted only to the Crown, as the Crown was the constitutional guardian of the public interest. Indeed, before 1972, PII was known as Crown privilege. Now PII is most frequently claimed either by a government minister or by the police, although claiming PII is not something which is limited strictly to the state as such. In the 1970s, the House of Lords held that the Gaming Board, a statutory body, and, in a later case, also the National Society for the Prevention of Cruelty to Children (NSPCC), a private, independent charity, could make claims to PII.[4]

While the law of PII has a long history, its modern development can be seen to have commenced with the seminal war-time decision of the House of Lords in *Duncan* v *Cammell Laird & Co. Ltd.*[5] This case concerned a submarine, *Thetis*, which had been built by the respondent shipbuilders under contract with the

---

2   See Minow, M., 'Stories in Law', in Brooks, P., and Gewirtz, P. (eds), *Law's Stories: Narrative and Rhetoric in the Law*, New Haven and London: Yale University Press, 1996, p. 33.
3   See *ibid.*, pp. 32–3.
4   See *R* v *Lewes Justices, ex parte Home Secretary* [1973] AC 388 and *D* v *NSPCC* [1978] AC 171.
5   [1942] AC 624.

Admiralty. In tests, the submarine sank and flooded, killing 99 men on board. A large number of actions for negligence were brought by various dependants of those killed. The plaintiffs requested discovery of documents from the shipbuilders, including the plans for the submarine, her hull and machinery. The Admiralty instructed the shipbuilders to refuse discovery and to object to the production of the plans on the ground that 'it would be injurious to the public interest that any of the said documents should be disclosed to any person'.[6] The case went to the House of Lords, where the question to be determined was what the circumstances were in which it could be claimed on behalf of the Crown that documents ordinarily required as evidence in a civil dispute could be validly withheld from production in court. The only speech in the House of Lords was delivered by Viscount Simon LC (although six other members of the House expressed their concurrence with him). There is clearly a separation of powers point here: was it appropriate, even in time of world war, for one Cabinet minister (the Lord Chancellor) to adjudicate on the propriety of a claim made by another (the First Lord of the Admiralty)? This is a point which was not apparently considered in the House of Lords at the time.

Even though one (albeit central) aspect of Viscount Simon's decision in *Duncan* v *Cammell Laird* has now been departed from, his speech still represents the foundation of the present approach to PII, at least in civil cases. His Lordship held that, as the Admiralty had wished, the documents should not be disclosed. His reasoning was that it is the minister who is charged with the responsibility of safeguarding the public interest, and if the minister has certified (as the First Lord of the Admiralty had done here) that the production of the documents would endanger the public interest, such an objection must be treated by the courts as being conclusive. The House of Lords in *Duncan* considered that the courts had no jurisdiction to go beyond the ministerial certificate: once a minister of the Crown claimed PII, such a claim would, as a matter of law, automatically be upheld by the courts: '. . . the practice in Scotland, as in England, may have varied, but the approved practice in both countries is to treat a ministerial objection taken in proper form as conclusive'.[7]

Having made this basic ruling, Viscount Simon went on to make two further points about PII which remain important. He stated first that PII could be claimed on two different bases: either because of the contents of a particular document, or because of the class of documents into which the document concerned fell, irrespective of its actual contents. In other words, the claiming of PII — the withholding of documents from the court — might arise for either of two reasons:

    (a)   either because the contents of a document, if disclosed, would be damaging to the public interest; or

---

6   *Ibid.*, at 626.
7   *Ibid.*, at 641.

(b) more controversially, simply because, even though the contents of the document were harmless, the document was the sort of document which as a matter of general policy should not be disclosed. These types of documents would include Cabinet papers, government departmental papers and such like.

These two different types of PII claims are known as contents claims and class claims. Viscount Simon also laid down an outline of the kinds of reasons why it would not be in the public interest for certain documents to be disclosed. In an important passage, he stated that

> it is not a sufficient ground that the documents are marked 'State documents' or 'official' or 'confidential'. It would not be a good ground that, if they were produced, the consequences might involve the department or the government in parliamentary discussion or in public criticism. . . . Neither would it be a good ground that production might tend to expose a want of efficiency in the administration or tend to lay the department open to claims for compensation. In a word, it is not enough that the minister of the department does not want to have the documents produced. The minister . . . ought not to take the responsibility of withholding production except in cases where the public interest would otherwise be damnified, for example, where disclosure would be injurious to national defence, or to good diplomatic relations, or where the practice of keeping a class of documents secret is necessary for the proper functioning of the public service.[8]

As we shall see, this is a passage which is worth quoting at some length as many of the phrases and sentiments expressed by Viscount Simon have since returned to haunt the subsequent development of the modern law of PII, a matter to which we can now turn.

PUBLIC INTEREST IMMUNITY AND JUDICIAL DISCRETION

In the period following *Duncan* v *Cammell Laird*, the government was increasingly indiscriminate in its growing use (and perhaps misuse) of PII, or Crown privilege as it then was. This led to substantial academic and other criticism, to two important government statements about future, more restricted use of PII, and eventually to two House of Lords decisions which changed — albeit not as radically as first appears to be the case — the course of PII law. It took the House of Lords two attempts rather than one because the first, in 1956, concerned Scotland, and the second, in 1968, related to England. We shall come to these cases

---

8   *Ibid.*, at 642.

shortly, but what of their background — growing use of, and growing worry about, PII?

Probably the most graphic example of what even the conservative *Law Quarterly Review* described as the 'evil . . . perpetuated' by *Duncan*[9] was the horrific case of *Ellis* v *Home Office*.[10] Ellis was detained in Winchester Prison, awaiting trial. He fell ill and was transferred to the prison's hospital wing. A warder left open all the doors to the individual cubicles in the hospital wing as the prisoners were slopping out, and another prisoner, who was in the hospital wing because he had a history of mental illness, entered Ellis's cubicle and hit him twice, severely, over the back of his head. Ellis required surgery as a result of his injuries, and he was left with a hole in the back of his head. After his release he secured a job, but was passed medically unfit for it. He fell back into crime and was later convicted of a serious offence for which he was sentenced to seven years' imprisonment.

Ellis sued the prison authorities for damages for negligence and for breach of the duty that was owed to him under the Prison Rules. He sought discovery of documents relating to the incident in which he had been injured, including police reports and prison medical records. The government claimed PII for these documents. The trial judge, Devlin J, dismissed Ellis's case, on the ground that the court could not examine the evidence that Ellis sought to rely on (because it had been subject to a claim for PII) and that Ellis was therefore unable to prove his case. In the course of dismissing the case, Devlin J expressed his grave concern about Ellis's inability adequately to test his case: 'I must express . . . my uneasy feeling that justice may not have been done because the material before me was not complete, and something more than an uneasy feeling that, whether justice has been done or not, it certainly will not appear to have been done.'[11] On dismissing Ellis's appeal, Singleton LJ held, in a ruling with which the other members of the Court of Appeal agreed, that:

> I cannot help feeling that if [the question of justice] had been considered in all its implications . . . it might well have been found that the disclosure of most of [the documents] could not have been fraught with any danger to the public interest, while it would have been desirable that they should have been disclosed to the advisers of this injured plaintiff for reasons of fairness and in the interests of justice.[12]

A further example, albeit not quite so controversial, of the over-use of PII in this period is the case of *Broome* v *Broome*.[13] A wife in a contested divorce served a

---

9   See Allen, C. K. (1953) 69 *Law Quarterly Review* 449.
10   [1953] 2 QB 135.
11   *Ibid.*, at 137.
12   *Ibid.*, at 144.
13   [1955] P 190.

subpoena on a Mrs Allsop, who was the representative of the Soldiers', Sailors' and Airmen's Families Association (SSAFA) in Hong Kong. It was thought that she would have to give evidence as to a number of letters, memoranda and records made by the SSAFA relating to the divorcing couple. The SSAFA dealt with family welfare and with problems of families in the armed services. The Secretary of State for War claimed PII in respect of the documents, and in respect of Mrs Allsop's oral evidence. As it turned out, the claim to privilege failed on the ground that it was not specific enough, but the court did hold that Crown privilege (or PII) could apply to the kinds of documents the case concerned, and that where the claim was made properly, the court could not override the claim.

These cases gave rise to considerable academic and other criticism. We have already seen the reaction of the *Law Quarterly Review*. The *Cambridge Law Journal* fumed away in a similar style.[14] Devlin J also wrote extra-judicially that 'unfortunately in practice [*Duncan*] has been regarded by government departments as almost a charter to withhold; and one suspects that the apprehension of a slight scratch is sometimes confused with real injury'.[15] In neither *Ellis* nor *Broome* was it at all clear what real damage would be done to the public interest if the evidence was allowed to be produced; yet, again in both cases, it was abundantly clear that grave damage could be done to the interests of justice if the evidence was not produced. It was this serious imbalance, and the courts' apparent inability to rectify it, which was the primary cause of concern.

In Scotland, these issues were resolved very differently. In *Glasgow Corporation v Central Land Board*,[16] the House of Lords held that the rule in *Duncan* v *Cammell Laird* did not apply north of the border. In this case, Glasgow Corporation sought a declarator (the Scottish equivalent of declaration) that certain decisions of the Central Land Board were *ultra vires* the Town and Country Planning (Scotland) Act 1947. Glasgow Corporation sought discovery of a number of documents held by the Central Land Board and by the Board of the Inland Revenue. The Central Land Board and the Board of the Inland Revenue objected to their production, and the Secretary of State for Scotland claimed Crown privilege. The questions for the House of Lords were, first, could privilege apply to documents held by the Central Land Board; secondly, if so, could the court look behind the ministerial claim to privilege, despite the rule in *Duncan's* case; and thirdly, if so, should the claim in this case be overridden or not?

The House of Lords unanimously held that as the Central Land Board was a servant of the Crown, privilege could apply in relation to documents in its possession. They went on to hold — also unanimously — that *Duncan* v *Cammell Laird*, despite statements in the speech of Viscount Simon LC in that case to

---

14   See Wade, E. C. S. [1954] *Cambridge Law Journal* 11.
15   See 'The Common Law, Public Policy and the Executive' [1956] *Current Legal Problems* 1, at 4.
16   1956 SLT 41.

contrary effect, did not change or affect the law of Scotland, and an inherent power remained in Scottish courts to override the certificate of a minister. Lord Radcliffe stated that in exercising this inherent power, courts are not engaging in any dispute with the minister's view of what is necessary in the public interest. Rather, the courts are merely recognising that there may be more than one aspect of the public interest which is relevant: 'the interests of government, for which the minister should speak with full authority, do not exhaust the public interest'.[17]

The documents in question in the case concerned the assessment of development charges. As Lord Radcliffe stated, 'nothing of high politics, diplomatic relations or state secrets can be involved'.[18] On the facts, however, the House of Lords decided that the documents would not assist the Glasgow Corporation in their action against the Central Land Board, and therefore the documents would not be ordered to be disclosed. In making the decision, though, Lord Radcliffe made a number of important points concerning the notion of withholding documents in the interests of 'the proper functioning of the public service' as Viscount Simon had put it in *Duncan* v *Cammell Laird*. Lord Radcliffe stated that:

> if it is to become accepted doctrine that this very general phrase covers everything, however commonplace, that has passed between one civil servant and another behind the departmental screen . . . I do not think that it will be a matter of surprise if some future judge in Scotland finds himself obliged to disregard the Crown's objection and to hold that disclosure can do much less injury to the interest of the public than non-production of a particular document may do to . . . the cause of justice. I am bound to say that I should myself have supposed Crown servants to be made of sterner stuff.[19]

As we shall see, subsequent English cases have also had to grapple with the thorny issue of what the proper functioning of the public service might require.

Later in the same year (1956) this general atmosphere of uncertainty and inconsistency as between English and Scots law, combined with the trenchant criticisms of the government's (mis)use of Crown privilege in cases such as *Ellis*, led the Lord Chancellor, Viscount Kilmuir, to make a statement in the House of Lords as to the government's policy on this area. Viscount Kilmuir rejected the notion that there was need for legislation and argued instead that:

> the proper way to strike a balance between the needs of litigants and those of government administration is . . . to narrow the class as much as possible by excluding from it those categories of documents which appear to be particularly

---

17   *Ibid.*, at 47.
18   *Ibid.*
19   *Ibid.*

relevant to litigation and for which the highest degree of confidentiality is not required in the public interest. We have carried out an extensive survey of this field, and have certain proposals.[20]

The proposals included the following: a large part of the litigation involving the Crown after the Crown Proceedings Act 1947 (which made no substantive difference to the law of Crown privilege) concerned road traffic accidents either involving government employees, or on Crown land. Viscount Kilmuir stated that the government would no longer claim privilege in road traffic cases. In addition, he said that the government would no longer claim privilege for ordinary medical records (which would prevent a recurrence of *Ellis*), but that privilege would still be claimed in respect of military medical records. Viscount Kilmuir also stated that privilege would not be claimed in criminal proceedings, an aspect of PII law which has become controversial more recently, and which is addressed towards the end of this chapter. The Kilmuir statement would not affect a case such as *Broome* v *Broome*, in respect of which the Lord Chancellor said that the work of the SSAFA's welfare officers 'is of the highest importance . . . and in the government's view it would be very unfortunate if it ceased to be protected by Crown privilege'.[21] It is important to understand the effect of the Kilmuir statement. It is not legislation. It is not legally binding on the government. It is merely a statement of what the government intended or desired to do. As Wade pointed out in his note on the statement, there could be no legal sanction against the government disregarding it.[22]

English law on this matter was not changed for over another decade, until the House of Lords decision in *Conway* v *Rimmer*.[23] This case concerned an action for malicious prosecution brought by a former probationary police constable against his former superintendent. Relations between the two officers were clearly bad. When another constable lost his torch, Conway was suspected of having stolen it; during investigations into the missing torch, the superintendent (Rimmer) told Conway that his probationary reports were adverse and advised him to resign from the police. Conway refused to resign. Rimmer then saw to it that Conway should be prosecuted for the theft of the torch (worth 15*s* 3*d*), but Conway's trial was stopped after the presentation of the case for the prosecution and a verdict of not guilty was returned. After the trial, Conway was dismissed from the police. He then brought his action for damages.

Conway sought discovery of a number of documents which were in Rimmer's possession, including four probationary reports which Rimmer had made during

---

20   197 HL Deb, col. 743, 6 June 1956.
21   *Ibid.*, col. 746.
22   See [1956] *Cambridge Law Journal* 133.
23   [1968] AC 910.

Conway's probationary period with the police. It was admitted that these documents were relevant to Conway's action, but the Home Secretary objected to their disclosure, certifying that they fell within a class of documents the production of which would be injurious to the public interest. The question for the House of Lords, as it had been in *Duncan* v *Cammell Laird*, was whether such a ministerial certificate was conclusive or not. All five Law Lords delivered speeches, and although in terms of the outcome they were unanimous, there are some important differences between them as regards the overall approach to PII.

The House of Lords decided that the rule in *Duncan's* case, that a ministerial certificate should be conclusive, should be overruled and that the court ought to be able to look behind such a certificate. Lord Reid held that although he had no doubt that *Duncan* was 'rightly decided', the House of Lords in 1942 were self-evidently preoccupied with cases where 'disclosure would involve a danger of real prejudice to the national interest'.[24] In times less driven by the emergency of war, a better approach, according to Lord Reid, would be for the court to accept that in cases where disclosure was resisted on public interest grounds there were two competing public interests at stake, and it was the court's role to balance them. On the one hand there is the public interest in ensuring the fair administration of justice, which would usually require full discovery and disclosure. On the other hand there is the public interest, as cited in the ministerial certificate, such as national security, confidentiality or the proper functioning of the public service, which would normally demand the withholding of the documents. The court's responsibility in such cases is to weigh these competing public interests and to determine, on the facts of the case, which one outweighs the other.[25]

As to precisely how the courts are to do this — how are they to know (or judge) which public interest outweighs the other in any particular case — Lord Reid was silent. If the effect of *Duncan* v *Cammell Laird* was to leave the question of PII entirely to the discretion of the minister, with no principles laid down as to how such discretion should properly be exercised, the effect of *Conway* v *Rimmer* was to leave the issue as one for equally unguided judicial discretion. In this, his decision in *Conway* v *Rimmer* is perhaps typical of Lord Reid's famous attempts in the mid- to late 1960s to reform various areas of administrative law: in *Ridge* v *Baldwin*[26] he swept away unnecessary restrictions as to when the rules of natural justice would apply, only to replace them with little more than case-by-case judicial discretion; and again in *Padfield* v *Minister of Agriculture, Fisheries and Food*[27] Lord Reid adopted much the same approach with regard to the test of legality in judicial review.

---

24   *Ibid.*, at 939.
25   *Ibid.*, at 940 and 952.
26   [1964] AC 40.
27   [1968] AC 997.

During the course of his speech, Lord Reid, although he departed from Viscount Simon's speech in *Duncan* on the issue of the conclusivity of the ministerial certificate, echoed and supported many of the other things that had been stated about PII in *Duncan*. For example, Lord Reid supported the notion that PII could be claimed on either contents or class grounds. He even went so far as to state that in his view there were 'certain classes of documents which ought not to be disclosed whatever their content might be. Virtually everyone agrees that Cabinet minutes and the like ought not to be disclosed until such time as they are only of historical interest'. The most important reason for this, according to Lord Reid, was that otherwise, disclosure would:

> create or fan ill-informed or captious . . . criticism. The business of government is difficult enough as it is, and no government could contemplate with equanimity the inner workings of the government machine being exposed to the gaze of those ready to criticise without adequate knowledge of the background and perhaps with some axe to grind.[28]

Conway v *Rimmer* may have been a reforming decision, but, as statements such as these make clear, it would be a mistake to parade the case as a great leap forward in the cause of open government and freedom of information. All *Conway* v *Rimmer* did was to modify the harshest effects of a rotten war-time precedent.

In addition to his support for Viscount Simon's approach to contents and class claims, Lord Reid also reinforced the spirit of *Duncan* v *Cammell Laird* on the issue of the candour argument. As we saw above, Viscount Simon laid down a number of the situations in which it would be appropriate for a claim to PII to be made. This list of situations ended with Viscount Simon's statement that documents could be withheld where it was 'necessary for the proper functioning of the public service'. This is the so-called candour argument that was roundly criticised by Lord Radcliffe in the *Glasgow Corporation* case. The idea here is that civil servants and other government officials will be frank and candid in their advice to ministers only if they know that such advice is and will remain confidential and will not at some point in the future be open to criticism and review in a court of law. The threat of future judicial scrutiny, it is said, is enough to inhibit the nation's civil servants and will result in advice which is somehow constrained and incomplete, rather than being full and free. As we have seen, this is a controversial argument, but it is one which Lord Reid had no trouble in supporting in *Conway* v *Rimmer*.[29] Other members of the House of Lords in that case were more critical of the candour argument. Lord Morris, for example, described it as 'a suggestion of doubtful validity'.[30] Lord Morris thought that if civil servants feared the

---

28   [1968] AC 910, at 952. See also Lord Upjohn at 993.
29   See his citing with approval the words of Viscount Simon: *ibid.*, at 952.
30   *Ibid.*, at 957.

possibility of future judicial scrutiny of their advice, this would encourage them to be more rather than less candid. Lord Pearce echoed Lord Morris's doubts as to the validity of the candour argument.[31]

The outcome of *Conway* v *Rimmer,* as far as the House of Lords was concerned, was that the documents were privately inspected by the court; and, in the words of Lord Reid, nothing was found 'in any of them the disclosure of which would . . . be in any way prejudicial to the proper administration of the [police] or to the general public interest'.[32] The House therefore ordered their disclosure to Conway.

In the 1970s, the House of Lords made two further decisions affecting the development of PII. Both of these cases concerned the question: who may claim PII? Is the claiming of PII limited to the state, or to central government or to ministers of the Crown? According to the House of Lords, it is not. In *R* v *Lewes Justices, ex parte Home Secretary,*[33] the Gaming Board was allowed to claim PII. This was also the case where the courts suggested that this area of law should now be known as PII rather than as Crown privilege. And in *D* v *NSPCC,*[34] the House of Lords further decided that PII could be claimed by the NSPCC, a private, independent charity. These cases are important in the context of the development of a legal notion of the state, or of the public sector, but they do not contribute greatly to the administrative law themes of PII, freedom of information and judicial discretion on which this chapter is focused.

TOWARDS GREATER OPENNESS?

The next case which does significantly affect our themes of judicial discretion and freedom of information is *Burmah Oil* v *Bank of England.*[35] Unlike *Conway* v *Rimmer, Burmah Oil* did concern high level government papers relating to the formulation of government policy on a sensitive issue: namely, the rescue by the Bank of England of a troubled company. The rescue plan involved, among other things, the company (Burmah Oil) selling stock it had owned to the Bank of England. Some months after the rescue plan had been put into effect, the company commenced legal proceedings against the Bank, arguing that it had been forced to sell its stock for an unconscionably and inequitably low price. The formulation of the rescue plan had involved weeks of sensitive negotiations between the Bank, the Treasury, the Department of Energy and Burmah Oil. In the course of its action Burmah Oil sought discovery of a number of documents emanating from or relating to these negotiations, and the Chief Secretary to the Treasury objected to the production of some of the documents on grounds of PII.

---

31   *Ibid.,* at 987.
32   *Ibid.,* at 996–97.
33   [1973] AC 388.
34   [1978] AC 171.
35   [1980] AC 1090.

By the time the case reached the House of Lords, only 10 documents remained subject to the claim to PII. These 10 fell into two categories, known as category A and category B. The former consisted of 'communications between, to and from ministers . . . and minutes and briefs for ministers and memoranda of meetings attended by ministers. All such documents relate to the formulation of the policy of the government'.[36] Category B consisted of communications between, to and from senior government officials. The PII claim in *Burmah Oil* was a class claim, based in the ministerial certificate on the candour argument: in the words of the certificate, 'it is, in my opinion, necessary for the proper functioning of the public service that the documents in category A and category B should be withheld from production. They are all documents falling within the class of documents relating to the formulation of government policy'.[37]

The question for the House of Lords was whether, applying the balancing exercise as described by Lord Reid in *Conway* v *Rimmer*, the overriding public interest lay in the documents being disclosed or withheld. The majority of the House held that they (the judges) should privately inspect the documents in question in order to determine whether the interests of justice outweighed those of confidentiality as outlined in the minister's certificate. Lord Keith, one of four judges in the majority, held that even though the documents in question in this case were high level government papers dealing with the formulation of government policy, this did not mean (contrary to what Lord Reid had stated in *Conway* v *Rimmer*) that the court could not authorise their disclosure. In an approach significantly different from that which had been adopted by Lord Reid, Lord Keith stated that 'it would be going too far to lay down that no document in any particular one of the categories mentioned should never in any circumstances be ordered to be produced'.[38] Lord Keith also poured scorn on the candour argument, on which the minister had relied in his certificate in *Burmah Oil*, stating that:

the notion that any competent and conscientious public servant would be inhibited at all in the candour of his writings by consideration of the off-chance that they might have to be produced in a litigation is in my opinion grotesque ... There can be discerned in modern times a trend towards more open governmental methods than were prevalent in the past. No doubt it is for Parliament and not for courts of law to say how far that trend should go. The courts are, however, concerned with the consideration that it is in the public interest that justice should be done ... This may demand, though no doubt only in a very limited number of cases, that the inner workings of government should

---

36   The words of the PII certificate signed by the Chief Secretary, quoted by Lord Wilberforce: *ibid.*, at 1109.

37   Quoted by Lord Wilberforce: *ibid.*, at 1110.

38   *Ibid.*, at 1134.

be exposed to public gaze, and there may be some who would regard this as likely to lead, not to captious or ill-informed criticism, but to criticism calculated to improve the nature of that working as affecting the individual citizen.[39]

While Lord Keith's views on open government and the 'grotesque' nature of the candour argument were not shared by the other Law Lords in the majority, the four majority judges did agree that they should privately inspect the documents in order to determine whether they should, on balance, be disclosed or not. In the event, the four judges considered that although the documents were relevant and material evidence in Burmah Oil's dispute with the Bank, they were not crucial and their absence from the litigation would not be unfair to Burmah Oil. In Lord Scarman's words, 'their significance is not such as to override the public service [i.e. candour] objections to their production'.[40] The House of Lords therefore ordered that they should not be disclosed.

Despite the fact that Burmah Oil did not gain discovery of the documents it had wanted, the majority view in the House of Lords in this case nonetheless represents the high watermark of judicial willingness to countenance a degree of openness towards claims to PII, even at a relatively high level concerning sensitive government papers. The House was not unanimous, however; and the dissent of Lord Wilberforce is significant and merits examination because it was his dissent, rather than the position of the majority, that heralded the way the House would seek to develop the law in future cases. In Lord Wilberforce's view, the claim to PII in *Burmah Oil* laid down in the ministerial certificate was *prima facie* a good one; and in the light of the concerns expressed by the minister in his certificate, before the court could privately inspect the documents concerned, the other side in the case (Burmah Oil) should first explain to the court exactly why it was in the public interest that the documents should be disclosed. Lord Wilberforce stated that:

a claim for PII having been made, on manifestly solid grounds, it is necessary for those who seek to overcome it to demonstrate the existence of a counteracting interest calling for disclosure of particular documents. When this is demonstrated, but only then, may the court proceed to a balancing process.[41]

This, he said, Burmah Oil had failed to do. Thus, Lord Wilberforce refused even to inspect the documents privately, holding against Burmah Oil because it had failed to establish the grounds on which he as a judge could overturn the ministerial certificate: the company had failed, in his view, to give him anything to weigh

---

39   *Ibid.*, at 1133–34.
40   *Ibid.*, at 1147.
41   *Ibid.*, at 1113–14.

against the public interest in the proper functioning of the public service that the minister had sought to rely on in his certificate.

Thus, in contradistinction to the views of Lord Keith, Lord Wilberforce had a good deal of sympathy with the candour argument. He stated of the candour argument that:

> it seems now rather fashionable to decry this, but if as a ground it may at one time have been exaggerated, it has now, in my opinion, received an excessive dose of cold water. I am certainly not prepared — against the view of the minister — to discount the need, in the formation of such very controversial policy as that with which we are here involved, for frank and uninhibited advice from the bank to the government, from and between civil servants and between ministers . . . To remove protection from revelation in court in this case at least could well deter frank and full expression in similar cases in the future.

Lord Wilberforce summed up his views with the ringing phrase: 'I do not believe . . . that it is for the courts to assume the role of advocates for open government'.[42]

SOUNDING THE RETREAT

Lord Wilberforce's position, in dissent in *Burmah Oil,* was largely followed by the House of Lords as a whole three years later, on the next occasion when PII was considered by their Lordships, in *Air Canada* v *Secretary of State for Trade.*[43] The background to this case was that the British Airports Authority (BAA) was in the process of making major improvements at Heathrow. Under the Airports Authority Act 1975, the Secretary of State had certain supervisory powers over BAA, especially as regards finance. He required BAA to pay for the improvements at Heathrow from its own internal revenues. In order to afford this, BAA increased its charges to airlines at Heathrow by some 35 per cent. Air Canada and 17 other international airlines challenged the increases in charges levied on them. One of their main arguments in the litigation was that although the Secretary of State did have certain statutory powers over BAA, these were powers which could be exercised only for legitimate purposes, i.e. the purposes which fell within the aims and objectives of the relevant Act (an argument based on *Padfield* v *Minister of Agriculture Fisheries and Food*).[44] Here, they asserted that the Secretary of State had exercised his statutory powers for an improper purpose — namely, as a way of reducing the public sector borrowing requirement. Clearly, in order to determine whether this had indeed been the Secretary of State's motivation, Air Canada

---

42   *Ibid.*, at 1112.
43   [1983] 2 AC 394.
44   [1968] AC 997.

needed access to documents containing communications between the Secretary of State, his colleagues and officials, and BAA. The government claimed PII for two categories of documents: first, for ministerial papers relating to the formulation of government policy (about 100 documents) and, secondly, for inter-departmental communications between senior civil servants. Just as in the *Burmah Oil* case, these were then class claims to PII based on the candour argument.

The judge at first instance decided that he should privately inspect the documents, but he stayed his order that the documents should be produced for his inspection, pending an appeal. The House of Lords unanimously dismissed Air Canada's appeal and held that the case even for private inspection, let alone public disclosure, had not been made out. Although unanimous as to this outcome, their Lordships differed as to what precisely the test adopted should be to determine whether documents subject to a claim to PII should be privately inspected or not. Lord Fraser ruled that, while it was not possible to lay down any uniform test, the party seeking disclosure 'ought at least to satisfy the court that the documents are very likely to contain material which would give substantial support' to its case and that without it it 'might be "deprived of the means of . . . proper presentation" of' its case.[45] Lord Fraser stated that 'the test is intended to be fairly strict', as courts 'should not be encouraged to "take a peep" just on the off-chance of finding something useful'.[46]

Lords Scarman and Templeman[47] took a slightly different view on the question of when the judge should inspect the documents. They felt that the documents should be privately inspected where they might assist *either* side in the litigation, or where they were necessary for disposing of the matter fairly, rather than only where the party seeking disclosure had established that the documents would assist *that party*. On the facts of the present case, this different emphasis made no difference to the outcome: all five Law Lords were agreed that Air Canada had not demonstrated to the satisfaction of the court that the documents should be inspected by the judge. The rather obvious question to be asked here is: if the party seeking disclosure does not have the documents in its possession, how can it establish the ways in which those documents might be useful to its argument? It is somewhat of a catch-22 situation.

PUBLIC INTEREST IMMUNITY IN CONTEXT: POLICE CASES

Taken together, the cases on which this chapter has thus far focused constitute the main body of PII law. The issue which remains to be explored is how this basic

---

45   [1983] 2 AC 394, at 435, citing *Glasgow Corporation* v *Central Land Board* 1956 SC (HL) 1, at 18, *per* Lord Radcliffe.

46   *Ibid.*, at 436. Lords Wilberforce (at 438) and Edmund-Davies (at 441) agreed with the approach of Lord Fraser.

47   At 445 and 449 respectively.

set of principles actually works in practice. In order to demonstrate this, two areas of topical interest will be highlighted: first, cases concerning the police; and, secondly, in the next section, criminal cases.

During the 1980s, the Court of Appeal developed a line of authority to the effect that the police could claim PII in respect of certain documents in their possession. This was controversial, especially in cases concerning complaints against the police lodged either by members of the public or by police officers. A number of cases concerned the status of witness statements which had been drawn up in connection with disciplinary police hearings. In *Neilson* v *Laugharne*,[48] the plaintiff sued the defendant Chief Constable alleging trespass, assault and false imprisonment by an officer of his force. There was an investigation under s. 49 of the Police Act 1964,[49] but this investigation found that there were no grounds for any disciplinary action to be taken against any of the police officers involved. In his action for damages the plaintiff sought discovery of a number of witness statements that had been drawn up for the purpose of the s. 49 investigation. The Chief Constable objected to the production of these statements, on grounds of PII, and the Court of Appeal unanimously accepted and upheld the police's objection on the ground that if such documents were to be allowed to be used in civil proceedings, this would discourage police officers and others from fully cooperating in the statutory investigation.[50] This is an argument closely related to the candour ('proper functioning of the public service') argument discussed above.

Neilson v *Laugharne* was reluctantly followed by a differently constituted Court of Appeal in *Hehir* v *Commissioner of Police of the Metropolis*,[51] and was further extended by the Court of Appeal in *Makanjuola* v *Commissioner of Police of the Metropolis*.[52] The facts of *Makanjuola* are similar to those of the *Neilson* case, except in *Makanjuola* the plaintiff sought discovery in civil proceedings against the police of a number of witness statements, including one which she herself had given. PII was claimed in respect of all such statements, including Makanjuola's own, and this claim was unanimously upheld by the Court of Appeal. According to the Court, the fact that the maker of the statement consented to its being disclosed could not override the claim to PII.

This line of authority was controversially applied in *Halford* v *Sharples*.[53] Halford was an Assistant Chief Constable. She complained of unlawful sex discrimination on the ground that she felt her promotion to Deputy Chief Constable was being unreasonably blocked. In the course of her proceedings against the

---

48   [1981] QB 736.
49   Now replaced by s. 84 of the Police and Criminal Evidence Act 1984.
50   See the judgment of Oliver LJ: [1981] QB 736, at 752.
51   [1982] 1 WLR 715.
52   [1992] 3 All ER 617. Although *Makanjuola* was reported only in 1992, it was decided in early 1989.
53   [1992] 3 All ER 624.

police, she sought discovery of a number of police complaints and disciplinary files from her own police force as well as from other forces. PII was claimed, and a majority of the Court of Appeal upheld the claim to immunity on the ground that all documents which depended on, referred to, or related to complaints and discipline in the police force — whether in the form of reports, correspondence, memoranda or notes between police officers, as well as statements and other evidence — were all included in a class of documents which was protected against disclosure for reasons of public interest. Ralph Gibson LJ dissented, on the ground that the police had not established to his satisfaction that on the facts the public interest in secrecy prevailed over the need for the documents in the trial of the sex discrimination issue.[54]

An exception to this general line of authority was established in *Commissioner of Police of the Metropolis* v *Locker*,[55] where it was held by the Employment Appeal Tribunal that, although PII attached to documents arising out of disciplinary hearings in the police, it did not attach to documents arising out of grievance proceedings. This rather odd state of affairs was altered again when the House of Lords considered the issue in *R* v *Chief Constable of the West Midlands Police, ex parte Wiley*.[56] In *Wiley*, the House of Lords overruled *Neilson*, *Hehir* and *Makanjuola*, ruling that a class claim to PII would no longer attach generally to all documents coming into existence in consequence of a complaint against or a disciplinary investigation into the police, although, where necessary, a contents claim could still be made.

Wiley is not the last chapter in this saga, however. In *Taylor* v *Anderton*,[57] the Court of Appeal held that although the House of Lords has now stated that PII does not attach to a class comprising witness statements concerned with police disciplinary hearings, the decision in *Wiley* did not relate to *reports* of investigations arising out of complaints against the police, which, according to the Court of Appeal in *Taylor* v *Anderton*, ought still to fall within a class that should be protected by PII.

These police cases demonstrate the importance of both of our themes. There is clearly little openness in the field of complaints against the police, an area where some degree of freedom of information might have been thought to have been more central than many others, for reasons not only of fairness but because of matters such as general public confidence as well. Similarly, the flexible way in which the judges have gradually shaped and reshaped the law of PII can also be seen from these police cases: the establishment of the basic position in *Neilson*,

---

54   *Ibid.*, at 652.
55   [1993] 3 All ER 584.
56   [1994] 3 All ER 420. Other aspects of this important case are considered in Tomkins, A., *The Constitution after Scott: Government Unwrapped*, Oxford: Clarendon Press, 1998, Ch. 5.
57   [1995] 2 All ER 420.

Hehir and *Makanjuola*; the exception in *Locker*; the reassessment in *Wiley*; and the continued development in *Taylor* v *Anderton*. But there is a third theme also demonstrated in these cases — namely, overall judicial reluctance unambiguously to advance claims of openness and greater freedom of information — a final theme to which we shall return in the final section of this chapter.

PUBLIC INTEREST IMMUNITY IN CONTEXT: CRIMINAL TRIALS

The most controversial use of PII in recent times has been the Conservative government's claims to PII in criminal trials, most notably (although not only) in a number of prosecutions concerned with alleged breaches of export law by companies trading with Iraq. The most famous of these trials was the aborted Matrix Churchill prosecution, the collapse of which in November 1992 was the immediate reason behind the government's establishment of the Scott Inquiry. A large part of the Scott Report, published in February 1996, considered the use and abuse of PII in the criminal context.[58] Although the use of PII in the criminal context (one might say the criminal use of PII) does not shed any new light on our administrative law themes, it is nonetheless worth considering briefly, if only to demonstrate another topical area where PII has a prominent role to play.[59]

In the Matrix Churchill trial, three directors of the company were being prosecuted on a charge of knowingly exporting goods with intent to evade export restrictions, contrary to the Customs and Excise Management Act 1979, s. 68(2). In their defence, the directors wanted to argue that they had had no intention to evade the restrictions: on the contrary, they had obtained licences for the exports from the Department of Trade and Industry (DTI) who had known all about (and indeed had encouraged) the nature of Matrix Churchill's trade with Iraq (i.e. that the exports could be and indeed were used for munitions manufacture). Clearly, in order to succeed with this argument, the Matrix Churchill directors needed access to DTI and other governmental papers which, they hoped, would establish that there had indeed been no deception. Four government ministers signed PII certificates which were used at the trial. Contents and class claims were made, on various grounds, including national security, the candour argument and commercial confidentiality. After several days of argument, the trial judge eventually ordered the disclosure of most of the documents, albeit with some of them being heavily blacked out (or 'redacted' as it was put). On the basis of the information contained in the documents, counsel for the defence was able to cross-examine key prosecution witnesses, most notably Alan Clark, the former Minister for Trade and

---

58   See Scott, Sir R., *Report of the Inquiry into the Export of Defence Equipment and Dual-Use Goods to Iraq and Related Prosecutions*, HC 115, London: HMSO, 1996, esp. vol. III.

59   For a fuller account, see Tomkins, A., 'Public Interest Immunity after Matrix Churchill' [1993] *Public Law* 650.

Minister for Defence Procurement, who appeared to change his evidence during cross-examination, as a result of which the prosecution was abandoned.

After the collapse of the trial, the government faced two charges: first, that it had no right to claim PII in a criminal case; and, secondly, that ministers were wrong in their claims to PII in any event. The government, and in particular the Attorney-General, Sir Nicholas Lyell, strenuously sought to refute these charges. They argued that there was judicial authority justifying the use of PII in the criminal context, and that in any event, ministers could not be criticised for having claimed PII, as they had a legal duty to do so. These arguments were examined and ultimately rejected by Sir Richard Scott in his report. On the issue of whether it was open to the government to claim PII in the context of a criminal trial, Sir Richard stated that although there was some authority in support of the view that PII could be claimed in criminal proceeding,[60] there was no clear judicial authority to support the government's class claims to PII in a criminal trial.[61] As to whether the government ministers who claimed PII in the Matrix Churchill case were under a legal duty to do so, as the Attorney-General had argued, Sir Richard Scott dismissed this view, describing it as one which was 'based on a fundamental misconception of the principles of PII law'[62] (see Radford, Ch. 2, p. 42 and Ganz, Ch. 3, p. 61 for further discussion of the Scott Report).

At first it was unclear precisely what the effects would be of the scathing criticisms contained in the Scott Report on the subject of government secrecy and misuse of PII. Scott's criticisms might have been strong, but his recommendations were comparatively limited. He recommended against legislation clarifying the principles of PII; he did not recommend that PII claims should be permitted only on a contents basis (although he did recommend that class claims should not be allowed in criminal cases); and he did not recommend that PII claims should in the future be based on something more compelling, and more exact, than the candour argument.[63] Depressingly, the government's initial reaction to the Scott Report's findings on PII was defensive, unhelpful and confrontational. It simply rejected Scott's views on PII law and continued to insist that in using PII claims in the context of a criminal trial, and in stating that ministers had been under a duty to claim PII, the government had done nothing wrong and had behaved impeccably throughout.[64] However, the government did institute a short consultation process on PII law and practice after the Scott Report was published, and in December 1996 the government made an important announcement in which it outlined a new approach to PII — one which for the first time really began to move PII out from the shadow of Duncan.

---

60   See R v Governor of Brixton Prison, ex parte Osman [1992] 1 All ER 108.
61   See Scott, op. cit. note 58 supra, paras G18.76 and G18.84.
62   Ibid., para. G18.54.
63   Although Sir Richard did appear to suggest this in a subsequent public lecture: see Scott, Sir R., 'The Acceptable and Unacceptable Use of Public Interest Immunity' [1996] Public Law 427.
64   For details, see Tomkins, A., The Constitution after Scott, op. cit. note 56 supra.

THE AFTERMATH OF SCOTT: A NEW APPROACH

While the government's new approach is limited to claims to PII made by the government itself (i.e. it does not extend to claims made by the police or by other non departmental public bodies) and is limited to England and Wales, it does represent a significant and welcome step in the right direction. The new approach outlined in the government's paper applies equally to civil and criminal cases.[65] The central point of the new approach is the abolition of the distinction between class and contents claims. Government ministers will no longer make claims to PII based on the contents of a document or on the class into which a document falls. In its announcement the government stated that the distinction between class and contents claims was 'no longer helpful'[66] and had become 'obscure'.[67] The government's new approach is that PII can be claimed only 'where disclosure of material could cause real damage to the public interest'.[68] This obviously raises the question of what 'real damage' means. Is the new approach a change merely of words, or will it also result in a change of practice? That the government chose late December to make its announcement (just a couple of days before the Christmas recess), and that the announcement was made merely by placing a short document in the libraries of the Houses of Parliament (rather than in a formally published command paper, for example), might indicate that the government was anxious to minimise publicity for its new approach. This was hardly an exercise in genuinely open government! No doubt the government was mindful that after nearly 18 years in power its new approach might be seen by some to represent an admission that past practice had been unacceptable — a view shared by the Scott Report and which only the previous February the government had strenuously denied, partly in order to save face and partly for the sake of rescuing the Attorney-General, Sir Nicholas Lyell, from that dreadful fate of ministerial resignation.

However, even if the form of the announcement was flawed, its contents give cause for greater optimism. As for defining what the new test of 'real damage to the public interest' might mean, the government took the view that 'it is impossible to describe exhaustively what that damage might be',[69] although some examples were given. A claim to PII would be justified if, for example, it would prevent harm to an individual (such as an informant), or if it would prevent damage to what the government slightly mysteriously called the 'regulatory process' or to international relations or to the nation's economic interests.[70] This is not an

---

65 *Attorney-General's Guidelines on Public Interest Immunity*, December 1996, paras 1.7–1.9.
66 *Ibid.*, para. 2.3.
67 *Ibid.*, para. 3.3.
68 *Ibid.*, para. 4.2.
69 *Ibid.*, para. 4.3.
70 *Ibid.*

exhaustive list: in the government's view no list could be complete — claims to PII would have to be considered on a case-by-case basis. As far as the candour argument is concerned, the government stated that this would also now be governed by the 'real damage' test. In contrast to the previous position (as endorsed, as we saw, by such senior judges as Lord Reid), the government now 'accepts that an approach to PII which claimed a kind of blanket protection for pre-defined categories of document would be wrong in principle'.[71] Inter-departmental papers and other internal government documents 'will not be the subject of a PII claim unless the responsible minister is satisfied that their disclosure would cause real damage or harm to the public interest in good government'.[72] Again, however, even the government's new approach leaves unclear precisely what this 'real' harm might be.

Overall, the changes announced by the government in December 1996 represent a remarkable improvement on the quite outrageous misuse of PII revealed by the Scott Report. No longer will government ministers make PII claims automatically. No longer will claims to PII be made solely because a document constitutes high level advice to ministers.[73] Moreover, those PII certificates which are signed by ministers will now have to 'set out in greater detail than before both what the material in question is and what damage its disclosure would, in the opinion of the minister, do'.[74] Ministers will, in short, have to be a good deal more open about their reasons for not being open.

CONCLUSION: TOWARDS GREATER FREEDOM OF INFORMATION

The new approach to ministerial claims to PII as outlined in the government's December 1996 announcement, makes it clear that PII is now an aspect of the controls on freedom of information which has to be seen (and operated) in the context of the government's *Code of Practice on Access to Government Information*. John Major's governments have done more perhaps than any other in recent times to advance the causes of freedom of information and open government. The central constitutional code of conduct for ministers, *Questions of Procedure for Ministers*, for example, even though it was first drawn up in the 1950s, was not published until 1992. In 1993 the government published a White Paper on *Open Government*,[75] and in April the following year the *Code of Practice on Access to Government Information* came into effect[76] (see also Radford, Ch. 2, p. 45).

---

71   *Ibid.*, para. 5.6.
72   *Ibid.*, para. 5.9.
73   See *ibid.*, para. 5.12.
74   *Ibid.*, para. 4.5.
75   Cm 2290, see Birkinshaw, P., *Freedom of Information: The Law, the Practice and the Ideal*, (2nd ed.) London: Butterworths, 1996, Ch. 5.
76   A second, slightly revised, edition of the Code came into effect on 1 February 1997.

This Code is extremely important. It applies to all bodies which are subject to the jurisdiction of the Parliamentary Commissioner for Administration (or ombudsman) under the Parliamentary Commissioner Act 1967. Under the Code, such bodies have an obligation, subject to a number of exemptions which are discussed below:

(a) to publish the facts and the analysis of facts which form the back-drop to government policy;

(b) to publish explanatory material on departments' dealings with the public;

(c) to give reasons for administrative decisions to those affected;

(d) to publish full information about how services are run, how much they cost, who is in charge, what complaints and redress procedures are available, what targets are set and what standards are achieved; and

(e) to release in response to specific requests information relating to government policies, actions and decisions. The commitment is to release information, not original documents.

Charges can be (and are) made by departments and other public bodies. Complaints under the Code are investigated first by the department concerned and then, where appropriate, by the ombudsman (via an MP in the usual way).

Part II of the Code lists 15 exemptions to the basic principle in favour of disclosure. Some of the exemptions are no more than one would expect and merely mirror provisions of the Official Secrets Act 1989, but others go well beyond. The exemptions are:

(a) defence, security and international relations;

(b) internal discussion and advice (the candour argument);

(c) communications with the royal household;

(d) law enforcement and legal proceedings;

(e) immigration and nationality;

(f) effective management of the economy and collection of tax;

(g) effective management and operations of the public service;

(h) public employment, public appointments and honours;

(i) voluminous or vexatious requests;

(j) information which already is, or is about to be, published;

(k) research, statistics and analysis;

(l) privacy of an individual;

(m) third parties' commercial confidences;

(n) information given in confidence; and

(o) information the disclosure of which is prohibited under statute.

The Code does not repeal any of the Acts of Parliament which, in addition to the Official Secrets Acts, provide for limitations as to government openness and publication of information.[77] Neither does it alter 'present practice covering disclosure of information before courts' (para. 10) such as PII. However, the Code does represent a positive, if limited, step towards more open government. The exemptions may be more broadly defined than one would ideally like; the powers of the ombudsman as to enforcement and publicity may be limited; and levels of public awareness (and use) of the Code may be disappointing,[78] but the picture is not an entirely bleak one. The government has at last accepted and acted on the basic principle of the importance of openness and freedom of information, and has strengthened Parliament's capabilities as regards holding the executive to account.

Parliament, in the form of the Select Committee on the Parliamentary Commissioner for Administration, has welcomed the government's Code. In an important report published in March 1996, the Committee outlined how the Code had been implemented and how it had operated in its first two years.[79] While the Committee was not without its criticisms and reservations (as to the lack of resources the government had committed to publicising the Code, and as to some of the overly broad exemptions in part II of the Code, for example), the unanimous report of the all-party Committee was largely positive, about both the need for open government and the contribution that the Code ought to make. In the committee's view, the Code is 'an important step forward which is already resulting in greater openness from government'.[80] In his evidence to the Committee, the Ombudsman, William Reid, agreed that the Code represented 'a pretty immense attitude change within the public service'.[81]

Certainly it appears that both Conservative and Labour governments have now moved on considerably from the disdain poured on notions of open government by leading judges in cases such as *Duncan* v *Cammell Laird* and *Conway* v *Rimmer*. This is borne out in the evidence of Roger Freeman MP, the Cabinet minister in John Major's government with responsibility for open government, who stated that

---

77   The White Paper which preceded the Code (Cm 2290) listed some 200 such Acts of Parliament which in many cases not only provide for limitations on openness, but which also attach criminal sanctions to acts of disclosure.

78   Only 41 complaints under the Code were made to the Ombudsman in the Code's first year. The Ombudsman stated in giving evidence to the Select Committee on the Parliamentary Commissioner for Administration that 'there remains a wholly insufficient level of awareness of the opportunities afforded by the Code to the citizen'. See Second Report from the Select Committee on the Parliamentary Commissioner for Administration, *Open Government*, HC 84, London: HMSO, 1996, para. 56.

79   This report was debated in the chamber of the House of Commons on 10 December 1996 (see *Hansard*, coll. 145*ff*). In addition to this report, the Ombudsman has also published a number of reports of adjudications he has made under the Code. The first four collections are published as HC (1994–95) 14; HC (1994–95) 606; HC (1994–95) 758 and HC (1995–96) 86.

80   *Op. cit.* note 78 *supra*, para. 127.

81   *Ibid.*, para. 23.

'it is very important [that] in government there should be a culture, a spirit of openness, because that makes for better decision making amongst civil servants and ministers,'[82] and further, that 'when you start saying, "well, we must only reveal the minimum amount of information possible to the public", and the presumption is that the public and Parliament do not have the right to know, you lead towards totalitarianism and political dictatorship'.[83] This modern executive approach is utterly different from and is much more embracing of openness in decision making than are the judicial precedents on PII which were examined above.

This has an important consequence. The Code is not a legal one enforceable through the courts. This should be seen as one of its main strengths. The story related in this chapter of the history and development of the modern law of PII has led us to a number of conclusions about freedom of information and judicial discretion. Probably the most important of these conclusions is the overwhelming feeling generated by reading the cases that, with a couple of bold exceptions (Lord Keith in *Burmah Oil* being the most notable, perhaps), English courts have not shown themselves to be terribly interested in or committed to freedom of information. The story of PII is that in our search for greater government openness we should not place too much reliance on judicial processes. Even when judicial steps in the right direction are made (as in *Burmah Oil* and in *Wiley*), it seems that they are often quickly circumvented, forgotten or erased (as in *Air Canada* and in *Taylor* v *Anderton*) and the judicial path to secrecy is more firmly marked out after a brief detour. The surprising and, for a lawyer, rather depressing lesson of the story related in this chapter is that it has been the executive branch rather than the courts which has done most in recent years to move towards greater freedom of information and more genuinely open government, albeit that the executive's actions (at least as far as PII is concerned) were initiated only after the prolonged prompting of an extraordinary three-and-a-half-year public inquiry.

If the judiciary were genuinely committed to ensuring open government and freedom of information, then the Lord Chancellor should never have been allowed to have decided *Duncan* v *Cammell Laird;* the judges should have insisted in that case that if the government objected to the disclosure of documents, then the Admiralty should have instructed the shipbuilders to concede liability and the government should have paid out compensation to the victims and their dependants. In a democracy the position should be that if the state is either unwilling or unable (by virtue of a rule of law) to produce evidence that is needed in a civil or criminal trial, then the case should be conceded or the prosecution abandoned. If judges are not prepared to go this far, then they should at least hear or see all the relevant evidence and hear argument on it in private.

---

82 *Ibid.*, para. 12.
83 *Ibid.*, para. 11.

One aspect of the decision in *Duncan v Cammell Laird* may have been overruled in 1956 and again in 1968, but until 1997 that case still cast a long, dark shadow over PII law and practice. That it was ultimately the government itself rather than the courts that — at last — initiated the move out of *Duncan's* shadow speaks volumes for the English courts' abject disregard for open government and for freedom of information. In a political climate in which once again freedom of information legislation is a real possibility, we would do well to remember the miserable part that the judges have played in English law's long struggle towards open government.

15

Civil Liberties and Judicial Review: Can the Common Law Really Protect Rights?*

Fiona Donson

SUMMARY

The traditional Diceyan approach to the protection of civil liberties in the UK has seen the role of the common law as crucial. In recent years, however, a growing level of concern has been expressed at the reduction of traditional liberties cut down by the dominance of parliamentary sovereignty. This chapter seeks to consider whether the courts are capable of establishing a renewed role for the common law in protecting civil liberties in judicial review applications, and in particular whether the adoption of fundamental human rights as a key element of the common law can provide an effective method of securing civil liberties.

INTRODUCTION: THE DICEYAN APPROACH TO PROTECTING CIVIL LIBERTIES

The traditional approach taken by the UK towards the protection of civil liberties is deeply rooted in our understanding of the common law in the constitutional context, as described by Dicey in *An Introduction to the Study of the Law of the Constitution*.[1] The protections that exist have been won and advanced by the common law. According to Dicey, the strength of the English constitution lay in the fact that it did not need to rely upon 'declarations or definitions of rights so

---

* The author would like to thank Professor Conor Gearty, Terry Woods and Peter Leyland for their comments on an earlier draft.
1 (10th ed.), London: Macmillan, 1959. First published 1885.

dear to foreign constitutionalists' as these could be, and were, capable of being suspended. Inherent in the British system, and lying at the heart of our approach today, is the idea that every subject is free to do what is not forbidden by law; and for Dicey it was exactly because such rights were not written down, but were upheld by judicial rulings and in particular the development of the common law, which made it more difficult for governments to take them away or reduce the liberties of people. The idea of the rule of law was central to this approach in that it required that no one could be punished without having first broken an express law.

The independence of the judiciary within the English constitution was therefore essential for the Diceyan approach to the protection of liberties, in that he saw their role as interpreting the language of Parliament and the executive which might result in them being 'disposed to construe statutory exceptions to common law principles in a mode which would not commend itself either to a body of officials, or to the Houses of Parliament, if the Houses were called upon to interpret their own enactments'.[2] However, the fact that parliamentary sovereignty meant that Parliament might overrule the common law and seriously undermine civil liberties was not addressed by Dicey. The problem at the heart of Dicey's approach is that by rooting the protection of civil liberties in a negative guarantee, it offers limited protections in the face of a legislature willing to create law limiting the population's liberties. As the residue of liberty decreases it leaves the courts in a position which requires them to protect civil liberties but offers little scope for action in the face of primary legislation.

The history of judicial review as a protector of civil liberties in the UK is vastly different, as a result of this constitutional approach, from that of the USA. Judicial review does not immediately seem to offer the potential for substantive constitutional adjudication. The early development of judicial review during the 17th century came from the desire of the courts to control 'inferior jurisdictions' and, where such authorities had treated an applicant in an unjust way, to provide adequate remedies.[3] However, as the power of Parliament grew and the actions of the executive multiplied, the ability of the courts to confront such power waned. It is only in the last few decades that the courts have once again faced up to the reality of political power, and sought to protect the interests and liberties of applicants from administrative power. As a result, the potential of judicial review to act as a protecting mechanism in the effort to reinforce civil liberties would appear to have grown. However, in this context the courts have not had a glowing record of intervention in aid of the public. There has been a consistent failure to

---

2   *Ibid.*, at p. 406.
3   See discussion in Craig, P.P., *Public Law and Democracy in the United Kingdom and the United States of America*, Oxford: Clarendon Press, 1990, Ch. 1 for more detail on the development of public law in the UK.

recognise civil liberties issues when they arise, for example the failure to develop ideas of privacy in the *Malone* case.[4] At times the common law has even been developed so as to diminish civil liberties, thus there has been the development of the tort of interference of rights of use of the highway by Scott J[5] in *Thomas* v *National Union of Mineworkers (South Wales Area)*,[6] when he transformed a tort which he admitted was concerned with 'activity which unduly interferes with the use and enjoyment of land', into one which could operate to protect other rights:

> All citizens have the right to use the public highway. Suppose an individual were persistently to follow another on a public highway, making rude gestures or remarks in order to annoy or vex. If continuance of such conduct were threatened no one can doubt that a civil court would, at the suit of the victim, restrain by injunction the continuance of the conduct. The tort might be described as a species of private nuisance, namely unreasonable interference with the victim's rights to use the highway.[7]

As Joan Small has pointed out in her discussion of the role of the courts in civil liberties cases:

> The judges have been placed, and to a large degree have helped to place themselves, in what some regard . . . . as an impossible position: guardians of human rights, but subject to parliamentary supremacy and under the strict injunction that they not make law, that they engage in common law adjudication, not legislation.[8]

The traditional approach to the protection of civil liberties through the common law, would therefore seem to be limited in its effectiveness. However, in recent years a number of factors have come to have a significant impact upon how the courts regard their role in relation to such adjudication. In particular, the influence of the European Convention on Human Rights (ECHR), and the European Union, has had the potential to cause a fundamental shift in the approach taken by the British courts in judicial review cases. Although the new Labour government has made a commitment to incorporate the ECHR into the law of the UK, until that policy is implemented it remains the case that the Convention, unlike the law of the European Union, is not part of the domestic law of the UK.[9] As a result it is currently not directly enforceable by the courts in this country although its

---

4   *Malone* v *Commissioner of Police of the Metropolis (No. 2)* [1979] 2 All ER 620.
5   As he then was.
6   [1985] 2 All ER 1.
7   *Ibid.*, at 22d.
8   Small, J., *The Courts and Civil Liberties*, London: Blackstone Press, 1996, at p. 87.
9   See discussion of *Brind* v *Secretary of State for the Home Department* [1991] AC 696.

principles have started to affect the way courts approach actions relating to fundamental human rights. In particular, the language of rights, although not entirely new to the High Court, has become far more prevalent in recent years.

In looking at recent trends and developments in the area of judicial involvement in civil liberties, this chapter will have regard to a number of different forums within which such changes have been developed. The case law itself shows a slow but not insignificant alteration in the approach of at least some of the judiciary when faced with difficult cases involving attempts to vindicate and enforce fundamental rights and freedoms. Moreover, this development mirrors a more dynamic debate which has been taking place amongst a small number of the judiciary and academic commentators, dealing with the question of what is the appropriate role of the courts in relation to judicial review in the area of rights-based actions. These two developments are not unaffected by the political climate and need to be considered in the light of relevant social and political factors.

WEDNESBURY UNREASONABLENESS: A PRACTICAL EXAMPLE OF HUMAN RIGHTS BASED JUDICIAL REVIEW?

Of the three main grounds of judicial review set out by Lord Diplock in *Council of Civil Service Unions* v *Minister for the Civil Service*,[10] that of irrationality (see also Fordham, Ch. 8 generally) has perhaps offered the most potential for development in the push towards a more active protection of civil liberties through the mechanism of judicial review. The principles which go to make up the modern understanding of irrationality require that the decision maker takes into account all relevant considerations and does not consider irrelevant ones. The *Wednesbury* unreasonableness test which lies at the heart of irrationality further allows the court to consider whether the decision maker has come to a conclusion that no reasonable decision maker could have reached.[11] While the traditional approach to *Wednesbury* review has been one of caution, requiring that the court emphasises its intention not to intervene in the substance of the decision,[12] an intervention which would require a political second-guessing of the 'correct' decision, recent pressures on judicial review would suggest that irrationality offers a ground which can provide a method of more invasive review.

Indeed, *Wednesbury* unreasonableness has long been seen as a concept open to development and manipulation. Its vague and circular definition has meant that it can be difficult to argue successfully in many cases, but it remains attractive to applicants who might just be successful in arguing it in their judicial review

---

10   [1985] AC 374.
11   The original test laid down by Lord Greene MR in *Associated Provincial Picture Houses Ltd* v *Wednesbury Corporation* [1948] 1 KB 223.
12   A position stressed by Lord Greene MR in his original decision, *ibid.*, at 228.

actions. However, a development towards substantive review through *Wednesbury* unreasonableness can perhaps be pinned down to the late 1980s, both in judicial decisions and in an academic approach that then took hold. Jowell and Lester, in their prominent article 'Beyond *Wednesbury*: Substantive Principles of Administrative Law',[13] criticised irrationality as being 'inadequate, unrealistic and tautologous' and argued that rather than continuing to rely on such a flawed concept, substantive judicial review should be developed openly. This development, they argued, should be based upon sound and understandable principles, for example on proportionality, and on principles of human rights.

Jowell and Lester identified a House of Lords decision which appeared to offer the potential for a change of direction for the courts, one that could take them towards substantive review. Although the traditional approach had been one which focused on 'remedies rather than the principles governing official action and individual rights', the House of Lords decision in *Bugdaycay* v *Secretary of State for the Home Department*[14] suggested a different focus. The case raised questions regarding the treatment of those seeking refugee status and required the court to consider that treatment in the context of the right to life claimed by the applicant.[15] Lord Bridge stated that the courts were entitled, within limits:

. . . to subject an administrative decision to the more rigorous examination, to ensure that it is in no way flawed, according to the gravity of the issue which the decision determines. The most fundamental of all human rights is the individual's right to life and when an administrative decision under challenge is said to be one which may put the applicant's life at risk, the basis of the decision must surely call for the most anxious scrutiny.[16]

and Lord Templeman took the view that:

. . . where the result of a flawed decision may imperil life and liberty a special responsibility lies on the court in the examination of the decision making process.[17]

Such an approach has been described as 'sub-*Wednesbury*'[18] and, as we shall see, has been enthusiastically argued by applicants in their attempts to challenge decisions which impact upon fundamental human rights.[19]

---

13   [1987] *Public Law* 368.
14   [1987] 1 All ER 940.
15   Under the 1951 Geneva Convention Relating to the Status of Refugees.
16   [1987] 1 All ER 940, at 952.
17   *Ibid.*, at 956.
18   Norris, M., '*Ex parte Smith*: Irrationality and Human Rights' [1996] *Public Law* 90. Note that there is also the concept of 'super-*Wednesbury*' which limits the ability of the courts to subject a decision to *Wednesbury* review. See decision of House of Lords in *Nottinghamshire CC* v *Secretary of State for the Environment* [1986] AC 240.
19   See discussion of *Ex parte Smith*, below.

In considering how irrationality should be developed to allow such critical review, Jowell and Lester made it clear that despite the fact that the European Convention was not incorporated into the law of the UK, it was nevertheless the case that:

> . . . the exercise of public powers should be subject to the presumption (in the absence of compelling statutory language to the contrary) that nothing may be done by a public body which infringes the rights and freedoms guaranteed by the European Convention. . . .[20]

This view has not been adopted by the courts, however, the House of Lords in *Brind* v *Secretary of State for the Home Deparment*[21] taking the view that such an approach would amount to entrenchment 'by the back door'[22] and that only Parliament should take the decision to incorporate the Convention (see also Craig, Ch. 12, pp. 278 *et seq* for some further discussion of this case in relation to the doctrine of proportionality.

Jowell and Lester concluded their article with a comforting reminder that they were not calling for the courts to 'usurp the functions of public authorities on matters of fact, judgment or policy'. To this end they stated that:

> Our argument comes into play when a public body acts under discretionary powers. The constitutional doctrines of separation of powers and the rule of law then insist that the discretion be exercised with fidelity to the objectives of the conferred powers. They also presume that the discretion will be exercised in accordance with those independent principles of justice that are appropriate for judicial application in all other areas of common law. In the interest of the integrity of the law, these principles should now be clearly articulated by the courts.[23]

As the House of Lords had already made clear in the *Brind* case, the courts have been reluctant fully to embrace the ideas put forward by Jowell and Lester. However, this is not to suggest that they have not been moving to a more open approach to substantive review. Indeed, much of the discussion that has come after Jowell and Lester's article[24] has been published by judges experienced in judicial review cases. Thus the House of Lords decision in *Bugdaycay* can be seen as a small, but ultimately not insignificant development which has been followed in later decisions.

---

20 *Op. cit.* note 13 *supra*, at p. 379.
21 [1991] 1 AC 696.
22 *Per* Lord Donaldson, *ibid.*, at 718.
23 *Op. cit.* note 13 *supra*, at p. 382.
24 A discussion that in no way entirely embraces their views.

However, it has been suggested by Martin Norris,[25] that the approach taken by the House of Lords in *Bugdaycay* has been misunderstood. He argued that Lord Bridge was in fact 'using the *Wednesbury* principle in the sense of a decision which was bad because the decision makers had "neglected to take into account matters which they ought to [have taken] into account"' as opposed to what he stated was the more 'modern sense of irrationality' which rests on the concept that the conclusion reached was one which was 'so unreasonable that no reasonable authority could ever have come to it'. Thus Norris pointed out that Lord Bridge came to the conclusion that the decision of the Secretary of State should be quashed as information concerning previous breaches of the Convention by Kenya had not been taken into account. Norris may well be technically correct to draw a distinction between the different types of *Wednesbury* unreasonableness. Nevertheless, such distinctions quickly get forgotten when courts begin to develop an area of the law in a new and more dynamic way.

In the move towards an altered *Wednesbury* test, the House of Lords decision in *Brind v Secretary of State for the Home Department*[26] built on the decision in *Bugdaycay*, although the court rejected the argument on the status of the ECHR in domestic legal proceedings. Lord Bridge — despite his conservatism on the incorporation point — was not willing to follow the traditional course of restrictive review in the face of a limitation on the fundamental right to freedom of expression. Thus his Lordship concluded that his decision did not:

> . . . mean that in deciding whether the Secretary of State, in the exercise of his discretion, could reasonably impose the restriction he has imposed on the broadcasting organisation, we are not perfectly entitled to start from the premise that any restriction of the right to freedom of expression requires to be justified and that nothing less than an important competing public interest will be sufficient to justify it.[27]

It can be argued that such an approach takes the court away from the traditional view of the court's role and requires that it considers in what way the decision interferes with human rights. However, it could be regarded as taking the court a step further, requiring it to inquire into whether the competing public interest is 'important' enough to overtake the fundamental right.[28]

Norris pointed out that Lord Bridge did not address himself as to whether this was the practical consequence of his reasons. However, Lord Ackner did conclude that it would be wrong to lower the threshold of irrationality as this could lead the

---

25 *Op. cit.* note 18 *supra*, considering the case of *R v Ministry of Defence, ex parte Smith* [1994] 4 All ER 427 (DC); [1996] 1 All ER 257 (CA).

26 [1991] 1 AC 696, challenging the decision of the Home Secretary to ban the broadcasting of words spoken by the representatives of proscribed organisations.

27 *Ibid.*, at 748–9.

28 An approach argued for by Laws J. See discussion below.

courts into the long-considered dangerous territory of substituting their view for that of the decision maker. Only Lord Templeman felt able to state that the traditional *Wednesbury* approach needed to be adjusted in order to deal with cases involving human rights. In considering the overall approach of the House of Lords, Norris concluded that three of the five judgments took a position that the court can undertake an enhanced level of scrutiny in cases affecting human rights, but that 'they leave the standard to be applied rather ambiguous'. By doing so, they left the position of *Wednesbury* review in this area uncertain and open to development towards a more substantive form of review or able to retreat back to the traditional approach.

Not all courts have therefore assumed that the decisions in *Bugdaycay* and *Brind* allow for a radical alteration in their jurisdiction. In particular, the case of *R* v *Secretary of State for the Environment, ex parte National and Local Government Officers Association*[29] suggests that the courts continue to be reluctant to move rapidly to adopt a new position. The Court of Appeal had to consider a challenge to restrictions made by statutory instruments upon the political activities of union members who worked in local government.[30] The union had argued that such restrictions were contrary to Article 10 of the Convention. Neill LJ (expressing the unanimous view of the court) not surprisingly pointed out that Article 10 was not part of domestic law, and as a result it was not necessary for decision makers to take into account its provisions in coming to their decision. However, he stated that 'where fundamental human rights including freedom of expression are being restricted the minister will need to show that there is an important competing public interest which is sufficient to justify the restriction'. In considering the decision as to competing public interests he stated that 'the court [was] only entitled to exercise a secondary judgment by asking whether a reasonable minister, on the material before him, could reasonably make that primary judgment'. However, in examining this process, and having considered in detail the judgment of the House of Lords in *Brind,* he concluded that:

> . . . as the law stands at present it seems to me to be clear that though the minister is required to justify the restriction imposed by reference to an important and sufficient competing public interest the court, when reviewing the minister's decision, is not entitled . . . to lower 'the threshold of unreasonableness' . . . In light of the decision in *Brind* . . . I am quite satisfied that it is not open to a court below the House of Lords to depart from the traditional *Wednesbury* grounds when reviewing the decision of a Minister of the Crown who has exercised a discretion vested in him by Parliament.[31]

---

29   (1992) 5 Admin LR 785 (CA).
30   The Local Government Officers (Political Restrictions) Regulations 1990.
31   *Ex parte NALGO* (1992) 5 Admin LR 785.

This decision can be interpreted as an attempt to rein back the sub-*Wednesbury* test. However, this has not stopped applicants arguing for a lower threshold test, with lawyers such as David Pannick QC — representing the applicants in *R* v *Ministry of Defence, ex parte Smith*[32] — emphasising the 'human rights dimension' of cases to that end. Pannick QC argued that in such cases the courts should be more ready to examine the merits of the case and to require its justification by the minister. At first instance, Simon Brown LJ considered the case law, including the conclusions of Neill LJ in the *NALGO* case, and found that he shared the view of Neill LJ that 'the threshold of unreasonableness' was not lowered. However, Simon Brown LJ went on to take a *Brind*-type approach when he stated that:

> . . . the minister on judicial review will need to show that there is an important competing public interest which he could reasonably judge sufficient to justify the restriction and he must expect his reasons to be closely scrutinised. Even that approach . . . involves a more intensive review process and a greater readiness to intervene than would ordinarily characterise a judicial review challenge.[33]

Thus Simon Brown LJ stated that the appropriate approach to be taken in a challenge to the blanket policy implemented by the Ministry of Defence of discharging anyone with homosexual orientation from the armed forces, was to use 'conventional *Wednesbury* . . . adapted to a human rights context'. It could be argued that there is little difference between the approach rejected by Simon Brown LJ and that which he ultimately used. The Court of Appeal, however, was bolder in its adoption of the argument put forward by the applicants when it followed the approach set out by Pannick QC that:

> The court may not interfere with the exercise of an administrative discretion on substantive grounds save where the court is satisfied that the decision is unreasonable in the sense that it is beyond the range of responses open to a reasonable decision maker. But in judging whether the decision maker has exceeded this margin of appreciation the human rights context is important. The more substantial the interference with human rights, the more the court will require by way of justification before it is satisfied that the decision is reasonable. . . .[34]

By taking this position the court was willing to adopt an approach which ultimately does lower the threshold of irrationality and thereby allows the court to consider substantive issues as well as the traditional procedural matters. Indeed, Lord

---

32   [1995] 4 All ER 427 (QBD).
33   *Ibid.*, at 445.
34   [1996] 1 All ER 257, at 263d.

Bingham MR went so far as to say that Pannick's approach, as adopted by the court, amounted to an 'accurate distillation' of the approaches found in both *Bugdaycay* and *Brind*.

It is clear that the judgments in *Bugdaycay* and *Brind*, which led up to the decision of the Court of Appeal in *ex parte Smith*, can be interpreted either way. Whether the courts are correct in interpreting the earlier cases as developing a lower threshold of review does not ultimately matter if the sub-*Wednesbury* test becomes widely adopted by courts dealing with cases concerning fundamental rights. Indeed, as the idea has become more acceptable to the courts, the language they have used in developing this lower threshold has taken on a more confident tone. Thus although Lord Bridge talked about 'anxious scrutiny' in *Bugdaycay*, Simon Brown LJ, although suggesting that he was not adopting an interventionist sub-*Wednesbury* approach, acknowledged a need for a 'more intensive review process' and 'a greater readiness to intervene'. The development of a confident language of substantive invasive review certainly suggests that the courts have been undergoing a significant shift in their consideration of judicial review cases in the human rights context. However, a pragmatic case law development of extended review in this area, responding to the difficulties involved in each separate case, will not necessarily achieve a coherent approach to substantive review. The call for a development of such review based upon clear principles, made by Jowell and Lester in 1987, is perhaps needed more than ever given that the courts are already engaging in such review in an open manner. The fact that the courts are more open about what they are doing does not diminish the very valid concern pointed to by Jowell and Lester:

> The reluctance to articulate a principled justification naturally encourages suspicion that prejudice or policy considerations may be hiding underneath *Wednesbury's* ample cloak.[35]

We must therefore consider the attempts currently being made to develop a theory that might underpin and justify this more ambitious form of review in the human rights context.

As the above discussion indicates, many of those judges who hear judicial review cases have begun to consider more clearly the impact of fundamental rights in the context of the cases brought before them. Rights are not new to the law of England and Wales, with the recognition and protection of private property by the courts being perhaps the most obvious example from the past. Nevertheless, the growing use of the language of rights and the courts' greater willingness to think more openly about the impact of such considerations are of fundamental import-

---

35 *'Beyond Wednesbury:* Substantive Principles of Administrative Law' [1987] *Public Law* 368, at 371–2.

ance, both in the context of the protection of civil liberties and in how public law itself will develop. The type of rights now being acknowledged by the courts are strong traditional rights found in the ECHR which, although largely uncontroversial in liberal democratic constitutions, do indicate a shift from the historical common law idea of rights. As a result of the movement in the courts' understanding of claims which should be protected by the common law, their designation as 'rights' has the potential to lead the courts into considering difficult questions. Thus Kennedy LJ recognised a right to freedom of expression protected by the common law in *R* v *Radio Authority, ex parte Bull*[36] and Sedley J has held that the common law recognises a right to life, a right not be subjected to inhuman treatment, and a right to freedom of movement in *R* v *Secretary of State for the Home Department, ex parte McQuillan*.[37]

HUMAN RIGHTS AND JUDICIAL REVIEW: A COHERENT APPROACH?

The mere recognition of fundamental rights and freedoms, and a movement in the direction of sub-*Wednesbury* review, does not in itself give us a clear idea of how judicial review will develop in this area. The history of the development of public law over the last 30 years has been one of dramatic expansion in order to meet equally dramatic developments in the functions of governmental power. If, by developing a sub-*Wednesbury* approach, the judiciary are simply responding to a set of political and constitutional circumstances which they feel have left civil liberties severely damaged under the traditional common law approach, some important questions have to be raised in order to challenge this new move, lest in the rush to develop the common law the underpinning of legal principles is quietly forgotten. Lord Lester sets out only half the picture when he concludes that:

> In *Brind* . . . the House of Lords have recognised again under the indirect influence of the European convention system that stricter judicial scrutiny of administrative decisions is called for where fundamental human rights and freedoms are involved. If one reads between the lines of their speeches one can see that they are here developing important constitutional and legal principles of administrative justice.[38]

In fact thus far in the development of judicial review in this area the case law has told us very little about the development of such principles. Courts have stated that the protection of fundamental human rights 'demands' a more intensive review in

---

36   [1995] 34 All ER 481.
37   [1995] 3 All ER 400.
38   Lester, Lord, 'English Judges as Law Makers' [1993] *Public Law* 269.

the context of acknowledged 'rights claims', but by developing such 'anxious scrutiny' under the guise of *Wednesbury* review the courts cannot clearly outline the basis upon which such scrutiny takes place. Is the *Wednesbury* test now one of proportionality in this context? Has the test actually changed in the human rights context, or is it simply one more element of the fundamental malleability of the common law? As the courts have slowly built up the confidence and belief in a sub-*Wednesbury* test they have yet to set out clearly in what way judicial review principles are developing in this area. Instead we must turn our attention from the case law to extra-judicial discussion, which suggests that some senior members of the judiciary are indeed engaged in attempting to develop new ways of thinking about the protection of rights.

Sir John Laws: the development of a higher order law?

Perhaps the strongest proponent of the development of a significant new approach by the judiciary in protecting fundamental rights is Sir John Laws (see also Leyland and Woods, Ch. 17, pp. 406–11 for a discussion of the similar position of T.R.S. Allan). He has consistently seen the role of the courts in cases where rights are at stake as being one where they should not be shy in standing up for the citizen against government power. Laws's starting point in 1993[39] was that fundamental human rights, and the principles found in the European Convention, could be protected directly in the law of England and Wales through the common law. To this end he proposed two possible stances which could be adopted by the courts — positions short of incorporation, but which would allow scope for the courts to take significant regard of Convention protections. These were that the courts should either use the Convention as a text to inform the common law, or develop public law in practice by reference to it. Considering such arguments, and the relationship between the EU and the Convention, Sedley J, concluded in *R v Secretary of State for the Home Department, et parte McQuillan*[40] that:

> Once it is accepted that the standards articulated in the convention are standards which both march with those of the common law and inform the jurisprudence of the EU, it becomes unreal and potentially unjust to continue to develop English public law without reference to them.[41]

In recent articles Sir John Laws has developed his view of the judicial role in modern democracies far beyond this modest consideration of how to protect rights.

---

39   Laws, Sir J., 'Is the High Court the Guardian of Fundamental Constitutional Rights?' [1993] *Public Law* 63.
40   [1995] 3 All ER 400.
41   *Ibid.*, at 422.

In 'Law and Democracy',[42] Laws took as his starting point the idea that a democratic constitution is in fact undemocratic if it gives all the power to elected government. Thus he saw the judiciary as having a fundamental role in the protection of individual rights. He argued that this role strengthens rather than weakens a country's democracy, and as a result adopts a liberal individual model of democracy. Although Laws made no direct reference to a theory of rights, his preference for a model which centres upon individuals and seems to reject the role of the state as protector of those individuals in their rights claims seems to suggest that he adopted Nozick's view of liberal theory which sees a society as consisting of individuals, each having their own interests and coming together only to develop society's rules.[43]

In having regard to the potential scope of judicial review to allow judges to undertake this task, without requiring the incorporation of the ECHR, Laws looked to the possible development of judicial review beyond the traditional constitutional and legal limits associated with public law in England and Wales. The solution for Laws arises in the development of the principles of unreasonableness and fairness which, he argues, are in fact judicial creations of standards of behaviour. Thus he concluded that a large part of the grounds of judicial review does not flow from the traditional source of judicial review, i.e. that public bodies must be kept within their limits of authority given by Parliament. In effect he rejected the *ultra vires* doctrine as the basis for judicial review,[44] declaring that unreasonableness and fairness 'have nothing to do with the intention of Parliament, save as a fig-leaf to cover their true origins. We do not need the fig-leaf any more'.[45] As a result, Laws concluded that the substantive principles of judicial review are judge-made; that they confine the scope within which discretionary decisions can be taken under statute; that the principles involved are 'morally colourless', amounting to 'ethical ideals as to the virtuous conduct of the state's affairs'; and that limits of the jurisdiction are set by the ideal that 'all public bodies should keep within the power which the law accords to them'. He is drawing out principles upon which judicial review is based which flow from an alternative rooting of judicial power. The concepts of acceptable 'standards of behaviour' and 'ethical ideals [of] virtuous conduct' offer alternative principles allowing a more dynamic and honest development of substantive review.

It would seem that Sir John Laws is looking for an extended power of judicial review in order that the judges can develop a systematic and principled protection

---

42   [1995] *Public Law* 72.

43   Nozick, R., *Anarchy, State and Utopia*, Oxford: Blackwell, 1972.

44   An argument I do not intend to get into here. For a detailed discussion of whether *ultra vires* remains the basis of judicial review, see Forsyth, C., 'Of Fig Leaves and Fairy Tales: The *Ultra Vires* Doctrine, the Sovereignty of Parliament and Judicial Review' (1996) 55 *Cambridge Law Journal* 122.

45   *Op. cit.* note 42 *supra*, at p. 79.

of what he sees as constitutional rights. He has argued that the concept of fundamental rights ought in principle to affect the extent to which democratic power is exercised, ensuring that such power is not 'absolute'; he takes freedom of expression as a central example. Only by guaranteeing such rights can a constitution 'honestly' maintain its credentials as an instrument allowing legitimate rule of a country.

Having concluded that the courts must therefore protect fundamental rights and freedoms for the sake of democracy in the UK, Laws reasoned that in order to achieve this we need a system of 'higher order law' which cannot be abrogated in the same way that ordinary laws can be by primary statute under the principle of parliamentary sovereignty. This is a position Stephen Sedley has described as 'a plea for judicial supremacism',[46] a view which, if correct, could seriously undermine a claim for rights protections via the courts in a country which has historically been cynical of claims by the courts to be protectors of the people. While recognising that democracy requires that the will of the people confers power, Laws restated that:

> . . . the fundamental sinews of the constitution, the cornerstones of democracy and of inalienable rights, ought not by law to be in the keeping of the government, because the only means by which these principles may be enshrined in the state is by their possessing a status which no government has the right to destroy.[47]

Thus the role of the courts, for Laws, is required by the theory that government operates under law. What is clear, however, is that he is unable to reject fully the criticism of Sedley; neither is it fully clear that he feels the need to do so.

Laws has, however, felt obliged to find some way of circumventing the apparent demands of parliamentary sovereignty. In order to do this he has called upon the work of Sir William Wade who, writing in 1955,[48] argued that parliamentary sovereignty is a judge-made principle. It is a constitutional norm which is 'in the keeping of the courts', a point Laws illustrated by referring to the fact that in recent years the judiciary have 'assumed the truth of the doctrine' and have required no argument on the point in court. He has therefore found himself able to come to argue that there is actually nothing to stop the courts ruling that a statute is invalid if it is inconsistent with fundamental rights or democracy. On this basis, Laws concluded that the doctrine of parliamentary sovereignty is conferred by a higher order law, and cannot be conferred by statute. As a result he has stated that a higher order law must also, 'of necessity', limit parliamentary sovereignty. From these

---

46   See discussion below.
47   *Op. cit.* note 42 *supra*, at p. 85.
48   Wade, H.W.R., 'The Basis of Legal Sovereignty' (1955) 14 *Cambridge Law Journal* 172.

arguments Laws concluded that Parliament possesses 'political sovereignty' but not 'constitutional sovereignty':

> Ultimate sovereignty rests, in every civilized constitution, not with those who wield governmental power, but in the conditions under which they are permitted to do so. The constitution, not Parliament, is in this sense sovereign. In Britain these conditions should now be recognised as consisting in a framework of fundamental principles which include the imperative of democracy itself and those other rights, prime amongst them freedom of expression, which cannot be denied save by a plea of guilty to totalitarianism.[49]

This approach fits with that suggested by T.R.S. Allan in his book *Law, Liberty and Justice: The Legal Foundations of British Constitutionalism*,[50] where he argued that legislation enacted to destroy some part of the fundamental element of the country's democracy[51] 'could not consistently be applied by the courts as law' on the basis that:

> Judicial obedience to the statute in such (unlikely) circumstance could not coherently be justified in terms of the doctrine of parliamentary sovereignty since the statute would violate the political principle which the doctrine itself enshrines. The practice of judicial obedience to statute obviously cannot itself be based on the authority of statute: it can only reflect judicial understanding of what (in contemporary conditions) political morality demands. The limits of that practice of obedience must therefore be constituted by boundaries of that morality. An enactment which threatened the essential elements of any plausible conception of democratic government would lie beyond those boundaries. It would forfeit, by the same token, any claim to be recognized as law.[52]

Lord Woolf, Master of the Rolls, has also expressed a view that fits within this understanding of parliamentary sovereignty in stating that the courts might be justified in refusing to recognise and give effect to legislative action which would undermine the rule of law by either removing or impairing the powers of the High Court to undertake judicial review.[53]

---

49 *Op. cit.* note 42 *supra*, at p. 92.
50 Oxford: Clarendon Press, 1993.
51 The example he gives is the removal of the vote from a substantial element of society on the basis that they were hostile to government policies.
52 Allan, *op. cit.* note 50 *supra*, at p. 282.
53 Woolf, Lord, '*Droit Public* — English Style' [1995] *Public Law* 57. See also Lord Woolf's judgment in *R* v *Secretary of State for the Home Department, ex parte Fayed* [1997] 1 All ER 228, where he held that despite the fact that statute explictly stated that reasons need not be given, fairness demanded the giving of such reasons.

The role the judiciary must play in the system as set out by Laws is that of 'the last resort' by which it seeks to guarantee that the framework is 'vindicated'. This does not mean that the judiciary can intrude into the affairs of Parliament, or that they should behave in a party political way. Instead Laws sees their role as being to 'protect values which no democratic politician could honestly contest: values which, therefore, may be described as apolitical'.[54]

Clearly the approach taken by Laws goes far beyond the current sub-*Wednesbury* form of review. It sets out an ambitious claim for a new form of judicial power and constitutional understanding. However, Laws has consistently failed to set out which rights and freedoms he sees as being fundamental and therefore as in some way operating as part of his 'higher order law'. The only example offered to the reader is that of freedom of expression. This can be seen as a somewhat easy option. When talking about fundamental constitutional rights, the argument for protecting the right to free speech falls neatly into the democratic ideal requiring important but widely accepted limits upon its operation.[55] It can be seen in the context of calls for open government and freedom of information legislation, and therefore lies at the heart of democratic protection. Freedom of expression is also well established in the jurisprudence of rights demanding little new thinking on the part of the judiciary. As an example of rights to be protected by higher order law it does not offer the reader any indication of where that leaves other potential rights, or whether Laws recognises a hierarchy of rights within the constitutional system.

Laws makes some attempt to offer an answer to these questions in his article: 'The Constitution: Morals and Rights'.[56] He identifies two competing sets of rights — the first are negative and are those rights embodying individual freedoms; the second are positive rights, in which he includes those that are advanced by policy the aim of which is to maximise 'human potential'. Laws recognises that there are tensions between the two types of rights, particularly where strains arise between the courts and Parliament. He also recognises that the reach of 'compulsory negative rights' is not fixed; that there are circumstances in which negative rights can be 'overridden by the claims of positive rights'; and that 'the enjoyment of negative rights very often depends on achievement or standards in the field of positive rights'.

According to Laws, the scope of the court's responsibility is to protect a 'class of compulsory, constitutional laws', those he designates as negative rights; while the government's role is to consider 'the class of optional laws', those being the positive rights, which may in some circumstances overrule the negative claims.

---

54 *Op. cit.* note 42 *supra*, at p. 93.
55 Although I am not suggesting that it is free from controversy! Thus issues such as pornography and hate speech give rise to difficult questions regarding the scope of freedom of expression.
56 [1996] *Public Law* 622. A version of a lecture he gave in honour of Lord Mischon at UCL.

However, Laws will go no further than making clear that in the negative realm he is considering the basic approach of minimal interference with people: 'Negative rights are founded on the moral rule that every individual is to be treated as an end, not a means. Hence the principle of minimal interference. . . .'[57] In this way Laws is building upon his previous works embodying a fundamental liberal approach to rights. In 'The Constitution: Morals and Rights' he makes direct reference to Kant in setting out his view that while the 'good constitution' recognises equal rights, the idea of equal rights 'is a consequence of man's shared morality, not a defining feature of it'. The sovereign autonomy of the individual is crucial to his approach therefore, with the individual being an 'end . . . never a means'.[58]

If the starting point for a just constitution lies with the recognition of the autonomy of the individual, Laws has argued that the rule of law embodies the notion of minimal interference in its idea of freedom. By taking an approach that the rule of law is substantive in nature, rather than formal, he can therefore conclude that it 'colours the substance of what the law should be'.

Sir John Laws recognises that a significant difficulty lies in how the tension between positive and negative rights is to be resolved. He has set out the starting point as being the assumption that there is 'a bias in favour of individual freedom' which requires that an 'objective justification' will be needed for the positive right to overrule it: '. . . freedom is not to be interfered with save so far as necessary to protect the rights — including the negative rights — and freedoms of others.'[59] The ability of positive rights to limit negative ones is set out by Sir John Laws as arising either where the limitation is justified because unrestricted enjoyment of the relevant right 'threatens, albeit indirectly, the conditions in which citizens generally may enjoy the freedoms guaranteed by negative rights', or where the gain for positive rights, when measured against the interference with negative rights, is substantial enough that the negative should give way to the positive. To illustrate the latter limitation Laws points to the system of planning control which has operated since the 1940s controlling the right to dispose of one's property. The individual's ability to do as he or she wishes with his or her private property is limited by the public interest requirements set out by government, which seek to control land use for the benefit of health, economic, community and environmental interests.

Laws recognised that some rights are weaker, and therefore less important, than others. Consequently, the assessment of what interference is justified will vary from right to right, and therefore from situation to situation. However, once again

---

57 *Ibid.*, at 633.
58 See Irvine, Lord, 'Response to Sir John Law' [1996] *Public Law* 636. Note that Laws's focus on Kant links in with his earlier discussion apparently following Nozick's liberal approach.
59 *Op. cit.* note 56 *supra*, at p. 634.

we are provided with little real explanation on the part of the author as to which rights he would view as necessarily strong and which are weak. To argue, as Laws does, that our understanding of rights comes from a shared morality is to fail to face up to the issue. In what way does a complex secular society have a shared morality which is identifiable and enforceable by the judiciary? Can it seriously be argued that we all share a common idea of what should be seen as being positive and negative rights? While Laws recognises that the boundary between the two is blurred, he understates the difficulties which will face the courts when having to decide such problems. As Lord Irvine has pointed out in his response to Laws:[60]

> Some may see the right to a good education as a positive right; others may claim that it is an essential component of, say, the right to freedom of speech, since without education, we are disabled from communicating our opinions to others effectively.[61]

Ex parte B — Substantive review in action
These difficulties were to face Sir John Laws in the courtroom when he had the opportunity to implement his approach in the particularly difficult case of *R* v *Cambridge Health Authority, ex parte B*.[62] B's father applied for judicial review of a decision by the health authority not to fund treatment offered to B, a 10-year-old girl, in the private sector following a decision that further treatment would not be in the child's interests.[63] In the High Court, Laws J attempted to subject the decision of the health authority to 'hard look' scrutiny. Thus his starting point for considering the challenge was that the jurisprudence of the common law of England had developed such that:

> . . . certain rights, broadly those occupying a central place in the European Convention on Human Rights and obviously including the right to life, are not to be perceived merely as moral or political aspirations nor as enjoying a legal status only upon the international plane of this country's convention obligations. They are to be vindicated as sharing with other principles the substance of the English common law. Concretely, the law requires that where a public body enjoys a discretion whose exercise may infringe such a right, it is not to be permitted to perpetrate any such infringement unless it can show a substantial objective justification on public interest grounds. The public body is the first

---

60 *Op. cit.* note 58 *supra.*
61 *Ibid.,* at p. 638.
62 (1995) 25 BMLR 5; [1995] 2 All ER 129 (CA).
63 The chances of the treatment being successful were regarded by the medics as being 'slim'. The cost to the authority of this 'extra contractual referral' was put at £15,000 for the initial chemotherapy, and a further £60,000 for a bone marrow transplant if the chemotherapy proved successful.

judge of the question whether such a justification exists. The court's role is secondary.[64]

To this end he argued that *Bugdaycay* and *Brind* 'pointed the way to a developing feature of domestic jurisprudence relating to fundamental rights which should be regarded as having a secure home in the common law'.

Concluding that the case dealt with B's 'fundamental right to life', Laws J, following his position that the common law should protect such a right, argued that *Wednesbury* unreasonableness was perhaps no longer the 'decisive touchstone' by which the legality of the decision should be judged. As a result he concluded that two questions should be considered by him: first, whether the respondent authority had taken a decision which interfered with the applicant's right to life; and, if he concluded that this had been the case, secondly, whether it had provided a substantial public interest justification for doing so. Although Cambridge Health Authority had argued that it was taking no positive act that violated B's right to life but had merely made a decision based upon the allocation of public funds, Laws J concluded that there was in effect no difference between a positive act and an omission when considering the obligations of a public body. Given that he had answered the initial question in the affirmative, Laws J therefore had to look at the reasons put forward by the health authority in support of its decision. The decision clearly affected the life chances of B, and a claim to the limitation of resources was, in his opinion, inadequate.

Cambridge Health Authority had argued that the treatment would not be an efficient use of resources as the authority's budget for funding extra contractual referrals was limited and therefore the needs of other patients, both present and future, had to be taken into account. However, Laws J dismissed such claims stating that 'merely to point to the fact that resources were finite told one nothing about the wisdom or the legality of the decision'. The authority had presented no evidence as to its budget and so, in the court's view, 'where the question was whether the life of a girl aged 10 might be saved by however slim a chance the responsible authority had to do more than toll the bell of tight resources'. What was expected of the authority was an explanation of the priorities that had led it to decide not to fund treatment. Laws J therefore granted *certiorari* and stated that the appropriate action to be taken by the authority was that it should re-take the decision in the light of his judgment.

By deciding that the fundamental issue at stake in the case was the right to life, it is not surprising that Laws J should have come to the conclusion that the health authority had not done enough to show that scarce resources should be a sufficient reason to overrule the right to life of a 10-year-old child. However, the case

---

64   (1995) 25 BMLR 5, at 12.

illustrates the particular problems inherent in the approach adopted by Laws J, both in his essays and in this judgment. Faced with a decision requiring a balancing of resources, medical ethics and public law, where the point at which the decision is taken does not fall easily to be identified within the typical approach taken by the court, the questions to be considered are particularly hard and require a strong and well accepted view of the appropriate role of the court. It might be argued that Laws J was adopting a proportionality test, considering whether the decision maker could justify its decision in a balancing process by ensuring that it did not do 'more harm than good' in coming to its conclusions. Clearly a more substantive approach to *Wednesbury* review can begin to resemble a proportionality test; but by adopting the mechanism without being honest about the process and considering the potential principles underpinning that approach, the review process is particularly difficult.

While Laws J at first instance had taken a bold approach to the difficult questions raised, the Court of Appeal ultimately adopted a more traditional view of its role in reviewing the decision of the health authority. Thus Sir Thomas Bingham MR concluded that Laws J had failed to recognise the realities of the situation before the court. The Court of Appeal found that the High Court had gone too far in requiring the health authority to justify its use of resources:

> . . . it would be totally unrealistic to require the authority to come to court with its accounts and seek to demonstrate that if this treatment were to be provided for B then there would be a patient, C, who would have to go without treatment. No major authority could run its financial affairs in a way which would permit such a demonstration.[65]

As a result of this approach, Sir Thomas Bingham MR found that he could not fault the decision making process of the authority and, although commenting that he felt great sympathy for B and her family, he clearly concluded that an attempt to involve the court in 'a field of activity where it is not fitted to make any decision favourable to the patient' was misguided.

The approach taken by the Court of Appeal was the traditional one that the court's role was to rule upon the lawfulness of the decision. Any decision on the allocation of resources was not one in which Sir Thomas Bingham MR felt the court should be involved. Thus whilst Laws J took a dramatic step towards substantive review in a hard case, the Court of Appeal confined itself to the traditionally limited grounds of review, rejecting even the *Brind* approach of requiring the decision maker to demonstrate that the decision was substantively justifiable to the court. A change in the approach of the courts which in some way

---

65   [1995] 2 All ER 129 at 137.

limits the level of discretion held by bodies such as health authorities is not a necessarily negative development. However, if this does occur the courts will of necessity become involved in hard questions, the like of which they have traditionally claimed to lack the expertise to deal with. It is not beyond the courts' ability to adopt a sensible approach to balancing and assessing the competing decisions which go to make up a discretionary decision making process. The European concept of proportionality, largely rejected in *Brind* because of its tendency to lead a court to consider the merits of a decision, offers a pre-existing mechanism, rooted in straightforward principles, which the courts could effectively utilise in difficult cases. However, although it has seen some acceptance in European law cases, it remains largely sidelined by the decision in *Brind*.[66]

Stephen Sedley: a left-of-centre perspective on substantive review

An alternative approach to substantive human rights review was offered by Sir Stephen Sedley, in his article 'Human Rights: a Twenty-First Century Agenda'.[67] He identified the developing culture of 'judicial assertiveness' as operating in a context where it compensates for 'and in places repair[s], dysfunctions in the democratic process'. Sedley concluded from the developments in recent cases that the courts could either draw back into the traditional form of review, or instead develop the role they have already started to adopt in the area of rights culture. However, Sedley did not wholeheartedly embrace rights adjudication as being a purely positive process, and therefore highlighted the view that the move towards the courts adopting a rights-based approach to judicial review is not without its dangers. Indeed, he acknowledged that 'human rights can be treated as commodities and, like commodities, appropriated by those who have the means to do so'. Thus, when considering why freedom of expression is always 'at the head of the queue for rights adjudication', he came to the conclusion that 'it is because for the mass media free speech is a valuable commodity and litigation a worthwhile investment in it'.[68]

Being cautious of the potential pitfalls that rights can throw up, Sedley focused on the idea of a 'rights instrument' operating 'to address in its terms the imbalances and appropriations of power which threaten the values — possibly even the meaning — of democracy'. To this end he argued that substantive equality before the law is the best method to protect democracy and to prevent 'the appropriation of legal rights and democratic processes for private and partial ends'. Sedley

---

66 The decision in *R* v *Secretary of State for the Environment, ex parte NALGO* (1992) Admin LR 785, was that other than in European law cases, and some limited contexts, when proportionality could be applied, it was not open to the courts to depart from the traditional grounds of judicial review when reviewing the exercise of a minister's discretion.
67 [1995] *Public Law* 386.
68 *Ibid.*, at p. 396.

therefore concluded that for the law to develop towards seriously protecting human rights, it would be necessary for 'the jurisprudence of substantive race and gender equality' to be developed:

> . . . so as to distinguish between the strong and the weak as claimants of fundamental rights and to avoid . . . a culture in which self-respect and human dignity depend upon being in a position to make strident, querulous and adversarial claims.[69]

Sedley therefore does not conclude that the traditional liberal model of rights protection will in itself solve the problems of inequalities within society. Given the current debate on the introduction of a bill of rights into the UK constitution, this is a suggestion rarely heard. As Sedley himself commented, 'It is . . . plain . . . as the end of the century approaches that the argument for a bill of rights for the United Kingdom is being won by its proponents'.[70] However, the danger of wholeheartedly embracing the liberal model of rights protection as a solution to the current problems in the context of civil liberties in the UK is that it potentially stifles debate about the general health of our democracy. While the incorporation of the ECHR is seen as the easiest solution to the status of human rights protection — especially given that UK citizens are already 'protected' by it in the international forum of the European Court of Human Rights — Sedley pointed to a bigger challenge facing the courts:

> The path I hope we shall follow in this country is therefore not simply that of the European Convention with its inevitable historical limitations, but that of a juridical culture which does not imagine that the poorest citizen is made equal to the richest corporation simply by according both the same rights; which does not co-opt the powerless into the opposition of the powerful to the state; which perceives the role of power in determining who gets to drink first and longest at the well; and which understands above all that in every society fundamental human rights, to be real, have to steer towards outcomes which invert those inequalities of power that mock the principle of equality before the law.[71]

Lord Irvine responds: is substantive review necessary?

Set against arguments that the courts might be justified in refusing to recognise and give effect to legislative action which would undermine the rule of law by either removing or impairing the powers of the High Court to undertake judicial review,

---

69   *Ibid.*, at p. 399, making reference to Waldron, J., *Nonsense on Stilts*, London: Methuen, 1987.
70   See discussion in 'Conclusion' below.
71   *Op. cit.* note 67 *supra*, at p. 400.

is the more traditional approach adopted by Lord Irvine, the Lord Chancellor. He starts from a position of judicial self-restraint, requiring the traditional deference to the sovereignty of Parliament. According to this approach, which combines both sovereignty and the separation of powers, it is a necessary part of the constitution that the powers which are given by Parliament to another body should not actually be exercised by the courts. This combines with the non elected nature of the judiciary to require the courts ultimately to defer to the elected part of the democratic system. While such arguments are strongly rooted in our traditional understanding of the nature of the UK constitution, they do not meet the concern, which arguably gives rise to the move towards substantive review, that the elected parts of the system are in fact failing to protect the fundamental rights and democratic interests of the people. Irvine dismisses what he considers to be the extreme nature of the claims made by the proponents of active review whom he regards as making:

> . . . an exorbitant claim that could only even be advanced were the courts ever to be presented with parliamentary decisions that were inconsistent with the fundamental tenets of a free democracy and therefore unworthy of judicial restraint.[72]

Are we therefore to conclude that if Lord Irvine was confronted with a particularly anti-democratic piece of government legislation he too would be willing to contemplate an extended form of judicial review? He does not answer such a question, preferring to deny the realistic possibility of such action. However, the difference between the traditional approach adopted by Irvine and that supported by those whom he sees as overreacting, may simply be a matter of degree. The level of concern and unhappiness on the part of Laws, Sedley, and Woolf may genuinely be seen as arising in a context within which they consider that there is no alternative but for them to act to protect the weak from excessive, 'unreasonable' public decision making in the realm of civil liberties. Irvine, as a political member of the legislature and member of the executive, sees the position as far less desperate and ultimately rejects the need for the judiciary to step in to repair and protect the democratic institutions of the UK. The courts, on the other hand, have found themselves regarding an executive in Parliament which has become less responsive and has been able to pass laws which have had a negative impact upon civil liberties. They therefore see themselves as being the final guardians of civil liberties, with the scope to develop their judicial review powers in a direction that will have an impact upon the situation — a development which has become necessary as a result of Parliament's own actions.

---

72   Irvine, Lord, 'Judges and Decision-Makers: The Theory and Practice of *Wednesbury* Review' [1996] *Public Law* 59, at p. 77.

The political context within which this legal and constitutional discussion is taking place emphasises and explains some of the current pressures being felt by the courts. The fall of the Soviet Union and the shift in the type of political debate which has followed the collapse of the Communist bloc — that being one in which political ideological differences have significantly declined — have seen many groups within society feeling marginalised and excluded from the democratic processes, regarding them as self-serving and unable to respond to alternative claims and pressures. As a result it would seem that an increasing number of such groups are seeking alternative mechanisms and processes to both protect and further their political and ideological ends. As political and democratic avenues have closed to such groups, the courts have been one of the few institutional routes left open to them.[73] The constitutional structures so praised by Dicey, and trusted by Irvine, appear to many, including many members of the judiciary, to be no longer able to function in order to protect democratic human rights.

CONCLUSION

The movement currently being made by the courts in the direction of substantive review, when considered in the light of political and legal developments, is fully understandable. While the impetus comes from frustration, it can also be seen as reflecting a new way of thinking that the courts have learnt from their experiences dealing with cases involving law from the European Union as well as the European Convention. If the ECHR is ultimately incorporated into the law of the UK, a commitment made by the Labour government, then some form of substantive judicial review in the rights context will become part of the law of the UK. In their consultation document *Bringing Rights Home*,[74] Jack Straw and Paul Boateng illustrate the dominance of liberalism in the current debate when they do not even feel it necessary to argue that incorporation will benefit civil liberties in the UK. As Professors Ewing and Gearty point out in their response to the Labour Party's paper,[75] such an assumption cannot be made with any certainty.

Recent case law which has utilised the Convention has not necessarily resulted in a move towards review which is sensitive to civil liberties claims. Thus the

---

73 The courts have at times been seen as one such route, for example in environmental litigation such as the challenges over the East London River Crossing — *Greenwich LBC and Others* v *Secretary of State for the Environment and Another* [1993] Times Law Reports 104 — and the M3 through Twyford Down — *Twyford Parish Council* v *Secretary of State for Transport* (1992) 4 JEL 273. A more dramatic, and arguably more successful, tactic has been the use of direct action. See, for example, the protests over the building of the M3 at Twyford Down; the Newbury by-pass; live animal exports.

74 See the Labour Party's Consultation Paper, *Bringing rights home: Labour's plans to incorporate the European Convention on Human Rights into UK law*, Jack Straw MP and Paul Boateng MP, published 18 December 1996.

75 Ewing, K., and Gearty, C., 'Rocky Foundations for Labour's New Rights' (1997) 2 EHRLR 146.

decision of the High Court in *Director of Public Prosecutions* v *Jones*,[76] that a prohibition order preventing the holding of trespassory assemblies within four miles of Stonehenge made under the public order provisions of the Criminal Justice and Public Order Act 1994 extended to any demonstration held in the area on the public highway, even if such a demonstration was peaceful and unobstructive. The court concluded that the provision did not infringe a person's right to assembly under the law of Britain, nor did Collins J think it was contrary to the freedom of assembly protection embodied in the ECHR.

The incorporation of the ECHR will offer a level of certainty as to the type of rights to be protected by the court, albeit that they are limited in nature.[77] Thus Ewing and Gearty point out that

> Despite carefully fostered appearances to the contrary, the European Convention is a deeply ideological document. Incorporation would guarantee supremacy to its narrowly individualistic view of society and would then make it impossible or extremely difficult to undermine or overthrow this ideology through the ordinary process. As such it represents the triumph of liberalism over socialism and as such fixes that triumph irrevocably into the constitution.[78]

However, the current attempts being made by the judiciary to find a solution to oppressive public decision making lead us into a pragmatic world of review where the nature and development of rights is uncertain and subject to the whims of judicial influence.

The common law has not had the best of records in protecting emerging concepts of rights, being forced to develop only when the push towards change has become irresistible.[79] In such a context, which rights should be considered strong and demanding of the highest protection are unclear. Sir John Laws's attempt to distinguish between positive and negative rights does not offer us any greater understanding of how the courts might approach the difficult questions which operate along the borderline.

Although Sir Stephen Sedley pointed to the fact that the Indian High Court has protected the right to 'an unpolluted environment', developed from the constitutional right to life, he also noted that such a move is based less on 'what a society can afford than on what it cannot afford'. However, it may take many cases before a court in the UK recognises that it can no longer deny a claim of a right to environmental justice. The experience of environmental protesters before the UK

---

76   (1997) 147 NLJ 162.
77   Although it would remain to be seen how the British courts would interpret and develop the concept of the 'margin of appreciation' in the domestic context.
78   *Op. cit.* note 75 *supra.*
79   See, for example, in the criminal context the decision of the House of Lords in *R* v *R* [1991] 4 All ER 481, overturning the marital rape exception.

courts in recent years does not suggest that there is an understanding on the part of the judiciary of what such a claim entails.[80] The courts are therefore left to uphold the *status quo* of the common law which they developed and which tends to reflect the dominant political ideology of the decision makers.[81]

Even when the courts attempt to ensure a balance between competing interests, they tend to fall within the traditional political processes and understandings. Thus in *R v Chief Constable of Sussex, ex parte International Traders' Ferry Ltd*,[82] Kennedy LJ considered the balance between ITF's freedom to trade and the public interest in preserving law and order. The court did recognise that the Chief Constable had had to also consider a third competing interest of animal rights, but did not appear to regard it as being of the same significance in its own consideration of the decision making process. However, when faced with difficult conflicts the courts may even fail to consider alternative claims. In *R v Coventry CC, ex parte Phoenix Aviation*,[83] the court protected the 'right to trade'[84] of the applicants, in the face of protests seeking to demand animal rights. While there is no doubt that a right to carry on one's own trade is a protectable right, the court made no reference, or any attempt, to consider in what context such a right might be limited by competing interests and rights.

A reluctance to see the courts undertake a developed substantive review process in the context of civil liberties may find its starting point in the fear that the courts cannot be trusted and that judges are out of touch.[85] However, recent developments in the area of judicial review, and the high profile battle between senior members of judiciary and Michael Howard, the former Home Secretary, over the previous government's policy on mandatory sentences for serious repeat offenders, have gone a long way to improve the reputation of the courts as fighters for rights. Nevertheless, the victory of liberalism over other ideological perspectives of democratic accountability does not necessarily lead to a conclusion that increased rights review will solve the problems of the UK constitution. A pragmatic development of the common law responding to rights claims in the judicial review context is a reactive and potentially limited process given the extent of the pressures within the democratic system. This is not to suggest that the courts

---

80   See, for example, the decision in *Twyford Parish Council* v *Secretary of State for Transport* (1992) 4 JEL 273. where the High Court held that the applicants should have 'suffered' before being allowed to rely upon the Environmental Impact Directive; a conclusion based upon a fundamental misunderstanding of the law of the EU.

81   Thus in the planning process it can be argued that the dominant ideologies operating in court decisions are those of private property and public interest. See McAuslan, P., *The Ideologies of Planning Law*, London: Pergamon Press, 1980.

82   (1997) *The Times*, 12 February (CA).

83   [1995] 3 All ER 37. Simon Brown LJ adopted an interventionist role in protecting and upholding the rule of law, in the same way the courts have been seeking to protect fundamental rights.

84   A right under European law.

85   See Griffith, J.A.G., *The Politics of the Judiciary* (5th ed.), London: Fontana Press, 1997.

cannot improve the status of civil liberties in many areas,[86] but rather that such an improvement will be fixed in a liberal perspective of human rights as interpreted by courts faced with complex polycentric disputes. Despite the desire of the courts to act in the civil liberties context to repair a damaged democratic system, the common law remains a deeply conservative law-making process. It could be argued that the courts are condemned inevitably to uphold the *status quo*, leaving the field open to others and that the actions of activists such as the anti-road protesters and the 'McLibel' defendants can therefore be seen as achieving more to champion and protect civil liberties and constitutional rights in the UK.

---

86 Thus in the House of Lords decision in *Derbyshire County Council* v *Times Newspapers Ltd* [1993] 1 All ER 1011, freedom of speech was protected by the common law to the same extent as under ECHR, Article 10, although it was a decision which was not based upon the existence of the ECHR.

16

Public Law History and Theory: Some Notes Towards a New Foundationalism: Part 1

Peter Leyland and Terry Woods

SUMMARY

Within the overall framework of an exploration of the possibility of a new grounding for administrative law, this chapter seeks to reassert the necessity of viewing public law in historical and theoretical perspective, a task which necessarily involves critically assessing the impact of Dicey and the functionalist response to his ideas.

INTRODUCTION

> When philosophy paints its grey in grey, then has a shape of life grown old. By philosophy's grey in grey it cannot be rejuvenated but only understood. The owl of Minerva spreads its wings only with the falling of the dusk.[1]

The deservedly famous remarks of Hegel, writing in 1821, point to the difficulties inherent in the theorisation of any area of human activity, including law. If legal history and theory are seeking to apprehend a reality lying outside of itself, an empirically existing reality of a working legal-administrative process, then how is this to be achieved? Is it indeed only too likely, as Hegel suggests, that any attempt

---

1 See Knox, T.M. (ed.), *Philosophy of Right*, Oxford: Oxford University Press, 1942, p. 13; also Inwood, M.J. (ed.), *Hegel: Selections*, New York: Macmillan, 1989, p. 287. See also Avineri, S., *Hegel's Theory of the Modern State*, Cambridge: Cambridge University Press, 1972.

to do so will always be in the position of running to catch up with ever-changing circumstances — capturing the world as a particular configuration in camera when this configuration has already (or is about to) come to an end? Can we ever give theoretical shape to administrative law in a form which will command both the attention and agreement of those working in the field? And scholars generally? Or is any such attempt doomed to failure, leaving us with theory as inevitably unrealised opportunity? Karl Marx criticised theoreticians for only interpreting the world, but the question for us is: can human reflection on what exists even do that?

What is our perspective on law?

At the outset, our own position is that more than lip service must be paid to the proposition that we should view the law in context. Law as such, *qua* law, does not actually exist severed from a clear relationship to historical, political, social, economic, philosophical, mythopoeic and aesthetic domains. That is, to situated and structured material and mental relationships. Each moment of legal consciousness unites a vision of law with a method of analysis. For example, Harlow and Rawlings note that a theory of the state underpins every paradigm of administrative law; Paul Craig and Martin Loughlin share this belief,[2] emphasising that reference to political theory, or political philosophy (we use the terms interchangeably), is vital. It will be necessary to consider the import of such assumptions below and in the next chapter.

This necessarily leads to a sceptical view of law, of the nature, assumptions and purpose of law in contemporary western societies, of the different presuppositions underpinning legal reasoning via the language games inherent to debates (or 'conversations') surrounding public law in particular. Given this historical, epistemological (claims to knowledge) and ontological (forms of existence) uncertainty, certain fundamental questions then arise. Namely, upon what foundations does public law actually rest? Are these foundations necessary, clear and consistent, or are they merely contingent and pragmatic? Does law stand to some extent outside social purpose, does it have autonomy, or is it part of that instrumental social purpose? Equally, if we must live with a plurality of perspectives, then how, if at all, can these perspectives be linked together as a coherent whole? Are they mutually informing or not? Are there hidden assumptions which pervade and colour theorising about the continent of law? We will need to keep in mind as we explore these, and other, questions that the history of law, including public law, may be as telling for its silences as for its revelations. For example, we will see that the very attempt to codify public law since Dicey, writing in the late 19th century, has been essentially constrictive and intimidatory, i.e. repressive of

---

2 Harlow, C., and Rawlings, R., *Law and Administration*, London: Weidenfeld & Nicolson, 1984, p. 1; Craig, P.P., *Administrative Law* (3rd ed.), London: Sweet and Maxwell, 1994; Loughlin, M., *Public Law and Political Theory*, Oxford: Clarendon Press, 1992.

thought by the very nature of the weight of historical condescension carried within its underlying assumptions.

Given these assumptions of our approach to law, including public law, how are they to be operationalised in this piece? We will make use of an essentially perspectival mode of analysis, one which accepts that every viewpoint is, whatever its claims to truth, shaped and moulded by a way of life, that of a particular time and place and set of circumstances. That there is no unmediated, non interpretative knowledge of reality. A method which seeks connections will be utilised here, as well as one which joins the search for a new foundationalism.

What is the framework of our analysis?

Every logic of analysis, every choice regarding the selection and significance to be assigned to the material in play, is invested with certain presuppositions. We begin by asserting the structural utility of two abstract and generally pervasive narrative framing traditions of thought: the Enlightenment; and the critics of that tradition, from the conservative counter-Enlightenment to contemporary debates centred around the validity or utility of 'postmodernism'. The first perspective is, for our purpose here, located in the work and influence of Kant and Hegel, through to Habermas' very recent writings on law. This is a tradition which has historically, to varying degrees, prioritised claims to truth, reason, rationality, objectivity and science, and one which informs the overwhelming body of public law scholarship discussed below. Here, for example, is a first tentative link to the contribution of Dicey and the positivistic separation of law from politics.[3] Accordingly, we spend some time, because of its continuing (and pervasive) influence, reviewing the history of the Diceyan position and how it has come to be subjected to much insightful academic criticism. The legal profession, the law school (as it has been constituted since the late 19th century) and public law theory are deeply imbued with a paradigm of law that emanates from Dicey and his colleagues, although, as we will see, there have been some notable exceptions to this project. The textbook writers largely continue to rely on this black letter-orientated orthodoxy, with the result that English law is largely perceived as a positivistic, rule-based discipline that ought to pay little or no heed to the historical contingencies of the moment. Yet, as we will see, so many 'objective' decisions are simply thinly veiled value judgments, inferences made from contested webs of belief.

We then briefly review the emergence of the 'functionalist' critique of Dicey's legacy. This social welfare perspective is commonly held to have its origins in the coming to maturity of the modern (20th century) administrative state, with its attendant instrumentalist-rationalist demands; and in the ideological conventions of a vaguely socialist/progressive tradition, perhaps exemplified by the Roosaveltian

---

3   Allan, T.R.S., *Law, Liberty and Justice*, Oxford: Clarendon Press, 1993, pp. 244*ff*.

'New Deal' of America in the 1930s. Here too, although we will have no space to analyse it in detail, administrative law was kitted out in new clothes to fit it for new social purposes. One incidental result of this has been that American administrative law theory had greater range and sophistication than its English counterpart, at least until very recently. This contemporary, home-grown efflorescence of conceptual-theoretical academic contributions to public law theory — including those of McAuslan, Allan, Lewis, Craig, Harlow and Loughlin — is discussed below as being significant both in itself and in relation to the individual contributions.

We end with a necessarily brief but (it is hoped) not overly simplistic review of the work of two internationally regarded theorists who attempt a theorisation of law from where the writers just noted leave off. The first of these, Jurgen Habermas, works within the broad parameters of the Enlightenment tradition. That is, he attempts to provide a rationalistic foundation for and an explanation of law's place within contemporary western society. We will need to ask whether this overarching theory can assist us in explicating the role of administrative law theory and administrative law proper, however defined, in its necessarily inextricably complex relationship to the whole. Similarly, for a generation which has witnessed the apparent fragmentation and dispersion of power and social relationships, there is a contrasting tradition, often described, but not unproblematically, as 'postmodern'. Postmodernism can be very schematically traced via the influence of Nietzsche, Wittgenstein, Derrida and Foucault. This tradition problematises the claims of Enlightenment thought and takes seriously the idea of perspectivism; accepting, to varying degrees and in varying senses of the terms, relativism, deconstruction and the challenge to rationality and objectivity. In sum, it is deeply suspicious of claims to have posited arguments on a secure foundation of truth. This must raise the question as to whether theories, such as we discuss here, have any purpose at all, so bringing us back to Hegel's initial disquieting proposition. We will take this tradition as being exemplified by the work of Michel Foucault. Foucault challenges every one of the propositions put forward by the rationalist tradition. Where they theorise a unifying discourse of progress and reconciliation, Foucault affirms, following Nietzsche, difference, diversity, agonism (in the sense of a conflictual relationship) and the necessary connection of claims to knowledge with the assertion of power. We will tentatively conclude with certain propositions regarding the future of public law theory.

PUBLIC LAW IN HISTORICAL AND THEORETICAL PERSPECTIVE

Introduction

Any piece trying to provide an overview public law as it has developed in England must begin with the figure of A.V. Dicey — because of his centrality to the subject, because of his continuing importance down to our own time.

It has been said of Dicey that, 'Dogmatically attached to the politics of his youth, he spent his later years attacking the phantoms of socialism'.[4] Yet, in the courts and the corridors of administrative power the spectre of his work has lingered like a mist over a dank tarn on a January morning, and his presence continues to exert itself in legal circles as the 20th century draws to a close. Despite this, for such an influential figure there is surprisingly little academic consensus about him. For example, there has been much sparring over how most usefully to categorise Dicey — whether he should be regarded as a 'conservative normativist', or as more of a 'liberal normativist'.[5] Similarly, there is some debate as to whether Dicey crafted a dogmatic model of the constitution centred around essentially frozen, timeless concepts such as the 'sovereignty of parliament' and the 'rule of law' that have fashioned the thinking of generations of lawyers and judges — a model, it is argued, that has told against the fertile development of public law scholarship and helped to undermine progressive politics and constitutional reform ever since[6] — or whether he simply wanted to provide a topical analysis of the 'British constitution' as he saw it in the late 19th century and intended no such implications to flow from his work.

We will see that no glib reconciliation of these positions is possible, for Dicey does not easily lend himself to stereotypical classification, but the best view would appear to be that he straddles many camps. He is neither a 'liberal' nor a 'conservative'; neither a simple utilitarian nor a follower of the historical school of Maine and Maitland.[7] He looks back to a Burkean tradition of conservative organic evolution, yet he also embodies a Millian liberal progressivist, legal-scientific strand. He resisted the method of deriving universal principles through a process of deductive reasoning, while also questioning the emphasis on inductive reasoning from the data to reasoned principles. Elements of all these are present in Dicey. The task for us, then, will be to determine how this fascinating and contradictory man and the widely varying responses to him can be assessed: Where do his ideas come from? What are his fundamental legal and political assumptions? How have they been put to use, and with what effect? What is his legacy? To what extent (if at all) does he manage to establish a link between law and political theory, and how far does his theoretical framework satisfy the need to identify the *locus* of power in the contemporary administrative state? These are the questions we must attempt to throw some light on below.

---

4   Sugarman, D., 'The Legal Boundaries of Liberty: Dicey, Liberalism and Legal Science' (1983) 46 *Modern Law Review* 102.

5   Loughlin, *op. cit.* note 2 and Craig *op. cit.* note 2.

6   McEldowney, J.F., 'Dicey in Historical Perspective — A Review Essay' in McAuslan, P., and McEldowney, J.F. (eds), *Law, Legitimacy and the Constitution*, London: Sweet & Maxwell, 1985, p. 57; and Harden, I. and Lewis, N., *The Noble Lie*, London: Hutchinson, 1986, pp. 4*ff.*

7   Stapleton, J., 'Dicey and His Legacy' (1995) 16 *History of Political Thought* 234, and McEldowney, *op. cit.* note 6 *supra*.

Dicey's legacy: reinventing the myth of the ancient constitution

In searching for the genealogy of his ideas, it becomes clear that Dicey has been widely regarded as propagating a conservative normativism because his theories offer us a received myth of English uniqueness, of evolving constitutional freedom and liberty derived from the constitutional struggles of the 17th century. O'Leary puts it succinctly:

> . . . He was a codifier and propagandist for a certain interpretation of British constitutional and administrative law, who tried none too successfully to blend the mythic 'ancient constitution' based on an organic common law which could not be traced to the sovereign with an unarticulated positivist conception of parliamentary sovereignty — which was justified as an expression of majoritarian will.[8]

In fact, Maitland at the turn of the century had already discerned the way the common law required an idealised, reified pseudo-historical justification as distinct from a fully reasoned one.[9] To achieve this Dicey turned back to among others, Burke and the common law tradition. And subsequent generations — including Barker, Oakshott and Hayek — have been influenced by Diceyan themes of English particularism and the benefits of time-sanctioned 'ordinary law' over rationalistically contrived and imposed legal systems.[10] Barker remarks, for example, that Dicey's equation of Englishness with 'legal-mindedness' projected an ideal of national belonging which was firmly rooted in a high degree of social detachment and personal autonomy.[11] This invention of a 'tradition' — a 'conceptive ideology', as Sugarman describes it[12] — has had many ramifications. Some writers have argued, for example, that the central doctrine of the 'sovereignty of parliament' is an invention of Dicey's, little more indeed than 'a dubious, dangerous and stultifying piece of theoretical speculation,[13] all too typical of Dicey's position where abstract concepts are created without any satisfactory empirical foundation and subsequently applied shorn of historical justification.

---

8   O'Leary, B., 'What Should Public Lawyers Do?' (1992) 12 *Oxford Journal of Legal Studies* 404, at 411.
9   Sugarman, D., 'Legal Theory, the Common Law Mind and the Making of the Textbook Tradition' in Twining, W. (ed.), *Legal Theory and the Common Law Mind*, Oxford: Basil Blackwell, 1986, p. 40.
10 Stapleton, *op. cit.* note 7 *supra*, pp. 239 and 246/7.
11 Barker, Sir E., *Political Thought in England 1848–1914*, London: Allen and Unwin, 1915, p. 255.
12 Sugarman, *op. cit,* note 9 *supra*, p. 54.
13 Walker, G. de Q., 'Dicey's Dubious Dogma of Parliamentary Sovereignty: A Recent Fray With Freedom of Religion' (1985) 59 *Australian Law Journal* (ed.) 276, at 284. See also Simpson, W.B., 'The Common Law and Legal Theory' in Simpson, W.B., *Oxford Essays in Jurisprudence* (2nd Series), Oxford: Oxford University Press, 1973, pp. 77 and 96.

Others have noted the borrowing from Bryce of the terminology of 'flexible' versus 'rigid' with the aim of enhancing English pride in what they had accomplished.[14]

This common law history of the constitutional settlement is utilised from Magna Carta, to the Bill of Rights of 1688 through to the 19th century, in order to establish that a legal system based on gradualism and the doctrine of precedents — of growth by nature rather than growth by design — is the very essence of the English nation. Thus it is that a reinterpretation of a myth of law is developed by Dicey, one balancing tradition with progress while embedding a symbolic function for the common law, one which is peculiarly English and, crucially, one placing law and lawyers at the core of English liberty and success. As Loughlin puts it, 'Law bolstered the moral order of society and judges, as custodians of those values, were deserving of respect and trust'.[15] In fact, this mission to enhance 'the peculiarities of the English',[16] to establish a 'conceptive' ideology, was, as Collini puts it, not one linked with the order of things, not an attempt to historicise the political character of law, but one linked to the order of meanings, with the language of law as myth.[17] The result of this mythologisation was that it enabled the English constitutional tradition to be appropriated, linked to nationalism, and distinguished from and propagated as being superior to that of France (which had incorporated the post-revolutionary Napoleonic codes, so creating a relatively authoritarian centralised state and a servile administrative law: the *droit administratif*). Indeed, as we shall see later, the French system was both misinterpreted and singled out for particular disapprobrium by Dicey;[18] although the *droit* was much less fully developed at the time Dicey was writing (as opposed to the time of actual publication). Despite his later work showing some moderation of his hostility[19] — in that he did recognise change and seek to reconcile 'the combined blessings of order and progress' — there is, nevertheless, a parochial evolutionary progressivism remaining at the heart of his work, in that law is inextricably linked in his own mind with the rise of the middle classes to prominence in 19th-century England.[20]

---

14   Trowbridge, H.F., *A V Dicey: The Man and His Times*, Sussex: Barry Rose, 1985, p. 140.

15   Loughlin *op. cit.* note 2 *supra*, p. 155.

16   Thompson, E. P., 'The Peculiarities of the English', reprinted in Thompson, E.P., *The Poverty of Theory & Other Essays*, London: Merlin, 1978.

17   See generally Collini, S., *Public Moralists, Political Thought and Intellectual Life in Britain 1850–1939*, Oxford: Clarendon Press, 1991.

18   Jowell, J., 'The Rule of Law Today' in Jowell, J., and Oliver, D. (eds), *The Changing Constitution* (3rd ed.), Oxford: Clarendon Press, 1994.

19   See, for example, the 8th ed. of Dicey, A.V., *An Introduction to the Study of the Law of the Constitution*, published in 1914 and Dicey, A.V., '*Droit Administratif* in Modern French Law' (1901) 17 *Law Quarterly Review* 302.

20   See Bogdanor, V., 'Dicey and the Reform of the Constitution' [1985] *Public Law* 652. For a defence of Dicey see Lawson, F.H., 'Dicey Revisited' (Parts 1 and 2) (1959) 7 *Political Studies* 109 and 207.

Defending the *laissez-faire* Whig tradition

Dicey can also be regarded as one variety of 'liberal normativist' because his ideas originate from a Whig tradition, with a strong emphasis on *laissez-faire* and on individual rights and freedoms. He thought very highly of John Stuart Mill's *On Liberty*: it has been well said that even his utilitarianism was Mill's not Bentham's.[21] Sir Ivor Jennings, for his part, situates Dicey firmly within this context: 'Just as Macaulay saw the history of the eighteenth century through Whig spectacles, so Dicey saw the constitution of 1885 through Whig spectacles. His principles were Whig principles'. Dicey did not understand this, according to Jennings, even though it coloured so many of his opinions, and indeed it was the rule of law, one of Dicey's central doctrines, 'which most obviously exhibits Dicey's Whigism'.[22] This was true of Dicey, despite the fact that by the 1890s any over-simplistic advocacy of 18th-century liberalism or early 19th-century *laissez-faire* libertarian doctrine — what has been well described as 'possessive individ-ualism'[23] — was becoming increasingly difficult in the face of the challenge of the 'New Liberalism', the critique of the Oxford Hegelians, Green, Bosanquet and Bradley, and the emergence of socialism as a countervailing ideology.[24]

One significant aspect of Dicey's endeavour was to assist in founding a rationalistic legal science which could sustain the individualistic bias of *On Liberty*, all the more because by 1915 it was clear even to Dicey[25] that the normative principles underpinning Mill's position, allowing for a distinction to be drawn between 'self' and 'other' regarding activities, was under threat. The law could serve, Dicey thought, not only to define self-regarding activity broadly, but also prevent any intrusion in such activity by the state, so maximising personal liberty. This classically liberal, essentially *laissez-faire* approach can also be employed to sever public from private spheres of law and may be seen to lead to a distinction being drawn between the 'public' (bad) and the 'private' (good). As we have already noted, Dicey himself was stridently opposed to any separate system of public law that could be equated with the French *droit administratif*.[26] Rather, any separation is related to a 'control' model of the public sphere by the ordinary courts utilising the (formal) principle of the rule of law. Therefore, within a Diceyan framework, the principal role of the courts is overwhelmingly negative:

---

21 Trowbridge, *op. cit.* note 14 *supra*, p. 243. See also Craig, P.P., 'Bentham, Public Law and Democracy' [1989] *Public Law* 652.
22 Jennings, Sir I., 'In Praise of Dicey' (1935) 13 *Public Administration* 123 at pp. 128 and 130.
23 Macpherson, C.B., *The Political Theory of Possessive Individualism: Hobbes to Locke*, Oxford: Oxford University Press, 1962.
24 See Lustgarten, L., 'Socialism and the Rule of Law' (1988) 15 *Journal of Law and Society* 25.
25 Dicey, A.V., 'The Development of Administrative Law in England' (1915) 31 *Law Quarterly Review* 148.
26 But see Dicey, *op. cit.* note 19 *supra*, 1901, for some modification of his hostility.

to prevent individual freedoms from being interfered with. It is apparent from this that what Dicey recognised in regard to fundamental ('residual') rights was extremely limited, and from a contemporary viewpoint entirely unsatisfactory. In fact it was closely associated with preventing any invasion of the liberties and property rights of Victorian gentlemen. For although Dicey did not ignore the claims of the working classes, his views were inevitably marked by an individualist emphasis on self-improvement *by* them not state aid *for* them (see below).

A much more obviously debilitating result of Dicey's positivistic, legal–scientific principles has been the divorce of law from politics (in the minds of academics and practitioners alike).[27] Nevertheless, this artificial distinction actually serves a political purpose, in that it gives credence to the belief that lawyers operate in a world removed from the wider social, economic and moral debates taking place outside their chambers. Similarly, Dicey's perspective serves not only to defend individualism, but also to critique the growth of the administrative state and the promotion of 'collectivism' (a term coming into general usage by the 1890s) as an ideology. As the historian Eric Hobsbawm remarks: 'The British jurist A.V. Dicey . . . saw the steamroller of collectivism, which had been in motion since 1870, flattening the landscape of individual liberty into the centralised and levelling tyranny of school meals, health insurance and old age pensions.'[28] Dicey opposed the use of law as an instrument of social policy: for example, he disapproved of the immunity of trade unions from being sued under the common law, provided by the passing of the Trade Disputes Act 1906, regarding this measure as an exception to the rule of equality before the law[29] in that it conferred special privileges on workers as a class. (More recent equal opportunities legislation could be criticised for much the same reason.)[30] This emphasis by Dicey is somewhat in contrast to that of Barker and Maitland, writing at around the same time, whose work recognised the emergence of the collectivist state and embryonic group pluralism, as well as (in Barker's case) the growing need for citizen redress against the state.[31] These themes of 'individualism' versus 'collectivism' run through the entire debate surrounding public law down to our own time, for example, in the work of F.A. Hayek,[32] where there is much grinding of teeth about the decline and ultimate disappearance of the rule of law. (Note also his conception of the untranslatable nature of Dicey's conception of the rule of law[33]).

---

27 Dicey, A.V., *Law and Opinion in England* (2nd ed.), London: Macmillan, 1905; see the Introduction at pp. xxxi and xxxii.
28 Hobsbawm, E.J., *The Age of Empire*, London: Weidenfeld & Nicolson, 1987, p. 103.
29 Dicey *op. cit.* note 27 *supra*, p. xliv.
30 See McEldowney *op. cit.* note 6 *supra*.
31 Stapleton *op. cit.* note 7 *supra*, p. 242.
32 *Ibid.*, pp. 248–9, and see Fennell R., '*Roberts* v *Hopwood*: the Rule Against Socialism' (1986) 13 *Journal of Law and Society* 401.
33 See Jones, H.W., 'The Rule of Law and the Welfare State' (1958) 58 *Columbia Law Review* 143, at 146 and 149.

In sum, Dicey's *laissez-faire* orientation left us with a legacy of ideas founded on the defence of individual liberty and property based on the common law, a tradition which, while encompassing prudent evolutionary reform, eschewed any radical liberal or socialist conception of the proactive state or a collectivist society. This ideology was to have the effect of leaving administrative law totally unprepared for the demands and needs of the post-1918 world.

The textbook tradition and the rise of the law school

Having seen that the account of our constitutional arrangements Dicey produced may be regarded as one aspect of the common law tradition, another strand in his thinking is that associated with rationalism, and particularly with his 'selective appropriation' of the work of Bentham, Mill and, above all, Austin.[34] It is one that seeks to provide a coherent account of law by means of a rational search for the fundamental principles underpinning it. As Dicey puts it: 'Law is rational and that rationality is revealed by principle.'[35] Austin in particular inspired his largely derivative attempt to provide a theoretically positivist framework of concepts which would allow constitutional law to be taught and imbibed as a coherent whole. By this pedagogy of legal formalism, with all extraneous matter such as political science or ethics excluded, students could concentrate their efforts upon the narrow and largely mechanical task of learning law as little more than a set of ascertainable rules. Moreover, once achieved, such knowledge would allow for any exceptions to the rules promulgated to be separated out from the basic professional function of legal education and marginalised. Therefore, the task of the teacher in a typical law school working within the expository tradition would henceforth be 'to arrange them [the rules] in their order, to explain their meaning, and to exhibit where possible their logical connection'.[36]

By what means did this stolid methodology come to be accepted as the conventional wisdom? Although Dicey himself did not originate such concepts, being rather a grand synthesiser than a genuine innovator, his essentially anti-historical focus on the present, on law as a science of rules, provided a rationale, however tenuous, at the right historical juncture. So it was that the legal mind came to focus upon the need for 'authority, and the newer the better'; while, for example, the historian would require 'evidence and the older the better'.[37] *The Law of the Constitution*, in particular, came to be 'elevated into almost biblical authority'[38]

---

34   Sugarman, D., 'A Hatred of Disorder: Legal Science, Liberalism and Imperialism' in Fitzpatrick, P. (ed.), *Dangerous Supplements: Resistances and Renewal in Jurisprudence*, London: Pluto Press, 1991, pp. 42*ff*.

35   Dicey, *op. cit.* note 27 *supra*, p. xxvii.

36   Jennings, *op. cit.* note 22 *supra*, p. 127.

37   Maitland, F.W., 'Why the History of English Law is not Written' in Fisher, H.A.L. (ed.), *Collected Papers*, Cambridge: Cambridge University Press, 1911, vol. 1, pp. 491 and 493.

38   Blackburn, R.W., 'Dicey and the Teaching of Public Law' [1985] *Public Law* 679, at 689.

and has provided *the* dominant theory in the teaching of constitutional and administrative law ever since, in both its conservative and liberal normativist variants — or at least until very recently. Dicey's doctrines have exerted a similarly powerful influence over the legal profession, inducing an insular, 'disciplinary tribalism'[39] around an essentially non scholarly (even anti-scholarly) black letter conception of the subject; while Dicey's conception of the 'rule of law', especially, has provided the leading self-legitimating judicial ideology for a century, strongly inhibiting fresh thinking and narrowing the horizon of critical reflection. Indeed, the concept has been authoritatively quoted in some of the key cases since 1945 where constitutional principles have been discussed, including *Burmah Oil* and *GCHQ*.[40] However, there are now some signs, even among the senior judiciary, that the ice is thawing; for example, see the recent contributions of Lord Woolf MR, Sedley J and Laws J (see Donson, Ch. 15 generally).

The main achievement of *The Law of the Constitution*, then, in the face of practitioner scepticism, was to provide a gloss of academic respectability for the study of public law, separating the 'is' from the 'ought' and thereby excluding from it as superfluous the contributions of philosophy, political science or any empirical sociological research. It did have claims to be empirical as well as conceptual, but the series of easy dualisms employed by Dicey which centred around the sovereignty of parliament and the rule of law, painted in bold colours and lacking nuance and subtlety alike, were, although functional to lawyers in an uncodified constitution like that of Britain, far removed from the particularistic and unsystematic practices of everyday social and legal life.[41] Nevertheless, this seductive functionality, operating via the convenient, implicit contradiction of parliamentary sovereignty, set against the (normatively based) rule of law, meant that it was possible to argue plausibly that laws once enacted by Parliament are removed from political controversy and simply subject now to the interpretation of the judicial branch through the concept of the rule of law. By this sleight of hand, Dicey's later adherents, for example Professor Wade,[42] might well find themselves in agreement with Lord Reid's view that an 'an ounce of fact is worth a ton of theory' and would claim to be non ideological (in the Marxist sense) as well as anti-theoretical. In fact, they rely upon a covert theoretical position based on a founding myth of the ancient constitution and the judiciary's place within it that depends upon Dicey more than any other single writer. Of course, any such argument for an independent normative discipline has long been questioned. Indeed, as we will see, later 'functionalist' critics, such as Jennings, Griffith and

---

39   Sugarman, *op. cit.* note 9 *supra*, p. 49.

40   *Burmah Oil* v *Lord Advocate* [1965] AC 65; *Council for Civil Service Unions* v *Minister for the Civil Service* [1985] AC 374. See Blackburn, *op. cit.* note 38 *supra*, p. 691.

41   Arthurs, H.W., *Without the Law: Administrative Justice and Legal Pluralism in Nineteenth Century England*, Toronto: University of Toronto Press, 1985.

42   Wade, H.W.R., and Forsyth, C.F., *Administrative Law* (7th ed.), Oxford: Clarendon Press, 1994.

McAuslan, as well as the American legal-realist and Critical Legal Studies schools, have demonstrated convincingly that many key judicial decisions are thinly veiled value judgments. If Dicey has achieved this extraordinary recognition as a *simplifier* — by suggesting that beneath the apparent complexity and irrationality of the law clarity could yet be found and engagement with the semantic confusions of the common law could be avoided[43] — is he more truthfully to be regarded, as one commentator memorably puts it, as a peddler of 'brilliant obfuscation'[44] rather than as a transmitter of light?

Yet despite wide-ranging academic criticism and the lack of reference to, or sympathy with, consumers of law as we would now understand the term, we come back to the attractiveness of Dicey's work, and that of many of his contemporaries such as Anson and Pollock, to the profession — to the idea of 'law' as something out there, a fetishised and reified symbol rather than a subjectively experienced empirical reality. Perhaps most significantly, the normative aspects of Dicey's account served to enhance the professional status of the law schools by the construction of a tradition, as well as the self-esteem of professionals because they could now regard themselves as being part of 'a closed model of rationality'.[45] This process of professionalisation, of the centralisation and unification of law and the legal profession, enables us today to view Dicey, at least on one account, as 'the self-satisfied belch of a common law system which had devoured its rivals'.[46]

Underpinning Dicey's legacy: The sovereignty of Parliament and the rule of law

We now need to take a more critical look at Dicey's model of 'self-correcting democracy'[47] which is constructed upon the twin pillars of the *sovereignty of parliament* and the *rule of law*. These are two concepts which offer, as we have already seen, at the same time both an appealing simplification and a reification of fundamental aspects of our constitutional arrangements. A simplification because it ties our constitution back to two basic principles;[48] a reification because although they are derived from fundamentally a-historical and a-sociological premises, they yet serve a political as well as a legal purpose.[49]

---

43 See generally Goodrich, P., *Languages of Law: From Logics of Memory to Nomadic Masks*, London: Weidenfeld & Nicolson, 1990.
44 Frankfurter, J., 'Foreword' (to a 'Discussion of Current Developments in Administrative Law') (1938) 47 *Yale Law Journal* 515, at 517.
45 Sugarman, *op. cit.* note 34 *supra*, p. 34.
46 Arthurs, H.W., 'Jonah and the Whale: the Appearance, Disappearance and Reappearance of Administrative Law' (1980) 30 *University of Toronto Law Journal* 225, at 237.
47 Craig, P.P., 'Dicey: Unitary, Self-Correcting Democracy and Public Law' (1991) 106 *Law Quarterly Review* 105, at 105.
48 Johnson, N., 'Dicey and His Influence on Public Law' [1985] *Public Law* 717, at 718.
49 Blackburn, *op. cit.* note 38 *supra*, p. 683.

The sovereignty of parliament

The idea of sovereignty originates from a tradition prior to Dicey, that of Hobbes and Austin.[50] A top-down hierarchical structure based on an image of 'imperium',[51] where the existence of sovereignty is, in effect, a necessary precondition for law itself to exist and have legitimacy, is borrowed from Austin, although Dicey criticised him for not distinguishing between political sovereignty (found in conventions) and legal sovereignty.[52] Missing the point that private law rules create options rather than lay down commands — in the sense that they are facilitative in essence rather than simply oppressive[53] — Dicey started by assuming that the highest authority should lie in an elected (at the time over half of men over 21 and no women had the vote) and omnicompetent Parliament. This majoritarian parliamentary monopoly on the power to legislate was to have two aspects: first, that Parliament could make and unmake any law; secondly, that no person or body could set aside the legislation of Parliament. In the absence of a written document, this principle was to be the ground rule, the source of ultimate legal authority in our constitution. But the seductive attraction of this doctrine was greatly augmented because it was also linked, in the eyes of many lawyers and politicians, with the legacy of Blackstone and Burke. A legacy where Parliament could be regarded as representing the mythic — not to say mystic — historical soul of the English people and their essential national identity. So it was that Dicey seized upon the *form* of modernity without the *content*. His conception is, therefore, not genuinely modern, as in America, where it is, theoretically at least, rooted in democracy and the ultimate sovereignty of the people. Here in Britain organic, historically derived and pluralistic traditions of authority are replaced by a single spurious basic norm of sovereignty, unquestionable by the judiciary. Thus modernity, as Carty argues, is turned from 'an intelligible history into a blind acceptance of "facticity"'.[54] Or, as Simpson puts it more starkly: 'The oracle spoke and came to be accepted.'[55]

Despite broad acceptance, on closer inspection the foundations of this influential edifice rest on both legal and political sand. In fact this was a lawyer's conception, an academic doctrine,[56] a doctrine of political theory with little evidence for it in

---

50   Hobbes, T., *Leviathan* (1651) (ed.) Tuck, R., Cambridge: Cambridge University Press, 1991 and Austin, J., *The Providence of Jurisprudence Determined* (1832), London: Weidenfeld & Nicolson, 1954.

51   Cotterrell, R., 'Judicial Review and Legal Theory' in Richardson, C., and Genn, H. (eds), *Administrative Law and Government Action*, Oxford: Clarendon Press, 1994.

52   *Ibid.*, pp. 24*ff.*

53   Tamanaha, B.Z., 'An Analytical Map of Social Scientific Approaches to the Concept of Law' (1995) 15 *Oxford Journal of Legal Studies* 501, at 533.

54   Carty, A., 'English Constitutional Law from a Postmodernist Perspective' in Fitzpatrick, *op. cit.* note 34 *supra*, p. 206 (an interesting essay overall).

55   Simpson, *op. cit.* note 13 *supra*, p. 961.

56   Heuston, R.F.V., *Essays in Constitutional Law*, London: Stevens, 1964.

history. Since Dicey's time, while many *obiter dicta* have served to buttress his theory, it has been argued that no court has ever upheld the doctrine in the face of an unmistakable attempt by Parliament to undermine fundamental constitutional doctrines.[57] Indeed, as Walker puts it, 'Dicey could not cite one single case in support of his absolutist and unbalanced view of the constitution, nor could he point to any reference to it in any statute or constitutional instrument'.[58] From the outset Dicey presents us with an abstract and over-simplified set of assertions which misconceive the place of Parliament in national affairs even at the time he wrote, for by the 1890s there were clear signs of executive domination over Parliament. Bagehot, for one, in *The British Constitution* had famously argued, as early as 1867, that parliamentary government had become Cabinet government. This has been elaborated further in the present century in terms of the 'Whitehall' as opposed to the 'Westminster' models of parliamentary liberal democracy. Contrary to Dicey's assumptions, it appears that majoritarian democracy is not 'self-correcting' after all,[59] and there is little evidence to support the idea that 'elective dictatorship' was ever unlikely in the UK, given the dominance of party politics by the third quarter of the 19th century and the growth of centres of power outside Parliament.[60] Although Parliament derives its legitimacy from the electorate, there is nothing to prevent any Parliament from passing laws which conflict with 'public opinion'. As Craig notes: 'Majoritarian tyranny was the great danger of the age, and the constitution provided no effective checks to prevent the encroachment of minority rights.'[61]

We have already said that, largely because of his reliance on Austin's positivistic conception of sovereignty, Dicey had no ready answer to these contradictions apart from putting his trust in a Parliament made up of English gentlemen and in the presumptions of the common law.[62] Prime Minister Ian Smith was driven to a similar conclusion regarding the contradiction between sovereignty and the rule of law after declaring independence unilaterally from the UK in Zimbabwe (then Rhodesia) in 1965. He, as much as Dicey, could not envisage survival of the rule of law unless government remained in 'civilised' (i.e., white) hands. Later in his life, Dicey was to recommend the device of the referendum to span the chasm. It would cure the problems of the British polity and the excesses of democracy, for example, in helping resist demands for egalitarian social policies, women's suffrage and Irish home rule.[63] However, in a period before the widespread use of mass empirical survey research, he consistently misjudged the consequences of

---

57 Walker, *op. cit.* note 13 *supra*, p. 276.
58 *Ibid.* See also Jennings, *op. cit.* note 22 *supra*, p. 129.
59 Craig, *op. cit.*. note 47, *supra*, p. 136.
60 *Ibid.*, p. 130.
61 *Ibid.*, p. 136.
62 McEldowney, *op. cit.* note 6 *supra*.
63 Trowbridge, *op. cit.* note 14 *supra*, pp. 289–90. See also Bodganor, *op. cit.* note 20 *supra*, p. 664.

public opinion and greatly overplayed its role. One wonders, did Dicey ever really pause to consider that the fundamental principles of *Law and Public Opinion* itself had been undermined by the changes he himself referred to in 1915? Or that the book had revealed clearly the contingent nature of any jurisprudential theories?[64]

It is also worth remembering here that Dicey and other Victorian public lawyers — such as Bryce, Anson, Maitland, Pollock and Maine — were deliberately contributing to a wider historical and political debate in society at the time. As McEldowney puts it:[65] 'The abstraction of simple principles from complex problems was the work of a lawyer but under the influence of a politician.' Dicey's conceptualisation of the principles of sovereignty and the rule of law accorded with a personal political agenda as a vociferous opponent of Irish home rule. For example, he could have emphasised (here we have a blend of legal and political sovereignty) the sovereignty of the Cabinet or government, but he chose to emphasise the sovereignty of Parliament instead. An all-powerful Parliament, including the monarch and the Lords, would act as a check on any Irish aspirations. Indeed, such a measure as Irish home rule might well violate the basic principles of the constitution, in much the same way as our membership of the European Community is alleged to have done since 1972.[66]

The rule of law

The 'Rule of Law becomes a banner under which opposing armies march to combat'.[67] This captures the fact that this second principle, too, is a multifaceted, political as well as legal entity, which can be defined and argued about in many different ways and with many different interests in mind. But, as with the sovereignty of Parliament, Dicey underplays any express political implications and regards it, in the tradition of private law remedies, as fundamentally a judicial control on the power of the executive, as a 'bridle for Leviathan'.[68] Dicey's second major principle, therefore — although again it did not originate with him[69] — acts, in principle at least, to qualify the unlimited nature of parliamentary sovereignty. The rule of law is defined in the *Law of the Constitution* as the supremacy of regular law over arbitrary power (the *Entick v Carrington* principle[70]); formal legal equality before the law (the basis of Dicey's criticism of the *droit administratif*);

---

64   Sugarman, *op. cit.* note 4 *supra*, p. 102.
65   McEldowney, *op. cit.* note 6 *supra*, p. 61.
66   Cosgrove, R.A., *The Rule of Law: Albert Venn Dicey*, London: Macmillan, 1980, p. 295; Trowbridge, *op. cit.* note 14 *supra*, pp. 138–40.
67   Griffith, G.J., and Street, H., *Principles of Administrative Law*, (5th ed.), London: Pitman, 1973, p. 22.
68   Arthurs, H.W., 'Rethinking Administrative Law: A Slightly Dicey Business' (1979) 17 *Osgoode Hall Law Journal* 1, at p. 3.
69   Arndt, H.W., 'The Origins of Dicey's Concept of the "Rule of Law"' (1957) 13 *Australian Law Journal* 117.
70   (1675) 19 St Tr 1030.

and the fact that the constitution is the result of the ordinary law of the land, a consequence of the rights of individuals as defined and enforced by the regular courts. For example, in *Derbyshire CC* v *Times Newspapers*,[71] Browne-Wilkinson LJ recognised that rights could be defended by the existence of fundamental presumptions of the common law, immune from interference except by express parliamentary action. Here, these would be used to defend the liberal right to free expression. The separation of powers theoretically underpinned these principles, with the courts playing a role in 'policing the boundaries'[72] of a jurisdiction established by Parliament after legislation has received the royal assent. Everyone, including the government and its agents, is subject to the ordinary law upheld by the courts. This meant that ordinary law predominated and that wherever possible discretionary powers were to be eliminated. Dicey therefore — like his 18th-century mentor Blackstone — 'dissolved the state into the various common law checks which were placed on it'.[73] On this view, which became the authoritative one in English legal circles (see, for example, the preamble to the Donoughmore Report of 1932), the rule of law provides a justification for intervention by the courts and a restrictive reading of legislative intent, especially where the defence of private property rights is concerned. (Compare the purposive approach advocated by the functionalist school discussed below.)

This perspective was famously contrasted by Dicey with the French system of administrative law, although he was mainly interested in it in order to display how fundamentally its basic principles conflicted with the rule of law as he understood it. Indeed, it has been said that, almost to the point of obsession, Dicey had a 'visceral suspicion'[74] of the *droit administratif*. Dicey focused on the separate system of administrative courts which existed and the immunities and special privileges he believed (dubiously even then) that these afforded to officials, and on the scope of executive discretion under the *droit* which potentially undermined the control function of the courts.[75] However, once again this is a point made in abstraction from the detailed analysis of the workings of government and administration, as the limitations of the English courts themselves were already exposed by the latter part of the 19th century in the face of the range of emerging institutions in the public sector; namely, those of the embryonic welfare state and the enormous growth in the statutory basis of the powers regulating the duties of public authorities, together with the administrative discretion conferred on officials. But Dicey was prevented from easily recognising either the nature or utility of these developments because resistance to a statutory (written) basis for the

---

71   [1992] 3 All ER 65.
72   Craig, *op. cit.* note 47 *supra*, p. 116.
73   Stapleton, *op. cit.* note 7 *supra*, p. 239.
74   Cosgrove, *op. cit.* note 66 *supra*, p. 98.
75   Arndt, *op. cit.* note 69 *supra*.

constitution as well as executive discretion is a central theme in his writings. He generally sought to deny the legitimacy of conferring regulatory functions on administrative authorities, failing to recognise that this is inevitable once government concerns itself with detailed provision of services, and that finding a balance between rule and discretion is central to the task of public administration in the new state. This is largely because he associated discretion with arbitrary power, and hence found it to be incompatible with the rule of law as he understood it.[76] In other words, a political prejudice of the Victorian era defined what purported to be a legal doctrine. This position has been described as 'pernicious'.[77] As we have seen, towards the end of his life Dicey to some extent modified his position, but still failed to come to terms with the view that statute-based wide discretion is a necessary and inevitable characteristic of modern government. In other words, there was excessive emphasis on limiting (controlling) power rather than on examining the *locus* of power itself; on the forms rather than on the empirical substance of administrative rule-making and its impact on society. An example is Dicey's failure to consider the full implications of the decision in *Local Government Board* v *Arlidge*,[78] for example, regarding the failure to apply basic standards of natural justice to statutory inquiries. A failure that Wade, for one, considers to be a missed opportunity.

This subconscious leitmotif, that anything like the *droit* was fundamentally alien to English freedom, has been described as 'one of the most potent political superstitions this century'.[79] Indeed, it is the belief that the spirit of *Entick* v *Carrington* remains at least partially intact which accounts for Dicey's enduring influence and popularity among sections of the senior judiciary and not a few academics. As Jowell recognises, the rule of law appears to many to provide an important form of 'institutional morality' and 'constrains the uninhibited exercise of governmental power' through 'unwritten principles' which are particularly important in a nation that lacks a written constitution.[80] However, even in the 19th century that Dicey was so confident of understanding, the role of the courts in making law and reviewing law-makers was marginal. It is even more so today. Nevertheless, some qualified support for the contrary proposition has come from the Marxist historian E.P. Thompson, in his class-based analysis of the 18th century *Black Acts*.[81] He argues that the old established language of the 'rule of law' was used by dissenting radicals, among others, to provide some inhibitions on the

---

76 Harden and Lewis (1986), *op. cit.* note 6 *supra*, pp. 45 and 195.
77 Arthurs, *op. cit.* note 68 *supra*.
78 [1915] AC 120. (*Note*: For a detailed discussion of Dicey and French administrative law, see Errara, R., 'Dicey and French Administrative Law: A Missed Encounter' [1985] *Public Law* 695.)
79 Blackburn, *op. cit.* note 38 *supra*, p. 690.
80 Jowell, *op. cit.* note 18 *supra*, p. 72.
81 Thompson, E.P., *Whigs and Hunters: The Origin of the Black Acts*, Harmondsworth: Allen Lane, 1975.

powerful and to afford some protection to the powerless. For Thompson, then, the rule of law is at once more acceptable to the commonsense understanding of the ruling classes and a medium through which incipient social conflict could find expression.[82] However, the whole idea of the 'rule of law' is both opaque and controversial, and other scholars do not follow Thompson's lead. Horwitz, for example,[83] argues that the rule of law is not an unqualified human good, for formal equality within the legal system can serve the interests of the rich and powerful in defending privilege and thwarting egalitarian legislation through the use of money and media to influence opinion. There must sometimes be a role for 'legitimate violence',[84] for example, in tilting law towards the cause of substantive equality and egalitarian redistribution. But here we have moved some way from anything Dicey as a common lawyer would have recognised or approved of. That is, that the rule of law is something which is fundamentally common to all nations or it does not exist.

Whatever the admonitions to the contrary, it is clear that while court-centred protection under the 'rule of law' is a commonplace requirement of good governance, this can never be wholly unqualified. In the first place, such an approach rests on the controversial assumption that the common law 'is a constantly evolving apparatus for protecting basic values'[85] operated through lawyer-dominated procedures — an approach which often marginalises the time, expense and procedural difficulties involved in exercising such rights, as well as the benefits afforded the citizen in making use of alternative institutional arrangements.[86] Moreover, on the evidence of the case law, it is hard to maintain that the rule of law protects either general or minority civil liberties against executive excesses, or that it provides relief when overbearing legislation is passed by Parliament. For example, the stirring speech of Lord Atkin in *Liversidge* v *Anderson*, cited by Allan as 'a fine illustration of adjudication in the common law tradition',[87] is surely simply a memorable dissenting judgment, and the liberties of the appellant were in the end not upheld under the common law by the court. Many other, more recent examples could be given, including *GCHQ*, the 'Spycatcher' litigation and the *Brind* case.[88] Thirdly, Dicey did not even mention the role of legislation in defending human rights and extending freedom for the many, as opposed to the essentially *individual* focus of the common law. Lastly, and

82 *Ibid.*, at pp. 266–7. See also Thompson, E.P., 'The Peculiarities of the English' in Thompson, E.P. (ed.), *The Poverty of Theory*, London: Merlin Press, 1978.

83 Horwitz, M.J., 'The Rule of Law: An Unqualified Human Good?' (1976) 86 *Yale Law Journal* 117.

84 Weber, M., 'Politics as a Vocation', in Gerth, H.H., and Mills, C.W. (eds), *From Max Weber: Essays in Sociology*, London: Routledge & Kegan Paul, 1970.

85 Allan, *op. cit.* note 3 *supra*, p. 15.

86 Gordon, R.W., 'Without the Law' (1987) 24 *Osgoode Hall Law Journal* 421, at 436.

87 Allan, *op. cit.* note 3 *supra*, p. 15.

88 [1985] AC 374; *R* v *Secretary of State for the Home Department, ex parte Brind* [1991] 1 All ER 469. See esp. Barendt, E., 'Dicey and Civil Liberties' [1985] *Public Law* 596.

decisively, as Gordon puts it: '. . . it encourages the more comfortable and privileged of us to hold the absurd delusion that the problem of domination in social life can be adequately solved by coating over the manifold hierarchies of political and civil society with a thin layer of judicial process'.[89]

Dicey: the end of an era?

'Thirty years later [than his earlier writings on the constitution] in his *Law and Opinion* . . . Dicey himself demonstrated the sociological sterility of his earlier chapter on the Rule of Law'.[90] These words of Felix Frankfurter, suggesting the insecurity of any conceptual framework in the context of historical evolution, give us an important clue to the understanding of Dicey's legacy. Dicey was indubitably a man of his time, a mid-Victorian legal scholar and incipient politician who is best viewed in relation to his contemporaries and to the task they individually and collectively set themselves of placing academic law on a firm foundation, one that would both enhance the status of legal education and be acceptable, indeed welcome, to the profession as a whole. Thinking of constitutional law in particular, Dicey, despite some degree of self-doubt, could be well satisfied with his achievements; he was held to be *the* eminent authority in almost all legal–constitutional circles before and, to a not inconsiderable extent after, 1914.[91] However, despite the obvious continuing utility of some aspects of the Diceyan legacy, it was not to be very long, as we have seen, before he stood condemned for the unreality of his inheritance, for its formalism and its mechanistic abstraction from real world legal and political analysis and practice. This view is well put in a recent article by Gavin Drewry: ' . . . his eloquently dogmatic and backward looking analysis cast a baleful shadow over legal scholarship for many years'.[92] Indeed, Maitland at the turn of the century already seems to grasp the essential features of this view. 'The traditional lawyer's view of the constitution has become very untrue to fact and to law . . . It seems to me impossible so to define constitutional law that it shall not include the constitution of every organ of government whether it be central government, whether it be sovereign or subordinate.'[93] The effect of these often biting critiques was a turn away from the essentially court-focused perspective of Dicey by a number of jurists and scholars, towards an investigation of the new role for government emerging after World War I as a result of the enormous expansion of commerce and industry after 1830. In

---

89 Gordon, *op. cit.* note 86, p. 436.
90 Frankfurter, F., 'Foreword' (to a Discussion of Current Developments in Administrative Law) (1938) 47 *Yale Law Journal* 515.
91 Sugarman, *op. cit.* note 4 *supra*, p. 102.
92 Drewry, G., 'Public Law' (1995) 73 *Public Administration* 41, at 45.
93 Quoted in Suzman, A., 'Administrative Law in England: A Study of the Committee on Ministers' Powers' (1932) 18 *Iowa Law Review* 160, at 162.

particular, of the impact of newly administrative–governmental structures — which Dicey called 'collectivism' — on our constitutional arrangements, on the citizen and on the functional place of law within this new paradigm. For what is administrative law now, they asked, if it is not housing, social security, planning, labour relations or local government, all the result of the hundreds of Acts of Parliament which had created the contemporary regulatory state. Judicial review today, for example, is largely concerned with disputes arising from such basic aspects of the state's role in modern society as social security and immigration control. This trend away from an elite judicial towards a more political–scientific and sociological–behavioural analysis in public law is exemplified by what is often termed the 'functionalist' school of thought, associated with some key figures. It is to this important movement that we must now turn.

A NEW WAY FORWARD: PUBLIC LAW AND THE FUNCTIONALIST CRITIQUE OF THE FORMALIST CONTROL PARADIGM

It will be useful to begin with a definition. The term 'functionalism' is used in many ways; two of which in particular are useful for our purposes. The first is that derived from sociological theory, namely, that of Comte and Durkheim, as well as the anthropologists Malinowski and Radcliffe-Brown. Its central tenet is that society is a system with interdependent and mutually supportive parts. Each of these parts has a function in the survival of the whole. The obvious analogy is with a biological organism. The work of the system theorists Niklas Luhmann and Gunther Teubner fits reasonably comfortably into this definition.[94] The second is associated with the American school of Realist Jurisprudence. This endorses scientific positivism and is empirical in orientation, eschewing abstract theoretical conceptualisation in favour of a distinct pragmatic bias. It asks what the *consequences* of law are, given that it is operationalised within and not apart from, an actually existing social system. This emphasis on what law does within an interest-driven set of competing power relationships is central to the functionalist analysis of public law discussed below.

The result of the persistent excavation of the foundations of the Diceyan legacy since the 1890s was that the period from 1918 to 1939 saw Dicey's ideas come under incisive and cumulative fire from Harold Laski, Ivor Jennings and William Robson, based at the London School of Economics. The *Modern Law Review* (founded in 1937) provided a new focus for an increasingly widely articulated dissenting perspective. In common with one facet of Dicey's work, the functionalist school were to pursue a highly rationalistic enterprise. But, by contrast, their

---

94 See Luhmann, N., *A Sociological Theory of Law*, London: Routledge & Kegan Paul, 1985; Teubner, G., *Autopoietic Law: A New Approach to Law and Society*, New York: Walter de Gruy 1988.

view has its origins in the more utilitarian notion of government associated with Bentham and the collectivist evolutionary socialism of Sidney Webb and the Fabian Society, founded in 1884. It was also strongly influenced by the realist school of jurisprudence. Legal realism is more obligated to sociology and the 'New Deal' policies of President Roosevelt in the USA during the 1930s. As these policies began to bite, fashioning the instruments of government and law to cope with the building of a modern legal–administrative state became much more attractive. This movement was to have considerable academic consequences in the UK. Adopting a sociological method, as Jennings advocated, became typical of the adherents of the functionalist view; social science and law together could facilitate progress and act as an expression of rational democratic government in the wider society.

The 'Great War' had resulted in a significant increase in the scope of government activity, and it ended with Parliament almost completing the task of at least formally democratising society, with the enfranchisement of all men over 21 and women over 30. The political, economic, social and cultural landscape had changed greatly. But the Diceyan view of the constitution nevertheless remained largely intact. What Robson termed the 'Dicey overhang' was particularly evident in Lord Hewart's *New Despotism*, first published in 1929. This amounted to a 'violent and undisguised attack upon the Civil Service',[95] an attack (according to Robson) supported by 99 per cent of the legal profession, because new developments 'could scarcely be expected to weigh with the predominantly upper-middle class, Forsytic and conservative legal mind'.[96] Robson viewed this work as not only representing the 'high watermark' of the Diceyan view 'with all its misconceptions',[97] but as providing the setting for the Donoughmore Committee. Indeed, he criticised the Committee's terms of reference for virtually determining its eventual recommendations, hence Robson's celebrated remark that 'The committee started life with the dead hand of Dicey lying frozen on its neck'.[98] In fact, these recommendations reveal a persistent underlying concern about creating administrative bodies that could act as rivals to the courts, coupled with the alarmist view that 'Shadows of the Star Chamber [had] beg[u]n to stalk the land'.[99] The upshot was that administrative discretion became a whipping post for the revival of the old order; radical initiatives were stillborn, the law was not adapted to take full account of new realities, and we continued to muddle through. For example, Robson lamented that the committee left the chaotic patchwork of ill-constructed tribunals untouched.

---

95 Robson, W., 'Administrative Law' in Ginsberg, M. (ed.), *Law and Opinion in England in the Twentieth Century*, London: Stevens, 1959, p. 196.
96 *Ibid.*, p. 349.
97 *Ibid.*, p. 196.
98 Robson, W., 'The Report of the Committee on Ministers' Powers' (1932) 3 *Political Quarterly* 351.
99 Robson, W., 'Administrative Law in England, 1918–1948', in Campion, G. (ed.), *British Government since 1918*, London: Allen & Unwin, 1950.

The starting point for functionalists, then, is to link constitutional and administrative law in a recognition of the new role for the liberal-pluralist, interventionist, administrative state; to ask what society's *needs* are and to discover how law might help to meet these pressing needs by a change in its role and self-perception. Although this is proposed without any general alternative theory being clearly articulated common to all adherents of the school (other than a vague neo-Marxist progressivism), any attempt to deal with the crisis of the old order required much more of an 'empiricist orientation', a determination to get on with the task at hand of ameliorative social reform and facilitating legislative intent to this end. Functionalists have not spent a great deal of energy reflecting on what law *is* but have concentrated rather upon discussing what government *does* with law. As Jones puts it, 'the state is not an end in itself but an instrumentality to be appraised in terms of its contribution to the welfare of the individuals who compose the national community'.[100] In tandem with the stress on what law can achieve, there is an implied relativism in such remarks as 'No theory of the state is ever intelligible save in the context of its time. What men think about the state is the outcome always of the experience in which they are immersed'.[101] Or that 'Law cannot transcend the relations it is intended to enforce. Its ultimate postulates are never self-determined, but given to it by the economic system of which it is the expression'.[102] Law and the state in this perspective arise and grow together, and each combines elements of political legitimacy as well as moral persuasiveness. This conflation of progressivism, relativism, positivism and empiricism gives rise to such comments as 'Social interests cannot be secured, or a social policy effected, by the application of abstract principles of justice as between man and man',[103] and to the predisposition towards an ideology in which 'the positive state is [seen as] the responsible state'.[104] And thus it follows that administrative law determines the organisation, powers and duties of all administrative authorities; that *all* aspects of public administration within the state need to be addressed in a new theory of institutions, one where (although some judicial oversight of administrative discretion is necessary) efficient public administration is regarded both as a work of professional expertise and as the best means for facilitating the delivery of agreed humane collectivist policy goals (along the lines of the Roosevelt precedent). Once again, Frankfurter puts it well: 'Ultimately, then, the concerns of administrative law are not less than the power and resourcefulness of democratic constitutional government: to fashion instruments and procedures capable of coping with some of the most perplexing but exigent problems of society.'[105]

---

100 Jones, *op. cit.* note 33 *supra*, p. 143.
101 Laski, H., *A Grammar of Politics*, London: Allen and Unwin, 1925, p. i.
102 *Ibid.*, at p. xxii. See also Ch. 10, p. 544.
103 Robson, W., 'Justice and Administrative Law Reconsidered' (1979) 32 *Current Legal Problems* 107.
104 Laski, H., 'The Growth of Administrative Discretion' (1923) 1 *Public Administration* 92, at 96.
105 Frankfurter, *op. cit.* note 90 *supra*.

Similarly, the 'amateurs' in Parliament and the senior judiciary were contrasted unfavourably with 'professional' civil servants (the emergence of which is viewed as one of the most significant institutional outcomes of democracy) and local government officials responsible for the implementation of statutory measures. Nevertheless, a significant strand of functionalist criticism has highlighted both the 'constant criticism of the administration [as being] essential to the success of the democratic adventure'[106] and the inadequacy of controls over legislation (or delegated legislation) prior to its enactment. Facing the growth of the new collectivist administrative state and the resultant proliferation of legislation, Parliament has proved inadequate to the task. While the legislature should not be regarded as being entirely distinct from the process of administration itself, effective mechanisms for scrutiny of the executive are vital for the health of democracy as well as for ensuring that legislation is well conceived and clearly drafted. This weakness, flowing from the dominance of party over Parliament, has given force to claims of 'elective dictatorship'. To take just two examples, the convention of individual ministerial responsibility has atrophied in the face of the development of new 'contracting' state formations; while the guillotining of legislation in the House of Commons can easily lead to the predominance of the executive over any opposition, however reasoned and measured the arguments. Nevertheless, while there is widespread agreement in this tradition that modern government needs to be open to scrutiny and that discretionary power should be made accountable, recent functionalist contributions continue to assert the desirability of democratic political responsibility through Parliament to any large-scale assertion of judicial control. But they would appear to lack any clear advice on how this might be achieved, other than that Parliament as a whole reasserts itself.

The 'politics of the judiciary' and the role of the courts

As we have already affirmed, a critical assessment of the role of the senior judiciary in particular has been a recurrent theme of the functionalist tradition. This preoccupation is best exemplified in a series of critical evaluations of their role by Harold Laski and J.A.G. Griffith. So that where Dicey and his supporters to this day place their faith in the rule of law upheld by judges, Griffith views the self-same principle as a form of mystification and one which serves to help facilitate the preservation of power in the hands of the status quo, largely because law can never stand in for politics.[107]

Several themes predominate. Judges are recognised, following the insights of American legal realism, as acting as inventive law-makers with all the implications that this suggests for democratic policy formation: 'The fiction that judges do not

---

106   Laski, *op. cit.* note 104 *supra*, p. 100.
107   Griffith, J.A.G., 'The Political Constitution, (1979) 42 *Modern Law Review* 1, at 15.

legislate has long since been abandoned by all who care for a conscious and realistic jurisprudence.'[108] If this is true, it should be explicitly recognised that the legislators on the bench should decide on the cases before them; not in the light of the abstract principles they have invented or their own prejudices, but in the context of their responsibility for the development of the policy of the democratically elected legislature. For Laski, as well as Griffith, the decision in *Roberts* v *Hopwood*[109] encapsulates the view not only that judges are covert legislators on the bench, but also, that there is a danger that they can be motivated by dated ideological prejudices, albeit probably unconsciously. Indeed, this famous case brings out the differences between the functionalist progressive perspective and that of the more traditional Diceyan view very clearly. Compare, for example, Laski's critique of the use of the word 'reasonableness' as it was interpreted in *Roberts* v *Hopwood*, with Wade's defence of the judgment as merely 'criticisms from literal-minded people'.[110] Or their view of *Local Government Board* v *Arlidge*, where Dicey's fears are downplayed by Laski — who regards the case as simply a striking indication of the new delegating state — while Wade regards it as missed opportunity for judicial control.

This general presupposition was channelled by Laski in particular into persistent criticism of the defective methods of interpretation employed by the judiciary, most notably in the field of administrative law. There is ongoing concern in his work that English judges act to circumvent the wishes of Parliamentary[111] through their narrow-minded literalism, with no understanding of policy or why this policy rather than another was chosen. For example, in legislation conferring rights on trade unions. Laski advocates a rejection of this narrowness and recommends that '[the court] should seek to discover the effect of the legislative precept in action so as to give full weight to the social value it is intended to secure'.[112] That is, that a *functional* test and not a *conceptual-analytical* one should be applied. The problem is that judges, given their preoccupation with private law rights, lack the necessary knowledge and expertise, or are unwilling to take account of the social or economic purpose lying behind the law; or indeed to recognise that many questions which purport to be purely factual are also matters of opinion. The judges should, rather, investigate the social aims of the legislation and develop a purposive approach to reasoning following in the wake of the example set by some of their American counterparts. The problem is that when faced with the

---

108   Laski, H., 'Judicial Review of Social Policy in England' (1925) 39 *Harvard Law Review* 832.
109   [1925] AC 578.
110   Laski, *op. cit.* note 108 *supra*; Wade, *op. cit.* note 42 *supra*, p. 421. See also Fennell, *op. cit.* note 32 *supra*.
111   Cooper, M., 'Administrative Justice and the Role of Discretion' (1938) 42 *Yale Law Journal* 577, p. 596.
112   Laski, H., 'Note by Prof. Laski on the Judicial Interpretation of Statutes', in *Report of the Committee on Minister's Powers*, Cmnd. 4060 (1932), Annex v, p. 137.

imprecision of terminology there has been a tendency, given the background and training of the common law, for judges to emphasise the rationality and coherence many of them perceive to be embodied in the very nature of law itself.

More recently J.A.G. Griffith has concentrated on analysing the overall contribution of the judiciary to the 'political constitution', and more specifically on that aspect of administrative law centred on decisions of the courts. In common with Laski and Jennings he adopts a realist perspective from which the courts are viewed both as part of the administration and as essentially unrepresentative of democratic popular opinion. Although a 'myth of neutrality' has been assiduously promoted for a century and more, law cannot be neutral for 'laws are merely statements of a power relationship and nothing more'.[113] Truth is grounded in experience and in practical conflictual power relations in society as a whole. Judges, therefore, inescapably have a creative role, but 'the courts have adopted a policy of intervening and of substituting their judgment of what is desirable — and that includes what is politically desirable — over wide areas of administrative activity and for a great variety of reasons'. This contention of Griffiths, that the judiciary are necessarily political, is supported by a detailed discussion of case law from the late 19th century down to the 1990s.

Griffith does recognise (like Laski) that law has a limited control function with a 'proper and adequate machinery . . . for ensuring that public bodies do not exceed their legal powers',[114] that they follow procedures set out by statute, and do not act arbitrarily or capriciously. This, for him, is in essence what the 'rule of law' means today. But this function can only ever be partially effective because public administration must have room for discretion, while laws cannot cover every eventuality. It follows that when exercising their review function the courts' tests for intervention should be narrow and precise, not vague and open to expansive definition like the terms 'illegality', 'irrationality' and 'procedural propriety' — terms which make it impossible to forecast the extent and limits of judicial review.[115] Griffith particularly disapproves of open-ended judge-made concepts such as 'fiduciary duty', which can be extended and restricted at will because of its very vagueness, describing the use of this concept in *Bromley* v *GLC*, for example, as a 'gross interference by the judiciary in the exercise of political responsibility of an elected local authority'.[116] The courts should keep their hands off unless decisions are clearly identifiable as arbitrary or capricious. However, his assessment of judicial prejudice is not reduced to a question of simple partisanship. The courts, he argues, are an integral part of the governmental apparatus, and

---

113   Griffith, *op. cit.* note 107 *supra*, p. 19. See also *The Politics of the Judiciary* (4th ed.), London: Fontana, 1991 and the revised edition (5th ed.), London: Fontana 1997; see also *Judicial Politics Since 1920*, Oxford: Basil Blackwell, 1993.
114   Griffith, *op. cit.* note 107 *supra*, 1979, p. 14.
115   Griffith, *op. cit.* note 113 *supra*, 1991, p. 146.
116   *Ibid.*, p. 131.

therefore cannot avoid making political decisions from a perspective of partiality as to what constitutes the 'public interest'. This is particularly true of 'the interest of the state (including its moral welfare); . . . the preservation of law and order, broadly interpreted; and . . . the promotion of certain political views normally associated with the Conservative Party'.[117] Griffith goes on to argue that just as politicians cannot be politically neutral, neither can judges. They arrive at the bench from a particular professional socialisation and educational background. As a group they support a remarkably homogeneous set of predominantly upper-middle 'class attitudes, beliefs and principles',[118] and are placed in particular positions where they are required to make political choices because of the nature of the issues which they are asked to adjudicate on. Griffith argues that his survey of the case law conclusively demonstrates that confronted with choices as to where the public interest lies, the senior judiciary can be shown to have supported 'conventional, established and settled interests' of a basically centre-right persuasion.[119] Perhaps this explains (because the whole political spectrum of debate has moved to the right over the last two decades) why the judiciary today appear so much more 'centrist' than 20 years ago.

One of the questionable features of Griffith's analysis is that he seems to leave little room for a perspective in which the judiciary play any role at all, other than the most strictly defined and narrowly constructionist. Even from a position sympathetic to Griffith, more radically inclined lawyers might regard his work on the politics of the judiciary as being essentially conservative. For he does not advocate any fundamental change but only some adjustment to the rules of the game, particularly — as we have already seen, in conjunction with many in the previous generation of functionalists — that Parliament, especially the House of Commons, should wake up and do its (political) job. Moreover, his work seems to be imbued with a sense of the 'war of each against all' in a pessimistic power-competition model of Hobbesian/Machiavellian proportions[120] — a model which leaves little room for speculation on alternative legal and constitutional–democratic arrangements. For example, Richard Rawlings questions the heuristic value of the idea of the 'political constitution' as a 'non legal' discourse of public controversy in the face of the *legalisation* of debates surrounding the ratification of the Maastricht Treaty, Britain's membership of the EC and the influence of the ECHR.[121] However, this is probably to misconstrue Griffith's purpose in simply deconstructing the cant and hypocrisy he perceives surrounds so much of the rhetoric of law and the 'trappings of democracy' — a good example,

---

117 *Ibid.*, p. 278.
118 *Ibid.*, p. 275.
119 *Ibid.*, p. 325.
120 See, for example, *op. cit.* note 107 *supra*.
121 Rawlings, R., 'Legal Politics: The United Kingdom and Ratification of the Treaty on European Union (Pt Two)' [1994] *Public Law* 367.

as we have already seen, is the rule of law itself. In this regard Griffith's modified positivist model has much in common with the strong emphasis on positivism, empiricism and nominalism found in the work of Foucault in Ch. 17.

Patrick McAuslan: participatory democracy and the new functionalism

Because of the positivist underpinning to the functionalist position and the resultant inhibition on thinking historically and speculatively, no thoroughgoing attempt to theorise the nature of administrative law and its relationship to society and the state as a whole took place from the 1930s until the early 1980s with the contribution of Patrick McAuslan. As he saw it, even in the 1970s[122] the focus of the courts was still on procedural aspects and private rights for individuals, the defence of property rights and '*away* from the issues of policy-formulation, the allocation of resources and collective decision making within the processes of collective consumption'.[123] In practice this meant that, despite the increased activism of the courts since the 1960s, largely because of the continuing influence of the private law model, the detailed application of the law to 'real world'[124] areas of such fundamental importance to the citizen as immigration, housing, education, the use of their powers by local authorities or access to judicial review, was neglected in administrative legal theory. This has now been rectified, to some extent at least;[125] but the persisting overhang of Donoughmore and Franks into the late 20th century had made us ill-equipped to deal with major clashes of policy and ideology in public law.

While adopting a broadly instrumentalist–functionalist orientation, from a position, influenced by Griffiths, which regards the constitution in the UK as merely 'a flag to drape over and conceal power',[126] McAuslan stresses more overtly the intimate connection between the political process and public law, so raising again the question of the proper role of law in society. What is it there for: What is it being used to achieve? How has it shaped attitudes and practices? To what extent should it be used to control governments? The operation of the legal system can help to create problems for collective social policy goals, or it can help to provide solutions. This perspective has the implication that the foundations for public law theory are to be found in the human sciences and in history; indeed, McAuslan does emphasise the central importance of theory, philosophy and ideology to administrative law. Law does not exist as a discrete entity in an environment all its own. It must constitute at least a part of the search for answers

---

122   McAuslan, P., 'The Plan, the Planners and the Lawyers' [1971] *Public Law* 247.
123   McAuslan, P., 'Administrative Law, Collective Consumption and Judicial Review' (1983) 46 *Modern Law Review* 1, p. 3.
124   MacPherson, C.B., *The Real World of Democracy*, Oxford: Oxford University Press, 1966.
125   See, for example, Hadfield, B. (ed.), *Judicial Review: A Thematic Approach*, Dublin: Gill & Macmillan, 1995.
126   McAuslan, P., 'Public Law and Public Choice' (1988) 51 Modern Law Review 703.

to questions about the nature of the economy, justice in society and the social purpose of government. Another feature of his work is that he argues for a more radical definition of democracy than that commonly found in the literature of the past (or present). Rather than incantations to the platitudes of representative and responsible (indirect) democracy, there is an urgency about the development of more openness to citizen choice and creative involvement by citizens in civil society and the governmental–administrative process. McAuslan, then, combines a stress on functionalist effectiveness with a normativist rights approach to participatory democracy.

In particular, in an influential article published in 1983,[127] McAuslan reaffirmed that the result of the lacuna in theorising already noted had been a lack of any coherent system of administrative law based on a single widely accepted framing perspective. Rather, as Robson and Mitchell had already pointed out, there had merely been a piecemeal growth of alternative dispute handling agencies added on to the core role of the courts. Writing against the background of what was by the 1970s conventionally regarded as a corporatist type state formation, there was a pressing need to step back and adopt a broad, critical perspective. Namely, the idea of 'collective consumption', a concept which covered both substantive and procedural aspects of law. Law should be used to implement a particular democratically validated concept of the public good. This approach is presented in an exemplary fashion in McAuslan's *Ideologies of Planning Law,* first published in 1980.[128]

McAuslan sets out an arresting and challenging thesis: that there are three basic ideologies which underpin judicial attitudes towards planning law:

> Firstly, the law exists and should be used to protect private property and its institutions . . . [s]econdly, the law exists and should be used to advance the public interest; [t]hirdly the law exists and should be used to advance the cause of public participation against both the orthodox public administration approach to the public interest and the common law approach of the overriding importance of private property . . .[129]

Notice also that he adopts a broad definition of planning, covering not only town and country planning itself, but also some elements of housing and roads, etc.

Pursuing his theme, McAuslan argues that the prevailing, dominant ideology of private property has its origins in the work of John Locke;[130] that of the public interest in the influential work of Bentham and Chadwick. However, these are far

---

127   McAuslan, *op. cit.* note 123 *supra.*
128   McAuslan, P., *The Ideologies of Planning Law,* Oxford: Pergamon Press, 1980.
129   *Ibid.,* p. 213.
130   See esp. MacPherson, C.B., *The Political Theory of Possessive Individualism: Hobbes to Locke,* Oxford: Oxford University Press, 1962.

from being co-equally regarded for there is an implied clash between the two ideologies, especially in the eyes of the courts, although McAuslan himself nevertheless discerns an underlying unity of interest between the two positions — to preserve the *status quo*. For they can combine, in perhaps uneasy alliance, to block moves to *participatory* democracy, moves that might necessitate a fundamental transformation of the ideological framework within which the debate is conducted. This radical democratic legacy is traced by McAuslan back to the writings of J.S. Mill. However, despite this democratic thrust, the tendency is for the professional ideology of the planners to predominate over such interests, because of the dominance of administrative–rationalist ideology in a direct relationship which subverts democratic accountability. Moreover, the law normally reinforces this bureaucratic/professional ethos, ultimately protecting capitalist private property interests through an implied ideology which works as an undercurrent to prevent knowledgeable discussion of the many issues involved and involvement of the plurality of interests concerned. McAuslan argues that, although the law is necessarily instrumentalist — in the end a tool for attaining political objectives — it should be so in the attainment of participatory democratic goals and values. Especially with regard to the interests of those who constitute the poorer, more marginal elements of society, rather than those who 'staff the command posts of society'.[131]

Specifically, focusing on the judiciary, he agrees with the functionalist school that they have tended to concentrate overmuch on the defence of private rights and regulative activity rather than acting in a facilitative, positive manner towards issues of collective consumption; indeed, to display a fear of democracy of a particular openly participatory variety. One unfortunate result of the over-insistence on individualising issues, of regarding them as issues of purely private concern, has been the misunderstanding of the policy conflicts involved; their necessary intermeshing with broader social, economic and political concerns. McAuslan asserts that these apparent clashes can be fully comprehended only by elucidating the underlying differences of approach that lie behind the disputes between the different agencies concerned with collective consumption, for example, disputes between central and local government, housing and planning and the individual rights of citizens.[132] Displaying a ready facility, a mastery of the legal material and case law in the field, he seeks to defend his perspective by means of an analysis of certain key legal battles of the 1970s, for example, *Norwich CC v Secretary of State for Environment*.[133] Most significantly perhaps, regarding *Bromley v GLC*,[134] McAuslan comments on the central issue of

---

131 See Mills, C.W., *The Power Elite*, New York: Oxford University Press, 1956.
132 For example, see *Coleen Properties v Minister of Housing and Local Government* [1971] 1 WLR 433; *Fairmount Investments Ltd v the Secretary of State for the Environment* [1976] 1 WLR 1255.
133 [1982] 1 All ER 737.
134 [1980] 1 All ER 129.

'fiduciary duty' that was raised in the case: ' . . . no concept could have been invoked which was better able to limit the growth of the processes of collective consumption than the fiduciary duty of local authorities to ratepayers'.[135] It converts a policy about collective consumption goals into one about the burden on individual ratepayers.[136]

A number of observations might be made of the approach by McAuslan. There are two basic concepts of ideology: one as false consciousness (stressed in the Marxist tradition); the other, that of any generally held perspective on the world (stressed, at least until recently, in the human sciences).[137] He appears to use it in the second sense. But just how precise is his definition of ideology or, indeed, of public law? Secondly, even if his analysis of judicial ideology was accurate at the time, does it still have heuristic value in the 1990s? Have personal and ideological changes in the senior judiciary undermined his position? It follows from these questions that we must raise the issue whether McAuslan emphasises sufficiently strongly that there is a need to test his claims empirically regarding judicial ideology. However, there are clear methodological difficulties in the way of such an approach.[138] Thirdly, McAuslan calls on academic legal study to abandon its narrow and parochial focus on rules and case-based analysis in favour of the utilisation of policy, theory and philosophy; for law to become part of the human sciences and the broader scholarly community. It must be said that there has not been a great deal of encouragement for his position since this rallying cry was made. Taking McAuslan's work as a whole, the functionalist perspective is refreshed, yet political and economic developments over the 1980s and 1990s have made the advent of such a conception of democracy as he proposes appear further away than ever. Subsequent theoretical work, as well as practical proposals for change, have taken public law in many different directions, leading to a sense of incoherence in the discipline.

CONCLUSION

It will be the task of Chapter 17 to analyse these developments with a view:

(a)   to arriving at some understanding of the different perspectives;

---

135   McAuslan, *op. cit.* note 123 *supra*, p. 18.

136   Note the similarity with Laski and Griffith above and the contrast with the public choice school today, an ideology which he regards as antithetical to the whole idea of the 'public interest'. This school has a direct affinity to contemporary developments in the law and economics approach, exemplified in the USA by the work of Richard Posner. Unfortunately, we have no space to discuss these here. See McAuslan, P., 'Public Law and Public Choice' (1988) 51 *Modern Law Review* 681; Posner, R., *Economic Analysis of Law* (4th ed.), Boston: Little Brown, 1992. For some recent reflections, see Goodhart, C.A.E., 'Economics and the Law: Too Much One-Way Traffic?' (1997) 60 *Modern Law Review* 1.

137   Eagleton, T., *Ideology: An Introduction*, London: Verso, 1991.

138   See generally Tamanaha, *op. cit.* note 53 *supra*.

(b)   to situating these (and other ideas which must remain off-stage because we do not have space to discuss them here) within some ultimate framework of analysis, one both empirical and normative in nature.

17

Public Law History and Theory: Some Notes Towards a New Foundationalism: Part 2: Some Contemporary Developments and a Sketch for the Future

Peter Leyland and Terry Woods

SUMMARY

Having provided an overview of influential contributions to administrative law theory since the late nineteenth century in Ch. 16, this chapter seeks to discuss a number of the more recent developments from a range of varying perspectives. These are contextualised within a broad framework of social and philosophical work from a number of the most original contemporary sources of theoretical debate. The chapter concludes with a necessarily brief sketch note towards a new foundationalism for public law generally.

INTRODUCTION

We asked at the outset of the last chapter whether theory could ever catch up with reality, however measured or defined. Whether Hegel's 'Owl of Minerva' could even fly as early as dusk? Is academic public law theory, in seeking a framing narrative for administrative law, capable of responding to this challenge; or is it little more than a spider playing games in a web of its own devising? First, in the long retreat from the conventional wisdom of black-letter textualism, public law theorising has been associated with sociology (the socio-legal movement), with economics (public choice theory) and with philosophy (e.g., Wittgenstein and Habermas). The result has been a degree of uncertainty, indeed confusion. But in the search for a new context for legal inquiry, for new critical, normative and practical guidelines, for a new theoretical paradigm, the most likely contender in the eyes of many has not been any of these but political theory. Given the inescapability of choice (including for the writers of this short piece), an analysis of the political context which frames and influences legal ideology and practice might well appear to be the most fruitful avenue of exploration. Secondly, the majority of the political theories to which the writers below have had recourse are a product of the Enlightenment project, of a desire to understand through reason and science (including the human sciences) the world around them with the ideals of optimism and progress underpinning the whole. They rest on many presuppositions, including utilitarian happiness, liberty, rights, fraternity and equality. In sum, on a plurality of values which are essentially liberal.

T.R.S. ALLAN: PUBLIC LAW AND LIBERAL NORMATIVISM

Allan is one of those who have had recourse to liberal political theory, and his work provides a striking contrast to the functionalist school in a period when it is widely seen to be running out of steam. The vacuum is filled by an anti-instrumentalist control model of unconstrained judicial review[1] in the guise of a highly rationalistic 'liberal normativism', a foundationalist perspective, of which he is a self-confessed adherent, advocating which beliefs we *should* hold rather than those we *do* hold about public law and constitutionalism. Influenced by the work of Fuller, Hayek and Dworkin (especially his theory of rights-based adjudication[2]) and working from an assumption that seeks to 'alleviate the stranglehold which legal positivism has placed on constitutional law',[3] Allan emphasises that 'the lawyer who seeks to evade philosophical questions condemns himself to work uncritically within a normative framework whose origins he may not understand and whose value judgements he may not even share'.[4] Legal interpretation must inevitably rest on underlying assumptions of political theory and liberal democracy,[5] but we need a new compass to help us find

---

1   Dyzenhaus, D., 'The Legitimacy of Legality' (1968) 46 *University of Toronto Law Review* 129, at p. 175.
2   Fuller, L.F., *The Morality of Law*, New Haven: Connecticut, 1969 (rev ed. Yale University Press); Hayek, F.A., *The Constitution of Liberty*, Chicago: Chicago University Press, and *Law, Legislation and Liberty*, London: Routledge and Kegan Paul, 1982; Dworkin, R., *Taking Rights Seriously*, London, Duckworth, 1977.
3   Allan, T.R.S., *Law, Liberty, and Justice: The Legal Foundations of British Constitutionalism*, Oxford: Clarendon Press, 1993, p. vii.
4   Quoted by Munro, C., review of Allan, in (1993) 14 *Legal Studies*, at p. 456.
5   Allan, T.R.S., 'Equality and Moral Independence: Private Morality and Public Law', in Loveland, I. (ed.), *A Special Relationship? American Influences on Public Law in the UK*, Oxford: Clarendon Press, 1995, p. 47.

the way forward — one which offers a critique of Blackstone; in particular, of Dicey's positivistic separation of law and convention and his doctrine of the supremacy of Parliament. By contrast, Allan seeks to conjoin law and a 'shared political morality'[6] within a broadened and deepened conception of the rule of law.

The result is that Allan's work represents a form of updated Diceyism, one which jettisons the authoritarian command model of Austin and English particularism, and strives to provide a renovated and coherent constitutional foundation for Dicey's theoretical model in contemporary circumstances. The common law of Dicey's imagination has no base or logical clarity; the theory underpinning the common law constitution is implicit not explicit, and a public lawyer in the orthodox tradition is working blind because of this lack of clarity. The result is that the common law borders on the mystical, a series of almost mythopoeic claims to legitimacy. Nevertheless, in the absence of a written document, we do arguably have some kind of common law constitution, and recognising this was Dicey's lasting insight.[7]

Allan believes that it is now imperative to provide a rights foundation to this theory inherited from the 19th century. The common law is flexible enough to provide for the same kind of protection as would be provided by, for example, a bill of rights on American or continental lines. We need to develop with sensitivity and imagination this inherent flexibility of the common law so that we may deal with contemporary dilemmas.[8] Allan himself is not predisposed in favour of a Bill of Rights in preference to these rich constitutional traditions which he regards as embodying rights prior to any legislative enactment. Indeed, parachuting in a codified document could be counterproductive, raising as many issues as it settles for the judiciary, politicians and society generally. To this end, as we have noted, he is attracted to the liberal political and legal theory of Dworkin where no distinction is made (unlike by Dicey) between legal and political principle; they are simply different names for legitimate constitutional behaviour.[9] It follows from this view that what is 'unconstitutional' is simply illegal: 'Dworkin's most important contribution to jurisprudence has perhaps been his insistence on the interconnection between law and morality, emphasising the role of the judge's political morality in his judgments about the law'.[10] Values as such are worthy of consideration; one identifies abstract ideals and sees how far they are approximated in practice. This court-centred focus of Dworkin incidentally helps to explain why Allan himself spends so much time discussing the work of the judiciary.

Dworkin's inclusive theory of 'law as integrity'[11] explains better (Allan believes) than either positivism or legal realism how cases are decided, with the appeal of

---

6   Allan, T.R.S., 'The Limits of Parliamentary Sovereignty' [1986] *Public Law* 614, at p. 621.
7   Allan, *op. cit.* note 3 *supra*, p. 4.
8   *Ibid.*, p. 10.
9   *Ibid.*, p. 72.
10 *Ibid.*, p. 100.
11 Dworkin, *op. cit.* note 2 *supra*.

the integrity principle lying in the idea of equality.[12] Unlike Dicey, who tended to marginalise the role of statute and accentuate the role of the common law, Dworkin sees the two as co-equal parts of an integrated system. Together these make up a 'community of principle'. However Allan argues that in England, unlike the USA, statute should always be subordinate because our rights are embodied in the common law developed through time by the courts in a flexible, adaptive manner. He also readily adopts from Dworkin his idea of a distinction between 'principle' and 'policy'. Rights are inclusive principles based on reason — and therefore potentially unlimited — while policies are goals. Legislation is primarily enacted to achieve goals rather than to recognise rights;[13] but rights derived from the rule of law should always 'trump' utilitarian considerations of the national interest.[14] A viewpoint such as this ultimately rests on the Kantian understanding that the human being has an inherent moral dignity and should never be used as a means to an end. Law, then, is a structure of 'rules of just conduct' independent of any purpose or policy. Policy goals are for the legislature; questions of principle (rights) for the courts. Rights must on occasion 'trump' other considerations because justice can be developed and encouraged if the idea of a rights-based rule of law becomes instantiated in the context of a society where such rights are accepted and widely commended.

The nature of public law, then, is as a system of rights; and the extent of judicial review in particular would be founded upon the *judicially* interpreted limit and enforceability of such rights.[15] By this process of reasoning we have, in principle at least, the means of distinguishing how the judicial process operates for the consideration of policy issues. For Dworkin, in the absence of rules (or where they are ambiguous) the ideal judge ('Hercules') will resort to legal principles (e.g., that one should not profit from one's crime); and where the principles themselves are ambiguous, the judge will resort to the background morality in society — an idea which Griffith,[16] as a positivist, caustically describes as 'nonsense at the very top of a very high ladder'. Allan puts it somewhat differently: interpretation is necessarily based 'on moral and political values which can serve to justify interpretation itself'.[17] These values are the bedrock values of justice, the rule of law and constitutional government itself. But can such an Archimedean stance ever be sustained in the face of cultural differentiation and the increasing complexity of the modern world?

---

12   Allan, *op. cit.* note 3 *supra*, p. 4.
13   Dworkin, *op. cit.* note 2 *supra*, p. 82.
14   Yet these can easily conflict: see *R* v *Cambridgeshire District Health Authority, ex parte B* (1995) 11 FLR 1055; BMLR 5 (DC); 1 WLR 898 (CA) and *R* v *Human Fertilisation and Embryology Authority, ex parte Blood* [1997] 2 All ER 687.
15   Allan, *op. cit.* note 3 *supra*, p. 7.
16   Griffith, J.A.G., 'The Political Constitution (1979) *Modern Law Review* 11. See also Allan, T.R.S., 'Citizenship and Obligation: Civil Disobedience and Civil Dissent' (1996) 55 *Cambridge Law Journal* 89, 90.
17   Allan, *op. cit.* note 5 *supra*, p. 73.

Given this scepticism, how does Allan argue the case for these principles to be incorporated in public law theory and constitutional practice? He begins by critiquing Dicey's model of parliamentary supremacy. *Pace* Dicey's assertions, legislative supremacy (or 'parliamentary omnicompetence') is *not* the foundation of the legal order. Rather, following Dworkin, 'that fundamental rule derives its legal authority from the underlying moral or political theory to which it belongs'.[18] (Compare Jurgen Habermas, below, where this is found in the 'life world' of intersubjective agreement.) Parliamentary supremacy is not devoid of political morality;[19] rather, it articulates the courts' acceptance of current British concepts of parliamentary democracy.

If it is not the supremacy of parliament, then, which concept *does* underpin our constitutional arrangements? Allan seeks to reassert the weight to be given to the rule of law over parliamentary supremacy based on a common law jurisprudence of equal rights for citizens (substantive as well as procedural) in order 'to defend a conception of the rule of law which emphasises the moral responsibility and independence of the ordinary citizen'.[20] Within the broader ideal of 'law as integrity', equality is viewed as being basic to liberty and democracy alike. Dicey's equality before the law is only one consequence of a 'deeper conception of the equality of citizens — an equality which forms the basis of our commitment to democracy itself'[21] and 'The rule of law is . . . an important part of a wider vision of political liberalism'[22] which seeks to balance 'the conflicting demands of authority and autonomy'[23] — part of a complex tapestry of constitutional principles where the citizen plays a role in 'the adoption of the laws, not only in their implementation'.[24]

At the same time, Allan supplements his emphasis, following Dicey, on the rule of law, and equality before the law in particular, with Hayek's stress on the separation of powers. The result is that the notion of the rule of law has been expanded well beyond Dicey's original position. In particular, the consequences of not accepting Dicey's positivistic distinction between law and politics (convention) result in a much-enhanced role for the courts in checking the powers of the state upon the basis of a continuous debate among a participating citizenry around which principles ought to be enshrined as the basis of the rule of law. As has been pointed out elsewhere, a very 'Protestant' perspective on our constitutional arrangements.[25]

---

18 Allan, *op. cit.* note 3 *supra*, p. 265.
19 *Ibid.*, p. 289.
20 *Ibid.*, p. 125.
21 Allan, *op. cit.* note 6 *supra*, p. 629.
22 Allan, *op. cit.* note 16 *supra*, p. 103.
23 *Ibid.*, p. 102.
24 *Ibid.*, p. 103.
25 Harden, I., 'The Fundamental Laws of the Kingdom', [1995] *Public Law* 298 (a review of Allan, 1993).

Nevertheless, despite the impressive range, appeal and lucidity of Allan's work, it begs many questions:

(a)   Allan's viewpoint is an idealised and reified, appellate court-centred view and is sociologically uninformed in that it does not address the functional realities of everyday law in action. The state is regarded as a neutral entity and there is no emphasis on the protection of collective (communal) rights, no class-based analysis of rights. Instead we are offered an individualised idea of rights and justice borrowed from liberal political theory. But this is a view from the top down, an analysis with precious little consideration of how the system appears from the bottom up. How does the less prosperous or poorly-educated litigant or applicant for a remedy view the system? What are the relevant connections? For whom is the system devised? Whose rights does it best serve?

(b)   A corollary of the neglect of the realities of the law in action is an idealisation of the common law and the role of the judiciary in enforcing rights. Indeed, the arguments inspired by Dworkin's work are highly abstract, part of a wider ambiguity as to which rights are to receive priority. Allan explains that the independent judiciary are not being celebrated by him; rather, the implication is that they are currently neglecting their constitutional duty.[26] Yet there are real problems in suggesting that judges might be expected to determine the limits of Parliament's power to make laws under a revitalised common law constitution[27] — in effect, to say what administrators should have said. Ultimately, there is a failure by Allan to articulate the means, resulting in an act of faith as far as the judges are concerned.[28] In effect, we are left with a form of judicial pragmatism which takes us no further, in that this is only another way of asking what the underlying presuppositions of judicial determination are, rather than what they should be.

(c)   Are rights to be treated as absolute, or can they be overridden to promote other social goods? In precisely what circumstances would the legal–political morality Allan articulates come into play? For Allan this appears to go back to John Locke, where obligation to obey the law is sundered by absolute dictatorial rule. Every man becomes his own judge before the decision whether to obey the law. Quite apart from the unreality of the choice, it may well be asked whether in such extreme circumstances the ruling authorities would take any notice whatever of what the courts think. In essence, Allan places too much trust in judges. In a pluralistic society of many competing and antagonistic values, who is to say, and from what perspective, that judges are better in finding a shared morality, deploying abstract philosophical principles to decide complex political and social questions? Even if judges do challenge on the grounds of rights being infringed,

---

26   Allan, *op. cit.* note 3 *supra*, Ch. 3.
27   Harden, *op. cit.* note 25 *supra*, p. 301.
28   *Ibid.*, p. 302.

given that there is always a choice to be made, Parliament may simply amend legislation. Over-reliance on the concept of the rule of law obscures this basic point. Indeed, false reassurance that such reified political and legal principles exist as a widely accepted practice can help to legitimise existing power relations.[29] For example, consider again the line of case law surrounding the question of the 'fiduciary duty' local authorities owe to their council taxpayers, from *Roberts* v *Hopwood* to *Bromley* v *GLC*.[30]

(d)   The role of legislation is de-emphasised[31] — for example, that on sex discrimination and race relations which provides a framework of coherent and enforceable rights for the citizen. Yet this is the framework under which judges already operate, and they have often been criticised for interpreting such rights restrictively, e.g., in *CRE* v *Prestige Group*.[32]

(e)   Does Allan succeed in defining the nature and role of the administrative law theorist in the new state formation which has emerged during the past 18 years? The nuts and bolts of accountability are altogether side-stepped in that nowhere does Allan clearly address the evolution of new forms of right or remedy — for example, citizen's charters, internal audit, the setting of league tables, external regulators, parents' power in schools — or the broader question(s) of historical change and evolution in our constitutional arrangements. This neglect can be compared with the work of Norman Lewis, below.

(f)   Allan seeks to embody in the jurisprudence of the courts timeless and universal moral principles; but in a situation where relations in society are always changing, is any such enterprise either possible or desirable? Ultimately, does the whole idea of a rights-based theory founder because of the problems inherent in clarifying the divide between 'public' and 'private' spheres central to almost all varieties of liberalism?[33]

NORMAN LEWIS: 'CHOICE AND THE LEGAL ORDER'

The work of Norman Lewis, particularly *Choice and the Legal Order: Rising above Politics*,[34] provides a further contrast with the approaches of both McAuslan and Allan. We have seen that the functionalist school attempted to reconcile law with the new pluralist and interventionist state, based on a vaguely socialistic consensus. Lewis has contributed something in the nature of a provocative

---

29   Gabel, P., 'Reification in Legal Reasoning' (1979) *Research in Law and Sociology* 3, at p. 25.
30   *Roberts* v *Hopwood* [1925] AC 578; *Bromley* v *GLC* [1983] 1 AC 763.
31   Allan, *op. cit.* note 3 *supra*, p. 4.
32   [1984] 1 WLR 335 (HL).
33   See the section on Harlow, below, and Berlin, Sir I., 'Two Concepts of Liberty', in Berlin, Sir I., *Four Essays on Liberty*, Oxford: Oxford University Press, 1969.
34   London: Butterworths, 1996. See also Lewis, N., 'Participation, Citizenship and the Constitution' (1996) 11 *Public Policy and Administration* 107.

manifesto which reflects a broadly centre-right cast of mind. His *raison d'être* is described as 'the construction of a vision for those committed to markets, choice, individual freedom and pluralism[35] — markets primarily because they represent the best allocative device we have; choice because it 'relates to human beings and their true identity';[36] freedom because the 'world is altered and shaped by human needs and aspirations[37] as consumer, as purposive searcher — a vision which is to issue in 'the "virtuous triangle" of individual, state and community'.[38] According to Lewis, the failure to formulate a coherent strategy has meant that while 'Privatisation, contracting out, the Citizen's Charter, the purchaser–provider split are all important ingredients of re-invented government . . . they have been developed almost independently without any real game plan being disclosed'.[39]

The change of emphasis during the 1980s, from a 'collectivist' towards an 'individualistic' market-orientated economy, is taken as the base line for this analysis. Lewis seeks a renovation of the constitutional framework and the place of administrative law within it for the 21st century.[40] A steering rather than a rowing metaphor is adopted to describe the role of the state, i.e. as representing a 'set of ideas', in that law, as well as social policy, should be used to guide and regulate choice within a market-led model. Lewis refers to the multi-faceted changes in perception and practices of government since 1979 which have been instrumental in the effort to limit the state's role in economic life. Such changes have, he argues, gone some way to marginalising parternalism as a force in history. However, the more extreme variant of 'New Right' atomised minimal state liberalism is rejected. Rights must exist for the benefit of all:[41] Lewis does not advocate reliance on market mechanisms alone, nor does he recommend the removal of the 'safety net' state. In essence, what we have here is a renovated social market model, common to Germany and some other European countries.

In agreement with many functionalists, Lewis is anxious to confront issues of public administration and delivery of services from the bottom up, by calling for devolved responsive institutions and decentralisation to people in their communities. The objective is 'pushing decision making . . . down to the lowest level where choice can effectively occur',[42] for 'To be market-players is to be freed from the tyranny of political centralisation'.[43] This would include moves to federalism. Indeed, a feature of this approach is the broad definition given to the administrative

---

35 Lewis, *Choice and the Legal Order*, note 34 *supra*, p. 6.
36 *Ibid.*, p. xi.
37 *Ibid.*, p. xii.
38 *Ibid.*, p. xiii.
39 *Ibid.*, p. 165.
40 *Ibid.*, p. 154.
41 *Ibid.*, p. 9.
42 *Ibid.*, p. 7.
43 *Ibid.*, p. 79.

state and a familiarity with the many government initiatives since 1979, for example, the implications of privatisation, contracting out, and the new public management. The 'Citizen's Charter', although flawed, is regarded as an example for others to follow. Similarly, freedom of access to information is a prerequisite for a rational system, according to Lewis, because perfect choice and participation rely upon perfect information.[44] This attempt to grapple with the ground rules for the operation of institutions in the public and private spheres can be contrasted with the 'court-centred' approach to administrative law favoured by Allan, above, or the recent work of Jurgen Habermas, below (although Habermas has influenced Lewis's work for some time).

At first sight, then, Lewis provides us with a modified functionalism, a critique of a remote, abstract, narrowly instrumental conception of law. Law should be facilitative in providing an enabling framework for interactive choice, not only in relation to policy but also in encouraging markets, high standards and quality assurance machinery. And there is full awareness of the potential of the courts as well as alternative dispute resolution, with an expanded role for ombudsman techniques being proposed, as well as incorporation of rights of participation by employees in company law.[45] This suggests a continuum between law and politics with the one blending into the other, involving an expanded jurisdiction for the courts — at one and the same time put in a control mode as 'long stops', while also acting as quality control devices with a social audit function. Under the new constitutional settlement, one aligned to choice, it is envisaged that a fresh balance would have to be struck between 'the legal as judicial, the legal as other instrumentalities and a reformed and devolved politics'.[46] However, despite appearances, closer examination reveals that a strong case for judicial suprematism is lurking beneath the surface.[47] In opposing arbitrary and capricious conduct by our rulers, Lewis pays homage to a conventional 'Diceyan view' of the rule of law and the separation of powers.[48] Not only is legal autonomy defended,[49] but judges preserve the power — issuing from a 'higher law' rooted in moral normativism — ultimately to trump political cards. But would not the suitability of the judiciary for this role inevitably be called into question? For if, following a new constitutional settlement, faith is placed in the judges, where would this new judical cadre come from; and would judges themselves be willing, let alone able, to take up such a challenge? It is far from clear that they would, or that they should, given that an

---

44   *Ibid.*, p. 143*ff.*
45   *Ibid.*, p. 109.
46   *Ibid.*, p. 143.
47   See also Laws, Sir J., 'Is the High Court the Guardian of Fundamental Constitutional Rights' [1993] *Public Law* 59; 'Law and Democracy' [1995] *Public Law* 72; 'The Constitution: Morals and Rights' [1996] *Public Law* 622.
48   Lewis, *Choice and the Legal Order*, p. 134.
49   *Ibid.*, p. 142.

extension of rights for some necessarily represents an exclusion of rights for others. Property rights are just such an example.

Lewis also deals with the relationship between the socio-political system and the market in some detail; but rather than considering different concepts and frameworks from first principles, he adopts an unsystematic 'pick and mix' approach . There is an assumption 'few will argue about'[50] that political freedom is linked to economic freedom and that the role of government should be subordinated to achieving classical markets and economic growth. This might involve incorporating market principles into the constitution, as is the case in Germany, or in the EC.[51] Lewis suggests that previous commitments to equality have been 'incompatible with a market economy'.[52] Yet at the same time there is explicit recognition of the philosophical incoherence of certain ideas emanating from the right[53] and that the rigours of competition are not always beneficial. For example, he observes that markets do not self-evidently guarantee either efficiency or choice; that the market system exhibits a tendency to accentuate inequality; and that tensions are generated between promoting efficient markets and regulating duties and rights.[54] There is express disapproval for the buying and selling of companies as if they were commodities in total disregard of the rights of workers and trade unions.[55]

Although Lewis's critical discussion of markets draws upon wide-ranging research evidence, this is often selected at random and applied out of context. For example, Will Hutton's work[56] is utilised; however, Hutton adopts an alternative approach to Lewis, a centre-left perspective, providing a comprehensive exposure of the shortcomings of British capitalism. An alternative 'stakeholder' economy of more active citizenship is proposed which decisively rejects the value system of the new right and its free market rhetoric of privatisation, primacy of individual choice, maximisation of shareholder value and the 'burden' of welfare and social costs. The stakeholder economy is based upon 'trust and reciprocity of obligation', viewed as a means for attaining greater productivity and social cohesion over the long term. On this view, a variant of welfare capitalism, social citizenship and economic membership are interdependent. The welfare state is regarded as a protective social instrument which provides 'boundaries to the operation of markets'. It needs not only to address inequalities in income and wealth because these bring inequalities in power and hence qualify freedom,[57] but also to promote

---

50 *Ibid.*, p. 41.
51 *Ibid.*, pp. 178*ff.*
52 *Ibid.*, p. 12.
53 *Ibid.*, see Ch. 7.
54 *Ibid.*, pp. 28*ff.*
55 *Ibid.*, p. 108.
56 Hutton, W., *The State We Are In* (2nd ed.), London: Cape, 1996; see also *The State To Come*, London: Vintage, 1997.
57 See Howarth, A., *Anti-Libertarianism: Markets, Philosophy and Myth*, London: Routledge, 1994.

social inclusion by long-term investment in high quality provision of education, training, welfare and pensions on a universalist basis.[58] From Hutton's standpoint, questions of political and economic accountability are crucial since the debate centres not simply on issues of wealth creation, 'choice' and 'efficiency', but on the sustainability of the social and natural environment. This last aspect is marginalised by Lewis's overly anthropocentric approach.

Despite the many insights offered by Lewis's work, this is a disappointing theory of constitutional change and the role of administrative law. It is philosophically thin (treating, for example, freedom as the essence of the individual) and insufficiently historically and sociologically informed. Moreover, it conspicuously fails to provide an intellectually credible justification for the new legal order that it proposes. Theoretical and social scientific concepts are referred to only obliquely with the result that Lewis appears to treat as self-evident many propositions about human beings and the nature of social existence which are, in fact, extremely controversial. Choice is celebrated, indeed elevated to be the fundamental right, and equated with freedom: '. . . the kind of legal order which gives centrality to choice as the guiding principle'.[59] In order to guarantee human rights 'proper' within this model, we are presented with a grand design for a constitution (an 'agreement citizens make and remake with each other to live out their lives in freedom'[60]) geared to facilitating the status of choice, conceived as a moral concept attaching to free-willing human beings, by nature 'choosing creatures'. But what does it really mean to have 'choice'? Lewis's account masks a host of complex questions; for example, he has no concept of ideology.[61] In fact, Lewis avoids examining how human beings are causally as well as meaningfully connected to their world; how ruling elites secure consent;[62] and how the choosing *conscious-ness* is shaped by experience and interaction with society — emphasising a consensus view of the way individuals are constituted rather than regarding them as products of division by class, ethnicity and sex, difference and conflict.

Further, although Lewis provides us with a wealth of detailed discussion of public and private institutions, including types of adjudication, no general mech-anism is proposed for distinguishing between and determining the *range* of choices that will inevitably arise in any society. Among consumers of commercial goods it is (relatively) straightforward to envisage selection based on preferences dictated primarily by ability to pay. Indeed, Lewis does[63] appear to argue that people should be free to spend 'their own' money, begging the central question about the *origin*

---

58   Hutton, *op. cit.* note 56 *supra*, pp. 306 and 340.
59   Lewis, *Choice and the Legal Order*, p. xi.
60   *Ibid.*, p. 8.
61   Eagleton, T., *Ideology: An Introduction*, London: Verso, 1991. Note: the concept of ideology is a complex one which we have no time to deal with here.
62   See, for example, Chomsky, N., *World Orders, Old and New*, London: Pluto Press, 1994.
63   Lewis, *Choice and the Legal Order*, pp. 4 and 12.

of any existing distribution. But, leaving this important fact to one side, any analogy with choice arising in regard to public services provision is much more difficult to sustain. How are the goals for education and healthcare to be set? What are they to be? How is value to be placed on the quality of such services? What happens if many citizens make the same choice and the resources available cannot meet demand? Who chooses, and why?[64] What if the exercise of choice results in opting out of the system of taxation and education altogether? What if choice results in discriminatory practices that conflict with the rights of others? Why should the right to choose prevail over other basic rights? Lewis gives us little real indication of how under a new constitutional settlement law will be capable of facilitating the resolution of such intractable questions or reconciling diverse social interests, for these are not simply about *choice* but predominantly about *access*. Such questions warn us that no prioritisation of choice as the ultimate benchmark is acceptable. It should be self-evident 'even among persons of goodwill'[65] that there is virtually no prospect of finding agreement for any such rights across the political spectrum, other than the most anodyne or those with so many qualifications as to be meaningless to the citizens most in need of them.

In sum, Lewis's quest for a new social consensus is mainly an exercise in wishful thinking. There can be no 'rising above politics' (or ethics) if we are to debate the future of public law meaningfully. Arguably it is far more true to say that to a certain extent institutions, including legal institutions, may need to be coercive (in the sense of Max Weber's term 'legitimate violences') if we are to shape our world in ways we think desirable.[66] And that people 'will seek to influence that world in accordance with a whole range of values'.[67]

The broader compass

While the writers discussed above focus their analysis on certain particular features of the socio-legal, other lawyers search for a more general account with the aim of situating public law/administrative law within a wider background framework of philosophy, history, and culture; in particular, of political theory.

PAUL CRAIG: A NEW FOUNDATIONALISM FOR PUBLIC LAW?

Unlike Allan, who attempts to provide us with an explicitly liberal-normative position underpinning the views we *should* hold, or Griffith, Craig embarks on a

---

64   See, for example, *R v Cambridge District Health Authority, ex parte B* [1995] 1 WLR 898 (CA).
65   Lewis, *op. cit.* note 63 *supra*, p. 150.
66   Weber, M., 'Politics as a Vocation', in Gerth, H.H., and Mills, C.W. (eds), *From Max Weber: Essays in Sociology*, London: Routledge & Kegan Paul, 1970.
67   Howarth, *op. cit.* note 57 *supra*, p. 103.

redrawing of the boundaries of public law theory from a determinedly 'neutral' position. That is, rather than engaging in a detailed theoretical or empirical elaboration of his own position, Craig seeks to provide a thoroughgoing description and explication of the underlying assumptions of public law theory. In his own words: ' . . . the approach which runs throughout my work: identify and assess the relevant background theory, consider the public law implications of it, and the political, social and economic background conditions within which it subsists.'[68] It follows from this, or is at least implied by it, that any version of administrative law theory is liable to be deeply flawed unless it is explicitly related to an informed sociological and political understanding of society and the state.

While highlighting the confusion that surrounds so much of the debate about the nature and purpose of administrative law and the role of theory within that debate — for example, regarding the influence of Bentham, who saw that such words as 'accountability' or 'control' presuppose a socio-political analysis — Craig argues that the position we espouse with regard to administrative law will be contingent on the nature of the (largely liberal) democratic theory we adopt in the society in which we live.[69] Accordingly, we will need to know the meaning of the theory(ies), what their normative presuppositions (in their own terms) are and their implications for public law. All the more is this generally the case because legal doctrines, as well as democratic theories, are readily malleable as well as manipulable, combinable and recombinable in diverse ways to reach a diversity of distinctive (sometimes self-interested) conclusions. Even the most radical, self-consciously critical option is a product of ideology, time and place, and hence cannot excuse us from thinking through its implications, beset as these will undoubtedly be with numerous vexed questions.[70]

In focusing down on the nature of the state and the role of law within it, Craig particularly emphasises the influence of political theory, because such knowledge allows us to elucidate what the presuppositions of public law are or should be. For example, that there is a selection of possible normative options to choose from if we wish to embody varying conceptions of citizenship within a functioning and interrelated system; what we mean by 'citizenship' is explicable only within the framework provided by a background political theory, liberal individualist or communitarian. The existence and validity of such a link between public law and political theory is exemplified for Craig in the work of Laski, for instance in his analysis of the forms of democratic participation by the community and the nature of the rights that individuals have in the broadest sense.[71] This would also be true, for Craig, of the work of Maitland, Barker, Rawls, and Dworkin, among others.

---

68 Craig, P.P., 'What Should Public Lawyers Do? A Reply' (1992) 12 *Oxford Journal of Legal Studies* 564.
69 Craig, P.P., *Administrative Law* (3rd ed.), London: Sweet & Maxwell, 1994, p. 3.
70 Craig, P.P., *Public Law and Democracy in the UK and the USA*, Oxford: Clarendon Press, 1990, p. 15.
71 Craig, *op. cit.* note 68 *supra*, p. 569.

Indeed, Dworkin's rights-based model is a good example of the questions raised for Craig by such a general theory. He has some pertinent doubts about any approach based on rights of a monolithic kind. Should such an approach be based on liberalism? If so, on a pluralist model or on a more republican version of rights? The problem is that these are sometimes in sharp conflict regarding the nature and extent of the rights to be accorded to the citizen. Craig argues that what matters regarding a rights-based, or any other, approach 'is that commentators [take] issue with the range and meaning of the political, civil, social and economic rights which ought to feature in any concept of citizenship. This is of course simply another way of articulating a background theory which one believes ought to underlie public law rights'.[72] Do not the consequences of all models of administrative law theory therefore 'only become evident if we are willing to articulate the theory of justice which underpins [them] and which serves to give colour and meaning to [their] constituent elements'?[73] The importance allotted to the concept of the rule of law as a component part of a theory of justice in both Dworkin and Allan is a good example of this.

But if it follows that which interests are accorded importance in any given theory will be crucial to the concepts that are developed, how are these interests to be balanced? Again, this is possible only through the medium of a background theory of rights, democracy, etc., which provides a rationale for helping us to define what is meant by freedom of speech, property and welfare rights. We can then with some degree of clarity go on ask how, and to what degree, society needs to change to accomplish the goals that are implicit in the respective theory(ies), and what institutional difficulties might lie in the way of their implementation. Take a market-based pluralist model as against a participatory democratic model;[74] there will be different conceptions of rights, accountability, citizenship, equality and society. It is only by exploring more specific proposals that content can be given to these principles.

We might argue, then, following Craig, that the real question is: what different notions of citizenship are in play? And what are the implications for administrative law of following one or other of these models, of granting participatory rights within very different economic, political and social circumstances?[75] For example, the view that administrative law can be founded upon the principles of market economics and efficiency, an argument found in the work of the Chicago School whose best known exponent is probably Richard Posner.[76] Other lawyers argue that the primary focus must remain justice, and that this may well not be easily reconcilable with an economic analysis of law.

---

72 Craig, *op. cit.* note 69 *supra*, pp. 23–4.
73 *Ibid.*, p. 40.
74 Craig, *op. cit.* note 70 *supra*, p. 7; *op. cit.* note 69 *supra*, pp. 33*ff*.
75 Craig, *op. cit.* note 70 *supra*, pp. 416–7.
76 Posner, R., *Economic Analysis of Law* (4th ed.), Boston: Little Brown, 1992. See also the remarks of Forbes J in *Pickwell* v *Camden LBC* [1982] 2 WLR 383.

Craig offers us an answer to the search for new foundations for public law by having recourse to political theory; but this approach, although attractive to many, is not without attendant difficulties of its own. For example, it might well be asked whether political theory really provides the answer. Does it offer more valid grounds, or a more comprehensive justification for administrative law than the Diceyan formula of a positivistic division between law and politics? Is the search for the normative foundations of any given theory of adjudication by the courts better satisfied by this method than by the time-honoured *ultra vires* principle based on parliamentary sovereignty and the rule of law? Martin Loughlin for his part[77] argues that while in *Public Law and Democracy* Craig focuses on the background of political theory and the ideals espoused therein, there are questions of fitness for purpose. Inspiration is drawn largely from the USA and not the Continent, but no explanation is given why this is so. Are the different jurisdictions truly commensurable, given their very different histories and cultural evolution?

Secondly, O'Leary[78] argues that in *Public Law and Democracy* Craig offers an overly abstract review of the literature without looking in any depth into the empirical practice of law. For example, the theories that Craig discusses have different empirical implications for the role of the judiciary, yet he provides no comparative analysis of the judiciary in respective legal systems.[79] Equally, that the stress on explicating a 'background political theory' provides for an insufficient focus on empirically lived experience, that there is no clear analysis of how theory is woven into an institutional setting. In articulating the desirability of explicating the background assumptions and prejudices that lie behind any given theory of administrative law, does Craig succeed in welding these together with experienced empirical realities into a cohesive whole? Does Craig actually operationalise his perspective? However, whether this is fair comment in the light of Craig's textbook on *Administrative Law*[80] is very much open to doubt. In defence of his own position, Craig comments[81] that the orthodox, taken for granted positivistic model rests upon presuppositions of its own, which are no less real for being so widely presumed rather than explained. That every theory has a conception of the good; that the relevance of explicating background theory(ies) is that these can give judges access to such background political theory or abstract theories of justices.[82] While, at the same time, stress on the meaning to be given to words such as

---

77 Loughlin, M., 'The Pathways of Public Law Scholarship', in Wilson, G.P. (ed.), *Frontiers of Legal Scholarship*, Chichester: John Wiley, 1995.

78 O'Leary, B., 'What Should Public Lawyers Do? (1992) 12 *Oxford Journal of Legal Studies* 404, pp. 405–6.

79 However, there are many problems involved in comparative analysis: see Legrand, P., 'How to Compare Now' (1996) 116 *Legal Studies* 232.

80 Craig, *op. cit.* note 69 *supra*.

81 Craig, *op. cit.* note 68 *supra*.

82 *Ibid.*, see p. 566, where Craig refers to Allan.

accountability, control or power allows us to escape from over-concern with external judicial control.[83]

More crucially, there are no general conclusions, only an 'agnosticism', as Loughlin puts it, to be found in Craig's work. Although it might be argued that, even if Craig has no *explicit* theory to offer, perhaps his work does not cease to suggest a way of seeing the theory and practice of administrative law. But why does Craig stop with political theory, and that of an overwhelmingly liberal perspective? Why no recourse to non liberal theory, for example the distinctively continental contribution of Jurgen Habermas? More seriously, is the project of seeking to explicate the background theory and substance of public law from the Archimedean position possible at all in the light of the critique of foundationalism by, among others, Michel Foucault (below)?

CAROL HARLOW: 'CHANGING THE MINDSET'[84]

Although not setting out with the intention to act as a theorist herself, in a series of articles Carol Harlow reviews some of the more recent contributions to the field. While assuming the relevance of a background theory and empirical sociology to an essentially functionalist approach, Harlow takes up the challenge of Patrick McAuslan in 1983 'that the time is ripe for a relook, a rethink and a rewrite on the evolution of our modern system of administrative law'.[85] In an earlier article,[86] Harlow discussed and amplified Griffith's critique of the judiciary while regarding it as the starting point for debate, not the conclusion of one. She now sees one of her central objectives to be 'the promulgation and discussion of ideas and issues central to public law; in particular, the establishment of a new, broadly conceived 'foreground theory' for public law,[87] including judicial review, especially in the light of the prevailing dearth of effective constitutional checks or open government legislation.

Harlow starts from the now familiar premise that one cannot understand the nature of law by assuming a 'classic' black-letter, formalist perspective, emphasising the anti-theoretical bias inherent in a tradition which pits the practical against the academic, the political against the legal. Rather than accepting this tradition of naive textual exposition of a set of applied legal rules, she, like others discussed in this chapter, asserts the necessary relationship between law and political and

---

83   Craig, P.P., 'Bentham, Public Law and Democracy' [1989] *Public Law* 407, at p. 427.
84   Harlow, C., 'Changing the Mindset: The Place of Theory in English Administrative Law' (1994)
 .   14 *Oxford Journal of Legal Studies* 419.
85   McAuslan, P., 'Administrative Law, Collective Consumption and Judicial Review' (1983) 46
      Modern Law Review 1, at p. 20.
86   Harlow 'Refurbishing the Judicial Service', in Harlow, C. (ed.), *Public Law and Politics*, London:
      Sweet & Maxwell, 1986.
87   Harlow, *op. cit.* note 84 *supra*, p. 422. (A term taken from O'Leary, *op. cit.* note 78 *supra*).

social theory, economics and the link to the human sciences: 'The truth is that the political nature of public law adjudication can neither be easily escaped nor disguised'.[88] Law, following functionalist assumptions, is essentially about the state, power and the achievement of political objectives, although every effort should be made not to blur the distinction between legal and political processes, for to do so 'could diminish law's problem-solving capacity and tarnish its image'.[89] However, a number of new possibilities for theorisation have recently opened up with the aim of understanding the implications of changes in government and administration since 1980. It is these recent developments, in particular, which Harlow seeks to review.

Given the low priority accorded to 'theory' by the time-honoured traditions of legal analysis, academics have a vested interest in justifying such work by providing it with a plausible and reassuring rationale. One such view of the task for theory within a renovated, albeit conservative, classical tradition has been that of establishing the abstract principles that lie behind a subject; that no legal *system* could simply comprise a mass of unrelated decisions. There must be some means of making sense of what there is and of providing some conceptual coherence for it. The task of an academic public lawyer put in these terms 'can then be defined in terms of the search for an overriding theoretical framework or conceptual unity'.[90] Implicit in this legal–political perspective is the suggestion, of Martin Loughlin, that the guidance, control and evaluation of governmental processes and performance should be the primary focus of administrative lawyers. Another variant of the control model, one better suited to Allan's approach, sees the task for academics as 'establishing the framework within which the judiciary evaluates the activities of government and administration'.[91] Both of these mark something of a break with the extreme form of 'black letter' subservience to the study of the judicial process viewed through the prism of judicial reasoning, an approach found mainly in the work of Sir William Wade. Yet a third perspective, of socio-legal derivation, has sought to focus on the 'law in action'; that is, any heuristically worthwhile theory must show a link, a relationship between theory and practice, between the law as a set of rules and the law as it is experienced as a set of outcomes in everyday life. Harlow notes that the work of the functionalist school has exposed the essentially fragmentary nature of everyday legal practice and undermined the still common assumption that law is a neutral force within society. One important question might then be: to what extent should theory be tested by empirical methods? Nevertheless, as we have seen, even if functionalist theories

---

88 Harlow, C., 'A Special Relationship? American Influences on Judicial Review in England', in Loveland, I. (ed.) *A Special Relationship? American Influences on Judicial Review in the United Kingdom*, Oxford: Clarendon Press, 1995, p. 91.
89 Harlow, C., 'Back to Basics: Reinventing Administrative Law' [1997] *Public Law* 245, at p. 256.
90 Harlow, *op. cit.* note 84 *supra*, p. 420.
91 *Ibid.*, p. 420.

tell us what law *does*, there remains the tendency to leave out what law *is*. Accordingly, any worthwhile contemporary theory will combine these two elements and not simply rest content with either a purely descriptive or an empirical analysis.[92]

However, despite her criticisms of the expository tradition, and unlike some of the other thinkers we have looked at, Harlow maintains that classical theory cannot be regarded as being simply outmoded. Whether he got it wrong or not, Dicey *has* provided the orthodox background theory of the constitution, and attempts simply to dislodge it are doomed.[93] Further, the practitioner orientation of the common law should not be underestimated because of the still overwhelming predominance of black letter traditionalism, together with the remaining similarities in contemporary political and social opinion with the views Dicey defended. The most reflective judges do provide valuable insights, but retain the focus on the role of the court in their perception of the subject. For example, Harlow points out that Lords Woolf and Slynn have made valuable but very much 'court-orientated' contributions in their Hamlyn lectures.

Given these background assumptions, then, there are different levels at which any theoretical debate needs to engage. Harlow prefers to conceptualise the terrain by drawing a distinction between what she refers to as 'shallow' and 'deep' theory.[94] The former seeks, following Holdsworth, to establish 'a system of principles and rules that [are] logically coherent, and yet eminently practical.'[95] It readily encompasses and combines the academic expository tradition of high-level conceptual clarification and, despite the critique offered by the functionalist school, the stress on the practical impact of law on the individual and society. The essential unity between these two positions is found by Harlow to reside in a more fundamental underlying agreement that law without conceptual clarity in its basic rules would be an absurdity. The latter, 'deep' theory seeks to offer 'an explanation of the function of law in general or public law in particular' in modern society. The first is exemplified for Harlow by the classical tradition of scholarship from Dicey and Pollock down to the present day, as well as by the movement for socio-legal research. The second by the work of Craig (we might add, for our purposes in this chapter, McAuslan, Allan, Lewis and Loughlin). 'Autopoiesis', as well as the work of Habermas and Foucault (discussed below), forms a yet more abstract layer of theoretical speculation about the role of law that might comfortably be placed under the sign of 'deep theory'.

The central question for Harlow is — set against the contemporary reality of the victory of the 'Model of Government' (the domination of Parliament by the executive) over the 'Model of Law' (the accountability of the executive to

---

92   *Ibid.*, pp. 420–2.
93   *Ibid.*, p. 426.
94   *Ibid.*, p. 421.
95   *Ibid.*, p. 421.

Parliament within a 'balanced constitution')[96] — where does the central deficiency in public law theory lie? The way forward for her is in a new 'foreground' theory that can capture the high ground. It must describe both the nature of modern society and the character of law within it,[97] with the key for Harlow being found in accessability and practical utility to the user. Certain strands of theory,[98] for example that of Luhmann and Teubner ('autopoiesis'), are rejected as too abstract and lacking in heuristic value for lawyers. However, to the question of *how far* this new theory should extend its ambitions into political science and philosophy, Harlow provides no clear answer.

Might an answer be found in America? Examining US influence on English legal culture and judicial review in particular,[99] Harlow refines American theorising into two paradigms of adjudication: The 'Public Interest Model' (legitimised by the political theory of popular participatory democracy in which pressure groups are able to use the courtroom as a platform for advocacy of what they consider to be the public interest, interests of a more or less openly political nature); and the 'Legal Process Model' (which looks to classic formalist methods of reasoned evaluation and adjudication, emphasising control and structuring of discretion via rule making throughout the system of government, as well as formalised legal rule making sometimes of a participatory kind, and which would necessarily involve the intrusion of legalism into the administrative process).[100] Each model aims at legitimation of judicial power. But, despite their superficial appeal, Harlow finds here too that 'There are no easy American answers',[101] not least because we must not delude ourselves into 'imagining a greater commonality than in fact obtains' between the two jurisdictions. There may indeed be a degree of incommensurability, given the different history, culture, traditions and goals of the USA.[102] This once again raises the issue of whether comparative analysis is worthwhile, or even possible.

The relevance of the public–private divide[103]

Another related aspect of Harlow's theoretical work, one she shares with Craig and others, is in calling for fresh thought to address the challenge to public law

---

96   *Ibid.*, p. 426.
97   *Ibid.*, p. 423.
98   Luhmann, N., *A Sociological Theory of Law*, London: Routledge & Kegan Paul, 1985; Teubner, G., *Law as an Autopoietic System*, Oxford: Basil Blackwell, 1993. See Harlow, *op. cit.* note 84 *supra*, p. 431.
99   Harlow, *op. cit.* note 88 *supra*.
100 *Ibid.*, pp. 87–8.
101 *Ibid.*, p. 94.
102 *Ibid.*, p. 80.
103 Harlow, C., ' "Public" and "Private" Law: Definition Without Distinction' (1980) 43 *Modern Law Review* 1.

presented by new types of state formation and the increasing complexity of civil society. One aspect of this which has concerned her for some time — one which serves to focus many of the issues raised above — is the distinction made for jurisdictional purposes by the courts, post-*O'Reilly* v *Mackman*,[104] between private and public law remedies (see Bamforth, Ch. 6 generally and Alder, Ch. 7).

There are two central aspects to Harlow's analysis. First, we now have many types of state (or quasi-state) formation and institutions, both at the national and the international level, none perhaps clearly 'public' or 'private' in their effects. These throw up new types of power relationships and organisation which inevitably impinge on the public interest, even if, for the purposes of administrative law remedies as currently conceived, they remain on the 'wrong' side of the public–private divide. New structures have been created since 1979 within the guiding principle of 'new public management — a triangular relationship between the public regulatory authority, service provider and citizen that, for example, the private law of contract is so ill-equipped to cope with that a law of public contracts may well be required.[105] Effectively, this may mean that the traditional control approach of public law is inadequate to conceptualise the remedies which ought to be available to the individual or group. Any comprehensive theory of administrative law must wrestle with these questions, as Harlow herself, working with Richard Rawlings, has attempted to do in recent work on how pressure groups utilise law to achieve longer-term collective goals and how the judiciary confront such pressures, defining three channels of communication for the groups to achieve these goals: 'drainpipe' (control), 'freeway' (accommodating) and 'funnel' (partial public interest model).[106]

Secondly, the public–private classification is, for Harlow, part of an insular tradition: 'It is nothing more than an attempt by the judiciary to conceal political issues behind a formalist facade and to shield from public criticism some highly executive minded decisions'.[107] At one level this is clearly linked into the Laski/Griffith tradition of analysis; at another to the myths of representative parliamentary democracy and the reality of social conflict underlying the nominal neutrality of the state. Accordingly, Harlow argues that there should be a *functional* rather than *organic* test of jurisdiction. We must ask: what are the *effects* of power, 'public' or 'private' on the citizen? The details have to be addressed not only at the macro level but also at the micro level of delivery of the service. What, indeed, is the basis for *any* conceptual divide between public and private law? Harlow offers a critique of the complex jurisdictional litigation resulting from the severance of one from the other post-*O'Reilly* and refers to the time-honoured utility of the classical model of remedies pre-1983. Perhaps, she reflects, we have

---

104   [1983] 2 AC 237.
105   Harlow, *op. cit.* note 103 *supra*, pp. 250*ff*.
106   Harlow, C., and Rawlings, R., *Pressure through Law*, London: Routledge, 1992, Ch. 7.
107   Harlow, *op. cit.* note 103 *supra*, p. 265.

gone on a long and unnecessary detour and that, given the new institutional forms of the modern state, we should revert to the old pre-1983 Anglo-American private law model, because 'the truth is that the "public"/"private" classification is wholly irrelevant to the organisation of modern society'.[108] This view is now even more justified with the development over the past 15 years of the 'contracting state.' In fact, it is clear today that perspectives based on 19th-century ideological perceptions of the nation state only ever became *contingently* outmoded, and that remoulding the contours of administrative law in response to contemporary societal change should, therefore, only ever be attempted with the maximum of flexibility and openness in mind. Accordingly, 'To function adequately in this new environment of international capitalism, legal systems may need to respond by collapsing not only the public/private divide but also the national/international dichotomy'.[109] Especially where, as today, 'the emerging boundaries are complex and hard to discern'.[110]

Harlow states that ultimtely 'no convincing holistic theory of public law has emerged . . . concerning respect for the background constitutional values of democratic society'. But one possible criticism of Harlow is that, like many of our commentators, she is unreflexive regarding the use of language. Can language ever be unproblematically used to found such a theory? Is such an enterprise possible, given the prevailing (and fashionable) critique of 'foundationalism'? And even if it can, should public lawyers seek a new *overarching* theory, one with links to history, philosophy and the human sciences; or should we, rather, look within law itself (defined as a sub-system of society) for an answer, as Jabbari argues?[111] If public law values are worth having and we have to fight for them, as Harlow contends, just how do we go about doing so? By pragmatic reform politics; or by something more openly radical, more comprehensive in its indictment of prevailing structures and values? We will return to these questions below.

MARTIN LOUGHLIN: THE SEARCH FOR A NEW UNIFYING THESIS

With Martin Loughlin's *Public Law and Political Theory*[112] we are on the terrain of one of the most wide-ranging attempts to situate public law in the context of history and society, working from the premise that to understand the social world

---

108 *Ibid.*, p. 256.
109 Harlow, *op. cit.* note 84 *supra*, p. 433.
110 Harlow, *op. cit.* note 88 *supra*, p. 94. See also Hutchinson, A.C., 'Private Rights/Public Wrongs: The Liberal Lie of the Constitution' (1988) 38 *University of Toronto Law Journal* 278; 'Mice Under a Chair: Democracy, Courts and the Administrative State' (1990) *University of Toronto Law Journal* 374.
111 Jabbari, D., 'From Criticism to Construction in Modern Legal Theory' (1992) 12 *Oxford Journal of Legal Studies* 507; see also Jabbari (1994) 'Critical Theory in Administrative Law' (1994) 14 *Oxford Journal of Legal Studies* 189.
112 Loughlin, M., *Public Law and Political Theory*, Oxford: Clarendon Press, 1992.

of complex causal and meaning relationships is always and everywhere a tangled and problematical task. Loughlin begins with the crisis in self-confidence of some public lawyers, that has surfaced over past decades with the realisation that the existing conceptual framework(s) of the discipline was inadequate to deal with the new challenges presented by the widespread belief that our existing constitutional arrangements were intellectually bankrupt.[113] This anxiety, as we have already seen, stemmed from developments in modern government over this century, particularly since 1979, with controversial shifts in the relationship between central and local government, developments in European Community law, and the growth of the 'quango state'. Yet there have not been any fundamental constitutional modifications to take account of this, nor, given that Loughlin decisively rejects the normative liberalism found in the approach of Allan, adequate responses in administrative law to challenge new complexities. Secondly, given that law is 'a broad and flexible framework which . . . provides little [sociological] insight into the nature of the system' (a good example would be local government),[114] is any kind of theory much help in understanding these matters?

How are we to trace the historical roots of this failure in public law theorising, and what is the status of current developments? Loughlin assents to the narrowing effect of Dicey's legacy, in that we still have a largely piecemeal foundation which leaves us with the unenviable choice of over-rigidity or an excessively pragmatic and unprincipled alternative — of law centredness or eclecticism.[115] And yet, even at ground level, we have seen that there is no agreed way of defining administrative law.[116] In the light of this uncertainty Loughlin presents two possibilities. First, a set of general legal principles that structure and limit the manner and nature of decision making by public bodies. Sir William Wade is a representative example of this control model of traditional analytical jurisprudence.[117] But acting from positivist assumptions of the separation of law and politics and public from private law, Wade helps to legitimate the *status quo* of a practitioner orientated, court-based discipline. For Loughlin, despite its apparent successes, at the heart of the critique of this narrow view is the very re-awakening of judicial interventionism in the 1960s which Wade praises, for this can include a self-satisfied complacency. Moreover, there has been no genuine attempt to get to grips with the key issues of:

(a)   the nature of the common law itself (non political, but how is it used by the courts?);

---

113   For example, see Harden, I., and Lewis, N., *The Noble Lie: The British Constitution and the Rule of Law*, London: Hutchinson, 1987.
114   Loughlin, M., 'Innovative Financing in Local Government: The Limits of Legal Instrumentalism' (Pt One) [1990] *Public Law* 372, at p. 373.
115   Loughlin, *op. cit.* note 112 *supra*, pp. 15–29 and 139–83.
116   Loughlin, M., 'Beyond Complacency' (1983) 46 *Modern Law Review* 666.
117   *Ibid.*, p. 667.

(b)   the nature of the judicial function (controversial judgments from the 1970s and 1980s); and

(c)   the nature of social reality and its relationship to law raised by the broader definition of the subject propounded by Robson, among others. In fact, Loughlin concludes that, in the 1960s, while the spirit that informs the principles of administrative law changed, the principles themselves remained much the same.[118] Judges still wallow in the superiority of the common law.

The alternative is a broader definition, essentially that of Robson, where administrative law is simply 'the law of public administration'.[119] This definition, essentially shared by Loughlin, is, in principle, one including any activity with a substantial degree of state involvement in it.[120] We have already seen that this school offers a firm challenge to the orthodox conception of Dicey. However, for Loughlin, the impact of the realist school is weakened because it still works uncritically within the framework of analytical positivism. Equally, there is too much focus on legislation and legal instrumentalism. The result is that this perspective has not qualitatively developed since the 1930s, with no serious analysis of law *qua* law, no theory of justice or of the role of legal tradition and its core values.[121] The upshot of these deficiencies is that many of the key determinants of the decision remain unarticulated under both control and functionalist perspectives.

What, then, is Loughlin's position when viewed against these dominant background assumptions? Beginning by firmly rejecting any approach which 'incorporates an implicit predisposition in favour of a particular type of interpretation which is compatible with a professionally prescribed view of the subject', he argues that 'A theoretical approach to public law must therefore be *interpretative, empirical, critical* and *historical*'.[122] *Interpretative* in that (congruent with an hermeneutic approach) we must focus not just on causal relations but on the meaning given to acts by the actors themselves within the system, so eroding the distinction between fact and value. Loughlin agrees with Craig that linking public law with political theory provides the most promising alternative model, in that it challenges the formal distinction between science and philosophy and assists in the task of rejecting any notion of a distinctively legal method.[123] *Empirical* in that law is rooted in the everyday (functional) realities of politics and government. We should not expect theory to provide us with new rational principles, for such legal–political conceptualisations will tell us little about the lived experience of the

---

118   *Ibid.*, p. 669.
119   *Ibid.*, p. 673.
120   *Ibid.*, p. 667.
121   *Ibid.*, p. 672.
122   Loughlin, *op. cit.* note 112 *supra*, p. 36.
123   Loughlin, *op. cit.* note 77 *supra*, p. 183.

system as structured daily events. Moreover, if law is a local discourse made up of shared understandings, then these, taken together, make up the constitutional traditions reflected in our institutions, texts, ceremonies and rituals.[124] Against rationalisers like Allan, who search for 'deeper' constitutional principles, Loughlin asserts that concepts are not items of knowledge or myths, but should be viewed as flexible tools for particular purposes.[125] *Critical* in that theory should attend to these realities and undertake a rational scrutiny of various interpretations of law and its relation to society. Lastly, any analysis must be *historically* aware: aware of how the present is shaped by the past, of how the past is shaped by the present. In sum, then, 'law is pragmatic and not philosophical, is a political rather than a propositional discourse, and is a local, cultural practice rather than a universal system that works itself pure' (i.e., from any taint of inconsistency). Indeed, it is this very inconsistency that makes it work.[126] It follows that we must look at law 'from principles which are internal to the practice', and that 'The ultimate test of law is that which is satisfactory in experience; law's truth is simply the truth that we can live by'.[127] So for Loughlin, 'the sceptical method which I am advocating may thus be viewed as an anti-foundational, anti-theoretical and anti anti-relativist method. And it is this positive method which I believe holds the best hope for the continuation of scholarly inquiries in public law'.[128] (Compare Habermas, below, and our conclusions to the chapter.)

How does Loughlin proceed to operationalise these assumptions? He wishes to open up an important range of issues for examination by constructing 'a map' of the subject.[129] This map is navigated by the use of a series of ideal-typical concepts, popularised in the work of Max Weber, in order to explicate the history of administrative law and its contemporary context. Although Loughlin recognises the limitations in such an approach, he nevertheless argues that 'Maps can guide even when they are grossly inaccurate because without a map there would be no way of focusing or organising one's journey'.[130] It is better to have some map than no map, and its value can always be pragmatically judged by how well you get around using it. He argues for the utility of two broad conceptual framing 'structures which shape the way we think about the subject': 'normativism' and 'functional-ism'. These two representations are permeated with historical and philosophical meaning about law, government and the role of the individual in the whole; and help us to 'explore the relationships between these styles of public law thought and the main (political) ideologies which have shaped constitutional politics', for

---

124   *Ibid.*, p. 185.
125   *Ibid.*, p. 184.
126   *Ibid.*, p. 182.
127   *Ibid.*, p. 185.
128   *Ibid.*, pp. 184*ff*. See in particular Rorty, R., *Consequences of Pragmatism*, Sussex: The Harvester Press, 1982.
129   Loughlin, *op. cit.* note 112 *supra*, pp. 37–57.
130   *Ibid.*, p. 37.

example the work of Dicey, Allan, and McAuslan.[131] Therefore, 'The task of theory must . . . be to bring to consciousness the assumptions secreted within such [normativist and functionalist] structures'.[132]

The *normativist* style, Loughlin argues, originates in the history of the ideal of the separation of powers and the rule of law, interpreted as control over government, and expresses a belief in the ideal of the autonomy of law from politics, from Dicey in the 19th century to Oakeshott and Hayek in the 20th century.[133] The stress on law's adjudicative function leads to a prioritisation of legal rules over legislation and conceptual clarity. On the other hand, the *functionalist* style is the only one of the two styles to break with the *internal* Diceyan rationalist project of serving the practitioner/judge and to focus its attention on the *external* sociological place of law within a complex society. These two styles, however abstractly, represent fundamental disagreements about the nature of human beings and how society ought to be governed.

There are two types of normativism: conservative and liberal. Conservative normativism is characteristic of the work of Oakeshott.[134] Liberal normativism[135] is linked with *laissez-faire* doctrine and the work of Hayek, although this is a broad category and includes many other variants. Allan and Dworkin would, for example, come into this category. In essence, it is individualistic and atomistic in conception, and characteristic of the private law model. For its part, functionalism,[136] as we have seen, upholds a more communitarian philosophy and is characterised by distrust of abstractions and a concern with effectiveness (instrumentalism). Its foundations rest in the sociological positivism of Auguste Comte and Emile Durkheim, Fabianism, the 'New Liberalism' of the 1890s and the pragmatism of Charles Pierce, William James and John Dewey.[137] Both conservative normativism and functionalism have an historically rooted abiding scepticism about any constitutional settlement based on the principle of individual rights. However, Loughlin's fear is that, owing to what he regards as the exhaustion of the functionalist style and changes in the perspective of some conservative normativists (e.g., Wade) toward the judicial role, all roads now point to the triumph of liberal normativism, with the principal challenge being based on the ideas of Dworkinian liberalism. We have already seen that Allan is much influenced by Dworkin's rights doctrine. Loughlin's own hope is for a modified and revitalised, less positivist and naive empiricist version of functionalism,[138] and he looks (in this

---

131   *Ibid.*, pp. 39–40.
132   *Ibid.*, p. 35.
133   *Ibid.*, pp. 60*ff*.
134   *Ibid.*, pp. 64*ff*.
135   *Ibid.*, pp. 84*ff*.
136   *Ibid.*, pp. 104*ff*.
137   *Ibid.*, p. 172.
138   *Ibid.*, p. 243.

work at least)[139] to the work of Niklas Luhmann and autopoiesis for some possible ways forward in the enterprise of contributing 'to the tasks of guidance, control, and evaluation in government', although how precisely this is to be effected within the new paradigm is left rather unclear.

Despite its imaginative richness, a number of criticisms have been made of Loughlin's work. For example, that he tends towards an over-historical determinism of ideas.[140] Is Loughlin's concentration on ideas and their influence on the nature and forms of public law too general, too immanent to law itself, too focused on Dicey and the inherititors of that tradition and lacking in sociological understanding of the history of state formations and their dialectical relationship with thought? Loughlin himself claims to be rooting ideas in life, but does he really succeed in this goal?

Craig,[141] for his part, develops this reasoning to argue that Loughlin has a tendency to lump together what are very diverse perspectives under the capacious conceptual frameworks of normativism and functionalism, thus eliding the differences that exist between theorists within these styles of thought. The heuristic value of the dichotomies that Loughlin employs is therefore placed in doubt. Craig stresses that, in fact, *all* the theories are normative. All recommend actions the functionalist school, as well as liberal normativists, have a strong view of society and what law should achieve in it. Liberal theory may be neutral about the *idea* of the state but not about what the state *does.* Compare, for example, the work of Hayek and Nozick[142] with that of both Dworkin and Allan, who have distinct interventionist, purposive ideals. Allan adds that Loughlin underplays certain similarities that exist between Dicey and Hayek.[143] Further caution is necessary over use of the term 'functionalist', viewed as 'tendentious and unhelpful' by Craig because it introduces an unnecessary rigidity: why cannot others, he asks, public choice theorists or libertarians for example, be regarded as functionalists in that they want to effectuate their own distinctive political conception? Are the dichotomies Loughlin employs too simplified and historically and sociologically thin to be other than very misleading? Or is it open to question whether this is something of a semantic dispute about meaning?

Another questionable feature of *Public Law and Political Theory* is: how *literally* does Loughlin use these terms? Are they intended to have ideal-typical analytical utility only, or are they intended to be more historically descriptive? The problem arises because the ideal-typical form is nowhere tightly defined in the book. If we regard an ideal-typical analysis (along Weberian lines) as being the

---

139   He may now have shifted his position: compare Loughlin, *op. cit.* note 77 *supra.*
140   Harlow, *op. cit.* note 84 *supra*, p. 426.
141   Craig, P.P., review of Loughlin, in (1992) 13 *Legal Studies* 275.
142   Nozick, R., *Anarchy, State and Utopia*, Oxford, Basil Blackwell, 1974.
143   Allan, T.R.S., review of Loughlin, in (1992) 109 *Law Quarterly Review* 495.

kind of project Loughlin is engaged in, as appears likely, then this is an important qualification of Craig's critique, in that these terms were never intended by Loughlin to mirror reality. He is, arguably, merely engaged in creating a conceptual formation that enables a more suggestive and insightful description of that reality to be made.

Lastly, however stimulating, even exciting, Loughlin's attempt to provide an synthesis is, it is deeply problematical whether any conclusive answer to the quest for a new theory is to be found in a modified functionalism, or by having recourse to any variant of systems analysis. The variety of legal thought we have encountered so far, with varying degrees of emphasis, has directed our attention to the relevance and range of public law theory in understanding law's place in the late 20th-century political, economic and social landscape. But is the role of law, and administrative law in particular, explicable outside of a yet more critical general account — one at the same time more philosophically and sociologically informed while yet sharing the commitment of the Enlightenment tradition to a free, just and humane political and social order? For this we need to go outside the work of lawyers, drawing as they do on the work of others, to the work of these theorists themselves, in particular that of Jurgen Habermas and Michel Foucault, for a framing narrative which moves beyond law's own self-understanding.

JURGEN HABERMAS AND MICHEL FOUCAULT: TWO PERSPECTIVES ON LAW'S PLACE IN THE MODERN WORLD

This quest for an integrative paradigm is one which Jurgen Habermas takes up. His work can be used to situate public law on a broad canvas, one that aims to provide an alternative both to the crisis of socialism and to the concept of the 'post-modern'; to develop a rationalistic theory of law to the most abstract level; and to pose vital questions regarding the interrelationship of administrative law and modern society, for example, the apparent disconnection of questions of administrative power and human rights, law and justice, morals and politics.[144] Arguably Habermas — already well known for his analysis of the 'legitimation crisis' of late capitalism and his theory of discourse ethics — represents the culmination of the attempt to chart the geography of emancipatory reason from the Enlightenment to the present.[145] His most recent work[146] in particular is arguably his most systematic attempt to date to accommodate existing tensions between individual and community, liberal and communitarian perspectives; to integrate law with history,

---

144 Bowring, B., 'Law and Injustice: Is there an exit from the postmodern maze?' (1996) 2 *Soundings* 213.

145 Habermas, J., *Legitimation Crisis*, London: Heinemann, 1976; Habermas, J., *The Theory of Communicative Action*, vols 1 and 2, Cambridge: Polity, 1984 and 1987.

146 Habermas, J., *Between Facts and Norms: Contributions to a Discourse Theory of Law and Democracy*, Cambridge, Mass: MIT Press, 1996 (for the UK ed., London: Polity Press).

philosophy and the human sciences. Here he avoids a purely normative approach like Allan's and posits some fundamental questions: how can rule-based legal forms of authority be legitimate; how to achieve a consensus on human rights; what can mediate between the plurality of voices endemic to modern complex societies; how can law avoid turning into an instrument of social control or cynical post-modern spectacle? He finds the answer not in basing law's legitimacy solely on its alleged derivation from autonomous legislative procedures, but in law's role within a constitutional democracy founded on universally acknowledged rational principles of a procedural kind, where truth is the outcome of *intersubjective* negotiation (debate) between social actors. In this enterprise he follows in the footsteps of (i.e. responds to) those who have made distinguished contributions to German legal theory, most notably Hegel and Weber.[147] However, as we will see, whether Habermas successfully achieves his objectives is open to doubt.

Habermas has emphasised for some time that in a world without an agreed framework of belief, following the collapse of traditional authority, and given the formidable complexity of modern society, the only form of shared belief that will be sustainable over the longer term and provide for the evolution of radical forms of democracy in a constitutional state is one arrived at via a theory of intersubjective 'communicative action'. The intimate social 'lifeworld' of everyday interaction by free human beings is the proper forum for such debate and the only means whereby we can resist 'colonisation of [this] lifeworld' by other potentially socially destructive forces of money and power, found in the economic and administrative 'sub-systems' of society respectively. Habermas is very conscious of the potentially totalising and alienating tendency of the systems rationality found in the contemporary capitalist state, via the modes of instrumental reason centred in the market economy and in the legal–bureaucratic professional forms of welfare organisation, which have been one outcome of the emergence of the modern state. How to overcome this tendency of Enlightenment thought, this invasion by

---

147   Hegel, G.W.F., *Philosophy of Right*, Oxford: Oxford University Press, 1942; Weber, M., *Economy and Society*, 2 vols, Berkeley: University of California Press, 1978. For further discussion see Murphy, W.T., 'The Habermas Effect: Critical Theory and Academic Law' (1989) *Current Legal Problems* 135; Bohman, J., 'Complexity, Pluralism and the Constitutional State: On Habermas' 'Faktizitat und Geltung' (1994) 28 *Law and Society Review* 897; Rehg, W., and Bohman, J., 'Discourse and Democracy: The Formal and Informal Bases of Legitimacy in Faktizitat und Geltung' (1996) 4 *Journal of Political Philosophy* 79: Alexy, R., 'Basic Human Rights and Democracy in Habermas' Procedural Paradigm of Law' (1997) 7 *Ratio Juris* 227; Dyzenhaus, D., 'The Legitimacy of Legality' (1996) 46 *University of Toronto Law Review* 129; Rosenfeld, M., (1995) 'Law as Discourse: Bridging the Gap Between Democracy and Rights' (1995) 108 *Harvard Law Review* 1163; Carlheaden, M., and Gabriels, R., 'An Interview With J Habermas' (1996) 13 *Theory, Culture and Society* 1; White, S.K., review of Habermas, in (1996) 24 *Political Theory* 128; Baynes, K., 'Democracy and the Rechsstaat: Habermas' Faktizitat und Geltung', in White (ed.) *The Cambridge Companion to Habermas*, Cambridge: Cambridge University Press, 1995; Deflem, M. (ed.), *Habermas, Modernity and Law*, London: Sage Publications, 1996.

instrumentalism?[148] How to preserve a privileged space for communicative democratic creative activity which is not entirely confined to the margins of the system,
and marginalisation by the system?

Habermas begins elucidating the interrelationship of law, politics and society by
attempting to overcome and reconcile two distinct traditions of thought about law,
both of which have coloured much of what has been said in the last chapter and
here:[149] the positivist effort to make the human world, including law, a subject of
scientific study, to provide causal explanations for human social action (itself a
product of the general over-estimation of science and a certain conception of a
correspondence theory of truth during the 19th and 20th centuries); and the
hermeneutic effort to critique this by asserting the irreducibility of human life to
causal explanation — human beings are self-reflexive, meaning giving creatures,
they *interpret* and act upon the world as well as being shaped by it. How can these
be reconciled? Sometimes human life is conditioned — social forces can appear
to be as determinant as nature — yet we can understand such forces and act so as
to change them. The role of theory might then be described as being somewhat
akin to a certain orthodox conception of psychoanalysis: to bring people to an
awareness of what forces are acting upon them in order to release the potential
inherent in their normative expectations; to make things knowingly happen. In
brief, Habermas takes on board Weber's unification of law and politics and Hegel's
critique of Kant's overly individualist reference for ethical choice. Rather, these
choices must be regarded as *emergent* entities, framed by history and by society.

Compared to 'traditional' and 'charismatic' forms of authority, modern law, as
an essential part of modern 'legal-rational' authority,[150] has two particularly
noticeable characteristics: it is positive (coercive and man-made), seen in legislation and in case law; and it contains an idealised normativity of a rights
guaranteeing nature. Thus we have a dualistic model — in modern society centred
on the concept of majoritarian democracy in the political domain (for example, the
UK Parliament). This gives us, via the separation of these two aspects, law as a
social force (positivistic 'facticity') and law as a bearer of moral reason, embodied
in principles of a universal nature (normative 'validity'). Law as command, where
people comply from fear or through the rational calculation of consequences to
themselves, and compliance from respect for law's validity — the idealised 'rule
of law' aspect. Both of these act together to legitimate the powerful state. We will

---

148   For a general critique see Adorno, T.W., and Horkheimer, M., *Dialectic of Enlightenment*,
      London: Verso, 1979.
149   Note that, in the space available to us, we can do little more than offer a short exposition (in
      many cases a paraphrase) of what is a long and densely written text. For this reason, for much
      of what follows, we are indebted to Habermas's own short but powerful summary of *Between
      Facts and Norms*, published as a 'Postscript' to the larger work. Available also in Deflem, *op.
      cit.* note 147 *supra*, pp. 135–51.
150   See Weber, *op. cit.* note 147 *supra*.

see that, for Habermas, in the modern world the two realms of facticity and validity have separated out; and that, given the current reality of endemic social complexity, the control element and the normative element can now only be held together in a stabilised long-term relationship by law. Such a relationship, however, must be reconstructed both sociologically and philosophically within the parameters of a new constitutional state.[151]

Given that law is part of the political system of power relations, the question is: what gives law its legitimacy, especially in contemporary structurally and ideologically fractured societies? In the absence of the traditional holding patterns of religion and natural law metaphysics after the 'Death of God',[152] and following the collapse of Soviet socialism post-1989, democratic legitimacy would now seem to be the *only* legitimacy currently available. It follows that law must found itself via democratic legitimacy. But how to do so; how to acquire it? The answer for Habermas is in abstract consensus; in a discourse theory of democracy of a procedural kind, one where all voices are heard. Such a constitution, the sum total of projects which Parliament, administration and judiciary end up dealing with all the time, is the only tenable one in modern societies.[153] This open and pluralistic (largely unsubverted by money and administrative power), universal, discursive, participatory-communicative answer to the formation of public opinion and will, allied to a system of human rights and an autonomous constitution of law, works to make outcomes 'reasonable' and thus 'legitimate'[154] because it puts them beyond any conventional morality and subjects them to a consensus theory of truth. So, for example, women's groups and the green movement can put new concepts of living into practice in a world of open communication, hoping to convince others of their relevance and worth and have them transmitted into legislative, administrative and judicially legitimated forms of life.

There are two considerations arising from this basic proposition raised by Habermas:

(a)   For social theory (sociology) law acts as a socially *integrative* mechanism and so (following Durkheim and Parsons) enhances social solidarity because it has the property of acting as a safety net, a transmission belt of failure to achieve social integration (witness the attempts of transsexuals to achieve legal rights arising from the private sphere). Law is able to transmit such rights 'in an abstract but binding form, to the complex and increasingly anonymous spheres of a functionally differentiated society',[155] so stabilising behavioural expectations between bearers

---

151   See generally White, *op. cit.* note 147 *supra*, 1996.
152   Nietzsche, F., *The Gay Science* (trans. W. Kaufman), New York: Vintage, 1887/1974, pp. 181ff.
153   See Carlheaden and Gabriels, *op. cit.* note 147 *supra*, p. 2.
154   See White, *op. cit.* note 147 *supra*.
155   Habermas, *op. cit.* note 146 *supra*, p. 318.

of individual rights. (Law then as communicative action both produces and applies legal norms.)

(b) For legal theory since Dicey law has held to the idea of individual self-determination, of law as a contract model (just as money represents a market model). This is true through Hobbes, to Kant, to Rawls and Dworkin. Habermas now argues that the *discursive* model of (communitarian) deliberation replaces the contract model. The legal community is not a social contract, rather it is a discursively achieved deliberative agreement, from the most formal level of structured discourse to the most informal diffused throughout society.[156] Law, then, is not exclusively a matter of control: it acts as a bridge between system and lifeworld, continuously translating needs from below in the lifeworld to political and administrative power structures, acting as a conveyor belt for citizens' demands, wishes, hopes and expectations; from the private to the public sphere, both of which in turn are part of a dynamic participatory democratic culture.

Yet there is a problem with this position: moral argumentation still often founds legitimating constitutional-democratic discourse (the language of human rights, for example). In essence it is Kantian (individual orientated); positive law must ultimately be subordinate to moral law. But for Habermas the connection between morality and law is much more complex: there is not simply a historically contingent relation between the rule of law and democracy, there is one of legal and factual equality. This is the (functionalist) welfare-state paradigm of egalitarian, redistributive democratic socialism; as developed from the new liberalism of the late 19th century and the progressivism of Roosevelt in 1930s America in reaction to the perceived weaknesses of the overly individualist model. So politics and law both now combine a private and a public dimension: a first generation *individual* rights discourse, and a second generation rights discourse of *social* entitlements fulfilling the promise latent in the legal–formal rights language of early modern liberal philosophy.

The democratic process, then, now bears the entire burden of legitimation, of the pressing need to secure both the 'private and public autonomy of legal subjects'.[157] We cannot arrive at these private rights or sustain them without public discourse and agreement, because law is not linked to abstract claims to rights, rather to pragmatic democratic consensus at any one time. Hence Habermas's *proceduralist* and deliberative (discourse) conception of law, democracy and politics: that of *communicative intersubjectivity*; not individual choice as prioritised by Norman Lewis, for the model of private law rights can offer no answer to problems of equal personal freedom in complex societies. Law *cannot* now draw its legitimacy from a higher order of religion, tradition or metaphysics, but only from the internal working out of communicative presuppositions (or perspectives)

---

156   Habermas, Postscript, in Deflem, *op. cit.* note 147 *supra*, p. 137.
157   *Ibid.*, p. 137.

in the social world — a world that provides far more space for democratic egalitarian politics than either Dworkin or Allan, for example, allow for. This approach represents, then, a strong critique of both positivism and functionalism: positivism because it cannot justify its own principles — for example, the sovereignty of Parliament (as a higher law or ground rule) rests on the concept that law is no more than a set of legitimate rules; functionalism because it is fundamentally an 'empiricist denial of any legitimacy beyond the contingency of legislative decisions'.[158] For Habermas this represents too sceptical a view of law and of the functional capacity of the legal system. We can see, therefore, that he takes the position that procedural standards (of an abstract, non specific, nature) must be agreed, must be stipulated in advance, if we are to reach agreement in a society without the kind of consensus taken for granted in more traditional and early modern polities.

So far we have seen that Habermas believes that there is an *internal* relation between law and democracy: that positive law cannot be subordinated to universal moral principles; that popular sovereignty and human rights are necessarily linked (presuppose one another); that democracy is grounded independently of any moral principle. His position is therefore a complex one. We have no space to do more than note this fact and here emphasise only two aspects of Habermas's nuanced and subtle approach. First, the argument that the moral law, by its very nature, seeks universality (the Kantian tradition). Secondly, that the legal community is overwhelmingly local and sociological, that it protects the bearers of rights only in so far as they acquire the status of bearers of such rights (compare rights for gays with those for transsexuals in Europe). Legal programmes and legislative enactments therefore raise not only moral but also pragmatic, empirical and ethical aspects.[159] This inevitably leads to compromise between interests so that the *process* of democratic will formation of the legislature depends upon the complexity of societal group interests, discourses, bargaining and events. That is, not just upon moral discourse of an abstract nature.

Habermas's discourse theory, then, steers precariously between positivism and natural law, tracing law's legitimacy back to procedural rationality and a qualified pragmatism; at base to 'an appropriate communicative arrangement'[160] not just the making of rules or attempts at moral containment. In fact, constitutional democracy is founded on a basic question, albeit one strongly skewed towards the search for consensus: '. . . what rights must citizens grant one another if they decide to constitute themselves as a voluntary association of legal consociates and legitimately regulate their living together by means of positive law'?[161] Natural law has,

---

158   *Ibid.*, p. 138.
159   Note, that for Habermas the term 'ethical', following Hegel, is defined more narrowly than 'moral'.
160   Habermas, Postscript, in Deflem *op. cit.* note 147 *supra*, p. 140.
161   *Ibid.*, p. 140.

in the context of a society which can find only weak agreement, been reformulated under new discourse–theoretic premises. In the absence of a higher law its place is taken by *intersubjective* understanding and choice: not individual; not collective, viewed as opposites (the classic liberal dilemma), but *conjoined* as positivity and normativity. Law then becomes 'both compulsory and compelling',[162] helping maintain consent in our fractured reality and effectively shrinking the tension between rights and democracy, reconciled now in the new procedural discourse paradigm. But reconciled, perhaps, at the cost of an idealised model of reflective consensual equilibrium which has small relation with actually experienced democracy anywhere.

We can now demonstrate why popular sovereignty and human rights presuppose one another. Remember that for orthodox liberal theory private autonomy is guaranteed by human rights in 'an anonymous rule of law' (see Allan, above), while democracy is constituted by self-legislation through popular majoritarianism. The problem is the time-worn Diceyan dilemma: majoritorian democracy can overturn anything, making the rule of law potentially an empty shell; an anxiety dating back to Locke's and Mill's fear of the 'tyranny of the majority'. While liberal individualism prioritises individual rights and the defence of private property, the republican/communitarian tradition of Rousseau, Hegel and Marx provides space for egalitarian redistribution and accords priority to the political community at the price of suffering from 'ethical overload' and falling into problems of system legitimacy arising from the inefficiency of administrative steering and from 'disturbances in the democratic genesis of law'.[163] Habermas, as we have seen, is sceptical of both positions. We need to reconcile private autonomy with public autonomy, to combine liberal and republican concepts, not least because politics, viewed as the values by means of which we govern ourselves, cannot be assimilated to a shared form of collective identity.[164] At base, law, morality, politics, etc., are part of an intersubjective will formation, 'a democratic procedure that grounds the supposition that the outcomes of political opinion and will formation are reasonable'.[165] It follows that private and public autonomy presuppose one another: there is a *constitutive* connection between law and politics. Within this 'intersubjectively exercised civic autonomy' citizens recognise each other as equals, and hence accord each other rights (reciprocally granted). There is a constitutional disciplining of power: discourse theory invests democracy with normative connotations stronger than liberalism, but weaker than republican/communitarian theories.[166] For Habermas, 'Rights against the state only arise as a

---

162 Outhwaith, W., *Habermas: A Critical Introduction*, London: Polity Press, 1994.
163 Habermas, *op. cit.* note 146 *supra*, p. 429.
164 Habermas, J., 'Three Normative Models of Democracy' No. 1 *Constellations*, Oxford: Basil Blackwell, 1994.
165 Habermas, Postscript, *op. cit.* note 147 *supra*, p. 142.
166 Habermas, *op. cit.* note 164 *supra*.

consequence of the process of differentiation in which a self-governing association of consociates under law becomes a legal community organised around a state'.[167] The result is that the very idea of a constitutional state can be described 'with the aid of principles according to which legitimate law is generated from communicative power and the latter in turn is converted into administrative power via legitimately enacted law'.[168]

Habermas now has to show that generalised deliberative politics has its own roots independent of any moral principle and that it extends well beyond orthodox party politics and the political system to the wider complex 'public sphere' of extensive communications,[169] of rational opinion and will formation within the complex conditions of modern society. This is the kernel of his *procedural* discourse principle of democracy, rational consent and the rule of law: that a consensus of all those who participate in rational debate is needed before legitimacy can be accorded to regulations and ways of life — 'Just those action norms are valid to which all possibly affected persons agree as participants in a rational discourse'.[170] This process of idealised speech and self-legislation, of democratic and communicative discourse, is anchored in law itself via legal institutionalisation so that, for example, agreement on legislative enactment should be reached with regard for universal moral principles of equal respect and 'completed through communicative and participatory rights that guarantee equal opportunities for the public use of communicative liberties. In this way the discourse principle acquires the legal shape of a democratic principle'.[171] Thus it is that the tension between facticity and validity is already built into moral discourse, as it is in the practice of speech and argument generally — in law it is simply intensified as it is operationalised and made into practical, workaday reality. (Remembering always that the discourse principle itself is 'situated at a level of abstraction that is still neutral *vis-à-vis* the distinction between morality and law'.[172])

Law is legitimated, therefore, 'not because it incorporates concrete, ethically right values, but because it relies on a procedurally conceived notion of rationality realized by democratic principles in legislation, jurisprudence and legal administration'.[173] This comes down to deliberative politics where there is no longer a need to demonstrate that it is *morally* required as well as functionally necessary that we organise life in complex societies by positive law. All that is required today is to show that:

---

167   Habermas, Postscript, *op. cit.* note 147 *supra*, p. 144.
168   Habermas, *op. cit.* note 146 *supra*, p. 169.
169   Baynes, *op. cit.* note 147 *supra*, p. 216.
170   Habermas, *op. cit.* note 146 *supra*, p. 107.
171   Habermas, Postscript, *op. cit.* note 147 *supra*, p. 144.
172   *Ibid.*, p. 146.
173   Deflem, *op. cit.* note 147 *supra*, 12.

the social substratum for the realization of the system of rights consists neither in spontaneous market forces nor in the deliberate measures of the welfare state but in the currents of communication and public opinion that, emerging from civil society and the public sphere, are converted into communicative power through democratic procedures.[174]

This is to regard law as a steering mechanism, a framework of regulations within which, for example, the political system works by fostering citizen participation, the role of political parties and curbs on the media; while the economic system is functionally assisted to operate smoothly via company law, contract law, consumer law, and labour law, with criminal law as a means of penalising interference with property rights.[175]

But it is not self-enclosed (as in systems theory), rather it is enveloped and enriched by the democratic and ethical life of a community of 'enfranchised citizens and a liberal political culture that meets it halfway'.[176] One where citizens are required, by the very nature of the processes of democratic life, to use their 'communicative and participatory rights with an orientation to the common good'; that is, they are 'politically called for but not legally compelled'. Law, then, can preserve its legitimacy only if citizens move from the role of private legal subject to communicative participants in the search for the common life of society. Constitutional democracy depends on such citizens who have the capacity for (i.e. are accustomed to) freedom and therefore the ability to found and refound claims to truth on something which cannot be created by administrative measures. Habermas's proceduralist conception of institutionalised democracy must, in its own terms, ultimately subsist on the foundation of a vibrant civil society of interacting citizens and an unsubverted (by money and instrumentalised concepts of power) political public sphere if it is to carry the burden of extensive normative expectations, 'especially the burden of a normatively democratic genesis of law'.[177]

But, it might be asked, what about interests and conflict, phenomena which can be dealt with only by means of the exercise of state power? Habermas's answer is that the discourse–theoretic approach is realistic to the extent that it 'shifts the conditions for a rational political opinion and will formation from the level of individual or group motivations and decisions to the *social* level of institutional processes of deliberation and decision making'.[178] This is what he terms a structural position: democracy functions to filter out issues and resolve conflicts leaving only valid inputs. But is his very demanding model of law workable in

---

174   Habermas, *op. cit.* note 146 *supra*, p. 442.
175   Rosenfeld, *op. cit.* note 147 *supra*, p. 1173.
176   Habermas, Postscript, *op. cit.* note 147 *supra*, p. 147.
177   *Ibid.*, p. 147.
178   *Ibid.*, p. 148.

societies like our own? Habermas argues that 'A reconstructive legal theory follows a methodology premised on the idea that the counterfactual self-understanding of constitutional democracy finds expression in unavoidable, yet factually efficacious idealisations that are presupposed by the relevant practices'.[179] That is, given freedom, equality of citizenship, debate, openness, the energies of competing ideas and interests, 'citizens must reach an understanding by following democratic procedures and publicly making use of their legally guaranteed communicative liberties'.[180] It is, therefore, the paradox and importance of law that it 'reduces the conflict potential of unleashed liberties through norms that can coerce only so long as they are recognised as legitimate on the fragile basis of unleashed communicative liberties'.[181] By these means forms of legitimate coercion are converted into a mode of social integration of the diverse individual and group action orientations of modern state formations. To put it slightly differently, social integration is reflexive; while law needs legitimation, it meets this need by the productive force of communication: '. . . law takes advantage of a permanent risk of dissensus to spur on legally institutionalised public discourses'.[182] This is what Habermas believes is salvageable from the wreck of socialism as a discourse of modernity: a vision of a radical participatory democracy within which law, including administrative law (defined as a 'principle of prohibiting arbitrariness in domestic affairs'[183]), assumes a crucial mediating function, helping to stabilise the tension between facticity and normativity, converting legitimacy into social solidarity. A theory which manages to be at the same time normative, universal, consensual, one founded on intersubjective and communicative reason.[184] This is a perspective based on decisively tilting the balance away from Hegelian, Marxist premises towards an argument founded on a Kantian transcendental procedure one which, while accepting the German constitutional state as a given, strives to discover the conditions of possibility of such a state. Therein lies both the innovatory and rigorous nature of Habermas's argument and its innate conservatism.[185]

Habermas's impressive edifice — his attempt to provide one of the most comprehensive theories of law in its relationship to the social and historical for some time — is, nevertheless, open to substantial criticism. For example:

(a)   The new procedural paradigm is too narrow and cannot provide an agreed measure for the resolution of the conflict Habermas identifies between facticity and validity, between private and public realms, between 'ego' and 'identity' politics, between the claims of reason and hope and the situated nature of the claims we

179   *Ibid.*, p. 148.
180   *Ibid.*, p. 148.
181   *Ibid.*, p. 148.
182   *Ibid.*, p. 148.
183   Habermas, *op. cit.* note 146 *supra*, p. 174.
184   *Ibid.*, see, for example, p. 409.
185   We are indebted to F. Bowring for this point.

actually make. The context of justification for his theory is established without substantive sociological analysis; while, within his model, power relations are abstract, idealised speech-communicative relations free from inequality. This variant on social contract theory, based on Habermas's turn in the 1980s to language as part of his quest for a grounding for the theory of intersubjective communication, offers too utopian a vision to have credibility. Is it not in fact too high a standard for *any* existent or likely democratic agreement, given ongoing tensions and the difficulty of mediating between them, let alone resolving them? Even with optimum conditions, we are likely to be able only legally to *institutionalise* such struggle(s), with any individual or group outcome depending upon the strength of the interests involved.[186]

(b)   Despite his democratic intentions and his belief in undistorted communication as a way to a continuous critique of truth claims, is Habermas's consensus theory too totalising — in danger of replacing a sometimes disturbing heterogeneity with a suffocating homogeneity? Does he answer at all satisfactorily Weber's pessimism about the role of reason in the modern administrative state? Further, is it not the case that any actually existing dialogue test, by its very nature and logic, is effectively one of unanimity? Stanley Fish comments that

> . . . participants must already agree as to what is appropriate and what is not; but agreement is supposedly the goal of the dialogue and if it is made a requirement for entry [as with Habermas] the goal has been reached in advance by rigging the context. Success is then assured but it is empty because impediments to it have been exiled in advance even though they surely exist in the world.[187]

(c)   For Foucault (see below), political and legal theory tends, in practice, to legitimate the state's sense of what constitutes order rather than the subject's freedom, for power lies at the heart of all relations. There can be no hierarchy without power, just as there can be no 'truth' (in the sense of an achieved paradigm of consensus) without coercion. Habermas frequently appears strangely complacent about the enormous costs to the individual or group of the oppressiveness of law; that law can destroy lifeworld integration as well as facilitate it. For example, what about the feminist critique of patriarchy, the gay critique of exclusionary mechanisms, or the clients' relation to administrative-legal institutions, where law can simply appear as an instrument of behavioural control? In a word, his analysis lacks all *ontological* depth.[188]

---

186   Alexy, *op. cit.* note 147 *supra*, p. 227.
187   Fish, S., 'Boutique Multiculturalism, or Why Liberals Are Incapable of Thinking about Hate Speech' (1997) 23 *Critical Inquiry* 378, at 391.
188   See, for example, Bowring, F., 'Communitarianism and Morality: In Search of the Subject' (1997) 222 *New Left Review*, pp. 110*ff.*

(d)   Habermas emphasises that as law has evolved it has become more general and abstract in nature and has reached into ever more spheres of public life; but generality and abstraction do not always mean more recognition of autonomy or rationality, as the debate over the coherence and purpose of judicial review played out in some of the chapters of this book well illustrates.

(e)   There is no extensive sociologically founded discussion in his new work of the material social and economic injustices, of the legal violence and cruelty inherent in market-based contemporary capitalist social formations. As Bowring asks: does Habermas have a tendency to equate existing social structures with rationality; despite contrary intentions, becoming little more than a defender of, an apologist for, modern Western law-based liberal democracies?[189]

(f)   Even assuming the consensus of a rational community, if we ask how the individual might *internalise* such a consensus we are immediately brought face to face with the likelihood that a reasoned argument will not take wing unless it resonates meaningfully within the context of a struggle for recognition of an individual's subjectively experienced form of life as a mode of social struggle. If this is so we should not ground critical theory in a theory of language but in some form of philosophical anthropology, in a broader conception of human life than can be captured by any linguistic theory; one centred not just on justice but on a stronger concept of the good viewed as the normative aspect of a critical theory allowing an argument to be made for a number of abstract conditions for every form of good human life.[190]

However, it is not Honeth, illuminating though his work is, but Foucault who takes the emphasis on irreducible struggle to an extreme. In this guise he stands as one of the most subversive of those who worked to deconstruct the Enlightenment project of emancipatory reason.

The critique of foundationalism: Michel Foucault and the micro-physics of power-knowledge

If Habermas represents the contemporary culmination of theoretical attempts to tie law to secure (or at least 'warrantedly assertable') foundations of knowledge, there is another tradition stemming most recently from the 1960s and originating in a very different model of life and the world. As Foucault himself puts it: 'It seems to me that there are two great families of founders. There are those who build [for our purpose Habermas], who lay the first stone, and there are those who dig and hollow out'.[191] The goal of Foucault 'has not been to analyse the phenomena of power, nor to elaborate the foundations of such an analysis. [The] objective,

---

189   Bowring, *op. cit.* note 144 *supra*, pp. 221–2.
190   See particularly Honeth, A., *The Struggle for Recognition*, Cambridge: Polity Press, 1995.
191   Lotringer, S. (ed.), *Foucault Live: Collected Interviews 1961–1984*, New York: Semiotext, 1996.

instead, has been to create a history of the different modes by which, in our culture, human beings are made subjects' (of the practice of power)[192] and to write the sociology and political history of productions of claims to truth,[193] including that of law:

> . . . a form of history which can account for the constitution of knowledges, discourses, domains of objects, etc., without having to make reference to a subject which is either transcendental in relation to the field of events or runs in its empty sameness throughout the course of history.[194]

Foucault, then, takes the metanarrative of the Enlightenment and turns it into a sharply *critical* enterprise, one which seeks to establish the proposition that, contra-Habermas, the conception of a society without unequal power relations can be only an abstract diversion; that there is no model of truth which is not traceable at the same time to relations of power; that the claim of knowledge to neutrality is merely an elaborate facade for interest associations.

In fact, two different worlds are in contention here: where Habermas is characterised by an emphasis on foundationalism, transcendentalism, objectivism and the search for truth (elements common in some degree to almost all varieties of administrative law theory discussed above), Foucault is characterised by perspectivism, scepticism, historicism, agonism and relativism. Crucial for both, however, is the relation of power to the 'institutionalisation of discourse' as practices.[195] They share in common the view of Max Weber and the Frankfurt School that modern forms of instrumental reason and bureaucracy, including legal bureaucracy, welfare bureaucracy and market forces represented by money, can lead to the reification of the forms of social life and undermine our subjective sense of freedom just as they provide the means for its continuation. Both support those forces who oppose 'colonisation of the lifeworld'. But where Habermas looks to complete the Enlightenment project through the medium of radical democracy — to subject the bureaucratic processes of modernity to intersubjective, universal communicative reason (the discourse model of democracy we have reviewed) where every particular outcome can be embodied in legal–institutional forms (including administrative legal forms) to defend human rights and limit excesses

---

192 Foucault, M., 'The Subject and Power', in Dreyfus, H.L., and Rabinow, P., *Michael Foucault: Beyond Structuralism and Hermeneutics*, Sussex: Harvester Press, 1982, p. 208.

193 Defined as: 'Truth is to be understood as a system of ordered procedures for the production, regulation, distribution, circulation and operation of statements. "Truth" is linked in a circular relation with systems of power which it induces and which extend it.' Foucault, M., 'Truth and Power', in Gordon, C. (ed.), *Power/Knowledge: Selected Interviews and Other Writings 1972—1977*, New York: Pantheon, 1980, p. 133.

194 Foucault, *op. cit.* note 193 *supra*, p. 117.

195 Richters, A., 'Modernity-Postmodernity Controversies: Habermas and Foucault' (1988), *Theory, Culture and Society* 611.

of power; where self-expression can be encouraged in a rational, ordered and consensual society of participatory democracy combining both individual autonomy and collective solidarity — Foucault, as 'the cartographer of power', holds to a very different, and much darker, conception of our present and our possible future.

Unlike Habermas, working within the Enlightenment narrative of the unfolding of human freedom, Foucault views the development of modern society as one of the creation of regimes of domination, constituting us within the grid of shifting relationships of power/knowledge. For him the project of Kant can be interpreted[196] only as a form of *permanent critique*; it must be separated out from the ideology of humanism and from the forms of instrumental reason embodied in the human sciences (including law) where every 'will to truth' becomes a 'will to power', where truth is always inseparable from the procedures establishing it as a definable and measurable object of investigation. Power relations cannot be analysed either from the perspective of the knowing subject, or from the viewpoint of centralised structures of state power — the juridical command model. Power is multiple, dispersed and productive (in the sense that it can create new discourses of power) and lies at the heart of every relationship individual and social. There can be no utopian society, either in theory or in practice. Law itself provides no answer to these dilemmas; indeed, it is deeply implicated in them, for the discourse of 'freedom' and 'rights' which courses through currently fashionable liberal sensibilities in public law theory is a chimera, one not universal but contingently historical, and always and everywhere contaminated by power with its baggage train of prohibitions and exclusions. Against the positivist model representing legal autonomy from power politics, law has to be analysed from *within* as an internally generated set of institutionalised disciplinary mechanisms of power/knowledge. This discourse only serves the 'normalised' society of domination by disciplines and 'dividing practices' (an example would be legal classification and delimitation of the person). The everyday practices of law, embodied in the prison and the courtroom, the asylum and the control of populations, are the costs of the very rationality and reason they strive to embody: 'We have entered a type of society where the power of law is not regressing but rather merging into a much more general power . . . that of the norm'[197] where 'legality combines with other discourses to form the individual as the *locus* of ever greater networks of administrative control.'[198] This concrete investment of the body by the techniques and tactics of domination amounts to 'polymorphous techniques of subjugation' where decision making processes develop their own particular political technolo-

196   Foucault, M., 'What is Enlightenment?' in Rabinow, P., *The Foucault Reader*, Harmondsworth: Penguin, 1984.
197   *Op. cit.* note 191 *supra*, p. 197.
198   Turkel, G., 'Michel Foucault: Law, Power and Knowledge' (1990) 17 *Journal of Law and Society* 170.

gies; for example, the social security system involves a hierarchy of observation of client conduct, the construction of spaces, an individualisation that facilitates surveillance and control, with law as its helpmate. Equally, the new stress during the 1980s on the discourse of new public management, of audit, quality, account-ability, customer service, performance indicators, aims and objectives and the like, represents nothing less than a powerful new regime of truth, a 'micro-physics of power'.[199]

Foucault, then, wishes to distance us from the norm and the discursive practices and strategies which give us the forms of 'individualisation' we live with and under. He does this, following Nietzsche, by means of a 'genealogical excavation':

> . . . it is not therefore via an empiricism that the genealogical project unfolds, nor even via a positivism in the ordinary sense of that term. What it really does is to entertain the claims to attention of local, discontinuous, disqualified, illegitimate knowledges *against the claims of a unitary body of theory* which would filter, hierarchise and order them in the name of some true knowledge and some arbitrary idea of what constitutes a science and its objects.[200]

There is no answer; in grand theory there is only resistance from below: the 'micro-politics' of agonism (of class, of gender, of ethnicity) which are ineradicable and lie at the very heart of collective life:

> It seems to me that the real political task in a society such as ours is to criticise them [i.e. the disciplines, including law] in such a manner that the political violence which has always exercised itself obscurely through them will be unmasked so that we can fight them.[201]

Unlike many of the 'post-modernists' and Habermas, therefore, Foucault's work is distinguished by a counter-hegemonic politics (a subversion of established para-digms, disciplines and concepts, an emphasis on the transforming experience in order to explore new relations with the self and others through points of resistance to the 'domination of truth') and the practice of power at the level of subjugation to bureaucratic modes of punishment.[202] The question then becomes not where does power emanate from, but how and upon whom is it practised?

Ultimately, for Foucault, the emphasis is not on how we can *theorise* law (including administrative law) in its relationship to state and society, but on

---

199 See McLennan, G., 'Post-Marxism and the "Four Sins" of Modernist Theorising [1996] *New Left Review* 218, at 53.

200 Foucault, *op. cit.* note 193 *supra*, p. 83 (emphasis added).

201 Quoted in Rabinow, P., (ed.), *The Foucault Reader*, Harmondsworth: Penguin, 1984, p. 6.

202 See esp. Foucault, M., *Discipline and Punish: The Birth of the Prison*, Harmondsworth: Penguin, 1977.

knowledge, power and the self: a three-fold scepticism and critique of law where
'truth' as an outcome of power simply becomes the pragmatic, negotiated outcome
among actors. Is the search for a theoretical grounding of administrative law, then,
little more than a persistent source of delusion; little more than an attempt to
conceal the reality of control via a succession of regimes of truth?[203]

CONCLUSION: ADMINISTRATIVE LAW THEORY: A NEW FOUNDATIONALISM?

To conclude, we would like to offer a brief outline of what we hope will appear
as a future article arguing for a new foundationalism for public law, one which
situates it within the context of an epistemologically and ontologically rich theory
of level distinctions of a structural–relational and normative kind.

We have now come full circle, from Hegel's doubts that it is impossible to
theorise retrospectively, only once events have occurred and the world has moved
on, to Foucault's disconcerting closing of the horizons of grounded theoretical and
normative speculation: both fundamentally act to question the assumption that a
foundationalist theory of law and society is either desirable or possible. Whether
we have recourse to the bulk of socio-legal work (vitiated to a not inconsiderable
degree by 'abstract empiricism') or to the more general offerings of Habermas and
systems theory (too abstract and rationalistic, too little related to law as understood
in academia, the profession or, more importantly, as experienced on the street; too
much stress on system autonomy rather than on human intentionality working
within structures that constrain them), there is no generally agreed paradigm for
research, no clear way (even no clear 'middle way') forward. Is there a possible
reconciliation? Among many contemporary writers in the field of public law liberal
political philosophy seems to be the most popular 'background theory'; but those
theorists used most often by lawyers are overwhelmingly Anglo-American in
orientation, largely individualistic in nature and all too often sex, race and class
blind. For example, the whole conception of the public–private divide is of
doubtful utility where women are concerned because so-called private bodies may
easily have a disproportionate impact on them.[204] Equally, those theorists tend to
be sociologically uninformed, not in currently prevailing socio-legal terms, but in
terms of what Wright-Mills called 'the sociological imagination'.[205] Another
instance is that, despite the glib rhetoric surrounding rights claims and the idea of

203   For a number of insights here we are indebted to Tony Beck — see Beck, A., 'Foucault and Law:
      the Collapse of Law's Empire' (1996) 16 *Oxford Journal of Legal Studies* 489. There is a large
      literature on Habermas and Foucault — for a recent example see Owen, D., 'Foucault, Habermas
      and the Claims of Reason' (1996) 9 *History of the Human Sciences* 119.
204   Goodman, R.E., Petit, P. (eds), *A Companion to Contemporary Political Philosophy*, Oxford: Basil
      Blackwell, 1993, p. 18.
205   Mills, C.W., *The Sociological Imagination*, Harmondsworth: Penguin, 1970.

equality before the law, research reveals that money and material interests generally use the courts to get their way.[206] And that administrative law itself, particularly judicial review, has very limited impact on the whole, emphasising 'the consequent inability of traditional legal remedies to cope with the major ways in which harm arises and is distributed in societies'.[207] The fundamental problem is that we do not live in the kind of societies made familiar by liberal individualistic philosophising (the 'communitarian' school of liberalism has more to offer) but in a world of hierarchy and inequality, a world memorably caught by the words of Elmer Schattschneider: '. . . the only flaw in the pluralist heaven is that the heavenly chorus sings with a strong upper-class accent'.[208] A meta-pluralist conception of law is now necessary, one which accepts that 'people's preferences are formed by politics [very broadly conceived] and not prior to it, where law and politics are socially constructed, and where law and politics are heavily normative modes of power, knowledge and truth.'[209]

What, then, might be the conditions of possibility of knowledge in a situation where, although ideas are indeed real in their consequences, the consequences are never quite those expected of them? And in the face of the decline in belief in the efficacy of the public sphere generally? We need a new framing narrative for administrative law because of the increasingly problematic role of the nation state in an interdependent global framework and, despite some argument to the contrary, because enormous potential power still resides in the hands of the state domestically, as regulator, facilitator and guarantor. Any new theoretical perspective needs to counter market fragmentation and the separation of public and private spheres with a reassertion of the priority of economic processes, not least because values like liberty, democracy and participation are substantially shaped by such processes. But we also need to be more sensitive, post-Foucault, to the way power intersects in a variety of complex ways, including symbolic ways, to shape identities and relationships between individuals, groups and institutions. Not, then, the vacuum of 'post-modernism' where incommensurability of language games (historical, ethical, political, legal and scientific) signal worlds in judgeless, relativised competition, where there is no universal vantage point from which we can survey and adjudicate between them; nor the complacency of liberal political philosophy. Administrative law (and public law generally) is necessarily historical, sociological and philosophical and, in a world of determinate structured

---

206 For example, see Gallanter, M.C., 'Why the "haves" come out ahead: speculations on the limits of social change' (1974) 9 *Law and Society Review* 95.

207 Campbell, T.D., 'The Contribution of Legal Studies', in Goodin and Pettit, *op. cit.* note 204 *supra*, p. 205.

208 *The Semisovereign People: A Realist's View of Democracy*, New York: Holt, Rinehart & Winston, 1960.

209 See the discussion in Eskridge, W.N. and Peller, G., 'The New Public Law Movement: Moderation as a Postmodern Cultural Form' (1990) 89 *Michigan Law Review* 707, at p. 738.

relationships which frame people's lives, always in any particular instance inevitably involves an amalgam of such influences. As we have seen, terms like 'justice', 'fairness' or 'the rule of law' have been assigned meaning, but these can be understood only by means of an excavation of the particular and the universal, by grasping the contingencies of history and its outcomes as well as the complex institutional framework and moral ideals which prioritise the just life (in Kant centred on the individual) or the good life (in Hegel and Marx centred on the historical community).[210]

How, then, might we go about the task of putting in place a framework, including a systemic conception of social change, which could provide the tools for this job? First, it is not clear that we need accept the recently fashionable critique of reductionism, essentialism or universalism.[211] Elements of all three of these remain necessary and valid components of any theory of administrative law. Secondly, we require a hierarchy of claims to knowledge, a theory of level distinctions which can assist us in the (admittedly formidable) task of analysis from the macroscopic down to the microscopic level.[212] Thirdly, legal analysis needs to escape from the trap of parochialism, and isolation from philosophy and the historical sciences, wherever it be found: from the eagle's eye view at mountain top or the frog perspective of base camp; or some supposedly intermediary position. A fresh (dialectical) synthesis is required, one which combines differences without seeking to elide them. This can be found in some combination of Hegel, Marx, Habermas and Foucault, together with the insights to be derived from the 'progressives/regressive' analysis of Jean Paul Sartre with regard to a person's place in history[213] and the 'Frankfurt School' with their reflections upon the ironies of the Enlightenment project where the urge to uniformity and sameness has been one outcome of modern 20-century bureaucratic, scientific-instrumental techniques (law pre-eminently among them).[214]

But finally, the time is passed when this could be enough, and it brings us to what should today form the ultimate framing narrative for administrative law (and public law generally) — namely, ecological (or 'deep green') legal theory, a view

---

210 See Shaw, J. and Salter, M., 'Towards a Critical Theory of Constitutional Law: Hegel's Contribution' (1994) 21 *Journal of Law & Society* 464.

211 See McLennan, G., 'Post-Marxism and the "Four Sins" of Modernist Theorising' (1996) 218 *New Left Review* 53, and Norris, C., *Reclaiming the Truth*, London: Lawrence and Wishart, 1996.

212 See, e.g., Rubin, G.L., 'The New Legal Process: The Synthesis of Discourse, and the Microanalysis of Discourse' (1996) *Harvard Law Review* 1393; Bhaskar, R., *Dialectic: the Pulse of Freedom*, London: Verso, 1993.

213 Sartre, J-P., *Search for a Method*, New York: Vintage Press, 1968. See generally Best, S., *The Politics of Historical Vision: Marx, Foucault, Habermas*, New York: Guildford Press, 1996 and Smith, T., *Dialectical Social Theory: From Hegel to Analytical Marxism and Postmodernism*, New York, Suny Press, 1993.

214 For example, see Adorno, T.W., and Horkheimer, M., *Dialectic of Enlightenment*, London: Verso, 1979.

which begins from the premise that humankind is inseparable from, indeed embedded in, the natural and social environment.[215] Administrative machinery worldwide, harnessed to capitalist economic growth and the despoilation of nature, has led human kind near to catastrophe.[216] And if 'Human history can only advance through a new relationship to the natural world from which it originated,' then ecological theory needs to prefigure and prioritise the legal-administrative require- ments necessary for a society of cooperation, decentralisation, participation, democracy, responsibility and balance.[217] This new holistic paradigm of *integrative ethics* will, if it is successful, ultimately have the most profound repercussions for law, as well as economics, politics and culture, for our institutional arrange- ments as well as the values of individuality and community. Adorno once commented that 'the value of a thought is measured by its distance from the continuity of the familiar'.[218] And that is what it should always be: the perpetual subversion of the conventional wisdom of the time.

In what can only be a prelude to a possible further article, we have sought to show: first, that exclusively intra-legal discourse about public law theory is inadequate; secondly, that any framework for a new foundationalism must come from philosophy, history and the natural and human sciences; thirdly, that this should combine both a structural–relational and a strongly normative element; fourthly, that the role of struggle and contest in a global framework needs to be recognised. Finally, Lee Marvin in 'Paint Your Wagon', commented in the song 'Wandering Star' that he 'never knew a sight that didn't look better looking back'; nevertheless, we have tried to look forward and tentatively offer something of a new paradigm for the future.

---

215 Capra, F., *The Web of Life: A New Synthesis of Mind and Matter*, London: Harper-Collins 1996; Dobson, A., *Green Political Thought* (2nd ed.), London: Routledge, 1995; and Zinneman, M.E., Contesting Earth's Future: Radical Ecology and Postmodernity, California: University of California Press, 1997.
216 For a recent example see Smith, R., 'Creative Destruction: Capitalist Development and China's Environment' (1997) 222 *New Left Review* 3. See also Beck, U., 'World Risk Society as Cosmopolitan Society?' (1996) 13 *Theory, Culture and Society* 1.
217 Best, *op. cit.* note 213 *supra*, pp. 272–3.
218 Adorno, T.W., *Minima Moralia*, London: New Left Books, 1974, p. 80–1.

Index